Contemporary Government and Business Relations

Contemporary Government and Business Relations

Second Edition

Martin Schnitzer

Virginia Polytechnic Institute

HOUGHTON MIFFLIN COMPANY   BOSTON
Dallas   Geneva, Illinois   Hopewell, New Jersey   Palo Alto   London

Printed in the U.S.A.

Library of Congress Catalog Card Number: 82-80075

ISBN: 0-395-31764-9

Contents

v

List of Diagrams

List of Tables

Preface

The purpose of this book is to fill a void in government and business courses: the lack of coverage of new areas of government regulation that directly affect business operations. Traditionally, books on government and business fail to show that government influence has expanded into a number of areas totally unrelated to antitrust policies and public utility regulation. In fact, most business firms are more likely to be affected by the federal government's environmental and affirmative action policies than by its antitrust policies. The federal government has expanded so greatly that today it has become the largest purchaser of business products. Moreover, the government's various fiscal agencies exercise a powerful indirect influence over business through their control of interest rates, discount rates, and other fiscal and monetary techniques.

The composition of this book reflects the many and diverse areas in which government and business interact. Chapter 1 is about how government affects business—in public finance, regulation and control, as an employer, and as an owner of industry. Chapters 2, 3, and 4 present the background of the development of government and business relations in the United States. Chapters 5, 6, and 7 cover industrial concentration and the application of antitrust laws. Chapters 8 and 9 deal with a subject of increasing importance, the multinational corporation. These chapters include discussions of the role of multinational corporations in détente, the application of U.S. and foreign antitrust laws to multinational corporations, and the increasing importance of direct foreign investment in the United States. Chapters 10 and 11 cover government regulation of the so-called natural monopolies. Chapter 11 focuses on the deregulation of the airline and natural gas industries. Chapters 12, 13, 14, and 15 deal with the subject of social regulation of business and include such areas as environmental policy, consumer protection, and affirmative action. Chapters 16 and 17 outline various ways in which government provides financial support to business. Chapters 18 and 19 discuss some of the economic issues confronting business including "Reaganomics" and the Japanese challenge.

Ben Jonson, the 17th century British poet and playwright, wrote "Time will not be ours forever." Operating within the constraints of time, I have tried to update this book to include as many changes as possible in a subject area that is prone to rapid change. I was able to include the January 1982 conclusion of major antitrust cases involving AT&T, IBM, and the breakfast food companies. However, events that happened after January 1982, such as the Braniff bankruptcy, were impossible to include. The state of the economy has received front and center attention from the Reagan Administration, and regulatory reforms have been placed on a back burner. Changes in the Clean Air Act, which has been in committee, have not taken place as of late May 1982.

M.S.

Contemporary Government and Business Relations

PART I

INTRODUCTION TO GOVERNMENT AND BUSINESS RELATIONS

In many ways it is correct to say that the future of the steel industry is made right here in Washington. We must regard the federal establishment as having a preeminent influence on capital investment decisions—preeminent and, unfortunately, unconstructive on many occasions. This is so because of a combination of two different aspects of Federal power: in the first place, it is broad and pervasive, affecting virtually every aspect of our business, and second, in many instances, the power is being exercised to meet special and often political objectives and not to achieve goals which will bring the greatest benefit to the nation in the long run.*

This statement by the president of Republic Steel defines quite well the significance of the relationship between government and business. Today no business firm is free from some form of government control. For example, a little more than a decade ago, most business firms were mainly unregulated private enterprises. They were free to design the kinds of products they pleased, subject to product acceptance. Marketing practices were also free from control, and pricing policies, depending on the size of the company, were geared to provide a high return on capital, based on a standard volume concept. But now, business firms are subject to detailed government regulations in which almost all phases of design, marketing, management, and at times even pricing policies are responses to specifications laid down in Washington. Therefore, the subject of business-government relations is even more important to students because there is an enormous interaction between these two major institutions in American society, and it is necessary to establish a framework within which a discussion of this interaction can take place.

*William DeLancey, president, Republic Steel Corporation, "The Federal Presence in Steel," speech delivered at Cold Finished Bar Institute Annual Meeting, Washington, D.C., December 4, 1975, pp. 2–3.

Chapter 1
The Influence of Government on Business

To use a botanical analogy, government and business are two genera of the social and economic system of the United States. Each of these genera contains species, such as federal, state, and local political bodies in the case of government, and corporations, partnerships, and proprietorships in the case of business. Sometimes there are even hybrid species, joint government/business or public/private enterprises such as the Communications Satellite Corporation (COMSAT). There is an interrelationship between these two genera because government provides the institutional foundation on which business rests, the legal framework within which it functions, and many of the instruments through which its activities are carried out. The economic system within which business functions is also shaped by government, and its performance depends on decisions that are made by government. The system's expectations of profit or loss depend to some extent on the policies adopted by central banking authorities to control the volume of credit and on the policies pursued by the federal government to balance its budget, to accumulate a surplus, or to run a deficit.

To be more specific, government relates to business in at least the following ways: it regulates the particular functions of all businesses, such as competition, foreign trade, product safety, the issuance and sale of securities, labor relations, and the impact of a business on the environment. Government participates in the management of the so-called public utilities by regulating entry, service, output, investment, prices, and other variables of the utilities' operation. Government also sells or regulates a wide variety of goods and services, including postal services, nuclear fuel, electricity, and police and fire protection. It taxes business, and it makes business a collector of taxes such as those levied on alcohol, gasoline, and tobacco. In addition, it purchases many kinds of equipment, supplies, goods, and services from business. Government also subsidizes some business enterprises, particularly those connected with farming and shipbuilding, and finances other enterprises through direct loans, loan guarantees, and insurance. Finally, and perhaps most important, government attempts to stabilize the economic environment within which business must operate through its use of fiscal and monetary policies.

3

The government's participation in America's business life has grown enormously. From the beginning of the republic in 1787, the federal government has been interested in promoting manufacturing, and it soon passed tariff laws to protect American business interests. Subsidies were used to develop canals, roads, and various forms of transportation, from which business benefited directly. As industrialization and business concentration increased, the government passed laws to regulate specific segments of business, for example, railroads, or to control business practices. This trend began in the latter part of the last century and continued, with some interruptions, until 1940. After World War II, government participation in business took the form of increasing consumption of a wide variety of goods and services, the bulk of which have been items considered essential for the national defense. One result of this process is that many industries and enterprises have become dependent on government spending.

In recent years in American society there has been a shift in emphasis from market to political decisions, largely in response to the increase in societal problems. Not much more than a decade ago, most business firms were largely unregulated, free to produce whatever kinds of products they pleased, as long as consumers would accept them. Today, these firms are subject to detailed government regulations in almost all phases of their operations. One example of this is the controversial affirmative action programs set in motion by the federal government, which apply to business firms and unions alike. Protection of the environment is another area in which the government has encroached on the activities of most business firms. The prime example of this is the automobile industry, which must now comply with emission control standards that require a radical reduction in the amount of hydrocarbons and carbon monoxide emitted by motor vehicles. Safety standards require automobile designers to accommodate various restraints, including seat belts and buzzer systems, and specifications for brakes, safety glass, and the padding of bumpers. Government constraints on business can be expected to increase in the future in accordance with new social and ideological demands.

For the purpose of organization, government intervention and participation in the American economy can be divided into four areas, which provide the subject matter of the remainder of this chapter. First, there is public finance, in which government is a purchaser of goods and services as well as a tax collector. Government economic stabilization policies may also be considered a part of this area. Second, government regulation and control prescribe specific conditions under which private business activity can or cannot take place. Government may interpose itself as a part of management in certain industries, such as public utilities, and regulate rates and the provision of services. It may also influence private business operations both directly and indirectly through antitrust and other laws. Third, government is the single largest employer in the American economy and, as such, competes directly with private industry for labor. The government also affects the level of wages and salaries. Fourth, government owns and operates business enterprises and is a major provider of credit. In fact, few, if any, changes in the market structure of the American economy have as much social and political significance as does this movement of government into areas previously reserved for private enterprise.

THE ROLE OF PUBLIC FINANCE

Public finance is the clearest and probably the most important example of the extent of government participation in the "mixed" economy of the United States. Taxes give the government control over the nation's resources and also affect the distribution of income. Government expenditures for goods and services divert resources from the private to the public sector of the economy. Through its own expenditures, the government has literally created business firms and whole industries, has conducted much of the basic research in certain industries, and has given impetus and direction to technological change. Indeed, the direct subsidies and indirect benefits offered business by government are too numerous to mention. In addition, preferential tax treatment is accorded to some firms and industries. So great is the impact of taxes and so great are the benefits of favorable tax treatment that businesses take great interest in and attempt to influence the writing of tax legislation. Examples of special tax treatment include the investment credit, depletion allowances, and accelerated depreciation.

The importance of the public sector to business can be explained in three ways. First, there is the general level of government expenditures and taxation in relation to the gross national product. Economists prefer, however, to use changes in the share of the gross national product taken off the market by the government rather than total government expenditures as a guide to the public sector's economic influence. Second, there is the actual composition of expenditures and taxes. For example, direct government expenditures for goods and services would have an impact on business different from that exerted by transfer payments, which return no equivalent value in either products or services. The composition of taxes is also important and in recent years more attention has been paid to the role of tax policies in promoting economic growth. Third, there has been a general acceptance of public policy measures designed to maintain a high level of employment, economic growth, stable prices, and other economic and social goals. Both fiscal and monetary policies have thereby come to be important to the management of the American economy.

The Level of Expenditures and Taxation

The importance of the federal government's budget to the business community cannot be overemphasized. The budget exerts an influence on the national economy and also on business regarding the level of expenditures and taxes, whether or not it is balanced, and the specific expenditures and taxes it authorizes. The federal budget tends to be the focal point of the presentation and implementation of the government's economic policy, and it is often used as a means of publicizing the government's policies toward particular sectors, groups of people, or industries, either in an attempt to improve the chances of success of the proposed measures or, at times, as a substitute for any specific measures. Moreover, the budget can be used to alter the level of economic activity. Taxes represent a withdrawal of income from the income stream, whereas government expenditures represent an injection of income into it.

The significance of the federal budget can be measured by its size in relation to the gross national product. Budgetary receipts for 1981 are estimated at $607.5 billion, and expenditures are estimated at $662.7 billion.[1] Most of these receipts come from many different tax sources. When these tax revenues are compared to the estimated gross national product for 1981 of around $2.8 trillion, it is apparent that the federal budget diverts around 20 percent of the gross national product from the private to the public sector. The budgetary outlays of around $663 billion take the form of direct expenditures for goods and services, most of which are provided by business firms, and of transfer payments and subsidies of various types, many of which also benefit business firms. Government purchases of goods and services also directly increase the total demand for output in the economy; government transfer payments and taxes exert a more indirect influence on total demand.

State and local government taxes and expenditures also have to be considered. In 1980, for example, total receipts, including taxes, for all levels of the government amounted to $834 billion, and total expenditures amounted to $869 billion. (However, some of the state and local government receipts are federal grants-in-aid.) In the same year, total government purchases of goods and services came to $534.8 billion, in comparison with a gross national product of $2.6 trillion. Of the total $534.8 billion, federal government expenditures for goods and services accounted for $198.9 billion, and state and local government expenditures accounted for $335.9 billion. It can be said that in regard to the actual purchase of goods and services, state and local governments have more of an impact on business than the federal government does.

---

1. *Economic Report of the President 1981* (Washington, D.C.: U.S. Government Printing Office, 1981), p. 315.

The economic influence of the public sector has intensified steadily throughout this century and has become particularly pervasive during the last thirty years. To some extent, this increase in influence can be attributed to a growing acceptance of the government's taking charge of public welfare. But in fact, government expenditures for the national defense have been the most important single factor in the growth of public expenditures during the last three decades. Indeed, in 1980 this type of expenditure accounted for about 25 percent of the total purchases of goods and services by all government units. Economic growth has also spurred a trend toward urban living. As a larger proportion of the nation's population has concentrated in urban areas, the inevitable result has been a greater demand for services that must be provided through the public sector. Increased industrialization has changed the size and complexity of business enterprises, and the government's regulatory operations have had to be expanded. But regardless of the causes, the growth of both the absolute and the relative importance of the public sector is clear, as Table 1-1 indicates. (The table excludes government transfer payments to individuals and business firms.)

Table 1-1 Government Expenditures on Goods and Services Compared to Gross National Product for Selected Years

Year	Gross National Product (billions of $)	Government Expenditures on Goods and Services (billions of $)	Federal (billions of $)	State and Local (billions of $)
1929	103.4	8.8	1.4	7.4
1933	55.6	8.0	2.0	6.0
1939	90.8	13.5	5.2	8.3
1945	211.9	82.3	74.2	8.1
1950	284.8	37.9	18.4	19.5
1960	506.0	100.3	53.7	46.6
1970	982.4	218.9	95.6	125.2
1975	1,528.8	338.4	123.1	215.4
1977	1,899.5	396.2	144.4	251.8
1978	2,127.6	435.6	152.6	283.0
1979	2,388.5	476.1	166.3	309.8
1980	2,627.4	534.8	198.9	335.9

Source: *Economic Report of the President 1981* (Washington, D.C.: U.S. Government Printing Office, 1981), p. 233.

The Composition of Expenditures and Taxes

The actual composition of taxes and expenditures is more important to business firms than the level of expenditures and taxes is. For example, national defense expenditures, which amounted to $117.8 billion in 1979, are very important to certain types of industries. In that year, Department of Defense expenditures for the procurement of various types of weapons amounted to $24.2 billion.[2] In addition to procurement expenditures, outlays for research and development came to around $11.9 billion.[3] Most of this expenditure helps the high technology industries. Operation and maintenance expenditures, including expenditures for ship and aircraft fuel, overhaul of ships, aircraft, other weapons, and medical supplies and services, also provide revenue for business firms.

Business firms are also the beneficiaries of other types of government expenditures, for example, shipbuilding. The cost of building a ship in the United States is about twice what it would be elsewhere, and if it were not for the subsidies and the various laws confining U.S. commercial shipping to American built and operated ships, there would be little shipbuilding in this country. Then there are the business development loans made by federal agencies at interest rates lower than those prevailing at the usual lending sources. The Economic Development Administration of the Department of Commerce offers low-cost loans to business firms that locate in areas of high unemployment.

There are many programs that directly or indirectly affect business. The federal government sponsors and encourages small businesses through the use of loans financed out of budget revenues. Housing programs, which are supported by the federal government through mortgage guarantees and subsidies, directly benefit the housing industry. Expenditures for education by all levels of government help a wide variety of industries. And certain subsidies are designed to produce more of a particular commodity than would be forthcoming if the regulation of its production were left exclusively to market forces.

The composition of taxes is important to business firms. Government expenditures are normally covered by taxes, including taxes on business, and thus, where taxes are levied determines ultimately who truly pays for government expenditures. Many of those who make public policy believe that variations in the rate of economic growth can be attributed to different tax systems. This means that tax measures designed to stimulate personal or corporate savings as well as capital intensive investment are used to accelerate growth. An example is the investment credit,

2. *The Budget of the United States Government, Fiscal Year 1979* (Washington, D.C.: U.S. Government Printing Office, 1980), p. 67.
3. Ibid., p. 77.

which has been used both in this country and abroad to stimulate investment in the capital goods industries. The investment credit, which is an inducement to increase the productive capacity of business firms, reduces the effective rate of the corporate income tax.

Taxes can be used manipulatively, granting exemptions and special tax rates to certain types of persons, corporations, or activities. An example is the corporate income tax, one of the most important taxes used by the federal government. The combined tax rate on all corporate income in excess of $100,000 is 46 percent,[4] though favorable treatment of particular types of income has been used to influence shifts in behavior. One such example is the provision in the corporate income tax law that allows firms in certain extractive industries to deduct an allowance for depletion before computing taxable income. This allowance has the effect of reducing the actual rate of taxes that these industries have to pay, one result of which is a tendency for additional capital investment to shift into this area.

Economic Stabilization Policies

It is the general consensus that the economic objectives of American society are full employment, price stability, economic growth, and a balance of payments equilibrium. Each goal is incapable of precise definition, and the attainment of one may not necessarily help achieve the others. A considerable amount of government intervention is necessary. This intervention takes two forms. First, the government sets and coordinates economic policy, and its various administrative decisions determine some of the boundaries or rules that business firms and other economic units must heed in their own planning and decision making. Second, the government participates more directly in the economy through the use of taxation and transfer payments to redistribute income and through its own purchases, which affect the allocation of resources. The growth of the public sector's economic role has made the government better able to act as the major stabilizing force in the American economy. The Employment Act of 1946 first gave congressional sanction to the idea that the federal government is responsible for the nation's level of income and employment.

Although it has many purposes, the federal budget's main intention is to provide a system of planning and control over government activities by the executive and legislative branches of government. In this respect, it is like an individual or a business budget. But, unlike the

---

4. The corporate income tax resulting from the Economic Recovery Act of 1981 is 17 percent of taxable income under $25,000 and goes up to 46 percent on incomes over $100,000.

budget of any other single economic unit, the federal budget, because of its sheer size—some $600 billion per year—exerts a potent influence on the nation's economy. And deliberately this influence is being directed more and more toward assisting the economy to attain and sustain high levels of employment and economic activity. Not only have the goals of growth and stability been incorporated into legislation such as the Employment Act of 1946, but there also has been a growing acceptance by the American public that it is both appropriate and necessary for the federal government to pursue these goals through macroeconomic instruments such as its fiscal policy, which is demonstrated by the specific content of both the tax and the expenditure sides of the budget, and its monetary policy.[5]

GOVERNMENT REGULATION AND CONTROL OF BUSINESS

The regulation and control of business is a second area in which government has become firmly entrenched. This sphere of public sector activity has developed sporadically. The demand for some form of government regulation or control arose as various crises or problems occurred. In the 1880s the trust movement threatened to envelop much of American industry, which brought about a demand for some sort of government control over the trusts, with the result that the Sherman Antitrust Act was passed in 1890. The Depression, which began with the stock market crash of 1929 and continued until the wartime mobilization of the early 1940s, was a crisis. In response, many new government agencies were created, most of which encroached in some way on the activities of business firms. By the end of the Depression, the federal government extensively regulated and controlled business. But after that time there was little increase in government intervention until the late 1960s and early 1970s when environmental protection, employment of minorities, and consumer protection became dominant issues.

Government regulation and control of business became necessary for several reasons, all of which are associated with certain failures of the market system. Over time, many industries came to be dominated by a relatively few large firms, instead of the many small firms that create the strict competitive conditions required for a pure market economy. In some cases, a single large firm or trust achieved control of a large part of an industry's productive capacity, or a few large firms were able

5. There is an indirect link between monetary policy and public finance through management of the public debt. The Federal Reserve can influence the composition of public debt through decisions concerning the types of debt to be purchased and sold in the conduct of open market operations.

to act together to achieve monopolistic control of output. Thus it follows that the results of operating under the conditions of monopoly or oligopoly can be quite different from those anticipated under the conditions that would prevail in a true market system. One reason is that firms operating under the conditions of monopoly or oligopoly have some control over output and are able, within limits, to ask a price that is not reflective of market forces.

The distribution of income and wealth can be considered a second flaw in the market system. In a purely competitive market economy, market forces are supposed to enable people to be compensated on the basis of their contributions to total output. In regard to reward for labor, those persons whose skills are scarce in relation to demand would enjoy a high level of income, whereas those persons whose skills are not scarce would not. But this concept of reward had to be modified when it became apparent that large incomes accrued to some persons not on the basis of their contributions to national output but through inherited wealth and other accidents of birth or through the exercise of special privileges. Moreover, capricious economic and social factors often impeded the most productive of individuals. The Social Darwinist concept of "survival of the fittest" made little sense when a depression caused millions of efficient and productive people to be out of work.

Finally, the market system, with its price mechanism, failed to furnish individuals or society with a satisfactory means for achieving certain wants, for example, the desire for a clean environment. Although great importance is attached to this want, it is difficult to achieve on the basis of price-cost relationships in the market. Initiative for the provision of a clean environment therefore falls to public agencies, which use controls that inevitably have a major impact on the operations of business firms. There are also certain services, such as education, that are not suitable for production and sale on a private basis and are provided by the public sector.

Because of these defects in the market, government regulation and control of economic activity has become a fact of life in the United States. Those phases of activity that have come under regulation include most forms of transportation, agriculture, public utilities and public utility holding companies, commercial and investment banking, insurance companies, monopolies and trusts, collective bargaining and other kinds of trade union activity, and the wages, hours, and working conditions of labor. In general, regulation and control of these and other areas are intended to prevent or eliminate abuses that occurred in the past as the United States evolved from a preindustrial to an industrial society. This evolution provided the historical setting for government activity in the economic realm.

Direct and Indirect Government Regulation of Business

It is necessary to differentiate between direct and indirect government regulation of business. The difference is really one of degree. In essence, the direct regulation of business makes the government part of the management of certain industries. The regulations imposed by the government restrict the managerial alternatives open to these industries. Public utilities are a case in point. They are closely regulated through rates that can be charged, areas to be served, and types of service to be provided. The rates, schedules, and routes of interstate carriers are also carefully regulated. The significance of direct regulation is that it is the government rather than private enterprise making these decisions.

The rationale for direct control is that certain types of industries vitally affect the public interest. In other words, they offer a particular type of service that is considered too important to society to be left to the vagaries of the market or to private enterprise to provide as it sees fit. An example is the provision of electric power to homes and industries, an absolute necessity if society is to function effectively. In other countries with economic systems similar to our own, industries directly affecting the public interest are owned and operated by their governments. But in the United States a natural monopoly is created instead by a state or federal government, usually when one or both of two conditions exist within an industry. First, economies of scale will occur if output is concentrated in one firm, with the result that one firm can supply the market more efficiently than two or more firms can; and second, unrestrained competition among firms in the industry is deemed by society to be undesirable. Industries included under the category of natural monopolies are transportation, electricity, gas, telephone service, and broadcasting. The government grants these industries an exclusive right to operate, in return for which the government imposes standards and requirements in the society's interest.

There are regulatory commissions on both the federal and state levels. The federal regulatory commissions are responsible for regulating public utilities and transportation in interstate commerce, and the state commissions regulate intrastate activity. The commissions carry out legislative and judicial functions under a broad grant of power from a state legislature or from Congress. They are called *independent agencies* because they are not supposed to be subordinate to any branch of government—executive, legislative, or judicial. Moreover, the federal regulatory commissions are made somewhat independent of political interference by having their members appointed for terms that extend beyond the term of the president. These commissions, of course, can exercise only powers specifically conferred on them by Congress.

Indirect regulation and control affect the character of private business operations differently than direct controls do. Laws that govern minimum wages, hours, and working conditions do not determine directly what a business firm can charge or the service it must provide. Within the constraints of these laws, business firms are free to operate as they see fit. Affirmative action programs also indirectly influence the character of business operations. Their objective is to promote the hiring and advancement of women and members of minority groups by pushing business firms in a given direction with respect to employment policies. The government's environmental protection policies force business firms to comply with certain antipollution laws that add to the cost of doing business. Nevertheless, in all these cases the business firms' basic objectives and operations are left intact; they are free to set prices, make profits, and produce what they want within the limits imposed by society.

One important area of government regulation is antitrust activity to prevent anticompetitive business practices. In general this activity has sprung from the concept that such practices interfere with the efficient operation of a competitive market economy and that the most effective method of regulation is to prevent them from occurring. Anticompetitive practices can be divided into several categories. First, there can be an industry in which a few firms are dominant and price competition is therefore minimal. Second, mergers between business firms can create an anticompetitive market situation. Third, anticompetitive business practices may entail certain types of market abuses such as price fixing and market sharing.

Government's Social Regulation of Business

Finally there is the government's social regulation of business—hiring of the handicapped, occupational safety, consumer protection, environmental protection, affirmative action, and so forth. Much of this type of regulation is the transfer of economic resources from a large number of people to a small number of beneficiaries. For example, the Occupational Health and Safety Administration's coke-oven standards protect fewer than thirty thousand workers, but it is paid for by everyone who consumes a product containing steel, that is, all of us. The Vocational Rehabilitation Act of 1973 compels employers with federal contracts of over $2,500 to take affirmative action to hire handicapped workers. Some incomes may go up as a result of social regulation, but other incomes may go down. A program designed to raise the occupational position of women and minorities automatically lowers the occupational position and income of some white males unless there is a constantly increasing real gross national product. In social regulation, there are economic pluses and minuses, with some groups winning and other groups losing.[6] Government has found it difficult to resist the temptation to do something for the benefit of some groups, even when this may be accomplished at a large cost to the rest of society.

Social regulation has changed business in several ways. There are a number of regulatory agencies whose goals are social in nature. Examples are the Equal Employment Opportunity Commission (EEOC), the Consumer Product Safety Commission (CPSC), the Environmental Protection Agency (EPA), and the Occupational Safety and Health Administration (OSHA). The rationale for these agencies is that the market system does not work to solve such problems as sex discrimination, externalities, and side effects. Pollution is an example of externalities. There was no price imposed on business for using the air or water to store or discharge its waste, and so the cost to society of polluting the air was not taken into consideration by market forces. Thus the federal government stepped in to impose regulation and to create the Environmental Protection Agency. It and other social regulatory agencies have come to have great influence on business for the simple reason that very few business firms can avoid dealing with them. Regulation has become all-pervasive, leading Senator Lloyd Bentsen of Texas to assert that "federal regulation has become America's number one growth industry," adding, "We write one page of law and get fifty pages of regulation."[7]

Social regulation also can be translated into two types of cost—paperwork and production. There is the paperwork cost of filling out government forms. Production costs include capital outlays for such items as pollution control devices and health and safety equipment, costs borne by business firms, consumers, and taxpayers. The Commission on Federal Paperwork was created by Congress in 1973 to assess and find ways to reduce government-mandated paperwork. The commission estimated that private industry spends between $25 billion and $32 billion annually on completing and filing federal reports.[8] Of these costs, approximately $15 billion is absorbed by the small business sector. There are over 4,400 different federal forms that the private sector must fill out each year, which takes an estimated 143 million hours of labor. State and local governments also have their paperwork requirements, which place an additional cost on business. Production costs, however, can be far more costly to business. In addition to capital costs, there are also personnel costs, and affirmative action, for example, may be expensive.

But we should point out that not all rules and regulations are bad. In some cases, it was necessary for the government to step in because business did not respond to such needs as safer working conditions, an

6. Lester C. Thurow, *The Zero-Sum Society* (New York: Basic Books, 1980), p. 10.
7. U.S., Congress, Joint Economic Committee, *Hearings on the 1979 Economic Report of the President* (Washington, D.C.: U.S. Government Printing Office, 1979).
8. U.S. Commission on Federal Paperwork, *Annual Report 1977*, p. 8.

improved environment, and safer products. Business had generally neglected its social responsibility and refused to consider those problems
that did not have a direct bearing on profits. Business also invited the
government to intervene in the market system when it sought controls
on costs and prices or restrictions that limited the entry of new competitors into some industries. It is ironic that business firms run to
Washington to seek protection from the Japanese and then complain
about all the mean things that the government has done to them.
Chrysler blames the government's envrionmental regulations for its inability to sell enough cars, and it and the other auto firms want import
quotas to keep out Japanese cars.

What is the optimum amount of government intervention in business
and the economy? Apparently in 1980 a majority of the American
voters believed that the optimum had been reached, as reflected in the
landslide victory of Ronald Reagan, who decried government interference in business. Economists as disparate in their views as Lester
Thurow and Murray Weidenbaum generally agree that much regulation
is wasteful and useless. Thurow, for example, questions the effectiveness and the need for most of the antitrust laws. Neither the public nor
most legislators know much about the trade-offs involved in government
regulation—the benefits received as opposed to its costs. The regulators
have no legislated incentives to use efficient means of social regulation,
and they are not subject to the competitive forces of the marketplace.
There is no punishment for mistakes made. New regulations are not
matched by the abolition of old regulations; to the contrary, old regulations persist long after they have outlived their usefulness but are held
in place by economic self-interest.

GOVERNMENT AS AN EMPLOYER

One measure of the public sector's size is the number of persons employed directly by governmental units. When the armed forces are
included, some 16 percent of the total labor force is employed directly
by the public sector, and it is likely that this percentage will increase in
the future, particularly at the state and local levels of government, since
the demand for social services is expected to increase. In addition,
numerous other jobs are related indirectly to government employment.
An army base, defense plant, or state university often supports the
economy of a whole town. In many areas, the public sector sets the
wage standards and competes against the private sector for labor
resources. But the productivity of the public sector is low in comparison with the productivity of the private sector, and as the public sector
expands relative to the private sector, productivity in general declines.
Unfortunately, many public-sector jobs are make-work and provide
little opportunity for creativity.

In the private sector, the profit and loss system encourages efficiency, and competition among business firms requires careful use of capital and other resources including labor. But both of these factors are lacking in government, for it is not in the business of making a profit or loss, nor is there a need to be competitive, because there is no competition among business units. There also is no reason to be productive: no government agency has ever gone broke. In fact, some observers have argued that agency managers are discouraged from improving production if such gains lead to budget cuts. Because the prestige of an agency manager is often measured by the number of employees the agency has, the fewer the employees, the lower its prestige is. Therefore, Congress or its state equivalent must take the place of the profit and loss system.

In a study on the federal government's productivity, Congress's Joint Economic Committee reached several conclusions.[9] First, if overall federal productivity were increased by 10 percent, personnel costs could be reduced by more than $8 billion without a cutback in services. Resources would then be free for use in the private sector. Second, the savings would be even greater if the productivity of the state and local employees were increased. Third, there is no relation between the growth of federal government employees' compensation and the growth of their productivity. The increase in the compensation of federal employees, particularly in recent years, has been quite promising, but unfortunately, it has not been accompanied by an equivalent increase in worker productivity. The Postal Service, for example, has had the highest average annual increase in yearly compensation, but one of the worst productivity records. Finally, although comparisons with the private sector are difficult to make, the available evidence suggests that productivity in the federal government sector has risen less rapidly than that in the private sector.

GOVERNMENT OWNERSHIP OF BUSINESS

Government ownership of business is quite limited in the United States in comparison with that of the other major Western industrial countries. In France, for example, the railroads, coal mines, and most of the banking system, airlines, electric power facilities, and insurance companies are state owned. The government also has a large interest in the petroleum and natural gas industries and in the production of motor vehicles and airplanes. In the United Kingdom, the coal mines, steel industry, railways, trucking, and the electric and gas industries are state owned. In Germany, government ownership is limited to the railroads, airlines,

9. U.S., Congress, Joint Economic Committee, *Productivity in the Federal Government* (Washington, D.C.: U.S. Government Printing Office, May 1979).

public utilities, and coal mines. But in all three countries, private enterprise is still dominant in that it employs by far the greatest percentage of workers and contributes the greatest part of the gross national product.

In the United States, all levels of government own and operate productive facilities of many kinds. Airports, but not railway terminals, are usually government owned. Governmental units own and operate the plants that provide water, gas, and electricity to thousands of cities and towns, as well as owning local transportation systems, heating plants, warehouses, printing companies, and many other facilities. The government also produces, either directly or indirectly, all our artificial rubber, atomic power, and many other goods, and it runs projects connected with reforestation, soil erosion, slum clearance, rural electrification, and housing. All of this does not mean that government ownership and operation is necessarily preferred to private. In many cases, the resources required were too large, the risks too great, or the likelihood of profit too small to attract private enterprise, and so the government was compelled to perform the tasks.

One example of this is the Tennessee Valley Authority (TVA), a major public enterprise for the production and distribution of electrical power in the southeastern United States. At one time, the area adjacent to the Tennessee River was among the most impoverished in the United States. Flooding and soil erosion were common, and most homes in the area were without electricity. The area was also generally unattractive to industry, and so TVA was created to erect dams and hydroelectric plants to provide electric power, to improve navigation on the Tennessee River, to promote flood control, to prevent soil erosion, to reforest the land, and to contribute to the nation's defense through the manufacture of artificial nitrates. It was opposed by private companies, in particular the utility companies, because it was empowered to sell electricity in direct competition with them, even though the utility companies in the Tennessee Valley area had never considered it profitable to provide any but the most minimal amount of service. TVA was also supposed to serve as a yardstick of efficiency, though government ownership and operation of power facilities do not always mean lower rates or greater efficiency. Opinion on TVA's efficiency is mixed: TVA is efficient compared with other government agencies, but not so compared with private business.

The federal government also owns and operates the Alaska Railroad Company. After several private railroads had gone bankrupt or had failed to run lines into the interior, in 1914 this government venture was undertaken to promote the development of the Alaskan territory. For administrative purposes, it is run by the Department of Interior. The Alaska Railroad Company owns and operates a number of minor business enterprises, but because of its low promotional rates and its sparsely populated service area, it has never been profitable; it failed even to earn its operating expenses until 1940. In more recent years, it has shown small net earnings, but these take no account of depreciation, and no interest is paid on the government investment. Nevertheless, the railroad is essential because it is the only link between sparsely populated areas and centers of population. Its importance has also increased with the discovery of oil on Alaska's North Slope.

Government credit programs are a gray area in that they do not involve outright state ownership of industry. Federal credit programs, however, do have an impact on private industry that should be mentioned. Direct, insured, and federally sponsored agency loans passed the $500 billion mark in 1980 and have continued to increase. These programs have three main functions: the elimination of gaps in the credit market, the provision of subsidies to encourage socially desirable activity, and the stimulation of the economy. The first two of these functions are microeconomic in that they are supposed to affect the types of activity for which credit is made available, the geographical location of that activity, and the types of borrowers who have access to credit. For example, Federal Housing Administration (FHA) and Veterans' Administration (VA) mortgage insurance programs have resulted in a greater demand for housing. The third function is macroeconomic in that federal lending affects the level of economic activity on a large scale, in particular, the gross national product and employment.

Federal loan insurance and guarantee programs are a key area of government involvement in credit markets. These programs, which in recent years have been growing much faster than direct federal loans and loans by federally sponsored agencies have, constitute an extremely important instrument through which the government can influence the amount and presumably the allocation of credit extended in the private market. Loan insurance generates private lending in insured areas, such as housing, by reducing the risks to which private lenders are subject. Two types of risk are reduced. The first is the risk of default, which is the risk that the borrower will not repay the loan. The second is the liquidity risk, which is the risk that market interest rates will rise during the life of the loan so that the lender will incur a capital loss if he or she sells the loan or will forgo some interest income if he or she retains it. Two types of loan insurance are used to reduce these risks: a government guarantee to pay off the loan should the borrower default and a government guarantee to buy the balance of the loan at par any time the lender requests it.

We also should mention the semipublic corporations in which ownership is divided between the private and public sectors. Examples are the Communications Satellite System (COMSAT), the Federal National Mortgage Association (Fannie Mae), the recently reorganized U.S. Postal Service, and the atomic energy program. These semipublic corporations were created for diverse reasons. COMSAT is an effort by the federal government to aid the private sector in developing a new and expensive technology, and Fannie Mae is a spin-off of a successful government activity that apparently no longer needed the special protection and aid of the government in order to survive. The reorganized postal service emerged from the failure of the public sector to perform a service efficiently, although the new service gives little evidence of functioning any better than the old one did. In the case of the atomic energy program, the federal government puts up all the money and has control over all major decisions, whereas private enterprise (General Electric) runs the nuclear facilities for a fixed fee. Workers on atomic energy projects are private employees rather than civil servants. This type of project affects the public interest and cannot be left to private enterprise to run as it sees fit.

As the scope of public enterprise broadens, it encroaches more and more on the economy as a whole. Even if government is not producing goods and services in direct competition with private industry, economic resources are being used by it. When transportation, power, housing, and large-scale credit operations come within the sphere of public activity, government is bound to have a considerable influence on the economy. Policies pursued in one field require some governmental coordination to ensure consistency in overall policy, because there are both microeconomic and macroeconomic effects on the economy. For example, federal credit programs stimulate the economy's output and income. A federal loan directly increases the purchasing power of the borrower, which can exert an expansionary effect on the gross national product. The borrower could use the entire amount of the loan to purchase newly created goods and services, and the result would be identical with an increase in government spending—a direct increase by the amount of the loan in one of the components of the gross national product. There would also be a multiplier effect: in the process of spending and respending, the loan would continue through the entire economy so that the ultimate effect would be to increase the gross national product by an amount greater than the loan.

SUMMARY

Some government intervention is necessary for the establishment of even the freest type of economic system. The very atmosphere for the conduct of business is created by the ability of government to establish and maintain private property, freedom of enterprise, money and credit, and a system of civil laws for adjudicating the private disputes of individuals. Such institutions make possible an elaborate system of private planning in which individuals, rather than the government, organize and direct the production of goods and services in response to the desires of consumers.

Government regulation of business has been established for a number of reasons. One reason is the failure of the market mechanism to allocate resources properly. When there is a breakdown in competitive market forces, monopoly, oligopoly, and otherwise imperfectly competitive market structures cause inefficient resource allocation and socially undesirable market performance. Antitrust policies are designed to deal with industry conduct, such as price fixing, and with industry structure that might foster monopolistic powers. There is also government regulation of the so-called natural monopolies—industries so large or so vital that competition is simply not feasible. Another area of regulation is the use of public resources such as air and water. There are two issues here: first, balancing the amount of tolerable pollution against the value of the goods or services produced and, second, choosing the appropriate instruments to minimize the cost of achieving this balance. Government regulation can also intervene between sellers and consumers in order to protect either or both from certain conditions that might emerge in the absence of regulation. Since research is expensive to conduct, the government itself often collects data rather than having the market participant do it. The government then uses the research data to determine whether or not a product should be available to the public. For example, it is unlawful to market certain drugs unless they have been approved by the Federal Drug Administration (FDA).

The government's intervention in the American economy during the Reagan administration may well decrease, as deregulation is one of the administration's primary goals. Former President Jimmy Carter made significant progress in deregulating certain industries—airlines, trucks, railroads, and financial institutions. The Reagan administration plans to reduce at least some of the pervasive social regulation that affects both large and small businesses. The core of the Reagan regulatory philosophy is that government intrusion in the private sector is justifiable only if it produces benefits that outweigh the costs and if the regulation chosen is the least expensive of the alternatives. This, of course, may prove difficult to do, particularly because there are so many special-interest groups, each convinced that its own benefit has been ordained by holy writ. A cumbersome federal bureaucracy may also circumvent the wishes of any president because often bureaucrats' personal interests are involved.

QUESTIONS FOR DISCUSSION

1. Discuss the various ways in which the activities of government have an impact on business.

2. Explain the reasons for the increase in the government's intervention in business affairs.
3. Government expenditures and taxes affect almost every business firm in the U.S. economy. Discuss this statement.
4. Explain the reasons for the increase in expenditures at all levels of government.
5. Too much government can hinder the efficient operation of the market economy. Discuss this statement.
6. What is meant by "interest group pluralism"?
7. There is a continuing shift from market to political decision making in the American economy. How does this affect business?
8. What is the rationale for the operation of the joint private/public type of enterprise?

RECOMMENDED READINGS

Ash, Roy L. *The Political World, Government Regulation, and Spending.* Los Angeles: International Institute for Economic Research, 1979.

Committee for Economic Development. *Redefining Government's Role in the Market System.* New York: CED, 1981.

Dunlop, John T. *Business and Public Policy.* Cambridge, Mass.: Harvard University Press, 1980.

Fox, Harrison, and Martin Schnitzer. *Doing Business in Washington.* New York: Free Press, 1981.

Haberler, Gothfried. *Challenge to a Free Market Economy.* Washington, D.C.: American Enterprise Institute for Public Policy Research, 1975.

Stigler, George. *The Citizen and the State.* Chicago: University of Chicago Press, 1975.

Thurow, Lester C. *The Zero-Sum Society.* New York: Basic Books, 1980.

U.S., Congress, Joint Economic Committee. *Productivity in the Federal Government.* Washington, D.C.: U.S. Government Printing Office, 1979.

Weidenbaum, Murray. *Business, Government, and the Public.* 2nd ed. Englewood Cliffs, N.J.: Prentice-Hall, 1980.

Winter, Ralph. *Government and the Corporation.* Washington, D.C.: American Enterprise Institute for Public Policy Research, 1978.

PART II
HISTORICAL BACKGROUND OF GOVERNMENT AND BUSINESS RELATIONS

Government regulation of business can be divided into three time periods. The first period, which is the subject of Chapter 3, lasted from 1870 to 1930. During this time, government intervention in the business sector tended to come in spurts and was essentially microeconomic in nature. This intervention was in the form of laws to regulate railroads and to curb the power of monopolies. Only when the competitive, self-adjusting market mechanism broke down did the government undertake to correct its most serious failings. The first laws to protect the interests of consumers were also passed during this period. Those laws regulating the railroads and monopolies usually were initiated by the state governments and only later by the federal government. Laws were also passed to improve the lot of laborers, particularly with respect to working conditions, and to tax income and wealth. But, for the most part, the laws directed against industrial concentration and the accumulation of wealth did not have very much effect, and by 1920 industrial concentration was more pronounced than it had been in 1880.

The second period covers the Depression of the 1930s, which was probably the most active period ever in business-government relations, and there was much legislation passed to stimulate business recovery. It was believed that certain defects in the business system were at least partly responsible for causing the Depression, and so laws regulating business were enacted in a number of areas, and the number of regulatory agencies multiplied. It was evident, when the decade of the Depression ended, that the federal government had begun extensive regulation of most segments of business activity. The Depression marked the decline of laissez faire and the advent of the mixed economy, which was reflected in increased governmental intervention in all spheres of business activity. The federal debt, which had been reduced to less than $2 billion by 1929, had increased to $40 billion by 1939. The machinery for the government's macroeconomic intervention was started during the 1930s and was completed with the passage of the Employment Act of 1946.

The third period of increased government control of business extends from roughly 1960 to the present. Prior to this period, most legislation affecting business was economic in nature. The Sherman Antitrust Act,

23

the Clayton Act, the Federal Trade Commission Act, the Robinson-Patman Act, and many other acts all dealt with specific economic issues: monopoly power, pricing, concentration of industry, and corporate economic power and its uses and abuses. The focus of more recent legislation, however, has been on the attainment of certain social goals: environmental protection, consumerism, minority employment, employment of women, job safety, and so forth. These goals are associated with a change in societal values that is characterized by the terms *rising entitlements* and *a better quality of life*. Examples of such legislation include the Clean Air Act of 1970, the Consumer Product Safety Act of 1972, and the Equal Employment Opportunity Act of 1972. This kind of legislation also has created a new type of regulatory agency that is broader based in its control over business activities and is more oriented toward accomplishing social objectives than the older regulatory agencies were. An example of this kind of agency is the Environmental Protection Agency, which can regulate any type of business that pollutes the atmosphere.

Chapter 2 provides a historical framework to explain why government intervention into business affairs became necessary. Because there was a concentration of economic power in many industries, terms like *competition* and *free enterprise* had ceased to have much meaning. In addition, there were great inequalities in the distribution of income and wealth, as there were no countervailing forces to big business. Labor unions were weak because they were denied due process under the law, and the authority of government was circumscribed by its adherence to the philosophy of laissez faire. The concentration of economic power in the hands of a few persons and corporations hindered the democratic process because it tended also to promote the concentration of political power, and many economic and political abuses ensued that worked to the detriment of the country's social welfare. These abuses angered the farmers, consumers, and small business owners, who felt at a disadvantage in comparison with big business, trusts, and the eastern banks. Organized pressure from these groups was the catalyst that eventually resulted in government intervention in the form of railroad regulation and action against the industrial monopolies.

Chapter 2
The Growth of Industrial Capitalism in the United States

This chapter and the two following it offer the historical background necessary to understand the reasons for government intervention into business affairs. Once this background has been presented, it will be possible to explore in some detail the role of government in the business world of today. It can be said that government and business relations as they existed in the late 1970s have followed a process of evolution that began in the last century as the United States began its transformation from an agrarian to an industrial society. Following the Civil War, industry became increasingly complex, and mass production techniques enabled producers to expand their output. The industrial capitalist began to rise above those who were so much a part of the American economy before that war—merchants, shippers, farmers, and small-scale artisans. The economic pendulum, which before the Civil War had favored competition among a large number of sellers, swung over to the large-scale industrial enterprise with an ever-increasing need for capital. Various business abuses followed that contributed to a decline in competition and an increase in the economic power of the large-scale business unit. Government regulation of business became an inevitable concomitant of these abuses.

In general, societies have numerous ways of organizing and performing their production functions. In economic and political terms, the possible range is from laissez faire capitalism through totalitarian communism. The American economy of today is by no means a pure laissez faire capitalist system but rather is a mixed capitalist system, since there are public enterprises, considerable government regulation and control, and various other elements that hinder the unrestrained functioning of market forces. But to understand how a capitalist system works, it is necessary to know something about its institutional arrangements.

CAPITALISM AS AN ECONOMIC SYSTEM

There are a variety of names used to describe an economic system that relies extensively on market arrangements. One is *free enterprise market economy*, a name suggesting that economic decisions are freely made by individuals without direct orders from others, including those who operate collectively in the guise of government. The essential element of free enterprise is the freedom of the individual to buy goods and services and to own and organize the means of production for private gain. Freedom of enterprise also refers to the right of individuals to select their own occupations or to invest their capital in whatever enterprise they choose. There is a libertarian element in this system that is easy to reconcile with the development of political democracy in the United States and in Western Europe, though self-interest, the profit motive for the entrepreneur, and the maximization of income for the workers and their families have probably been even stronger rationales for freedom of enterprise.

Another name for a market economy is *capitalism*, a term emphasizing the importance of private nongovernmental ownership of the agencies of production and also indicating the existence of certain rights of persons who own property. An individual has the right to acquire property, to consume or control it, to buy and sell it, to give it away as a gift, and to bequeath it at death. Private property encourages accumulation and serves as a stimulus to individual initiative, both essential to economic progress. In addition to private ownership of property, there are other institutional arrangements: profit—the paramount motive keeping people competing to organize production and supply the market—the price system, and consumer power which, when expressed in the marketplace, affects what and how much will be produced.

The Profit Motive

The kinds of goods produced in an economy that relies on market arrangements is determined in the first instance by managers of business firms who are directly responsible for converting resources into products and determining what those products will be, guided, of course, by the actions of consumers in the marketplace. The profit motive is the lodestar that draws managers to produce goods that can be sold at prices that are high in relation to the costs of production. In private enterprise, profit is necessary for survival; anybody who produces things that do not, directly or indirectly, yield a profit will sooner or later go bankrupt, lose ownership of the means of production, and so cease to be an independent producer. There can be no other way. Capitalism, in other words, uses profitability as the test of whether any given thing should or should not be produced, and if it should, how much of it should be produced.

The Price System

Individuals and business firms under capitalism are supposed to make most types of economic decisions on the basis of prices, price relationships, and price changes. The function of prices is to provide a coordinating mechanism for millions of decentralized private production and distribution units. Usually the prices that prevail in the marketplace determine what kinds and quantities of goods should be produced and how they should be distributed. Price changes are supposed to adjust the quantities of goods that the buyers are willing to purchase to the quantities of these goods available for the market. It is through the mechanism of prices, rather than through a comprehensive national economic plan, that scarce resources are allocated to various uses. The interaction between the price system and the pursuit of profits is supposed to keep economic mistakes down to a reasonable level. Profits, which depend on the selling price of goods and the cost of marketing them, indicate to business firms what people are buying. A product that commands high prices draws business firms into that industry; low prices check production by causing business firms to drop out. In general the conditions of supply and demand determine price and guide production. A small supply raises price, and a large supply lowers price.

Consumer Sovereignty

In countries operating with a market economy, consumers are important because their preferences in the marketplace decide what and how much will be produced. These preferences will be expressed through the price mechanism that operates on supply and demand for goods and services. In a capitalistic system, any consumer can obtain almost any good produced if he or she is able and willing to pay for it. If consumer demand for color television sets is great relative to the supply, prices will be higher than costs of production, and in response to demand, existing firms will expand, new firms may choose to enter the market, and eventually, the output of color television sets will be equal to the demand. But if consumer demand is for less than the existing supply of television sets, prices will fall below costs, firms will stop producing sets, and supply eventually will adjust to demand.

But consumers are unequal in their ability to bid for goods and services, because incomes are not distributed equally. The question "For whom are goods produced?" is resolved by the price system operating in the marketplace. Some consumers have more money than others and can bid higher for certain goods. Because this may seem unfair, it should be pointed out that in a capitalist free market system, supply and demand largely determine the distribution of income to individuals.

Labor, as an agent of production, is rewarded according to its productivity. If it is scarce in relation to the demand for it, then its productivity is high and it can command a large income; if it is abundant relative to demand, then its productivity and income will be low.

Modifications of Capitalism

For many years, the idea persisted that the government in a capitalist system, however it might be organized, should follow a policy of laissez faire with respect to economic activity. That is, its activities should be limited to the performance of a few general functions for the good of all citizens, and it should not attempt to control or interfere with the economic activities of private individuals. Laissez faire assumes that individuals are more or less rational beings and better judges of their own interests than any government could be.[1] The interests of individuals are closely identified with those of society as a whole, and the individuals in the system, in relentlessly pursuing their own ends, contribute, whether or not they are aware of it, to the maximization of the social welfare. The government needs only to provide a setting or environment in which these institutions can operate freely. This the government was supposed to do by performing only those functions that individuals could not do for themselves—to provide for the national defense, maintain law and order, and construct roads, schools, and public works.

The advanced capitalist economies of today represent a radical departure from laissez faire. In the operation of capitalist economies, problems have arisen that seemed impossible for private individuals to resolve and whose impact on their lives necessitated governmental intervention. As a result, government regulation is a fairly common feature of economic life under capitalism. Consumers are not left to depend entirely on competition to furnish them with foods and drugs of acceptable quality and purity; there are laws that provide certain standards in these matters. Nonetheless, capitalistic societies have never been willing to extend complete freedom of enterprise to any individual; that is, it has always been recognized that an individual selecting the field of activity that would be most profitable might well choose something antisocial. In such cases, government has not hesitated to step in with restrictions. In general, government intervention is intended to prevent or eliminate abuses and to enable the capitalistic system to operate more nearly like the ideal, theoretical model.

1. The term *laissez faire* originated in France, possibly as early as the first half of the eighteenth century, and was later developed by Adam Smith as a rule of practical economic conduct. See Adam Smith, *The Wealth of Nations* (London: T. Nelson & Sons, 1891), bk. IV, especially p. 286. Laissez faire was a reaction to the stringent government restrictions imposed in earlier times by mercantilism.

THE INDUSTRIAL DEVELOPMENT OF THE UNITED STATES

The years between the Civil War and World War II saw the introduction and growth of government as a regulator of business. Before the Civil War, the United States was largely a nation of small businesses and farms. The business units were small and were usually owned by individuals or small groups of persons, and business enterprises generally found their outlets in trade, banking, land speculation, mining, and transportation ventures such as canals, turnpikes, and railroads. The modern factory system with its automatic machinery, standardized products, rationalization of operations, and wage labor was just beginning to make its appearance, and government intervention in the economy was minimal. At the federal level, the government was responsible only for the national defense, the postal service, tax collection and tariff administration, the mint, land grants, and other rather specialized areas of activity. State governments regulated banks, levied taxes, and made loans to business firms for various types of ventures, including canal building.

The Influence of the Civil War on Industrial Development

The Civil War was important for several reasons. First, it marked a turning point in the economic development of the United States. The war hastened the coming of the Industrial Revolution, gave unionism its real beginning, and greatly increased agricultural productivity. For the North, victory meant the establishment of public policies favorable to the rising financial and industrial interests, and a precedent was set for direct federal intervention in the economy when an income tax was imposed for the first time. For the South, defeat meant the change of its entire economic system: the dominant planter aristocracy was overthrown, and slavery was abolished. Although industrial development there was retarded for a long period after the Civil War, the South was eventually able to develop a much more diversified economy than had existed before the war.

During the Civil War, northern business firms began to prosper from the stimulus of increased government expenditures, and both agriculture and manufacturing benefited from an unusual demand for goods and services both at home and abroad. The industries that led in the expansion were those most closely related to war activities—munitions, iron, canvas goods, locomotives and all types of railroad equipment, food, and clothing. Wartime needs led to the use of production methods that hastened large-scale mass production, with the attendant danger that the developing American industries would overextend themselves and still be unable to compete with established European producers. Therefore, these industries were protected by tariffs granted by Congress. When the war was over, the factories and mills that had been producing for the war effort were converted to providing goods for civilian consumption. As has always been the case in time of war, civilian goods were in short supply and had to be replenished after the war was over.

One area of direct government intervention in the economy was in the financing of the war. The North resorted to extremely heavy taxation: the first federal income tax was imposed during the war but was repealed in 1870.[2] The income tax was first levied at a rate of 3 percent on all incomes over $800 per year. By 1865, the personal exemption had been lowered to $600, and the rate of taxation rose to 10 percent on incomes over $5,000. In 1817, the federal government had discontinued the use of excise taxes, but an act in 1861 imposed low and moderate taxes on a large number of items rather than high taxes on a few luxuries and necessities for which the demand was unchanging. These excise taxes were also levied on business firms, including railroads, banks, and insurance companies. The federal government also borrowed over $2 billion through the issuance and sale of bonds. Various banking houses benefited particularly from the purchase and sale of these bonds. Revenues were also derived from the sale of public lands and from the printing of paper money. The Civil War greatly increased the role of government in the economy and established a precedent for later intervention.

Development of Industry, 1860–1900

Industrialization after the Civil War accelerated. In 1860, for example, the value of pig iron output in the nation was $20.9 million; by 1870 its value had increased to $55.7 million, and in 1880, its value was $89.3 million.[3] Capital invested in manufacturing increased from $1.1 billion in 1860 to $2.8 billion in 1880. The value of manufactured

2. The primary difficulty centered on the question of whether legally the income tax was direct or indirect. In 1872 the Civil War tax was held to be indirect and thus valid, though the need for the tax had passed. A direct tax would have been unconstitutional if not apportioned among the states according to population. As a consequence, the Sixteenth Amendment was enacted in 1913 to give Congress the right to levy taxes on incomes without apportionment on the basis of population.
3. These data come from Louis M. Hacker, *The Triumph of American Capitalism* (New York: Simon & Schuster, 1940), app. A, pp. 437–438. There was no inflation in the American post–Civil War economy; therefore, rise in value reflects rise in output.

products tripled during this time period. Agriculture, too, was undergoing a process of mechanization and expansion; the increasing emphasis on cash crops helped provide exportable goods from which to pay interest and dividends on the imported capital that was furthering industrial growth. In 1860 the value of manufactured agricultural implements was $20.8 million; by 1880 their value had increased to $68.6 million.

The impetus for industrial development continued unabated during the rest of the century. As a result of the greater industrial productivity, the national wealth increased and the standard of living rose. There were many factors favoring industrial development in the United States, not the least of which was an abundance of natural resources. Other important factors were the opening up and development of the West, an abundance of capital, particularly foreign, and an increase in the labor supply, mainly through immigration.

The Opening of the West

The opening of the West to settlement was of paramount importance to industrial development. In 1860 the great area between the Mississippi River and the frontiers of California and Oregon contained only 1 percent of the nation's total population. But by the end of the century, the region was largely settled, the decisive factor in its development being the transcontinental railroads which facilitated the westward movement of settlers and the marketing of produce and raw materials. The West provided a ready-made market for the products of industry, and agricultural machinery, barbed wire, and other types of steel products were shipped westward from mills and factories based in Chicago and Pittsburgh. New industries, based on cattle and minerals, also sprang up in the West. For two decades after the Civil War, the cattle industry was dominant in the area from Texas to Montana. With the expansion of the cattle industry, the meat-packing industry moved westward, with centers at Chicago, St. Louis, Kansas City, and Omaha. The mining industry, aided by the transcontinental railroad linking the West to the East, also grew when deposits of silver, gold, and copper were found in Nevada, Arizona, and Montana. Mining created a demand for specialized equipment such as steam turbines and dynamos, and the cattle and mining industries contributed to the railroads' increased need for locomotives and rolling stock.

The opening of the West also spurred the development of agriculture. The expanded area under cultivation raised the need for mechanization, and the greater use of scientific methods of farming contributed to productivity. Federal land policies also encouraged the settlement of the West. The Homestead Act, passed in 1862, gave a farmer the right to obtain title to 160 acres of public land merely by living on it for five years and cultivating it.[4] The western regions lent themselves to large-scale farming, and industry benefited from the need for various sorts of machines. New inventions were introduced, the most important of which were the Marsh Harvester, patented in 1858, which cut reaping time in half, and the twine binder, invented in 1878, which increased eightfold the speed of harvesting. But mechanization was something of a mixed blessing: although it increased farm income and output, it also made it more difficult for persons with little capital to go into farming, and it encouraged overproduction.

Capital Investments

Capital investment expenditures are very important because of their impact on an economy's productive capacity: investment expenditures provide for the acquisition of capital goods, the procreative element in any industrial society. The function of capital goods is to produce other goods and services. Capital is necessary for determining the rate of economic growth, which depends to a great degree on how rapidly productive capacity is being expanded. An increase in capital not only raises productive capacity but also creates income and employment in the process. This is true because capital goods are purchased in the market and income and employment are created when they are produced. But even though capital helps maintain the level of employment, the higher the rate of growth of capital is, the greater productive capacity becomes, and the more difficult it becomes to attain full employment and full capacity production. Business recessions became a more and more familiar phenomenon in the period between 1860 and 1900.

In the United States the market for capital funds grew very slowly before 1860, but the Civil War stimulated the expansion of the investment market, and additional facilities were needed for the transfer of funds from savers to borrowers as industry expanded and the government struggled to finance the war. After the war was over, new markets for capital investment were created by the development of the West's resources. A rapidly increasing population also offered almost unlimited opportunities for capital investment. To some extent the United States was in the same position as Brazil is today—having many resources waiting to be developed, a growing population, and a government favorably disposed toward industrial development. The United States became a huge free-trade market area, in which domestic producers were

4. The significance of the Homestead Act has been overrated. Much of the best land in the West had already been given to the railroads or purchased by land companies.

protected from foreign competition through government support, which took the form of tariffs and trade barriers, at the same time that American manufacturers were also able to build up an export market.

At first American investors were unable to meet the demand for capital, and until the twentieth century, foreign investors contributed most of the money required for the United States' economic development. Without large amounts of foreign capital the railroads could not have been built as rapidly as they were: though the profits realized by American businesses were large, they were not enough to meet the demand of the railroads for capital, which also supplied an outlet for the investment of foreign funds. European capitalists and capitalist institutions were interested in finding investment outlets for their loanable funds that would return higher rates of interest than they received from domestic investments. In most cases, portfolio rather than direct investments were made. It has been estimated that a total of $400 million in American securities was owned by foreign sources in 1860; the figure had risen to $1.4 billion in 1869 and to $4.0 billion by the end of the century.[5] In addition to stimulating railroad development, foreign capital also contributed to the growth of the mining and steel industries. But foreign investment also was partly responsible for the United States' becoming a debtor nation, a position that it did not relinquish until World War I.

Immigration

Capital is not the sole source of economic growth; labor, too, is important, as no industrial development is possible without an adequate supply of labor. And an abundant labor supply was available during this period of industrial development, for millions of immigrants came to the United States from all over Europe in the hope of finding a better life, though for many this expectation did not materialize. From 1860 to 1900 the population of the United States increased from 31.4 million to 76.0 million. Of this increase of 44.6 million, the natural increase in the population accounted for 29.5 million and immigration for 15.1 million. This immigration continued unabated until 1920 when quotas were set to restrict the influx of foreigners, particularly Asians, into this country. From 1860 to 1920 the total increase in the U.S. population amounted to 74 million persons, of which the natural increase accounted for 45 million and immigration for 29 million.[6]

5. Hacker, *The Triumph of American Capitalism*, p. 402.
6. U.S. Department of Commerce, Bureau of the Census, *Historical Statistics of the United States, Colonial Times to 1957* (Washington, D.C.: U.S. Government Printing Office, 1960), pp. 8, 56.

Immigration also contributed to the natural increase, since the American-born children of immigrants were counted as part of the natural increase total.

Immigration provided a large, continuous flow of cheap, unskilled labor that was used to build roads, railroads, and homes for an expanding population and to run the mills and factories of a rapidly growing industrial system.[7] The majority of immigrants were unskilled or became unskilled workers who not only facilitated industrial expansion but also provided a cushion of labor for agriculture during periods of depression. They accepted wages and jobs that native workers would not, and in their extreme poverty and ignorance of anything better, they became prey to exploitation. Their low wages kept labor costs low in relation to other costs and enabled business firms to earn increased profits, a part of which went into the savings necessary for capital formation. In assessing the contribution of the immigrants during the period from 1860 to 1920, it can be said that their economic contribution was the creation of reserves of cheap, unskilled labor and the expansion of the consumer market.

Other Factors Contributing to Industrial Development

The Civil War encouraged the development of manufacturing in the United States, for peace brought prosperity and an industrial boom to the North and caused the South to turn its attention to manufacturing. As was true again in the post–World War I period, economic prosperity ushered in a series of innovations and inventions that influenced industrial development. Thomas Edison invented his phonograph in 1877 and his electric lamp in 1878. Numerous other patents during this period also pertained to electricity, laying the foundation for the coming electric age. Already in 1880 there were more than 70 plants in the United States manufacturing electric apparatus and supplies. Alexander Graham Bell's telephone and George Westinghouse's air brake led to other new industries. By 1880, there were 148 telephone companies in operation, with 34,000 miles of wire and 59,000 receiving stations. The technical advances made in this period made possible greater productivity, better quality, and the standardization of products. In fact, by 1880, standardized interchangeable parts were commonly used for much machinery, and standardized products were being manufactured in abundance.

7. Immigrants employed in industry were concentrated in the mining and manufacturing industries. In 1910, male foreign-born workers constituted 48 percent of all male workers in coal mining, 65 percent in copper mines, 46 percent in meat packing, 67 percent in iron mining, 76 percent in the clothing factories, 51 percent in blast furnaces and steel rolling mills, and 49 percent in textile mills.

INDUSTRIAL CONSOLIDATION AND THE DECLINE OF COMPETITION

The period from the end of the Civil War to around 1890 can be called the golden age of laissez faire capitalism. Business had just about everything its own way. The government, in particular the federal government, did nothing to intervene until business abuses of the market system became so prevalent that intervention in some form became necessary. Business, after a period of fierce competition, was characterized not only by the rise of the corporation as the dominant business unit but also by the growth of large-scale production and the beginning of business combinations. These combinations, of which the trust was the most important, were organized to eliminate competition and to regulate output and thereby stabilize prices, control production, and acquire greater profit. They were united under one central management of a large number of production units either turning out the same product or operating different stages of the process necessary to prepare the final product for market.

The growing concentration of economic power also created another problem—extremes of poverty and wealth. The new aristocracy of the country was made up of wealthy entrepreneurs and business leaders whom some called *robber barons.* The prototypes of the industrial capitalists were John D. Rockefeller and Andrew Carnegie. They epitomized the Protestant work ethic, successful in a competitive race in which victory went to the swift and resourceful. They also were not particularly scrupulous, taking advantage of every loophole, corrupting government officials, and bribing rivals' employees in a no-holds-barred effort to ruin competitors. But they were supported by a philosophy that helped explain and justify their preeminent position—the philosophy of Social Darwinism. To put it simply, Social Darwinism was the application of Darwin's biological theory to economics.[8] It was the "survival of the fittest" principle applied to the business world. The Carnegies and the Rockefellers reached their positions through a competitive selection process, proved themselves the fittest, and were therefore entitled to the fruits of their labor. Society was the beneficiary of their efforts. Social Darwinism opposed government intervention in the operation of the economy and upheld industrial capitalism as a system in which each contributing group received a just reward.

There is some merit in Social Darwinism. Carnegie, Rockefeller, and others of their type possessed certain attributes that encouraged

8. Social Darwinism was conceived by the English philosopher Herbert Spencer. His disciples in the United States were William Graham Sumner and John B. Clark. Sumner, a professor of moral philosophy at Yale, had a particularly strong influence on American thought.

success.[9] They were energetic, shrewd, and resourceful men who worked hard and expanded their business by plowing back profits. But there also were hard-working people at the opposite end of the income spectrum. In 1890, Marshall Field's income was calculated at $600 an hour; his shopgirls, earning salaries of $3 to $5 a week, had to work over three years to earn that amount.[10] The working conditions for most of the workers were deplorable—a twelve-hour day, seven-day work week was not uncommon. Wages were low, and there was no government intervention in the form of laws designed to provide unemployment benefits, worker's compensation, or any form of social security taken for granted in the industrial societies of today. There were no child labor laws—children of eight and even younger worked in the mills and coal mines. Social and economic inequities divided the United States, and by 1890, 1 percent of the population owned as much of the nation's wealth as the entire remaining 99 percent did.

The Decline of Competition

Edward Bellamy, a social critic of the time and the author of the well-known utopian novel *Looking Backward*, offers some rather incisive insights into the industrial society that existed in the United States during the latter part of the last century.[11] He feared the consequences of the ever-increasing concentration of business in the hands of fewer and fewer individuals—individuals who were responsible neither to society nor to government. He saw that smallness was no remedy for bigness, however, and that if the concentration of business continued, government control would be the only means of protecting the public from exploitation. The following excerpt from *Looking Backward* summarizes conditions as they existed at the time:

> The next of the great wastes was that from competition. The field of industry was a battleground as wide as the world, in which the workers wasted in assailing one another, energies which, if expended in concentrated effort would have enriched all. As for mercy or quarter in this warfare, there was absolutely none of it. To deliberately enter a field of business and destroy the enterprises of those who had occupied it previously, in order to plant one's own enterprise on their

9. Hacker, *The Triumph of American Capitalism*, p. 401.
10. Cited in Otto L. Bettman, *The Good Old Days—They Were Terrible* (New York: Random House, 1974), p. 67.
11. Edward Bellamy, *Looking Backward* (New York: NAL, 1963). The main protagonist in the story is a wealthy young Bostonian named Julian West who is transported in time from the year 1887 to the year 2000. There has been a complete transformation of society during the interval.

ruins, was an achievement which never failed to command popular admiration. . . .[12]

This description of competition during the late nineteenth century was not far from the truth. Competition among companies took many forms, including physical violence. For example, an independently owned railroad, the Albany and Susquehanna, had been constructed between Albany and Binghamton, New York. One of its major objectives was to haul coal between the Pennsylvania coal fields near Binghamton and the New England users of coal beyond Albany. The line was adjacent to the territory served by the Erie Railroad, which saw the desirability of possessing the Albany and Susquehanna. First the Erie tried to buy a majority of the shares of stock in the line but failed. It then attempted through legal maneuvering to gain a clear majority on the line's board of directors but failed in this, too. The Erie finally tried by armed assault to gain control of the Albany terminus of the line but was repulsed, though it did succeed in taking the line's facilities at the Binghamton end. The Albany and Susquehanna planned to retaliate by sending out several hundred men from Albany to retake the terminus. The Erie Railroad sent out its own men from Binghamton. The trains carrying the two factions met head-on, and passengers in both trains were killed. A battle between the two groups of men ensued. The Erie group lost and retreated, tearing up tracks and bridges as they went. Only then did the Erie group give up trying to gain control of the Albany and Susquehanna.[13]

The market system, if working well, can produce many generally good results. It can play on self-interest to produce results in the interest of others. It can use the lures of profits, income, and material rewards to induce individuals and business enterprises to behave in ways that are supposed to benefit others. The market system does not, however, eliminate all the disadvantages of economic interdependence among persons and groups. At times it is a hard taskmaster, exacting heavy penalties on those who fail to conform to its demands. Thus there are not only winners under a market system but losers, too, and many manufacturers learned the hard way that competition can have the effect of reducing prices and profits. At least to some extent, the more some win, the more others lose. A business, for example, may lose its local market to a distant rival now able to compete because of a new mode of transportation. Therefore business firms began to seek ways to make sure that they, rather than someone else, were the

12. Ibid., pp. 156–157.
13. For a detailed description of this and other practices, see Matthew Josephson, *The Robber Barons* (New York: Harcourt, Brace, & World, 1934). The Erie Railroad was controlled by the Erie Ring, a combination put together by Jay Gould.

winners. In the absence of laws and government regulation to force them to play the free enterprise game by the rules, it became easy for business firms to circumvent competition through collusive practices and various forms of combinations.

Modern technology was partly responsible for the decline of competition. As mentioned previously, there were numerous inventions after the Civil War that made possible the use of highly specialized and sometimes quite elaborate and complex machinery. Efficient ways to organize production in large units were also being discovered. One outcome of this was an increase in the average size of many businesses and a decline in the numbers of firms in many industries. Many of these larger firms had a considerable investment tied up in durable and highly specialized equipment. Interest, maintenance, and depreciation costs were incurred regularly whether or not the equipment was being used. Fixed costs were beginning to be very large and therefore very important for some firms. When the volume of output was below capacity, additional amounts of product could be produced without any increase in fixed costs and, therefore, with relatively little total additional cost. In these circumstances, the managers of these firms were eager to find ways to sell all of the output that could be produced at full capacity.

A third factor leading to the decline of competition was the business cycle. As the United States became an industrial nation, there were more and more periods of boom and bust. During a business depression, competition for survival led to falling prices and output. Business firms learned that the reductions in the price of goods they offered for sale often did not encourage consumers to buy more of them, particularly when the demand for the goods was inelastic, in other words, when a change in price was accompanied by a less than proportionate change in the quantity demanded. The small increases in the volume of sales of these goods also were accompanied by declining profits. An advantage of the business combine or monopoly was that output could be controlled and prices stabilized. Business consolidation was facilitated by the depressions. In the depression of 1893, Andrew Carnegie was able to take advantage of his competitors' economic distress to acquire a wide variety of holdings. He bought iron deposits, ore ships, ports, docks, warehouses, and railroad lines to link his coal, coke, limestone, furnaces, and mills into a single chain. The end of that depression saw the Carnegie Company, which later become the United States Steel Corporation, in control of the heavy-steel field and the fixer of prices for the finished-steel manufacturers.

Devices for Achieving Monopoly Power

The era of industrial expansion that began after the end of the Civil War resulted in two related developments important to policy. The first was a trend toward the concentration of production in the hands of a limited number of firms. This was in part a logical concomitant of changing technology: as the technically optimum size of firms grew larger, some firms went under. The high proportion of fixed costs associated with the elaborate equipment that the new technology had made possible increased the efforts of each firm to take over the market sales of other firms. In many industrial fields competition was virtually unimpaired, but in others a few enterprises came to dominate enough of the market to allow them to control prices. The second development, which had more important implications for public policy, was a trend by business firms to limit competition through various types of combinations designed to promote monopoly power.

These combinations usually came in cycles. The first cycle, which lasted roughly from 1870 to 1890, used the pool and the trust as monopoly devices.[14] The pool was devised first but was superseded by the trust, which proved to be a more effective type of combination. A wave of federal and state antimonopoly legislation, culminating with the Sherman Antitrust Act, made the trust a rather unpopular vehicle for combination. The trust began to decline in popularity, and by the end of the last century the holding company had achieved dominance. The second cycle was the period of the holding company. There was an intensive phase of consolidation facilitated by the holding company device that lasted from 1897 to 1903. A third cycle of industrial combination occurred during the 1920s, when mergers in the form of holding companies or outright mergers between companies were used to consolidate and reduce the number of firms in new industries such as radios, automobiles, and electrical appliances. The fourth cycle of the combination movement came after the end of World War II and continued into the 1950s and was characterized by horizontal and vertical merger arrangements.

We should emphasize that the results of various business combinations were often disappointing. There were many reasons for this. Combinations were unable to increase profits or even to perpetuate them in industries that were subject to stagnation, but on the other hand, accelerated growth in a new industry created an industrial climate in which combinations were able to prosper. Industrial combinations were also affected by the vagaries of the business cycle and were often incapable of forestalling sharp decreases in profits in years of general business depression. When combinations acquired unmanageable financial structures that subjected them to fixed charges above their minimum earnings capacity, they were often unable to adapt themselves readily to new situations. Many of the earlier combinations were made up of equal producers who sought to curb the excesses of cutthroat

14. The terms *pool* and *trust* are discussed on p. 40.

competition by allocating production and fixing prices; sooner or later, however, most such arrangements ended in failure because one of the participants violated the agreements. The large corporation had to appear first, based on horizontal and vertical integration, before combinations could be really effective. Finally, combinations did not automatically guarantee competent management.

Pools

The pool was used widely in the 1870s among the railroads and in some manufacturing companies. Under this arrangement, all or most of the producers of some good or service reached an agreement, usually informally, to share customers, sales, profits, or territories in some fashion. In this way, they hoped to avoid price reductions and the more ruthless kinds of competition among themselves. Pooling arrangements took a number of forms. Two railroads could decide to divide freight revenues evenly, regardless of which one actually transported the freight. For example, in the 1870s, the five or six railroads that controlled the shipment of anthracite coal in the five counties of northeastern Pennsylvania divided the total shipment among themselves. Some pools attempted to corner the market for a given product, though too often, pooling agreements were violated soon after their initiation when one or more of the parties would find it irresistible to undercut the others. There also were other reasons for the short duration of the pools. There was competition from a large number of small firms operating in local markets that made pooling agreements ineffective, and the pools could not adapt rapidly to changing market conditions.

Trusts

In the 1880s trusts came to replace or exist alongside pools as the primary means for eliminating competition. Under a trust arrangement, owners of a controlling interest in all or most of an industry's firms would agree to entrust their ownership shares to the control of one or a few people, called trustees, and to receive trust certificates in return. These certificates were issued on the basis of the amount of stock held in trust, and the board of trustees controlled the business policies of the combination. The trustees would direct all firms in the trust as though they were one large firm. With monolithic power, they confronted the competition. They maximized profits, not by being best, but by being biggest. Trusts had a highly centralized form of management in which the trustees were able to elect members of the board of directors of the operating companies whose common stock was deposited with them.

Although the trust eventually gave way to other arrangements, it first gave its name to the general government campaign against monopolies.

The trust par excellence was the Standard Oil Trust formed in 1879, forever to be associated with John D. Rockefeller. By 1884, Standard Oil was selling more than 80 percent of all the oil that flowed out of domestic wells. It controlled not only the refining of petroleum but also its retail sales. The trust was organized to eliminate competition at these two levels of operation. In areas in which the competition with the products of other oil companies was keen, the trust reduced the retail prices of its products in order to attract customers from competing retailers. In many cases, these outlets were unable to compete and sold out to Standard Oil. In areas in which there was no competition, Standard Oil would charge artificially high prices. The trust also tried to control the transportation of petroleum. It was able to negotiate secret rebates from railroads, which were eager to carry Standard's petroleum, and it was even able to force one railroad to give it a rate of ten cents a barrel and to charge other companies thirty-five cents a barrel, of which twenty-five cents went back to Standard Oil.[15]

Holding Companies

Holding companies replaced trusts as a device to ensure the firms' survival and to prevent economic warfare among them. A holding company is a corporation that has among its assets shares of stock in other corporations. Controlled corporations are subsidiaries of the holding company, which may be a managing company or an operating company. Those who control a holding company are able through their ownership of stock in other companies to dictate business policies. Competition among companies can be controlled by the holding company. As a direct corporate entity, it can issue stock and it can borrow money through the issuance of corporate bonds. The proceeds from the sale of either or both of these types of securities have often been used to purchase common stock in other holding companies, thus creating a pyramid arrangement. In the 1920s, pyramiding corporate issues in public utility companies channeled power and control over vast corporate empires into the hands of a few utility magnates.

Mergers

The merger was another device used to eliminate competition. Mergers may take several forms. One company may purchase the physical assets

15. Ida M. Tarbell, *The History of the Standard Oil Company* (New York: McClure, Phillips, & Co., 1904).

or the shares of stock of a previously competing company. Two companies may exchange their stock, and a new company may be formed to buy up the assets or shares of two or more older companies. The General Electric Company, the American Sugar Refining Company, and the International Harvester Company all were early results of mergers. The results of mergers are similar to those of holding companies. The power to make decisions about such things as production techniques and selling arrangements is transferred to a single group of persons, among whom coordination is achieved largely by central command. The merger was somewhat impractical as a method of controlling large industries, as it required the consent of each class of security holder to the merger and involved complex negotiations on the terms of exchange.

Mergers also can be classified on the basis of horizontal and vertical arrangements. A horizontal merger is one between firms engaging in the same or similar activities—a union of railroads, bakeries, or shoe manufacturers, for example. There is nothing illegal about a horizontal merger unless it is used to restrict competition, which all too often has been the case. A vertical merger is one between firms engaging in different parts of the producing and selling process. An example would be the union of a shoe manufacturer and a shoe retail store. A steel mill could acquire a coal mine and use its entire output in its own furnace. In a vertical merger, various phases of the production and distribution process are integrated. Again, there is nothing illegal about a vertical merger unless it can be demonstrated that competition is lessened. During the last century, both types of mergers were common, and there were no laws that controlled their impact on competition. The merger arrangement itself did not guarantee success, for profits were often affected by other factors, including business recessions, over which a combination had no control.

Cartels

Cartels are international associations of firms in the same industry established to allocate world markets among their members, to regulate the prices in those markets, to eliminate competition, and to restrict output. The cartel arrangement was less a product of the time period that produced the trust and the holding company than of a later period when business firms had more global operations. Most of the cartels have been made up of companies in the production of chemicals, electrical equipment, and synthetic products like plastics. Their control is usually over the cross-licensing of patents, which has often led to worldwide control of production and trade by what almost amounts to a private government. The cartels may also control the use of trademarks, with each cartel member granted the exclusive right to use a trademark in its own territory.

Interlocking Directorates

An interlocking directorate is an arrangement in which one person sits on the board of directors of two or more companies. In a complex network of many interlocking directorates, it is possible for the interlocked firms to eliminate or reduce competition. The interlocking device has been used not only by industrial firms but also by banks. The latter would place one of their members on the board of directors of companies with which they did business, and in this way, the banks were in a position to dictate corporate policy and to regulate competition. Thus, supposedly independent firms collaborated rather than competed with each other. Although it is now illegal for one person to serve on the board of directors of two companies that produce the same goods and services, interlocking directorates are still used, with interlocks between competitors and between companies and their suppliers or customers.

Anticompetitive Business Practices

A variety of anticompetitive business practices began during the last century, and many still remain in effect. As laws were passed to correct existing abuses, new abuses would arise. Some of the devices used to eliminate competition are presented below. It should be emphasized that trusts, pools, and other monopoly arrangements were originally devised to circumvent some of the more ruthless kinds of competition. But this certainly did not mean that the trust was free from anticompetitive business practices; if anything, it refined them.

Preemptive Buying

One tactic that has been used to eliminate competition is preemptive buying. Using this technique, a company would buy up all the supplies or resources needed to make its product. The company does not necessarily need all that it buys, but in this way it can deny vital supplies to its competitors. In the last century, the Southern Pacific Railroad, in an attempt to ensure for itself a monopoly on rail transport eastward out of the state of California, bought up land and constructed rail lines in the few suitable passageways through the Sierra mountains. It did this not to provide services through these places but to block the construction of competing lines. More recently (during the 1920s and

1930s), the Aluminum Company of America (Alcoa) acted in a similar fashion. According to the government charges levied against it, Alcoa acted to acquire bauxite deposits, water power sites, and plants in excess of its needs with the intent of denying their use to competitors.[16]

Exclusive Sales Arrangements

In exclusive sales arrangements, manufacturing companies agree to allow distributors and retailers to handle their products only if they agree not to handle similar products made by other manufacturers. A case in point is the American Tobacco Trust, a trust comparable in power and ruthlessness to the Standard Oil Trust. During the latter part of the nineteenth century, the trust controlled distributors at the wholesale and retail levels by offering large discounts to jobbers who agreed to handle exclusively the products of American Tobacco. A commission of 2.5 percent was paid to jobbers who agreed to sell only to the retail trade and at prices fixed by the trust. If they agreed to handle only the products of the trust, they received an additional 7.5 percent commission. The objective of the arrangement was to leave no room for the products of other tobacco manufacturers. American Tobacco was able to do this because of its economic power: it almost completely controlled the supply of cigarettes and other tobacco products.

Tying Agreements

Tying agreements are somewhat similar to exclusive sales arrangements. In a tying agreement, a company requires a buyer to purchase one or more additional products as a condition for purchasing the desired product. For the tying agreement to be successful, the desired product must have few substitutes and also be relatively less interchangeable than the tied item. In one well-known case, the International Salt Company, which had patents on two salt dispensing machines, would lease the machines only if the lessee would agree to buy all salt to be used in the machine from International Salt. The United Shoe Machinery Company once compelled shoemakers to purchase other materials and intermediate products from it as a condition for purchasing shoe machinery, which limited the other sellers of the tied products from competing in the market. But the courts have generally disallowed tying agreements in which the end result is the lessening of competition, particularly when the tied product is a legal monopoly such as a patent.

16. Robert F. Lanzilloti, *The Structure of American Industry: Some Case Studies*, ed. Walter Adams, 3rd ed. (New York: Macmillan, 1961), chap. 6.

Patent Control

In order to stimulate invention, patents are granted by the federal government, which give exclusive control over articles and processes for seventeen years. These legal grants of monopoly privilege sometimes have been used to establish and maintain a monopolistic position. Patent rights are property and can be rented with conditions of use specified. They thus have formed the basis of agreements to maintain prices, allocate markets, and restrict production. Patents promote invention by granting temporary monopolies to inventors, but they have often had the effect of subverting competition. An example of this was the Ethyl Gasoline Corporation, jointly owned by Standard Oil of New Jersey and General Motors, which held the patent on tetra-ethyl, "antiknock" gasoline. It licensed all refiners and eleven thousand independent retail distributors, forcing them to agree to maintain a price differential over ordinary gasoline and to follow the big oil companies' price policies before they would be allowed to make and use tetra-ethyl.

Price Discrimination

Discriminatory pricing policies are almost too numerous to describe. One example is the basing point system. In order to avoid giving mills located near a consuming center an advantage in obtaining business, steel corporations adopted the idea of selling all iron and steel products, except rails, at delivered prices only. The delivered prices were the sum of the base price added to the cost of transportation from Pittsburgh to the destination, regardless of the origin of the shipment or the actual freight cost. Thus the "Pittsburgh-plus" system was born. Prices were quoted on the basis of Pittsburgh, even though the product may have been made in Chicago. Buyers in the Chicago area, for example, were required to pay $7.50 a ton in phantom freight—the freight "plus" from Pittsburgh—on steel produced in Chicago by the local subsidiaries of U.S. Steel. In 1948 the Supreme Court declared that the basing point system was a monopolistic form of pricing.

In attempting to eliminate competition, business firms have also used predatory pricing practices. Firms with several products or with sales in more than one market area were able to use predatory pricing. A firm with a chain of grocery stores, for example, might lower prices at one of its outlets that was in close competition with an independent grocery store. It could sustain the resulting temporary losses at the one outlet by relying on the profits it received from other outlets. In this way, the chain could drive the independent store out of business. Then it could raise its prices in what had become its own local monopoly. Firms with many products used similar tactics to eliminate rival firms with one product. Price discrimination occurs when a seller charges different prices to the same or different buyers for the same good. This in itself is not necessarily unfair, for it may be more economical for a firm to sell in bulk, and those economies can be passed on to the consumer. But often discriminatory pricing has been used to undercut the competition of other firms.

Business firms also have resorted to price fixing. This approach has always been tempting because firms can reduce or even eliminate the risk of economic loss. The power to fix prices requires having the power to control the market. Price fixing may take two forms, overt collusion between business firms to set prices or price leadership, in which one firm sets the price. Collusion may occur when several firms agree to fix bids on government contracts, with each firm taking its turn in submitting the lowest bid. In some industries there is a relatively small number of firms, and one dominates the market by virtue of its size and economic power. The dominant firm acts as the price leader, and the others set their prices accordingly, either because of fear of the consequences if they do not or because of the benefit of the price stability that will occur if they do. Price competition disappears, and often the prices are higher than they would be in a competitive market. The potential harm to competition from adopting the same prices as those of the industry leader is as great as that stemming from an outright conspiracy to fix prices.

Reciprocal Agreements

Reciprocal agreements are arrangements in which firms agree to purchase certain products from each other. This kind of thing happens all the time, and there is nothing inherently wrong with reciprocal agreements unless the end result is the lessening of competition. This may well happen. Company A may refuse to buy products from Company B unless it in turn agrees to buy Company A's products. Company A may be able, through the volume of its purchases, to compel Company B to reciprocate by buying its products, and Company A can threaten to purchase its goods elsewhere unless such an arrangement is made. In one case, Consolidated Foods was able to use its buying power to force its suppliers to purchase products from one of its affiliates. In another case, General Motors told the railroads that unless they bought locomotives from General Motors, GM would take its shipping business to other lines. In both cases, the courts found these activities to constitute a substantial lessening of competition and ordered them stopped.

FINANCE CAPITALISM

American capitalism can be divided into three distinct phases: merchant capitalism, industrial capitalism, and finance capitalism.[17] Merchant capitalism prevailed from 1790 to 1840 and was based largely on plantation agriculture, shipping, banking, and trading. The merchant capitalists of New England, for example, made their money in shipping. Then, in the first quarter of the nineteenth century, they founded the turnpike, canal, and river improvement companies of the region; later they established savings banks and life insurance companies. By 1840 the rudiments of industrial capitalism had been established. The textile industry was established in New England, which also became a center for industries producing small metal products. The introduction of machinery and government subsidies and a desire to be economically independent stimulated the development of industrial capitalism. By the time of the Civil War the factory system was in place, and the corporate form of business organization had become common. After the Civil War, the industrial development of the United States progressed rapidly, and the inclination toward large-scale production and integration of manufacturing accelerated rapidly. Finance capitalism, the third phase, began toward the end of the last century.

Origins of Finance Capitalism

Acquiring capital goods, such as machines, to use in production requires the existence of investment credit. Capital goods are produced and delivered to the user at a particular time, but they offer their benefits over an extended period of time. Someone must be willing to finance the production of the capital goods and to wait to receive the benefits the capital goods create. This function is performed by the "savers" of the economic system. Individuals may invest their savings directly in productive facilities or in the securities of corporations that will use the funds in their own production of goods. When there are large numbers of savers and of firms that desire to obtain funds for investment purposes, there is a need for an intermediary to bring together the savers and the borrowers. In a capitalistic system this function is usually performed by investment bankers. Corporations obtain large quantities of long-term capital funds by selling their securities with the assistance of investment bankers. These bankers underwrite and distribute the securities, eventually getting them into the hands of insurance companies, banks, investment trusts, and individual investors.

17. Hacker, *The Triumph of American Capitalism*, pp. 418–494.

Investment banking is relatively new. In the first half of the nineteenth century, the few securities issued were sold mainly through private banks to a few wealthy individuals here and abroad. Later, the Civil War stimulated investment banking. To finance the war, the North utilized taxation, the issuance of paper money, and borrowing. In all, the federal government borrowed $2.6 billion through the issuance and sale of bonds. But there had to be a link between the potential buyers and the seller of these securities. Agents were appointed by the secretary of the treasury, Salmon P. Chase, to stimulate public sales of the bond issues. Jay Cooke, a Philadelphia banker, was particularly successful in marketing the bonds. He organized a campaign that went beyond institutions and appealed directly to individuals to buy the bonds. Cooke was given monopoly privileges in the sale of the bonds, privileges that were criticized and subsequently canceled.

After the Civil War, investment banking expanded to meet the need to mobilize capital for the growth of corporate enterprise.[18] At first, private banking concerns handled many of the bond issues, some specializing in one class of bonds, such as railroad or public utility bonds, and others handling a wide range of stocks. Such concerns became the great investment banks to which the large corporations turned to market their security issues. These investment banks were essentially go-betweens, buying securities from corporations and governmental units and selling them to investors. Individually or, if the security issue were large, in groups organized as a syndicate, the investment banks were prepared to underwrite an issue so that a corporation could be certain of having funds when they were needed. Aided by branches or correspondents all over the country, they created a broad market in which to dispose of the issue.

Abuses of Finance Capitalism

As the investment banks became stronger, their aims became more ambitious. They came to have more and more control over the agencies of savings—insurance companies, trust companies, and savings banks. At the same time, they began to expand their influence into industry by exercising some control over the sources of demand for investment funds, and a hierarchical system of investment banks evolved. At the top were a few groups that controlled the marketing of most large issues and were likely to be represented on the boards of directors of the issuing corporations. Less important firms would handle smaller issues. The growth and profits of investment banking were such that large commercial banks came to organize or affiliate with investment

18. Chester W. Wright, *Economic History of the United States*, 2nd ed. (New York: McGraw-Hill, 1949), pp. 594–598.

banks. The investment banks' financial resources grew to the point at which they were able to buy the stock of industrial firms or set up competing firms.

The investment bankers, or finance capitalists, operating out of their banks were more effective than the industrial capitalists had been in stultifying competition. Capitalism became a more impersonal arrangement, in that the finance capitalists were removed from the production process. Profit became the prime desideratum of production, something to be made at all costs. This is not to say that the industrial capitalists such as the Carnegies and the Rockefellers were averse to profits but that there were other reasons for their drive for success—the creative efforts of skill and production. The finance capitalists utilized various types of monopoly controls to assure profits. Production was limited, inventories withheld, prices fixed, security markets rigged, and the judicial and legislative process perverted. With their funds, finance capitalists were able to manipulate credit to control industrial concerns and railroads. Indeed, in direct competition with Andrew Carnegie, the finance capitalists were able to acquire the Carnegie Steel Company and to assimilate it into their own United States Steel Corporation.

The House of Morgan

John Pierpont Morgan was supposed to have told a friend, "If you have to ask how much it costs to operate a yacht, you can't afford to own one." Although this statement may have been apocryphal, the man was not. He was to banking what John D. Rockefeller was to oil and Andrew Carnegie was to steel; he may not have had their wealth, but he probably had much more economic and financial power, for the investment banking house of J. P. Morgan and Company had the funds that industry needed for expansion. These funds were used to vitiate competition rather than to promote it. Morgan and Company gained control over the financial affairs of corporations as a condition of issuing investment credit. It achieved this control by having one or more of its members appointed to the boards of directors of corporations with which it did business, ostensibly to ensure the safety of the securities issues. By 1920, J. P. Morgan and Company, together with its dependents and allies, held directorships in corporations with net assets of some $74 billion, or about one-fourth of the total of American corporate assets at the time. This power was held by some 167 representatives of the banking house who, in turn, held some 2,450 interlocking directorates in corporations.[19]

19. U.S. Congress, Senate, National Resources Committee, *The Structure of the American Economy* (Washington, D.C.: U.S. Government Printing Office, 1939), pp. 306–317.

Foreign Investments

As America's need for investment capital was fulfilled, investment bankers turned to foreign outlets. Under the aegis of finance capitalism, funds poured out of the United States into Cuban sugar plantations, Mexican silver mines and oil fields, and Canadian railroad construction. The halcyon period of foreign investment was the period between 1900 and 1914. In 1897, American investment abroad amounted to $685 million; by 1908 the total amount had increased to $2.5 billion, and on the eve of World War I, the amount was $3.5 billion.[20] Most of these investments were direct rather than of the portfolio type. These foreign investments were significant because their return helped the United States reverse its position from that of a debtor nation to that of a creditor nation. This final transition came after World War I.

It can be said that the modern multinational corporation has its roots in this time period, with United Fruit operating in Central America, Standard Oil in Mexico, Anaconda Copper in Chile, and other American corporations operating all over the globe. Certain occurrences were harbingers of events that would come much later. A precedent was established for the alleged machinations of the Central Intelligence Agency (CIA) and International Telephone and Telegraph (ITT) in Chilean internal affairs that led to the overthrow of the Allende government in 1973. United Fruit, with the help of the State Department, did the same kind of thing in Costa Rica, Nicaragua, and Honduras at the beginning of this century. The United States was not at all hesitant to use gunboat diplomacy to protect American investments abroad, particularly in Latin America. Mexico is an example, in which the United States supported the dictator Porfirio Diaz, and he in turn lavished mining and petroleum concessions on American business firms. This was agreeable to both sides until the Mexican Revolution of 1910. Then, through the connivance of the American ambassador to Mexico, General Victoriano Huerta was able to depose President Francisco Madero, who had taken office after the revolution. In 1914, to protect American interests, the United States sent its marines to Vera Cruz.

SUMMARY

Since the Civil War industrial concentration and monopoly power have grown steadily in the United States. The opening of the West, immigration, and the inflow of foreign capital contributed to its rapid industrial development between 1865 and 1900. During this period, there was a

20. Cleona Lewis, *America's Stake in International Investments* (Washington, D.C.: Brookings Institution, 1938), pp. 605–606.

decline in business competition attributable in part to the rise of large-scale production, which permitted the more efficient utilization of resources with the result that firms became larger and fewer in number. The desire for profits, which can be increased by eliminating or restricting competition also contributed to industrial concentration. A series of monopolistic devices designed to restrict competition were introduced, the earliest of which, the pool and the trust, appeared in the 1870s and 1880s and were followed later by the holding company. These combinations were not restricted to one field but extended to manufacturing, mining, transportation, public utilities, and trade. The concentration of economic power and the frequent abuse of that power gave rise to the antitrust movement and to the desire to regulate business more closely.

As the industrialization of the United States progressed, the leaders of industry became dependent on investment bankers for funds, and thus the control of industry passed more and more into the hands of a few large investment banking houses. This system of organization became known as finance capitalism. These banking houses were able to acquire an inordinate amount of economic power. An oligarchy of several New York banking firms, including J. P. Morgan and Company, dominated finance capitalism. Their control extended into industry through the ownership of securities and through the interlocking directorate device. In 1904 the Morgan and Rockefeller banking interests controlled six railroad combinations with a total capitalization of $10 billion. Finance capitalism spread to other parts of the globe in search of new investment outlets. Until the 1890s the United States, preoccupied with its national development and having no surplus capital for investment abroad, had little interest in foreign affairs, but finance capitalism forced the foreign policy of the United States into a new phase.

QUESTIONS FOR DISCUSSION

1. What is the function of profit in a market economy?
2. What were some of the factors that contributed to the industrial development of the United States?
3. The philosophy of Social Darwinism was used as a rationale to justify the accumulation of great wealth by Carnegie, Rockefeller, and other of the great industrial magnates of the nineteenth century. Define Social Darwinism, and explain how it was used as a justification by such magnates.
4. Discuss the factors that led to the decline of competition in many industries during the latter part of the nineteenth century.
5. Differentiate among the following types of business combinations: pools, trusts, and holding companies.

6. What is meant by *finance capitalism*, and with what institution is the term associated?
7. Discuss the differences in attitude toward business held by the finance capitalists, such as Morgan, and the industrial capitalists, such as Carnegie and Rockefeller.

RECOMMENDED READINGS

Faulkner, Harold U. *The Decline of Laissez Faire, 1897–1917*. New York: Holt, Rinehart & Winston, 1951, chaps. 5, 8, 15.

Hacker, Louis M. *The Triumph of American Capitalism*. New York: Simon & Schuster, 1940.

Hofstadter, Richard. *Social Darwinism in American Thought*. Boston: Beacon Press, 1968.

Josephson, Matthew. *The Robber Barons*. New York: Harcourt, Brace & World, 1934.

Kirkland, Edward C. *Industry Comes of Age: Business, Labor, and Public Policy, 1860–1897*. New York: Holt, Rinehart & Winston, 1961.

Sinclair, Andrew. *Corsair: The Life of J. Pierpont Morgan*. Boston: Little, Brown, 1981.

Smith, Adam. *The Wealth of Nations*. London: T. Nelson and Sons, 1891, bk. IV.

Tuttle, Frank W., and Joseph M. Perry. *An Economic History of the United States.* Cincinnati: South-Western Publishing Co., 1970, chaps. 16, 17.

Wright, Chester W. *Economic History of the United States*. 2nd ed. New York: McGraw-Hill, 1949, chaps. 33, 34, 35.

Chapter 3
Government Regulation of Business, 1870-1930

Industrial and railroad monopolies were formed around 1880 and have continued into this century. The primary reason for the creation of this type of combination was the manufacturers' desire to restrict or eliminate competition and thus to establish monopoly prices. This was done by the business monopolies' control of supply. A monopoly price is likely to be higher than a competitive price, for the monopolist can limit supply and in this way prevent prices from falling to the level determined by competition. A second reason for the combination was the development of the business cycle. As recessions became more severe, business firms merged to achieve some sort of control over the market. A third reason for the monopolies was that those organizing them hoped they would achieve the economies of the trust: a trust could almost always secure raw materials more cheaply than would be possible in a state of competition, and it could often save money by vertically integrating so that it was assured of an ample supply of raw materials at cost.

RAILROAD REGULATION

In his novel *Giants in the Earth*, O. E. Rolvaag describes the coming of the railroad to South Dakota:

> One fine day a strange monster came writhing westward over the prairie, from Worthington to Luverne; it was the greatest and most memorable event that had yet happened in these parts. The monster crawled along with a terrible speed, but when it came near, it did not crawl at all; it rushed forward in tortuous windings, with an awful roar, while black, curling smoke streaked out behind it in the air. People felt that day a joy that almost frightened them; for it seemed now that all their troubles were over, that there could be no more hardships to contend with—at least, that was what the Sognings solemnly affirmed. For now that the railway had come as far as this, it wouldn't take long before they would see it winding its way into Sioux Falls.[1]

1. O. F. Rolvaag, *Giants in the Earth* (New York: Harper & Row, Pub., 1927), p. 327.

Few inventions have had more impact on American life than the railroad. To the farmers, the railroads brought many blessings. They enabled the farmers to get their produce to market, supplied them with agricultural implements, catalogues, and other accoutrements of the outside world, and ended rural isolation as passenger trains connected the farms with the cities. The railroads contributed to the development of mass transportation and distribution and to large-scale corporations in their modern form. They also helped urbanize the American economy by carrying laborers and supplies to newly built factories in the cities. Many railroad innovations and inventions improved the economy, for example, the Pullman car and the creation of a standard gauge, which enabled the integration of the nation's rail system. Methods of financing and promoting railroad expansion also influenced the economy. Railroad securities were one of the largest outlets for the American peoples' savings. State and local governments also extended financial aid to the railroads in the form of loans, grants, and property tax exemptions. Most of the railroads tended to rely on bonds for financial expansion; however, the heavy fixed interest charge they incurred often led to financial disaster.

The railroad industry had many of the same characteristics of industrial capitalism described in the last chapter—increasing costs leading to large-scale production, keen competition, and a resulting tendency toward monopoly. But it was in the railroads that the country first encountered the problems that arise under such conditions. There was a period of competition that eventually degenerated into a struggle for the survival of the fittest. One condition that contributed to undesirable practices by the railroads was the high ratio of fixed to operating costs. In addition, the railroads' total fixed costs bore no relation to the volume of traffic once these fixed costs had been incurred or once the railroads had been constructed. Rate wars were common, and in response, railroad operators began to expand and consolidate their holdings in order to operate more efficiently and to secure greater profits. The earliest type of combination is exemplified by the railroad empire created by Cornelius Vanderbilt, who bought control of the competing lines operating from New York City to Albany and from Albany to Buffalo, and out of them formed the New York Central system.[2] A later form of railroad combination was the pool, formed to apportion business, fix rates, and thus avoid ruinous competition. For example, the five or six railroads that controlled the shipment of anthracite coal in northeastern Pennsylvania allocated to each of themselves certain percentages of the total shipment of coal. Fines were collected from those railroads that exceeded their allocations, and in

2. Matthew Josephson, *The Robber Barons* (New York: Harcourt, Brace & World, 1934), pp. 134–138.

turn, the money from the fines was distributed among the railroads that had carried less than their allocated portions of coal.

Reasons for Railroad Regulation

In the railroads' early days, the prevailing government policy was one of aid rather than regulation. The promise of swift transportation, industrial development, and access to market enhanced the value of the railroads, and the public interest was identified with the railroads' interests. But there were a number of abuses, resulting in part from cutthroat competitive practices in which railroads disregarded the interests of the consumers and shippers. Rate discrimination was one abuse, which entailed setting different rates for different places, for different commodities, or for different firms. Railroads charged more for short hauls than for long hauls, and rates were higher between local, noncompetitive points. Deviations from published tariffs were a common means of rate discrimination, and in addition, rebates were given to favored shippers and localities. One of the reasons for these practices was the high ratio of fixed costs to operating costs. Traffic attracted by charging rates that brought in anything at all over operating costs was better than no traffic at all; at least it brought in something to help defray fixed costs.

Immediately after the Civil War, the farmers and small businessmen began pressing for railroad regulation. The farmers were particularly hard hit because they were absolutely dependent on the railroads, which, unregulated by any government body, practiced various forms of price discrimination, the money from which often went to pay dividends on watered stock. The prices for agricultural products fluctuated widely in domestic markets, and a high protective tariff prevented foreign manufactured goods from competing effectively with American manufactured goods, whose prices remained high. The farmers' discontent coalesced in the Grange movement, which became an important political force at the state level.[3] The Grange wanted the regulation of railroads to bring about lower freights and fares and to ban discriminatory rates for different places and persons. It also wanted cheap money, an income tax, and a reduction of the protective tariff except on agricultural products. But the Grange's main impact was on the passage of laws to regulate the railroads.

3. Broadus Mitchell, *American Economic History* (Boston: Houghton Mifflin, 1947), p. 697.

State Regulation of Railroads

The Grange, together with its allies—merchants and other small businessmen who also resented rate discrimination—gained control of a number of midwestern state governments and enacted a series of regulatory laws since known as *Granger legislation*.[4] In 1871 Illinois created a railroad and warehouse commission authorized to fix maximum rates for intrastate freight and passenger service on the railroads, as well as rates for storing grain in public warehouses and grain elevators. The commission was empowered to prosecute when a railroad charged a higher rate for a short than for a long haul over the same line in the same direction. In 1871 the Minnesota legislature prescribed maximum rates for passengers and freight and appointed a railroad commissioner to enforce the railroad laws. In 1874 a board of railway commissioners was authorized to fix maximum rates. The Iowa Railroad Act of 1874 followed the Minnesota model of setting maximum rates, with provisions for a railroad commission empowered to reduce rates below the maximum when that could be done without injury to the railroad. Wisconsin and other states followed the Minnesota and Iowa examples.

Munn v. Illinois, *1877*

One important result of the states' regulation of the railroads was the landmark decision of the Supreme Court in the *Munn* v. *Illinois* case.[5] Munn, who owned and operated a grain elevator in the state of Illinois, challenged the right of the Illinois legislature to establish the maximum rates he could charge farmers for storing their grain. He contended that the state had no right to pass legislation that infringed on the rights of the private property owner. Losing his case in the Illinois Supreme Court, he appealed, and the case went to the United States Supreme Court.

In 1877 the Supreme Court upheld the constitutional right of the state of Illinois to fix maximum charges for the storage of grain in grain elevators, since the business was one "clothed with a public interest." In other words, the public interest took precedence over private property rights. The emphasis of the decision was on the power of legislatures to fix rates, and it was immediately applicable to the railroads, since they were public in nature.

The states' regulation of the railroads was generally unsuccessful. One reason was that as the political power of the Grange began to decline, the railroads were able to lobby for the repeal or emasculation of

4. Ibid., p. 701.
5. *Munn* v. *Illinois*, 94 U.S. 113 (1877).

the state railroad laws. In 1874 the Minnesota legislation was modified and made more acceptable to the railroads, and in 1878 the Iowa law was similarly modified. In Iowa and in other states, the railroads were able to convince the state legislatures that restrictions would inhibit the flow of capital necessary for investment. It also became apparent that state laws did not give enough authority to the state commissions to enable them to enforce the law. But despite the commissions, many railroads continued to maintain pools and charge discriminatory rates in direct violation of state laws. Above all, without federal control, the state commissions were powerless to correct most of the railroads' abuses. As long as most traffic was intrastate, there was no pressure on Congress to act under the interstate commerce clause of the U.S. Constitution. But as the railroads spread across the nation, the federal government was finally forced to take action.

Federal Regulation of Railroads

The farmers' anger regarding railroad abuses also affected the federal government. The railroads continued to combine and strengthen, and the farmers continued to find themselves exploited, suffering from high rates and rate discrimination. Stock watering and manipulation and bribing of state legislatures injured a further section of the population. Between 1875 and 1880, pooling arrangements spread rapidly all over the United States. Whenever competition promised to regulate railroad rates through supply and demand, the pool was used to preserve dividends on watered stock and interest on fixed obligations. To a certain extent the railroads were caught up in a frenetic round of speculation and overbuilding, and they resorted to frequent issues of common stock to provide investment funds. Competition on interstate rail routes brought rate wars: in one year, the rate for fourth-class mail from New York to Chicago fell from $1.80 a pound to $.25 a pound.[6] In turn, the rate wars, particularly on trunk lines, led to the first pooling arrangement in 1874 when, at the Saratoga Conference, the owners of the Erie, Pennsylvania, and New York Central railroads met to devise a means for suppressing competition in trunk line traffic.

But the pools, far from being a remedy for the evils of excess competition, only aggravated the problem they attempted to cure. The high rates they were able to maintain often attracted the attention of speculators and led to the creation of rival roads. After prolonged railroad wars, in which competing promoters neglected the interest of the shippers and all others, E. H. Harriman achieved control of the Union

6. Chester W. Wright, *Economic History of the United States*, 2nd ed. (New York: McGraw-Hill, 1949), p. 597.

Pacific and Southern Pacific, and James J. Hill, with Morgan backing, gained control of the Great Northern and the Northern Pacific. The New York Central and the Pennsylvania Railroad established a community of interest between themselves; the Pennsylvania Railroad obtained stock control of the Baltimore and Ohio and the Norfolk and Western, and the New York Central acquired the Lake Erie and Western and leased the Baltimore and Albany. These two major roads also controlled the Chesapeake and Ohio. These railroad combinations were possible because stock ownership had become so diffused that often a comparatively small block of shares was sufficient to give one railroad decisive control over the management of another railroad.

The Interstate Commerce Act of 1887

The Interstate Commerce Act was the culmination of a series of cases that had taken place over a period of almost twenty years. As mentioned earlier, many farmers and small businessmen had joined the Grange movement, and state legislatures, supported by the Grange, had enacted laws regulating railroads. These laws were tested in the courts in a series of cases known as the Granger cases. The most important, *Munn* v. *Illinois*, established the right of a state legislature to regulate the rates of concerns that affected the public interest. Other Granger cases established that the regulation of railroads by state legislatures was not subject to judicial review and that in the absence of federal legislation, state legislatures could enact laws that indirectly affected interstate commerce. But these rights were abrogated in the Wabash Case of 1886, in which the United States Supreme Court ruled that a state did not have the power to regulate rates for transporting freight entirely within state boundaries if the transportation within the state was part of an interstate movement.[7]

The Interstate Commerce Act was the first major federal regulatory act, stating that all interstate freight and passenger traffic was subject to federal regulation. Among its more important provisions were:

1. It created an Interstate Commerce Commission consisting of five members appointed by the president and approved by the Senate. The terms of office were set at six years.

2. It made it unlawful for railroads to charge a higher rate for short hauls than for long hauls on shipments on the same line in the same direction.[8] This removed one of the major grievances of the shippers,

---

7. *Wabash, St. Louis & Pacific Ry. Co.* v. *Illinois*, 118 U.S. 557 (1886).
8. One railroad charged more to ship coal from Bessemer, Alabama, to Birmingham, Alabama, a distance of 11 miles, than from Bessemer to Pittsburgh, Pennsylvania, a distance of 594 miles.

because the railroads had discriminated against way points on their lines in order to recoup losses incurred between main points.

3. Pooling traffic was forbidden, as was the division of either net profits or aggregate proceeds among the railroads.

4. Schedules of freight rates and passenger fares had to be made public, and increases in such rates and fares could be made only after ten days' advance public notice had been given. One of the worst abuses by railroads had been their keeping rates secret.[9] Rates would change from day to day, and shippers often had no idea of what a shipment would cost. Secrecy also permitted the railroads to charge whatever the traffic would bear.

5. The Interstate Commerce Commission could hear complaints, and it was given the power to initiate investigations of the common carriers' management policies.

But for the most part, the Interstate Commerce Act was ineffective. The Interstate Commerce Commission had little power; it had to look to the courts to enforce its rulings. Court decisions took a long time to be reached and often went against the commission. Railroad officials would plead the Fifth Amendment and refuse to answer the questions put to them by the commission. During litigation, the railroads were able to continue the same practices or abuses of which they had been accused. Court decisions denied the commission the right to establish the reasonable maximum rates that a carrier could charge in interstate commerce, and lastly, the railroads also could obtain a temporary injunction to suspend the new rate prescribed by the commission.

The Hepburn Act, 1906

For all practical purposes, the Hepburn Act was more important than the Interstate Commerce Act, as it marked the beginning of effective railroad regulation. The jurisdiction of the Interstate Commerce Commission was broadened to include express companies, sleeping car companies, pipe lines, railroad facilities, and other types of transportation such as private cars and industrial railroads. The so-called commodities exchange clause attempted to prevent the railroads from engaging in other businesses and to eliminate the opportunities for discrimination implied in a dual carrier-shipper status. Other provisions of the Hepburn Act were as follows:

1. Railroads were forbidden to give free passes to passengers other than officers, employees, and their families. Exceptions were made for persons engaged in charitable work. A common practice of the railroads

9. William Z. Ripley, *Railroads* (Boston: Ginn, 1915), I, 355-357.

had been to give free transportation to politicians, thus creating a conflict of interest.[10]

2. Rate-making power was granted to the Interstate Commerce Commission, which now could declare existing rates to be unjust and unreasonable and could also set maximum rates.

3. The commission was authorized to prescribe uniform accounting practices to be used by the railroads. This provision was important because in the past the railroads had used different accounting methods to mislead investors and rate-making commissions.

4. The number of members on the commission was increased to ten, and the term of office was increased to seven years.

5. Sanctions against discrimination were strengthened by subjecting to stiff penalties the givers and recipients of rebates and all those departing from published tariffs.

Mann-Elkins Act, 1910

The Mann-Elkins Act extended the authority of the Interstate Commerce Commission to include telephone, telegraph, and cable and wireless companies engaged in interstate commerce. Thus, gradually, limited governmental intervention evolved into extensive federal regulation of railroads and other common carriers. The Mann-Elkins Act's most important provision was to grant the commission the authority to administer the long- and short-haul clause of the Interstate Commerce Act of 1887. It was declared unlawful for a railroad to charge a higher rate for traffic moving a shorter distance over the same line in the same direction than for traffic moving a longer distance, the short haul being considered included in the longer. Previous court cases had virtually nullified the effectiveness of the long- and short-haul clause. In 1897 the Supreme Court, overruling the Interstate Commerce Commission, ruled in a case dealing with domestic rates that competition among railroads might be important in dissimilar circumstances and so justify lower rates for longer hauls.[11]

Results of Railroad Regulation

Federal regulation, however, had little impact on the consolidation of railroads into large combinations. In the 1890s and early 1900s, the

10. This was and remains a common practice in many countries. In the early 1920s, Adolf Hitler, although the leader of only a minor political party, was entitled to free railroad passes, which he used to travel about and promote his doctrine of national socialism.
11. *ICC* v. *Alabama Midland Railway Co.*, 168 U.S. 144 (1897).

process of combination continued as large railroad operators secured control of smaller competing lines, either through direct purchase and lease or through the holding company device. By 1906 the great period of railroad combination was over, and seven large railroad organizations had come to own two-thirds of the nation's railway mileage and to receive about 85 percent of the railroads' total earnings.[12] Finance capitalism also was involved, for the investment banking houses supplied the funds to finance these combinations. The Vanderbilt railroad system, through the New York Central Railroad, dominated the routes from New York to the Great Lakes and Chicago. The Pennsylvania Railroad and its affiliates controlled the routes from Baltimore and Philadelphia to Pittsburgh and westward. J. P. Morgan built a system extending from New York to the Southwest, with connections from Florida to the Great Lakes and from the Atlantic to the Mississippi. In the Mississippi valley region, Jay Gould's Erie Railroad and the Rock Island combination controlled nearly 32,000 miles of track. James J. Hill's Great Northern combination and its affiliates monopolized all the railroad lines in the Northwest, and the central and southern transcontinental railroads were controlled by Edward H. Harriman and his associates.

There were other defects in railroad regulation. The Interstate Commerce Commission was not authorized to regulate the issuance of securities: railroads were often overcapitalized, and their financial standing was weakened during business recessions. Indeed, excessive overcapitalization contributed to the bankruptcy of such railroads as the New Haven and the Frisco. Although the commission had the power to set maximum rates, it lacked control over the railroads' financial structure, according to which the rate level was decided. Regulation of rates carried with it the need to regulate financial abuses, a power the commission did not have. In sanctioning rate increases designed to help weak railroads, the commission often inadvertently bolstered the financial position of strong railroads, giving them high profits that led to more financial speculation. Finally, the commission's position was defensive; it could protect shippers from rate discrimination, but it could not ensure adequate rail service, efficient management, and the development of transportation facilities to meet national needs.

GOVERNMENT REGULATION OF TRUSTS

As was mentioned in the last chapter, the enormous growth in the size of business units, often with consequent damage to competition, took

12. Mitchell, *American Economic History*, p. 703.

place in the period following the end of the Civil War and continued unabated until the end of the century. To circumvent competition, various types of business combinations were formed—the pool, the trust, and the holding company. These combinations engaged in various forms of abuses that aroused the general public. Freedom of enterprise was threatened as combinations were able to restruct entry into many business fields. Consumers were at the mercy of the trusts, for through control over markets, they were able to set prices on many basic necessities. In particular, there was public resentment against the Standard Oil Trust and the Sugar Trust. The former was criticized for its goal of monopoly and for the practices it used to eliminate competition; the latter was charged with fixing prices and eliminating competition. The Standard Oil, Sugar, and other trusts were able to apply political pressure to achieve their goals; for example, the Sugar Trust engineered the passage of protective tariffs to protect itself against foreign competition, and then it was free to raise the domestic prices of sugar.

The Influence of Populism

Although public indignation by itself was not enough to enact antitrust laws, the same political force was present that had contributed to the passage of federal and state laws to regulate railroads. Even though the influence of the Grange had declined by 1880, various farm-labor parties, the most important of which was the Farmer's Alliance, were created as part of the general political movement known as populism. Populism expressed the anger of the farmer, the factory worker, and the small businessman against the trusts, railroads, and big banks. The trusts, they felt, overcharged them for the necessities of life they had to buy, the railroads overcharged them for what they had to transport, and the banks charged them usurious rates when they had to borrow. These groups felt that the politicians of both the major political parties represented vested business interests; therefore, it would be better for them to elect their own representatives. The farmers, together with the nascent labor movement, were able in the decade between 1880 and 1890 to elect many senators, congressmen, and state legislators supporting their interests. A national third party, the Populist Party, emerged in the presidential election of 1892.[13] Pragmatic Republican and Democrat politicians took notice and concluded that the best way to defeat a competing political movement was to incorporate some of its more important ideas.

13. The Populist Party gained twenty-two electoral votes and over a million popular votes in 1892.

State Antitrust Laws

We should emphasize that the state courts rather than the state legislatures were the first to regulate trusts under the provisions of common law, which is a system of unwritten law not necessarily expressed in written statutes. Until 1889 there were no state laws covering industrial combinations and trusts, but there was a large body of common doctrine on which courts could rely. It was established early in English law that contracts or agreements in restraint of trade were void and, therefore, unenforceable. English common law was carried over into United States law and generally accommodated the rising American antitrust movement; in fact, the state courts used the common law to outlaw trusts. In what is probably the most important common law antitrust case, the Ohio Supreme Court in 1892 declared the Standard Oil Trust to be illegal.[14] The state charged that the Standard Oil Company of Ohio had violated the law by placing the control of its affairs in the hands of trustees, nearly none of whom were residents of the state. In its decision, the court ruled that the Standard Oil Trust, domiciled in New York, exerted a virtual monopoly over petroleum production, refining, and distribution all over the country and ordered the Standard Oil Company of Ohio to dissociate itself from the trust.

The first antitrust laws were enacted by the states rather than by the federal government because the impact of populism was felt first at the state level. In 1889 the state of Kansas passed a law outlawing trusts, which were defined as combinations formed to restrict trade, fix prices, or prevent competition. In the same year, similar laws were passed in Michigan, Tennessee, and Texas. By 1895 seventeen states had passed various types of antitrust laws. These laws varied considerably in content, but almost all forbade monopolies and combinations in restraint of trade and provided criminal penalties and administrative machinery for prosecution. In addition, they attacked particular forms of agreements and specific practices that were thought likely to bring about control of the market. The state antitrust laws, however, were limited, because in the American system of government the states can regulate only intrastate commerce.

Federal Antitrust Laws

The application of common law to business combinations did little to slow down their growth. Remedies were difficult to enforce and rarely succeeded in restoring competition. Too, these applications of common law were statewide only, and a large combination could operate in

14. *State* v. *Standard Oil Company*, 49 Ohio 137 (1892).

other states even after being declared illegal in one. States varied in their interpretation and application of the law, and there was no all-encompassing federal law. State antitrust statutes were at best in an embryonic stage and applied only to intrastate commerce. Thus the movement toward industrial concentration was viewed with concern by many people, and this concern crystallized in the populist reform programs. In 1888 both the major political parties referred in their presidential platforms to the dangers inherent in trusts, and in 1890 the Sherman Antitrust Act was passed, during President Benjamin Harrison's administration.

The Sherman Antitrust Act

The Sherman Antitrust Act is the most important of all of the federal antimonopoly laws, and it probably is one of the most important measures ever passed by Congress.[15] It marks a milestone in government and business relations, for after its passage there was no turning back to a period of complete laissez faire capitalism. It marked the end of an era. Even with its loopholes and ambiguities, the act was cordially disliked by business, for its passage meant that business's fight to maintain a laissez faire economy, unfettered by federal intervention, had failed. With the passage of the act, the federal government began the long task of controlling business.

The two main provisions of the Sherman Act are:

1. Section 1—All contracts, or combinations in the form of a trust or in some other form, and all conspiracies in restraint of trade or commerce among the several states or with foreign nations are declared illegal. Every person who makes any such contract or engages in any such combination or conspiracy shall be deemed guilty of a misdemeanor and, on conviction thereof, shall be punished by fine not exceeding five thousand dollars or by imprisonment not exceeding one year, or by both said punishments, at the discretion of the court.

2. Section 2—Every person who monopolizes, or attempts to monopolize, or combine or conspire with any other person or persons to monopolize any part of the trade or commerce among the several states or with foreign nations shall be deemed guilty of a misdemeanor and, on conviction thereof, shall be punished by a fine not exceeding five thousand dollars or by imprisonment not exceeding one year, or by both said punishments, at the discretion of the court.

The enforcement of the Sherman Antitrust Act was entrusted to the Justice Department. In 1903 a special antitrust division was created just

15. The Sherman Antitrust Act will be discussed in more detail in Chapter 6.

for this purpose. The punishments for violating the act are spelled out in Sections 1 and 2. Section 4 provides for the use of civil suits, giving the attorney general the right to enforce the act by using civil proceedings to prevent and restrain violations. Dissolution, divestiture, or divorcement procedures can be used to prevent combinations and to promote competition. Another civil remedy is to use an injunction, which is a restraining order issued by a judge, to prevent unfair business practices. A third method of court action against violators of the act is given in Section 7, which provides for damage suits by private parties injured by other private parties acting in a manner forbidden or declared to be unlawful by the act. If successful in their suit, the injured parties can recover three times the amount of damage sustained.

Application of the Sherman Act, 1890–1900   The application of the Sherman Act can be divided into two periods, 1890 to 1900 and 1900 to 1911. There is some overlap between the two periods, but this is because during the first period neither the federal government nor the courts were eager to enforce the act. When action was taken against trusts and other combinations, the government often lost its case, and in the 1890s the holding company succeeded the trust as the most effective means of combining the activities of several companies under the same control. There were many kinds of holding companies, but they all had in common the control of subsidiaries through the ownership of voting stock. Frequently a pyramid of operating and holding companies was formed by separate tiers of holding companies.

The Sherman Act had some success, however, in two areas for which it was not intended, the labor unions and the railroads. The first use of the Sherman Act in regard to the railroads came during the Pullman strike of 1894, when the federal government used injunctions to end the strike.[16] Eugene V. Debs, the leader of the Pullman strike, was enjoined by an order obtained by the federal government from continuing a workers' boycott of handling Pullman cars that, the government alleged, interfered with interstate commerce. After the Pullman strike, the lower courts issued injunctions against unions when there was evidence of damage, threatened or actual, to the employer's business. But in rejecting an appeal regarding one of these actions, the Supreme Court upheld the use of injunctions against the unions on other grounds, declining to rule on the applicability of the Sherman Act. In 1908, however, the Supreme Court did place union activities under the act in the Danbury Hatters' Case.[17] In this case, a labor union had been convicted of restraint of trade in interstate commerce when it organized a secondary boycott. The Supreme Court upheld the conviction and awarded triple damages to employers involved in the boycott.

16. *U.S.* v. *Debs*, 64 Fed. 724 (1894).
17. *Loewe* v. *Lawlor*, 208 U.S. 274 (1908).

The government also won two cases, one against a railroad combination and the other against a manufacturer's pooling agreement. The first case involved the Trans-Missouri Freight Association, which consisted of a number of railroads engaged in interstate commerce.[18] The purpose of the association was to establish and maintain rates, rules, and regulations on interstate freight traffic south and west of the Missouri River. The issue in this case was whether or not the Sherman Act applied to railroad combinations. The Supreme Court ruled that the act did, and the combination was dissolved. The second case involved the application, for the first time, of the Sherman Act to manufacturing. This was the Addyston Pipe and Steel Company case, which included six companies, all engaged in the manufacture of cast-iron pipes.[19] Under a pooling agreement, the companies divided the United States into three parts—reserve cities, free territory, and pay territory. Orders from reserve cities were reserved for certain companies, and none of the other companies was permitted to do any business there. Any company could sell in free territory, but pay territory, in which high transportation costs gave a company some monopoly power, was assigned by secret auction. In 1899 the Supreme Court declared the pool illegal.

Application of the Sherman Act, 1900–1910 In the beginning, the Sherman Act did very little to slow the growth of business combinations. If anything, the trend toward business consolidation accelerated, as indicated in Table 3-1. By the turn of the century, after ten years of

Table 3-1 Recorded Mergers in Manufacturing and Mining, 1895–1912

Year	Mergers	Year	Mergers
1895	43	1904	79
1896	26	1905	226
1897	69	1906	128
1898	303	1907	87
1899	1,208	1908	50
1900	340	1909	49
1901	423	1910	142
1902	379	1911	103
1903	142	1912	82

Source: U.S. Department of Commerce: Bureau of the Census, *Historical Statistics of the United States, Colonial Times to 1957* (Washington, D.C.: U.S. Government Printing Office, 1960), p. 572.

18. *U.S.* v. *Trans-Missouri Freight Assn.*, 166 U.S. 290 (1897).
19. *U.S.* v. *Addyston Pipe and Steel Co.*, 175 U.S. 211 (1899).

enforcement of the antitrust act, the number of industrial combinations in the United States with capital of $1 billion or more had increased from ten to three hundred.[20] This growth was achieved with the help of banks and holding companies. Between 1898 and 1901, during which time more than one hundred trusts were formed, there was only one minor antitrust suit brought before the Supreme Court. The E. C. Knight decision not only had limited the effectiveness of the Sherman Act, but it also had called into question the very power of the federal government to deal effectively with trusts.

During President Theodore Roosevelt's administration, there was a complete turnabout with respect to the enforcement of the Sherman Act, though Roosevelt himself was ambivalent toward big business combinations. He was an internationalist who believed that the great corporate combinations were a potent factor in international trade and that there was a need to find markets abroad to take care of the constantly growing surplus of American production. Roosevelt also believed that industrial combinations were the natural consequences of economic and technical development. On the other hand, he was well aware of the abuses of combinations, and being a political pragmatist of the first order, he was attuned to the public outcry against big business. Possessed with a sense of the theatrical, he inveighed against the "malefactors of great wealth." In 1903 he asked for and received from Congress a Bureau of Corporations; armed with the power of subpoena, it was to investigate all corporations engaged in interstate commerce and to use public disclosure of the facts as an instrument of discipline. In the ten years of its existence, the bureau contributed much to the economic knowledge of American industry, especially in its studies of meat packing, oil, tobacco, and steel.

But there was also substance as well as style in Roosevelt's stance against the trusts. Altogether there were forty-four antitrust cases during his administration.[21] Action was taken against the Standard Oil Trust, the American Tobacco Trust, and the DuPont Powder Trust. Lesser combinations were attacked in the meat-packing, salt, paper, licorice, elevator, naval stores, and furniture industries. The Sherman Act was also used against a number of railroad combinations, including the Northern Securities Company. In fact, the Northern Securities Company case was the hallmark antitrust case during the seven and a half years of the Roosevelt administration.[22]

20. U.S. Department of Commerce: Bureau of the Census, *Historical Statistics of the United States, Colonial Times to 1957* (Washington, D.C.: U.S. Government Printing Office, 1960), p. 558.
21. John D. Clark, *The Federal Trust Policy* (Baltimore: Johns Hopkins Press, 1931), p. 137.
22. *Northern Securities Co.* v. *U.S.*, 193 U.S. 197 (1904).

The Northern Securities Company Case, 1904

The Northern Securities Company was a holding company for three large railroads—the Northern Pacific, the Great Northern, and the Chicago, Burlington, and Quincy. Some of the nation's largest finance capitalists and railroad tycoons were involved in its formation—J. P. Morgan and Company, the Rockefeller interests, James J. Hill, and E. H. Harriman. To Morgan, the holding company combination represented stability and the removal of wasteful competition. The holding company acquired, by giving its own stock in exchange, more than nine-tenths of the stock of the Northern Pacific and three-fourths of the stock of the Great Northern. The effect of this arrangement would have been to end competition between those two railroads; the former stockholders in the two roads, as common stockholders in the holding company, would have an interest in preventing competition.

The federal government instituted a suit to have the Northern Securities Company dissolved as a combination in restraint of interstate commerce and the railway stock returned. The case reached the U.S. Supreme Court, which by a vote of five to four, ordered the company dissolved. The case was significant because it condemned the holding company as a method of control over previously competing companies, and it included this type of stockholding within the scope of the commerce clause.

Two landmark antitrust cases were initiated during Roosevelt's second term in office, but the final decisions were not reached until 1911 when William Howard Taft was president. These cases involved the Standard Oil Company and the American Tobacco Company. Taft believed that the Sherman Act, if properly enforced, would effect a desirable economic policy with regard to competition. Seventy-eight antitrust suits were instituted during Taft's administration, compared with only sixty-two during the entire previous period from 1890 to 1908.[23]

The Standard Oil Case, 1911

The Standard Oil Company had reorganized itself as a holding company after the Ohio decision of 1892. This holding company, the Standard Oil Company of New Jersey, was given voting control over the other companies of the Standard Oil group, and it exchanged its stock for the stocks of the firms that formerly had been controlled by the Standard Oil Trust. Through this process of exchange the holding company obtained $97 million in stock, practically the same amount of trust

23. Clark, *The Federal Trust Policy*, p. 145.

certificates as had been issued at the time the Standard Oil Trust was
dissolved in 1892. Standard Oil of New Jersey had massive economic
power. In 1906 the Bureau of Corporations reported that about 91 percent of the refining industry was either directly or indirectly under
Standard control.[24] In 1904 the Bureau of Corporations reported that
Standard Oil controlled 85 percent of domestic sales of refined oil.[25]
In the same year, the total production of refined oil in the United
States was 27.1 million barrels; of this total, Standard Oil and its affiliates produced 23.5 million barrels, or around 86 percent of domestic
output.[26]

Some indication of the Standard Oil Trust's economic power can be
seen in Table 3-2. This table presents the ratio of net earnings to the
value of Standard Oil's property for the period from 1890 to 1906. The
net earnings of Standard for the ten years ending in 1906 averaged over
25 percent of the average value of its property. During the same ten-year

Table 3-2 Dividends and Profits of the Standard Oil Company,
1890–1906

Year	Percent Rate of Dividends	Percent of Net Earnings to Capital Stock	Percent of Net Earnings to Property
1890	12.0	19.7	17.6
1891	12.0	16.8	13.8
1892	12.2	19.7	15.4
1893	12.0	15.9	11.9
1894	12.0	16.0	11.6
1895	17.0	24.8	17.3
1896	31.0	35.0	23.5
1897	33.0	48.8	27.6
1898	30.0	48.8	27.6
1899	33.0	48.8	27.6
1900	48.0	57.0	27.6
1901	48.0	53.7	25.1
1902	45.0	66.3	29.2
1903	44.0	83.5	32.4
1904	36.0	62.6	21.7
1905	40.0	58.4	18.7
1906	40.0	84.5	24.6

Source: *Brief for the United States*, 1, No. 725 (1909), 6; 2, 8-9.

24. *Brief for the United States*, 1, No. 725 (1909), 8.
25. Ibid., p. 9.
26. *Brief for the United States*, vol. 2, p. 18.

period, the ratio of net earnings to capital ranged from 48.8 percent to 84 percent, the average for the period being over 61 percent. The ratio of dividends to capital ranged from 30 percent to 48 percent, with the average for the period being over 40 percent. The ratio would have been much higher if allowance had been made for the fact that Standard was overcapitalized by $30 million.

Theodore Roosevelt distinguished between "good" trusts and "bad" trusts. A good trust was one that gained its position through economies engendered by large-scale operations short of complete monopoly and took no unfair advantage of competitors or consumers. A bad trust competed unfairly and abused its monopoly power. Standard Oil was in the latter category. It had perpetrated a number of abuses on competitors and consumers.[27] It had secured rebates and other discriminatory favors from the railroads, and it had bribed railway and other employees for information about competitors. Through its ownership of most of the oil pipelines in the United States, Standard controlled the flow of crude oil and was able to fix prices. The independent refiners were unable to obtain crude oil except from Standard itself, and Standard would allow them only as much crude oil as it chose and thus was able to prevent them from expanding their business. Standard allocated sales areas among its subsidiaries so as to eliminate competition among them. Because of the rebates and other favors it obtained from the railroads, Standard was able to sell oil in competitive areas at prices that were profitable to it but that left no profit for its competitors. And then when it had eliminated the competition, Standard raised its prices.

In 1911 the U.S. Supreme Court unanimously affirmed a circuit court decision to dissolve Standard Oil.[28] The brief leading to the dissolution of Standard Oil was filed on November 15, 1906, and it charged the company with conspiracy to restrain trade and commerce in crude oil, refined oil, and other products of petroleum in interstate and foreign commerce.

In its decision, the Supreme Court ordered the transfer by the holding company back to the stockholders of stock that had been turned over to it in exchange for holding company stock. Each owner of one share of stock in Standard Oil of New Jersey received securities in thirty-three companies and, in addition, retained stock in the parent company, which continued as a producing concern. Since a few persons owned a large proportion of the stock of Standard Oil of New Jersey, the decree resulted in giving these same persons a controlling interest in all thirty-four companies. The effect of the decision was to divide Standard Oil into a series of companies, each of which was supreme in a

27. Ida M. Tarbell, *The History of the Standard Oil Company* (New York: McClure, Phillips & Co., 1904).
28. *U.S.* v. *Standard Oil of N.J.*, 221 U.S. 106 (1911).

given geographical area. Nothing was done by the Court to create competition within a geographic sales area.

The American Tobacco Case, 1911

The American Tobacco Company was also a "bad" trust. Before 1890 there was competition in all branches of the tobacco trade: snuff, plug, cigarettes, and cigars. The Tobacco Trust differed from its contemporaries in that it was formed to hold property, whereas the others held securities. It exchanged its shares directly for the plants, business, brands, and good will of the five companies that manufactured cigarettes. The trust was originally formed as a horizontal combination, but then it expanded and absorbed the MacAndrews and Forbes Company, which had an almost complete monopoly of the manufacture of licorice, a substance used in processing tobacco. Other concerns that did not process tobacco but made related products were bought by the trust, including those that manufactured tin foil, the cotton bags in which tobacco was packed, and wooden boxes. The trust controlled the companies that made the machinery used in the manufacture of tobacco and those that held the patents for such machines.

The American Tobacco Trust was formed to check a decline in the price of tobacco products, and this it set out to do by controlling competition in foreign markets as well as domestic ones. A cartel was formed to control foreign markets, and the trust used its large financial power to eliminate domestic competition. In 1899 it bought and closed thirty competing companies engaged in the manufacture, distribution, and sale of tobacco. Price wars were entered into freely in order to force the manufacturers of competing cigarette products to agree to terms set by the trust. The trust also required vendors, stockholders, and employees to promise to use only its products. While buying up the tobacco companies, American Tobacco also seized the plug tobacco trade. It approached the leading manufacturers of plug tobacco and sought to bring about a combination of plug tobacco interests. Failing in this, it simply tried to ruin the competition by lowering the price of its plug tobacco below cost. It was successful.

The American Tobacco Company had nearly complete control of the tobacco industry, as indicated in Table 3–3. In 1891 the trust produced about 89 percent of the cigarettes and small cigars in the United States. But by 1897, its percentage share of output had slipped to 80 percent. It reversed this decline by acquiring some of its competitors, in particular the Liggett and Myers Company in 1899. By 1899 the percentage share of the trust was back to what it had been in 1890. Although the trust's share of production declined again to 82.3 percent in 1906, it was back to 86.1 percent by 1910. In the production of cigarettes alone,

American Tobacco was even more dominant, controlling about 90 percent of the total output of cigarettes in the United States from 1891 to 1906.

The way American Tobacco gained control over the output of plug and twist tobacco was rather spectacular. In 1891 it had only 2.7 percent of the total market. But its monopoly of the cigarette business aided the company's expansion into the plug and twist tobacco market, since its monopoly profits could be used to gain control of other markets. By 1898 American Tobacco had become the nation's single largest producer of plug and twist tobaccos. In 1899 it acquired Liggett and Myers and R. J. Reynolds, and its share of the market jumped to 56.0 percent. American Tobacco's percentage share continued to rise as it bought out competitors, shut down their plants, and discontinued their brands. We should also add that in 1900 American Tobacco controlled 60.1 percent of the output of pipe tobacco and 80.0 percent of the output of snuff; by 1910 these percentages had increased to 76.7 and 96.5 respectively.

Table 3–3 Total Domestic Output of Cigarettes and Little Cigars, Plug and Twist Tobacco, and the Percentage Made by the American Tobacco Co., 1891–1906

	Cigarettes and Little Cigars		Plug and Twist Tobacco	
Year	Output (000,000)	Percent	Output (000,000)	Percent
1891	3,137	88.9	166	2.7
1892	3,282	87.9	171	3.5
1893	3,660	85.3	147	5.9
1894	3,620	86.5	160	5.6
1895	4,237	87.3	167	12.4
1896	4,967	83.4	153	20.1
1897	4,927	80.0	182	20.9
1898	4,842	84.6	165	23.0
1899	4,367	89.0	170	56.3
1900	4,255	88.1	175	62.0
1901	4,505	87.1	173	67.7
1902	4,820	82.8	189	71.2
1903	5,327	82.1	186	76.9
1904	5,881	86.6	176	78.2
1905	6,309	83.9	172	80.7
1906	7,427	82.3	182	81.8

Source: *Report of the Commissioner of Corporations on the Tobacco Industry*, pt. 1, "Position of the Tobacco Combination in the Industry," February 25, 1909, pp. 49, 325.

In 1907 the government initiated a suit against the American Tobacco Company, charging it with violations of Sections 1 and 2 of the Sherman Act. The lower courts dismissed the suit, but the government appealed the case to the Supreme Court. In May 1911 the trust was dissolved by order of the Court.[29] The dissolution did very little to promote competition in the tobacco industry, as subsidiary companies of the American Tobacco Company were reorganized into new companies. The American Snuff Company, which had a monopoly on the manufacture of snuff, gave part of its facilities to two new snuff companies, George W. Helme and Weyman-Burton. American Tobacco gave to its common stockholders the stock it held in R. J. Reynolds Company, a manufacturer of plug and pipe tobacco. American Tobacco was then split into three full-line companies making cigarettes, small cigars, plug, pipe, and fine-cut tobacco. These companies were American Tobacco, Liggett and Myers, and P. Lorillard.

In 1913, two years after the dissolution, these three companies produced 91.0 percent of the United States' little cigars and 84.7 percent of the plug tobacco. The three snuff companies controlled 97.3 percent of the total output of snuff. The seven companies controlled a larger percentage share of the country's tobacco business than did the trust that had preceded them. Moreover, the common stock in these companies belonged to substantially the same people as had owned the American Tobacco Company.

Rule of Reason

The Standard Oil and American Tobacco cases represent a landmark in the Court's interpretation of antitrust laws. In these cases the legal concept of "rule of reason," that is, the guidelines by which to distinguish good trusts from bad trusts, was drawn up. In the mind of the Court, the size and power of a combination created only the presumption of an attempt to dominate an industry. What was needed was proof that predatory acts had been committed, such as price discrimination, allocation of markets, or other devices designed to achieve market dominance, before the Sherman Act could be applied. In other words, size could be achieved through the normal methods of industrial development or through the commission of predatory acts designed to eliminate competition. Only the latter, the Court believed, imposed unreasonable restraints on competition.

Thus, the Supreme Court's decisions in these two cases virtually amended the Sherman Act by holding that it condemned only unreasonable restraint of trade, despite the text of the statute. A degree of

29. *U.S.* v. *American Tobacco Co.*, 221 U.S. 106 (1911).

combination in the public interest, but not abusive monopoly power, was permissible. But the Court failed to define just what constituted predatory and unfair acts, and so it became necessary to define more explicitly what predatory or unfair practices were, and this Congress attempted to do in 1914 with the passage of the Clayton Act.

Passage of the Federal Trade Commission and Clayton Acts

Two major antitrust acts were passed in 1914, the Federal Trade Commission Act and the Clayton Act.[30] Both were designed to strengthen the Sherman Act by adding teeth to its enforcement provisions. By 1914 the Sherman Act, through judicial interpretation, had lost much of its efficacy. There was no legislation to prevent holding companies, interlocking directorates, price discrimination, or other abuses designed to lessen competition, and the trend toward concentrating economic power in the hands of a few business firms and investment banks continued unabated. The Sherman Act was surrounded by a cloud of uncertainty because it failed to state precisely which kinds of abuses or actions by business were prohibited. The Sherman Act emphasized the punishment of abusers without being specific about the abuse; the Federal Trade Commission and Clayton acts tried to define and prevent abuses. In particular, the acts were aimed at the practices of unfair competition, including price discrimination, exclusive and tying contracts, and interlocking directorates.

The Federal Trade Commission Act, 1914

The Federal Trade Commission Act was passed in September 1914, replacing the Bureau of Corporations with the Federal Trade Commission, consisting of five members, each holding office for seven years. The commission was made independent of the president, and it was hoped that it would be a specialized new body that would aid in law enforcement and would supervise and apply guiding rules to the competitive system. Application of the Sherman Act to specific competitive practices had proved unsatisfactory to business groups and the general public, as the victims of predatory acts felt that the law should intervene before such acts had been committed. As well, many business people wanted clearer guidelines as to what constituted unfair methods of competition. The rule of reason seemed to leave excessive

30. The Federal Trade Commission Act and the Clayton Act will be discussed in more detail in Chapter 6.

discretion to the courts in condemning or approving business practices. Moreover, each antitrust decision covered a number of specific practices, and it was impossible to know whether any given practice could be condemned if employed alone.

The Clayton Act, 1914

The Clayton Act was passed almost concurrently with the Federal Trade Commission Act and was an attempt to modify the Sherman Act by specifying unfair business practices and thus eliminating some of the uncertainty introduced by the concept of rule of reason. The Clayton Act outlawed specific abuses such as charging different prices to different buyers in order to destroy a weaker competitor. This abuse, prohibited in Section 2, was called "primary-line" or "sellers-level" price discrimination. Other prohibited abuses included tying contracts that made the lease or sale of a product conditional on the lessee's or purchaser's use of associated products sold by the same manufacturer, and exclusive dealership arrangements in which one firm induced another not to deal with the former's competitors. Corporations were prohibited from acquiring stock in competing concerns if such acquisitions would substantially reduce interstate competition. In addition, the Clayton Act forbade interlocking directorates in competing concerns engaged in interstate commerce whose capital amounted to more than $1 million, and the act provided for triple damage suits for private citizens.

SUMMARY

Industrial and railroad monopolies were created around 1880 and continued into this century. The primary reason for instituting the various types of combinations was the manufacturers' desire to restrict or eliminate competition and thus to establish monopoly prices. This was done by having business monopolies control supply. A monopoly price is likely to be higher than a competitive price, for the monopolist can limit supply and by this means prevent prices from falling to the level they would if determined by competition. A second reason for establishing monopolies was the hope of those organizing them that they would thus achieve the economies of the trust. This is because a trust can almost always secure raw materials more cheaply than would be possible in a state of competition. A trust can often save money by vertically integrating so that it is assured of an ample supply of raw materials at cost. A trust is also supposed to achieve certain economies of production through specialization of plant and machinery and also of business talents.

Federal and state regulation of business began with the railroads. Because of the abuses of the power vested in corporate railroad management, the shippers demanded relief. The first laws to regulate railroads were passed during the 1870s. In 1887, the first federal law, the Interstate Commerce Act, was enacted, creating the Interstate Commerce Commission and making illegal pooling agreements among the railroads. Subsequent railroad acts strengthened the regulatory power of the Interstate Commerce Commission. The Hepburn Act of 1906 broadened the jurisdiction of the commission to include express companies, sleeping-car companies, pipe lines, and railroad facilities. The so-called commodities clause attempted to prevent the railroads from engaging in other businesses and to eliminate the opportunities for discrimination implicit in a dual carrier-shipper status. The Mann-Elkins Act, passed in 1910, strengthened the Interstate Commerce Commission in two important respects: it revitalized the long- and short-haul clause, and it gave the commission the power to suspend proposed changes in rates, pending an investigation of their reasonableness.

There was a complete transformation of American economic life between the end of the Civil War and the turn of the century. Rapid industrial expansion was accompanied by the use of various devices by business firms to limit competition and to control markets. These devices, which resulted in large business combinations, were the pool, the trust, and the holding company. The anticompetitive practices of these combinations eventually led to popular support for the passage of antitrust laws, the first and most important of which was the Sherman Act of 1890. Little use was made of that act, however, during the first ten years after its passage. Decisions by the Supreme Court impeded enforcement of the law, and the federal government itself was often lukewarm to the public regulation of business. In 1914 two more antitrust laws were passed, the Clayton Act and the Federal Trade Commission Act. The Clayton Act prohibited certain corporate practices when they reduced competition and created monopolies. The Federal Trade Commission Act established a commission empowered to investigate corporate practices in interstate commerce and to issue "cease and desist" orders to corporations engaged in unfair practices.

QUESTIONS FOR DISCUSSION

1. What prompted the railroads to form combinations such as pools?
2. What was the significance of the *Munn* v. *Illinois* decision?
3. Discuss why railroad regulation was generally ineffective in preventing the continuing consolidation of the railroads.
4. Discuss the reasons why common law was unable to prevent the development of the trusts.

5. Discuss the methods used by the American Tobacco Company to gain control over the tobacco industry.
6. Discuss the legal concept of rule of reason.
7. The Sherman Act created certain problems of interpretation that required the passage of the Federal Trade Commission and Clayton acts. What were these problems?
8. What is primary-line price discrimination?
9. How can a tying contract reduce competition?

RECOMMENDED READINGS

Brandeis, Louis D. *The Curse of Bigness: Miscellaneous Papers*. Pt. II, "Industrial Democracy and Efficiency." Pt. III, "The Curse of Bigness." New York: Viking, 1935.

Burns, Arthur. *The Decline of Competition*. New York: McGraw-Hill, 1936.

Chandler, Alfred D. Jr., ed. *The Railroads: The Nation's First Big Business*. New York: Harcourt, Brace & World, 1965.

Clark, John D. *The Federal Trust Policy*. Baltimore: Johns Hopkins Press, 1931.

Jones, Edward. *The Trust Problem in the United States*. New York: Macmillan, 1921.

Mitchell, Broadus. *American Economic History*. Boston: Houghton Mifflin, 1947.

Ripley, William Z. *Trusts, Pools and Corporations*. Boston: Ginn, 1916.

———. *Railroads*. 2 vols. Boston: Ginn, 1915.

Chapter 4

Extension of Government Control over Business: The New Deal to the Present

During the Depression decade of the 1930s, government regulation and control of business greatly expanded. By the end of the decade, much of the legislative framework for government's current relations with business had been completed. Direct government regulation was extended over the electrical power and airline industries. Antitrust laws were strengthened by the passage of new legislation, including the Robinson-Patman Act, and consumer protection, particularly in the area of false or misleading advertising, also was improved with the passage of the Wheeler-Lea Amendment. A number of changes were made in the banking system, including the creation of the Federal Deposit Insurance Corporation to insure individual deposits against loss in the event of a bank failure. The position of the individual investor was also improved by federal legislation designed to regulate the securities market. As well, there was direct government intervention to support business. In 1932 the Reconstruction Finance Corporation was created and financed by the federal government to make loans to business firms in economic difficulty. The first effort at national economic planning occurred in 1933 when the National Industrial Recovery Act was passed. The federal government also entered the mortgage market through the creation of the Home Owners Loan Corporation to refinance the mortgages of financially distressed homeowners.

Other New Deal measures had a more indirect impact on business. The National Labor Relations Act, passed in 1935, greatly enhanced the bargaining power of unions and made them a countervailing force to business. New Deal efforts to regulate hours, wages, and working conditions culminated in the passage of the Walsh-Healey Act and the Fair Labor Standards Act. The Walsh-Healey Act illustrated the leverage that the federal government could use to enforce compliance with an economic or social goal. It required business firms with federal contracts for $10,000 or more to limit working hours to eight per day or forty per week and to pay wages that were no less than the industry's minimum. The Fair Labor Standards Act enacted minimum wages and maximum hours for labor engaged in interstate commerce or in the production of goods sold in interstate commerce. In the area of social welfare, the Social Security Act provided for federal pensions for persons sixty-five years and older and for survivors' benefits to widows and orphans. The cost of social security was financed in part by a payroll tax on employers.

Until the 1960s most of the government legislation affecting business was economic. Within the past fifteen years, however, the pattern of legislation has changed to reflect shifts in societal values. These shifts have occurred in several areas—ecology, consumerism, civil rights, and women's liberation. The legislative approach that has been used attempts to influence private decision makers to achieve specific social ends. New government regulatory agencies have been created in such areas as affirmative action, consumer protection, and environmental protection, and their regulatory efforts have cut across virtually every form of private industry. Changes in societal values also have caused an increase in the amount of federal funds allocated for social welfare programs. The federal government, through a variety of programs, has made a commitment to alleviate social inequalities but, in the process, has drastically altered the distribution of the federal budget. In 1950 federal budget outlays for social welfare amounted to one-fourth of the total outlays; by 1981 the outlays for social welfare had increased to one-half of what had become a much larger total of the budgetary outlays.[1]

THE GREAT DEPRESSION

The Great Depression was an economic and social catastrophe with no previous parallel in American history. Prior to the 1930s, there had been periods of unemployment and falling prices, but they were rarely of long duration, and they were generally followed by a reasonably prompt recovery. But all this changed with the Great Depression, which began with the collapse of the stock market in the fall of 1929 and continued until 1941, when preparation for war eventually created full employment in the American economy. Prolonged mass unemployment became the norm for the decade of the 1930s—at its worst, 25 percent of the labor force was out of work.[2] But the Depression meant more than unemployment; it also meant idle production capacity, loss of profits, business bankruptcies, a fall in the standard of living, decreases in the value of property, the closing of many banks, and considerable social unrest. It can be said that the Depression did more to reshape the American economic system than any other event of the nineteenth or twentieth centuries, with the possible exception of the Civil War, for the government's efforts to alleviate it changed the market system.

1. *The Budget of the United States Government, 1982* (Washington, D.C.: U.S. Government Printing Office, 1981), p. 480.
2. *Economic Report of the President, 1976* (Washington, D.C.: U.S. Government Printing Office, 1976), p. 380.

The Causes of the Depression

Economists disagree on the causes of the Great Depression.[3] One theory suggests that during the 1920s many business firms enlarged their productive capacity at a rate that was too rapid to be sustained into and through the 1930s. These businesses expanded by ordering and installing new equipment, building additional floor space, and adding to their inventories of materials and products. As long as the spending continued, jobs were plentiful and times were prosperous. Indeed, the 1920s was a period of prosperity, with the mass production of the automobile stimulating the development of a number of related industries. But beginning in 1929, business firms discovered that they had been creating too much productive capacity, and consequently, they decreased their spending. Workers who had jobs necessitated by the previous expansion were discharged or required to work fewer hours for lower wages. Earning less income, these workers inevitably spent less. A cumulative decline in employment, earnings, and income, in spending on the expansion of productive capacity, and in expenditures on products ensued.

Still, the Depression might have been avoided, at least in part, if the market system had functioned the way it was supposed to. In an ideal market economy, the forces of supply and demand should have caused price readjustments, and there should have been a series of reactions to price changes. Consumer and capital goods in oversupply would have declined in price, and those types of labor and other resources in oversupply would also have declined in price. The fall in the price of consumer goods would eventually have induced buyers to purchase larger quantities of them, and the fall in the price of labor would have prompted business firms to hire more labor. In other words, an ideal market system would have been self-correcting because all markets were assumed to be competitive and labor and capital able to go wherever needed. Competition among sellers or buyers would have set an equilibrium price that would have cleared the market of any surplus product or resource.

It can be argued that the pattern of response was defective. There was resistance to reducing prices, because business firms held monopolistic power over their products and chose not to permit their prices to fall. Instead, they restricted the volume of physical output of their products to amounts that could be sold at prices higher than would prevail in a purely competitive market. Holding companies controlled large segments of the utilities and railroads and curtailed investment in operating plants in order to maintain dividends, the interruption of

3. John Kenneth Galbraith, *The Great Crash* (Boston: Houghton Mifflin, 1972), chap. 9.

which meant default on bonds and the collapse of the holding company structure. Unionized labor, although at that time lacking the economic power of big business, did try to resist wage cuts, even though the consequence was unemployment. Income was also distributed unequally, with the top 1 percent of all income earners in 1929 receiving 14.5 percent of the total income and the top 5 percent receiving around a third of the total income.[4] This unequal income distribution meant that the economy was dependent on a high level of investment or a high level of luxury consumer spending, or both.

The Depression's Effect on Public Policy

Regardless of the cause or causes of the Great Depression, however, forces were set in motion that produced an increase in federal economic and political power unparalleled in scope and purpose. As the Depression grew worse, public policy was pushed far beyond the traditional regulatory techniques that had been devised for railroad regulation and antitrust. The principal concern became the stability of the nation's whole economy; the problems that called for action transcended the boundaries of any single industry. Public policy was increasingly forced to cope with the broader issues of large-scale unemployment and poverty and with ways of stimulating production and new investment. The Depression also changed the country's political and social milieu. Politically, as the prestige of corporate managers and financiers declined, the federal government became more sensitive to the claims of labor, farmers, and small business firms. President Franklin D. Roosevelt's New Deal provided a vehicle for the organization of these groups, thereby counterbalancing the power of the large business firms. In addition, the New Deal instituted new laws to regulate business.

When Franklin D. Roosevelt became president in March 1933, the nation was near economic collapse. Industry was operating at less than half its full capacity, the rate of unemployment had reached 25 percent, prices were at their lowest point during the whole Depression, the banking system was on the verge of disintegration, and the gross national product of the country had declined 50 percent from its 1929 level. A number of economic measures were enacted, some of which were temporary and cosmetic, but others of which permanently restructured the American economy. New Deal measures related directly to business can be divided into several broad categories: increased regulation and control of industry, reforms of the banking system, closer government control of the securities market, regulation of public utilities and airlines, and consumer protection.

4. Maurice Leven, Harold G. Moulton, and Charles Warburton, *America's Capacity to Consume* (Washington, D.C.: Brookings Institution, 1934), chap. 5.

GOVERNMENT REGULATION OF BUSINESS

It should not be assumed that increased government intervention in business began with the New Deal, for some changes were initiated by the Hoover administration. In the early stages of the Depression, President Herbert Hoover followed the traditional policy of laissez faire and waited for the self-correcting forces of the market to work. Gradually, however, he began to use governmental powers and influence to relieve economic distress.[5] The Reconstruction Finance Corporation was organized to assist banks, railroads, insurance companies, and other enterprises that were threatened with insolvency. The federal government contributed $500 million in capital, and the corporation was empowered to borrow an additional $1.5 billion through the sale of debenture bonds. The creation of the corporation put the federal government in the business of making loans to private firms and set a precedent for a later time when the government would decide to make loans to firms faced with bankruptcy, such as Lockheed and Penn Central. By 1933 the Reconstruction Finance Corporation had advanced over $2 billion to business, and during the Roosevelt administration it was enlarged so that it could also make loans to newly created public financial institutions. During its twelve-year life the corporation lent $50 billion to businesses.

New Deal Experiments in Industrial Self-Regulation

The Depression continued and deepened in spite of President Hoover's efforts to end it. The few corrective measures that the Hoover administration undertook proved insufficient to check the economic decline or to alleviate the economic and social distress that had followed. The industrial production index fell from 125 in June 1929 to 67 in March 1932, and many businesses and banks were ruined.[6] By March 1933 the industrial production index had sagged to 59, and business bankruptcies were accelerating. Ironically, competition was stimulated, for in an effort to survive, sellers were lowering prices in order to move their products. Wage rates also were being lowered in order to cut costs. A downward spiral of price and wage cutting exacerbated the problem of business failures because consumers were not buying: they could not because their wages had been cut. Furthermore, large business firms,

5. Herbert Stein, *The Fiscal Revolution in America* (Chicago: University of Chicago Press, 1969), pp. 6-26.
6. U.S. Department of Commerce, Bureau of the Census, *Historical Statistics of the United States: Colonial Times to 1957* (Washington, D.C.: U.S. Government Printing Office, 1960), p. 74.

burdened with heavy fixed costs, did not want price competition. So the Roosevelt administration decided that the federal antitrust laws should be suspended during this national emergency and that prices should be stabilized or even raised through legalized monopoly action. If this was done, then wages also could be raised and the purchasing power thus increased would stimulate prosperity.

The National Industrial Recovery Act, 1933

The National Industrial Recovery Act (NIRA) was an early exercise in national economic planning. It was divided into two main parts: Title I declared Congress's intention to promote the organization of industry to create cooperative action among trade groups and to induce and maintain unity between labor and management under government sanctions. Under Title I, trade associations could formulate codes of fair competition, as approved by the president, that would be exempt from antitrust laws. The act also created the National Recovery Administration, to which codes of fair competition were sent for approval. After being approved by the NIRA and signed by the president, the codes became law. Most of the codes had provisions for fixing minimum prices and for open-price filing, with waiting periods before new prices could go into effect. Section 7a of Title I required that every code of fair competition must grant the right of employees to organize and bargain collectively through unions of their own choosing and pledged that every code would include maximum hours and minimum wage provisions. Title II of the act provided for the establishment of a Public Works Administration which was to set up a program of public works and construction.

The purpose, then, of NIRA was to relax antitrust policies designed to promote competition and instead to permit business firms to modify or even to eliminate competition. The devices used included restricting an industry's total production and assigning quotas to individual producers. Although deliberate attempts to reduce competition and restrict output were socially unjustifiable, it was felt that once the industrial system was stabilized, an economy of abundance would result. But the NIRA did not work as well in practice as it did in theory. One effect it had was the creation of a price structure unfair to the interests of consumers. It was also felt that the codes of fair competition were breeding monopolies, and large firms did engage in price fixing under the codes. Moreover, the degree of government control necessary to prevent abuses of the codes was immense, beyond what business and the general public was willing to accept. In May 1935, in the Schechter Poultry case, the Supreme Court held the NIRA to be unconstitutional on the grounds that it had provided for an unconstitutional delegation of legislative power to the president in his code-making authority and that the wages and hours of employees working in local plants were not subject to regulation, because the processes of production did not come under the constitutional meaning of interstate commerce.[7]

Revival of Antitrust Policies

With the end of the NIRA, there was renewed interest in enforcing measures designed to promote competition and to halt various types of price-fixing arrangements. There now was a new trend in American business, namely, the development of large-scale organizations in the area of distribution. Of particular importance was the creation of chain stores. Chain stores were organized around the turn of this century in order to take advantage of discounts that were offered to them by manufacturers in return for purchasing in volume. Chain stores also standardized the packaging and labeling of consumer goods, which tended to lower production costs. The next step was the introduction of self-service, so as to lower the cost of handling goods. Particularly during the 1920s, chain stores began to multiply, and their impact on retailing and wholesaling was significant: many types of specialty stores disappeared entirely or became much fewer in number. And as chain stores increased, the wholesale function of the marketing process was absorbed by the chain itself, and independent wholesale outlets were eliminated.

Chain stores were the focus of independent stores' resentment, which was partly caused by the various forms of price discrimination used by the chains.[8] One form of price discrimination was the manufacturers' awarding discounts for volume purchases by the chains that could not be justified on the basis of a lower cost for selling and delivering the larger quantity. A second form of discrimination took the form of "loss leaders." The chains would often sell nationally advertised products or unbranded staples familiar to the buying public at a price below cost. These loss leaders would entice buyers into the chain stores where they would buy other products as well. The device had a particularly deleterious effect on single-line independent stores, which might lose their entire trade to multiline chains using the same line of merchandise as a loss leader. Independent druggists and tobacco stores were particularly hurt by the loss leaders employed by drug and food chains. A third form of price discrimination was what is called whip-

---

7. *Schechter* v. *U.S.*, 295 U.S. 495 (1935).
8. The history of the anti-chain store movement is summarized in Frederick M. Rowe, *Price Discrimination Under the Robinson-Patman Act* (Boston: Little, Brown, 1962), pp. 8–11.

sawing. When a chain, or any large seller, operated in several geographic markets, prices were cut in one market but maintained in others. This device was used to eliminate local sellers who, unlike the chains, could not make up a portion of their losses in other geographic areas. The chains also had a competitive advantage in that manufacturers would grant advertising and promotional allowances for large-scale purchases— allowances that were not granted equally to independent buyers.

We should also point out that the Depression created all sorts of demands for government assistance to small business firms. The growth of the large chain stores, such as A & P and Peoples Drugs, placed great competitive pressures on individual firms engaged in distribution, particularly the independent retail groceries and retail drug stores, and also attracted the general hostility of the state legislatures, which enacted legislation to regulate the chains. To some extent A & P became a symbol similar to what Standard Oil had been in an earlier time. But there is some doubt that the charges of anticompetitive practices leveled against the chains were entirely justified, for there was an ease of entry into both the grocery and retail drug industries that tended to negate the idea that chains had monopoly power in any field of distribution.[9] There is no reliable evidence of widespread monopoly abuses by the chains during the 1930s, and the Federal Trade Commission, in a study of chain-store practices, largely exonerated the chains from the charges of anticompetitive business practices made against them.[10]

The Robinson-Patman Act, 1936

The Robinson-Patman Act is commonly known as the "Chain Store Act." It is an amendment to the Clayton Act, in particular to Section 2, which had sought, among other things, to outlaw price-cutting practices by large firms that were designed to eliminate competition from smaller firms. But Section 2 had not been widely used, even though the Federal Trade Commission had on occasion attempted to apply it to discriminatory discounts and to geographical discrimination resulting from the use of basing-point price systems, under which uniform delivered prices were charged regardless of the origin of the shipment. In one case, the commission condemned a manufacturer who granted discounts to chains for the combined purchases of their separate stores while refusing to grant a similar privilege to associations of independent stores, even though selling costs did not vary between the two.[11] The commission was rebuffed in its attempt by a circuit court of appeals, on the

9. Richard A. Posner, *The Robinson-Patman Act* (Washington, D.C.: American Enterprise Institute for Public Policy Research, 1976), pp. 34–36.
10. FTC, "Final Report on the Chain Store Investigation," Senate Document No. 7, 74th Cong., 1st sess., 1935.
11. *National Biscuit Co.* v. *FTC*, 299 Fed. 733 (1924).

grounds that the Clayton Act applied only to the reduction of competition in the seller's own line of commerce.

The most important provision of the Robinson-Patman Act is Section 2(a), which amends Section 2 of the Clayton Act to prohibit what is called secondary-line price discrimination. This refers to the sale of the same good to different buyers in the same geographic area at different prices when there is no cost difference. Although the impact of this kind of discrimination is felt in the competition among the buyers for the discriminating seller's favor, it does permit a seller to show that lower prices to some buyers are based on cost differences related to different methods or quantities involved in the sale or delivery of the product. Section 2(a) also prohibits any form of price discrimination when the end result is to lessen competition, when it tends to create a monopoly in any line of commerce or when it injures, destroys, or prevents competition with any person who either grants or knowingly receives the benefits of such discrimination. Not only restraint of competition but also injury to competitors became a test of illegality.

The remaining subsections of the amended Section 2 of the Clayton Act enacted new prohibitions that were not included in the original Clayton Act. For example, the payment of brokerage fees when no independent broker was involved became illegal. This was designed to eliminate the practice of some chains of demanding the regular brokerage fee as a discount when they purchased directly from the manufacturers. This was compensation that normally went to a broker, traditionally a seller's agent who assembled the output of a number of small producers for shipment to the distributor. Advertising allowances also were prohibited. These were normally made for point-of-sale advertising of goods manufactured by the seller and sold at retail by the buyer. These could no longer be given unless the allowances were made on equal terms to all competing purchasers. Advertising allowances and the remission of brokerage fees were considered to be forms of secret rebates secured because a buyer was in a strong position to extract them from a seller. The Standard Oil Trust was thought to owe its rise to a monopoly position—and its continuance in that position—in part to its ability to extract secret discounts from the railroads. The authors of the Robinson-Patman Act felt that price discrimination in the form of secret brokerage fees or advertising allowances should be forced into the open, where it would come under Section 2(a).[12]

The Miller-Tydings Act, 1937

A second New Deal Act was related to the Robinson-Patman Act in that it, too, pertained to distribution. This was the Miller-Tydings Act, which

12. Posner, *The Robinson-Patman Act*, p. 38.

exempted resale price-maintenance agreements from the Sherman Anti-trust Act. The antitrust laws had condemned price-fixing agreements among retailers, as well as agreements between a manufacturer and his distributors to fix resale prices. But the states had passed fair-trade laws legalizing resale price–maintenance agreements, which made it possible for a manufacturer to fix by contract the minimum wholesale or retail price of branded or trademarked products as they moved to the con-sumer. Small independent retailers supported the fair-trade laws on the grounds that they offered protection against the large chain stores, which could offer brand merchandise at a lower price. The Depression and the growth of chains and cut-rate stores crystallized the efforts of both the independent retailers and the wholesalers to obtain the legali-zation of resale price maintenance, first at the state level and then at the federal level. Approval by the states made the commodities sold in interstate commerce subject to the limitations of the federal antitrust laws; hence the passage of the Miller-Tydings Act.

The Miller-Tydings Act was an amendment to the Sherman Act and legalized resale price–maintenance agreements covering branded goods shipped in interstate commerce in any state permitting such agreements in intrastate trade. The amendment also provided that the making of resale price–maintenance contracts was no longer to be regarded as un-fair competition under Section 5 of the Federal Trade Commission Act of 1914. The act was not made applicable in states without fair-trade laws and applied only to products in open competition with others of the same type. It permitted the manufacturer or distributor of a branded product to set the minimum retail price at which that product could be sold, thereby eliminating price competition for the good at the retail level. One argument for Miller-Tydings was that it protected the brand image of a particular product by preventing it from being sold in a discount or bargain-basement store below a set price. But it raised prices above the competitive level that would ordinarily prevail and denied consumers the opportunity to obtain the best products at the lowest prices; therefore, resale price-maintenance laws were finally repealed by Congress in 1976.

FEDERAL REGULATION OF THE SECURITIES MARKET

The stock market crash of 1929 was a traumatic experience for many Americans. Millions of investors lost their savings, and many were forced into bankruptcy. After a decade of unprecedented prosperity, during which investors speculated feverishly in stocks, hoping for quick profits, in 1929 the economy began to sour. By autumn the indexes of industrial and factory production and turned downward. The stock

market, which is a mirror of economic conditions, began to reflect
investors' deepening concern about the state of the economy. On
October 24, 1929, over 12 million shares were traded on the major
exchanges. October 29 was the most devastating day in the history of
the stock market; 16.4 million shares changed hands, as the average
price of fifty leading stocks fell forty points.[13] This crash was followed
by repeated declines in stock prices throughout the period from 1929
to 1932; the average value of fifty industrials fell from $252 to $61 per
share, that of twenty railroads from $167 to $33 per share and that of
twenty public utilities from $353 to $99 per share.[14]

Business Abuses of the Securities Market

The stock market crash eventually brought to light many corporate
abuses that had occurred during the 1920s.[15] Some of these abuses involved the issuance of securities to the general public. Business firms
were caught up in the general optimism of the time, and, undoubtedly,
American capitalism was at its productive best: automobile production
alone increased from 2.3 million new cars in 1921 to 5.4 million in
1929.[16] The general public, traders on the exchanges, and investment
trusts found the stock market an appropriate vehicle for investment,
and the demand for securities was high. To capitalize on the demand
for securities, business firms would often continue to issue stock until
it was so "watered down" as to be almost worthless in book value.
Another abuse was the use of various accounting methods to overstate
the value of assets or to understate the extent of liabilities. Many business firms issued stock far beyond their need for financing and would
use the proceeds to invest in the stock market through loans to brokers.
The public also lacked adequate information to make rational buying
decisions, for firms often did not reveal relevant data or, when they did,
often misrepresented the facts.

There were other abuses that were not necessarily related to business
firms. Insiders on the stock exchanges who could learn about corporate
earnings in advance were able to make financial gains by manipulating
the market. They would run up the price of stocks to induce buying by
the general public and then sell out, thus causing prices to decline. They
would also depress the price of stocks by selling "short," thus prompt-
ing the public to sell. Then, of course, they would repurchase the stocks
at a lower price. Brokers were usually unlicensed and unregulated, and
their records were not subject to inspection.

13. Galbraith, *The Great Crash*, pp. 103–110.
14. Ibid., p. 146.
15. See U.S., Congress, Senate, Committee on Banking and Currency, *Stock Ex-
    change Practices*, 73rd Cong., 2nd sess., 1934.
16. Galbraith, *The Great Crash*, p. 7.

Banks, too, were guilty of unsound practices with respect to the stock market, for they often made loans to brokers and investors to buy securities. When the stock market crashed, the banks were caught short because they were unable to recoup their loans and to pay their depositors on demand.

Investment banking practices also contributed to the stock market crash. Senate hearings conducted from 1932 to 1934 revealed many instances of irresponsibility and abuse of trust by investment bankers, particularly in the flotation of foreign securities, which often turned out to be worthless. Investment banks would get large underwriting margins for handling the securities; the public enthusiastically purchased them; competition among banks to handle the securities was keen; and the bribery of foreign officials was a way of life. In one case, the son of the president of Peru was paid $450,000 for services rendered to a New York investment bank in the flotation of a $50 million loan for the Peruvian government.[17] No attention was paid to the fact that Peru had a bad debt record, with defaults on previous loans, and an unstable economic and political situation. A similar pattern held true for other Latin American countries. About one-half of all foreign securities floated by investment banks ended in default. The Depression particularly wrecked havoc on the Latin American countries, for their economies were almost wholly dependent on world prices for their exports.

The distribution of domestic securities by investment banks often did not fare much better. It is estimated that American investors lost some $25 million on worthless domestic and foreign securities acquired from 1923 to 1929.[18] One source of abuse, since terminated by legislation, was in the interrelationship of commercial and investment banking. Large commercial banks would organize affiliated investment companies and use them to speculate in stock and to manipulate the market price for securities. In numerous instances, investment bankers sponsored the flotation of issues that created unsound and unsafe corporate structures. In fact, the promoters of business mergers and consolidations during the 1920s were often investment bankers, who would profit from the result because these mergers would create new securities for flotation. Perpetual option warrants were issued, which enabled the sponsoring banker to purchase common stock at a fixed price over an unlimited time. In 1929, for example, J. P. Morgan and Company received, for $1 apiece, 1,514,200 option warrants on United Corporation stock.[19] Within two months Morgan and Company was in a position to sell these warrants at $40 each, and it netted a profit of $60 million.

17. Ibid., p. 187.
18. U.S., Congress, Senate, Committee on Banking and Currency, *Regulation of Securities*, Senate Report No. 47, 73rd Cong., 1st sess., 1933, p. 2.
19. U.S., Congress, Senate, Committee on Banking and Currency, *Stock Exchange Practices*, p. 115.

Securities abuses were particularly prevalent in public utility holding companies, which were used to centralize management and control. A holding company would acquire control of public utility operating companies, and often of other holding companies, which controlled yet other holding companies. The end result resembled a pyramid, with the operating companies as the base. These operating companies were controlled by a first-degree holding company because it had a controlling interest in the common stock. First-degree holding companies were in turn controlled by second-degree holding companies in a similar manner; and over these, at the top of the pyramid, was a single holding company. In all instances control was obtained by acquiring a controlling interest in the common stock. This controlling stock constituted the entire assets of each holding company. These holding companies were utilized to siphon off funds from operating utilities into the holding companies and their subsidiaries. Holding companies would charge their operating companies excessive fees for services rendered; these fees were listed as part of the operating companies' expenses and were passed on to consumers in the form of higher utility rates. State agencies encountered great difficulty in controlling operating companies whose policies were determined by corporate officials outside state jurisdiction.

Public utility holding companies were particularly affected by the stock market crash, as the unsound financial structures of many made them vulnerable to a decline in the economy. The companies were overcapitalized, and the properties of the operating companies were overinflated in value. From September 1929 to April 1936 a total of fifty-three holding companies with combined securities of a par value of $1.7 billion went into receivership or bankruptcy.[20] In addition, twenty-three other holding companies were forced to default on interest payments. The loss to stockholders also was catastrophic. It is estimated that the stockholders who held stock in the Middle West Utilities Company, a public utility holding company put together by Samuel Insull, lost $4 billion during the period from 1929 to 1932.[21] Stock in the Middle West Utilities Company declined from $57 a share in the summer of 1929 to $.25 a share in 1932. The stocks of other public utility holding companies fared no better. From September 1929 to April 1932, the stock of the Associated Gas and Electric Company declined from $65 a share to $.50 a share.[22]

20. Herman H. Trachsel, *Public Utility Regulation* (Chicago: Richard D. Irwin, 1947), p. 396.
21. Ibid., p. 398.
22. Ibid., p. 399.

Reforms of the Securities Market

The stock market crash, and the abuses that led up to it, created a need for reforms in the securities market. A series of laws were passed to achieve such reforms, beginning with the Securities Act of 1933, which prohibited the public sale of securities in interstate commerce or through the mails unless detailed information concerning the securities had been filed with the Federal Trade Commission. In 1934 the Securities and Exchange Act extended federal regulation to the securities market through the creation of the Securities and Exchange Commission (SEC), with which information about securities had to be registered. In 1935 the Public Utility Holding Company Act extended the power of the commission into the field of public utility holding companies. Subsequently, the commission was given broadened authority with respect to over-the-counter markets, was enabled to participate in corporate reorganizations, and was authorized to regulate trust indentures and investment trusts.

The Securities Act, 1933

The Securities Act, or, as it is commonly known, the Truth-in-Securities Act, was passed in 1933. Its objective was to protect the unwary investor from the sale of fraudulent securities through the mail and by door-to-door salesmen, who peddled "get-rich-quick" schemes in, among other things, Florida real estate ventures and Nevada silver mining stock. Various states had enacted legislation, later called blue-sky laws, to regulate the sales of securities. The laws varied widely in their scope and character, with some providing penalties for fraud and others requiring the registration of security salesmen, but not the registration of securities. State laws were limited in their effectiveness, as they did not have adequate provisions for enforcement. Thus more comprehensive federal legislation became necessary to protect the public.

The important provisions of the Securities Act are:

1. The heart of the act is the requirement that new securities offered for sale in interstate commerce, unless exempted, must be registered with the Securities and Exchange Commission (SEC). The registration statement must contain all the information about the issuing company and its business that the SEC considers necessary to the investors' interest. Although the requirements for different types of issuers vary, they generally include a full description of the kind of business conducted, the services or products sold, the physical assets owned, the identity of the directors and officers, detailed financial statements for

the past three years, the terms of the issuer's contract with investment bankers, and many other details.

2. There are penalties for failure to comply with the registration requirements. The issuer, and almost anyone in a position of authority or responsibility in connection with a registered issue, may be held liable for damages suffered by investors as a result of false statements in the registration statement, an omission of a material fact, or the failure to state a fact necessary to keep another stated fact from being misleading.

The Securities Exchange Act, 1934

As mentioned previously, there were widespread and flagrant abuses in the securities markets during the 1920s. Through such abuses, prices of securities were either pushed up or forced down for the benefit of those in control, with corresponding losses for investors. Uncontrolled margin requirements, in which a buyer puts up only a small percentage of the cost of securities and has his or her broker use the purchased securities as collateral for loans to finance the rest of the cost, caused much speculation and accentuated the instability in the stock market. When market prices declined, there was a deflationary spiral in which falling prices reduced collateral values, causing loan liquidations, which put a further downward pressure on prices.

The major provisions of the Securities Exchange Act are:

1. It created the Securities Exchange Commission, consisting of five members appointed by the president with the consent of the Senate, and each holding office for five years. The terms are staggered so that a new member is appointed each year.

2. The act condemns a number of manipulative practices and gives the SEC the authority to check their use. Manipulation of stock prices in any manner is outlawed. Corporate directors, officers, and insiders are not permitted to sell their company's stock short, and they must make public any intent to exercise stock options. Willful violation of an unfair practice is punishable by a fine of not more than $10,000 or imprisonment for not more than two years, or both. Persons engaged in manipulative practices can be sued for damages by injured parties. In addition to the penalties of a fine and imprisonment, the SEC may revoke the registration of the security.

3. A third major provision of the act is that all securities listed on national security exchanges must be registered with the SEC by the issuer. This is very much like registration under the Securities Act, in that a statement must be filed containing detailed information about the issue and the issuer. But this provision extended the federal requirement for full disclosure of information to many securities listed on the

exchanges that had never been registered under the Securities Act. The financial reports contained in the registration of securities must be in a form prescribed by the SEC and must be audited independently. Furthermore, registration statements must be kept up to date by filing annual reports with the SEC.

The Public Utility Holding Company Act, 1935

There were several reasons for the passage of the Public Utility Holding Company Act. One was to protect investors from a recurrence of what had happened during the 1920s, namely, the loss of billions of dollars in the collapse of the public utility holding companies. Another reason was the inability of state regulatory commissions to exercise any effective control over rate making. The magnitude of the holding company systems put them beyond the reach of the state commissions. The ease with which inflated property values could be worked into the rate base and the lack of access to holding company books led state commissions to accept almost any valuation put on properties by the holding companies. Proponents of public utility holding company regulation also wanted to reduce the concentration of control of the electric and gas industries. In 1930, for example, the nineteen largest holding company groups received 77 percent of the gross revenues for electricity in the United States, and in 1932 thirteen holding companies controlled three-fourths of all privately owned public utilities.[23] This concentration, it was felt, circumvented the natural processes of a free enterprise economy.

The Public Utility Holding Company Act declared gas and electric holding companies to be responsible for the public interest because of the sale of their securities in interstate commerce and because of their use of the mails. So the following provisions are applicable to their issuance of securities:

1. The act requires public utility holding companies to register with the Securities and Exchange Commission. The registration statement must include copies of the charter or articles of incorporation, partnership agreements, trust indentures, and similar documents. The statement must also show the organization, financial status, directors and officers, bonus and profit-sharing arrangements, balance sheets, and related information. Unless a holding company is registered, it is unlawful for it to sell, transport, or distribute gas or electricity across state lines.

2. A public utility holding company, as defined by the act, is one that directly or indirectly owns 10 percent or more of the voting stock of a public utility or of another holding company.

23. Galbraith, *The Great Crash*, p. 106.

3. The act also has an antipyramiding provision, in that it requires the dissolution of holding companies above the second degree. In other words, there can be no more than two tiers of holding companies above the operating companies; the first-degree holding company, which controls the operating companies directly through stock ownership, and the second-degree holding company, which controls the first holding company.

4. The act also requires the SEC's approval before holding companies or their subsidiaries can issue any security and also before they can acquire additional public utility assets or securities. Furthermore, the assets or securities of a holding company or an operating utility may not be acquired unless the SEC finds that such an acquisition will serve the public interest by leading to the development of a more efficient and better-integrated public utility system. The SEC may also prescribe terms and conditions for such an acquisition, including the price to be paid, in order to protect the interests of consumers and investors.

Reforms of the Banking System

The collapse of the banking system was one of the cataclysmic results of the Depression. In 1929 the banking system was inherently weak, in part because of the large number of speculative loans made by bankers during the 1920s and in part because of the large number of independent banks that were free from any form of government control.[24] When the economy collapsed, these loans went into default, as the market value of the borrowers' goods or the value of their collateral declined. When debtors defaulted on their loans, banks were unable to satisfy the demands of depositors who came to claim their deposits. Whenever one bank failed, it would act as a warning to depositors to go to their other banks and withdraw deposits. Thus, one bank failure would lead to other bank failures, and these spread, dominolike, throughout the country. As income, employment, and property values fell as a result of the Depression, bank failures quickly became epidemic, and the eventual collapse of the entire banking system became a very real possibility. In March 1933 President Roosevelt declared a moratorium on bank operations until ways could be found to resuscitate the banking system. Congress passed an Emergency Banking Act providing for the inspection of banks and the reopening of solvent banks under license.

24. Paul Studenski and Herman E. Krooss, *Financial History of the United States* (New York: McGraw-Hill, 1952), chap. 25.

The Glass-Steagall Act, 1933

The Glass-Steagall Act was an effort by the Roosevelt administration to place the banking system under more centralized government control. The act was designed to strengthen the commercial banks, weaken the connection between speculation and banking, and give added powers to the Federal Reserve system. The more important provisions of the act are:

1. It created the Federal Deposit Insurance Corporation (FDIC) to guarantee deposits up to $2,500. The purpose of this guarantee was to prevent "runs" on banks by depositors who were fearful of losing their money. The FDIC was made available to all commercial banks and was financed by a subscription of $150 million from the U.S. Treasury and $139 million from the surplus of the Federal Reserve banks. Member banks were assessed one-half of 1 percent of their total deposits.

2. It required commercial banks to give up their securities affiliates and to abstain from investment banking. It also limited the investment securities that member banks in the Federal Reserve system could have in their investment portfolio.

3. In order to prevent a recurrence of speculative transactions in corporate securities, real estate, and commodities that were financed by member banks of the Federal Reserve, officers of reserve banks were charged with keeping informed about the uses being made of member bank credit and with reporting such information to the Board of Governors of the Federal Reserve Bank. In cases of continued misuse of member bank credit, the board was authorized to deny such banks further use of Federal Reserve Bank credit facilities.

4. An Open Market Committee was created, whose membership was to consist of the members of the Federal Reserve board of governors and five other persons, not more than one of whom could be selected from any one Federal Reserve district. The committee was given stricter control than had existed in the past over the credit policies of the Federal Reserve system's member banks.

The Banking Act of 1935

The Banking Act of 1935 marked a further extension of government control over banking. With the passage of this act, the banking structure became inseparably connected with federal government monetary and fiscal policy, and the Federal Reserve and the Treasury were operated in tandem. The act is also important because it provided for certain forms of centralized credit and monetary controls. The basic provisions of the act are:

1. It made the president's power to appoint and remove members of the Federal Reserve Board practically unlimited. The old Federal Reserve Board was dissolved and replaced by a board of governors composed of seven members appointed by the president, each for a period of fourteen years.

2. The board of governors was given broader rediscounting power and mandatory power over legal reserve requirements against customer deposits. For example, the board could set reserve requirements against demand deposits anywhere within the range of 7 to 14 percent for country banks, 10 to 20 percent for city banks, and 13 to 26 percent for reserve city banks. Each reserve bank was required to restate its rediscount rate every two weeks, and approval of the rate had to be obtained from the board.

REGULATION OF PUBLIC UTILITIES

As mentioned in Chapter 3, public utility regulation began in the 1870s when various states passed special laws and granted charters for the railroads. The first federal law regulating the railroads was the Interstate Commerce Act of 1887, which created the Interstate Commerce Commission. Subsequent acts reinforced the powers of the commission. The regulation of transportation was expanded to include motor carriers, first at the state level. State regulation of trucks and buses, which was introduced in the 1920s, was at first concerned with safety, physical characteristics of vehicles, licensing of drivers, and the number of hours that a driver might operate. Soon, however, the states began to regulate the rates and services of common carriers. In order to prevent the evasion of such regulation, these controls were extended to contract carriers. But the impossibility of the states' regulating interstate motor carriers led to the federal regulation of motor carriers, through the Motor Carrier Act of 1935.

Government regulation of the electric power industry also began at the state level. As with the railroads, early public policy was largely promotional, primarily concerned with encouraging the development of the industry. Later, as abuses ensued, particularly in the form of high rates, consumer dissatisfaction laid the groundwork for state regulation. Starting in 1907, regulatory commissions were established in New York and Wisconsin and spread rapidly to other jurisdictions. With the growing importance of interstate transmission of electricity, federal intervention became inevitable. In 1920 the Federal Power Commission (FPC) was established, with the authority to issue permits or licenses for private and public power projects involved in interstate commerce. In 1935, by which time about 18 percent of all generated electric power was used in interstate commerce, the authority of the FPC was extended to cover the regulation of rates, earnings, financial transactions, and accounting practices. In 1938 control over the interstate transmission of natural gas was also placed under the FPC. As well, the FPC obtained planning control over all river basins.

The New Deal and Public Utility Regulation

The large-scale entry of the federal government into the field of public utility regulation began with the New Deal. This was not primarily a result of any change in the government's philosophy; it was merely a recognition of the forces of the time. The utility industries had crossed state lines and were beyond the power of the state regulatory commissions. The rapidly growing communications industry had always been national or international. At the same time, the arrival of the air age introduced a new facet to the regulation of transportation, and two important acts were passed, the Motor Carrier Act of 1935 and the Civil Aeronautics Act of 1938, which created a major regulatory commission, the Civil Aeronautics Board.

The Motor Carrier Act of 1935

The Motor Carrier Act of 1935 extended the jurisdiction of the Interstate Commerce Commission to motor carriers engaged in interstate commerce. But the ICC cannot interfere with the exclusive rights of the states to regulate intrastate motor carriers, and permission from the ICC to engage in interstate commerce does not thereby convey any right to do intrastate business. The act established different degrees of regulation for common carriers, contract carriers, private carriers, and transportation brokers. A common carrier may operate only under a certificate from the ICC, after a finding that it is able to perform the proposed service and that the proposed service is required for public convenience and necessity. Rates and fares must be published and must not be discriminatory. The ICC is also charged with enforcing safety standards. Although general publication of rates is not required, minimum rates must be made public and filed with the ICC, which can prescribe minimum but not maximum rates. Private carriers, not available for hire and carrying their own goods, are subject only to controls over hours of service for employees, safety, and equipment. Brokers must be licensed by the commission.

The Civil Aeronautics Act, 1938

After 1918 the federal government had indirect control over air routes and types of planes allowed through its granting of conditional airmail contracts. The Air Mail acts of 1934 and 1935 gave the postmaster general the power to regulate schedule frequencies, departure times, stops, speed, load capacity, and so forth. Regulation of air transportation, however, culminated in the passage of the Civil Aeronautics Act, which created the Civil Aeronautics Board and gave it regulatory authority over entry, routes, rates, airmail payments, and subsidies of common carriers. The Civil Aeronautics Board is authorized to issue what is called a certificate of convenience and necessity, which gives an air carrier the right to serve a particular route. Rates had to be approved by the board and had to be published and observed. Pooling, combinations, intercorporate relations, and abandonment of services were subject to control, but the CAB had no authority over security issues. The Civil Aeronautics Act was modified by an executive order in 1940 that created within the Department of Commerce a Civil Aeronautics Authority (CAA), which maintains the national airway system, plans and administers the airport program, and enforces safety, licensing, and traffic control regulations.

Communication facilities were also made subject to federal government control. The first federal regulation of communications was authorized by the Post Roads Act of 1866, which encouraged the construction of telegraph lines. In 1888 Congress gave the Interstate Commerce Commission the power to require telegraph companies to interconnect their lines. Regulation of rates and practices of communications carriers was introduced in the Mann-Elkins Act of 1910, which also extended certain provisions of the Interstate Commerce Act to cover wireless service. When the radio became the principal form of mass communications, regulatory problems arose, for the ICC had really been created to regulate railroads, not telephone and telegraph services and radio broadcasting. So in 1927 Congress created the Federal Radio Commission and in 1934 passed the Communications Act.

The Communications Act, 1934

The Communications Act, 1934, created the Federal Communications Commission (FCC) to regulate interstate and foreign commerce in wire and radio communications. The commission replaced the Federal Radio Commission and was given the jurisdiction over communications that was previously held by the ICC. The FCC has control over the telephone and telegraph industries and radio and television broadcasting. The latter is not a utility, and its regulation is based on the principle of competition. The FCC has power over rates, services, accounts, interconnections, facilities, combinations, and finances. For example, the FCC grants licenses to radio stations, assigns them frequencies, fixes their hours of operations, and prevents interference among stations. With respect to rates, the FCC has control over interstate and foreign rates of telephone and telegraph companies, but not over broadcasting charges. Telephone and telegraph companies must file their rates with the FCC and make them available for public inspection. Notice must be given of rate changes. If a new rate is filed, the commission may suspend it for a period not exceeding three months and hold hearings on its reasonableness. The burden of proving reasonableness is on the company.

The Federal Power Act, 1935

The Federal Power Act of 1935 gave the Federal Power Commission jurisdiction over securities, combinations, and the interstate rates and services of all interstate electric utilities. The commission was also empowered to make special studies of electric rates, the interstate transmission of electricity, national defense problems, and other matters. A corollary act, the Natural Gas Act of 1938, enlarged the commission's responsibilities by also giving it jurisdiction over the interstate transportation and wholesale sale of natural gas. These powers were similar to those exercised over the nation's interstate electric utilities. In subsequent acts, the commission was authorized to make water basin studies and was given control of the Tennessee Valley Authority's accounting and use of bond proceeds.

THE NEW CYCLE OF GOVERNMENT REGULATION OF BUSINESS

As mentioned previously, government regulation of business tends to move in cycles or waves, usually in response to some crisis. After the end of World War II and for a period extending through the middle of the last decade, government policies toward business were largely concerned with enforcing the laws that were passed either before or during the Depression. In 1946 the Employment Act was enacted, reflecting the widespread belief that the chief postwar problem would be deflation, depression, and mass unemployment. The passage of the Employment Act was significant in that it marked formal acceptance of the fact that the leadership in preventing this problem would have to come from the federal government and that the federal budget was to be the key instrument in regulating the economy. In 1951 the Celler-Kefauver Act was passed to amend Section 7 of the Clayton Act. This act prohibits the acquisition by one corporation of the assets as well as the stock of another corporation when the effect of the acquisition would be to reduce competition substantially or to create a monopoly. The Celler-Kefauver Act resulted from congressional concern about the greater number of corporate mergers in the late 1940s which increased industrial concentration in the United States.

A new wave of federal government regulation of business began during the 1960s and continued into the 1970s. This cycle is marked by the appearance of social goals in business legislation: eliminating discrimination in employment, ensuring better and safer products for the consumer, reducing environmental pollution, creating safer working conditions, and so forth. These goals resulted in the creation of a number of new federal agencies with regulatory functions—the Consumer Product Safety Commission, the Environmental Protection Agency, the Equal Employment Opportunity Commission, the Federal Energy Administration, the Occupational Safety and Health Administration, and a myriad of others. These new agencies follow a fundamentally different pattern from that of the older regulatory agencies such as the Interstate Commerce Commission. They are broader in scope and they are not limited to a single industry. Their jurisdiction extends throughout most of the private sector and, at times, into the public sector as well. There are advantages as well as disadvantages in this type of federal regulation. An advantage is that the wide range of these agencies makes it impossible for any one industry to exercise a controlling influence on their activities. A disadvantage is that these new types of agencies are concerned only with the limited segment of operations that falls under their jurisdiction. This limitation often results in a lack of concern or understanding on the part of an agency about the effects of its actions on an entire company or industry.

The recent government legislation is the subject of Chapters 8, 9, 10, and 11. Most of the legislation falls into three categories—consumer protection and safety, environmental protection, and equal employment opportunities. These laws have specific objectives—reduction of product hazards, elimination of job discrimination, environmental cleanup, and so forth. Many of these laws are meritorious on the surface, but they are not without their costs. For example, the basic purpose of the Occupational Safety and Health Act of 1970 is to achieve a higher level of job safety. This act places the responsibility for safeguarding an individual's well-being on the employer. In some cases, investment in employees' safety and health can add up to a considerable part of an industry's total capital spending. In 1972, 8 percent of the capital investment of the textile industry and 12 percent of the capital

investment of the steel industry went to comply with safety requirements,[25] an expense that will presumably be passed along to the consumer. It is also true that if money did not have to be spent on health
and safety, it could be spent on something else. Resources used for one
thing are not available to be used for anything else.

Consumer Protection

Several consumer protection laws were enacted between 1962 and 1975.
These laws, and a brief summary of what they are supposed to accomplish, are presented in Table 4-1. They are a manifestation of a consumer movement that has fluctuated in intensity from the beginning of
the twentieth century but that has never coalesced into an organized
pressure group. Occasional waves of popular indignation and, more frequently, identity of interest between consumers in general and better-
organized groups have produced several kinds of special government
protection for the consumer—protection against adulteration or misrepresentation of foods, drugs, and cosmetics; labeling of consumer
products; product safety; and so forth.

Environmental Protection

Concern about the quality of the environment, which has come from
the ecology movement, is a second area that is currently affecting government and business relations. Although laws to protect the environment against industrial pollution have been on the books for many
years, it was not until the 1970s that the major legislation was passed.
Protection of the environment is partly a reflection of changing societal
values, the new emphasis on the quality of life as opposed to mindless
material consumption. More and more citizens have come to object to
the increasing annoyances and assaults on health and aesthetic sense
that result from various forms of pollution. The probability that pollution creates health hazards, some of which may endanger life itself, and
the possibility that pollution may in time upset the balance of nature
to such an extent that earth can no longer support human life, also
creates anxiety and has led to demands for stringent regulation of pollution. Unfortunately, the issue of environmental protection has become
entangled with emotion, and ascertaining the true effects of pollution
has become difficult.

25. Murray L. Weidenbaum, *Government-Mandated Price Increases* (Washington,
    D.C.: American Enterprise Institute for Public Policy Research, 1975), p. 51.

The most important pollution laws are quite new. The Air Quality Act of 1967 directed the federal government to establish atmospheric areas for the country and created the Presidential Air Quality Advisory Board. The Clean Air Act Amendments of 1970 set air quality standards and required that by 1975 new cars be virtually pollution-free.[26] The National Environmental Policy Act of 1970 created a permanent Council on Environmental Quality, consisting of three members and a

Table 4-1 Consumer Protection Laws, 1962–1975

Year of Enactment	Law	Purpose
1962	Food and Drug Amendments	Require pretesting of drugs for safety and effectiveness.
1965	Cigarette Labeling Act	Requires labels disclosing hazards of smoking.
1966	Fair Packaging and Labeling Act	Requires producers to state what a package contains and how much it contains.
1967	Wholesome Meat Act	Offers to states federal assistance in establishing inspection standards.
1968	Consumer Credit Protection Act	Requires full disclosure of terms and conditions of finance charges in credit transactions.
1968	Wholesome Poultry Products Act	Increases protection against impure poultry.
1970	Public Health Smoking Act	Extends warnings about hazards of cigarette smoking.
1970	Poison Prevention Packing Act	Authorizes creation of standards for child-resistant packaging of hazardous substances.
1972	Consumer Product Safety Act	Establishes commission authorized to set safety standards for consumer products.
1975	Consumer Product Warranty Act	Establishes warranty standards to which business firms must adhere.

26. These amendments have subsequently been amended several times.

professional staff, whose functions are to advise and assist the president
in environmental matters. The act also requires all federal agencies to
consider the effect on the environment of all their actions. In 1970 the
Environmental Protection Agency was established to enforce the environmental protection laws and to assume responsibility for environmental functions previously given to other federal agencies. In 1972 the
Water Pollution Control Act was passed to regulate the discharge of industrial pollution into navigable waters, and in the same year the Noise
Pollution and Control Act was passed to regulate the noise limits of
products and vehicles. In addition to these major laws, a number of
minor laws, mostly concerned with relatively limited matters such as
the effluents from navigable vessels, have also been enacted.

Affirmative Action

A third new area that touches the operations of business firms is
affirmative action. This also reflects a shift in societal values, which
was prompted by three movements: the civil rights movement, the
women's liberation movement, and an increased emphasis on egalitarianism. The civil rights movement was begun to end economic and social
discrimination based on race or color. Because a large proportion of
minority members have among the lowest incomes in our society, the
movement also advocates the concept of entitlement, based on the idea
that since society over time has deprived certain groups of their rights,
the members of these groups are now entitled to compensatory incomes
and education, more representation at all levels of management, and so
forth. The women's liberation movement is somewhat similar to the
civil rights movement. It asks for the elimination of sex discrimination,
and it also advocates entitlement. Egalitarianism is somewhat more difficult to define. Essentially, it rejects merit as a desideratum for promotion and reward and instead stresses equality of result. An example is
the use of mandatory quotas for minority groups, including women, in
hiring and promotion policies, education, and job training.

These movements have resulted in the passage of laws that affect
business. In 1963 the Equal Pay Act was passed to eliminate wage differentials based on sex when the type of work performed by either sex
was the same. In 1964 the Civil Rights Act was enacted to eliminate
job discrimination based on such factors as sex, race, color, or religion,
and it created the Equal Employment Opportunity Commission to investigate charges of job discrimination. In 1967 the Age Discrimination
in Employment Act was passed to prohibit job discrimination against
persons aged forty to sixty-five. In 1972 the Equal Employment Opportunity Act broadened the authority of the Equal Employment Opportunity Commission so that it could sue employers accused of job discrimination. In addition to these laws, a series of executive orders have

extended the authority of the federal government to cover business personnel practices. It is these executive orders that are the framework for affirmative action, which seeks to redress any racial, sexual, or other imbalance that may exist in an employer's work force. Affirmative action applies to all nonconstruction contractors and subcontractors of the federal government and to all government entities.

SUMMARY

Legislation affecting government and business relations tends to come in cycles. One cycle occurred during the Depression of the 1930s, when much of the existing government regulatory framework was created. New Deal legislation, for the most part, was crisis oriented. The banking system was in a state of collapse, and so it was necessary to pass laws to preserve and support banking. Abuses in the securities market contributed to the stock market crash of 1929, and a thoroughgoing reform of the market followed. Massive unemployment and an increase in business failures stimulated a shift in emphasis in government antitrust policy and a reliance on a form of state planning under the National Industrial Recovery Act, which was to influence market conditions in ways previously prohibited by the antitrust laws. But the desire, especially of small business firms, for protection against the rigors of competition was reflected after the demise of the NIRA in their pressure for such measures as the Robinson-Patman Act. The New Deal also provided a vehicle for the organization of labor and other groups, thereby counterbalancing the power of big business. The federal government assumed greater responsibility for the functioning of the economy and for overall coordination of economic activity.

The second cycle of government-business legislation began in the 1960s but has run its course. This cycle was the result of several factors, including ecology, consumerism, and civil rights. Legislation was concentrated in three areas—consumer protection, ecology, and employment. A new set of regulatory agencies was created that has had a rather broad effect on business, in that their functions are not limited to a specific industry. With the new legislation, no business firm can operate today without contending with a multitude of government restrictions and regulations. Moreover, virtually every major department of a typical industrial corporation in the United States has one or more counterparts in a federal agency that controls or strongly influences its internal decision making. As will be pointed out, government regulation can have many adverse effects on business and consumers—a stultification of incentives and innovations by business and an increase in the costs that consumers pay for products, as government regulation increases the cost of production. Because such costs are not the result of any measurable output, they are reflected in a lower rate of productivity.

QUESTIONS FOR DISCUSSION

1. In what ways did the New Deal change business-government relations?
2. The National Industrial Recovery Act represented an attempt by the Roosevelt administration to relax the antitrust laws. Was it successful?
3. Discuss the reasons for the passage of the Robinson-Patman Act.
4. What is meant by *whipsawing* and *loss leader*?
5. Distinguish between primary-line and secondary-line price discrimination.
6. What is the function of fair-trade laws?
7. Describe the activities of the Securities Exchange Commission.
8. The epidemic of bank failures between 1929 and 1932 can be attributed to basic defects in the banking system. Discuss.
9. Explain the reasons for the New Deal's regulation of air and motor carrier transportation.
10. Discuss the purposes of the Communications Act of 1934 and the Federal Power Act of 1935.

RECOMMENDED READINGS

Allen, Frederick Lewis. *The Big Change: America Transforms Itself, 1900–1959.* New York: Harper & Row, Pub., 1952, chap. 10.

Elias, Erwin A. "Robinson-Patman: Time for Rechiseling," *Mercer Law Review*, 26 (1975), 689–697.

Galbraith, John Kenneth. *The Great Crash.* Boston: Houghton Mifflin, 1972.

Mitchell, Broadus. *Depression Decade: From New Era Through New Deal.* New York: Rinehart & Co., 1941.

O'Connor, James F. *The Banking Crisis and Recovery Under the Roosevelt Administration.* Chicago: Callaghan & Co., 1938.

Posner, Richard A. *The Robinson-Patman Act.* Washington, D.C.: American Enterprise Institute for Public Policy Research, 1976.

Rowe, Frederick M. *Price Discrimination Under the Robinson-Patman Act.* Boston: Little, Brown, 1962.

Studenski, Paul, and Herman E. Krooss. *Financial History of the United States.* New York: McGraw-Hill, 1952.

PART III
INDUSTRIAL CONCENTRATION AND ANTITRUST

The concentration of industry in the hands of a few firms is an established practice in the United States and other major industrial countries, though attitudes toward industrial concentration vary from country to country. In the United States there is a deeply rooted tradition that holds that monopoly is bad and that competitive conditions ought to be the rule rather than the exception in most parts of the economy. There is a belief that certain, identifiable unfair business practices interfere with the efficient operation of the competitive marketplace and that the most effective method of regulation is to prohibit those harmful practices. It is not surprising that by statute and common law our legal system has been concerned with the maintenance of a competitive market system. Among other things, competition in itself is thought to promote research and development, maximize productivity, enhance the position of the small business person, prevent excessive concentrations of economic power, and eliminate arbitrary barriers to market entry. Thus, competition is a multifaceted concept, with both economic and legal connotations. It may be used to describe both the economic structure of a particular nation and certain aspects of rivalry among business firms.

Antitrust policy in the United States has had an uneven course. Historically, enforcement has had political overtones, with laws coming as a result of congressional reaction to a problem considered pressing at the time. The Sherman Act was passed in 1890 in response to public (including business) reaction to the economic power of the trusts. Congressional action was helped along by the Populist Party, which had threatened to preempt some of the support of the major political parties. Because laws in the antitrust field so often were enacted as a result of congressional reaction to a particular problem at a given time, it has meant that antitrust policy has moved in spurts, with long interim periods during which there has been little activity. The last major antitrust law, the Celler-Kefauver Act, was passed in 1950 when Congress opposed the use of asset acquisition to concentrate power in certain industries.

Too often the analysis of antitrust and industrial organization issues has been based on assumptions that our economy is essentially stable and that fundamental factors such as consumer demand and effective barriers to entry will not vary significantly over time. Within our operating economic system are many divergent, concurrent groupings of activities, each carrying with it radically different implications for regulatory policy. Government policymakers, and for that matter the general public, have no clear idea of what they want, partly because of the economic and social heterogeneity of American society, which makes improbable a legitimate consensus on any goal. There are a number of goals that are related in one way or another to antitrust policy. One is technological efficiency and progress. Is it necessary to have large firms to achieve this goal, or would several smaller, more competitive firms be more efficient? Another goal is economic growth. There are many advantages to large-scale production, but is bigness itself necessary for economic growth? Other economic and social goals also complicate the area of antitrust.

The United States' antitrust policy also must be considered within the 1980s' framework of global market competition. Once unassailable U.S. industries are losing their edge over foreign competitors and will face increased competition during this decade. The mystique of American management superiority has been shaken by such events as the rise of the Japanese in the world auto industry. International considerations come to the fore in reference to U.S. antitrust laws, particularly when multinational firms are concerned. American antitrust policies, like other national policies pursued unilaterally in a world of multinational firms, could have hitherto unconsidered effects. A tough antitrust policy, with mainly domestic competition objectives, could undermine the strength of American firms in world markets, because foreign competitors play the game by different rules. Attitudes toward industrial concentration are different in such countries as Germany and Japan and the degree of antitrust enforcement also varies, and national policies that encourage monopoly in the hope of gaining a competitive advantage in world markets may work to the detriment of American business firms.

Chapter 5
Industrial Concentration in the United States

The trend toward industrial concentration in the United States began in the last century when many industries came to be dominated by a few relatively large firms or even by only one firm. By 1884 Standard Oil was selling more than 80 percent of the oil that flowed out of American wells. In 1891 the American Tobacco Company produced 88 percent of the total output of cigarettes, and by 1901 the U.S. Steel Corporation controlled 65 percent of the nation's steel capacity. This concentration continued unabated into the twentieth century. In 1914, firms with an annual output valued at a million or more dollars constituted only 2.2 percent of the total number of manufacturing firms, but these few firms employed 35.3 percent of all manufacturing workers and produced, in value, 48.7 percent of all manufactured products.[1] In part this concentration was an inevitable concomitant of a rapidly developing industrial society in which the use of large specialized machines and facilities and assembly-line methods of production necessitated large firms. But industrial concentration was also a result of the drive for market power made possible by liberal corporation laws and ineffective antitrust enforcement, particularly with respect to mergers.

In the 1920s, there was an extraordinary expansion of the merger movement; between 1922 and 1929, 1,245 manufacturing and mining firms disappeared through the process of consolidation and merger.[2] To a considerable degree, the merger movement in the 1920s was stimulated by changes occurring in the economy as a whole, in particular, the mass production of the automobile and the growth of the electrical appliance and broadcasting industries. General Motors became the leader in the automobile industry through a series of mergers with other auto firms. Size came to have certain advantages from the standpoint of using modern marketing methods and, therefore, was a consideration in the development of mergers. The kinds of items that were being produced almost guaranteed large industries. Automobiles cannot be

1. Solomon Fabricant, *The Output of Manufacturing Industries, 1899–1937* (New York: National Bureau of Economic Research, 1940), pp. 84–85.
2. U.S. Department of Commerce, Bureau of the Census, *Statistical Abstract* (Washington, D.C.: U.S. Government Printing Office, 1968), p. 485.

produced by one or two employees; they require a large manufacturing plant. Financing was also easier for large enterprises because it was possible for them to use different methods to raise capital.

Industrial concentration in the United States was accentuated by events during and immediately after World War II. Large corporations emerged from the war in a much stronger position, whereas small businesses were weakened. War contracts had been given mainly to large firms, most likely because large firms had the capacity to mass-produce the thousands of airplanes and tanks necessary for the war effort. Indeed, the United States' industrial might was probably the decisive factor in the Allied victory over the Axis powers.[3] War contracts were instruments of economic power that guaranteed their holders markets and sizable profits, gave them priority in obtaining parts and raw materials, and gave them the right to take advantage of favorable depreciation and tax carry-back provisions. During the war the federal government spent about $600 million a year on industrial research, over one-third of all the research funds going to large corporations. And even when the large firms subcontracted work, three-fourths of their subcontracts went to other large firms. The federal government also financed new production facilities, which also benefited the largest corporations most.

The same conditions of industrial concentration prevail in the United States today as in the past. Typically, large firms have become larger through mergers. A case in point is a comparison of *Fortune* magazine's 500 Largest U.S. Industrial Corporations between 1955 and 1979. Of the top 500 in 1955, only 262 were still around to be included in the 1980 list.[4] Most of the departed 238 were acquired by mergers or acquisitions by other large firms; only four of them actually went out of business. But the big firms did not necessarily get bigger, and some that were small firms in 1950 ended up making *Fortune*'s 500 in 1979. In 1955 Occidental Petroleum's total sales were $3,000; by 1979 sales were $9.6 billion and Occidental was among the 50 largest industrial firms in the United States.[5] Conversely, there was some slippage among the very large firms. Of the top 100 largest firms in 1950, 59 remained by 1979, but Swift, now known as Esmark, fell from its fifth position in 1955 to forty-second in 1979.[6] There has also been an industry shift, with basic industries such as rubber and steel declining in industrial importance. In 1955 the basic industries accounted for 43 percent of *Fortune*'s 500 total sales, but by 1979 the basic industries accounted for 30 percent of total sales.

3. The author saw some old destroyed Sherman tanks rusting in a farm field in eastern Poland, some of the thousands of tanks sent by the United States to the Soviet Union in World War II.
4. *Fortune*, May 5, 1980, p. 88.
5. Ibid., p. 89.
6. Ibid., p. 90.

In the 1960s and 1970s there arose a new form of business combination called the conglomerate, a disparate union of unrelated companies. A majority of American business units are of the simple horizontal type, the union under one central management of two or more firms that turn out exactly the same type of product. Other combinations are of the vertical type, the union under one central management of two or more plants that operate different stages of the production process necessary to prepare the final product for the market. Conglomerates, however, are multiproduct, multimarket companies that are the result of an amalgam of unlike companies. The conglomerate became the most popular combination when companies hastened to acquire other companies with different markets. Pepsi-Cola and Pizza Hut and Philip Morris and Seven-Up are examples of conglomerate acquisitions. The oil companies, too, have attempted to become conglomerates, as seen in Mobil's takeover of Montgomery Ward. There are even those who predict that by the end of the current decade there will be only two hundred major industrial companies in the United States, all conglomerates.[7]

THE EXTENT OF CONCENTRATION BY INDUSTRY

The extent of concentration in the United States varies considerably by industry. In some industries, one large firm is clearly dominant, in that it contributes 50 percent or more of the total output. General Motors, with over 60 percent of America's domestic output of automobiles is an example. In other industries, a few firms may account for the bulk of sales, with no one firm clearly dominant over the others. An example of this is the codominance of the tobacco industry by R. J. Reynolds Industries, Philip Morris, and American Brands. There are industries that have little or no concentration and thus approximate a market situation called pure competition, in which no seller produces more than a negligible share of market supply. The shoe and clothing industries are examples.

Concentration by Firm Size

Table 5-1 presents a division of firms based on number of employees, payrolls, and value added by manufacturing and capital expenditures. The data are for 1977. Firms employing one thousand or more workers accounted for 1.5 percent of all manufacturing firms, but 27.8 percent of the total employment in manufacturing, 35.5 percent of the total value of payrolls, 34.8 percent of value added by manufacturing, and

7. *Fortune*, February 11, 1980, p. 199.

Table 5-1 Distribution of Industry in the United States by Class Size for 1977 (Establishments and employees in thousands; money figures in millions of dollars)

Item	Total	Under 20	20–99	100–249	250–999	1,000 & over
			Employee Size—Class of Establishment			
Establishments	351	237	78	22	12	2
Employees	18,515	1,206	3,489	3,336	5,393	5,191
Payroll	242,032	13,713	38,693	37,772	66,248	85,609
Value added by manufacturing	585,166	30,081	89,829	92,232	172,607	200,417
Capital expenditures	47,459	1,377	4,280	7,812	13,337	17,001

Source: U.S. Bureau of the Census, 1977 Census of Manufacture, Concentration Ratios in Manufacturing, General Summary Report, Table 4, May 1981.

36.0 percent of new capital expenditures. But these percentages show a decline when compared with earlier statistics for 1967, which were as follows: employment in manufacturing, 32.8 percent; total value of payrolls, 39.1 percent; value added by manufacturing, 38.0 percent; and new capital expenditures, 38.3 percent. In 1977, approximately 4 percent of all American industrial firms produced about half of the value added by manufacturing and of all new capital expenditures.

In recent years, there has been no discernible major trend toward a greater concentration of output from a smaller number of firms; in fact, there appears to be a decline. Using 1954 as a base year, firms with one thousand or more workers employed 32.6 percent of the labor force in manufacturing, compared with 27.8 percent in 1977. The percentage of payrolls provided by these largest firms declined from 37.3 percent of the total in 1954 to 35.5 percent in 1977; the contribution to new capital expenditures by the largest firms decreased from 38.3 percent in 1954 to 36.0 percent in 1977; and value added by manufacturing declined from 37.0 percent in 1954 to 34.8 percent in 1977. On the other hand, the contribution to new capital expenditures by the largest firms decreased slightly, from 38.3 percent in 1954 to 38.2 percent in 1977. Value added by manufacturing increased from 37.0 percent in 1954 to 38.0 percent in 1977.

Table 5-2 outlines the largest companies' percentages of total value added by manufacturing over several time periods, with 1947 as the base. The trend during the entire period is toward greater concentration of output. The largest 50 companies, as measured by their contribution to value added by manufacturing, contributed 17 percent of value added in 1947 compared with 24 percent in 1977. But from 1954 to 1977 the percentage share of the largest 50 companies remained virtually constant. The largest overall relative gain was made by the second largest 100 companies. From 1963 to 1977 there was very little change in the percentage shares for all groups. It is important to note that the largest 50 companies contributed more to the total value added by manufacturing in 1947 and 1977 than the next largest 150 companies did.

Table 5-3 compares the shares of value added by manufacturing, employment, value of shipments, and capital manufactures held by the 200 largest manufacturing companies for two periods, 1977 and 1967. The dominance of the 50 largest firms is apparent. In 1977 the 50 largest firms accounted for 24 percent of the total value added by manufacturing; the next 50 largest contributed only 10 percent; and the next largest 100 firms accounted for 10 percent. The 50 largest companies employed 16 percent of all manufacturing workers in 1977; the next largest 150 companies employed 15 percent. The 50 largest companies accounted for 25 percent of the total value of shipment in that year in comparison with 20 percent for the next largest 150 companies. With regard to new capital expenditures, the 50 largest firms were

Table 5-2 Percent Share of Largest Companies of Total Value Added by Manufacturing, 1947 to 1976

Value Added by Manufacturing	1947	1954	1958	1963	1966	1967	1970	1972	1977
Largest 50 companies	17	23	23	25	25	25	24	25	24
Largest 100 companies	23	30	30	33	33	33	33	33	33
Largest 150 companies	27	34	35	37	38	38	38	39	39
Largest 200 companies	30	37	38	41	42	42	43	43	44

Source: U.S. Bureau of the Census, 1977 Census of Manufacture, *Concentration Ratios in Manufacturing*, Table 1; May 1981, p. 7.

Table 5-3 Share of Value Added, Employment, Payroll, Value of Shipments, and Capital Expenditures Accounted for by the 200 Largest Companies: 1977 and 1967

Company Rank Group Based on Value Added by Manufacturing		Value Added by Manufacturing	All Employees		Production Workers			Value of Shipments	Capital Expenditures, New
			Number	Payroll	Number	Man-hours	Wages		
50 largest	1977	24	16	25	16	17	24	25	28
	1967	25	20	25	18	18	23	25	27
51st to 100th largest	1977	9	7	8	6	7	7	9	11
	1967	8	6	7	5	6	6	9	13
101st to 150th largest	1977	6	5	5	5	5	5	6	6
	1967	5	4	5	4	4	4	5	6
151st to 200th largest	1977	4	4	4	4	4	4	4	5
	1967	4	3	3	3	3	3	4	4
200 largest	1977	44	33	42	31	32	40	45	49
	1967	42	34	40	30	31	37	43	51

Source: U.S. Bureau of the Census, Census of Manufacture, 1977, *Concentration Ratios in Manufacturing*, Table 4; May 1981, p. 9.

Table 5-4 Percentages of Industry Output Produced by the Four Largest Firms in High and Low Concentration Industries (Output measured by value of shipment)

	Percent of Industry Output Produced by Four Largest Firms
High Concentration Industries	
Motor vehicles and car bodies	93
Household laundry equipment	89
Cereal breakfast foods	89
Cigarettes	84
Sewing machines	83
Organic fibers	78
Primary aluminum	76
Photographic equipment	72
Tires	70
Malt beverages	64
Motor vehicle parts and accessories	62
Metal cans	59
Aircraft	59
Soap and other detergents	59
Low Concentration Industries	
Petroleum refining	30
Pharmaceutical products	24
Canned fruits and vegetables	22
Men's and boys' suits and clothes	21
Radio and TV equipment	20
Millinery	19
Meat packing	19
Fluid milk	18
Sawmills	17
Poultry dressing	16
Wood household furniture	14
Fur goods	11
Concrete products	9
Women's and misses' dresses	8

Source: U.S. Bureau of the Census, 1977 Census of Manufacture, *Concentration Ratios in Manufacturing*, Table 7, May 1981, pp. 12–61.

responsible for 28 percent of the total in 1977 compared with 21 percent for the next largest 150 companies. There was very little change in the firms' relative shares in each classification for the two periods 1967 and 1977, which supports a point made in Table 5-2, namely, that industrial concentration, as measured by various criteria, seems to have stabilized.

Concentration Based on Share of Industry Output

A common measure of industrial concentration is the total output of an industry's four largest firms. Table 5-4 compares the output of the four largest firms in a number of high and low concentration industries. The extent of concentration is lowest in the clothing industry and highest in the aluminum industry. A high degree of concentration, however, does not necessarily mean there is a monopoly or a general lack of competition. The data on concentration presented in Table 5-4 do not give any information about the kind of market that exists for particular goods or the degree of competition that prevails. Size by itself does not always give a firm control over markets.

But there have been shifts in the extent of concentration by industry over time, and some have shown a decline. The four largest cigarette companies were responsible for 89 percent of the value of shipment in 1935 and 84 percent in 1977.[8] The four largest petroleum producers accounted for 38 percent of the value of shipment in 1935 and 31 percent in 1977. In 1947 the four largest producers of gypsum accounted for 85 percent of the value of shipment in comparison with 80 percent in 1977. On the other hand, there has been an increase in concentration in other industries. The four largest producers of food machinery controlled 18 percent of the value of shipment in 1947 and 23 percent in 1977. The four largest producers of malt liquor had 11 percent of the value of shipment in 1935 and 52 percent in 1977, and the four largest producers of wines, brandy, and brandy spirits accounted for 26 percent of the value of shipment in 1947 and 49 percent in 1977.

THE ISSUES IN INDUSTRIAL CONCENTRATION

In some industries, a certain amount of industrial concentration apparently is inevitable, as some types of business organizations lend them-

8. U.S. Bureau of the Census, Census of Manufacture 1977, *Concentration Ratios in Manufacturing* (Washington, D.C.: U.S. Government Printing Office, 1981), pp. 12-61.

selves to large-scale production. For example, there are industries in which the product itself is highly complex and can be constructed only by a large and diversified organization. Automobiles and computers are an example. There also are industries in which the product is large in size, requiring complex equipment for construction and large capital investments, for example, shipbuilding and locomotives. Then there are industries that require a large capital investment, particularly in plants and equipment. The steel industry is an example of this. There are many good reasons for manufacturing iron and steel on a large-scale basis, one of the most important being the tremendous financial outlay necessary to secure blast furnaces, steel furnaces, and other equipment. Finally, there are industries in which a natural resource is required that is available only in limited amounts and in specific geographic locations. Examples of this are the lead and petroleum industries.

Industrial concentration may also be an inevitable concomitant of advancing technology in all major industrial countries, regardless of their ideologies. For example, data show that for the same industries, concentration ratios are generally higher in other Western countries than in the United States; that the foreign industries in which concentration is high are generally the same as those in which concentration is high in the United States; and that the industries that are not highly concentrated in foreign countries are generally the same as the unconcentrated industries in this country. For example, in West Germany, three chemical companies produce 87 percent of all chemical products, and each company is larger than Du Pont, the leading American chemical company.[9] The West German electrical equipment company Siemens produces 58 percent of all its electrical equipment; the French aluminum firm Pechiney Ugine Kuhlmann produces 90 percent of France's aluminum products, specialty steels, and nonferrous metals such as titanium and zirconium;[10] and in Japan two automobile companies account for 85 percent of all Japanese automobile production.[11] These data strongly suggest that fundamental technological and economic factors determine somewhat the degree of concentration of industries in all market economies.

The extent of industrial concentration is even higher in the advanced Communist countries than in the United States.[12] To some

9. Statistisches Bundesant, *Statistisches Jahrbuch für die Bundesrepublik Deutschland, 1980* (Wiesbaden: W. Kohlhammir Verlag, 1980), p. 315.
10. Ministerie de L'Economie et des Finances, *Statistiques Français 1979* (Paris, 1979). Among all capitalist countries, the greatest degree of industrial concentration may be in France. This also is true for banking.
11. Bureau of Statistics, *Japan Statistical Yearbook, 1979* (Tokyo: Office of the Prime Minister, 1979), p. 47.
12. Frederick L. Pryor, "An International Comparison of Concentration Ratios," *Review of Economics and Statistics*, 54 (May 1972), 130–140.

extent the centralized planning characteristic of Communist states necessitates the concentration of output into large production units. The organization of industry has to be considered a basic part of the economic and political organization of the state, and there is a constant effort to combine industrial and agricultural enterprises into larger units to increase output so as to support the population and to export to world markets. In the German Democratic Republic (East Germany), one of the Communist superpowers, the largest one hundred industrial enterprises, or about 1 percent of all enterprises, produced 45 percent of its total industrial output in 1979.[13] In Poland the tractor combine URSUS produces 100 percent of all its tractors, and in Hungary the combine RABA produces all its heavy-duty trucks, tractors, and railroad equipment.[14] The high degree of concentration in centrally planned economies is evidence that large-scale operations and the concentration that accompany them do yield economies of scale.

Industrial concentration also can transcend national boundaries. Large American firms acquire foreign firms, and large foreign firms acquire American firms. As competition becomes global, additional economies of scale may be created. A *Business Week* article suggests that by the end of the current decade, conceivably only five automobile companies will be left in the world—two American, one Japanese, one French, and one German. Perhaps this is the final extension of an evolutionary process that began with the creation of the automobile industry when there were literally hundreds of firms turning out autos for the populace who could afford them. Social Darwinism will have been applied to the auto industry when the final survivors can be counted on one hand. This world trend may be irreversible, regardless of the product, and laws, antitrust and otherwise, will have to be restructured within a global frame of reference.

There are certain advantages to large-scale production. An expansion of a firm's production units often permits greater specialization in the use of both labor and capital equipment. Overhead costs can be spread over a larger output, which results in a lower unit cost. Economies can result from new, lower minimum cost combinations of production factors, that is, land, labor, and capital. The basic change is not a variation in population factors; more of all factors are used, and the total output increases at a faster rate than does the increase in production factors. Specialized labor and capital equipment frequently can be added to a production unit only in large, indivisible amounts, and because of the

13. Staatliche Zentralverwaltung für Statistik, *Statistisches Jahrbuch der Deutschen Demokratischen Republik, 1979* (East Berlin: Staatsverlag der DDR, 1979), pp. 125–135.
14. Martin Schnitzer, *U.S. Business Involvement in Eastern Europe* (New York: Praeger, 1980), pp. 81, 103.

indivisibility of specialized factors, they cannot be used profitably in small-scale operations. In many industries, smaller business units may well result in higher unit costs, and hence the answer to the problem of monopoly may not necessarily be the breaking up of large firms. Market power can be based on underlying economies of scale and technological or managerial leadership, and in some cases large firms are the price of efficiency and innovation.[15]

Industrial concentration also carries with it certain problems. In a competitive market economy the interests of producers and consumers coincide because the way to larger profits for the former is through greater efficiency, price reductions, and increased volume of sales, all of which naturally benefit the latter, too. In a monopolistic market, or one approaching this state, profits may be maximized at the expense of the consumer by selling a smaller quantity of goods at a higher price than under competitive conditions. The existence of monopoly power also means that the spur to efficiency and technical progress that competition provides is often lacking. There is evidence to indicate that small- or medium-sized firms are often more innovative than large firms. For example, in the steel industry, the oxygen converter was introduced in this country by McLough Steel, one of the smallest steel producers. Most of the innovative developments in the automobile industry were made by small companies, most of which were eventually absorbed by other companies. Packard developed the automobile air conditioner; Pierce-Arrow, automatic power braking; Studebaker, the power-operated windshield wiper; Hudson, the sedan body; Reo, the gear shift on the dash; Nash, a pressured fresh-air heating system; and Duesenberg, four-wheel brakes, both mechanical and hydraulic.

Small firms are often put in the position of having to innovate in order to survive. From this comes a willingness to take risks. Big firms, like big government, can be so encrusted with bureaucracy that there is more of a desire to maintain the status quo than to be experimental. Besides, experimentation usually requires approval from someone in the hierarchy of the organization. This can be disturbing, for often no one in the hierarchy wants to be held responsible in the event of failure. Often it is much easier to absorb a smaller company that has already made the innovation and has survived the risk of failure.

Industrial concentration can and has resulted in the growth of unfair business practices designed to eliminate competition and exploit consumers. In fact, price fixing and other forms of collusion have all too often been characteristic of markets in which a few firms are dominant. Moreover, the interlocking directorate arrangement can further the

---

15. In a case involving Alcoa, the Supreme Court was unwilling to split up the company for fear of losing substantial economies of scale in production and research and development.

effects of concentration. The interlocking directorate, in which one person serves on the board of more than one firm, is prohibited by Section 8 of the Clayton Act. But the section has not been actively enforced, and the few attempts that have been made to carry out its provisions have resulted in judicial emasculation. For example, the officers of one company who are not its directors may serve as the directors of a competitor. In addition, Section 8 prohibits interlocks only when two companies produce the same items. Potential competitors may have interlocking directorates, and interlocks among buyers and sellers, manufacturers, bankers, and others are permissible. So there can be interlocks among the largest industrial firms and the largest banks and insurance companies, and interlocks among firms producing closely related products. One study found that the 50 largest industrial firms had interlocks with 134 other firms producing in the same product class, and another study found that 49 commercial banks had a total of 768 interlocking directorates with 286 of the 500 largest industrial corporations.[16]

Industrial Concentration and Profits

On the basis of the economic models of oligopoly and monopoly, high profits can be regarded as a putative indicator of economic power. Certainly in an oligopolistic industry the barriers to entry of new firms are considerable, and therefore, it is logical to assume that profits should be higher in industries dominated by a few firms than in industries that come closer to approximating conditions of pure competition. This may ignore the fact that profit also could result from a firm's superior efficiency. But there is still the premise that there is a direct relationship between the extent of concentration in an industry and its rate of profit. The empirical basis for this premise seems to be somewhat contradictory, with some studies indicating a direct relationship, others not.

One study that indicated a link between market concentration and the rate of profit was made by Joe Bain in 1951.[17] In this study he found that industries with market concentrations of 70 percent or more had higher average profit rates than the less concentrated industries did. In those industries in which the eight largest firms were responsible for

16. U.S., Congress, House, Committee on Banking and Currency, *Commercial Banks & Their Trust Activities: Emerging Influence on the American Economy,* Washington, D.C., 1968, vol. 1.
17. Joe S. Bain, "Relation of Profit-Rate to Industry Concentration: American Manufacturing, 1936–1940," *Quarterly Journal of Economics,* 65 (August 1951), 293–324.

70 percent or more of value added by manufacture, the average rate of profit for the period between 1936 and 1940 was 11.8 percent; in other industries with lower concentration rates the average rate of profit was 7.5 percent. The rate of profit was higher than this, though, in some of the least concentrated industries used in the study. For example, in industries in which the eight largest firms contributed 10 to 20 percent of value added, the average rate of profit was 17.0 percent compared with an average rate of profit of 5.8 percent in industries in which the four largest firms contributed 60 to 70 percent of value added. But there were some problems associated with the study. First, the time period (1936–1940) was short, and second, the sample of industries (sixty-eight were examined) also may have been too small to be representative.

Another study of the relationship between market concentration and profit was made by George Stigler in 1963. Concentrated industries in the study were defined as those in which the four largest firms produced 60 percent or more of output. Industries in which the four largest firms produced less than 50 percent of output were defined as unconcentrated. Sixty-eight industries were used in the study, fourteen of which were concentrated and fifty-four unconcentrated. Several different time intervals were used. As shown in Table 5–5, the results of the study indicate no clear relationship between the extent of industrial concentration and the profit rate.

There are other studies that also indicate no apparent relationship between the extent of industrial concentration and the rate of profit.[18] Yale Brozen elaborated on the Bain study and found that the industries with the highest profit rates at the time of the study (1936–1940) subsequently expanded at a higher rate, and then their profits fell toward the average of all manufacturing industries. Conversely, firms in those industries with low profit rates during the period of the study subsequently expanded at a lesser rate, and their profits then rose toward the average for all manufacturing industries. This would seem to indicate that competition was present in both types of industries. In a second study, Brozen expanded the sample of forty-two industries used by Bain to more than eighty and also included more individual firms.[19] The study, which added the years 1963 through 1969, did not indicate a correlation between industrial concentration and the rate of profit.

18. See Yale Brozen, "The Persistence of 'High Rates of Return' in High Stable Concentration Industries," *Journal of Law & Economics*, 14 (October 1971), 501–512; Stanley Ornstein, "A Multiregression Analysis of the Concentration and Profits Relation," *Journal of Business*, 45 (October 1972), 519–541; and Harold Demsetz, "Industry Structure, Market Rivalry, and Public Policy," *Journal of Law & Economics*, 18 (April 1973), 1–9.
19. Yale Brozen, "Bain's Concentration and Rates of Return Revisited," *Journal of Law & Economics*, 14 (October 1971), 351–369.

Table 5-5 Concentration and Profits, 1938–1957

| Time Interval | Profit Rate | |
	14 Concentrated Industries	54 Unconcentrated Industries
1938–1941	6.51%	5.25%
1942–1944	6.23	7.68
1945–1947	7.30	10.01
1948–1950	9.11	8.02
1951–1954	6.33	5.05
1955–1957	7.05	5.44

Source: George J. Stigler, *Capital and Rates of Return in Manufacturing* (Princeton, N.J.: Princeton University Press, 1963).

For example, the average rate of profit in the industries in which the four largest firms contributed 10 to 20 percent of total output in 1963 and 1969 was 9.4 percent, as compared with 9.9 percent for the industries in which the four largest firms contributed 60 percent or more of output.[20]

Using *Fortune*'s 500 Largest U.S. Industrial Corporations as a reference, it is also apparent that the largest firms are not necessarily the most profitable ones. Chrysler, which is one of the largest corporations in the world and ranks in *Fortune*'s top 10, has distinguished itself by being the top money loser for the years 1958, 1974, 1978, 1979, and 1980. Bethlehem Steel, Anaconda, Boise Cascade, Lockheed, and Celanese all have been top yearly money losers. Using various measures of profitability, very few of the really large firms show up as performing exceptionally well. It is usually firms that are somewhere in the middle in terms of size that make the highest profits. This is indicated in Table 5-6 which uses one measure of profitability, total return to investors, for a ten-year period, 1970 to 1980. Only one firm, Boeing, ranked among the top 100 on *Fortune*'s list. Conversely, General Motors and Texaco, which have ranked among the top 5 corporations over this period, ranked 383 and 216 in total return to investors.

Concentration and Price Inflation

It would be logical to assume that price inflation is at least partly a concomitant of the large industrial firms' market power. In fact, the

20. Ibid., pp. 355–361.

Table 5-6 Total Return to Investors for the Ten Best Performers Among *Fortune*'s 500, 1969–1979

Company	Sales Rank	Average Annual Return
Dorchester Gas	430	42.6%
NVF	330	41.6
Trinity Industries	467	37.3
Nucor	482	37.2
Bally Manufacturing	398	35.1
Boeing	30	34.3
National Semiconductor	307	33.3
Smith International	356	33.2
Teledyne	132	32.2
Baker International	224	32.1

Source: *Fortune*, May 4, 1981, p. 345.

whole theory of cost-push inflation is based on the idea that large business firms and unions have the economic power to pass along price and wage increases to the general public. The theory holds that when unions force wages up, business firms will react by raising prices to cover the higher costs that result. This, of course, is impossible in a pure competitive market situation because any firm that raised its price would quickly incur a decline in sales and profits. For that matter, unions would not exist or would not influence wages in a competitive labor market, and so it would be impossible for any one seller of labor to have an impact on wages by withholding his or her services. In the absence of pure competition, however, oligopolistic firms could either engage in some form of collusion to raise prices in response to rising costs or, failing in this, react to changes in cost or in demand by altering their rate of output rather than their price. A decrease in output would exacerbate inflation.

There have been several studies to test the hypothesis that there is a direct relationship between industrial concentration and price changes. One study by DePodwin and Selden, based on a census of industry for the period between 1953 and 1959, found that only a small percentage of price changes could be attributed directly to industrial concentration.[21] Another study by Weiss found that between 1953 and 1959 industrial concentration and price changes were positively related, but

21. H. J. DePodwin and R. T. Selden, "Business Pricing Policies and Inflation," *Journal of Political Economy*, 71 (May 1963), 110–127.

between 1959 and 1963 they were unrelated.[22] A third study by Phlips, who used data on countries belonging to the European Economic Community, indicated that for European industries the relationship between price change and market concentration also was either negative or insignificant.[23] Apparently, there is no broad statistical support for the idea that there is a direct link between inflation and industrial concentration. In fact, there may be an inverse relationship between the degree of concentration and the extent of price increases.

Industrial Concentration and Competition

Though comparatively few American industries operate under strict textbook competitive conditions, we should not jump to the conclusion that there is no competition at all. Competition can exist in a number of forms. Competitors in an industry compete with each other on the basis of quality and product differentiation. They compete for customers with firms in other industries that produce other families of products intended for the satisfaction of the consumer's same general need, and they compete with firms in completely unrelated industries for the limited incomes of all consumers. Competitors in any industry compete with each other and with firms in all other industries for the scarce agents of production. The firms in any given industry also compete on the basis of technology; that is, they continually try to improve machines and methods of production that will both lower their own costs of production and render obsolete the machines and methods of their competitors. Even large firms, which do not have much competition within their own industries, must compete with firms in other industries for the consumers' limited funds and for the supplies of the scarce agents of production.

There also is international competition, for many American firms compete globally. The plight of Chrysler in particular and the automobile and steel industries in general indicate that there is plenty of competition in the world, particularly from the Japanese. The American automobile industry, an oligopoly if there ever was one, lost $4 billion in 1981, with most of that loss coming from increased imports of cars from the Japanese auto industry, also very much an oligopoly. Obviously, there is competition, with the Japanese winning and the Americans losing and asking for changes in the rules of the game,

22. Leonard Weiss, "The Role of Concentration in Recent Inflation," in *The Competitive Economy*, ed. Yale Brozen (Morristown, N.J.: General Learning Press, 1974), pp. 204–210.
23. Louis Phlips, *Effects of Industrial Concentration: A Cross-Section Analysis for the Common Market* (Amsterdam: North-Holland Publishing Co., 1971).

namely, U.S. government protection against Japanese automakers. Large companies, be they Chrysler or U.S. Steel, have to compete as ferociously as many small firms do in order to survive in markets that are now international, against competitors from countries that have different attitudes toward bigness and competition. In Japan, competition is fierce, but it is a "survival of the fittest" competition, with no help for the losers. And if the winners become larger in the process of winning, there is no government objection.

The number of American business firms, large and small, is rising both absolutely and in proportion to population. For example, in 1910 there were 2,923 corporations per one million persons; in 1968 the number was 7,936 per one million persons; and in 1976 there were 9,800 corporations per one million persons.[24] The number of business enterprises in the United States grew from 3,114,000 in 1945 (one per forty-six persons) to 7,950,000 in 1976 (one per thirty-nine persons). Individuals with self-employment income grew from 7,377,000 (one per nineteen persons) in 1945 to 14,700,000 (one per fifteen persons) in 1977.[25] This all reveals that the American economy is becoming less oriented toward manufacturing and more oriented toward service, with the result that the overall opportunity for the independent entrepreneur is growing. The proportion of manufacturing employment relative to total employment declined from 34 percent in 1967 to 30 percent in 1976.[26]

INDUSTRIAL CONCENTRATION—BANKING

Chapter 2 discussed how, as the industrialization of America progressed, the leaders of industry became more and more dependent on investment bankers for funds. With this development the control of industry and railroads passed into the hands of the bankers. The railroads offer a prime example of how the system of finance capitalism grew. At one time or another between 1890 and 1910 the bulk of American railroads went through insolvency into receivership. Usually, an officer in the company or someone designated by an investment bank was appointed receiver, and the railroad securities would then be given to the investment bank for safekeeping. The security holder would be bypassed, and the receiver and a committee appointed by the bank would work up a reorganization plan with a new set of securities issued by the reorganized

---

24. U.S. Bureau of the Census, *Statistical Abstract of the United States, 1981* (Washington, D.C.: U.S. Government Printing Office, 1981), p. 553.
25. Ibid., p. 279.
26. U.S. Bureau of the Census, *1977 Census of Manufacturing*, "General Summary Report," April 20, 1981.

company and put under the control of the bank in the form of a voting trust. The original security holders would have no choice but to accept the plan of the bank.

Investment bankers continued to acquire control over corporate affairs in the American economy. In 1937 the Temporary National Economic Committee reported on eight investment interest groups that had combined industrial, railroad, and public utility firms with financial organizations in informal communities of interest. The so-called Morgan-First National interest group contained thirteen industrials, twelve public utilities, five major railroad systems, and five banks.[27] The combined companies had total assets of over $30 billion. The second, or Kuhn-Loeb group, was composed of five major railroad systems, two other railroads, one utility, and one bank, with combined total assets of almost $11 billion. The smallest of the eight interest groups controlled companies with assets of almost $2 billion. In all cases, it is likely that the investment banking houses exercised control and power far beyond that which was necessary and appropriate to the conduct of their business.

Market Structure of Banking Today

The bank concentration in the United States is substantial. In 1978 the 10 largest commercial banks held 27 percent of all commercial bank deposits; in 1955 the 10 largest banks held 22 percent.[28] The 25 largest commercial banks, out of 14,200, held 36 percent of bank deposits in 1978 compared with 29 percent in 1955. The 25 largest banks had almost the same amount of bank deposits in 1978 as the remaining 14,175 banks did—$462 billion compared with $489 billion. The concentration can also be translated on a more local basis. In New York City the 3 largest commercial banks held 51 percent of the city's total bank deposits; in Los Angeles the 3 largest banks held 70 percent of all deposits; and in San Francisco the 3 largest banks held 78 percent of all deposits.[29] In smaller cities the degree of concentration sometimes was higher. For example, in Phoenix, Arizona, the 3 largest banks held 90 percent of the total deposits. When holding companies are included, the degree of bank concentration is even higher. Together, holding compa-

27. Temporary National Economic Committee, Monograph No. 20, *Investigation of Concentration of Economic Power* (Washington, D.C.: U.S. Government Printing Office, 1941), p. 33.
28. Edwin B. Coe, *Bankers Desk Reference: 1980 Handbook* (Boston: Warren, Gorham and Lamont, 1981), p. 213.
29. William G. Shepherd, "The Banking Industry," in *The Structure of American Industry*, ed. Walter Adams, 5th ed. (New York: Macmillan, 1977), p. 346.

nies controlled around two-thirds of the nation's commercial bank deposits. The new holding companies, especially among the largest banks, have expanded their assets into new lines of business activity.

Similar patterns of bank concentration prevail in other major industrial countries. In West Germany, 3 banks control 68 percent of all commercial bank deposits and hold two-thirds of all common stock shares held by the German banking system. Two banks, the Deutsche Bank and the Dresdner Bank, have a majority stock interest in 58 German companies and have a holding above 25 percent in another 131 companies.[30] In Japan the degree of bank concentration is even greater than it is in the United States and West Germany. The 3 largest commercial banks account for one-third of the total fund resources of all financial institutions, public and private. The Japanese commercial banks own one-third of the total wealth of Japan, and 70 percent of all industrial bonds are owned by the commercial banks.[31] In France the degree of bank concentration may be even more pronounced, with 4 commercial banks controlling 90 percent of all bank deposits, and given France's combination of free enterprise and government control, French commercial banks are important to French economic policy.[32]

Issues of Bank Concentration

There are certain advantages that accrue to large-scale bank operations, one being that economies of scale can be effected. Large bank operations also have specific scale advantages. They can hire highly specialized experts, such as economists and engineers, whose expertise can provide a bank with greater knowledge about a client's prospects. Specialists also can improve large banks' portfolio management. Economies of scale can prevail in relationships between two or more large banks; large accounts can be divided among several banks; and risks can be pooled. In addition to scale advantages, there may be pecuniary advantages in favor of large-scale banking relationships, as large banks often have inside access to information of value to their clients. In addition, their size can allow them to offer capital to their clients at a lower cost. Access to expensive computer technology also can improve the nationwide clearing functions of large banks.

On balance, however, the disadvantages of bank concentration to the public interest tend to outweigh the advantages.[33] Economies of scale

30. Data on the West German banking industry can be found in the *Annual Report of the Deutsche Bundesbank.*
31. Data on the Japanese banking system can be found in the Bank of Tokyo, *The Financial System of Japan, 1980*, pp. 27–35; and *Mitsubishi Bank Review*, 10 (May 1980), 165.
32. French bank statistics can be found in *Statistiques Français 1979*. p. 44.
33. Shepherd, "The Banking Industry," pp. 335–361.

from bank concentration appear to be minimal, and the extent of bank concentration is tighter than social economies would require. Banking legislation, in particular the Bank Merger Act of 1960, has done little to curb mergers and check concentration in banking. To some extent, there is a tacit agreement among banks on such matters as price fixing and terms of service, and unspoken agreements not to encroach on each other's area are common. The interest rate spread between bank loans and borrowings reflects a degree of monopoly: interest differentials against smaller borrowers exceed the differences in costs and risks, and the structure of interest rates discriminates in favor of large client firms. Innovation in the banking system has been slow, and most banks tend to absorb new technology at a relatively slow pace. In fact, most innovations have been introduced by firms outside the banking system. Computer handling was prepackaged by computer firms, and sidewalk push-button transaction units also are an outside innovation.

INDUSTRIAL CONCENTRATION—COMMUNICATIONS

A study by the *Washington Post* of the newspaper industry indicates that within two decades, virtually all of the daily newspapers in America will be owned by less than two dozen major newspaper conglomerates. A generation ago, nearly every American city had two or more daily newspapers. Almost every small town had its weekly newspaper, locally owned and operated. But today, most city newspapers have the same owner and thus no competition, and 72 percent of the daily newspaper circulation is controlled by companies that publish two or more dailies. Weekly newspapers also have become part of the newspaper chains; today, it is rare to find a locally owned, independent weekly newspaper. Newspaper companies own commercial radio and television stations as well. In fact, the *Washington Post* itself owns *Newsweek* magazine, various television stations, and a daily newspaper in Trenton, New Jersey. All this leads to the problem of a single newspaper having a monopoly of news and information, since many of the daily papers are owned by a single newspaper publishing chain whose owners' political views are reflected in their daily newspapers.

The communications industry has more forms of communication than newspapers, however. CBS, the leader in the broadcasting industry, owns Holt, Rinehart & Winston, a major book publishing company, and ABC also owns movie theaters and publishing houses. Thus, there is much cross-pollenization in the communications industry, with newspaper chains owning magazines and television stations, broadcasting companies owning book publishing companies and movie theaters, and book publishing companies owning magazines and television stations. There also is a trend toward concentration in the publishing industry, facilitated in part by high advertising and publishing costs. Whether all of this is good or bad is a matter of opinion. Economies of scale can result from this concentration, and firms such as General Cinema have been able to revive the once moribund movie theater by combining pictures in three or four locations or studios under the same roof. But again there is the matter of concentration of communication leading to control over information.

INDUSTRIAL CONCENTRATION—RETAILING

The general store was once the most important retail outlet in America. But as the country became urbanized and living standards increased, the general store was supplanted by more specialized stores—grocery stores, dress shops, shoe stores, drug stores, and so forth. Until the 1930s and early 1940s, the majority of these stores were owned by local merchants who were someone's next-door neighbor. But all of this has changed: the local drug store is now part of the Peoples Drug chain; the local grocery store is now a Winn-Dixie; and the locally owned department store has gone the way of a Sears Roebuck or a K Mart store. These changes are not necessarily bad; they reflect the continuing change in the evolution of distribution and the transformation of America from a rural to an urban society. Economies of scale can be effected by mass volume sales, and lower prices redound to the consumers' advantage.

There also is concentration in retailing. In 1960 the ten largest retailing firms accounted for 56.4 percent of the total retail sales among *Fortune*'s fifty largest retail companies.[34] In 1979 the ten largest retail firms accounted for 54.5 percent of the total retail sales among the top fifty. The top twenty retail firms accounted for 74.4 percent of the top fifty's total sales in 1960 and 73.7 percent in 1979. But there were many shifts in and out of the top ten and top fifty. McDonald's and Eckert Drugs were not in the top fifty in 1960, but both were in 1979. K Mart was not in the top fifty in 1960 but ranked third in total sales in 1979. In general, the top fifty were not particularly profitable, with three losing money in 1979 and seven others earning less than 1 percent on total sales. The best performer, McDonald's, earned 9.9 percent on sales, and the average return on sales for the top fifty was 2.2 percent. Sears Roebuck, the largest of all retailing firms, had a return of 4.6 percent on sales in 1979, and Safeway, the second largest, had a return of 1.0 percent.

34. *Fortune*, July 14, 1980, pp. 154-155.

SUMMARY

The American economy is characterized by the control of a large share of the output in particular industries by comparatively few large business firms. This, however, is not a phenomenon limited solely to the United States, for similar patterns of industrial concentration also exist in other capitalist and socialist countries. Whether this is good or bad from the standpoint of public policy really depends on the particular country's attitude toward competition. To some extent industrial concentration is a logical concomitant of modern national economic systems. Large business size has certain advantages, one of which is the mass production of one or a few products, such as automobiles or rubber tires. In addition, there can be economies in mass production, including division of labor and specialization in particular operations, and also economies in large-scale buying and selling. Large companies, representing a large and varied organization and having many scientific specialists, are in a position to develop and implement the most advanced technology. Large firm size also enables the reduction of risk and the offsetting of losses through diversification.

But there also are problems in industrial concentration. Large firm size may restrict competition and impede the rate of capital investment, and the economies of scale associated with large firms are limited. Up to a certain point, increasing the size of a single plant brings lower average unit costs. But beyond this point, greater size in a single plant brings disadvantages and results in higher unit costs. Large firms also do not necessarily excel in productive efficiency in comparison with medium or small firms. And increasing corporate size can create managerial problems, for the top management of a large firm cannot know all the details of the business and must rely on the reports of their subordinates. Such persons are frequently reluctant to jeopardize their careers by taking risks or trying uncertain methods. Finally, large firms in certain situations can exercise discretionary power over prices and entry into market. It is this power to engage in restrictive practices that forms one of the bases of American antitrust policy, which is the subject of Chapter 6.

QUESTIONS FOR DISCUSSION

1. It is evident that industrial concentration is not an American phenomenon. What does this suggest for public policy toward industrial concentration?
2. What is meant by *economies of scale*?
3. It is argued that industrial concentration is an irreversible trend that is occurring in all industrial society. Do you agree?

4. Why is industrial concentration higher in the socialist countries than in the capitalist countries?
5. Compare the extent of concentration in the West German and U.S. commercial banking systems.
6. What are the advantages and disadvantages of large-scale production?
7. Can it be demonstrated that there is a direct correlation between profit and the extent of concentration in a particular industry?
8. The influence of banks in a modern industrial economy, such as the United States, extends beyond normal bank functions. Discuss.
9. Should large newspaper companies be allowed to own television and radio stations?
10. Has it been demonstrated conclusively that there is a direct relationship between industrial concentration and inflation?

RECOMMENDED READINGS

Adams, Walter, ed. *The Structure of American Industry*. 5th ed. New York: Macmillan, 1977.

Brozen, Yale. "The Antitrust Task Force Deconcentration Recommendation." *Journal of Law and Economics*, 13 (October 1970), 279–292.

Caves, Richard E., and Masu Vekasa. *Industrial Concentration in Japan*. Washington, D.C.: Brookings Institution, 1976.

Demsetz, Harold. *The Market Concentration Doctrine*. Washington, D.C.: American Enterprise Institute for Public Policy Research, 1973.

Lustgarten, Steven. *Industrial Concentration and Inflation*. Washington, D.C.: American Enterprise Institute for Public Policy Research, 1975.

McGee, John S. "Economies of Size in Auto Body Manufacture." *Journal of Law and Economics*, 16 (October 1973), 248–253.

Penn, David W. "Aggregate Concentration: A Statistical Note." *Antitrust Bulletin*, 21 (Spring 1976), 91–98.

Scherer, Frederick M. *Industrial Market Structure and Economic Performance*. 2nd ed. Boston: Houghton Mifflin, 1980.

Chapter 6
Antitrust Policies in the United States

Antitrust legislation in the United States rests on two premises. The first is the English common law as it evolved through court decisions over a long period of time. In general these decisions held that restraint on trade or commerce are not in the public interest. In interpreting the common law, courts in both England and the United States ruled that contracts or agreements to restrain or attempt to restrain trade were illegal. The second premise is the belief that competition is an effective regulator of most markets and, with a few exceptions, that monopolistic practices can be stopped by competition. This premise is based on the economic theory espousing pure or perfect competition as the ideal, since according to the theory, competition forces firms to be efficient, cut costs, and receive no more than normal profits. The theory assumes that in a state of pure or perfect competition, economic decisions would be made on the basis of prices, price changes, and price relationships, all of which are determined by the market-related forces of supply and demand.

Ideal competition of the pure or perfect type does not exist, nor can it, given the impact of modern technology and the economies of scale resulting from this technology. Modern attitudes toward industrial concentration assume that when a few firms dominate an industry they are in a position to set prices higher than would prevail in more competitive pricing situations, and they are able therefore to gain profits higher than total competition would allow. It is presumed that concentration and competition are inversely related. So what is desired is some form of competition that would require sellers in a given industry to compete against each other in terms of prices. In addition, there should be no natural or artificial barriers to entry so that there will be a flow of sellers in and out of markets that will reflect market changes. Each seller would then be limited in his or her ability to control prices.

Unfortunately, competition has many facets, and it is likely to mean different things to different individuals. And as an objective of national economic policy, it may have even more meanings. Thus, many of the federal regulatory laws are concerned with different definitions of competition and, consequently, may not necessarily be totally compatible with one another. The American economy is characterized by its heterogeneity, and no one model or set of normative criteria can be used to explain or evaluate overall economic performance. Therefore, the issue for those responsible for regulatory policymaking must necessarily be to determine whether consumers have realistic alternatives, rather than to engage in a quixotic search for perfection in marketplace competition.

A REVIEW OF ANTITRUST LAWS

Although we discussed the major antitrust laws, with the exception of the Celler-Kefauver Act of 1950, in Chapters 3 and 4, our aim then was largely to set them in their historical context. Now we shall review these laws in some detail, for they are complex and are constantly subjected to changes in interpretation, although not changes in principle. The laws contain sweeping provisions directed against private restraints that might threaten a competitive market economy. There has been no meticulous itemization of these restraints by Congress, because it is possible for a specific type of conduct to be prohibited in most settings, although it could be in the public interest to permit it in others. For example, defining an illegal monopoly as a firm seeking to control 90 percent of the output of a product might be justified for large producers of basic commodities competing in a national market, but such a determination would be unrealistic for the only movie theater in a small town. To catalogue a list of antisocial restraints invites evasion by ingenious firms, for what is applicable to one industry may not be applicable to another.

The Sherman Act

The Sherman Act is, of course, the original and most basic of the antitrust laws. Its most important provisions are summarized here.

Section 1—combinations, agreements, or conspiracies in restraint of trade—prohibits agreements, express or otherwise, conspiracies, or combinations between two or more persons, who may be individuals or corporations, that unreasonably restrain the trade or commerce of the United States. This trade or commerce may be domestic, interstate, or foreign. This section's provisions are relevant only if the facts—when weighed by the courts—reveal either an unduly restraining effect on trade or an intent so to affect it.

The Supreme Court has held that certain types of agreements, conspiracies, or combinations are in and of themselves so restrictive of competition as to be conclusively presumed unreasonable restraints of trade. In other words, the Court has declined to inquire into whether or not such arrangements cause any public injury or are justified for business reasons and has not considered the amount of interstate trade and commerce affected so long as it is clearly beyond a small level. Any of these arrangements is unlawful if it limits the import of products into the United States or the export of products from the United States, or impedes commerce within the United States. The government need not prove any more than that the parties to such arrangements have in fact entered into them. Among these offenses, called per se violations, are the following:

1. Price fixing: This is any agreement or understanding between two or more competitors to fix, stabilize, or in any way affect the price of a product. What the courts are concerned about here is the inhibition of price competition. Arrangements that tamper in any way with the price structure have been determined to constitute price fixing.

2. Division of customers, markets, and volume of production: This pertains to agreements or understandings between two or more corporations to divide or allocate the markets in which each will sell a product, or arrangements to divide, limit, or maintain the production of a given product at a certain level. The courts have consistently struck down arrangements between two or more competitors in which they agree to divide customers, allocate markets, or in any way control the output of goods.

3. Boycotts or concerted refusals to deal: An agreement or understanding among competitors to boycott or refuse to deal with any third party is unlawful. Moreover, a single seller may not agree, directly or indirectly, with one or more of its independent distributors to refuse to deal with anyone else desiring to purchase the product for sale.

4. Tie-in sales: Any type of tying arrangement may be a per se violation, for example, when the tied product is patented or the seller has a dominant economic position in the sale of the product. Unlawful tie-in sales usually occur when the seller seeks to force or induce a buyer to purchase one or more less desirable products in order to purchase the desired product over which the seller has significant economic control.

In addition to the per se violations discussed above, the courts have applied what is termed a rule of reason approach to deciding which other types of conduct may be unlawful under Section 1 of the Sherman Act. As a general proposition this rule results in legalizing certain types of conduct, even though there is some restraint of trade, when the restraint is ancillary to the main business purpose of an arrangement. In this situation a corporation may defend a challenged course of conduct on the ground that there is a sound business justification for it and that any restraint of trade is ancillary or incidental to the main business purpose. Under this rule, the legality of business conduct may be determined on the basis of the duration of the agreement, the percentage of the market affected by it, the relative bargaining power of the parties involved, and the size of the geographic market affected.

Section 2—monopolies—prohibits any single company from monopolizing, or attempting to monopolize, any part of interstate trade and commerce in any relevant market. A relevant market is defined both by the geographic area in which a product competes and by the products with which the product in question can reasonably be interchanged in its end use. This section also makes it unlawful for two or more competing firms to agree to or to conspire to monopolize any part of trade or commerce. No exact minimum percentage of a relevant market has been fixed by the courts as constituting monopoly; the real test is whether a company has the power to control prices or to exclude competition. If that power is proved, the company is a monopolist. Note that Section 2 prohibits even attempts to monopolize; that is, a company could violate the law if it engaged in conduct intended to result in monopoly even if it did not succeed.

The Clayton Act

The Clayton Act is more substantive than the Sherman Act in that it is not directed at conduct that may result in a general restraint of trade or competition, but rather at certain specific practices that manifest a substantial probability of creating a restraint—mergers, exclusive dealerships, interlocking directorates, tying agreements, and so forth. In passing the Clayton Act, Congress stated that its objective was to promote competition through general prohibitions, whose specific meaning must be decided case by case in proceedings brought in the courts and before the Federal Trade Commission. The act itself provides no criminal penalties, but the mere probability of an act's having an adverse effect on competition is enough to constitute a violation and subject a company to injunctions and other restrictions on its conduct of business. A summary follows of the more important practices proscribed by the Clayton Act.

Section 2—price discrimination—attempts to foster competition by specifically prohibiting price discrimination, in which a seller charges different prices to two or more buyers of the same or similar grades of commerce when the end result is to reduce competition substantially in a line of commerce. The type of discrimination in which one seller tries to undercut rivals by charging lower prices for the same good when there is no economic rationale for doing so is called primary-line discrimination. The original purpose of Section 2 was to forbid all kinds of price discrimination, including both area price discrimination and the receipt of railroad rebates, in which Standard Oil allegedly had been involved in the antitrust case of 1911. But other provisos of Section 2 allow primary-line price discrimination if it is justified by cost savings or by the necessity to meet in good faith the equally low prices of a competitor.

Section 3—exclusive dealing and tying agreements—prohibits tying arrangements, as, for example, when a seller makes the purchase of another product a condition for purchase of a product over which he or she has significant or dominant control. This section also forbids exclusive dealing agreements, as, for example, when a seller induces a buyer not to deal with the former's competitors. The test of the illegality of a tying arrangement or exclusive dealing agreement is whether its effects may lessen competition substantially or tend to create a monopoly in any line of commerce in any section of the country. But tying agreements are allowed when a seller can prove that the tied product is necessary to maintain the reputation of the desired product and that exclusive dealing arrangements can be legitimately motivated by economic necessity, for example, when a utility needs to enter into a long-term contract for fuel supplies.

Section 7—mergers and acquisitions—amended in 1950 by the Celler-Kefauver Act, prohibits any corporation engaged in commerce from acquiring the assets or stock of another corporation when the effect may be to reduce competition substantially or to create a monopoly in any line of business and in any section of the country. It should be emphasized that Section 7 applies to firms engaged in either interstate or foreign commerce. There is little question that the acquisition by an American firm of a major interest in a foreign firm that threatens actual or potential competition to United States' firms would be scrutinized, as well as any joint venture by an American firm and a competing foreign firm. Section 7 exempts from its application, however, those acquisitions in which one of the two parties is an individual or a partnership or the acquired firm is not engaged in interstate commerce. The section also exempts the acquisition of stock when it is made solely for investment and therefore is not used to restrain trade, or the acquisition of assets by any corporation not subject to the jurisdiction of the Federal Trade Commission.

The Federal Trade Commission Act

The Federal Trade Commission Act supplements the Sherman and Clayton acts by using sweeping prohibitions of unfair methods, acts, and practices to foster competition. It provides that these prohibitions are to be interpreted and enforced in administrative proceedings brought by and before the Federal Trade Commission, subject to review by the courts. Section 5 of the act empowers the FTC to prevent unfair methods of competition and unfair or deceptive acts or practices in or affecting commerce. Generally, this section is used to stop practices before they develop into other violations of the antitrust laws. As a consequence, the FTC has used it to attack alleged price fixing that would not necessarily be a violation of the Sherman Act, as well as mergers, tie-in sales, exclusive dealing, and other actions that the commission deems are unfair methods of competition. For example, a suit was brought in 1972 against the major cereal companies for alleged price fixing, even though the FTC admitted publicly that there was no charge of agreement or conspiracy, which would be essential to a Sherman Act case. The suit has since been dropped.

It can be said that Section 5 has been interpreted to go further than the other antitrust laws do to reach all unfair business practices, whether or not they have an impact on competition. Section 5 gives to the FTC and the courts the power to prohibit present and potential trade restraints proscribed by the Sherman and Clayton acts and also allows the commission to proceed against other antisocial conduct. The current aim of the commission's enforcement activities under Section 5 is both to protect fair competition and to assure that the consumer is not subjected to unfair or deceptive practices, without regard to their effect on competition. One example of the latter is the commission's attack on false or misleading advertising.

The Robinson-Patman Act

The Robinson-Patman Act is designed to deter discrimination in price or price-related benefits, such as backhauls or promotional allowances, in sales to competing buyers. The act amended Section 2 of the Clayton Act to forbid price discrimination against purchasers of like grade and quality by a firm selling commodities in interstate commerce when the effect may be to lessen competition substantially, to tend to create a monopoly, or to prevent or destroy competition with any firm. Section 2 does not impose liability if the difference in price charged to buyers is based on methods of manufacture, sales, or delivery. Section 2 also permits price differences to buyers when it is necessary to meet, but not to beat, competition. But the Federal Trade Commission has refused to accept savings in manufacturing costs as a justification for quantity discounts. Large orders may enable a seller to use otherwise idle capacity and to schedule operations over longer periods. But though the seller with idle capacity may be willing to grant quantity discounts so great that price covers little more than marginal cost, the FTC has set up average total cost, not marginal cost, as its standard. Put in another way, overhead costs must be spread evenly over all units produced so that each buyer bears a proportionate share of the total costs. The burden of proof of cost saving is on the seller.

The implementation of Section 2 as amended by the Robinson-Patman Act has varied considerably over time. There has been some difficulty in drawing the line between discriminatory price cutting to injure competition and discriminatory price cutting to meet competition. The burden of proof of intent to injure competition was placed on the Federal Trade Commission, which then had to demonstrate that competition actually had been injured. In a case involving Standard Oil of Indiana, the Supreme Court ruled that even though competition was injured, a seller might justify price discrimination by showing that the lower price was made in good faith to meet the lower price of a competitor.[1] Quantity discount provisions of the act have been applied by the commission and the courts so as to minimize the advantage of large buyers. The Supreme Court has not ruled quantity discounts to be illegal per se, but individual cases have fared poorly. An example is the Morton Salt case of 1948, in which the Morton Salt Company granted discounts to large-quantity buyers.[2] The commission contended that this practice discriminated against small buyers, but Morton Salt argued that its quantity discounts were available to anyone. The Supreme Court supported the commission and held the discounts to be illegal on the ground that few buyers were in an economic position to avail themselves of the quantity discount; therefore, the fact that the discounts were available to all was irrelevant.

The Celler-Kefauver Act

The Celler-Kefauver Act was passed in 1950 to plug a loophole that had opened in Section 7 of the Clayton Act. Section 7 specifically forbade the acquisition of one firm's stock by another firm when the end result was to reduce competition substantially in interstate or foreign commerce. But over time, the courts had generally emasculated this provision through judicial interpretation: in 1926 the Supreme Court distinguished between acquisition of stock and acquisition of assets, holding the latter to be beyond the reach of the Federal Trade Commission even if the merger of physical assets had been based on an illegal acquisition of voting stock. Moreover, the Supreme Court in several other cases had held that such mergers were not illegal under the Clayton Act if a corporation used its stock purchases to acquire assets before the FTC issued a complaint or before it issued its final order banning the stock acquisition. Thus the number of mergers based on the acquisition of firm assets steadily increased, and it was not until the late 1940s that federal legislation to plug the loophole was considered seriously. There had been a wave of post–World War II mergers, leading to the fear by Congress that greater industrial concentration would lead to a significant decline in competition.

1. *Standard Oil Co.* v. *FTC*, 340 U.S. 231 (1951).
2. *FTC* v. *Morton Salt Co.*, 334 U.S. 37 (1948).

Section 7 of the Clayton Act was amended to make it illegal for one corporation to acquire the stock or assets of another corporation when the end result might be to lessen competition substantially or tend to create monopoly. Celler-Kefauver also tightened the constraints against business mergers by making a merger illegal if there was a trend toward concentration in an industry, thereby creating a presumption of tendencies toward monopoly. It delineated markets more narrowly by defining them as "a line of commerce" in any section of the nation. The intent of Congress in passing the Celler-Kefauver Act was that competition be maintained. Small firms that merge to improve their competitive position are generally not challenged, but mergers that would ordinarily be allowed in nonconcentrated industries may well be challenged if a large firm acquires a small competitor. For example, Alcoa, which accounted for 27.8 percent of all aluminum conductor production, acquired Rome Cable, whose market share was 1.3 percent.[3] The merger was disallowed in 1964 on the grounds that Alcoa would increase its market share through the acquisition and thus competition would be substantially reduced, since Rome had been an aggressive competitor in the aluminum conductor field. It has been said that Celler-Kefauver has virtually stopped horizontal and vertical mergers between large companies.[4]

Exemptions from Antitrust Laws

The Sherman Act, as well as other antitrust legislation, is applicable in principle to all forms of private business enterprise carried out in interstate and foreign commerce. The Sherman Act itself makes no exceptions and declares that every restraint of trade and commerce is unlawful. There are, however, certain industries and organizations that are exempt from the antitrust laws. The reasons for exemption are as varied as are the industries and organizations exempted. Each exemption is supposed to accomplish some specific objective, which, in the minds of a particular group, is necessary to its interests. Over time, there have been moving forces, or interest groups, that demanded relaxation of the antitrust laws. Some of the more important industries and organizations and the reasons for their exemption from antitrust laws are presented below.

Labor Unions

Section 6 of the Clayton Act exempts labor unions from antitrust laws. There were two main reasons for this exemption. First, the Sherman

3. *U.S.* v. *Aluminum Co. of America*, 377 U.S. 271 (1964).
4. George J. Stigler, "The Economic Effects of the Antitrust Laws," *Journal of Law and Economics*, 9 (October 1966), 235–236.

Act had been used on occasion to break up labor unions. In the Danbury Hatters Case of 1908, for example, a labor union was convicted of restraint of trade when it organized an interstate boycott against the hat manufacturers of Danbury, Connecticut.[5] The court found the members of the union liable for triple damages of $240,000 for the boycott. The end result of the conviction was the dissolution of the union. Second, it was felt that labor had a bargaining position far inferior to that of business; therefore, collective action by labor was necessary to improve this position. Today, labor unions retain their exempt status as long as they do not combine with nonlabor groups to effect restraint of trade.[6]

Natural Monopolies

The so-called natural monopolies exist in those industries that possess special conditions inherent to the nature of their operations that would make competition self-destructive and hence incompatible with the public interest. Since they provide a service that is indispensable to the public, however, they are subject to government regulation in the interest of the public. Such industries include transportation, electricity, gas, telephones, and broadcasting. A public utility is usually given a monopoly over a particular area. The purpose is in part to prevent the wasteful and duplicating competition that prevailed at one time. During the nineteenth century the railroads built duplicating lines in a desire to surmount their competition. The end result was cutthroat competition and a great waste of resources.

In return for its control over a given service area, a natural monopoly is subject to the regulation of rates, services, and other functions by federal and state agencies to ensure the protection of the public interest. Regulation is designed to prevent a public utility or an airline from making too much profit. Because these industries are so strictly regulated, there is no particular need to subject them to antitrust laws.

Export Trade Associations

The Webb-Pomerene Act of 1918 specifically exempts export trade associations from the Sherman Act. The rationale for this exemption was the existence of cartels and monopolies in other countries that were actively engaged in international trade. Countries such as Germany and the United Kingdom encouraged the formation of these cartels as a

5. *Loewe* v. *Lawlor*, 208 U.S. 274 (1908).
6. *U.S.* v. *Hutcheson*, 312 U.S. 219 (1941).

matter of public policy. The purpose of the Webb-Pomerene exemption
was to enable American firms to compete more effectively with foreign
companies belonging to cartel arrangements. The act permits the formation of export associations, which are required to file outlines of their
organization with the Federal Trade Commission. The commission is
then supposed to investigate association activities to see that there is no
violation of the law, since the Webb-Pomerene Act was intended to
promote competition rather than collusion in the world markets.

Agricultural Cooperatives

Agricultural cooperatives were exempted by the Clayton Act from antitrust laws provided they issued no capital stock and were not run for a
profit. The Capper-Volstead Act of 1922 amended the Clayton Act to
allow the formation of cooperatives issuing capital stock, and it also
legalized action by the members of a cooperative marketing association
to enhance the prices of their products. The Capper-Volstead Act provides agricultural producers with a substantial exemption from antitrust
laws in giving their associations the power to set prices. However, this
power has limits, for the price must not be increased unduly. A single
cooperative association also may enter into contracts with many farmers that require them to market their products only through the association.

Other Exemptions

There are also other exemptions from antitrust laws. Transoceanic
shipping rates established by shipping conferences have for years been
exempted from the antitrust laws on certification by the U.S. Maritime
Board. Combinations and mergers were sanctioned by Congress in the
case of the railroads in 1920, telephone companies in 1921, motor carriers in 1935, and water carriers in 1940. Rate agreements and pooling
arrangements among airlines, when approved by the CAB, have been
allowed since 1938. Combinations of marine insurance companies were
exempted from the antitrust laws in 1920. There is also an antitrust
exemption for small businesses in that the Small Business Act of 1953,
as amended, provides that voluntary agreements may be made by small
business concerns for joint programs in research and development and
for joint participation in national defense contracts. The McCarran Act
of 1945 partially exempts insurance companies from the antitrust laws
in that it leaves their regulation up to the states. The Reed-Bulwinkle
Bill of 1948 specifically authorizes the Interstate Commerce Commission to approve railroad traffic association agreements with respect to

rates and fares. The Miller-Tydings Act and the McGuire Act extended antitrust exemptions to retailers so as to maintain resale prices. But the Consumer Goods Pricing Act of 1975 repealed these provisions, mainly because they sanctioned a form of price fixing that was having a perceptibly adverse effect on consumer purchasing power.

State Antitrust Laws

As mentioned in Chapter 3, the first antitrust laws were passed by the states in the latter part of the last century. The development of trusts and other kinds of business combinations created much popular discontent, which was translated into state laws. Kansas enacted the first antitrust law in 1889, and at least thirteen states had antitrust laws prior to the passage of the Sherman Act in 1890. The first state laws came from the farming states in the Midwest, in which populism was influential. In fact, the Sherman Act was intended to supplement, rather than supplant, state power. The federal courts were supposed to cooperate within the limits of their constitutional power with the state courts in curbing and controlling any form of business combination that threatened American commerce.

By 1900 thirty states had antitrust laws which varied in content but, in general, restricted monopolies and combinations in restraint of trade, prohibited specific unfair business practices, and provided criminal penalties and other sanctions. These laws fell into disuse after the turn of the century, however, and the enforcement of antitrust was left almost entirely to the federal government. There were several reasons for the decline in state activity. First, state antitrust law was attacked and often invalidated on the grounds of vagueness. Second, the laws were subjected to a prolonged series of constitutional challenges. State statutes were often attacked on equal protection and due process grounds. Third, the courts set severe restrictions on the extraterritorial jurisdiction of state enforcement efforts. Fourth, the enforcement of state laws was generally haphazard and poorly financed, and it was difficult for the states to deal with national or international economic institutions through their limited jurisdiction.

State antitrust activities picked up during the 1960s and accelerated even more during the 1970s. From 1970 to 1974, twelve states, one territory, and the Commonwealth of Puerto Rico enacted or reenacted antitrust statutes.[7] This resurgence of antitrust enforcement can be attributed to a number of factors: protecting state and local governments from the collusive bidding practices practiced by some business firms; combating the efforts of organized crime to take over legitimate

---

7. Unpublished data furnished by the Antitrust Division, Department of Justice.

business interests; and protecting the general business community from the predatory actions of a few firms. In some states, organizations of small businesspersons lobbied successfully for the state's enforcing its own antitrust laws once again. There was also a growing belief that the federal government could not and should not bear sole responsibility for the enforcement of antitrust. And there was an increasing recognition that the state attorney general, as the people's advocate, must combat abuses of the marketplace through antitrust as well as consumer protection programs. Finally, there had been a great growth in state procurement of goods and services and a concomitant belief that a vigorous antitrust program could save money on government purchases.

State antitrust laws differ significantly in form and content, but there are several basic legislative patterns that have been followed. Many state laws are modeled on the broad provisions of the Sherman Act. For example, the Hawaii law states that every combination in the form of a trust, every contract or conspiracy in restraint of trade or commerce in the state or in any section of the state, is illegal. Other state laws specifically forbid trusts or combinations to fix prices or to limit the quantity of articles. Some states have laws condemning price discrimination when done with the intent of injuring competition. Finally, many states have legislation similar to that adopted by Texas in 1889, which outlaws certain defined trust practices. There are also states that have no antitrust laws. To some extent, this is a matter of definition. West Virginia, for example, is considered not to have an antitrust law, although it does have an antitrust law limited to food, fuel, and other necessities of life.

State antitrust laws can be regarded as a supplement to federal antitrust laws. They are of some importance because there is some business that is strictly intrastate. In the federal system, the regulation of intrastate or local commerce is left to the states, and within this area state governments perform the same kind of economic regulation that the federal government performs at the national level. Moreover, the Department of Justice and the Federal Trade Commission prosecute only a small fraction of the complaints they receive, and their efforts are concentrated on the restraints and abuses that are national in scope. This leaves to the states jurisdiction over a wide area of economic activity within intrastate commerce, for example, the production and sale of food and beverages, fuel oil, lumber, used cars, hotel and housing facilities, building and road construction, recreational facilities, local transportation, and banking services. The same kinds of abuses and anticompetitive business practices can occur locally as well as nationally, and so state governments also have such functions as prohibiting false advertising and preventing monopoly and unfair competition.

APPLICATION OF ANTITRUST LAWS TO MARKET POWER

Antitrust laws can be applied to the market power that has been achieved by a particular firm. This dominance can be achieved in a single product market or in a geographic market. One problem that has arisen over time is that there has been no set test of market power within a particular relevant competitive market. In applying Section 2 of the Sherman Act a variety of tests can be used. One is the existence of a specifically monopolistic intent. Another is the committing of specific anticompetitive acts, and a third is the attainment of what is considered an illegal absolute or relative size. The last test comes the closest to meeting the economic test of a monopoly. However, in applying Section 2 of the Sherman Act, the courts have been unable to rely on the economic model of monopoly because it is based on the concept of one firm being protected from the entry of others into the market in the absence of competitive products and, thus, does not represent a practical legal standard.

Antitrust Laws as Applied to Monopolies

In applying the antitrust laws, especially Section 2 of the Sherman Act, the courts have not used a clear definition of monopoly that is based on economic concepts. Generally, they have focused their attention on predatory acts, exclusion of competitors, conspiracies to monopolize, and the impact of mergers on competition. In particular, enforcement of the monopoly section of the Sherman Act has been based on determining whether or not the industry structure in question rose out of some wrongdoing. Under the act, monopoly and the offense of monopoly have two characteristics: the actual possession of monopoly power in a market and the maintenance of that power or its willful acquisition.

The Standard Oil and American Tobacco cases discussed in Chapter 3 were landmark cases. Although both companies were monopolies in terms of size and market power, it was their abuses of size and power that got each into trouble. In the case of American Tobacco, it was found that the company's extensive financial power had been used to cut prices in one area while maintaining them elsewhere in order to drive out competitors. The company also spent millions of dollars to buy up competitors' plants, merely to close them down. Tying agreements were used to bind vendors and employees to American Tobacco. The sins of the Standard Oil Trust already have been mentioned. Among many other acts, the trust had bribed railway employees for information about competitors and had allocated sales areas among its subsidiaries so as to eliminate competition among them.

In deciding these two cases the Supreme Court essentially distinguished between good and bad trusts. Large firm size in itself was not illegal; what was illegal was the commission of predatory acts. The Supreme Court adopted the famous rule of reason. Since the Sherman Act did not specifically define those acts that were in restraint of trade, the courts had to do so. Rule of reason meant that in applying a statute condemning restraints on trade, a court could use flexibility and discretion. Two criteria were used to determine the kind of business practice that would be in violation of the Sherman Act. First, there had to be unworthy motives or predatory acts designed to harm competitors, and second, there had to be such overwhelming control of an industry that competition really had ceased to exist.

The U.S. Steel Case, 1920

Later, during the 1920s, the Supreme Court, acting under the rule of reason doctrine, held that the existence of monopoly power that was not abused did not violate the Sherman Act. The U.S. Steel case of 1920 is an example of the application of the rule of reason doctrine.[8] U.S. Steel, then the nation's largest industrial enterprise, was a holding company formed in 1901 to merge concerns that were themselves amalgamations of smaller companies. It had been set up to forestall a threat of overexpansion and ruinous competition at a time when other manufacturers of heavier semifinished products had been about to integrate forward into the finished lines, and other manufacturers of finished products had made plans to integrate backward. The U.S. Steel Corporation brought under its control in one financial unit a series of corporations that had already secured control over the principal plants in their respective lines of business in the steel industry. These and other acquisitions gave U.S. Steel control of 65 to 75 percent of all lines of steel manufacturing in the country and also over 80 percent of the best iron ore reserves, bringing together major companies that were themselves competing with one another.

The Justice Department brought action against U.S. Steel in 1912, accusing it, among other things, of a conspiracy to fix prices in the steel industry. The corporation had made it a practice to meet with its competitors to set a price. Prices set at these meetings became the official prices for all iron and steel products. When U.S. Steel changed prices, its competitors followed suit. In 1920 the Supreme Court reached a final decision in the case and refused to allow a dissolution of the company.

---

8. *U.S.* v. *U.S. Steel Corporation*, 251 U.S. 417 (1920).

There were several reasons for the Court's decision. One was that the meetings of U.S. Steel and its competitors had been discontinued before the government suit. In its approach to competition, a majority of the Court emphasized the legal rather than the economic concept. Competition had not been restrained, for U.S. Steel had made no efforts to suppress other companies by unfair means. The Court also held that the corporation did not have sufficient power to control prices in the industry and ruled that size in itself did not constitute a violation of the Sherman Act. What was required to violate the act were overt predatory actions. The decision of the Supreme Court gave rise to the so-called abuse theory of monopoly. In other words, in the absence of abusive market practices, the Sherman Act did not make mere size an offense.

The Alcoa Case, 1945

The Alcoa case is considered a landmark case in that it broke sharply with antitrust cases of the past.[9] In this case, Judge Learned Hand, speaking for the Supreme Court, declared monopolies illegal per se, thus abandoning the rule of reason. A government suit had been initiated in 1937 charging that the Aluminum Company of America (Alcoa) had violated Section 2 of the Sherman Act by monopolizing virgin aluminum production. At the time of the suit, Alcoa controlled over 90 percent of the production of aluminum ingots. It had become a monopoly originally through its exclusive control over patent rights and then by its control over bauxite deposits and generation sites for the hydroelectric power needed in aluminum manufacture. Moreover, Alcoa was able to anticipate and forestall virtually all competition in the production of aluminum ingots by stimulating demand and producing new uses for the metal. Thus, it was difficult for the company to hold that it was a passive beneficiary of a monopoly that had come about from an involuntary elimination of competitors by automatically operating market forces.

The significance of the Alcoa case lies in the identification and condemnation of monopoly in and of itself, without respect to abuses, predatory acts, injuries to competitors, or intent to monopolize. In initiating the suit, the Justice Department asked for the dissolution of Alcoa. A district court ruled in favor of Alcoa, finding no abuse of power. The case was then appealed, and Judge Hand ruled against Alcoa. The test of a monopoly, he emphasized, is the existence of that size that gives a firm the power to fix and manage prices. Alcoa's control of 90 percent of all aluminum ingots was sufficient in itself to constitute monopoly power. The mere existence of such a monopoly

9. *U.S.* v. *Aluminum Co. of America*, 148 F. 2d, 416 (1945).

gave the firm as much or more power to fix prices as would an illegal combination or contract among several firms. Monopoly power, even though not abused, was now to be considered a violation of the Sherman Act. The good behavior of the company, which prior to 1945 would have been an acceptable defense to the court, was no longer valid, for Congress, according to the Supreme Court, in passing the Sherman Act, did not condone "good" trusts and condemn "bad" trusts; it forbade all. Therefore, Alcoa was required to divest itself of certain facilities, which were given to other aluminum companies in order to encourage more competition.[10]

Subsequent court decisions have not reversed the thinking advanced in the Alcoa case. At the present time, the judgment of monopoly is based on such factors as the number and strength of the firms in the market, their effective size from the standpoint of technological development, their ability to compete with similar domestic and foreign industries, and the public's interest in lower costs. But the Alcoa case also indicated that the courts would not apply Section 2 of the Sherman Act to a firm with overwhelming market power when that position was "thrust upon" the defendant. This meant that a firm could achieve market power legitimately in one of several ways. It could acquire its position through historical accident, by lawful use of government-granted patent protection, or by uncontrollable marketplace factors.

ANTITRUST LAWS AS APPLIED TO MERGERS

A company can attain a preeminent position in a market in two ways, through internal growth over time or through mergers. Usually, however, market dominance has been reached through mergers. Mergers have accounted for most of the concentration existing in many industries. In fact, the largest two hundred industrial firms, as measured by the value of assets, acquired about two-thirds of the assets of all merged firms with assets of $10 million or more during the period from 1948 to 1970.[11] During the same period the two hundred largest firms consummated around four thousand mergers with firms that had combined assets of over $50 billion.[12] Many of the two hundred largest firms in

10. There was a second Alcoa case in 1950. The Justice Department accused Alcoa of price fixing and asked that the company be required to divest itself of more facilities. The court decision favored Alcoa this time, however, on the grounds that there was strong competition in the industry.
11. Betty Bock and Jack Farkas, *Relative Growth of the "Largest" Manufacturing Corporations* (New York: National Industrial Conference Board, 1973), pp. 24–36.
12. Federal Trade Commission, *Economic Report on Corporate Mergers* (Washington, D.C.: U.S. Government Printing Office, 1969), chap. 7.

1947 were also absorbed in mergers: out of the two hundred largest firms in 1947, almost half had lost their corporate identity through mergers by 1970.[13] The outcome was an increase in the asset positions of a number of large firms and an increase in the share of corporate manufacturing assets held by the two hundred largest corporations from around 42 percent in 1947 to 61 percent in 1970.[14]

Development of Mergers

Mergers tend to come in cycles, the first coming around the turn of the century. The Sherman Act had little effect on curbing industrial concentration in the first decade after its passage, and in fact, from 1898 to 1902 there were some 2,653 mergers, with capitalization amounting to $6.3 billion.[15] By 1900, after ten years of enforcement of the Sherman Act, the number of industrial combinations in the United States with capital of $1 billion or more had increased from ten to three hundred.[16] The catalyst in the merger movement was the economic depression between 1893 and 1896. The merger was one way to protect against a decline in economic activity, for if a firm could gain control over competing plants in its principal lines of industry, it would have a better opportunity to fix prices and control output. The mergers consummated at the turn of the century were in such industries as petroleum, iron and steel, copper, sugar, lead, and salt.

There was a second cycle of mergers during the prosperous 1920s, with the peak in 1929, when some 1,245 mergers were formed.[17] During that entire decade there were 6,818 mergers,[18] primarily in the mass-production and entertainment industries—automobiles, automobile parts, motion pictures, movie theaters, and appliances. The mass production of the automobile effected certain economies of scale that could be best achieved through mergers. Vertical mergers often consisted of the acquisition of medium-sized firms that could produce such things as parts and components used in the automobile industry. The stock market itself had an influence on the merger movement of the 1920s. This was a period of rapidly rising security prices, which pro-

13. Federal Trade Commission, Bureau of Economics, staff report.
14. Ibid.
15. Temporary National Economic Committee, Monograph No. 21, *Competition and Monopoly in American Industry* (Washington, D.C.: U.S. Government Printing Office, 1940), p. 88.
16. Ibid., p. 105.
17. Jesse W. Markham, "Survey of the Evidence and Findings in Mergers," in National Bureau of Economic Research, *Business Concentration and Price Policy* (Princeton, N.J.: Princeton University Press, 1955), p. 157.
18. Ibid., p. 156.

vided a ready opportunity for selling new securities to brokerage houses and to the general public, and mergers themselves were a way of stimulating speculative interest in securities. Promoters encouraged many mergers for the express purpose of securing promotional profits: in combining various firms, the promoters increased the firms' asset valuations and secured for themselves substantial numbers of securities.

A third cycle of mergers began in the middle 1950s and continues to the present. During the Great Depression the merger movement was practically moribund, with only 87 mergers in 1939. There was an increase in mergers during World War II, peaking at 419 in 1946 and declining to a low of 126 in 1949. Beginning in 1954, however, the number of mergers started to grow at a rather rapid rate. In 1954 the number of mergers was 387; by 1963 the number had increased to 1,018, and a peak of 2,407 was reached in 1968.[19] The Federal Trade Commission reported that the number of manufacturing and mining firms acquired between 1955 and 1973 was 20,084.[20] There was a significant increase in the number of conglomerate mergers, a movement that cut across different types of industries—manufacturing, mining, banking, insurance, trade, and the service areas. The reasons for the continued growth of mergers are varied and include the desire to meet foreign competition, the need to control the various stages of product flow, the need to diversify, and the need to improve access to credit. Certainly a widespread, unstated motive may be the desire to restrict competition. An acquiring firm also can gain from a merger by securing the acquired firm's personnel, marketing facilities, and trade reputation.

During the third merger cycle there has been a decline in the horizontal and vertical types of mergers and a rise in the conglomerate form of merger, as shown in Table 6-1. Figures are confined to firms with total assets of $10 million or more. Conglomerate mergers accelerated even more quickly during the middle 1950s and increased to the point that by 1978 most mergers were of the conglomerate type. One reason for the conglomerate's popularity is that the Celler-Kefauver Act virtually stopped the horizontal and vertical mergers. But the conglomerate merger seems to have leveled off in recent years, apparently because of changes in tax laws discouraging the use of debt in acquisitions, as well as threats of legal action. Moreover, the experience of conglomerate firms has shown that diversification by external acquisition has been more difficult to manage than diversification developed internally.

The antitrust laws generally oppose the expansion of one corporation with substantial market power through the acquisition of the stock or assets of another company that also has substantial market power. The objective, of course, is to preserve competition among buyers and

19. Federal Trade Commission, *Economic Report on Corporate Mergers.*
20. Ibid.

Table 6-1 Horizontal, Vertical, and Conglomerate Mergers,
1970–1978 (Concerns with assets of $10 million or more)

Year	Horizontal and Vertical	Conglomerate
1970	12	79
1971	8	51
1972	24	36
1973	25	39
1974	24	38
1975	7	52
1976	18	63
1977	30	69
1978	27	83

Source: Federal Trade Commission, Bureau of Economics, *Statistical Report of Mergers and Acquisitions, 1978*, p. 110.

sellers. Mergers combining a large firm and a small but rigorous competitor, moreover, also can be challenged. A large firm competing in the sale of alternative forms of a product or representing merely a potential source of the same product can be barred from merging its business with a substantial existing producer of that product. For example, in an antitrust case involving the Continental Can Company, the question was whether the acquisition of a glass container manufacturer by a metal can producer was an acquisition within the same lines of commerce.[21] The Supreme Court reversed a district court's decision that two separate relevant product markets were involved and ruled that the merger was within a single glass and metal container line of commerce. Antitrust decisions also have applied the potential competition doctrine to mergers. In a case involving the Pabst Brewing Company, which wanted to acquire the Narragansett Brewery so as to enter the New England beer market, the merger was disallowed on the grounds that the potential competition between the two companies would be thus eliminated.[22]

But not all mergers of competitors are prohibited, nor, for that matter, are all joint ventures in which two companies acquire the assets or stock of a third company. Small competitors in industries with low concentration can merge without risk of challenge, particularly if competition is somehow increased. Both large and small firms can acquire another firm when it is of little or no competitive significance or when it is a failing company for which there is no alternative purchaser. Joint

21. *U.S.* v. *Continental Can Co.*, 378 U.S. 441 (1964).
22. *U.S.* v. *Pabst Brewing Co.*, 384 U.S. 546 (1966).

ventures also may go unchallenged, particularly if they are essential to the development of new technology and entrance into new markets. Mergers and joint ventures are not necessarily challenged even if large companies are involved. The key factor in a challenge is the restraint of competition. The number of cases involving mergers initiated by the Justice Department and the Federal Trade Commission under Section 7 of the Clayton Act is a small fraction of the total number of mergers consummated yearly.

Horizontal Mergers

Of the three kinds of mergers, a horizontal merger has the most immediate effect on competition. The unification of two firms producing the same product will increase concentration within an industry, no matter how small the firms are. The merger may be insignificant with respect to its effect on competition, or it may be patently anticompetitive. In a horizontal merger there is the question of what constitutes an anticompetitive share of the total market. The factors considered are the number of firms, the degree of industry concentration, the conditions of entry, and product characteristics. There is no set minimum market share that can be declared illegal. The Brown Shoe case illustrates some of the points that have been weighed in horizontal merger cases.

The Brown Shoe case of 1962 was a landmark case with regard to the application of the Celler-Kefauver Act.[23] In 1955 the Justice Department challenged the acquisition of the Kinney Shoe Company by the Brown Shoe Company, charging violation of Section 7 of the Clayton Act as amended by Celler-Kefauver. At the time of the acquisition, Brown was the third largest shoe retailer and the fourth largest shoe manufacturer in the United States, and Kinney was the eighth largest shoe retailer and the twelfth largest shoe manufacturer. Brown and Kinney between them had about sixteen hundred retail shoe store outlets but produced only about 5 percent of the total national output of shoes. The Justice Department, however, challenged the merger on the grounds that competition would be lessened substantially both vertically and horizontally—vertically because Brown Shoe would use the Kinney retail outlets to sell Brown Shoes exclusively, thus excluding independent firms from using the same outlets, and horizontally because the former retail store competition between the Brown and Kinney shoe companies would be eliminated. The vertical arrangement was in effect a tying agreement, which was declared illegal under the Clayton Act.

There were also other issues in the Brown Shoe case. An important one, often considered in merger cases, was the determination of the

23. *Brown Shoe Co.* v. *U.S.*, 370 U.S. 294 (1962).

relevant market area. In order to determine a merger's effect on competition, the relevant market area can be subdivided into a geographic market and a product market. The latter is determined by the reasonable interchangeability of products or the cross-elasticity of demand between the product itself and the substitutes for it. A high cross-elasticity of demand for a product is evidence of a lack of control over prices. Within the product market are well defined submarkets whose boundaries may be defined by examining industrial customs and practices. With respect to the vertical arrangement in the Brown Shoe case, the relevant geographic market was the United States, and the product market was various lines of shoes, each with individual characteristics that rendered it noncompetitive with the others. The geographic market involved in the horizontal aspect of the merger was cities with a population of ten thousand or more and their environs in which both Brown and Kinney retailed shoes through their own outlets. The horizontal product market was men's, women's, and children's shoes sold in all retail shoe stores.

We should emphasize that there were both horizontal and vertical aspects to the Brown-Kinney merger. There was a horizontal combination at both the manufacturing and the retail outlet level. The ruling of the district court, which was upheld by the Supreme Court, was that the merger at the manufacturing level was too insignificant to affect competition adversely. But at the retail level the ruling was different. It was ruled that as a result of the merger, competition was lessened in those cities in which both Brown and Kinney had retail outlets. In some 118 cities with populations of ten thousand or more, the combined retail outlets exceeded 5 percent of the total market. Even though there was a lack of concentration in the shoe retailing industry, it was felt that a merger resulting in 5 percent market control could have an adverse effect on competition, particularly since future merger efforts by Brown's competitors might be encouraged. It was also ruled that a vertical restraint existed, specifically that Brown would use its control to force its shoes into the Kinney retail stores, thus excluding other manufacturers and resulting in the vertical foreclosure of about 2 percent of the shoe market. Brown was then forced to divest itself of Kinney, which it sold to the F. W. Woolworth Company.

Vertical Mergers

The basic problem in applying the antitrust laws to vertical mergers is that since direct competition is not involved, it is difficult to apply such criteria as market shares or percentage of total productive assets. This is true because in a vertical merger, the firms operate at different stages of the production or distribution process. Somehow it has to be demonstrated that the merger has an anticompetitive effect. In the Brown Shoe case, the Supreme Court was concerned that independent shoe manufacturers would be denied access to retail shoe store outlets because of the number of retail stores that Brown-Kinney would control after acquisition. Generally, action against vertical mergers is taken when the result is likely to raise barriers to entry in an industry or is likely to foreclose equal access to potential customers or suppliers.

A case involving the Du Pont Corporation illustrates the application of Section 7 of the Clayton Act to a vertical merger, even though technically the merger was never consummated.[24] In 1919, when General Motors was just getting a major start in the automobile industry, Du Pont acquired ownership of 23 percent of its stock. The primary issue in the case, which was initiated by the Justice Department in 1949, was whether or not Du Pont had used this stock ownership to ensure a market for many of its products, including automobile finishes, fabrics, and chemicals. As General Motors had become dominant not only in the automobile industry but also was first in sales among all industrial corporations in the United States, its link with America's largest chemical company was significant with respect to the alleged anticompetitive effects of the stock acquisition. In this case, the complaint was originally issued some thirty years after the stock acquisition, which shows that Section 7 can be applied to both past and current mergers.

In 1956 the Supreme Court reversed a ruling by a lower court and ordered that Du Pont divest itself of its General Motors stock. Even though Du Pont and General Motors were not competitors, Du Pont enjoyed a commanding position as a General Motors supplier in a particular line of commerce, namely, automotive finishes and fabrics. In 1946 Du Pont supplied 67 percent of General Motor's requirements for automotive finishes and in 1947, 68 percent. In fabrics, Du Pont supplied 52 percent in 1946 and 38 percent in 1947. The Court ruled that anticompetitive effects were created by the stock acquisition because Du Pont was able to use its stock to become the primary supplier of General Motors in these two fields, thus negating the principle of free competition and creating an element of monopoly.

Conglomerate Mergers

Conglomerate mergers do not entail firms in direct competition with each other, nor are there usually any extensive vertical relations between the firms. These mergers can be divided into three categories— market extension, product extension, and pure conglomerate. Market extension is a merger in which a conglomerate wants to get a toehold in

24. *U.S.* v. *Du Pont and Co.*, 353 U.S. 588 (1956).

a particular industry through the acquisition of an existing firm within the industry. A product extension merger is one firm's acquisition of a second business producing a product closely related to the acquiring firm's product line. The classic example of a product extension merger, which was eventually disallowed, was when Procter & Gamble, the United States' largest manufacturer of household cleaning supplies, entered the liquid bleach market through the acquisition of Clorox.[25] The products were complementary in use, employed the same methods of distribution and advertising, and were sold to the same customers. The pure conglomerate merger is a merger of two totally unrelated firms. In all three types of conglomerate mergers, the problem in applying Section 7 is to prove that the acquisitions have an anticompetitive effect on business.

In 1969 the Justice Department filed suit against International Telephone & Telegraph (ITT), America's largest corporate conglomerate, to force it to divest itself of the Hartford Fire Insurance Company and two other subsidiaries.[26] This case deserves special attention for several reasons, the most important of which is the cumulative economic impact of ITT's merger activity, which accelerated between 1960 and 1970. In 1960 ITT had total assets of $924 million, sales and revenues of $811 million, and 132 thousand employees. Before World War II, the company had operated almost exclusively as a telephone, telegraph, cable, and wireless public utility, primarily in the Caribbean area. After the war, it expanded into the manufacturing of telecommunications equipment in Europe, then in Latin America, and eventually in certain countries in the Pacific. Limited manufacturing operations in telecommunication and defense-related electronics were also established in the United States. Starting in 1960, however, ITT diversified rapidly through the acquisition of several corporations, and by 1970 it had assets of $6.7 billion, sales and revenues of $6.4 billion, 392 thousand employees, and an after-tax profit of $353 million.[27] In 1970, its utility operations, which were at one time its major source of revenue, accounted for only 4 percent of total revenue. The company operates in several general areas: telecommunication equipment and operation; industrial and consumer products; consumer services; business and financial services; and defense, electronic, and space systems. It obtains the bulk of its revenue from overseas sales.

From 1960 to 1970, ITT acquired through mergers companies with total assets equaling about $4.4 billion. A list of some of ITT's major acquisitions is presented in Table 6–2. The companies acquired by ITT

25. FTC v. Procter & Gamble Co., 386 U.S. 568 (1966).
26. U.S. v. International Telephone and Telegraph Co., 324 F. Supp. 19 (1970).
27. Moody's Industrial Manual, 1971, p. 2770.

were not in direct competition with one another, nor were there any extensive areas of vertical relationship among the firms. The acquired companies were neither competitors nor customers of ITT; rather, it turned its attention toward the acquisition of industrial products manufacturers, as well as finance and insurance companies. For the most part, the acquisitions were in the fields of commercial heating and furnaces, air conditioning systems, industrial controls, and industrial pumps. The mergers also included a rather diverse collection of other kinds of companies, including Avis, the automobile rental company; Canteen Corporation, which makes vending machines; and Sheraton Corporation, one of the largest owners of hotels and motor inns.

The Justice Department initiated action against ITT in 1969 for two reasons. First, it wanted to press for an early Supreme Court test to determine whether existing antitrust laws covered conglomerate mergers. There was a feeling that the ITT mergers would encourage the existing trend of large corporations to acquire dominant firms in concentrated markets, thereby increasing the concentration of control of manufacturing assets. The ITT acquisition of the Hartford Fire Insurance Company is a case in point. With assets of $1.8 billion, the Hartford Fire Insurance Company was one of the five largest fire and

Table 6-2 Selected Major Acquisitions of ITT, 1960-1970

Company Acquired	Year	Assets*	Product Line
Cannon Electric	1963	31.5	Electrical connectors
General Control	1963	32.4	Automatic industrial controls
Bell & Gossett	1963	26.9	Pumps and heating equipment
Aetna Finance Co.	1964	90.1	Consumer finance & insurance
Avis, Inc.	1965	49.0	Automobile rental
Howard W. Sams	1966	19.5	Book publishing
Levitt & Sons	1968	91.0	Residential construction
Continental Baking	1968	186.5	Baking
Sheraton	1968	283.0	Hotels and motor inns
Thorpe Finance	1968	120.2	Consumer financing
Rayonier	1968	291.7	Chemicals
Canteen Corporation	1969	140.9	Vending machines
Grinnell	1969	184.5	Sprinklers & power plant piping
Hartford Fire Insurance	1970	1,891.7	Fire and casualty insurance

*In millions of dollars

Source: FTC *Economic Report on Corporate Mergers; Moody's Industrial Manual;* and *Moody's Bank & Finance Manual.*

casualty insurance companies in the United States. In 1966 Hartford wrote 6.4 percent of all net premiums written for fire insurance in the whole fire and casualty insurance industry; 5.9 percent for extended coverage; 4.9 percent for homeowner's multiple peril; and 4.9 percent for commercial multiple peril.[28] Second, ITT was the leading acquiring company of the 1960s, having acquired over one hundred other American and foreign companies. The impact of these acquisitions was reflected in the assets, sales, and profit rank of ITT in comparison with other manufacturing firms from 1961 to 1970. In 1961 ITT ranked twenty-ninth among all major manufacturing firms in value of assets; in 1970, it ranked ninth. In 1961 ITT ranked forty-seventh in total value of sales; in 1970 it ranked eighth, and in profit ITT ranked fiftieth in 1961 and tenth in 1970.[29]

Three separate acquisitions of ITT were challenged by the Justice Department. The first was the acquisition of the Canteen Corporation; the second was the acquisition of the Grinnell Corporation; and the third was the acquisition of the Hartford Fire Insurance Company. The government's case against these mergers was based on several forms of alleged competitive damage—reciprocity, geographical foreclosure of markets, financial resources, and the combination of the automatic sprinkler (Grinnell) and fire insurance (Hartford) business. The record of the ITT-Canteen case documented how ITT promoted reciprocity with banks. Another example was the ITT-Sheraton purchases of Philco-Ford television sets in return for Ford's use of Sheraton hotel rooms and services. As for geographic foreclosure of markets, it was felt that the acquisition of Grinnell, a major producer of automatic sprinkler systems, would enable ITT to capture a dominant position in an expanding foreign market. ITT also had the financial resources through its acquisition of various finance companies such as Aetna to promote the sales of automatic sprinklers. Finally, there was the interrelationship between Grinnell and Hartford, for insurance rates are related directly to the presence of automatic sprinkler systems. There was the possibility that Hartford agents would recommend Grinnell sprinkler systems to their customers, thus eliminating competition from a segment of the sprinkler market.

There were three judgments in the ITT case:

1. In the judgment involving the Canteen Corporation, ITT was ordered to divest itself, within two years, of all its interest, direct or indirect, in the company.

2. ITT was ordered to divest itself, within two years, of all its interest, direct and indirect, in the fire protection division of Grinnell.

28. Stanley E. Boyle, "*U.S.* v. *ITT*—Incompetence, Irrelevance and Confusion," *Antitrust Bulletin*, 19 (Summer 1974), 345.
29. Ibid., p. 337.

3. ITT was ordered to divest itself, within three years from the final judgment, of all its interests, direct and indirect, in Levitt, Avis, and Hamilton Life or, alternatively, of all its interests, direct or indirect, in Hartford.

ANTICOMPETITIVE BUSINESS PRACTICES

Anticompetitive business practices cover a multitude of sins—price fixing, reciprocity, exclusive dealing, price discrimination against buyers or sellers, territorial restrictions, tying agreements, interlocking directorates, boycotts, and other coercive practices. Each device can be used to restrain competition. For example, the aim of a price-fixing agreement, if effective, is the elimination of one form of competition. The power to fix prices, whether or not it is reasonably exercised, includes the power to control the market. Reciprocity can also be used in restraint of trade, when a buyer uses his or her power to compel sellers to purchase from him or her as a condition for doing business. Any restrictive agreement can be regarded by the government as a conspiracy of firms that results in a restraint of trade among separate companies. It is usually understood to entail some direct or indirect, overt or implied, form of price fixing, output control, market sharing, or exclusion of competitors.

Application of Antitrust Laws

As mentioned earlier in this chapter, the antitrust laws apply to various forms of restrictive agreements. Section 1 of the Sherman Act has been used to prohibit both vertical and horizontal price-fixing agreements. With respect to price fixing, the courts have applied, with few exceptions, an ansolute prohibition. Pricing discrimination would generally come under Section 2 of the Clayton Act as amended by the Robinson-Patman Act. This legislation attempts to foster competition by prohibiting both primary-line and secondary-line price discrimination. Tying agreements, if used in restraint of trade, would come under Section 1 of the Sherman Act and Section 3 of the Clayton Act. Reciprocity that leads to restraint of trade would come under the Clayton and Sherman acts. With the onset of the conglomerate merger, there has been an increase in reciprocal arrangements. Until the conglomerate appeared, a business firm usually had little opportunity to furnish goods to its supplier, because the latter generally had little need for what the firm was producing. The conglomerate changed this because frequently at least one constituent of the buyer's conglomerate produced some item needed by the supplier. In one case, Consolidated Foods, a major food processor and retailer, acquired Gentry, a manufacturer of dehydrated onion and garlic, and then attempted to persuade its suppliers to buy the Gentry products.[30] The merger was set aside.

The Electrical Equipment Case, 1961

The Electrical Equipment case of 1961 is a good example of a restrictive business practice, specifically price fixing by a number of firms in the electrical equipment industry.[31] Agreements to fix prices violate Section 1 of the Sherman Act and are illegal per se, for they vitiate the essence of competition in the marketplace. The case involved a conspiracy by a number of companies, including General Electric and Westinghouse, to fix prices and rig bids in the sale of heavy electrical equipment to private and public utilities. Markets were also divided up among the companies, with General Electric and Westinghouse getting the biggest shares. The conspiracy had been going on for a period of nearly twenty-five years, and the companies were accused of fixing prices and rigging bids on the sale of $7 billion of heavy electrical equipment between 1953 and 1960.

The conspiracy followed an elaborate pattern. Executives of the various electrical equipment companies would meet at conventions, hotels, and private homes to work out arrangements to divide markets and to rig bids on contracts. The companies literally would take turns in submitting low bids. The executives used false names and blank stationery to correspond and phases of the moon to determine which company would put in the low bid on a contract. Using the phase of the moon system, each firm knew when to bid high or to bid low, taking its turn in rotation as the low bidder. With twenty-nine different companies taking part, including the two largest, the conspiracy was about as complete as possible. This meant that over the period of the conspiracy, millions of extra dollars were charged to utilities and their customers. The conspiracy directly or indirectly affected almost every dam built, every power generator installed, and every electrical distribution system set up in the United States. Eventually, the TVA became suspicious of the similarities of a series of bids and notified the Justice Department.

The fines, penalties, and loss of business prestige resulting from the outcome of the suit, which was initiated by the Justice Department,

30. *U.S.* v. *Consolidated Foods*, 380 U.S. 592 (1965).
31. *U.S.* v. *General Electric et al.*, 209 F. Supp. 197 (1961). For discussions of the case see John G. Fuller, *The Gentlemen Conspirators* (New York: Grove Press, 1962); and Walter Jensen, "The Light of the Moon Formula—Some Whys and Wherefores," *Western Business Review*, 5 (May 1961), 27-33.

were enormous. Both the Clayton and Sherman acts provide for triple civil damage suits by private citizens. Both fines and jail sentences are provided for in the Sherman Act. Conviction by a federal court led to the thirty-day imprisonment of seven executives, the greatest number of jail terms ever in an antitrust proceeding, and suspended thirty-day jail sentences for twenty-one other executives. A total of $1.9 million was levied in fines against both the companies and their executives. In addition, by the end of 1967, a series of private triple damage suits filed against the major companies involved had cost General Electric $225 million and Westinghouse $125 million. Although the victims of the electrical equipment–price-fixing conspiracy were able to recover hundreds of millions of dollars, the triple damage remedy generally has not been an effective tool for victimized individuals. Private plaintiffs have often found antitrust litigation too costly and time consuming to be effective for them.

ANTITRUST AND PATENTS

Patents

The patent is a seventeen-year monopoly created by statute. It confers on its holder exclusive rights to processes and products, monopoly power that the government deems appropriate as a means of encouraging inventive initiative. The legal monopoly of a patent can protect only the invention claimed in the patent, nothing else. However, patents have formed the basis of various forms of agreements that have had the effect of restricting competition in the marketplace. Attempts to extend the reach of the patent monopoly beyond its proper scope can lead to charges of misuse of the patent, which can prevent the patent owner from enforcing his or her patent against parties injured by the misuse, or to an antitrust violation if the misuse has had or may have the requisite anticompetitive effect. The antitrust laws place the following types of restrictions on a patent monopoly:

1. An arrangement under which the grant of a license is made conditional on the purchase of unpatented supplies from a specified source is merely a form of illegal tie-in sale because the patent is practically a per se violation of Section 1 of the Sherman Act. In rare cases, if there are legitimate technical considerations in using the patented invention, it may be legal to require the licensee to buy special or specially adapted supplies.

2. An attempt by a patent owner to fix the price at which the licensee may sell articles manufactured under the license is very narrowly restricted and in practice is almost impossible to justify.

3. The right of the patent owner to license the patent for specified uses may in some circumstances be legal, although as a general rule it is very suspect under the antitrust laws. Licenses may be limited geographically in rare situations, but it is almost impossible to do so without running afoul of the law.

4. The practice of package licensing, in which a licensee accepts a license in a package deal, is proper only when the licensee voluntarily accepts the package; otherwise, it is an illegal tie-in situation.

5. The accumulation of patents in a company's portfolio is not in itself illegal, although the purchase of patents may be illegal under the merger provisions of Section 7 of the Clayton Act.

Various sharing devices such as the cross-licensing of patents or the pooling of patents for mutual benefit are not held to be illegal as such, but they generally are declared to be illegal when in the eyes of the courts, they are used as a means of eliminating competition among patent owners and licensees. For example, the Justice Department has challenged long-term agreements between two leading American and Japanese electrical equipment manufacturers, Westinghouse and Mitsubishi, covering both patents and know-how.[32] Each firm has a license to the technology of the other, and each is prevented by the agreement from selling products that use the technology of the other. The broad result has been to keep these two large electrical equipment manufacturers out of each other's home markets—an important consideration for the United States, given the concentrated nature of the electrical equipment market and its history of anticompetitive business practices.

Trademarks

Trademarks are also subject to the antitrust laws, particularly when they are used in restraint of trade. The purpose of a trademark, as originally conceived, was to identify the origin or ownership of a product. They are a vitally important component of the operating marketing mix of most successful business firms. Business firms have come to regard trademarks as a strategic device for establishing product differentiation and, through advertising, strong consumer preference. The use of a trade name, which is a form of trademark, for a wide variety of products will cause the name to become associated intimately with the overall image of the particular business. In this way firms have sometimes been able to establish a degree of market control that has remained substantially unchallenged for many years. An example is

---

32. *U.S.* v. *Westinghouse Electric Corp.*, Cic. No. 70-852-SAW (April 22, 1970).

Coca-Cola, which has achieved worldwide recognition. There is nothing wrong with trademarks, provided they are not used to restrict competition in a particular market. There are several types of trademark abuses that violate the antitrust laws:

1. Tying agreements in which a trademark owner ties the use of the trademark by other parties to the purchase of goods not normally sold under the trademark.

2. Exclusive dealing arrangements in which the trademark owner is able to persuade users to purchase its product to the exclusion of others. For example, General Electric was able to persuade government procurement agencies to establish specifications requiring the use of Mazda bulbs. It licensed Westinghouse to use the name but denied its other licensees the same right.

SUMMARY

The antitrust laws of the United States are based on the idea that the most beneficial national allocation of goods and services is attained by encouraging effective competition in the marketplace. To achieve this goal, these laws have been used to attempt to prevent certain business practices considered economically harmful. The laws are designed to maintain a competitive industrial structure by challenging monopoly power, whether achieved through internal growth or through mergers. The laws also are directed at specific business practices considered anti-competitive. These practices have been defined by the courts over a period of time and have become an integral part of the legal environment in which the modern business manager must operate. Obeying the antitrust laws is not always simple. The laws are complex, and there is often a hazy line between legal and nonlegal conduct. In most cases the marginally legal acts that a business manager engages in are not challenged, but there is always the risk that some action will violate a government regulation.

QUESTIONS FOR DISCUSSION

1. Should labor unions be subject to the antitrust laws?
2. Discuss the rule of reason doctrine as it was applied to the U.S. Steel case of 1911.
3. What is a conglomerate merger? Give examples.
4. How can a vertical merger be anticompetitive? Give examples.
5. How can a conglomerate merger be anticompetitive when, by definition, it involves noncompeting and nonrelated firms?

6. What is meant by a per se violation of the Sherman Act?
7. Why are certain industries exempt from the antitrust laws?
8. What is a product extension merger? Give an example.
9. Under what conditions can a cross-licensing agreement be illegal?

RECOMMENDED READINGS

Areeda, Phillip. *Antitrust Analysis*. 2nd ed. Boston: Little, Brown, 1974.

Asch, Peter. *Economic Theory and the Antitrust Dilemma*. New York: John Wiley, 1970.

Backman, Julius, ed. *Business Problems of the Seventies*. New York: New York University Press, 1973.

Kintner, Earl. *An Antitrust Primer*. 2nd ed. New York: Macmillan, 1973.

Markham, Jesse W. *Conglomerate Enterprise and Public Policy*. Boston: Harvard University Graduate School of Business Administration, 1973.

Scherer, Frederick M. *Industrial Market Structure and Economic Performance*. Chicago: Rand McNally, 1973.

Shepherd, William G. *Market Power and Economic Welfare*. New York: Random House, 1970.

Van Cise, Jerrold G. *The Federal Antitrust Laws*. 3rd rev. ed. Washington, D.C.: American Enterprise Institute for Public Policy Research, 1975.

Williamson, Oliver. *Markets and Hierarchies: Analysis and Antitrust Implications*. New York: Free Press, 1975.

Chapter 7
The Present State
of Antitrust

Opinions as to the effectiveness of antitrust policies vary widely.[1] There are those who think that antitrust legislation generally has been ineffective in curbing the concentration of industries. Competition has lessened, according to this argument, and market control by a few firms has brought them excessive profits, which in turn have contributed to inflation. Some other critics of antitrust policy are concerned about mergers between companies in unrelated fields. The acquisition of Montgomery Ward by Mobil Oil is an example. Still other critics equate bigness with badness. They feel that large firms increase their power at the expense of the individual and of smaller and less organized groups. There is suspicion about size and its relationship to the power and politics of society; and a belief exists that the primary purpose of antitrust is to perpetuate and preserve—in spite of any cost in efficiency and consumer welfare—a system of governance for competitive free enterprise. The well-publicized earnings of a few oil companies have also focused attention on antitrust. For the third quarter of 1979, Mobil Oil reported a 131 percent increase in earnings over the same quarter for 1978.[2] A feeling has developed among consumer groups and at least a part of Congress that new antitrust laws are needed to regulate the oil industry.

On the other hand, many antitrust observers feel that a combination of market forces, antitrust laws, and competition have provided restraints on prices and excess profits in most industries. They feel that industrial concentration in itself does not necessarily mean a lack of competition. In this view, the notion that increasing the number of competitors in an industry will add to competitive pressures is conjectural. There is nothing to prove that it is the number of competitors that guarantees efficiency or increases the likelihood that decision making will be improved. Bigness cannot be equated with badness, and

1. For a summary of these opinions, see Joint Economic Committee, paper no. 1, "Antitrust Law and Administration: A Survey of Current Issues," vol. 3. Inflation and Market Structure, 94th Congress, 2nd sess., 1976, pp. 17–22.
2. Oil company earnings are volatile. Gulf Oil reported a 20 percent decline in earnings for the first quarter 1981.

in the absence of proof to the contrary, why ban it?[3] Bigness is often a result of efficiency, and efficiency contributes to economic growth. Did International Business Machines (IBM) attain its present pre-eminent position by ruthlessly crushing its competitors (as alleged by the Justice Department in a lawsuit that began in 1969) or because it was more efficient than its competitors? IBM contends the latter. In a final argument, these observers point out that empirical studies indicate that profit rates are not significantly affected by whether industries are concentrated or not concentrated.

Historically, the United States has been ambivalent in its attitude toward competition. The antitrust laws may have had good effects on the behavior of the steel and automobile industries, but these good effects have been offset by government measures designed to protect the steel and auto industries from foreign competition. The reference price system was designed to keep foreign steel out of the United States, and the automobile industry has wanted import quotas placed on Japanese cars. Thus, policy is contradictory. Competition is fine as long as it is a matter of General Motors versus Ford, but not fine if it involves a foreign competitor and the foreign competitor wins. American consumers thus are denied freedom of choice and maximum satisfaction. General Motors and Ford have become part of a worldwide competitive industry and must deal with their competitors; protection is not the way to handle the problem.

Also, competition within the American antitrust rubric has meant price competition—nothing more, nothing less. But obviously, there are other areas of competition, such as that of quality, for example. Rightly or wrongly, Governor Hugh Carey of New York reflected the sentiments of many Americans when he compared American-made cars to disposable tissue. Japanese cars often cost more than American cars, but they sell because of their perceived image of quality. Moreover, although there are some industries that may approximate the textbook norm of millions of small competitors, each feverishly engaged in pure competition, there is one catch: little price competition actually exists. The legal and medical professions are examples. Doctors compete in reputations, not prices. Then, too, there are customers who would rather shop at Neiman-Marcus or Bloomingdale's, even though they could probably get the same product at one-third the price at a discount store. Nonprice forms of competition can be as useful and valid as price competition.

In any event, the time is not propitious either for increased enforcement of existing antitrust laws or for the passage of new laws. The public is generally disenchanted with government and particularly with

3. "New Thrust in Antitrust," *Time*, May 21, 1979, pp. 62–67. In a symposium on antitrust sponsored by *Time*, most of the experts were of the opinion that there is no proof that bigness is bad.

regulation. Many people have evinced the wish to "get the government off our backs." This disenchantment was translated in part into the election of Ronald Reagan in 1980.[4] But although the Reagan victory is unquestionably a prime contributing factor to the current antitrust climate, there are also other factors. The decline of the United States in many world markets has led to an examination of our antitrust laws within an international framework. In foreign trade, the United States suffers from its restrictive antitrust laws, for they hold American companies overseas to standards tougher than those competing firms must meet. Foreign laws and attitudes toward antitrust are different from ours. Governments in Europe and Japan are urging that some of their own big firms merge in order to sharpen their ability to compete in world markets. Thus some people in Congress feel that the United States should not force its companies doing business abroad to adhere to antitrust standards tougher than those of the countries where they have to operate.

REAGAN ANTITRUST ENFORCEMENT

Antitrust enforcement tends to come in cycles. The first enforcement movement came early in the century, during the trust-busting period of Theodore Roosevelt. A series of antitrust suits were initiated, culminating with the landmark Standard Oil and American Tobacco cases of 1911. Then enforcement of antitrust was largely quiescent until the economic catastrophe of the 1930s. During this period, the Robinson-Patman Act was passed, and some effort was made to apply the laws to business monopolies. During World War II, largeness became a virtue, since it was partly the mass production of armaments that enabled the United States and its allies to defeat the Axis powers. After the war, a spate of mergers prompted new interest in antitrust enforcement. The Celler-Kefauver Act was passed in 1950 and was followed by a series of antimerger cases, including the Du Pont–General Motors case of 1956, the Brown Shoe case of 1962, and the Philadelphia National Bank case of 1963. Mergers in the 1960s and 1970s often took the form of conglomerate combination of companies in different, often unrelated, industries. In the late 1970s and early 1980s, a combination of inflation and a lagging stock market left many stocks underpriced, selling well below the book value of their assets. This has encouraged corporate takeovers.

The Reagan administration has been accused by its critics of being

---

4. The Reagan administration came very close to shutting down the antitrust division of the Federal Trade Commission, which would have left only the Justice Department to enforce antitrust.

pro-big business, and the criticism extends into the area of antitrust enforcement. The resolution of three major antitrust cases in early 1982 indicates to some extent the attitude of the administration toward antitrust. Bigness, in itself, is not equated with badness. (This goes against the precedent established in the Alcoa case of 1945 when Justice Learned Hand ruled that Alcoa's dominant share of the aluminum market was in itself proof that the company was anticompetitive.) Bigness is accepted as desirable when economies of scale are effected. Also, bigness now has to be relative to a global environment: American banks are big, but so are French banks. In addition, bigness is not regarded necessarily as proof of monopoly power; perhaps it resulted from a company's greater efficiency which was translated into lower prices for consumers.[5]

In this chapter, five cases illustrate the Reagan administration's antitrust policies. Three of the cases can be legitimately called monopoly cases; the other two involve mergers. The monopoly cases concerned (1) IBM, which was accused by the Justice Department of attaining undue market size, of pricing discrimination, of buying scientists and engineers from competitors, and of entering into tying agreements; (2) the cereal companies—Kellogg, General Foods, and General Mills— which were accused by the Federal Trade Commission of having a shared monopoly; and (3) the AT&T case, which was probably the most important, given the company involved, since the Standard Oil and American Tobacco cases of 1911. The merger cases included Du Pont and Conoco, where no antitrust litigation was involved, and Schlitz and G. Heileman, a proposed merger of two brewers which was opposed by the Justice Department. The first case was a vertical merger which was accepted by the government even though the two firms were among the largest in the United States. The proposed merger of the two brewers was a horizontal merger which was rejected on the grounds that it was anticompetitive.

Monopolies

In January 1982, three very important antitrust cases finally came to an end. The Justice Department called off the two largest antitrust suits it had ever brought, those against IBM and AT&T, and the Federal Trade Commission dropped its suit against the big three cereal companies. The only clear winners in the suits were the lawyers who received $600 million in legal fees from IBM alone during the thirteen-year period of the suit. It can also be argued that AT&T came away a winner,

5. Edward Meadows, "Bold Departures in Antitrust," *Fortune*, October 15, 1981, pp. 188-192.

even though the government got most of what it wanted. The cereal company case, if nothing else, was an exercise in semantics. Its end was a landmark setback for the government's novel antitrust theory that a group of companies can "share" a monopoly, thus turning an oligopoly into a monopoly.

The IBM Case, 1969–1982

The IBM case was once called by *Time* "the case of the century."[6] Even allowing for a certain amount of hyperbole, it was the most significant antitrust case since the landmark Standard Oil and American Tobacco cases of 1911.[7] IBM is one of the corporate giants, and the issue in the case was its dominant position in the computer–data processing industry. In 1980, IBM's total sales amounted to $25.9 billion in comparison to total industry sales of $52 billion.[8] In contrast, the next nearest competitor, Sperry Corporation, had sales of $5.4 billion. IBM's return on sales for 1980 was 13.1 percent compared to 10.3 percent for the industry as a whole; its average return on sales for the 1970s was 13.8 percent compared to an average of 9.8 percent for the industry.[9] IBM also fared well among *Fortune*'s 500 Largest Industrial Corporations, ranking 14th in return on sales in 1980. It was the only firm among the top 20 largest U.S. industrial corporations to also rank in the top 20 in return on sales. Exxon, the leader in sales, ranked 288th in return on sales.[10] IBM is a true multinational corporation in every sense of the word. Its foreign business accounted for 54 percent of total sales in 1980 and 49 percent of earnings. It operated in seventy-nine countries and derived about 80 percent of its total revenue from the sales of information processing equipment.

This case was the third the Justice Department initiated against IBM. In 1932, it accused IBM and Remington Rand of combining to restrain trade in tabulating machines and punch cards by entering into agreements in which they agreed to adhere to minimum prices as fixed by IBM for the rental of tabulating machines and to require customers to purchase their punch cards from the lessor or pay a higher price for the rental of machines. IBM and Remington Rand agreed only to lease and not sell tabulating machines. The companies canceled their agreements before going to trial.[11] In 1952 the Justice Department once again sued

6. *Time*, May 21, 1979, p. 65.
7. *U.S.* v. *International Business Machines Corporation*. Civil Action No. 69, civ. 200, U.S. District Court for the Southern District of New York, January 17, 1969.
8. Arnold Bernhart & Co., Inc., *The Value Line*, March 13, 1981, p. 1107.
9. Ibid., p. 1066.
10. *Fortune*, May 5, 1981, p. 324.
11. 13 F. Supp. 11, affirmed 298 U.S. 131 (1934).

IBM, charging that it had violated Sections 1 and 2 of the Sherman Act by attempting to monopolize interstate commerce in the tabulating industry. The complaint alleged that IBM owned more than 90 percent of all of the tabulating machines in the United States, and manufactured and sold about 90 percent of all tabulating cards. The suit was settled in 1956 by a consent decree.[12]

The Justice Department, in a case begun in 1969 and resolved in 1982, accused IBM of monopolizing the multibillion-dollar computer business through a variety of unfair and anticompetitive business practices. The Justice Department accused IBM of price fixing, tying agreements, and announcing products embodying new technology far in advance of their actual availability. Specifically, IBM was accused of using lease arrangements with its customers to raise barriers against other companies seeking to enter markets and submarkets of the computer industry. IBM was alleged to have monopolized interstate trade and commerce in tape drives, memory drives, and add-on memory devices for the purpose of restraining or attempting to restrain its competitors from entering the market. The company was also alleged to have restrained or attempted to restrain competitors from entering or remaining in the general-purpose digital computer market by introducing selected computers with unusually low profit expectations in those segments of the markets where competitors had or appeared likely to have unusual competitive success. IBM was accused of dominating the educational market for general-purpose digital computers by granting exceptional discriminatory allowances in favor of universities and other educational institutions.

These and other offenses, the Justice Department charged, had the following effects:

1. IBM monopolized and continued to monopolize the general-purpose digital computer market in the United States.

2. Actual and potential competition in the manufacture and marketing of general-purpose digital computers in the United States was restrained.

3. Competitors of IBM were improperly deprived of the opportunity to earn competitive profits on their general-purpose digital computers, and actual and potential competitors were discouraged from entering or continuing in the business of manufacturing and marketing general-purpose digital computers.

The IBM antitrust case was filed by the Justice Department on January 17, 1969. The trial began on May 19, 1975, in the U.S. District Court for southern New York. The government suit charged IBM with violating the antitrust laws by monopolizing the general-purpose digital

12. Civil Action 72-344 (1956).

computer industry. IBM argued that it had not used anticompetitive practices and had not attained a pre-eminent position in the computer industry. IBM accused the Justice Department of using a narrowly circumscribed concept of the computer market. Among other relief requested by the Justice Department was the divestiture by IBM of whatever business and properties the court might consider necessary to dissipate the effects of IBM's allegedly monopolistic activities and to restore competitive conditions in the general-purpose computer industry. It might be added in this connection that IBM's total revenues from the sale or lease of general-purpose digital computers in the United States increased from $507 million in 1961 to $15.1 billion in 1980. In 1980, IBM's share of total industry revenue was approximately 50 percent. Its nearest competitor in 1980 had revenues amounting to 10 percent of the industry total.

IBM's defense was that size alone could not be termed illegal, and that its leadership in the computer industry had been achieved by the kind of enterprising effort that, in a free economy, should meet with reward rather than punishment. There is some merit to this defense. Logically, if competition is allowed free reign, some are going to win and some are going to lose, and usually there are going to be more losers than winners. IBM contended that what the Justice Department was saying in the suit was simply that those who have won must be broken up so the race can start over again. It might be added that a breakup of IBM into smaller competing units would not, in itself, have been likely to make the path easier for the existing competition. The proposed remedy of the government to subdivide IBM into smaller units conceivably could have created a pattern in which once again the industry would come to be dominated by a single firm.

In dropping the IBM case on January 8, 1982, the Justice Department said that although IBM might have controlled as much as 75 percent of the computer markets during the 1960s, its position had been achieved in an entirely legal way.[13] Actually, IBM now faces more competition instead of less. In its own immediate industry, its market share has slipped considerably as new competitors have entered the field.[14] At the end of 1980, there were thirty-one firms listed in the computer–data processing industry. Nine entered the market in the last fifteen years, and six of the nine entered the market during the 1970s. IBM also will now go head to head against AT&T in the communications market. In addition to computers, IBM, through a partnership, Satellite Business Systems, is already competing with AT&T for consumer dol-

13. In 1980, IBM had 68 percent of the large general-purpose computer market, 34 percent of the small-business computer market, 11 percent of the personal computer market, and 3 percent of the minicomputer market.
14. *The Washington Post*, January 9, 1981, p. 1.

lars. In the broad field of high-technology communications, there are such competitors as ITT, RCA, and General Telephone and Telegraph. Last, and most important, there are the Japanese. It is conceivable that they can do to the United States high-technology industries what they have already done to the United States auto industry. The struggle for dominance of a new generation of memory chips is already over, with the Japanese the winners.[15] In fact, in the Mitsubishi Report of 1979, the Japanese cite the weakness of IBM and state that companies such as Fujitsu will be fully competitive.[16]

The AT&T Case, 1974–1982

The AT&T case, perhaps the most important antitrust case of all time, was also resolved in January 1982. Not since the breakup of Standard Oil in 1911 has there been a more complex and potentially revolutionary restructuring of an American corporation, which happens to be the largest in the world. In 1980, AT&T had total assets of $137 billion, and its total operating revenues amounted to $51 billion.[17] In contrast, the next largest public utility, General Telephone & Electronics, had assets of $21 billion and operating revenues of $10 billion. In fact, AT&T's assets and operating revenues were larger than the nine next largest public utilities combined. The company's stock is owned by more stockholders than any other company in the world, and the stock has always been regarded as the bluest of the blue chips.

In its suit against AT&T, the Justice Department sought to separate ownership of AT&T's local operating phone companies, its long-lines department, and its equipment-manufacturing subsidiary, Western Electric, which by itself ranked nineteenth among the five hundred largest industrial corporations in the United States. This presented the anomaly of a regulated public utility owning an industrial firm not subject to regulation. The Justice Department charged that AT&T subsidiaries bought equipment from Western Electric even when other companies were developing better and cheaper equipment. It contended that AT&T set unreasonable restrictions on the connection of terminal equipment produced by other companies. The Justice Department also believed that AT&T either refused to deal with competitors of its long-lines department who wanted to connect with local phone networks or subjected them to discriminatory terms and prices. Finally, the Justice Department wanted a realignment of AT&T's research unit, Bell Laboratories.

15. *Fortune*, December 14, 1981, p. 52.
16. Jean-Jacques Servan-Schreiber, *The World Challenge* (New York: Simon & Schuster, 1981), pp. 190–194.
17. *Fortune*, May 31, 1981, p. 124.

AT&T contended that the government was attacking policies the company developed under comprehensive state and federal regulation. The company argued that its policies were reasonable responses to regulation and were subject to change by the regulators, and therefore should be immune from antitrust laws. It maintained that restrictions on some equipment connection was necessary to protect the telephone network from harm. It defended its opposition to competitors in long-distance service as a way to prevent "cream-skimming" by competitors —taking the most lucrative lines of business, and leaving AT&T as a utility, with an obligation to supply the most costly services. AT&T also contended that competition in the communications industry increased dramatically during the 1970s. A side argument, which was advanced by the Department of Defense, was that fragmentation of AT&T might well prove detrimental to the interest of national defense. The company argued that its telecommunications system produced an important contribution to the nation's missile, defense, space, and scientific programs.

The results of the historic settlement were as follows:

1. AT&T must divest itself of the local telephone services of its twenty-two Bell System operating companies.
2. Western Electric, Bell Laboratories, and the long-distance division of AT&T will be retained by AT&T. All intrastate long-distance service will be turned over to AT&T by the local companies.
3. AT&T no longer will be barred from offering unregulated nontelephone service, thereby opening the way for the corporation to enter the computer processing and information service business.
4. Local telephone companies divested by AT&T will be required to share their facilities with all long-distance telephone companies on the same terms.
5. Local companies will be barred from discriminating against AT&T competitors in buying equipment and planning new facilities.
6. AT&T shareholders will retain stock in AT&T and will be issued proportionate values of shares in the local exchange companies.
7. The Justice Department will have visiting rights at the local operating companies to interview employees and review the books.

AT&T now becomes a competitor in the broad field of high technology, ready to take on such multibillion-dollar corporations as IBM, ITT, RCA, and General Telephone and Electronics. There are also Japanese firms that are becoming more important every year in the high-technology area. In the field of telecommunications, AT&T, through its Bell Laboratories, has developed or is in the process of developing phones that use miniature display screens to identify the source of a call before the receiver is answered, and phones that can edit out and block preselected callers from reaching a person's number.

Keeping IBM intact sets up a fight between it and AT&T for the telecommunications market of the 1980s. The restructured AT&T will also
be able to enter the highly profitable computer and information industries, such as cable television and electronic newspapers. But working
against AT&T is its lack of marketing expertise; as a regulated monopoly, the company never really had to sell anything. There is also the
problem of management continuity resulting from the divestiture of its
local operating subsidiaries where most of its managers were trained.

The main issue as far as consumers are concerned will be the cost of
local phone service. Prior to the breakup of AT&T into separate corporate entities, AT&T charged premium prices for long-distance service in
order to hold down the cost of local calls. By divesting itself of its
twenty-two local operating companies, AT&T has relinquished its role
as the main supplier of telephone service.[18] There is concern that rates
for local services will rise sharply. Most likely to incur higher costs are
people in rural areas where telephone equipment is often old and the
number of subscribers is low. The rates will depend to some extent on
AT&T divestiture plans. The settlement gives AT&T wide latitude in
deciding whether it will spin off its twenty-two operating companies
into one large operating company, many little ones, or a smaller number of large regional telephone companies. The division of AT&T assets
among these companies will affect local telephone rates. The more
assets given to the operating companies, the higher local rates will tend
to be. This is because regulated telephone rates are computed to give
the telephone company a specific rate of return on its investment,
which is known as its rate base.

The Cereal Manufacturers Case, 1972-1982

In May 1972, the Federal Trade Commission initiated antitrust action
against the four largest manufacturers of breakfast cereals—Kellogg,
General Mills, General Foods, and Quaker Oats.[19] The case was important for several reasons. First, the case involved an oligopoly market
situation. In 1972, these four firms accounted for 91 percent of the
market in ready-to-eat cereals. Kellogg, with sales of $300 million, ac-
counted for 45 percent of the market;[20] General Mills, with $141
million in sales, had 21 percent of the market; General Foods, with $92
million in sales, had 16 percent of the market; and Quaker Oats, with

18. AT&T has eighteen months from January 1982 to divest itself of its operating
    companies.
19. *FTC* v. *Kellogg et al.*, File No. 711 0004, 1972. Quaker Oats was dropped
    from the case.
20. Data on cereal companies is from FTC, *Antitrust and Trade Regulation Report*,
    no. 547, January 25, 1972.

$56 million in sales, accounted for 9 percent of the market. Second, the FTC was not claiming any conspiracy or predatory acts on the part of the companies. It was trying to prove, instead, that a lengthy list of long-standing industry practices are anticompetitive and permit the companies, whose market shares went from 68 percent in 1940 to 91 percent in 1972, to share monopoly power. Third, it was charged that the shared monopoly violated Section 5 of the Federal Trade Commission Act. It marked an attempt to attack oligopolistic structures and mergers that occurred before passage of Celler-Kefauver through the use of Section 5.

The specific anticompetitive business practices of the cereal manufacturers were as follows:

1. Unfair methods of competition in product promotion and advertising. Specifically, by means of statements and representations contained in their advertisements, the cereal companies implied to children that their cereals would enable them to perform the physical feats depicted in the ads. In fact, ability to perform depends on many factors, most totally unrelated to eating cereal. Also advertisements were used to represent, directly or by implication, that consuming the ready-to-eat cereals would result in loss of body weight without adherence to a reduced calorie diet. This has not been demonstrated in fact. Advertisements also represented, directly or by implication, that failure to eat the cereals resulted in the failure of athletes or others to reach their full potential.

2. Brand proliferation, product differentiation, and trademark promotion. During the period 1950–1970, the four companies introduced around 150 brands, mostly trademarked, of cereals. The companies produced basically the same ready-to-eat cereals and then emphasized and exaggerated trivial variations, such as color and shape, primarily through advertising. Trademarks were used to conceal the basic similarities and to differentiate the cereal brands. Proliferating brands, product differentiation, and trademarks were all promoted by extensive advertising. The end result, the FTC claimed, was to create high barriers to the entry of other firms into the ready-to-eat cereal market, because brand names were so indelibly, and unfairly, impressed upon the minds of consumers.

3. Control of shelf space. Kellogg, the leading cereal company, controlled display space for the ready-to-eat cereal sections in many retail grocery outlets. Kellogg's services included the selection, placement, and removal of cereals and the allocation of space to other cereal producers. The other major cereal companies, the FTC claimed, acquiesced in and benefited from the Kellogg shelf space program because it benefited and perpetuated their market shares through the removal or controlled exposure of other breakfast food products. It was alleged that

through such services Kellogg and the other major cereal companies interfered with the marketing efforts of other firms.

4. Acquisition of competitors. The FTC claimed that through the acquisitions of competitors in the past, the four companies heightened the monopoly structure of the industry. One of the effects of these acquisitions was the elimination of significant sources of private-label ready-to-eat cereals. For example, in 1943, General Foods acquired Jersey Cereal Company, a substantial competitor in the sale of private-label cereals.

The FTC asked for the following remedies. It wanted three new companies spun out of industry leader Kellogg; one for Special K, one for Product 19 and Cocoa Krispies, and one for either Rice Krispies or Sugar Frosted Flakes. General Mills would have been required to spin off one new company and give the new unit its Wheaties brand. General Foods would also have been required to spin off a company. Together with the divestitures, the companies would have had to license their trademarked brands for production by other companies without royalty payments. A third proposed remedy was that the four major cereal companies not be allowed to license brands among themselves.

One problem with the cereal manufacturers' case was that only Kellogg makes breakfast cereal exclusively. General Foods and General Mills produce breakfast cereals, and also a wide variety of other products as well. General Foods sells Gaines Dog Food and Kool-Aid, and is in the process of acquiring Oscar Mayer, a meat-packing firm. General Mills does more than produce Wheaties. It owns a toy company (Kenner), a game company (Parker Brothers), and a restaurant chain (Red Lobster), and like General Foods, produces a wide variety of food products. Moreover, Kellogg, General Foods, and General Mills are part of the rather broad-based food processing industry, which includes about fifty good-sized companies, including Beatrice Foods, Best Foods, Nabisco, Standard Brands, United Brands, and other well-known firms.[21] There is heavy emphasis on brand products, like Planters Peanuts, Maxwell House Coffee, and so on, and thus advertising is important. There is also a substitution effect. Thus, breakfast cereal is one part of the product mix of a large industry, although it is circumscribed in terms of a given market.

In oligopolistic industries, the presence of homogeneous products, such as breakfast foods, may induce two types of anticompetitive business behavior—product differentiation based on little except advertising, and consciously parallel pricing policies theoretically explained by the so-called kinked demand curve in the economic model of oligopoly. There is nothing wrong with product differentiation per se. What was alleged in the cereal suit was that the large cereal manufac-

21. On April 21, 1981, Nabisco and Standard Brands decided to merge. The new firm is called Nabisco Brands.

turers came up with so many different forms of essentially similar breakfast foods, differentiated primarily by advertising, that competition was in effect locked out of the cereal market. Smaller firms could not afford the expensive advertising campaigns necessary to break into the market. Parallel pricing practices means that if one firm in an oligopolistic industry raises its price and others do not, consumers will quickly shift to purchasing the less expensive products. Conversely, if one firm lowers prices and the others do not follow, all the firms that do not lower their prices could lose their business. Consequently, all firms are almost certain to follow with lower prices, so that they all end up with the same share of the market, but selling at a lower price. Thus the demand curve for an individual firm operating under oligopoly is kinked, which means it is elastic above and inelastic below the prevailing market price. This means that if a firm raises its prices above the kink, sales will fall off rapidly because other firms are not likely to follow suit; if prices are lowered below the kink, sales will expand little because other firms will also lower their prices.

The theory of shared monopoly applied in the cereal manufacturers' case was an untried economic concept with a weak foundation. The theory asserted that a small number of firms may violate the antitrust laws simply by virtue of possessing substantial market shares. Merely the structure of the industry makes out the cause of action, and no collusive or otherwise illegal conduct need be demonstrated. However, the likelihood of acceptance of the shared-monopoly concept was small. In the 1980 presidential campaign, both Reagan and Carter expressed opposition to the FTC suit against the cereal companies. The Reagan administration proposed eliminating the FTC's antitrust authority, but did not do so. Equally significant was the opposition in Congress. Congressman Howard Wolpe of Michigan introduced a bill to place a moratorium on the cereal case.[22] The bill had eighty-one cosponsors of all political persuasions. The moratorium was to remain in place until Congress defined *shared monopolies* and suggested judicial remedies. The case was dropped by the Federal Trade Commission in late January 1982 after an FTC judge recommended the suit be dismissed.

Mergers

A spate of merger activity involving major companies occurred from 1975 to 1981. There were fourteen mergers in 1975 in which the purchase price of the acquired firm was in excess of $100 million; 1980

22. H.R. 2509 was introduced on March 12, 1981. It also might be added that, at their 1980 convention, the AFL–CIO Executive Council expressed opposition to the FTC suit, claiming that divestiture would cost 2,600 union cereal workers their jobs.

saw ninety-four mergers with a similar purchase price of acquired firms.[23] Some mergers have involved the exchange of a considerable amount of money. For example, Standard Oil of California made an offer in early 1981 of between $3.9 billion and $4.3 billion for Amax, a mining conglomerate, and Standard Oil of Ohio also made a multi-billion dollar offer for Kennecott Copper. Joseph E. Seagram and Sons, of Canada, the world's largest distiller and wine producer, offered $2 billion for St. Joe Minerals, a leading United States producer of zinc and lead. But mergers are not limited to big industrial firms; banks, savings and loan associations, and even individual investors may get into the act. A large number of mergers can be expected to take place among hard-pressed savings and loan associations. Government regulators have loosened restrictions on such mergers to prevent bankruptcies.

Table 7-1 presents examples of mergers consummated during the period 1974–1981. The acquiring company is usually a big, well-capitalized firm with strong cash flow and a need for changing its product mix. Philip Morris is a case in point. Hoping to duplicate its enormous success with Miller Brewing, the company bought Seven-Up. Dart and Kraft emerged from the combination of Kraft, a food-products company, and Dart Industries, a maker of housewares. These mergers also involve the acquisition of United States firms by foreign firms.

Du Pont–Conoco: The Merger of the Century

For several weeks in the summer of 1981, the American public was treated to a business version of the old-fashioned melodrama. Who would acquire Conoco? Would it be mighty Mobil Oil, the second largest company in the United States? Would it be the world's largest liquor firm, Seagram of Canada? Would it be Du Pont, the largest chemical firm in the United States, or a dark horse, like Texaco, the fourth largest company in the country? Each day provided another possible winner for Conoco's hand, which would depend to some extent on which firm could raise the most money. Finally, on August 5, 1981, a merger was consummated between Du Pont and Conoco—a merger that would be the largest in the history of the United States. Du Pont had purchased 47.3 million shares of Conoco's stock, or 55 percent of the shares outstanding, at a cost of over $7 billion. To celebrate their victory, Du Pont officials uncorked five cases of Dom Perignon 1970 champagne ($100 per bottle). Seagram won the consolation prize by acquiring 27 million shares of Conoco stock, thus becoming the second largest stockholder in the new Du Pont. But the stock purchase took Seagram out of bidding for any other oil company in the near future.

23. *U.S. News and World Report*, April 6, 1981, p. 79.

Table 7-1 Examples of Corporate Mergers Consummated During the Period 1974–1981

Acquiring Firm	Main Product	Acquired Firm	Main Product
Philip Morris	cigarettes	Seven-Up	soft drinks
Pepsi-Cola	soft drinks	Pizza Hut	pizza
Reynolds Industries	cigarettes	Del Monte	food products
Consolidated Foods	food products	Hanes	hosiery
Dart	housewares	Kraft	food products
Imperial Group	cigarettes	Howard Johnson	motel
Grand Metropolitan	conglomerate	Liggett Group	cigarettes
Mobil Oil	oil	Montgomery Ward	chain store
Standard Oil of Ohio	oil	Kennecott	copper
Wheelabrator-Frye	pollution control equipment	Pullman Inc.	railroad equipment
Bendix Corporation	aircraft equipment	Warner & Swasey	machine tools
Nabisco	food products	Standard Brands	food products
Du Pont	chemicals	Conoco	oil
U.S. Steel	steel	Marathon	oil
Coca-Cola*	soft drinks	Columbia Pictures	movies

*January 1982.

Source: Data compiled by the author.

In 1980, Conoco ranked 17th among American corporations, with total sales of $18.3 billion; Du Pont ranked 21st, with sales of $13.6 billion.[24] The combined sales would have placed the new Du Pont 7th in total sales in 1980, right behind Ford Motor Company. When the value of total assets are used as a measure of corporate size and strength, Conoco ranked 54th in 1980, with assets valued at $11.0 billion, and Du Pont ranked 65th, with assets valued at $9.6 billion. Combined assets would have placed Du Pont 26th in size in 1980, behind the Travelers Insurance Company. Using net profit as a third measure of corporate performance, Conoco ranked 15th in 1980, with net profits of $1.0 billion on sales of $18.3 billion; Du Pont ranked 22nd, with net profits of $716 million on sales of $13.6 billion. Combined profits would have placed Du Pont 9th in 1980. It is necessary to emphasize, however, that the size of profits is not the same thing as return on sales. Finally, in terms of market value of common stock, Conoco ranked 21st in 1980, with a value of $7.0 billion, and Du Pont ranked 25th, with a value of $6.2 billion. When combined, total market value would have put Du Pont 12th in 1980, ahead of Texaco, but behind General Motors.

Statistics are only a part of the total picture, however. Conoco is not only an oil producer, it is also the second largest producer of coal in the United States. Du Pont sells everything from synthetic fibers and insecticides to cookware coatings and auto paints. But for the company that invented nylon and Teflon, growth has come mainly from in-house research and innovation rather than through mergers. It was interested in Conoco because petroleum is the raw material for 80 percent of its products. Like all chemical makers, Du Pont has been badly hurt by the surge in oil prices since 1973. Now the company will have its own supply of crude oil. In 1980, Conoco produced 374,461 barrels of oil a day worldwide, of which 36 percent came from United States wells. Du Pont scientists will be able to help Conoco develop new techniques for boosting the yield from oil wells and converting coal into synthetic fuel. The acquisition of Conoco may also strengthen Du Pont's position in the world markets, a position that has come under attack from the West German chemical giants—Bayer, Hoechst, and Badische-Anilin, all of which are larger in sales volume than Du Pont.

The Du Pont–Conoco merger has revived a debate, to put it mildly, about the American economic system, which can be traced to the beginning of the industrial age. Is there something wrong—even sinister —about concentration of corporate power? Since the passage of the Sherman Antitrust Act in 1890, antitrust advocates have opposed

24. Data taken from Forbes Annual Directory Issue, *The Nation's 500 Largest Companies Ranked Four Ways*, May 11, 1981, pp. 215–256. Forbes includes all corporations, industrial and insurance companies, utilities, and banks.

mergers on the grounds that they reduce the number of competitors and thus make it easier for big companies to dominate markets. Moreover, mergers, if unchecked by any restraint, could conceivably reach a point where public confidence in the United States economic system is seriously undermined. On the other hand, there is the contrary opinion mentioned earlier that bigness in business does not necessarily mean badness. Competition can be just as effective between a half-dozen firms as between forty or four hundred firms. Chrysler will attest to that. There are those who argue that mergers can promote efficiency, which is the indispensable ingredient in a healthy economy. The efficient company wins and the less efficient competitor dies in a contest ultimately determined by consumers.

Of course, not all mergers promote efficiency, and there is a limit to the "big-is-beautiful" antitrust philosophy which appears to be the hallmark of Reagan's policy. Mobil Oil's proposed takeover of Conoco did not meet with Justice Department approval on the grounds that the merger would have been horizontal. Both were in the same industry; more important, Mobil Oil ranked second in total sales among all United States corporations in 1980. Texaco's proposed bid for Conoco also would have run into Justice Department resistance. Seagram based its sales pitch for a Conoco takeover on the grounds that it would be approved by the Justice Department, for Seagram and Conoco were not in competition with each other in any area of operation. But Conoco's executives saw no way that a large oil company could rationally be integrated into a liquor company. Du Pont and Conoco overlap because of a minor Conoco chemical division that could easily be spun off as a condition for government approval. The merger of Du Pont and Conoco can be considered vertical in that in gives Du Pont a secure supply of oil, gas, and coal as raw materials for its production of plastics, synthetic fibers, and other products.

There are a number of peripheral issues involved in the Du Pont–Conoco merger. First, Du Pont had to borrow $3 billion to finance the purchase, which more than doubled its debt load. Mobil and Texaco also established lines of credit, resulting in a diversion of credit that could have been put to other uses. The benefit of the merger must be weighed against alternative gains that could have resulted from loans for other purposes. Small business firms might have used some of the credit that went to Du Pont. Second, inflation in the cost of construction has encouraged companies to buy existing factories rather than build new ones, and to acquire mines rather than dig their own. Companies may not want to risk establishing new ventures. They might rather acquire firms with an already profitable track record. Buying undervalued oil on the stock market is far cheaper than finding it. Measured by the stock market prices for their shares, most oil companies have long been depressed relative to the underlying value of their assets. It is estimated that it costs $10 a barrel to find oil and $6 a barrel to refine it compared to stock market oil at $5 a barrel.

The number of mergers between large companies may well increase in the future. A combination of inflation and slow economic growth has increased the desire to merge among United States business firms. The real rate of return on the value of company assets has declined significantly in recent years—from 15.8 percent in 1965 to 9 percent in 1979 —and profits are decreased by the ever-rising cost of maintaining and building plants and equipment. As a result, companies may seek higher returns by investing in other companies. The mergers will probably involve some oil companies, with the large ones after smaller ones—Mobil Oil after Cities Service, and so on. Mobil, Texaco, and other international oil companies have watched OPEC gain control at the wellhead of most of the world's oil supply, and they wish to acquire safer domestic sources of oil. Mobil and Conoco were not actually direct competitors, for 63 percent of Mobil's total revenue in 1980 was derived from foreign sales. Mobil Oil and Texaco are cash-rich companies, with an extensive line of credit that makes them prime candidates to acquire other firms.

It is difficult to adopt a consistent merger policy, because each merger is different in terms of its impact on the economy. Unquestionably some mergers can effect economies of scale, whereas others could prove to be disasters. Mobil Oil's acquisition of Montgomery Ward is a case in point. Mergers of the Du Pont–Conoco type also have to be considered within the frame of reference of a global economy—something that critics of United States merger policies conveniently ignore. One question should be, will the merger improve the United States balance of payments and provide more effective competition against the Europeans and Japanese? Certainly the United States economy of today is a million light years removed from the economy that existed when the Sherman and Clayton acts were passed. The same holds true for the rest of the world, where half of the countries that exist today were not around when the Clayton Act was passed in 1914.

Schlitz Brewing, G. Heileman Brewing, and the Herfindahl Index

The beer industry is a classic example of industrial concentration that has developed over an extended period of time. As late as 1947, there were some four hundred breweries in the United States; by 1981, the number of breweries left was less than a hundred. Most of the beer companies had been absorbed by other beer companies, while some had discontinued their operations. By 1981, the beer industry was dominated by two brewing companies, Anheuser-Busch, with sales for the year of $3.8 billion out of total industry sales of $10.7 billion, and Miller Beer, which is actually owned by Philip Morris, with sales of $2.1 billion.[25] The combined sales of the two brewers amounted to around 55 percent of total industry sales. Moreover, the trend was toward increased market dominance by the two companies, with Anheuser-Busch projected to have 41 percent of the beer market by 1986 and Miller, which has the financial resources of Philip Morris to support it, projected to have a market share of 24 percent. Advertising is important in the marketing of beer, and both Anheuser-Busch and Philip Morris have the financial resources to sponsor athletic contests and remind the viewers of the enjoyment to be derived from drinking Michelob or Miller Lite.

Conversely, the Joseph Schlitz Brewing Company, which has long been a part of the brewing industry, with a name identification that goes back to the turn of the century, has fallen upon hard times, now relying on its president, Frank J. Sellinger, to tout the glories of Schlitz beer on television commercials. In 1981, Schlitz's sales amounted to $880 million, or around 8 percent of total beer sales for the year. Moreover, projected sales for 1982 and for subsequent years up to 1986 are at best expected to remain constant. The projected sales for the 1984–1986 period are estimated to be around 6 percent of total sales for the industry, down from the 15 percent share of the market the company had in 1970. With declining sales relative to total market sales, Schlitz has found it more difficult to finance advertising to increase its share of the market.

The G. Heileman Brewing Company enjoyed considerable success during the 1970s, advancing to fourth place in the brewing industry by the end of the decade. Through a number of acquisitions, including Carling and Falls City, the company became the dominant beer marketer in the Midwest. In 1972, Heileman had $107.9 million in total sales; by 1981, sales had increased to $820 million. The company increased its barrelage growth at twice the industry average during the 1972–1981 period, and profits increased 700 percent since 1975. Although brewing is its main line of economic activity, Heileman also derives part of its sales from its ownership of baking companies and a metal parts company. Because Heileman was an aggressive merchandiser of beer, the company proposed an acquisition of Schlitz, whose stock was selling at around book value, and offered Schlitz stockholders $17 a share for stock selling for $11.

The proposed merger was challenged by the Justice Department, which announced it would go to court to oppose it. Since Schlitz was

25. Data taken from Value Line Investment Survey and Standard & Poor's Industrial Surveys, The Beverage Industry, and the 1977 Census of Manufacturing, *Concentration Ratios in Manufacturing* (Washington, D.C.: U.S. Government Printing Office, 1981), Table 7, p. 15.

unwilling to challenge the government's decision, the proposal was dropped. In challenging the proposed merger, the Justice Department set new guidelines concerning mergers and industrial concentration. The department divided industries into three categories—least concentration, middle-range concentration, and high concentration. Least concentration is defined as a four-company share of 50 to 55 percent of the total industry market, middle-range concentration includes a four-company share of around 55 to 75 percent of concentration, and high concentration includes a four-company share of 75 percent or more of the market. The beer industry itself falls within the middle range as Table 7–2 indicates. However, extent of concentration has increased over time. Although no data is available for 1980, an estimate of 70 percent for the four largest companies is reasonable.

The critical test for two companies wanting to merge works this way: a figure corresponding to the market share of one company is multiplied by that of the other and the result is doubled. If the final total is more than 100 and the market fell into the middle range of concentration, then the Justice Department is likely to block the merger. In the highly concentrated range, the Justice Department will likely challenge a merger scoring 50 to 75 by this calculation. In the case of Schlitz and Heileman, the decision process worked as follows: based on 1980 statistics, Schlitz had 8.3 percent of industry total, based on value of barrels shipped, compared to 7.3 percent for G. Heileman. Multiplying 8.3×7.3 and doubling the total provides an index of 122. Since the beer industry comes close to being classified as a highly concentrated industry, the total of 122 placed the proposed merger of Schlitz and

Table 7–2 Concentration in the Brewing Industry (Based on Value of Shipment for the Four Largest Companies, 1935–1977)

Year	Percentage of Shipment
1977	64
1972	52
1970	46
1967	40
1963	34
1958	28
1954	27
1947	21
1935	11

Source: U.S. Department of Commerce, Bureau of the Census, 1977 Census of Manufacturing, *Concentration Ratios in Manufacturing* (Washington, D.C.: U.S. Government Printing Office, 1981), Table 7, p. 15.

Heileman into the danger zone. This proposed merger never material-
ized.[26] However, in April 1982 Stroh's made a successful bid for Schlitz.

The department also plans to use a mathematical index called the
Herfindahl Index that can take into consideration larger numbers of
companies and their relative sizes in determining market concentration.
The index is obtained by squaring and summing the market shares of a
given number of firms.[27] If there is only one firm, the index would attain its maximum value of 1.0 or 100 percent, because the one firm
would be a pure monopoly. If four firms have an equal share of the
market, the Herfindahl Index would be .25 $(.25)^2 + (.25)^2 + (.25)^2 +
(.25)^2$. By squaring market shares, the Herfindahl Index is weighted
more heavily in favor of firms with large market shares than firms with
smaller market shares. If one firm has a 50 percent market share and
four other firms each have an equal share of the remaining 50 percent,
the Herfindahl Index would be .313 $(.50)^2 + (.125)^2 + (.125)^2 +
(.125)^2 + (.125)^2$. The value of the index decreases toward zero as the
number of firms of equal size increases in an industry. Thus, the larger
the share of market that is controlled by one firm, the larger the index
and the greater the concentration. However, it is necessary that the
market share of the largest firm be measured accurately.

SUMMARY

The French diplomat Talleyrand once made the comment, "treason—it
is a question of the times," which is perhaps appropriate to antitrust
policy in the 1980s. The days of evil corporate dragons for the trust
busters to slay appear gone. No new major antitrust cases were filed
when Jimmy Carter was president, and the Reagan administration has
also relaxed antitrust enforcement, particularly in the area of mergers.
This, in itself, is not necessarily bad. In fact, it is conceivable that bigness can improve the United States competitive position abroad. It is
argued that rules and regulations largely written nearly a century ago no
longer apply to the international business world of today. The important competition in many markets is not among American firms, but
between United States and foreign companies. Such actions as splitting
off the Chevrolet division from General Motors, which the FTC considered as recently as 1976, seem archaic at a time when the United States
automobile industry is losing out to Japan. Antitrust must now be examined within the framework of a world business environment.

26. *The Wall Street Journal,* November 16, 1981, p. 4.
27. The Herfindahl Index is discussed in more detail in Frederick M. Scherer, *Industrial Market Structure and Economic Performance* (Boston: Houghton
Mifflin, 1980), pp. 58–59; and Eugene M. Singer, *Antitrust Economics and
Legal Analysis* (Columbus, Ohio: Grid Publishing Co., 1981), p. 22.

The recent dispositions of five cases have illustrated the current attitude toward antitrust. The Justice Department dropped its thireen-year suit against IBM on the ground that although it had controlled as much as 75 percent of the computer markets in the 1960s, it had achieved that position legally. It was also apparent that the company faces strong competition now, both nationally and internationally. The AT&T case, perhaps the most important of all time, was resolved with the company divesting itself of its local operating services and retaining Western Electric, Bell Laboratories, and its long-distance division. The cereal manufacturers' case, involving Kellogg, Generals Mills, General Foods, and, originally, Quaker Oats, was dropped, thus laying to rest the government's theory that the market oligopoly was a shared monopoly.

In two merger cases, the Justice Department approved the Du Pont–Conoco merger—largest in the history of the United States. It foreshadowed increasingly likely mergers between large companies in the future. In the case of the Schlitz Brewing and G. Heileman Brewing companies, the Justice Department challenged their proposed merger, and the plan was dropped. The department in this case set new guidelines concerning mergers and industrial concentration. In addition, the department plans to use a mathematical index called the Herfindahl Index which will help determine the relative sizes of companies and thus their market concentration.

QUESTIONS FOR DISCUSSION

1. What is a kinked demand curve? What is its significance with respect to oligopoly?
2. What were the issues involved in the IBM case?
3. What is a basic defect of United States antitrust policy as revealed in the IBM case?
4. Discuss the concept of shared monopoly as it was applied to the cereal companies.
5. What are some of the reasons for the declining interest in antitrust enforcement?
6. Why is the AT&T settlement one of the most important antitrust decisions of all time?
7. Discuss the antitrust policy of the Reagan administration as it applies to corporate mergers.
8. Discuss the attitude of the Reagan administration toward the long-held antitrust view that bigness is bad.
9. Discuss the Du Pont–Conoco case. What are some of the important issues?
10. What is the Herfindahl Index?

11. It is likely that the AT&T and IBM settlements will create more competition in the high-technology area rather than less. Explain.
12. Discuss some of the results of the AT&T case.

RECOMMENDED READINGS

Bloom, Paul N. "The Cereal Companies: Monopolists or Super Marketers?" *MSU Business Topics*, Summer 1978, pp. 41–49.

Bork, Robert. *The Antitrust Paradox*. New York: Basic Books, 1978.

Demsetz, Harold. "Economics as a Guide to Antitrust Regulation." *Journal of Law and Economics*, 19 (August 1978), 371–384.

Goldsmith, Harvey J., H. Michael Mann, and J. Fred Weston. *Industrial Concentration: The New Learning*. Boston: Little, Brown, 1974.

Mitchell, Edward J., ed. *Vertical Integration in the Oil Industry*. Washington, D.C.: American Enterprise Institute, 1976.

Nelson, Phillip. "The Economic Consequences of Advertising." *Journal of Business*, 48 (April 1975), 213–241.

U.S. Federal Trade Commission. *Statistical Report on Mergers and Acquisitions, 1978*. Washington, D.C.: U.S. Government Printing Office, 1980.

U.S., Senate, Committee on the Judiciary. *The Petroleum Industry*, pts. 1, 2, and 3. Hearings before the Subcommittee on Antitrust and Monopoly, 94th Congress, 1st sess., 1975.

PART IV
SOCIAL REGULATION OF BUSINESS

The point was made in Part II that there have been three major cycles in the government's regulation of business. The first cycle occurred in the last century and involved the passage of antitrust laws to control monopolies and railroad laws to regulate anticompetitive railroad practices. This cycle continued into the early part of this century and culminated in the passage of additional antitrust laws (Clayton Act) and laws to regulate the sale of electric power. The second cycle came during the Depression of the 1930s and was mainly reformative, including reforms of the banking system and the securities market to prevent abuses that had contributed to the collapse of the stock market and the banking systems. The legal environment for the labor unions was thus greatly improved, and the unions then became a countervailing force to business. The third cycle of regulation began in the late 1960s and early 1970s and was social in nature. We are currently in the process of digesting this social regulation, which includes the protection of the environment, consumer protection, and the safety and health of the labor force.

Social regulation, unlike the traditional rate-setting regulation for public utilities, is not subject to the market forces and public opinion that can limit costs. The public reaction to rising utility rates, for example, has been an important constraint on public utility commissions. The disparity between intrastate and interstate airline tariffs increased the pressure to deregulate the interstate airlines. Because the price of such regulation is visible, it invites a political response. As well, when prices are set above the cost of production, many customers will shop for alternative sources of supply. Thus a decision of the Interstate Commerce Commission to allow value-of-service pricing for interstate trucking and generally to permit interstate truck rates to exceed the cost of service led shippers to find other, unregulated forms of transportation. Similarly, improperly set toll rates induced large users of communications to establish their own microwave systems or to obtain them from non-Bell carriers.

The corrective forces of the market and public opinion do not exist in most areas of social regulation. A businessperson has no alternative but to comply with a mandatory standard if the regulatory agency has sufficient enforcement tools. The cost of health, safety, and environmental standards is not directly observable; therefore, the public cannot separate the mandatory costs from the other costs incurred in producing a pound of aluminum or a ton of paper. Social regulation often entails some aspect of human health or safety that can be used by a regulatory agency to incite strong emotional support for its actions, no matter how extreme or costly they may be. After all, who could be so callous as to be opposed to protecting workers from exposure to a cancer-producing agent? What all of this means is that much social regulation cannot be subject to rational economic analysis, even though it is costly and inefficient. A peripheral example is the national social security program, which is in some danger of running out of funds in the near future. Revising it, as President Reagan has attempted to do in order to make the fund more solvent, is tantamount to defiling the holy places in Mecca.

During the 1970s the federal government extended its involvement in the market system, directing more and more of its effort toward cushioning individual risks and regulating personal and institutional conduct. The cumulative impact of its actions have strongly affected business. In some cases, this was necessary because business was not responsive to public demands for such measures as safer working conditions; in other cases, actions were taken because business became an easy target for the discontent of many special interest groups. There was a conflict between a political system that emphasized public well-being and economic equality and a business system that adhered to a utilitarian goal of efficiency. Government social regulation proved to be quite costly, and people came to believe that somehow costs were never taken into consideration and little attention was paid to finding alternative ways of achieving the same social goals. The Carter administration did try to apply sunset measures to regulation of all types and to new procedures that would require federal agencies to show that their rules were beneficial to the economy and society as a whole. It is anticipated that the Reagan administration will increase these efforts.

Many regulatory changes can be expected from the Reagan administration, particularly in those rules and regulations that do not help business. An unfettered business, like Prometheus unbound, is supposed to save the economy, solve all social problems, restore the virtue of hard work, and create a new "Golden Age." But earlier business indifference and inaction contributed to many social problems that government then had to try to solve. President Calvin Coolidge once said, "The business of America is business," and many business firms still accept this as an article of faith. It still is not known how business will respond to such problems as protecting the environment and employing minorities without some form of coercion like the threat of losing government contracts. Also, as evident in the Chrysler bail out, restrictions on Japanese autos, and import quotas to protect the steel industry, business is not at all hesitant to ask for government help when its own ox is being gored.

Chapter 8
Issues of Social Regulation

Social regulation is broad based in its objectives and enforcement. It encompasses such areas as occupational health and safety, equal employment opportunity, consumer product safety, and environmental protection, areas that have specific social goals—a cleaner environment, safer consumer products, employment of minorities, and so forth. A number of important regulatory commissions, most of which were created during the 1970s, function to enforce the laws designed to achieve these social goals. The most important commissions are the Consumer Product Safety Commission, the Occupational Safety and Health Administration, the Equal Employment Opportunity Commission, and the Environmental Protection Agency. The jurisdiction of each of these relative newcomers extends mostly to the private sector and at times to productive activities in the public sector. Each of these agencies and commissions has a rather narrow range of responsibility, however. For example, the Equal Employment Opportunity Commission is responsible only for employment policies in a given firm or industry, whereas the CAB is responsible for all the activities of the airline industry.

Social regulation has an enormous impact on business firms, both large and small. Not much more than a decade ago, most business firms were unregulated private enterprises. They were free to design and produce the products they pleased, subject only to consumer acceptance. Marketing practices were subject to management and control, and pricing policies were devised to yield a rate of return on capital based on a standard volume concept. Antitrust laws did not apply to these business firms except as a deterrent to engaging in certain practices. Public utility regulation ruled only public utilities, and about the most interference any business firm could expect from Washington was with respect to bookkeeping involving social security and payroll taxes. Business leaders, of course, complained about Washington, thinking that even this amount of interference was excessive, but by and large they were free to manage with few constraints. A businessman could even hire and promote his mother-in-law if he saw fit.

But times have changed, and in instance after instance business firms, both large and small, have been made accountable to the public through legislative action or court action, rather than through voluntary action. In great part, the fault was that of business in failing to recognize the changes in American society or, more often, in recognizing the changes but not responding. Another reason was the rise of special interest groups that did not hesitate to alter the political decision-making process to achieve their own goals. The end result was that business firms have become subject to a wide variety of social regulations in a short period of time. By 1980 they were ruled by detailed government regulations under which almost all phases of their operation were affected. No longer do business firms have complete control over personnel practices: government affirmative action policies have to be considered. Marketing policies have to take into account the possibility of product recall. Today, each auto company now publicly recalls hundreds of thousands of automobiles if serious defects have to be corrected. In many companies, each division has a counterpart agency in Washington with which it must deal—personnel and the EEOC, production and OSHA.

REASONS FOR SOCIAL REGULATION

Justification for social regulation is based partly on the belief that imperfections in the market system are responsible for various social problems. In a market economy, the price mechanism gives individuals no opportunity to bid against the production and sale of certain commodities and services that they regard as undesirable. There may be many people who would be happier if they could prevent the production and sale of, for instance, alcoholic beverages or the emission of noxious fumes from a chemical plant, and who would be glad to pay the price if given the opportunity to do so. But there seems to be no way that the market-price mechanism can take these negative preferences into account. The only way that this can be done is through government action that places controls on the output of both public and private goods deemed deleterious to the public interest.

A second reason for the onset of social regulation is the externalities created by technological advances. Pollution is an externality because one individual can impose a cost on another without having to pay compensation.[1] This other individual then demands government protection in the form of regulation that prohibits or limits the actions of the first individual. As our society has become more technologically advanced and congested, one group's meat becomes another group's poison. Airports are necessary to facilitate rapid transportation, but their creation brings the attendant airplane noise which damages the environment of those persons who live near them. Thus these persons

1. Lester C. Thurow, *The Zero-Sum Society* (New York: Basic Books, 1980), p. 124.

will coalesce into a group demanding noise abatement measures. Coal is an important, and often the cheapest, source of fuel in the United States, but there are externalities involved in the mining of it—black-lung disease for the miners plus the despoliation of the environment, particularly after strip mining. Competitive markets are no solution at all to these externalities: a competitive firm will generate as much, or more, smoke than a noncompetitive one does.[2]

A third reason is the preoccupation with the quality of life. Following World War II, the main concern of most Americans was getting a job and buying a car and a house. Memories of the 1930s' Depression were still fresh, and so their requirements were few. But as both money and real incomes rose, these basic wants were satisfied, and they turned their interest to the quality as opposed to the quantity of life. By the late 1960s many persons had achieved a level of real income at which they could afford to be concerned about such issues as a clean environment. What fun was it to go to the beach for a vacation if the beach was polluted? This concern about the quality of life extended into other areas as well. Unlike the consumers of the past, who were interested more in the quantity of production to fulfill basic needs, consumers now have come to expect goods and services of better quality and at lower prices; and thus laws have been passed in such consumer areas as product warranty and product safety.

A fourth reason for social regulation was a general disenchantment with the American system, resulting from the new social concerns that developed during the latter part of the 1960s. This disenchantment with the system was manifested in several issues. Environmentalists and other groups accused business firms of neglecting their social responsibility to the poor and disadvantaged. Business was also the target of individual crusades, such as Ralph Nader's highly publicized efforts to spearhead improvements in such areas as automobile safety. The criticism of existing institutions, including business, permeated all sections of society. The discontent of the late 1960s did indeed facilitate the passage of social regulation: most of the major social regulatory commissions, such as the EPA and OSHA, were created in the early 1970s and the principal environmental laws also were passed then. There also were important consumer laws enacted in the early and middle 1970s, the Consumer Product Safety Act of 1972 and the Consumer Product Warranty Act of 1975.

Entitlement was a fifth reason, reflecting the changes in social values. The increase in economic growth during the 1950s and 1960s created what Daniel Bell has called a "revolution of rising expectations."[3]

2. Ibid., p. 125.
3. Daniel Bell, *The Cultural Contradictions of Capitalism* (New York: Basic Books, 1976), p. 275.

Translated into entitlement, it means that anyone who wants to work should be entitled to a job, even under government auspices if necessary. Anyone who is sick is entitled to medical care, and anyone who wants an education should have it. But, more important, entitlement has come to be expressed on a group basis, particularly in the areas of civil rights and social rights. To put it simply, entitlement has come to mean some form of compensation for a particular group. Because society over time deprived particular groups of their rights, those groups are now entitled to higher incomes and equal representation at all levels of the decision-making process, and there are demands that these disadvantaged groups —blacks, women, and specified national minorities—be given quotas or preferential treatment in hiring. Only in that fashion, it is argued, can these historical injustices be redressed. Attention to merit is regarded with suspicion; proportional representation is more important.

To some extent entitlement is linked to the egalitarian movement that has long been popular in the United States, particularly in the late 1960s. The concept of equality has meant different things throughout American history. The Jeffersonian concept of equality was more at-tuned to the relationships among a particular group of people, namely, property owners. In other words, there was an equality of the elect. The Jacksonian idea of equality was somewhat simpler. In essence it was that any person was just as good as the next one, that no one should put on airs, for that would be emulating the effete aristocracy in England. In fact, spitting on the floor was probably as good a way as any to demonstrate one's democratic and egalitarian instincts. On the positive side, this kind of equality came to mean the opportunity to get ahead regardless of one's origins. The egalitarianism of the late 1960s also was antielitist; in fact, *elitism* became a pejorative term for any social philosophy opposed to the notion that rigorous egalitarianism was a democratic imperative. Equality was defined in terms of equity; hence the emphasis on equality of result.

THE ADMINISTRATIVE AGENCIES

Almost every type of American business enterprise falls within at least the indirect influence of a number of administrative agencies. It is im-portant to study these agencies and their functions, though first some general points should be made. Administrative agencies, regardless of responsibility, acquire their authority to act from the legislative branch of government. They do most of the day-to-day work of government, and as a consequence, they make many significant policy decisions. Ad-ministrative agencies can be divided into two categories: the independ-ent regulatory commissions and those agencies that are part of the executive branch of government. In many areas of domestic policy formulation, independent agencies exercise more control, although different economic and political needs have produced administrative agencies exercising vast legislative and adjudicative powers that cannot be classified as independent regulatory agencies. Many executive agencies perform regulatory functions as part of their broader responsibility. Administrative functions can be divided into legislative, judicial, and executive categories and are performed by all types of agencies, although the agencies themselves may differ in the reasons for their creation, their principal goals, and their organizational structures.

Most regulatory agencies that function within the executive departments possess both quasi-legislative and quasi-judicial powers, just as the independent regulatory commissions do. The power to make rules and regulations has been delegated to these agencies by legislative fiat. The only important difference between an agency rule and a law enacted by a legislative body is that the rule may be slightly more susceptible to attack because it was not made by elected officials. Administrative agencies can also implement policy or legislation through a process of initiating and settling specific cases. They also engage in administrative adjudication, which includes procedures used in deciding cases. For many types of cases the procedures are carefully outlined: hearings are frequently prescribed, records are required, and so on. Furthermore, there often are elaborate provisions for judicial review, which suggests that if the agencies overstep the boundaries of legitimate authority, redress can always be secured in the courts. However, the scope of the judicial review of particular administrative agency decisions is limited, the logic being that the agency rather than the court is supposed to be the expert in the field in which it has been empowered to act.

Administrative agencies, as agents of Congress, reflect group demands for positive action. They are not supposed to be arbiters like the courts, but rather, they should be activists and initiate policy in accordance with their policy interests. For example, when the Federal Trade Commission (FTC) ferrets out deceptive business practices, either through its own investigation or through information gained from an outside source, it initiates action in the name of the FTC against the party involved. It then adjudicates the very case it initiates. If the case reaches a formal hearing and goes to a hearing examiner for an initial decision, it is not at that point subject to commission control. But after the examiner renders the decision, the commission may reverse it. The result is that the FTC can control the decisions rendered in most of the cases it initiates.

Sanctions

Government intervention in business carries with it the threat and the actual application of sanctions in order to achieve desired economic and social outcomes. When industry survival, industrial externalities such as pollution, or both, are of concern, sanctions may often be positive, taking the form of subsidies, tariffs, and tax incentives. When the target is the undesirable behavior of firms or groups of firms within an industry, negative sanctions are often used to induce compliance. These negative sanctions can designate noncompliance either as a criminal offense requiring the imposition of fines, imprisonment, or both, or as a civil offense involving the deprivation of the right or privilege to engage in economic transaction through the loss of licenses, permits, and franchises. For example, the Clean Air Act of 1970, which is administered by the Environmental Protection Agency, subjects willful polluters to fines of up to $50,000 a day and jail sentences of up to two years. Plants can be shut down and permits to operate canceled if pollution continues. Citizens and interest groups have the right to sue in federal court to force polluters, including the federal government, to cease and desist pollution practices.

In applying negative sanctions, the intent is to use the coercive powers of the state in order to obtain compliance. This is done by announcing to society or its components, including business, that various actions are not to be carried out and to ensure that fewer of them are. Business firms have no other choice but to comply with a mandatory standard if the regulatory agency has sufficient enforcement tools. In addition, the regulatory agencies are expected to amass facts, to apply the law to these facts, and to impose the appropriate sanctions when noncompliance is found. Thus, the intent and process of regulation is more like adjudication than other types of political action. It can be said that violators of economic regulation differ from violators of criminal law only in the degree of responsibility for societal harm that is attributed to them by policy makers, regulators, and the community as a whole. Firm owners and managers are generally held responsible only for their actions, which are often technical and morally neutral.

The Major Social Regulatory Agencies

Subject to the Reagan administration's approval for their continued existence, the following social regulatory agencies stand in the forefront: the Consumer Product Safety Commission (CPSC), the Environmental Protection Agency (EPA), the Equal Employment Opportunity Commission (EEOC), and the Occupational Safety and Health Administration (OSHA). These and several others of the alphabet-soup variety, in particular the Federal Trade Commission (FTC), are authorized to make rules that have the force of law; in other words, they have quasi-legislative powers. They also possess quasi-judicial power in that they settle disputes and hear and decide on violations of statutes of their own rules. Finally, much of the work of these agencies is administrative, including investigating firms in a particular industry, determining if formal action should be taken, and negotiating settlements.

The Consumer Product Safety Commission (CPSC)

The Consumer Product Safety Act of 1972 created the five-member CPSC, which functions as an independent regulatory commission. The commission is regarded by its critics as the most powerful regulatory agency in Washington.[4] It has jurisdiction over more than ten thousand consumer products and has the power to inspect facilities where consumer goods are manufactured, stored, or transported. The commission can also require all manufacturers, private labelers, and distributors to establish and maintain books and records and to make available additional information as it deems necessary. It can require the use of specific labels that set forth the results of product testing. The greatest impact that this requirement has is in the production process, in which the design of numerous products must conform to federal standards. Since safety standards are formulated at various governmental and independent testing stations, a manufacturer may find that a finished product no longer meets federal standards, and product lines may have to be altered drastically.

The Environmental Protection Agency

In July 1970, President Richard Nixon submitted to Congress a reorganization plan to create an independent environmental protection agency. The organization was approved, and the EPA was created in the executive branch. Functions that formerly belonged to the Department of the Interior relating to studies on the effects of insecticides and pesticides in the United States were transferred to this agency. Also transferred were functions originally belonging to the Department of Health, Education and Welfare (now the Department of Health and Human Services), including the creation of tolerance norms for pesticide chemicals under the Food, Drug, and Cosmetics Act. The EPA was given supervision over air pollution standards as set forth in the Clean Air Act

4. U.S., Congress, Joint Economic Committee, *Hearings on the 1979 Economic Report of the President*, 96th Cong., 1st sess., 1979, p. 32.

of 1970 and its subsequent amendments. The EPA also was given jurisdiction over water pollution control programs, particularly those set
forth in the Water Pollution Control Act of 1972, including the setting
of water quality standards. The jurisdiction of the EPA later was extended to apply to the Noise Control Act of 1972, and it became responsible for setting noise emission standards for products that have
been identified as major sources of noise. The EPA now has jurisdiction
over all the major federal environmental laws passed during the last
decade.

The Equal Employment Opportunity Commission (EEOC)

The EEOC was created by the Civil Rights Act of 1964 as an independent commission, and its enforcement authority was greatly increased by
the Equal Employment Opportunity Act of 1972. The EEOC now has
the power to investigate and act on a charge of a pattern or practice of
discrimination, whether filed by or on behalf of the person or group
claiming to be aggrieved or by a member of the commission. The EEOC
has the right to initiate civil suits against employers, labor unions, and
any group accused of practicing employment discrimination. As well,
private individuals and groups have the right to sue under Title VII of
the Civil Rights Act of 1964. The EEOC also can investigate company
records to see whether a pattern of discrimination exists and to subpoena company records if necessary. Every employer, labor union, and
organization subject to the Civil Rights Act and subsequent executive
orders must keep records that can determine whether unlawful practices have been committed, and they must furnish to the EEOC a detailed description of how persons are selected to participate in job-
training programs.

The Federal Trade Commission (FTC)

Few regulatory agencies have had more effect on business than the
FTC has. It was created by the Federal Trade Commission Act of 1914
with the intent of preventing unfair business methods of competition.
It was given the power to prevent persons or corporations, except banks
and common carriers subject to the various acts that regulate interstate
commerce, from using unfair methods of competition in commerce. It
was also given the power to investigate the practices of business combinations and to conduct hearings. It was authorized to issue cease-and-
desist orders and to apply to a circuit court of appeals to enforce them.
A violation is punishable by contempt of court. In addition to cease-
and-desist orders, the commission was given the power to negotiate

terms of agreement, known as consent decrees, violations of which are cause for court action. The commission was also given joint responsibility with the Justice Department for enforcing certain prohibitions that pertain to various forms of price discrimination.[5]

The FTC has come to be an all-purpose agency. It administers not only the antitrust laws of the United States but a wide variety of other laws as well. The Wheeler-Lea Act of 1938 authorizes the FTC to protect the public by preventing the dissemination of false or misleading advertisements with respect to food and drugs. Various labeling acts are also under the FTC's jurisdiction. The Wool Products Labeling Act and the Fur Products Labeling Act are examples. The McCarran Insurance Act of 1948 gives the commission partial jurisdiction over the insurance industry. This responsibility is complex because it varies according to the differences in state law. Then there is the Consumer Credit Protection Act of 1968 or, as it is more commonly called, the Truth-in-Lending Act, which requires that borrowers be made aware of basic information about the cost and terms of credit. Finally, there is the Consumer Product Warranty Act of 1975, which provides minimum disclosure standards for written consumer product warranties and defines federal content standards for these warranties. The act also extended the FTC's consumer protection powers to cover local consumer abuses when state or local protection programs are inadequate.

The FTC is currently one of the most controversial regulatory agencies in Washington. It often has been accused of either insufficient regulation or regulation too oriented to the needs of a given industry and not to the needs of the public. It also has been accused of too much regulation, with the result that the individual and the economy —in fact society as a whole—are stifled. This condemnation has been strengthened because critics have been able to point to specific instances in which the FTC has not performed well. Congress has recently voiced its criticism of the FTC, taking the position that it has overstepped its authority. It has accused the FTC of excessive paternalism and of overzealousness in its enforcement efforts. The attempt of the FTC to regulate "kid vid," the content of and advertising on cartoons and children's programs, also has drawn criticism. Congress has threatened to curb the authority of the FTC unless it tones down the intensity of some of its activities, reflecting Congress's current antiregulatory sentiments.

5. The FTC has jurisdiction over Section 2 of the Clayton Act, which covers what is called primary-line price discrimination, and over the Robinson–Patman Act, which amended Section 2 to prohibit secondary-line price discrimination. This refers to the sale of the same good to different buyers in the same geographic area at different prices when there is no cost difference.

The Occupational Safety and Health Administration (OSHA)

OSHA was created as an agency of the Department of Labor to administer the Occupational Safety and Health Act of 1970. The purpose of the act is "to assure safe and healthful working conditions for working men and women."[6] It requires employers to comply with safety and health standards promulgated by OSHA. In addition, every employer is required to furnish for each of his or her employees a job "free from recognized hazards that are causing or are likely to cause death or serious physical harm."[7] Although this "general duty" clause might appear to be an all-encompassing requirement for the provision of safety, it was clearly Congress's intent that the clause be limited in scope and relied on infrequently. "Recognized hazards" were defined in the congressional debate as those that can be detected by the common human senses, unaided by testing devices, and that are generally known in the industry as hazards.[8] Further, a firm can be penalized under the general duty clause only if the unsafe condition has been cited by an inspector and the employer has refused to correct it in the specified time.

Rightly or wrongly, OSHA has been the bane of many an employer's existence. Its reach and authority are considerable. If inspection discloses a violation, an employer can be cited and ordered to comply within a specific abatement period and may be fined. Serious violations, those that create a substantial probability of death or serious physical harm, must be fined up to $1,000 for each violation, but fines for lesser violations, although permitted, are not required. Deliberate or repeated violations may result in a civil penalty of $10,000 for each violation, and the failure to correct a violation within a prescribed period may result in a fine of $1,000 per day. The only criminal penalties for violations of standards are imposed on deliberate violations that lead to the death of an employee; in these cases, a fine of up to $10,000 and a jail sentence of up to six months are authorized.[9] Employers may and do appeal cited violations to OSHA—a three-member body appointed by the president. Its rules have often been capricious and have conflicted with the rules of other regulatory agencies,[10] but efforts have been

6. Robert Stewart Smith, *Occupational Safety and Health Act* (Washington, D.C.: American Enterprise Institute for Public Policy Research, 1976).
7. Occupational Safety and Health Act, Section 5a.
8. U.S., Congress, Senate, Committee on Labor and Public Welfare, *Legislative History of the Occupational Safety and Health Act of 1970*, 92nd Cong., 1st sess., 1971.
9. Smith, *Occupational Safety and Health Act*, p. 12.
10. A president of a small company complained, "The United States Department of Agriculture requires that our kitchen floors be washed repeatedly for sanitary purposes, yet OSHA rules that the floors must be dry. What is a man to do?" Cited in *Wall Street Journal*, September 21, 1979, p. 20.

made to make OSHA more efficient. The number of rules and regulations have been reduced, and some employers have been exempted from its jurisdiction.[11]

IMPACT OF SOCIAL REGULATION

Social regulation affects business and society in several ways. First, income is redistributed; resources are transferred from one income group to another. Second, there are both paperwork and compliance costs. Finally, social regulation influences business organization. Management must be responsible for the internal monitoring of company operations, including the hiring and promotion of personnel, personnel safety, product evaluation, and other areas. It also is subject to liabilities and restrictions; for example, management has to assume responsibility for product safety.

Income Redistribution Effects

Social regulation results in the redistribution of income. One example is environmental protection. Although most Americans generally favor a clean environment, the issue itself is primarily the preserve of the upper middle classes.[12] Lower-income groups do not rank a clean environment high on their list of priorities because it often threatens their income-earning opportunities, the loss of jobs if plants close. The steel companies argue that high environmental costs impede their ability to compete in world markets, which also may be translated into job losses for some steel workers. For the lower-income groups, basic needs have to be satisfied, and the quality of life does not become important until real incomes rise. For those Americans who can afford boats, summer homes, and trips to the beach, a clean environment ranks as a prime desideratum; for those Americans who cannot afford these things, a clean environment means little.

There is also a transferral of income from society as a whole to a small number of beneficiaries. For example, OSHA's coke-oven standards protect fewer than thirty thousand workers but are paid for by everyone who consumes a product containing steel, that is, nearly all of us. The EPA's oxidants standards protect people with respiratory problems and its mine safety regulations protect miners, but both at the expense of the general population.[13] These goals, although desirable, have

11. *Economic Report of the President, 1981* (Washington, D.C.: U.S. Government Printing Office, 1981).
12. Thurow, *The Zero-Sum Society*, pp. 104–105.
13. Robert W. Crandall, "Curbing the Costs of Social Regulation," *Brookings Bulletin*, 15 (Winter 1979), p. 2.

few trade-offs because special interest groups often are able to lobby effectively for particular objectives without considering them. The cost is not borne by these groups alone, but by the general public which usually is not aware of possible alternatives. What has happened is that the regulators avoid imposing costs on any group that can organize political pressure, and therefore it is easy to promulgate excessively costly regulation and charge it to the general public.

Costs of Social Regulation

The British playwright Oscar Wilde once said, "A cynic is a person who knows the price of everything and the value of nothing."[14] Obviously there are many benefits to be derived from social regulation—cleaner air and water, less noise, safer products, safer working conditions, and better employment opportunities for minorities. Few people would argue for the complete elimination of all forms of regulation. Rather, the objection is to a sometimes willy-nilly and often capricious application of social regulation. Little attention was paid to costs when many of the laws were passed. Since few citizens can possibly know how much alternative policies will cost them in terms of fewer resources for buying food, shelter, or medical care, the decision to minimize the economic costs of social regulation seldom seems to the administrators of regulatory agencies to be the politically most prudent one. Thus, they often end up choosing a needlessly expensive regulation or a very tight standard that cannot be justified by its benefits and costs. There is no mechanism to compel the regulators to compare the possible economic trade-offs of the different ways of achieving a given regulatory goal.

There have been many estimates of the costs to the private sector of government regulations. Some estimates include both economic and social costs, and others focus on various types of costs, individual areas of regulation and specific industries. These estimates come from several sources and are not limited to right-wing ideologues who wish to eliminate all forms of regulation.

1. A study prepared for Congress's Joint Economic Committee estimated that in fiscal 1979 the cost to the public of compliance with federal regulations was $102.7 billion—$4.8 billion for the administrative costs of the regulatory agencies and $97.9 billion for the compliance costs by the private sector of the American economy.[15] This

14. *Lady Windermere's Fan*, act 1.
15. U.S., Congress, Joint Economic Committee, Subcommittee on Economic Growth and Stabilization, *The Costs of Government Regulation of Business*, 95th Cong., 2nd sess., 1978.

study also attempted to determine the costs in 1976 for specific regulations. Consumer safety and health regulation costs were found to be
$6.6 billion, occupational safety regulatory costs to be $4.5 billion, and
environmental regulatory costs to be $8.4 billion.

2. For all businesses to comply with pollution abatement control
requirements, the Council on Environmental Quality estimated the incremental cost in 1977 to be $12.8 billion.[16]

3. Edward Dennison of the Brookings Institution estimated that the
incremental costs of protecting the environment and safety and health
of workers in 1975 was $10.5 billion, $9.5 billion of which was attributed to environmental regulations.[17] He also found that in 1975 these
factors resulted in a 0.5 percent annual reduction in growth of output
of net national product per unit of output.

4. Paul Sommers of Yale University determined the annual cost of
regulation to have been between $58 billion and $73 billion in 1977.[18]
He also estimated regulatory costs for eleven sectors of the economy,
which were grouped into three categories—economic; environmental;
and health, safety, and product quality regulation. By far the largest
regulatory cost to society came from the regulation of health, safety,
and product quality, set at between $30 billion and $45 billion.

5. A study for the Business Roundtable prepared by the accounting
firm of Arthur Andersen and Company measured direct incremental
costs incurred by forty-eight companies in complying with the regulations of six federal agencies in 1977.[19] These agencies were the Environmental Protection Agency (EPA), Equal Opportunity Commission
(EEOC), Occupational Safety and Health Administration (OSHA), Department of Energy (DOE), Employee Retirement Income Security Act
(ERISA), and Federal Trade Commission (FTC). Incremental costs
were defined as the direct costs of those actions taken in compliance
with a regulation that would not have taken place in the absence of
regulation. Incremental costs represent a portion of the costs of regulation to society. There also may be secondary effects on both business
and society, lower productivity being one example.

Table 8–1 shows the total incremental costs of the forty-eight companies mentioned above. By far the most expensive area was the en-

16. U.S., Congress, Joint Economic Committee, *Government Regulation:
    America's Number One Growth Industry, Notes from the Joint Economic
    Committee*, 10 (May 16, 1978), 2.
17. Ibid., p. 3.
18. Paul Sommers, *The Economic Costs of Regulation: Report for the American
    Bar Association* (New Haven, Conn.: Yale University, Department of Eco-
    nomics, 1978).
19. Arthur Andersen and Company, *Cost of Government Regulation Study: Re-
    port for the Business Roundtable* (New York: Business Roundtable, 1979).

vironmental regulations imposed by EPA: $2 billion of the total cost of $2.6 billion. The firms in the study noted that these incremental costs were either passed on to consumers in the form of higher prices or to shareholders in the form of diminished equity. There were also secondary effects which included lower productivity of labor, equipment and capital; delays in construction of new plants and equipment; misallocation of resources; and lost opportunities. Many companies felt that the costs of the secondary effects, although difficult to compute, were much higher than the incremental costs. Oil and gas companies cited delays that affected the whole economy. An example is the Trans-Alaska Pipeline, which was delayed over four years and whose cost of construction was estimated by one of the companies to have increased $3.4 billion owing to inflation during this period.[20]

In measuring the cost of regulation, it is necessary also to consider the concept of opportunity cost, which is defined as the value of the benefit that is lost as a result of choosing one alternative rather than another. This is an important concept, because the real cost of any activity is measured by its opportunity cost, not by its outlay cost. Thus, if resources are used to control pollution, society gives up all of the other goods and services that might have been obtained from these resources. If resources were not scarce, there would be no opportunity cost. But resources are scarce, and they do have alternative uses. So, for example, resources devoted to the manufacture of pollution control

Table 8-1 Incremental Costs of Regulation Imposed by Government Agencies

Agency	Cost (millions)
EPA	$2,018
EEOC	217
OSHA	184
DOE	116
ERISA*	61
FTC	26
	$2,622

*ERISA is not an agency. It is the Employee Retirement Income Security Act.

Source: Arthur Andersen and Company, *Cost of Government Regulation Study: Report for the Business Roundtable* (New York: Business Roundtable, 1979), p. 19.

20. Ibid., p. 27.

equipment might have been used to manufacture houses instead. Put in a strictly environmental context, opportunity cost means that when water is allocated for recreational uses, it carries with it the cost of sacrificing other activities that also require water use. Whether it should so be used, therefore, depends not only on whether the intended use is good but also on whether it is better than the other uses to which the resource could be put.

Impact of Social Regulation on Business Organization

The chairman of the Council of Economic Advisers Murray Weidenbaum has identified a "second managerial revolution."[21] (The first was noted by Adolphe Berle and Gardiner Means more than four decades ago.[22]) These observers of the American corporate scene were referring to the divorce of the modern corporation's formal ownership from its actual management, which occurred when the corporate form of management superseded the Carnegies, Fords, and Rockefellers of the world and became the dominant business unit by the end of the last century. In the corporate system, the owner of industrial wealth was left with only a symbol of ownership, and the power, responsibility, and substance that had been an integral part of ownership in the corporate beginning were transferred to a separate managerial group into whose hands their control fell. In other words, Standard Oil is no longer both owned and operated by the Rockefellers; rather, it is operated by a managerial class, completing the separation of ownership and management.

The second managerial revolution, according to Weidenbaum, came when the locus of the decision-making process shifted to Washington. This shift was particularly pronounced in the early 1970s, when the federal government took on the unprecedented tasks of coordination and priority setting, thus shifting the professional manager selected by the corporation's board of directors to a vast cadre of government regulators who can influence and often control the key decisions of the typical business firm. For example, management has had to accept responsibility for the internal monitoring of company operations, including the hiring and firing of personnel, personnel safety, product evaluation, and so forth. Government regulation changed the process of production, one reason being that an increased share of investment became unproductive. Distribution has had to be geared to the possibility of product recalls, and labeling and advertising have had to be recon-

21. Murray L. Weidenbaum, *Government Mandated Price Increases* (Washington, D.C.: American Enterprise Institute for Public Policy Research, 1975), p. 88.
22. Adolphe A. Berle and Gardiner C. Means, *The Modern Corporation and Private Property*, rev. ed. (New York: Harcourt Brace Jovanovich, 1968).

sidered. Affirmative action has had an impact on employment policies that call for special recruitment, training, and facilities for the benefit of women, minorities, and handicapped persons. Government regulation has also changed international business operations, and the executives of many American corporations complain that government regulations have adversely affected international competition.

During the 1970s, the pace of government regulation increased, particularly in the areas of health, safety, and environmental protection. Many of these regulations brought with them substantial costs in paperwork and production. The Commission on Federal Paperwork estimated that in 1977 private industry spent between $25 and $32 billion on completing and filing federal reports.[23] One company, Goodyear Tire and Rubber, in one week produced 345,000 pages of paper, weighing 3,200 pounds, to meet one new regulation of the Occupational Safety and Health Administration.[24] Many of the problems of regulation have stemmed from the original laws written by Congress. Statutes proliferated without incorporating appropriate incentives for regulators to consider the economic consequences of their actions. Many regulation costs are unnecessary, the result of needless and expensive duplication that has produced little more than higher business costs and prices. Congress now is leaning toward less regulation, with liberals joining conservatives in agreeing that better alternatives to detailed rules and regulations that pay no attention to cost should be developed.

Regulatory Budget

Some economists argue for a regulatory budget,[25] asserting that social regulation is the only institution without a budget constraint. In most American institutions, the use of resources is constrained, at least to some extent, by a budget. Households, firms, most government agencies, and the military services are operated within budgetary limitations. Only the regulatory agencies are not subject to limits imposed by a budget, and thus there is no mechanism that forces agency decision makers to trade off expenditures on one goal for outlays on another. Without a budget, regulators may proceed as if the resources they command have no other social value, as if the resources used in one way could not be devoted to other uses. For example, the resources used for

23. U.S. Commission on Federal Paperwork, *Annual Report, 1977*, p. 8.
24. *Wall Street Journal*, October 28, 1980, p. 1.
25. U.S., Congress, Joint Economic Committee, *Regulatory Budgeting and the Need for Cost-Effectiveness in the Regulatory Process*, 96th Cong., 1st sess., August 1979, pp. 15–22; and Crandall, "Curbing the Costs of Social Regulation," p. 4.

environmental protection could also be used to enhance the quality of life by enlarging the supply of food, shelter, and clothing. A mechanism is needed to ensure that society has enough environmental protection but that in the process it does not fail to satisfy most of its other needs.

Society would gain from a regulatory budget in two ways. First, the imposition of a regulatory budget would require congressional action on the size of the federal budget, which would focus attention on the benefits of regulation. Would the EPA, for example, be given the right to command, for instance, $30 or $40 billion per year without some evidence that it is offering the public an equal value in the form of a safer, cleaner environment? Without some attempt to measure benefits, it would be difficult to argue for $30 billion rather than $25 billion. Second, subjecting regulators to a budgetary constraint would compel them to choose the wisest way of using the nation's resources and to recognize that a dollar spent in the pursuit of one objective is a dollar withdrawn from fulfilling other objectives. A regulatory budget would require each regulator to make trade-offs among various policies. Soon, each agency's management would begin demanding staff estimates of alternative standards and of the cost of different degrees of regulatory stringency because each decision would affect the value of regulatory options available elsewhere. Cost-benefit analysis would become an important tool for regulators, not just a concept to be avoided if possible.

Regulatory Reform Under President Carter

President Carter's Executive Order 12044 on Improving Government Relations issued in March 1978 marked an attempt to bring better management to the regulatory process. It contains the requirements for economic impact analysis and sets the criteria for identifying significant regulations that necessitate regulatory analysis. The requirements cover those regulations that cost the economy $100 million or more annually or that produce a noticeable increase in costs or prices for individual industries, levels of government, or geographic regions. As an adjunct to the executive order, President Carter also established an interagency Regulatory Analysis Review Group (RARG) to assist agencies in improving regulations. It is composed principally of representatives from the executive branch agencies with regulatory responsibilities and is supposed to concentrate on those regulations that impose especially large costs or that promise to be precedent setting. The Council on Wages and Price Stability (COWPS) also was given statutory authority to intervene on its own behalf in regulatory proceedings. It can provide estimates of the costs and benefits of proposed regulations and can suggest alternatives that may not be provided during the course of rule making.

Regulatory Reform Under President Reagan

In 1960 candidate John Kennedy campaigned for the presidency of the United States by promising to get the economy moving again; twenty years later, candidate Ronald Reagan promised to get the government off the people's backs. As president he apparently enjoys the support of many people who feel that government has intruded too much into private affairs.[26] We may expect drastic actions in the area of social regulation. The Reagan administration, armed with a mandate to curtail the federal regulatory burden on business, will make a potentially lasting imprint on the activities of dozens of executive branch and independent agencies. Through appointments, executive orders, and legislation, the administration may well reshape the whole regulatory process and the agencies that enforce the nation's consumer, energy, environmental, health and safety, and equal employment laws. It may dismantle such agencies as the Consumer Product Safety Commission and devote more attention to cost-benefit analysis and to making the managers of regulatory agencies take greater heed of regulatory balance. There also is support for sunset legislation that would result in the automatic expiration of federal regulatory rules, and in the above-mentioned regulatory budget.

In the next three chapters, we shall discuss three areas of social regulation: consumer protection, environmental protection, and equal employment opportunity. For the most part, these areas are the product of the third cycle of regulatory activity that occurred during the late 1960s and early 1970s. There were several factors that contributed to their development. There has been a more rapid rate of social change in the last fifteen years than ever before, and the importance of the individual often has been subordinated to the interests of a group. Economic minorities argue that group parity is fundamental to economic and social justice and that an optimum distribution of income is more than an optimum distribution of income among individuals. Many forces—urbanization, which brought pollution, entitlements, and so forth—accelerated the transition of government from its old role to a more participatory new one.

26. A Harris Poll found that 77 percent of the public agreed that excessive government regulation was a cause of low U.S. productivity (*Washington Post*, January 11, 1981, p. L5). A Yankelovich poll of May 1981 indicated that 62 percent of those persons polled felt that the government should stop regulating business and protecting consumers.

Table 8-2 Number of New Major Social and Economic Regulatory
Laws Passed by Congress by Time Periods

Time	Economic Laws	Social Laws	Total
Pre–1900	4	6	10
1900–1909	1	5	6
1910–1919	10	8	18
1920–1929	5	10	15
1930–1939	23	23	46
1940–1949	6	12	18
1950–1959	14	13	27
1960–1969	18	35	53
1970–1979	45	80	125

Source: Joint Economic Committee, Congress of the United States, *The Economy of 1981: A Bipartisan Look*, 97th Cong., 1st sess., 1981, p. 290.

SUMMARY

Social regulation has become an important part of our economic system, given market imperfections that have created such problems as
pollution. But social regulation has also become very expensive because
the regulators have not had to consider the costs of achieving a given
regulatory goal, and this has often led them to choose an expensive
regulation or a tight standard that could not be justified by benefits and
costs. Estimating the benefits of environmental or health and safety
regulations may not be easy, but it is necessary at least to attempt to
measure the effects of regulation in a manner that allows a comparison
with the costs.

Social regulatory agencies are beholden to a given constituency: EPA
to the environmentalists, EEOC to the civil rights groups, and OSHA to
organized labor. The lobbying pressures from these groups can be great;
yet the public is unaware of any trade-offs, and a small group can be
protected at the expense of the public.

QUESTIONS FOR DISCUSSION

1. What are incremental costs?
2. What is opportunity cost?
3. Discuss how government social regulations affect business operations.

4. What is a regulatory budget?
5. What is meant by *entitlement* and *egalitarianism*?.
6. Discuss the two types of administrative agencies.
7. Discuss the use of sanctions as a way of controlling business.
8. Explain how social regulation can have an income redistribution effect.
9. What is cost-benefit analysis?
10. How do federal regulatory activities influence the economy?

RECOMMENDED READINGS

Arthur Andersen and Company. *Cost of Government Regulation Study: Report Prepared for the Business Roundtable.* New York: Business Roundtable, 1979.

Committee for Economic Development. *Redefining Government's Role in the Economy.* New York: CED, 1979.

Crandall, Robert W. "Curbing the Costs of Social Regulation." *Brookings Bulletin,* 15 (Winter 1979), pp. 1–3.

Lilly, William, and James Miller. "The New Social Regulation." *The Public Interest,* (Spring 1977), pp. 14–28.

Smith, Robert Stewart. *Occupational Safety and Health Act.* Washington, D.C.: American Enterprise Institute for Public Policy Research, 1976.

Sommers, Paul. *The Economic Costs of Regulation: Report for the American Bar Association, Commission on Law and the Economy.* New Haven, Conn.: Yale University, Department of Economics, 1978.

Thurow, Lester C. *The Zero-Sum Society.* New York: Basic Books, 1980.

U.S., Congress, Joint Economic Committee, Subcommittee on Economic Growth. *The Costs of Government Regulation of Business.* 95th Cong., 2nd sess., 1978.

U.S., Congress, Joint Economic Committee, "Environmental Regulation: America's Number One Growth Industry." *Notes from the Joint Economic Committee,* 95th Cong., 2nd sess., May 16, 1978.

U.S., Congress, Joint Economic Committee, *Regulatory Budgeting and the Need for Cost-Effectiveness in the Regulatory Process.* 96th Cong., 1st sess., 1979.

Chapter 9
Consumer Protection

Government regulation of business accelerated in the late 1960s and early 1970s, particularly in new areas and areas that received little attention in the past. New federal regulatory commissions were created with which business firms now have to contend. There is a significant difference between the new form of regulation and the older, more formal regulation that is much more circumscribed in its application to business. The new regulation is broad based and applies to firms in many industries. For example, the Environmental Protection Agency is responsible for implementing controls that apply to all firms that in any way pollute the environment. The Consumer Product Safety Commission has jurisdiction over more than ten thousand products and is authorized to set mandatory safety standards for a number of industries. The older regulatory commissions focus on controlling a specific industry. Thus the Federal Energy Regulatory Commission is responsible for regulating oil pipelines, and the Securities and Exchange Commission is responsible for regulating the securities market.

The newer regulation is much more social in its orientation and has several forms.[1] First, there is government intervention between sellers and consumers to protect the latter from conditions that might emerge in the absence of regulation. To protect consumers, it has been made unlawful for a firm to market certain drugs until they have been approved by the Federal Drug Administration. Likewise, the Consumer Product Safety Commission is authorized to establish mandatory standards and require the labeling of products that have been found to be unsafe. Second, government regulates the use of so-called public resources. Social costs and benefits are balanced most closely in the regulation of the environment, by balancing polluting uses against nonpolluting uses and by choosing the appropriate instruments to minimize the cost of achieving this balance. Third, government regulation is used to redistribute income among social groups. The federal government's affirmative action program is an example of this. Its purpose is to upgrade hiring and promotion opportunities for women

1. Alfred L. Seelye, "Societal Change and Business-Government Relationships," *MSU Business Topics*, 23 (Autumn 1975), 3-5.

and members of minority groups in order to change the occupational mix of the labor force.

Although laws to protect consumers from various forms of abuse have been on the books for a number of years, in the 1960s and 1970s there was a renewed interest in passing new laws, which have been quite comprehensive in their application to business. This interest could be attributed to a consumer movement that, although somewhat amorphous, had its impact in the passage of such laws as the Consumer Product Safety Act of 1972. Consumer protection covers a rather broad category of laws that must be separated on the basis of objectives—laws protecting the consumer against the adulteration or misbranding of foods, drugs, and cosmetics; laws requiring truthful disclosure, including protection of the consumer against false or misleading advertising; and laws governing product safety. Before examining them, we shall discuss the rationale for government protection of the consumer.

CONSUMER SOVEREIGNTY AND FREEDOM OF CHOICE

In a capitalistic market economy, consumer sovereignty is an important institution because consumption is supposed to be the basic rationale of economic activity. As Adam Smith said, "Consumption is the sole end and purpose of all production; and the interest of the producer ought to be attended to only as far as it is necessary for promoting that of the consumer." Consumer sovereignty assumes, of course, that there is a competitive market economy in which consumers are able to "vote" with their money by offering more of it for products that are in demand and less of it for products that are not in demand. There will be shifts in supply and demand in response to the way in which consumers spend their money. In competing for the consumers' dollars, the producers will produce more of those products that are in demand, for the price will be higher, and fewer of those products that are not in demand, for the price will be lower. Production is the means; consumption is the end. Those producers that effectively satisfy the wants of the consumers are rewarded by large monetary returns, which in turn enable them to purchase the goods and services they require in their operations. On the other hand, those producers that do not respond to the wants of the consumers will not remain in business very long.

Freedom of choice is linked to consumer sovereignty. In fact, one defense of the market mechanism is the freedom of choice it offers consumers in a capitalistic economy. Consumers are free to accept or reject whatever is produced in the marketplace, and thus they are paramount, since production ultimately is oriented toward fulfilling their desires. Freedom of choice is consistent with a laissez faire economy. It is

assumed that consumers are capable of making rational decisions, and in
an economy dominated by a large number of buyers and sellers, this assumption has some merit. Since the role of the government is minimal,
the principle of caveat emptor, or "let the buyer beware," governs consumer decisions to buy.

These statements, however, should be qualified in regard to the position of the consumer in the current marketplace.[2] First, the statements
assume some sort of parity between consumers and producers, at least
with respect to product knowledge. They also assume that consumers
are capable of making rational, dispassionate choices in the marketplace
based on information about a particular product. True consumer choice,
taking into account that the buyer must be wary, is all very well in a
society in which consumers are generally equipped with at least the
minimum of technical information necessary for enlightened choice.
Indeed, in a far less complex time than the present, it was possible for
consumers to be relatively well informed about products and markets.
In the last century the range of products from which consumers had to
choose was small. The products were generally simple and were in
everyday use. Intelligent buyers had the expertise to make a reasonable
evaluation of the products, and if they needed credit, the sources to
which they could turn, although limited, were at least well known. Consumers in the last century were faced with few choices that were not
within their range of personal experience.

Today the situation is different. Consumers are confronted with
many products and not enough information to make the most rational
or optimum choice. The average person, in fact even the most intelligent, has neither the ability nor time, nor probably the inclination to be
an expert in the intricacies of the many products that industry provides.
Differences in the qualities of goods are a mystery to many consumers.
If consumers do recognize differences in the quality of certain goods,
they face the almost impossible task of determining whether or not a
given item is sufficiently superior to another article to justify a higher
price. The relation of price to quality is further complicated when retailers sell the same article at different prices or when merchants offer
at so-called bargain prices articles that are in reality set at their regular
price or even higher. Even in purchasing relatively simple products,
such as food, consumers are confronted with added considerations such
as weight, color, and chemical substances.

Probably the most important qualification is that producers influence
the choice of consumers. First, producers take the initiative in changing
the techniques of production that increase the variety and volume of
consumer goods. Second, producers use skilled marketing methods,

2. Robert L. Birmingham, "The Consumer as King: The Economics of Precarious
    Sovereignty," *Case Western Reserve Law Review*, 20 (1969), 354–367.

including advertising, that influence the consumer's choice of goods. It can be argued that the purpose of advertising is to provide product information for the consumer, but it also can be argued that the purpose of advertising is to entice consumers into buying products that, for the most part, they do not need. The so-called educational benefit of advertising may be designed merely to stimulate conspicuous consumption, such as a new car every year or the emulation of certain living standards. Consumers are goaded into maintaining superficial appearances at the expense of more fundamental needs. The overall effect of the producers' influence on consumers cannot be determined accurately; there are both gains and losses to consumers.

The market and price mechanism never asks consumers to specify for which commodities and services they would like the scarce resources of society used. The most important choices are made by business managers who decide what commodities and services should be placed on the market, and consumers can choose among only those options offered to them by the managers. Consumers are not totally passive, however; they can exercise a considerable degree of selectivity despite the persistent advertising aimed at them. So there is some freedom of choice, and it is related to the range of alternatives available. Different market structures may determine the degree of choice. For example, the responsiveness of the market to consumer demands will be less than ideal when monopolistic elements are present, whereas a competitive market structure necessarily has to be more responsive to consumer demands. The consumer, although less sovereign than capitalist theory would have it, does have more freedom of choice than in a centrally planned economy, such as in the Soviet Union. There the state reduces choice to a minimum by presenting only a narrow and biased range of alternatives.

GOVERNMENT AND THE CONSUMER

The laws protecting the consumer are of infinite variety, but it is possible to divide them into several categories. The first includes laws designed to protect consumers from the adulteration, misbranding, or mislabeling of food, drugs, and cosmetics. In fact, the original focus of government consumer regulation was in this area. Its first piece of consumer legislation, the Food, Drug, and Cosmetics Act of 1906, was passed in response to public demands to curb these abuses. The second category includes laws to protect consumers from unfair competition, such as false or misleading advertising or various forms of product misrepresentation. Of particular importance in this category is the Wheeler-Lea Amendment to the Federal Trade Commission Act. The third category of consumer protection laws is product safety, and it has become even more important in recent years. In essence, the purpose of product safety legislation is to protect the consumer from himself or herself. Implicit in product safety legislation is that the concept of consumer sovereignty is inadequate if there are external costs in a product's consumption or production, or both, that the consumer does not account for in the consumption decision. As a result of this market failure, the government has intervened in order to control product quality standards and regulations so as to upgrade product quality and repairability.

Both the federal and state governments participate in consumer protection. The Federal Trade Commission Act of 1914 created the Federal Trade Commission to protect both business and consumers against unfair competition. The commission has since expanded its responsibilities so that it is now the primary regulatory agency concerned with consumer protection. Some of the acts that the FTC administers are the Wheeler-Lea Act of 1938, the Wool Products Labeling Act of 1939, the Fur Products Labeling Act of 1951, the Textile Fiber Labeling Act of 1958, the Cigarette Advertising and Labeling Act of 1966, the Fair Packaging and Labeling Act of 1966, and the Consumer Product Warranty Act of 1975. The FTC also has jurisdiction over certain provisions of the Packers and Stockyard Act, as amended in 1958. In addition, Section 6 of the FTC Act gives the commission the right to collect and make available to the public factual data about various business practices. The FTC has investigated the meat-packing, cereal, oil, and telephone industries, chain stores, and farm implements.

Pure Food, Drugs, and Cosmetics Legislation

The passage of pure food and drug laws was related directly to the consumers' welfare. In the last century hygienic standards were very low, and many sellers, particularly in the cities, sold goods that were not fit for human consumption. Adulteration of foodstuffs was a common practice among the bakers and grocers of the 1880s, who met the growing demands of an increasing population by diluting their raw materials with a variety of additives.[3] Milk was often diluted with water, and to improve the color of milk from diseased cattle, dealers often added chalk or plaster of paris. Meat and other perishable goods were displayed on unrefrigerated racks, subject to the vagaries of the weather. Spoilage was common, but the meat was still sold to the public. Fruit was not covered by inspection laws and rotted on the counters. *Harper's Weekly* in 1872 stated that in the markets of New York City there were cartloads of decayed fruit, which, if eaten, would almost

3. Cited in Otto L. Bettman, *The Good Old Days—They Were Terrible* (New York: Random House, 1974), pp. 77–85.

certainly cause death.[4] Even the growth of the food canning industry did not necessarily reduce the danger of spoilage, for chemicals often were used to mask the signs of food decay. In fact, many American soldiers died during the Spanish-American War from eating decayed meat packaged in tin cans.

State and local governments were the first to pass laws to protect the consumers' interests. Sanitary regulations, inspection of weights and measures, and the like were established public functions at the beginning of the nation's history. State laws to protect consumers against the adulteration of food and drugs were first passed in Virginia in 1848 and in Ohio in 1853. As production methods became more sophisticated, leading to the development of large-scale food and drug enterprises, state regulation did not work as efficiently. Products sold in interstate commerce were difficult to subject to state regulation, and as the problem of consumer protection became more complex, federal action became inevitable. One catalyst for this action was *The Jungle*, written by Upton Sinclair in 1906, which described conditions in the meat-packing industry. Here is one of its more graphic descriptions:[5]

> It was only when the whole ham was spoiled that it came into the department of Elzbieta. Cut up by the two-thousand-revolutions-a-minute flyers, and mixed with half a ton of other meat, no odor that ever was in a ham could make any difference. There was never the least attention paid to what was cut up for sausage; there would come all the way back from Europe old sausage that had been rejected, and that was mouldy and white—it would be dosed with borax and glycerine, and dumped into the hoppers, and made over again for home consumption. There would be meat that had tumbled out on the floor, in the dirt and sawdust, where the workers had tramped and spit uncounted billions of consumption germs. There would be meat stored in great piles in rooms; and the water from leaky roofs would drip over it, and thousands of rats would race about on it. It was too dark in these storage places to see well, but a man could run his hand over these piles of meat and sweep off handfuls of the dried dung of rats. These rats were nuisances, and the packers would put poisoned bread out for them, they would die, and then rats, bread, and meat would go into the hoppers together.

The Pure Food and Drug Act of 1906

There is no question but that *The Jungle* was one of the reasons for the passage of the Pure Food and Drug Act. Theodore Roosevelt read the

---

4. Ibid., p. 88.
5. Upton Sinclair, *The Jungle* (New York: Doubleday & Page, 1906), p. 321.

book and was as aroused by its disclosures as was the general public. He immediately ordered an investigation of the meat-packing industry, and a pure food bill that had been bottled up in Congress took a new lease on life and was passed with only a few opposing votes. The Pure Food and Drug Act is considered to be the first significant piece of consumer protection legislation in the nation's history. Its main provisions were:

1. The federal Food and Drug Administration was formed to administer and enforce the provisions of the act.

2. The law prohibited interstate commerce in adulterated or misbranded foods and drugs. Adulteration was defined as the hiding of damage or inferiority through artificial color or coating, the addition of poisonous or other deleterious ingredients injurious to health, and the inclusion of decomposed or diseased animal or vegetable substances. Foods and drugs were declared to be misbranded if their packages or labels bore statements that were "false or misleading in any particular" or if one were sold under the label of another. Food also was considered misbranded if its weight or measure was not plainly shown, as were drugs if their packages or labels bore false claims of their curative effects.

3. Such acts were made criminal offenses, with a fine of up to $200 for a first offense and $300 or a year's imprisonment for subsequent offenses.

The results of the Pure Food and Drug Act were mixed. A revision of food and drug laws followed in almost every state, generally bringing state definitions into line with the federal model. The act was reasonably effective in barring the extremes of dangerous adulteration, and it was later strengthened by the authority given to the Federal Trade Commission to enforce fair business practices. But there were many loopholes in its enforcement. Publicity was used to sway public opinion, but publicity was not always forthcoming when corporate managers threatened to withdraw their advertising from the public press when it printed information unfavorable to their corporations. The enforcement of the act also was hindered by a lack of adequate funding from Congress. In addition, the location of the Food and Drug Administration within the Department of Agriculture until 1940 meant that it was sometimes subjected to pressures from certain segments of the department's clientele.

The Food, Drug, and Cosmetics Act of 1938

The Food, Drug, and Cosmetics Act of 1938 strengthened the Pure Food and Drug Act of 1906. It expanded consumer protection by enlarging the range of affected commodities, broadening the definitions of adulteration and misbranding, increasing penalties, and making special provisions for particularly dangerous substances. Cosmetics and therapeutic devices also were included in its terms. Food was defined as adulterated if it contained any poisonous or deleterious substances; if it was colored with coal tars not approved by the Food and Drug Administration; if it was prepared under conditions that might result in contamination with filth or injury to health; or if it was packed in containers composed of substances that might make it injurious. The definition of adulterated cosmetics was similar to that for food, with special provisions for coal-tar hair dyes. However, no provision was made for the establishment of standards for cosmetics, and the disclosure of ingredients was not required.

Other provisions of the Food, Drug, and Cosmetics Act of 1938 were:

1. A food sold under the name of another had to be marked clearly as an imitation, and foods bearing proprietary names had to be labeled with the common or usual name of the food and with each ingredient.

2. Containers so formed or filled as to be misleading were prohibited.

3. Dietary food had to contain such information about its vitamin, mineral, and other properties as the secretary of agriculture determined to be necessary for consumer protection.

4. The Food and Drug Administration was authorized to inspect factories producing food, drugs, and cosmetics and was empowered to license manufacturers and establish standards of sanitation for granting licenses when the processing of foodstuffs might involve a risk of contamination that would make it a menace to public health.

5. Drug firms developing new drugs were required to obtain approval from the Food and Drug Administration before putting them on the market, and the FDA was authorized to deny approval of drugs that either had not been tested or had been found to be unsafe.

6. Certain drugs had to carry a warning of their habit-forming qualities, and drug labels were required to contain adequate directions for use, warnings against unsafe dosage, and disclosure of ingredients involving special dangers to the user.

7. Penalties were increased, amounting to a year's imprisonment or a fine not exceeding $1,000 for a first offense, with subsequent offenses entailing imprisonment of up to three years and fines of up to $10,000. Injunctions against the continuance of prohibited actions also were authorized.

Drug Amendments of 1962

The Food, Drug, and Cosmetics Act of 1938 was amended in 1962 to extend the authority of the Food and Drug Administration, particularly in the area of drugs. The initial impetus for changing the 1938 law came from hearings begun in 1959 by Senator Estes Kefauver's Antitrust and Monopoly Subcommittee.[6] Underlying these hearings was a belief that the prevailing regulation permitted the introduction of new drugs of dubious efficacy which were sold at high prices. This was said to result from a combination of patent protection for new chemical formulas, consumer and physician ignorance, and weak incentives for physicians to minimize patient drug costs. It was argued that drug companies devoted inordinate amounts of research to the development of patented new drugs that represented only a minor modification of existing formulas. The companies would then exploit the patent protection through expensive promotion campaigns in which extravagant claims for the effectiveness of the new drug were impressed on doctors. Even when patent protection was weak, as for new products that were combinations or duplicates of existing chemical formulas, consumer ignorance and weak cost-minimization incentives made artificial product differentiation an attractive market strategy.

The hearings characterized much drug innovation as socially wasteful. The waste was said to arise from product-differentiation expenditures in an imperfectly competitive market permeated by physician and consumer ignorance. Product-differentiation expenditures were incorporated in prices that therefore did not reflect the "true value" of the drug to the consumer. It was argued that only in hindsight would doctors or patients discover that claims for new drugs were exaggerated; consumers would have been better off if they had used the lower-priced old drugs instead of the new drugs. They would have paid less for a treatment at least as effective as what they received. It was apparent that accurate information about new drugs would be provided only if the federal government regulated the manufacturers' claims of effectiveness. Thus the primary feature of the 1962 amendments to the 1938 act is that a manufacturer must prove to the satisfaction of the FDA that a drug has the curative powers the manufacturer claims for it. No drug can be put on the market unless it is approved by the FDA, which also can remove a drug from the market if it has evidence that it carries a threat to health.

Other Food and Drug Laws

The Meat Inspection Act of 1907 was a companion to the Food and Drug Act of 1906. It provided that a veterinarian from the Department of Agriculture must inspect the slaughtering, packing, and canning

6. Sam Peltzman, *Regulation of Pharmaceutical Innovation: The 1962 Amendments* (Washington, D.C.: American Enterprise Institute for Public Policy Research, 1974), pp. 8–27.

plants that ship meat in interstate commerce. The use of adulterates to hide meat decay or to color the meat was prohibited. Animals had to be inspected before slaughter and the carcasses after slaughter. The Wholesome Meat Act of 1967 amended the 1907 act. It is designed to force states to raise their inspection standards to those of the federal government. If the states failed to meet federal standards within two years after the passage of the act, the Department of Agriculture had the right to impose federal standards. The Poultry Products Inspection Act of 1957 gave the Department of Agriculture the right to inspect poultry sold in interstate commerce. In addition, the department was to supervise the sanitation and processing of poultry for sale in interstate commerce. The Wholesome Poultry Act of 1968 offers federal aid to the states so that they can establish their own inspection programs for intrastate poultry plants and meet federal inspection standards. States were given two years to comply with federal standards. Those intrastate poultry-processing plants that posed a health problem were to be cleaned up or shut down.

There are some weaknesses in enforcing the existing pure food and drug laws. One is that the FDA is given far less money than are those agencies with smaller responsibilities but greater political support. The FDA, like many older, well-established agencies, has been accused by consumer interest groups of being more concerned with maintaining the status quo than with protecting the consumer. The increased use of chemicals in many foods and cosmetics has raised some hazards to health and has strained the capacity of the FDA. Chemicals may be added to foods without prior tests: only when the FDA has investigated and found the chemical to be unsafe may its use be banned. Only a small fraction of all the establishments processing or storing foods, drugs, and cosmetics can be inspected in any one year, and an even smaller fraction of their products can be tested. In many cases, gross adulteration of food, such as visible filth or decay, goes undetected until noticed by the consumer.

Advertising and Other Forms of Disclosure

A second area of government involvement in consumer protection is the various forms of disclosure such as advertising and warranties. This area is rather broad, but generally the practices that come under its purview are covered by Section 5 of the Federal Trade Commission Act of 1914, which gives the FTC the right to prevent unfair competitive practices, including those that affect consumers adversely. A rather common practice over the years has been false or misleading advertising. But a study of advertising by no means takes in the entire subject of disclosure. First, there are various product labeling requirements designed to protect consumers against misrepresentation and fraud. There also are laws designed to protect consumers against excessive credit charges. Since 1969, federal law has required that creditors disclose to borrowers basic information about the cost and terms of credit. Finally, there are consumer product warranties. Consumers usually are not aware of the warranty coverage on purchased products until after the sale is consummated and some defect or problem with the product directs their attention to the terms of the warranty.

The rationale for advertising is that for markets to work effectively, buyers must have accurate information about the quality and other characteristics of products offered for sale. Otherwise, the market is unlikely to enable consumers to make purchases maximizing their welfare within the limits of their resources. The provision of information about products is of fundamental importance to a market system. Without individuals or firms producing and selling product information to consumers, most of the information about products would have to be generated by the sellers and, to a lesser extent, by the consumers. As a result of the increases in the complexity and variety of products and in the value of people's time, there has been a major shift from consumer to seller in the comparative advantages of supplying consumer product information. But this increased reliance on sellers for information about products does not mean that the information disseminated will be truthful. A seller's general purpose is to provide information that, if believed, will induce consumers to buy this product in preference to other sellers' products.

There are several market situations that can predispose a seller to use false or misleading information about a product:[7]

1. The first situation is monopoly. This market arrangement is conducive to the use of false or misleading advertising for two reasons. First, there is little likelihood of effective consumer retaliation when the deception is discovered, for the consumer has no close substitutes to which he or she can turn; and, second, the incentive of other sellers to correct false advertising is weak, for the false claim is unlikely to have much impact on them. By definition there is no very close substitute for a monopolized product, and so any sales loss will be a small one distributed among the producers of a variety of distant substitutes.

2. Another market situation is oligopoly, in which a few sellers practice product differentiation through advertising. One seller, in an attempt to gain a competitive advantage over rivals, may make false claims about his or her products. False claims aside, a certain level of industrial concentration is necessary before it becomes profitable for a

7. Richard A. Posner, *Regulation of Advertising by the FTC* (Washington, D.C.: American Enterprise Institute for Public Policy Research, 1974), pp. 22–24.

firm to engage in large-scale product promotion. By and large, it is only the largest firms in an industry that can afford the high costs of advertising, particularly on television. A good example of concentration is the cereal industry, with the three largest firms—Kellogg, General Foods, and General Mills—together accounting for about 85 percent of total industry sales. Advertising is a way of life to the cereal industry, for some form of product differentiation is necessary to facilitate consumer choice among a myriad of products. Thus, each company is compelled to make exaggerated claims for its cereals in order to maintain its market position and to achieve some payoff on advertising expenses, which amount to around fifteen cents out of every sales dollar.

3. A third market situation is created when the performance of a product is highly uncertain, making false claims difficult to challenge, or when the seller can terminate business quickly and at low cost. The first category covers many restorative services, ranging from automobile repair to medicine, and the second includes various "fly-by-night" operations in which the seller does not have a substantial investment that would be jeopardized if customers, having discovered the falseness of the seller's claim, ceased to deal with him or her.

The Federal Trade Commission Act and False Advertising

The first demands for the control of advertising came at the turn of this century, as a result of the false claims made by the many charlatans who populated the food and drug industries. Although the early postal laws were meant to deal with the wholesale distribution of false advertising by mail, it was not until 1914, when the Federal Trade Commission Act was passed, that broad federal legal weapons against false or misleading advertising came into existence. As mentioned earlier, Section 5 of the act declared that unfair methods of competition in commerce were unlawful and gave the Federal Trade Commission the authority to prevent persons or corporations from using unfair methods of competition in commerce. So preoccupied were the framers of the act with the commission's role in supplementing antitrust enforcement that the intended role of the commission as an agency for protecting consumers against fraud was left wholly undefined. The intention of Section 5, however, went deep, for it authorized the commission to proceed against various forms of antisocial business conduct over and above the unfair practices proscribed by the Sherman and Clayton acts, for example, price fixing and boycotts.

The FTC did attempt to prosecute consumer fraud cases. To circumvent objections that a mandate to prevent unfair methods of competition did not include efforts to protect consumers, the commission claimed that the fraudulent practice harmed the honest competitors of the defendant by diverting sales from them. In 1931 the Supreme Court overturned an FTC ruling that Raladam, the manufacturer of Marmola, cease and desist from representing its product as a remedy for obesity.[8] The Court found misrepresentation common among vendors of such nostrums and concluded that no damage had been done to Raladam's competitors. The Court held that in the absence of proof of such an effect, the FTC could not act against consumer fraud. This decision led to proposals to amend the original Federal Trade Commission Act.

The Wheeler-Lea Amendment

In 1938 the Wheeler-Lea Amendment to the Federal Trade Commission Act changed Section 5 to direct the FTC to prevent "unfair or deceptive acts or practices" as well as "unfair methods of competition," thereby making it the commission's explicit duty to protect consumers against fraud in the form of false or misleading advertising when no harmful effect on other sellers can be established. The amendment also forbids specifically false or misleading advertisements for food, drugs, cosmetics, and therapeutic devices sold in interstate commerce. The term *false advertising* means an advertisement, other than labeling, that is false or misleading in a material sense. When injuries to health ensue from customary or advertised uses of the commodity being falsely advertised, the advertiser becomes subject to the same criminal penalties as those under the Food, Drug, and Cosmetics Act of 1938. The importance of Wheeler-Lea is that it made of equal concern before the law the consumer who may be injured by an unfair trade practice and the merchant or manufacturer injured by the unfair methods of a dishonest competitor.

With Wheeler-Lea, it has become possible to prosecute for deceptive advertising without having to show that competition has been restrained. The amendment, however, has failed to define what is "unfair" or "deceptive" with respect to a practice, nor does it have any provisions for monetary damages, compensatory or punitive. The commission's inability to award monetary reparations to victimized consumers has had two effects. First, it has weakened the consumer's incentive to lodge complaints of deception with the commission, and second, it has weakened the seller's incentive to comply with the statutes enforced by the commission. The only consequence of violation is that if apprehended and successfully prosecuted, a fraudulent seller will be prevented from continuing, or repeating, the violation. But the seller is permitted to keep any of the profits obtained during the period of violation.

8. *FTC* v. *Raladam Co.*, 283 U.S. 643 (1931).

Enforcement Proceedings

As mentioned earlier, there is only one standard procedure by which the FTC can act to prevent deceptive practices such as false advertising, but it can encourage and promote voluntary compliance. That is, the commission will, in certain instances, settle cases by accepting adequate assurance that a given business practice has been discontinued and will not be resumed. The FTC also can make a formal complaint against a business firm engaged in deceptive acts and practices. The business firm, which is the respondent, or accused party, is given an opportunity to enter into a consent settlement without formal litigation. If the respondent decides to contest the complaint, the matter is set for trial before an administrative law judge, or hearing examiner, appointed by the FTC. The commission and the respondent each are represented by their own attorneys. At the conclusion of the hearings, the judge issues his or her findings and an initial decision, which, if it goes against the prosecution, can be appealed to the full commission. The respondent can also appeal if the decision goes against him or her. A judicial review of the commission's decision is available only to the respondent.

The Wheeler-Lea Amendment provides that if a respondent plans to appeal an order of the commission, he or she must do so within sixty days, or the order becomes final and binding. If the respondent is judged guilty, either by the administrative law judge or the full commission, an order is entered directing him or her to cease and desist from the unlawful conduct. Like an injunction, it need not be wholly negative in its terms: it may spell out particular requirements that the respondent must follow. Once the cease-and-desist order has become final, either because the court of appeals has affirmed the commission or because the respondent has not sought a judicial review, any subsequent violation of the order subjects the respondent to contempt proceedings and a civil penalty of up to $5,000 for each day of continuing violation or for each separate offense. This fine—technically a civil rather than a criminal penalty—is enforced through federal court actions brought by the Department of Justice.

Deceptive advertising takes many forms. One example is a Rise Shaving Cream commercial of about a decade ago, in which the manufacturer, Colgate-Palmolive, claimed that the cream had such a softening effect that even the toughest beards could be shaved. To prove this point, Rise was applied to sandpaper and then a razor was used to "shave" the sandpaper. The lesson to be learned was that if Rise could soften sandpaper, it could soften any beard. What the public did not know, however, was that the sandpaper had been soaked for a number of hours in water before the "test" was made. Naturally, the sand did not adhere to the paper after the soaking. But perhaps the classic example of deceptive advertising is that of Geritol, the ubiquitous patent drug and elixir that was supposed to cure "iron-poor blood," among a myriad of other things.

The Geritol Case

Actually the Geritol case was a series of running battles, dating back to 1962, between the FTC and the J. B. Williams Company, the makers of Geritol, Femiron, and other so-called elixirs, and the Parkson Advertising Agency, a wholly owned subsidiary of the company, over claims made about the therapeutic effects of the elixirs, in particular Geritol.[9] The FTC had ruled that television commercials and newspaper advertising falsely represented that all cases of tiredness, loss of strength, run-down feeling, nervousness, and irritability indicated a deficiency of iron and that the best remedy for these symptoms was Geritol. The case culminated in 1973 when a U.S. district court ruled that the company had consistently and flagrantly violated the FTC's orders to cease and desist deceptive advertising of Geritol. The court fined the Williams Company $456,000 and the Parkson Agency $356,000.[10] The total fine of $812,000 was the largest ever levied for violating a cease-and-desist order of the FTC. The Justice Department had initiated the suit in 1970 at the request of the FTC. The suit had asked for $1 million in civil penalties—a minimum of $5,000 for each of one hundred occasions on which commercials were run on network TV in direct violation of a series of cease-and-desist orders by the FTC.

The FTC voiced a number of complaints about the Geritol commercials. One pertained to a television ad in which a husband is depicted as "just too tired to budge."[11] He takes Geritol and then is shown dancing with his wife. While the man is dancing, the announcer states, "In only one day Geritol iron is in your bloodstream carrying strength and energy to every part of your body." Another television commercial depicted a winter scene, complete with the sound of howling wind.[12] The announcer asks, "As a result of winter weather, have you been in bed with a cold, flu, or fever? After such an illness, if you suffer from iron-poor blood, you may find that recovery is slow. To get back your normal strength fast, when this is your problem, you should build up iron-poor blood. Therefore, take Geritol three times a day." The obvious implication is that winter illnesses may cause iron-poor blood and that Geritol would speed recovery by curing this deficiency.

---

9. The material on the Geritol case can be found in FTC Complaints, Orders, Stipulations, *Drug Preparation* (17339) Final Order to Cease and Desist, Dkt. 8547, 1965, pp. 22490–22498.
10. *Washington Post*, October 17, 1973, p. 3.
11. FTC Complaints, p. 22492.
12. FTC Complaints, pp. 22292–22293.

These were only two of many Geritol commercials that came under attack by the FTC. The first ad involving the rejuvenation of the husband was rejected by the hearing examiner on the grounds that the company falsely represented that Geritol would increase the strength and energy of every part of the body within twenty-four hours—a statement also made in the ad and reflected in the transformation of the tired husband into Fred Astaire. Clinical evidence established the fact that in persons suffering from iron deficiency, the time lapse between taking Geritol and any appreciable increase in strength and energy was more like two weeks than twenty-four hours. In the second ad, the examiner agreed with the FTC's contention that the Williams Company falsely claimed that Geritol would speed recovery from winter illnesses. As the courts have held, the important criterion in determing whether an advertisement is false and misleading is the net impression it is likely to make on the general public.[13] Clinical evidence has established that winter illnesses such as a cold, flu, or fever will not cause iron-poor blood, contrary to the ad's implication. The Williams Company was also charged with falsely representing that the vitamins contained in Geritol contributed to the effectiveness of the product in the treatment or relief of an existing deficiency of iron or iron-deficiency anemia.

Other Disclosures

Advertising is by no means the only problem in the area of disclosure. In fact, the FTC is responsible for administering several laws regulating various types of disclosure. The Wool Products Labeling Act of 1939 is an example. The purpose of the act is to protect merchants and consumers against deception and unfair competition with regard to articles made from wool. Many abuses prompted the passage of this act. Reused wool was sold as new wool, and products sold as "all wool" often contained less than 5 percent wool. The act of 1939 provided that all-wool garments must disclose on a label attached to the merchandise the percentage of each fiber contained in the product. The Fur Products Labeling Act of 1951 was passed to protect consumers from the mislabeling of furs, such as rabbit fur being called mink. Manufacturers are required to attach labels to a garment showing the true name of the animal that produced the fur and indicating whether the fur is bleached or dyed. The Textile Fiber Products Identification Act of 1958 covers the labeling of textiles and fibers, and its purpose is to protect consumers by requiring a disclosure on the label and in advertising of the exact fiber content of all textile fibers other than wool marketed in interstate commerce. All products must have a label that shows the

13. Posner, *Regulation of Advertising by the FTC*, p. 25.

exact fiber content, the identity of the product, and the name of the manufacturer.

Then there is the Cigarette Labeling and Advertising Act of 1966, which requires that cigarettes sold in interstate commerce be packaged and labeled with the warning that cigarette smoking may be hazardous to health. The Consumer Credit Protection Act of 1968 or, as it is more commonly called, the "Truth-in-Lending Act," requires that creditors disclose to borrowers basic information about the cost and terms of credit. The purpose of these disclosures is to encourage competition in financing by making debtors aware of specific charges and other relevant credit information, thus encouraging them to shop for the most favorable terms of credit.[14] Before the act was passed, borrowers had no way of knowing the true percentage rate that they were being charged for credit. Often they believed the rate of interest was far less than what they actually paid, for creditors had ways to obfuscate the issue by using a variety of methods in quoting rates. The effect of using a variety of methods in quoting rates was to make it impossible to compare the rates of competing creditors. The act restricts the garnishment of wages by creditors and provides penalties for exorbitant credit charges.

One form of disclosure that has been the center of consumer discontent is the warranty. There often are problems confronting a consumer attempting to have a product repaired under warranty. Often a warranty fails to cover a particular part, or it fails to cover the cost of labor. State laws on warranties have conformed to the Uniform Commercial Code (UCC), which follows the theory of the common law that a product when sold carries with it the promise that it is fit for ordinary use. the UCC provides that a sale by a merchant is accompanied by an implied warranty of title and an implied warranty of merchantability together with any express warranties, oral or written, that the seller makes as part of the sale. The UCC has followed the theory of the common law that a buyer and seller may bargain freely over the terms of the warranty and sale. Consequently, the UCC allows a seller to disclaim, limit, or modify the warranties implied by law, provided he or she does so in a clear and conspicuous manner. A purchaser may recover damages for breach of warranty under the UCC, including incidental and consequential damages.

A warranty is a promise, either express or implied. An express warranty is usually, although not always, in the form of words, written or oral, that affirm a fact or make a promise relating to the goods. The buyer must be able to rely on the affirmation of fact or promise as the basis for the purchase. Sometimes it is difficult to distinguish between

14. U.S., Congress, House, Committee on Banking and Currency, *Report on Consumer Credit Protection Act*, 90th Cong., 1st sess., 1967.

an express warranty and sales puffery. An implied warranty is a promise that is based on the law itself, and hence its existence does not depend on the words or actions of the seller.

Consumer Product Warranty Act of 1975

The Consumer Product Warranty Act is important for two reasons. First, it provides minimum disclosure standards for written consumer product warranties and defines federal content standards for those warranties. Second, it strengthens the capabilities of the Federal Trade Commission to function as the protector of consumer rights when deceptive warranties and other unfair acts and practices are found to exist. The act came about because consumers had become increasingly dissatisfied with product warranties and had resorted to the courts for redress. Generally this dissatisfaction centered on such problems as the purchase of a product that turned out to be a "lemon," delay in making repairs, excessive labor charges, failure of companies to honor guarantees, unscrupulous service operators, and the consumer's lack of power to compel performance.

The act is one of the most sweeping consumer protection bills passed by Congress in recent times, and it has had a significant impact on business, particularly in the area of marketing. Its major provisions can be divided into two categories—those that pertain specifically to product warranty and those that involve important amendments to the authority and power of the Federal Trade Commission.

1. Product Warranty Provisions. A written warranty is defined by the act as any affirmation of fact, promise, or undertaking in writing that becomes part of the basis of the bargain between a supplier and a purchaser. Hence, a written warranty could be created by point of sale advertising or by other media advertising if the affirmation is in writing. The act defines a deceptive warranty as one that contains an affirmation of fact, false or fraudulent representations, or promises or descriptions that would mislead a reasonably prudent person exercising due care; one that fails to contain enough information to prevent its terms from being misleading; or one that uses the terms *guarantee* or *warranty* when other terms limit the breadth and scope of the protection apparently granted so as to deceive a reasonable person.

In order to increase the product information available to purchasers, prevent deception, and promote competition in the marketplace, any warrantor offering a written warranty for a consumer product must disclose the terms and conditions of the warranty in simple and easily understood language. The FTC is directed to require that the terms and conditions of consumer product warranties be made available to consumers before the product is sold. The commission also is authorized to determine the manner and form in which such warranty information is presented so that it will not mislead the average customer when the warranty is found in advertising, labeling, point of sales representations, or in other written information.

As a result of the act, there are a number of items that warrantors must disclose, including the product or parts covered; the identity of the party or parties to whom the warranty is extended; a statement of the exceptions and exclusions from the terms of the warranty; a statement as to what the warrantor will do, at whose expense, the work that will be done, and the period of time the warranty will last, assuming that the product fails to conform to the written warranty; a brief summary of the legal remedies available to the consumer; the time during which the warrantor will fulfill the obligations under the warranty; the characteristics or the properties of the products or parts not covered by the warranty; and the step-by-step procedure the consumer must follow in order to obtain performance of any obligation under the warranty.

2. Amendments to the Authority of the Federal Trade Commission. The consumer protection powers of the Federal Trade Commission were extended by the Consumer Product Warranty Act. Title II of the act amends the original Federal Trade Commission Act to read "in or affecting commerce" in place of simply "in commerce." Although the interstate commerce clause has been interpreted to forbid federal regulatory control over purely local matters, this new jurisdictional clarification allows closer supervision of borderline gray areas formerly beyond the commission's competence. As a result, the commission may move against local consumer abuses when state or local consumer protection programs are ineffective or when dishonest operators quickly move their base of operations from one location to another before authorities can take action. Local abuses are especially common in large population centers where the poor and uneducated are concentrated, making them targets for fraudulent schemes.

The FTC's powers to prescribe rules regulating unfair or deceptive practices were extended to apply to national banks, member banks of the Federal Reserve System, and banks insured by the Federal Deposit Insurance Corporation. With respect to defective warranties, the commission has the power to seek injunctions against offenders and to represent itself in litigation. Before the passage of the act, the commission was compelled to rely on cease-and-desist orders to seek compliance with its rulings. In the past, firms were able to circumvent these orders with some impunity through the use of delaying tactics and procedural technicalities. Fraudulent practices often were continued for years after orders were issued. As a result, consumers suffered losses over protracted periods of time. In addition to its injunctive authority, the FTC can initiate civil suits against offenders that knowingly engage in an act or practice determined to be unfair or deceptive. Also subject to civil actions are offenders that knew or reasonably should have known that their acts or practices were forbidden. Each violation can draw a penalty up to $10,000.

Product Safety

Until recently, national product safety legislation consisted of a series of isolated statutes designed to remedy specific hazards existing in a narrow range of product categories. Moreover, enforcement authority was divided among a number of federal agencies. For example, the Flammable Fabrics Act of 1953 was passed after serious injuries and deaths had resulted from the ignition of clothes made from synthetic fibers. The act prohibits the sale of highly flammable apparel and empowers the FTC to issue appropriate rules and regulations, to conduct tests, and to make investigations and reports. Enforcement measures include cease-and-desist orders, seizure of offending goods, and criminal penalties of a year's imprisonment or fines of up to $5,000 for willful violations. Tests of flammability are established by the Bureau of Standards. The act was amended in 1967 to cover interior furnishings, fabrics, and materials as well.

There is also the Federal Hazardous Substances Labeling Act of 1960, which mandates warnings on the labels of potentially hazardous substances such as cleaning agents and paint removers and which is administered by the Food and Drug Administration. The Child Protection Act of 1966, also administered by the FDA, prevents the marketing of potentially harmful toys and other articles intended for children. The FDA is supposed to remove the potentially dangerous products. The National Traffic and Motor Vehicle Safety Act of 1966 is related specifically to automobiles. Under its provisions, safety standards were set for new automobiles, which include such features as an impact-absorbing steering wheel and column, safety door latches and hinges, safety glass, dual braking system, and impact-resistant gasoline tanks and connections. Tires must be labeled with the name of the manufacturer or retreader and with certain safety information, including the maximum permissible load for the tire. The Public Health Smoking Act of 1970 extends warnings about the hazards of cigarette smoking, and the Poison Prevention Packaging Act of the same year authorizes the establishment of standards for child-resistant packaging of hazardous substances. In 1971 the Lead-Based Paint Elimination Act was passed to assist in developing and administering programs to eliminate lead-based paints.

The Consumer Product Safety Act of 1972

The Consumer Product Safety Act is one of the most important laws
with a direct impact on business to be passed in a long time. Fragmentation of legislation and generally ineffective controls over product
hazards prompted the federal government to introduce new product
safety legislation to protect the consumer. The act was a result of congressional findings that unsafe consumer products are widely distributed,
and hence, consumers are frequently unable to anticipate and guard
against the risks entailed in their use. Findings presented before the
Senate Committee on Commerce indicated that more than 20 million
Americans are injured by consumer products annually.[15] Of this total,
110,000 persons are permanently disabled, and 30,000 lose their lives.
The annual cost to consumers is around $5.5 billion. It has been esti-
mated that 20 percent of these injuries could have been prevented if the
manufacturers had produced safe, well-designed products.

The origins of the Consumer Product Safety Act are in the common
law in that the manufacturer or seller is liable for injuries to a buyer or
other individuals caused by a defective or hazardous product. The common law imposed liability on a broad group of persons involved in the
marketing process, including suppliers, wholesalers, and retailers. Many
product liability cases have been based on the landmark case of *Mac-
Pherson* v. *Buick Motor Company*, which held that the manufacturer of
an automobile with a defective wheel is liable for negligence, even
though the customer had no direct contact with the manufacturer.[16]
Liability is assumed for injuries to the consumer when the results of
such injury are reasonably foreseeable, regardless of whether the product itself is dangerous or harmful. A consumer need not have to prove
that a manufacturer was guilty of negligence.

Provisions of the Act

The Consumer Product Safety Act is broad in scope and affects those
consumer products not already regulated by the federal government.
When compared with earlier consumer-oriented legislation, the act not
only possesses more effective legal and administrative sanctions but also
allows an application of safety standards. Its basic provisions are:

1. It created a five-member Consumer Product Safety Commission,
which functions as an independent regulatory agency. A major function

15. U.S., Congress, Senate, Committee on Commerce, *Hearings on National Com-
     mission on Product Safety*, 91st Cong., 2d sess., 1972, p. 37.
16. *MacPherson* v. *Buick Motor Company*, 217 N.Y. 382, 111 N.E. 1050 (1916).

of the commission is the gathering and dissemination of information related to product injuries. In addition, the commission is empowered to create an advisory council of fifteen members to provide expert information on product safety.

2. Section 14 of the act requires manufacturers to conduct a testing program to assure that their products conform to established safety standards. After the products are tested, a manufacturer must provide distributors or retailers with a certificate stating that all applicable consumer product safety standards have been met. Section 14 also holds the manufacturer accountable for knowing all safety criteria applicable to the product and requires that safety standards must be described in detail. The manufacturer also is obligated to maintain technical data relating to the performance and safety of a product. This information may have to be given to the consumer when purchasing the product.

3. The Consumer Product Safety Commission also can require the use of specific labels that set forth the results of product testing. This requirement will have its most significant impact on the production process, in which the design of numerous products must conform to new federal standards. Since safety standards will be formulated at various governmental and independent testing stations, a manufacturer may find that a finished product no longer meets federal standards, and product lines may have to be altered drastically.

4. Section 15 requires a manufacturer to take corrective steps if he or she becomes aware that a product either fails to comply with an applicable consumer product safety rule or contains a defect that could create a substantial product hazard. The manufacturer has to inform the Consumer Product Safety Commission of the defect. If, after investigation, the commission determines that a product hazard exists, the manufacturer, or distributor or retailer for that matter, may be required to publicize the information to consumers. The commission can compel a manufacturer to refund the purchase price of the product, less a reasonable allowance for use, or to replace the product with a like or equivalent product that complies with the consumer product safety rule.

5. Section 16 gives the commission the power to inspect the facilities in which consumer goods are manufactured, stored, or transported. The commission also can require all manufacturers, private labelers, and distributors to establish and maintain books and records and to make available additional information as it deems necessary.

The Consumer Movement

Consumerism as a movement can be divided into three distinct cycles. The first cycle began around the turn of the century and was concerned with pure food and drug laws. The second cycle began in the 1930s and included the passage of several disclosure laws designed to protect consumers against fraudulent advertising, mislabeling, and so forth. The third cycle began in the late 1960s when product safety laws were passed to protect consumers. But the term *consumer movement* is used rather loosely here, for unlike other movements of the past such as the Grange movement, which pertained only to farming, the consumer movement was actually a conglomerate of disparate interest groups, each with its own set of concerns but able to coalesce and form temporary alliances on particular issues. Included were labor unions, consumer cooperatives, senior citizens' groups, credit unions, consumer education organizations (such as Consumers Union), and other organizations with related interests. This coalition of interest groups is expressed from time to time in efforts to bring pressure on business and government to pass consumer laws. But coalitions often lack cohesiveness, and consumers, unlike environmentalists, have no well-organized, well-financed lobby to push for their interests.

DECLINE OF CONSUMERISM

The last cycle of consumerism reached its apogee around 1975 with the passage of the Consumer Product Warranty Act. More consumer protection laws were passed between 1965 and 1975 than between 1890 and 1965. Consumer groups also lobbied for a federal consumer protection agency that would have had the authority to represent and advocate consumer interests before federal agencies and courts, and a bill to create such an agency was introduced in Congress. In 1975, the legislation to create an independent consumer agency within the executive branch of government, designed to represent consumers' interests, was passed by both the House and the Senate but was vetoed by President Gerald Ford. When Jimmy Carter was elected president in 1976, he promised to create a consumer protection agency along the lines proposed by Congress. But the legislation introduced to create the agency failed to clear Congress, showing that consumerism as a viable political factor had already begun to lose its force.

There were several reasons for the decline of consumer regulation. First, a mood favoring deregulation had begun to develop in Congress, a feeling that there was already too much regulation and less, not more, was needed. In 1978 measures designed to deregulate the airline and natural gas industries cleared Congress and were approved by President Carter. Second, consumerism lacked an effective spokesperson. Ralph Nader, the self-appointed advocate of consumerism, began to lose the influence he once had had, when he took on other social issues. He also lost his influence with Congress when he published his own ratings (mostly bad) of its members. Third, many felt, including the respected senator from North Carolina, Sam Ervin, that consumers could be over-protected. They believed that consumers had to assume some responsibility for their actions and that they were intelligent enough to make rational choices. Fourth, and most important, was the ability of business to organize and lobby effectively against any proposed legislation it did not like. There is no question but that effective business lobbying was the catalyst that killed the consumer protection agency, even though impartial observers considered it to be unnecessary.

Business has traditionally disdained government, being preoccupied with its own affairs. As special interest groups began to organize and lobby effectively for legislation they wanted, business decided it could no longer remain aloof.

Most legislative and executive policy decisions have been implemented by persons acting under the influence of groups. As our country has become more institutionally complex, the ability of the federal government to reflect the interests of all citizens and groups of citizens has become more diffused. Our system has many access points—Congress, the courts, regulatory agencies, and the executive office of the president—to which groups can present their views. And so business began to organize and lobby with a vengeance. It created political action committees (PACs) to raise campaign funds for politicians, and in the 1980 congressional campaign, the funds provided by the PACs were the single largest source of political contributions. So it is that special interest groups, including business, help write the legislation and shape the government rulings that affect everything from the price of gasoline to the care of the sick. As long as we have a democratic system of government, there will be people and groups seeking favors.

The Reagan Administration and the Consumer Product Safety Commission

The Consumer Product Safety Commission faces a somewhat uncertain future under the Reagan administration, particularly with its emphasis on deregulation. There are those in the administration who propose the commission's outright abolition, but in lieu of that, measures have been introduced in Congress to eliminate its independent status and place it, as an executive agency, under the jurisdiction of the Department of Commerce.[17] It would be required to use cost-benefit analysis in setting industry regulations and also to encourage industry-imposed voluntary standards. But it is likely that the Consumer Product Safety Commission will retain its independent status at least through the end of fiscal year 1982. Its appropriations have been cut by 30 percent for fiscal

17. S.1155 introduced May 6, 1981.

year 1982, though in all likelihood, the CPSC will survive but will become an executive branch agency, like the Food and Drug Administration which is under the jurisdiction of the Department of Health and Human Services.

The achievements of the Consumer Product Safety Commission appear to be mixed. Its supporters contend that its regulations have made the marketplace safer for consumers. The CPSC claims that it has prevented 1 million injuries and 150 deaths annually by the recall of hazardous products such as hair dryers, paint strippers, and toys with parts that can be swallowed by small children.[18] Business has argued that the CPCS lacks the knowledge and experience to weigh hazardous regulation, and in 1976 the U.S. General Accounting Office cited the CPSC for inefficient management and poor enforcement. In 1978 a White House panel recommended authorizing the CPCS for a short period and then either abolishing it or reorganizing it, but these recommendations were rejected by President Carter. The CPSC did not improve its reputation when a former chairman stated, "If a company violates our statutes, we will not concern ourselves with its middle-level executives; we will put the chief executive in jail. Once we do put a top executive behind bars, I am sure that we will get a much higher degree of cooperation."[19] Needless to say, this statement did little to foster better business-government relations.

A Return to Caveat Emptor?

Opponents of consumer protection regulation have raised some valid arguments. They have claimed that regulation laws increase the cost of goods, limit the freedom of individuals to make significant choices by themselves, and lead to bigger, more expensive, and restrictive government. Bureaucratic inefficiency also impedes the effective operation of a market economy. But although less regulation may appear desirable, there is the danger that the pendulum will swing too far. Reliance on voluntary standards set by business firms may be a good idea, but will it work? The new federalism proposed by the Reagan administration would place more reliance on state agencies to protect consumer interests, but the effectiveness of state agencies can vary considerably. The principle of caveat emptor (let the buyer beware) was relevant to a time period, perhaps the 1880s, when the consumer could be expected to know more about a product. A carriage was constructed from a few

18. U.S., Congress, House, *Hearings before the Appropriations Committee*, 97th Cong., 1st sess., April 3, 1981.
19. Gerald R. Rosen, "We're Going for Companies' Throats," *Dun's Review* (January 1973), 36.

parts that the buyer probably also could have assembled. The principles of power and locomotion were simple; and if the buyer needed credit, the sources that he or she could turn to, although limited, were well known. The consumer faces a much more sophisticated world today.

SUMMARY

One of the fundamental tenets supporting a market economy is consumer sovereignty, which is based on the idea that ultimate decisions as to what will be produced rest with the consumer. This presupposes that consumers have the information necessary to make rational choices in the marketplace. If this is true, then consumer expenditures guide resource allocation into chosen products. But in a complex industrial society it is difficult for consumers to have the expertise necessary to distinguish among the many products. In addition, consumers are subject to the external pressures of advertising. It can be argued that consumers are led by advertising to make product choices on the basis of subjective factors—conspicuous consumption, envy, and emulation of one's peer group, for example. Therefore, laws have been passed to protect consumers against those practices considered deleterious to their interests.

Consumer protection reached a new peak in the late 1960s and early 1970s when the federal government began to increase its support of consumer welfare. This reflected the mood of the times, with consumer interests coalescing into group pressure for the passage of new laws. Business firms often have lacked innovation or have been slow to respond to consumers' needs. But in the minds of many, regulation in the consumer area was carried too far and proved to be costly and inefficient. The basic issue before the public today is whether consumers can be better protected by relying on voluntary standards set by business; transferring responsibility to state consumer protection agencies; relying on existing federal agencies such as the Food and Drug Administration; or allowing consumers to act for themselves.

QUESTIONS FOR DISCUSSION

1. What are some of the reasons for the increase in consumer legislation over the last fifteen years?
2. What is meant by *consumer sovereignty*? Are consumers really sovereign?
3. Discuss the provisions of the Pure Food and Drug Act of 1906.
4. What is considered false or deceptive advertising?

5. What control does the Federal Trade Commission have over false or deceptive advertising?
6. In your opinion, is more consumer protection legislation needed today?
7. What philosophy did Congress adopt for controlling rates of credit in the Truth-in-Lending Act?
8. Discuss the provisions of the Consumer Product Safety Act of 1972.
9. There are costs as well as benefits in consumer protection legislation, but the costs are often overlooked. Discuss.
10. Discuss the impact of the consumer movement on business.

RECOMMENDED READINGS

Bowers, Patricia F. *Private Choice and Public Welfare*. Hinsdale, Ill.: Dryden Press, 1974.

Brunk, Max E. "Consumerism & Marketing." In *Issues in Business & Society*. Ed. George Steiner. New York: Random House, 1972.

Campbell, Rita Ricardo. *Food Safety Regulation: A Study of the Use and Limitations of Cost-Benefit Analysis*. Washington, D.C.: American Enterprise Institute for Public Policy Research, 1974.

Hermann, Robert O. "Consumerism: Its Goals, Organization, and Future." *Journal of Marketing*, 34 (October 1970), 55–60.

Jentz, Gaylord A. "Federal Regulation of Advertising." *American Business Law Journal*, 6 (January 1968), 409–427.

Jordan, William A. "Producer Protection, Price Market Structure and the Effects of Government Regulation." *Journal of Law & Economics*, 22 (April 1972), 151–176.

Lodge, George C. *The New American Ideology*. New York: Knopf, 1975, chap. 8.

Peltzman, Sam. *Regulation of Automobile Safety*. Washington, D.C.: American Enterprise Institute for Public Policy Research, 1975.

Posner, Richard A. *Regulation of Advertising by the FTC*. Washington, D.C.: American Enterprise Institute for Public Policy Research, 1974.

Rados, David L. "Product Liability: Tougher Ground Rules." *Harvard Business Review*, 47 (July–August, 1969), 144–152.

Weidenbaum, Murray L. *Government-Mandated Price Increases*. Washington, D.C.: American Enterprise Institute for Public Policy Research, 1975.

Chapter 10

Environmental Policies and Their Impact on Business

The quality of the environment emerged as one of the most important economic and social issues of the 1970s. In the United States, concern about pollution, expressed for years by scientists and conservationists, eventually spread to the general public. In addition to the personal experiences of many with foul air, bad water, excessive noise, overcrowding of the cities, and disappearing landscapes, concern about the environment also grew from Malthusian warnings about the population explosion. There is some question as to whether or not the existing resources of the planet Earth are capable of sustaining the everburgeoning population, and so zero population growth became one of the shibboleths of the 1970s.

To a certain extent there is a conflict between the rate of economic growth and the quality of the environment. Economic growth means increased output, higher living standards, and greater employment of resources, including labor. Economic growth, since it results in increased output, produces a number of harmful by-products that damage the environment—smoke and fumes from more cars, litter from more cans and containers, and the pollution of lakes and streams from the increased effluvia of factories. Questions are being raised about the environmental damage or external diseconomies that more and more appear to be part of the price paid for a rising real gross national product. Critics contend that in recent years growth has so damaged the environment as to cast doubt on the presumed advantages of economic growth. They also challenge the conventional notion that growth expands the range of choices available to consumers and so improves their economic welfare. As more goods and new types of goods appear on the market, older goods no longer are available, and therefore, consumers may not really have more choices of goods.

Pollution of the environment, however, is common to all advanced industrial countries, regardless of their ideologies. In the Soviet Union, untreated or inadequately treated industrial effluents have polluted rivers and lakes, and the practices that allow this have even elicited some criticism from the Soviet press.[1] The Soviet Union's neglect of

1. See Keith Bush, "Environmental Problems in the USSR," *Problems of Communism* (Washington, D.C.: U.S. Information Agency, July–August 1972), pp. 21–32.

the consumer in another area—that of automobile production—can be considered an environmental "plus" factor, since the lack of cars inadvertently preserves the quality of air in the cities. Of all the major industrial countries, Japan, given its small land area and crowded cities, has the worst pollution problem. The Japanese rate of economic growth has been the fastest of all industrial countries. Pollution has been an end result, and the Japanese now have chosen a slower rate of growth and an industrial location policy aimed at the dispersion of industry in the hope of halting the spread of pollution.

Pollution is by no means a recent phenomenon. In fact, in one form or another, pollution probably has existed throughout recorded times. In the United States, pollution as we know it today is a by-product of the North's industrialization, which was stimulated by the Civil War. Industrial cities, such as Chicago and Pittsburgh, were cited by foreign visitors to the United States early in this century as being particularly foul.[2] The largest assemblage of stockyards in the world added a mephitic flavor to Chicago's air; natural drainage was nonexistent, flooding was habitual, and the surface of the Chicago River was so thick with grease that it looked like a liquid rainbow.[3] If anything, Pittsburgh was worse. The steel mills along the Monongahela River constantly poured a residue of waste into the river, which washed down into the Ohio and other rivers. Soot from the mills presented a cleaning problem. Around the turn of the century, Pittsburgh's residents were forced to spend each year $1.5 million on extra laundry work and $750,000 for extra cleaning.[4] But many persons saw pollution as a good omen, a portent of better things to come and a sign of industrial prosperity.

PROBLEMS AND CAUSES OF POLLUTION

Pollution is a dramatic and controversial subject, made so by the fear that humankind may permanently damage the balance of nature. Modern civilization's capacity for manipulating and modifying nature and the rapidity with which new means and methods of production are being discovered and implemented make it necessary to look for rational solutions for environmental problems. But before solutions can be identified, the problems and causes of pollution must be explored. The subject of pollution is complex and cuts across many disciplines—biology, geology, chemistry, sociology, and economics. Attempts to alleviate one environmental problem sometimes have created others that

2. Rudyard Kipling, *Actions and Reactions* (New York: Doubleday & Page, 1909).
3. Louis Mumford, *The City in History* (New York: Harcourt, Brace & World, 1961), p. 469.
4. Ibid., p. 474.

are even more troublesome. Too, since the quality of the environment is not subject to market forces, allocational efficiency is difficult to attain.

Problems of Pollution

Like most economic problems, the problem of the environment is primarily one of choice. Air and water, as commodities, generally have been free because supply has far exceeded demand. And since they have been free, there has been no need to establish property rights or other procedures for deciding on their use. Resource allocation presented no problem of who would get what, for there was no scarcity of these particular resources. As demand has grown, however, the supply of clean air and water has become inadequate, and it is necessary to find ways of allocating these scarce resources among different uses, that is, ways to use them more efficiently. Because of their mobility, it is much more difficult to attach property rights to air and water than to land. Indeed, even in the case of land, the mere establishment of property rights is not necessarily enough to guarantee the best use.

Clean air and water can be considered a public good, and patterns of using them have evolved in the absence of clearly defined and enforced property rights. It is difficult for a private individual to lay claim to a particular level of quality in a given lake or air stream. In such cases an individual usually cannot identify his or her water or air, nor can that person purchase identifiable packages of these goods. Though one person's activities affect another's enjoyment of these resources, there is no recourse through property rights for protecting these assets. Thus, in the absence of property rights, other forms of control over the use of air and water have to be imposed. The form of these controls determines their effectiveness and also influences the operations of business firms. The main purpose of these controls is to keep air and water reasonably clean so that nobody will be affected adversely, either by being exposed to harmful substances or by having to incur unreasonable costs to render air and water sufficiently clean for consumption.

One problem of pollution is that it entails social costs that are not measured in terms of prices. In a market economy, resources are allocated on the basis of the price mechanism. These resources, land, labor, and capital are reflected in the money costs to producers of goods and in turn are incorporated in the sales price of the goods. There can be certain adverse side effects generated in the process of production that are not reflected in the money cost of production but, nevertheless, become real costs to society. Pollution is a social cost of production that the market system does not indicate and may include noneconomic as well as economic costs. The problem, therefore, is to develop mechanisms for protecting resources when the internal or private costs to firms differ substantially from their costs to society at large. In the absence of a price mechanism, this can be settled only through the political process.

There are several public policy approaches that can be used to control pollution—direct regulation; charges for emissions, including taxes; and subsidies. Combinations of these approaches also can be used. Each approach has advantages and disadvantages, and it is impossible to say which is best, as there are different kinds and sources of pollution, many of which are not well understood. Hence, a method of control that might effectively curb air or water pollution might not be suitable for reducing noise levels or the misuse of land.

Regulation

Legislation can be used to establish appropriate standards for air, water, noise, and land use: the Clean Air Act of 1970 sets standards for air quality, and there is similar legislation for water. In addition, regulation can require licenses, permits, zoning regulation, and registration. The formulation of air and water standards implies a value judgment about the reasonable degree of control that can be achieved through regulation. A rationale for regulation is that similar standards are established for all business firms. Requiring every steel mill to meet similar effluent standards is deemed to be fair not only among individual firms but also among communities. Proponents of uniform or similar standards contend that unless these standards are applied everywhere, the rules will be neither fair nor effective in reducing pollution. Firms that are polluting in one area would move to locations where standards are lower, and firms in areas with high standards would be treated unfairly. Communities with high standards also would be at a disadvantage in attracting and holding industry, and pollution would continue to come from communities with low standards.

An objection to regulation is that it leads to rigidities and, in many cases, unwieldly and inefficient forms of control. For example, if uniform emission standards are used, certain problems can result. One is that there are differences among firms in the same industry and differences in environmental conditions among geographic areas. Different firms have different requirements in the use of the environment. The discharge of waste into a river is an example. Some firms want to discharge more waste because their cost of waste treatment is higher; other firms may have lower costs. A firm might be permitted to discharge more waste if the damage done by such waste is lower because few or no people live downstream from the point of discharge. Environmental conditions also may vary considerably among geographic areas, and these differences will be reflected in the prices of the goods produced. An area with natural resources that absorb waste discharges may be prevented from using this absorptive capacity because of uniform national standards for environmental quality. Thus, a law that sets a standard on pollution levels may cause a misallocation of resources.

Emission Charges

Another method of controlling pollution is to levy emission charges in the form of taxes or fees against polluters. For example, in copper smelting, sulphur oxides are among the principal pollutants produced. Rather than requiring copper companies to reduce the sulphur oxides by a given percentage, they could be taxed according to the amount of sulphur oxide they actually do release into the atmosphere. Each polluting firm could then decide for itself how much control it wants to provide. A firm that, for one reason or another, has higher costs for control presumably would release more pollutants than a firm with relatively low control costs. Emission charges would become part of a firm's costs of operation and would cause the firm to calculate both the costs of waste and the costs and benefits of pollution abatement. Since emission charges would take advantage of differences in control costs among polluters, it would be possible to reach an average air standard at a lower cost to society than would be possible by applying a uniform emission standard through law. Another advantage of emission charges is that the government could charge lower emission fees in sparsely populated areas and higher fees in more densely populated areas, thus spreading pollution more evenly throughout the country and encouraging industrial dispersion. This would have the net effect of decreasing total pollution. As well, the fees would provide revenue that could be used for various social purposes, including the construction of waste treatment facilities or research on pollution abatement.

The implementation of a tax or any form of use charge requires an evaluation of the damage done by the emission of an incremental quality of pollution at any given time or place. After this evaluation, an emission charge is assessed to the responsible parties based on the amount of damage. Presumably, those firms with the capabilities to reduce emissions at a cost that is less than the pollution charge will do so, and the proper amount of abatement will be obtained by the means that are the least costly. If the tax or charge is too low, it will not be an adequate inducement to reduce the wastes disposed, and if the price is too high, it will impose more control than is necessary and will be uneconomic in its effect. The experience gained through using some sort of charge might resolve this problem; however, charges have yet to be tried extensively, even though numerous task forces and studies have specifically recommended their experimental use.[5]

Subsidies

A third public approach to pollution control would be to award subsidies to business firms to defray the cost of compliance with pollution control standards. A rationale for such subsidies is that business firms are being forced to treat their effluents at least in part so that others may benefit, and therefore, they should be compensated for the benefit. Subsidies could take several forms. First, a tax credit might be given to compensate for the cost of acquiring pollution abatement equipment. This credit would be deducted from the tax a firm would pay on net income after total business deductions. Thus, a $100 tax credit for pollution control equipment would reduce by $100 the amount of tax due. Second, outright cash payments could be made to reduce the level of pollution. Third, accelerated depreciation allowances could be used to reduce the cost of pollution control equipment. Specifically, accelerated depreciation would permit business firms to write off the cost of equipment in a shorter time period than would standard depreciation provisions, increasing the cash flow of these firms in the process. Fourth, state and local governments could allow property tax exemptions on pollution control equipment.

Subsidies do have disadvantages.[6] If firms are given aid for their cost of waste treatment or for the purchase of pollution abatement equipment, there is less pressure on them to find alternative ways of dealing with the pollution problem. Subsidies in the form of tax relief that are based on the purchase of abatement equipment favor waste treatment that is capital intensive. A firm must respond to varying consumer tastes, which means manufacturing different products that in turn give rise to different forms of waste. Subsidies for capital equipment reduce its cost to the firm and encourage the firm to substitute fixed for variable costs, and economic inefficiency in waste treatment may result. It also can be argued that subsidies, particularly if they are financed out of general tax revenues, violate the benefit principle of equity. According to this principle, the cost of pollution control should be part of the cost of production, and consumers who buy products should pay the antipollution costs just as they pay for labor, capital, and other inputs.

5. Tax Foundation, *Pollution Control: Perspectives on the Government Role* (New York: Tax Foundation, 1971), pp. 11-25.
6. Hugh H. Macauley, "An Evaluation of Subsidies for Water Pollution Abatement," in *The Economics of Federal Subsidy Programs*, pt. 8, U.S., Congress, Joint Economic Committee, 93rd Cong., 2d sess., 1972, pp. 1018-1039.

The traditional and most common way of dealing with pollution has been direct legal regulation. When confronted with a problem such as polluted air, the instinctive reaction of government, be it federal, state, or local, is to pass a law ordering the problem to stop. But there are obstacles to the effective regulation of pollution, one being the interstate regulation of both air and water pollution, because each can overlap state jurisdictions. So if one state sets standards of control, another state may nullify its efforts by not taking similar action, which requires the federal government to take responsibility for setting interstate pollution standards. But the federal government has hesitated to act on interstate pollution for fear of usurping state and local prerogatives, and therefore, federal laws generally have required states either to draw up acceptable standards for air- and water-pollution control or be forced to accept federal standards.

Reasons for Pollution

The reasons for pollution are varied and cannot be attributed solely to the operations of business firms, as some critics of American society contend. One reason is the concentration of population in the United States and in other industrial countries into urban areas. The geographic distribution of population densities and the volume of pollution have an important relationship to each other. More than half the people in the United States live in 1 percent of the total land area; two-thirds live in 9 percent of the area. On this basis, the United States is one of the most overpopulated countries in the world. Such clustering of population greatly intensifies the problem of pollution: the very process of living generates wastes—wastes that, for the most part, nature can cope with efficiently until population density becomes quite high. Thus, at least part of the pollution problem can be attributed to the concentration of a large population in a relatively small land area. The larger the population is, the greater the volume of waste it will create—all other things being equal.

A second reason for pollution is the widespread affluence of Western industrial society. This affluence has created effluence, since many people have the money to demand a wide variety of goods and services, while discarding articles that often are still usable. In the United States and other advanced countries, millions of cars and billions of bottles and cans are junked annually. Demand patterns have shifted to require more convenience goods and services. Parents who themselves walked to school transport their children by auto day after day. In the past, one automobile was enough for most families; today, two cars per family is very common. The increased demand for creature comforts is also a part of the changing lifestyles. Few churches today would expect their congregations to keep cool on a summer's day with paper fans from local funeral parlors as in the past, even though the generation of electricity to operate air conditioning may add to the pollution of the environment.

A third reason for pollution is industry itself. Undeniably, dramatic examples of industrial pollution can readily be found, in part because much of this pollution is highly visible. One has only to look at the effluvia dumped into the rivers and lakes near any industrial city. Lake Erie is an excellent example, for it is one of the most polluted water areas in the world, polluted by industrial wastes from Cleveland's steel mills as well as industries in other cities. Moreover, today's rapidly advancing technology constantly creates new problems of pollution; the very processes that improve the ordinary person's lot as a consumer may have the reverse effect on the ecological balance. As an example, when most steelmakers changed from open hearth methods to the more efficient oxygen process, the demand for scrap metal dropped, since the oxygen process mainly uses iron ore and taconite pellets. Consequently, the incentive for junk dealers to salvage old cars became so low that some dealers actually insisted on being paid for accepting the vehicles. The inevitable result of this was that cities began to face the expensive chore of disposing of old automobiles. This raises the question as to who the polluter is: the steelmaker who changed to a new process, the auto manufacturer who builds a car that fails to disintegrate readily, or the auto owner who behaves in an antisocial way by abandoning the car.

Government is the fourth source of pollution. Localities must contend with two major kinds of potential pollutants: sewage and solid wastes such as garbage, sometimes on an incredibly large scale. All too often, localities have taken the most economical approach, letting raw sewage pour into the nearest river and dumping the garbage at the city dump and then burning it, thus polluting the air. In addition, cities that operate their own public utilities and conduct other quasi-business activities are often as guilty of polluting the environment as their counterparts in private industry are. A city that operates a public utility is going to use the same fuels and emit the same fumes as does a privately owned public utility. Federal government facilities also have contributed to pollution. In 1968, for example, out of 387 federal installations located throughout the country, 126 burned refuse in the open, and 140 used fuels with a high sulphur content, emitting chemicals or vapors into the air.[7]

Pollution also may emanate from other sources. One source is agriculture, which adds to pollution in several ways: wastes from feedlots,

7. Secretary of Health, Education and Welfare, *Air Pollution Abatement by Federal Facilities*, Senate Document 91-10, 91st Cong., 1st sess., pp. 1-3.

fertilizers containing nutrients that nourish algae in water, pesticides, and sediments carried by erosion. Drainage from mines accounts for a significant part of the water pollution in many parts of the country. Watercraft wastes and oil spills contaminate beaches and harbors. But the problems of pollution are not confined solely to air and water. There are also other types of pollution, such as noise and radiation, and in fact, noise abatement has become one of the more important environmental issues.

GOVERNMENT ROLE IN POLLUTION CONTROL

There are several government activities regarding the protection of the environment. Both the federal and state governments have become regulators, establishing laws, setting standards, and monitoring and supervising compliance. Thus, the Clean Air Act as amended in 1970 provides standards of air quality; there is similar legislation for water. The government also offers special tax assistance and subsidies by underwriting or engaging directly in research related to environmental problems. Virtually all the states now have enacted legislation that establishes a legal basis for controlling the sources of pollution. Besides writing laws to regulate pollution and provide subsidies, the government has also had to cope with its own harmful by-products.

Federal legislation for pollution control dates back as far as the turn of the century, when the Refuse Act of 1899 prohibited the discharge of waste materials into navigable waters. The Oil Pollution Act of 1924 forbade the discharge of oil into coastal waters, and in 1948 the Water Pollution Control Act was passed. Asserting that pollution problems were better handled at the local level, the act nonetheless authorized the Public Health Service to coordinate research, provide technical information, and, on request from the states involved, provide limited supervision of interstate waterways. The Water Pollution Control Act of 1956, along with amendments in 1961, 1965, 1966, and 1970, considerably extended federal involvement, both regulatory and financial, in water pollution control. The Water Quality Act of 1965 created the Water Pollution Control Administration, which almost immediately was transferred to the Department of the Interior. Responsibility for air pollution, however, remained with the Department of Health, Education and Welfare (now the Department of Health and Human Services).

Federal laws concerned with air pollution were first instituted in 1955, when Congress authorized technical assistance to states and localities, as well as a research program. In 1963 the Clean Air Act was passed to give states grants both to improve pollution control programs and to provide for federal enforcement in interstate pollution cases. The 1963 act also expanded federal research, particularly in connection with pollution from motor vehicles and from the burning of coal and fuel oil, and emphasized the need for controlling pollution from facilities operated by the federal government. A 1965 amendment authorized federal regulation of motor vehicles through standards that became effective in 1968. In 1966 an amendment broadened the federal aid program, making grants available for state and local control programs. The Air Quality Act of 1967 directed the Department of Health, Education and Welfare to delineate broad atmospheric areas for the entire country, as well as air quality control regions. The act continued and strengthened most of the provisions of the earliest legislation and provided for special studies of jet aircraft emissions, the need for national emission standards, and labor and training problems. The 1967 law also established the Presidential Air Quality Advisory Board.

The Clean Air Act of 1970

Probably the most important of all federal laws governing pollution is the Clean Air Act of 1970, which contains a series of provisions that have a direct impact on the operations of business firms. The more important provisions are:

1. The act required that by 1975 new cars be virtually pollution-free and specified that emissions of hydrocarbons and carbon monoxide gases had to be 90 percent less than levels permissible in 1970. At the insistence of the automobile manufacturers, who contend that compliance is a costly proposition, the date was extended to 1981. The act also requires manufacturers to offer a fifty-thousand-mile warranty on automobile emission control devices and establishes strict controls for fuel additives.[8]

2. The 1970 act also sets national standards for air pollution, with the states required to establish and enforce programs that meet national standards within four to six years. The federal government has the right to establish minimum ambient air standards for the entire country.

3. Willful polluters are subject to fines of up to $50,000 a day and jail sentences of up to two years.

4. The act gives all citizens and groups the right to sue in federal court to force polluters, the U.S. government included, to cease and desist pollution practices. This allows class action suits, which permit

8. It should be noted that compliance dates and emission standards have been changed since 1970. In August 1977, Congress agreed to modify auto emission standards for American-manufactured cars that were to take effect in 1980. In April 1982, amendments to the Clean Air Act were being considered by Congress.

citizens to sue when they believe that some action taken by other parties adversely affects them.[9]

5. The act authorized $1.1 billion for state agencies to use over a three-year period for air pollution research and established the Federal Office of Noise Abatement and Control.

The Clean Air Act of 1970 was amended in 1977 to provide some flexibility in the enforcement of the act, which had used legislatively set goals and rigid guidelines to force compliance. The act required the Environmental Protection Agency, which was created in 1970,[10] to establish national safe-concentration levels for major air pollutants, such as carbon monoxide, hydrocarbons, and lead,[11] and set 1975 as the deadline for meeting these standards. State governments were to draw up plans for cleaning up the air within their borders by this time. But most states could not meet the deadline. If an industry, particularly the auto industry, was unable to meet the deadline, the EPA was allowed to grant it a one-year extension, but only if it found that the industry was making serious efforts but could not comply for technical reasons. It was the industry's responsibility to find a solution and pay for it. The amendment to the Clean Air Act was designed mainly to give automobile companies more time to comply with auto emission standards. In places where automobile pollution is particularly heavy, cities were given until 1987 to bring air quality into line with national standards.

The Clean Air Act directed the Environmental Protection Agency to set national ambient air quality standards for pollutants covered in the act. It also authorized the EPA to set two types of standards, primary and secondary, without considering the cost of compliance. Primary standards were to protect human health with an added margin of safety for vulnerable segments of the population, like the elderly and infants. Secondary standards were to prevent damage to such things as crops, visibility, buildings, water, and materials. The EPA was also directed to determine maximum emission limits for plants and factories, called new source performance standards. These standards were to be set on an industry-by-industry basis for states to use as a guideline in deciding on more specific emission restrictions for individual factories. Regions that violated standards for any of the pollutants covered by the act were designated as nonattainment areas for those pollutants, and the states had to limit new construction of pollution sources until the air in these

9. On December 17, 1973, the Supreme Court refused to allow persons to bring class action suits unless each individual in the class action has an interest of at least $10,000 in the matter. This applies only to federal courts.
10. The functions of the EPA were discussed in Chapter 9.
11. There are seven major air pollutants as defined by the Clean Air Act: carbon monoxide, hydrocarbons, lead, nitrogen dioxide, ozone, particulates, and sulphur dioxide.

regions was brought up to federal standards. Companies wanting to build plants in these regions were required to install equipment that limited pollution to the least amount emitted by any similar factory elsewhere in the country.

The Water Pollution Control Act of 1972

The Water Pollution Control Act amends previous acts pertaining to water pollution, including the Water Quality Act of 1970, which extended federal control standards to oil and hazardous substance discharges from onshore and offshore vessel facilities. The Water Pollution Control Act is divided into five categories: research and related programs, grants for construction of treatment works, standards of enforcement, permits and licenses, and general provisions. Responsibility for the enforcement of the act is vested in the EPA and in state governments. Some of the more important provisions of the act are:

1. Manufacturers are required to monitor discharges at point sources of pollution and to keep records of the results of their efforts to reduce water pollution. The EPA or the state is authorized to inspect records to determine whether or not the act is being violated.

2. The act extended federal water pollution control to all navigable waters. When there is a violation, EPA can issue an order requiring compliance or notify the appropriate state of the alleged violation. If the state does not begin an appropriate enforcement within thirty days, the EPA can issue a compliance order requiring the violator to comply with a conditional or limited permit, or it can bring a civil action or begin criminal proceedings.

3. The act provides both civil and criminal punishments for violators. Civil punishments can range up to $10,000 per day of violation. For willful or negligent violations, criminal penalties can be imposed. Penalties for the first violation include fines of $2,500 to $25,000 per day and imprisonment for a period of up to one year; for subsequent violations, the penalty is fines of up to $50,000 per day of violation and imprisonment for a period of up to two years.

4. Both the Clean Air Act and the Water Pollution Control Act give citizens the right to bring suits to enforce standards set under the acts. Anyone having an interest that is or may be adversely affected by pollution may sue in the judicial district in which the offending source is located, and the U.S. district courts are given jurisdiction without regard to citizenship or amount in controversy.

5. The act declares as a national goal the ending of discharge of pollutants into all navigable waters by 1985.

The Noise Control Act of 1972

Although air and water pollution have been the targets of corrective legislation for a long time, recent efforts have been directed at abating noise in order to create a quieter environment. The Noise Control Act of 1972 places noise in the formal category of a pollutant. Congressional findings indicated that inadequately controlled noise presented a danger to the health and welfare of the nation's population, particularly in the urban areas. Noise adversely affects human blood pressure and heartbeat and causes other detrimental physiological changes.[12] Although its immediate consequences are usually transitory, sustained noise can accumulate in an almost imperceptible manner, causing permanent injury to the human body. Harmful noise is often difficult to isolate, since the degree of annoyance depends on the individual's response to the source of irritation.

The Noise Control Act offers federal regulatory guidelines for controlling noise pollution. Though primary responsibility for control of noise rests with state and local governments, federal action provides national uniformity of treatment. The act is intended to facilitate the establishment of federal noise emission standards for commercial and consumer-oriented products and to allow the federal government to preempt the field of noise control, though not depriving the states of local control and autonomy. The provisions of the act are:

1. The act's most important provision is noise emission standards for a wide variety of product categories. The act is designed to control and abate aircraft noise and sonic boom as well as establish railroad, aircraft, and motor carrier emission standards. The EPA is required to establish noise emission standards for newly manufactured products that have been identified as being major sources of noise. Such standards will limit the noise emissions from each product, as necessary to protect the public health, safety, and welfare. Effective noise emission standards have to be established for all products identified as major noise sources within eighteen months after the passage of the act.

2. Criminal sanctions under the act parallel those of the Clean Air and Water Pollution Control acts. Fines of up to $25,000 per day of violation or imprisonment for up to one year, or both, are authorized for the first offense. Subsequent offenders are liable for fines of up to $50,000 for each day of violation or for imprisonment of up to two years, or both. Each additional day of violation constitutes a separate offense.

3. The act also authorizes citizens to sue in the federal district courts for any violations of noise control requirements. Citizens are also per-

12. Robert A. Baron, *The Tyranny of Noise* (New York: St. Martin's Press, 1970).

mitted to sue the administrator of the EPA for an alleged failure to perform his or her duties under the act and also the administrator of the Federal Aviation Administration for similar reasons.

4. Technical assistance can be given to state and local governments to develop and enforce ambient noise standards.

5. The act authorizes labeling requirements for any product that emits noise capable of adversely affecting the public health and welfare or that is sold on the basis of its effectiveness in reducing noise. When a product is labeled, purchasers or users must be informed as to the level of noise the product emits or its effectiveness in reducing noise, whichever the case may be.

Other Environmental Legislation

The Toxic Substances Control Act of 1976 gives the EPA broad regulatory authority over chemical substances during all phases of their life cycles, from before their manufacture to their disposal. It directs the EPA to make an inventory of the approximately 55,000 chemical substances in commerce, to require premanufacture notice to the EPA of all new chemical substances, and to enforce record-keeping, testing, and reporting requirements so that the EPA can assess the relative risks of chemicals and regulate them. In December 1980 the Comprehensive Environmental Response, Compensation, and Liability Act became law. This legislation created a $1.6 billion fund for the cleanup of both spills of hazardous substances and inactive hazardous waste disposal sites. The Resource Conservation and Recovery Act of 1976 requires the safe disposal of hazardous wastes. Regulations define hazardous waste and establish standards for generators and transporters of hazardous wastes, as well as permit-requirements for owners and operators of facilities that treat, store, or dispose of hazardous wastes. A waste generator has to prepare a manifest for hazardous wastes which is to track movement of the wastes from the point of generation to the point of disposal. If a waste is hazardous, it must be properly packaged and labeled.[13]

13. In 1979 the Justice Department and the EPA filed the largest environmental suits to date. The suits charged the Hooker Chemical Company, its parent company Occidental Petroleum Corporation, and Olin Corporation with violating pollution laws and endangering human health at Love Canal and three other sites at Niagara Falls, New York. The government is seeking $125 million—$68 million from Hooker for cleanup at three sites, $50 million from Hooker and Olin for cleanup at the fourth site, and $7 million from Hooker for reimbursement of federal funds already spent to clean up the Love Canal area.

COSTS OF POLLUTION CONTROL

The subject of the environment is very controversial, although it is almost impossible to argue against a clean environment. Suggestions that perhaps environmental laws should be modified to make them less costly to business or that perhaps more public land should be opened up for mineral exploration elicit the wrath of environmentalist groups and their supporters. If there is a complaint that a certain environmental requirement may cost a firm $10,000 a year per worker, the response may be that the possibility of cancer is reduced or the length of life of the worker is increased. The response does not address the wisdom of the rule, nor does it consider more viable alternatives, but it is virtually impossible to argue against it in any public forum. Since most persons are unaware of the cost of alternative environmental policies, there is little incentive for legislators or regulators to select the type of regulation that has a trade-off—a balancing of benefits and costs —so as to rationalize the resources being consumed. Thus it is desirable for us to discuss some of the issues related to environmental regulation.

Opportunity cost is part of environmental regulation. The money spent for cleaning up the environment could have been spent in modernizing industrial plants in order to meet foreign competition. Costs need to be weighed against benefits, a task that is enormously complicated. Environmental trade-offs can be either economic or social. A social goal is clean air and water in a community, but an economic cost is the loss of jobs when a plant shuts down as a result of compliance costs. An economic goal is the discovery of more domestic energy sources in order to reduce dependence on OPEC oil. A social cost is the strip mining of coal or the oil leakage from offshore oil drilling onto beaches. Social goals can create economic costs, and economic goals can create social costs. It is necessary to be aware of all the costs and benefits—social as well as economic—in order to be able to make prudent decisions about resource allocation.

In addition to opportunity costs and economic and social trade-offs, there are the actual monetary outlays related to pollution control. The Council on Environmental Quality has estimated that during the ten years from 1979 to 1988, spending in response to federal environmental regulations will amount to $518 billion.[14] Of this total, $229 billion will be spent to satisfy air pollution control requirements; $170 billion will be spent to fulfill water quality requirements; and the remainder will be spent to satisfy other pollution control standards. This spending, which is presented in Table 10-1, includes only federally mandated pollution control requirements. There are also expenditures made in

14. Council on Environmental Quality, *Eleventh Annual Report* (Washington, D.C.: U.S. Government Printing Office, 1981), p. 395.

Table 10-1 Estimated Pollution Control Expenditures, 1979–1988 (billions of dollars)

Program	Total Cost
Air pollution	
Public	$ 19.5
Private	279.6
Water pollution	
Public	84.3
Private	85.4
Solid waste	
Public	4.6
Private	10.8
Toxic substances	8.2
Drinking water	2.7
Noise	6.9
Pesticides	1.2
Land reclamation	15.3
Total	$518.5

Source: Council on Environmental Quality, *Eleventh Annual Report*, December 1980, p. 394.

response to state and local environmental regulations, as well as voluntary expenditures. The spending on all environmental programs, either voluntary or in response to federal, state, or local regulations, is estimated at $735 billion between 1979 and 1988.[15] Air pollution expenditures will account for nearly half of the total. Solid waste disposal expenditures will probably cost $101 billion, both for compliance with the Resource Conservation and Recovery Act of 1976 and, more importantly, because most of the spending on solid waste disposal is either voluntary or in response to state or local environmental regulations.

Pollution Control and Its Impact on Business

Pollution control costs are by far the most important regulatory costs imposed on business. There is the incremental cost that, as mentioned previously, is the cost of anything that has to be done to comply with a regulation that would not have been done without that regulation. Emission control devices, such as smokestack screens, are an example.

15. Ibid., p. 396.

Paperwork costs are also part of the incremental costs. In addition to the incremental costs of regulation, there are also secondary effects that incur costs to business and to society. These costs may exceed the incremental cost of compliance. Examples of secondary effects are opportunity costs, changes in productivity, and costs of regulatory-imposed delays. One example of a regulatory-imposed delay is the Trans-Alaska Pipeline, which was delayed over four years. In those four years, the cost of construction is estimated to have increased by $3.4 billion owing to inflation during this period.[16] Payments for imported crude oil that North Slope production would have displaced augmented the nation's trade deficit by some $20 billion. Scrubbing for sulphur dioxide emissions can impose a penalty on efficiency and require additional capital expenditures to compensate for the efficiency loss.

Table 10-2 shows the incremental costs for the forty-eight companies included in a study made by the accounting firm Arthur Andersen and Company. The costs reflect clean air and clean water regulations, but not the cost of toxic substances control regulations, which are expected to increase in the future. The incremental costs for the forty-eight companies amounted to around $2 billion, or 77 percent of all incremental costs associated with various regulations with which the companies complied in 1977. There was a disparate effect of environmental regula-

Table 10-2 Incremental Costs of Federal Environmental Regulations to 48 Companies for 1977

Regulation	Cost (millions)
Auto emissions	$ 631
Water treatment	590
Ambient air standards	454
Air program new source performance standards	93
Water pretreatment standards	39
Oil pollution prevent	39
Paperwork	36
Other	136
Total	$2,018

Source: Arthur Andersen and Company, *Cost of Government Regulation Study: Report for the Business Roundtable* (New York: Business Roundtable, 1979), p. 25.

16. Arthur Andersen and Company, *Cost of Government Regulation Study: Report for the Business Roundtable* (New York: Business Roundtable, 1979), p. 27.

tion on individual companies, with public utility, chemical, primary metals, and transportation equipment companies paying the bulk of the cost.

The Environmental Protection Agency has made some efforts to reduce the cost of environmental regulation. It introduced the "bubble concept," which is based on the idea that it is often possible to reduce emissions of a given pollutant from one source far less expensively than from another. Thus, instead of compelling each source to meet a certain standard, a "bubble" is placed over the plant or geographic area, and private decision makers are allowed to decide the best way to meet the standard for the area at the lowest cost. The EPA also is experimenting with the use of marketable permits. It has suggested, for example, an overall limit on fluorcarbon production, and hence fluorcarbon emissions, combined with the creation of a market for buying and selling emission rights. Such an approach would permit the continued use of fluorcarbons in those products that consumers value most but eliminate the need for the EPA to determine essential and nonessential uses. Finally, the EPA is attempting to fit the regulations to the organization being regulated. The burden of compliance, particularly paperwork compliance, falls disproportionately on small business firms. The Regulatory Flexibility Act of 1980 requires the federal government to estimate the cost of new regulations for small business firms and to review existing regulations to see whether the burden can be reduced.

Cost Shifting

It cannot be assumed that the cost of pollution control will automatically be passed on to the consumer. Business firms, of course, will regard this cost as a part of the total cost of doing business and will attempt to shift it forward to consumers via price increases, backwards to stockholders in the form of lower dividends, or to workers in the form of lower wages. Consumers, faced by inflation and unemployment, may very well react by simply not buying the product. A good example may be found in the automobile industry in 1981. In increasing the price of its cars to compensate for labor, materials, and other costs, including pollution control, the industry found that consumers scaled down their expectations and refused to pay the higher prices. The result was one of the worst periods in automobile sales since the Depression. Faced with a need for capital, most companies are not too likely to compensate for increased pollution control compliance costs by cutting dividends, and the existence of strong labor unions in many industries precludes the possibility of compensating for costs through lower wages to employees.

The actual extent to which prices change in a given market as a result of the inclusion of pollution control costs in production will depend on a complex set of variables, including the elasticities of demand and supply and the degree of monopoly in a given market. If the demand for a product is absolutely or relatively inelastic, then consumers will purchase the same or similar quantities at a higher price than the original equilibrium price. There is an inelastic demand for a product when there are few, if any, available substitutes and the product is inexpensive—the smaller the fraction of total expenditures consumers allocate for a good is, the more inelastic the demand for it is likely to be. Thus, all other things being equal, firms confronted with an inelastic demand for their product would be able to incorporate pollution control costs into a higher price for the product, and with the quantity demanded decreasing at a rate slower than that of the increase in price, consumers would incur the cost of pollution control. On the other hand, if the demand for a product is absolutely or relatively elastic, then an increase in price to cover the cost of installing pollution control equipment will be accompanied by a more than proportional decrease in the quantity demanded, and revenue will fall. In this situation, rather than raise prices, a firm would have to absorb the pollution control cost itself.

It is also necessary to consider the total output or supply of a product. When a business firm has to purchase pollution abatement equipment, this represents an addition to toal fixed costs and average fixed costs at all levels of output. Marginal costs also will increase. Firms with sharp increments in costs associated with small increases in output will be less likely to shift pollution control costs forward because of the declining margin of profit gained on incremental amounts sold, as compared with firms experiencing less rise in their incremental costs. The firm with steeper incremental costs has more to lose by sacrificing its marginal units of production than do other firms. We should emphasize that this is for a short period. In the short run a firm can vary its output but not its plant capacity and hence will have some variable and some fixed costs. In the long run a firm can vary not only its output but also its plant capacity and therefore has no fixed cost. In the short run a firm may have to absorb at least some of its pollution control costs itself.

The nature of the industry also will affect cost shifting. In general, the more competitive a market is, the more difficult it will be for firms to pass pollution control costs on to consumers. Because not all firms within a competitive market are required to reduce pollution, a firm confronted with abatement may not be able to pass its cost forward to consumers. In this case, the abatement cost may result in a reduction in employment and output in the firm's effort to maintain normal profits. But if all firms are required to reduce pollution, shifting of the cost to consumers becomes easier. In industries characterized by oligopoly the market situation is somewhat different. In most other market situations, including monopoly, price is determined by how firms react to their cost situation in light of the individual firm's demand curve. The sum of these reactions gives the supply response, which, in combination with total market demand, sets the price. In oligopoly, however, the situation is not so simple, primarily because the individual firm cannot act without considering the reactions of its rivals. Thus demand, as seen by the individual firm, is not independent of the reactions of rival firms, as it is in other market situations. The precarious position of the individual firm under an oligopoly gives it an incentive to move in concert with other oligopolistic firms or to follow a price leader.

There are not many monopolies in the United States, primarily because there are few commodities or services for which there are absolutely no acceptable substitutes. But local or regional monopolies of various kinds are relatively common. In controlling its affairs, a monopolist must heed the demand curve for its product. A monopolist tends, under any given conditions of demand and productive capacity, to limit output to the volume at which the marginal cost of producing the good is equal to the marginal revenue derived from its sale. Since such an output is ordinarily well short of that at which the price just covers the average cost of production per unit of output, it follows that the productive results of operations under conditions of monopoly are quite different from those prevailing under competitive conditions. The monopolist has more leverage and more opportunity to push the cost of pollution control onto consumers by simply readjusting output to a different point on the demand curve for its product and charging a higher price. It is possible that a monopolist might be constrained from raising prices by the fear that such action would lead to government regulation.

In the case of natural monopolies, for example, public utilities, the cost of air and water pollution control equipment is considerable. In 1980, the electric utilities' estimated capital outlays for pollution control was $3.3 billion—the highest expenditure by any industry.[17] However, the price a public utility can charge is determined by a regulatory commission. The utility would include pollution abatement as a fixed cost of operation, which would be part of its rate base. State regulatory commissions, confronted by rising political pressures from consumer groups, are not proving to be very malleable when it comes to granting rate increases to public utilities. But for the most part, pollution control costs to utilities are reflected in higher electric and gas rates to consumers, who are thus bearing the major share of the cost of cleaning up the environment.

The market mechanism through which changes in prices tend to reflect the inclusion of pollution cost can be illustrated with a simple diagram of market price determination. (See Diagram 10-1.)

17. Council on Environmental Quality, p. 394.

In the diagram, DD and SS represent the respective demand and supply curves before the imposition of pollution cost. Market price is at P_1 and output at Q_1. After the cost, the supply curve shifts to $S_1 S_1$, the vertical distance between SS and $S_1 S_1$ representing the cost of installing pollution control devices. Since demand (DD) is less than perfectly elastic, the price in the marketplace has risen by less than the full cost of pollution control, in other words, the distance $P_1 P_2$. This means that the cost is borne partly by the consumer and partly by the producer; the exact manner in which the cost is divided depends on the relative elasticities of demand and supply.

The costs to business of compliance with pollution control requirements may be overemphasized, as there also are benefits to business aside from the aesthetic value of a clean environment. Fulfilling pollution control requirements do increase business's expenditures. Installing

Diagram 10–1 Market Price Determination of Inclusion of Pollution Control Cost

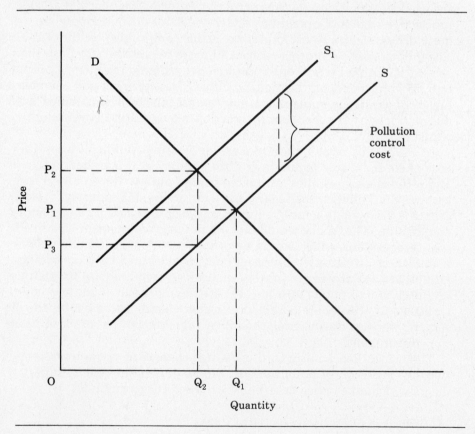

and maintaining pollution control equipment necessitate additional bricklayers, electricians, iron workers, operating engineers, carpenters, and plumbers. Additional off-site labor is required to produce or transport the materials and equipment used in the actual construction of a project, as well as the engineering and technical labor needed to design, plan, and evaluate the operational performance of the pollution control systems. There also are jobs created in the pollution abatement industry. All of this can stimulate employment. Nonetheless, this increased employment also can be offset by the closing down of plants that cannot comply with the cost of cleaning up the environment.

Benefits are much more difficult to quantify than costs, particularly in the environmental area. Regulators are also not compelled to examine economic trade-offs in choosing the best way to achieve a regulatory goal, and it has not been determined to what extent the regulators must demonstrate the benefits of their actions and the relationship of these benefits to the costs of regulation. In 1980 the U.S. Supreme Court handed down a decision that is somewhat relevant to regulatory costs and benefits.[18] The Court upheld in part a ruling by a lower court in favor of the American Petroleum Institute, that the Occupational Safety and Health Administration (OSHA) could not tighten its standards limiting workers' exposure to benzene without first conducting a cost-benefit analysis of the proposed change. OSHA, the lower court had ruled, failed to prove that there was a "significant risk of harm," according to the old standard, that would justify the proposed revision. The Court did not rule on whether benefits had to be completely and precisely quantified or had to bear some reasonable relationship to costs.

THE ENVIRONMENT AND ECONOMIC TRADE-OFFS

There is a conflict between the need to find new energy sources and the desire to clean up the environment. The energy shortage in the United States, coupled with its dependence on foreign sources of oil, makes the discovery of new fuels mandatory. Another problem is the belief that pollution can be attributed directly to the society's preoccupation with economic growth. It is argued that the level of pollution is indeed linked to an increase in real gross national product: more goods result in more pollution. As a solution, some persons advocate zero economic growth. Conversely, other groups feel that an increase in the rate of economic growth is necessary to reduce inflation and to increase job opportunities for minorities. Environmentalism is an economic issue in which one

18. *American Petroleum Institute* v. *Occupational Safety and Health Administration*, 581F.2d493 (5th Cir. 1978).

group wants a particular type of goods and services that may be different from what another group wants, and thus there are trade-offs between them.

Energy and the Environment

The aforementioned conflict between the need for new sources of energy and the desire for a clean environment is a problem for both business and society. The American economy is faced with a shortage of sources of energy, particularly oil. High prices, shortages, and supply disruptions have been serious and have contributed to the currently high rate of inflation in this country. Rising standards of living have caused the per capita use of oil to double since 1940. Oil is the most important source of primary energy in the United States, accounting for 45 percent of its total energy consumption. Oil is the only fuel that can serve all parts of the transportation sector—a market that accounts for nearly one-quarter of all domestic primary energy consumption. Coal and natural gas are also important primary energy sources, with coal supplies adequate for several hundred years at current consumption rates. Energy independence—particularly with enormous coal reserves, potential new sources of oil, and the development of new sources of energy, for example, nuclear, solar, and wind—appears to be possible, at least from a resource standpoint. However, there is some opposition to each approach to energy independence. Coal can be cheap to mine and consume when there is no concern for environmental standards, but quite expensive to mine and consume when there are strict environmental controls. Environmentalists want coal mined and burned safely and cleanly without disturbing the topography at either end.[19] The opposition to coal development also applies to oil. Environmentalists criticized the Alaska pipeline on the grounds that its construction could ruin the permafrost and that breaks in the pipeline could damage the environment and kill the wildlife. The general public is split on the environment-energy issue. A CBS News–*New York Times* poll asked, "Which do you think is more important—producing energy or protecting the environment?" Forty-one percent believed energy to be more important, and 43 percent favored the environment.[20] A trade-off is needed to provide some middle ground between the two alternatives.

19. Lester C. Thurow, *The Zero-Sum Society* (New York: Basic Books, 1980), p. 38.
20. News Release: CBS News/*New York Times* Poll, April 10–14, 1980.

Economic Growth and the Environment

Another problem is the apparent conflict between economic growth and the environment. Economic growth is generally defined as the rate of increase in an economy's real output or income over time. Environmentalists contend that economic growth must be curtailed in the name of ecological sanity.[21] They feel that the level of pollution is a direct concomitant of economic growth—as real gross national product increases, so does pollution. The social costs of pollution have been high, as affluence associated with a rising gross national product has increased. Environmentalists regard the world as an ecosystem whose natural resources are not infinite and which it is possible for humans to waste or despoil through imprudent actions. Therefore, environmentalists argue that it is necessary to de-emphasize economic growth. Since population is a variable that influences the rate of economic growth, environmentalists feel it is necessary to introduce worldwide birth control measures to lower the birth rate. Otherwise, the world will not be able to support the billions of people that are projected to be born during the coming decades.

Supporters of economic growth contend that a constantly increasing real gross national product is necessary to maintain a high level of employment and to improve living standards. This is especially true as long as the population continues to grow. In the United States, the rate of unemployment has been high for several years, a problem that has been compounded by the fact that the size of the labor force is constantly expanding. Thus, it is necessary to absorb new entrants into the labor force by providing more employment opportunities. If the economy does not grow, there is no way in which the rate of unemployment can be reduced and new job seekers can be absorbed into the labor force. Further, the nation will not be able to obtain the resources to solve its social problems—to provide the schools, medical care, hospitals, and other things it needs. There also is a conflict between environmentalists and other groups whose increased aspirations are being translated into a demand for a greater share of both money and real gross national product—public employees' unions, civil rights groups, and so forth. So a lower growth rate could exacerbate the problem of unemployment and create social unrest among those groups that are caught in the syndrome of rising expectations.

21. Hazel Henderson, "Ecologists versus Economists," *Harvard Business Review*, 51 (July–August 1973), 28–30.

SUMMARY

Problems related to environmental pollution have attracted widespread attention only in recent years. This is not to say, however, that pollution is a relatively new phenomenon; on the contrary, pollution was a part of the American industrial and municipal scene during the last century. Recognition of this fact was expressed in the Refuse Act of 1899, which prohibited the discharge of waste into navigable waters. Nevertheless, most laws governing pollution are of recent vintage. The basic Water Pollution Control Act dates only from 1948, and the first Clean Air Act dates from 1956. The most important laws governing pollution were passed during the 1970s—the Clean Air Act of 1970 and the Water Pollution Control Act of 1972, both of which are amendments to the basic acts, and the Noise Control Act of 1972, which adds an entirely new dimension to the whole area of pollution control, with noise considered for the first time to be a major environmental pollutant.

Improving the quality of the environment will be very expensive, at least for business. For example, the passage of the Clean Air Act of 1970 has forced many design changes in automobiles to reduce their polluting emissions. It cannot be assumed that business firms can pass the cost of pollution control on to product users. The automobile industry itself offers an example, as consumers have proved reluctant to purchase higher priced cars that included the cost of installing pollution control equipment.

For some industries and firms, the amount of pollution control costs will vary widely from the average. The chemical industry is likely to spend nearly four times this average for water pollution control, but the machinery industry is likely to spend less than one-fourth. Finally, pollution control costs appear to have an adverse impact on small firms operating at the margin.

Apart from the cost of pollution control, there are other problems that confront business firms. One problem is the regulatory infrastructure that has been built up at the federal and state levels of government to administer pollution control laws. Business firms have to deal directly with these regulatory agencies in order to conform to pollution abatement requirements. But there is more to regulation of the environment than conformance to required standards of abatement. Government also is making an effort to control other areas that are in some way related to environmental pollution—land use, energy, and urban transportation. All encroach directly on business operations. Land use in particular has an impact on business location. Local governments have adopted controls over the use of land that require the dispersion or isolation of new factories and power facilities from centers of population. Local control over urban transportation designed to meet air quality standards would also affect industrial dispersion and business costs. Even the energy crisis is unlikely to alter materially the total impact of clean air requirements on industry.

QUESTIONS FOR DISCUSSION

1. What are some of the causes of pollution?
2. Emission charges have an advantage over direct regulation of pollution in that there is less interference with the market mechanism. Discuss.
3. In your opinion, have increased pollution control costs contributed to inflation?
4. Discuss the provisions of the Clean Air Act of 1970.
5. How is the term *opportunity cost* applied to the cost of cleaning up the environment?
6. Is there a conflict between the goal of economic growth and the goal of a clean environment?
7. How do environmental regulations interact with the development of such sources of energy as coal and offshore oil?
8. What is the impact of required investments in pollution control facilities on the market for capital funds in the United States?
9. In your opinion, should the strip mining of coal be prohibited?
10. Discuss how tax incentives can be used to encourage the use of pollution control devices and to influence plant location.
11. In the final analysis, who ultimately bears most of the costs of cleaning up the environment? Discuss.

RECOMMENDED READINGS

American Institute of Certified Public Accountants. *Measurement of Corporate Social Performance*. New York: AICPA, 1977.

Arthur Andersen and Company. *Cost of Government Regulation Study: Report for the Business Roundtable*. New York: Business Roundtable, March 1979.

Brace, Paul. *Glossary of the Environment*. New York: Praeger, 1972.

Commoner, Barry. "The Environmental Costs of Economic Growth." In *Economics of the Environment*. Ed. Robert Dorfman. New York: W. W. Norton & Co., Inc., 1977.

Council on Environmental Quality. *Environmental Quality—1981: Twelfth Annual Report*. Washington, D.C.: U.S. Government Printing Office, 1981.

Crandall, Robert W. "Curbing the Costs of Social Regulation." *Brookings Bulletin*, 15 (Winter 1979).

Fox, Harrison W., and Martin Schnitzer. *Doing Business in Washington*. New York: Free Press, 1981, chap. 7.

Frieden, Bernard J. *The Environmental Protection Hustle*. Cambridge, Mass.: MIT Press, 1979.

Henderson, Hazel. "Ecologists versus Economists." *Harvard Business Review*, 51 (July–August 1973), 28–36.

Kneese, Allen V., and Charles L. Schultze. *Pollution, Prices, and Public Policy.* Washington, D.C.: Brookings Institution, 1975.

Marcus, Alfred. "The Environmental Protection Agency: An Experiment in Regulatory Reform." In *The Politics of Regulation*. Ed. James O. Wilson. New York: Basic Books, 1980.

Ruff, Larry E. "Federal Environmental Regulation." In *Case Studies in Regulation*. Ed. Leonard W. Weiss and Michael W. Klass. Boston: Little, Brown, 1981.

Segel, Frank W., and Frederick J. Dreiling. "Pollution Abatement and Control Expenditures." *Survey of Current Business*. Washington, D.C.: U.S. Department of Commerce, February 1978, pp. 12–16.

Seneca, Joseph J. *Environmental Economics*. Englewood Cliffs, N.J.: Prentice-Hall, 1979.

Thurow, Lester C. *The Zero-Sum Society*. New York: Basic Books, 1980, chap. 5.

Chapter 11

Equal Employment Opportunity Policies and Their Impact on Business

As mentioned earlier, the newer type of government control differs from the older, more formal type of government regulation of business. It is directed more toward achieving the various social goals of particular interest groups. More important to business is that these controls cut across virtually every kind of private industry. Thus, the Environmental Protection Agency or the Consumer Product Safety Commission really has a much broader area to regulate than does the Civil Aeronautics Board, which governs only one industry. The impact of these newer agencies is extensive. Environmental controls apply to all companies, as do requirements for consumer product safety. Moreover, these and other agencies have attempted to bring about social change through the government procurement process—a leverage that few business firms can resist.

A third area of the government's social control of business is affirmative action, which is the federal Equal Employment Opportunity Commission's term for hiring and promoting women and nonwhites. Because business firms are required to meet affirmative action goals, the federal government has intervened in their personnel practices. The purpose of affirmative action is to ensure equal employment opportunities for all individuals, regardless of race, sex, religion, or national origin. To put it another way, sex, color, and age cannot be used as criteria to deny hiring or promotion. Noncompliance by employers with affirmative action goals can lead to severe penalties; for example, American Telephone and Telegraph had to pay $75 million in 1973 to employees who charged that discrimination had deprived them of past promotions and raises.

To a considerable degree, affirmative action policies are linked to what Daniel Bell has called a "revolution of entitlement."[1] It used to be that economic growth brought rising expectations, which meant simply the desire for higher material living standards. But modern society has come to believe that each person is entitled to at least a minimum and decent standard of living, including the right to a job, protection against the various vicissitudes of life—unemployment,

---

1. Daniel Bell, *The Cultural Contradictions of Capitalism* (New York: Basic Books, 1976), pp. 232-236.

sickness, accidents, and old age—and the right to certain social ameni-
ties, such as decent housing. This revolution of rising entitlement has
also spread to the areas of civil rights, political rights, and social rights.
Disadvantaged groups—blacks, women, and others—demand preferential
treatment, arguing that only in this way can historical injustices be redressed. Equality of opportunity is no longer sufficient in itself;
equality of representation is the desired goal.

Affirmative action is a broad subject, and it is necessary to distinguish its basic concept from its many laws and regulations. Federal
agencies and the courts have applied the concept of affirmative action
differently. For example, the courts have not gone as far as the administrative agencies in forcing numerical goals and timetables on employers. Affirmative action programs are designed to resolve enormous
problems, and their policies touch both employers and society. It is not
easy to determine what affirmative action actually means to society,
but in this chapter we shall examine its concepts, intentions, and actual
effects.

DISCRIMINATION AND THE DISTRIBUTION
OF INCOME

The rationale for government intervention in employment policy and
education is that equal opportunity is a basic desideratum of the
American democratic system—everyone should have the same opportunity to achieve material success, the usual goal. When opportunity is
equal, the competition and market forces determine one's worth in the
marketplace. The idea behind equality of opportunity is that if everyone is given the same, or substantially the same, starting position in a
race, the winners will have achieved their rewards through merit rather
than through any favored position. Reward will be based on merit, and
the result will be a society based on the principle of meritocracy.[2]
Logically, if everyone is given the same opportunity and there is no
discrimination based on sex, age, or other factors, the rewards should
be distributed fairly uniformly, without much difference between the
sexes or among races.

Equality of opportunity has worked better in theory than in practice, however, though the United States has probably done a better
overall job of encouraging this equality, particularly by offering mass
education, than any other country has. The problem is that there are
a number of impediments in the path of achieving true equality of opportunity. Clearly, if there is discrimination—on the basis of sex, color,

2. Daniel Bell, "On Meritocracy and Equality," *The Public Interest*, 29 (Fall 1972),
18–21.

religion, or any criterion outside professional qualification—there is no genuine equality of opportunity. And equality of opportunity is only a part of the total picture, for in the United States it is linked to the distribution of income. In part, income inequality is based on natural differences among individuals' abilities, and neither Congress nor the Supreme Court can change the fact that some people can run faster and jump farther than others. But sometimes there are differences in income based on sex, race, and age that have little or no relation to ability. First, therefore, we shall discuss the distribution of income in the United States in order to explore in some depth these income differences.

The Distribution of Personal Income

The median and mean are absolute values used to measure the central tendency in any distribution. In 1979 the median household income in the United States was $16,533, and the mean household income was $19,620.[3] Household income can be broken down further into family and nonfamily incomes. The median income for family households in 1979 was $19,801, and the median income for nonfamily households was $8,519. But because these statistics do not tell us much about the distribution of personal income in the United States in 1979, we shall analyze income distribution based on such economic and social factors as sex, race, and age. There are marked disparities in income distribution that are related to these characteristics, and these are the crux of affirmative action policies. Our age is an age of group consciousness, with each group arguing that income parity is necessary to achieve economic justice.

Sex

In 1979 the median income of households headed by a male was $20,140, and the median income of households headed by a female was $8,510.[4] The mean income of households headed by a male was $22,844, and the mean income of households headed by a female was $11,387. The median income of single men was $13,365, and their mean income was $15,897; conversely, the median income for single women was $10,000, and their mean income was $12,095. There are

3. U.S. Department of Commerce, Bureau of the Census, Current Population Reports, *Monthly Income of Households in the United States: 1979*, March 1980, pp. 1-4.
4. Ibid., p. 41.

several reasons for these differences in income based on sex. A greater percentage of males was in the labor force in 1979, and a greater percentage of males worked full time in 1979. There also were more males in the higher-paying occupations. For example, over one-half of all working women were in the relatively low-paying clerical and service occupations. As we would expect, men outnumbered women by a ratio of three to one in the management, professional, and technical areas. Finally, long-term comparisons of the median incomes of full-time workers, based on sex, reveal that in 1947 the median income of women was 59 percent of the median income of men, compared with 58 percent in 1979.

Race

There also are differences in the distribution of income based on color or race. In 1979, the white household median income was $17,330, and the black median household income was $10,220, or 59 percent of the white median income.[5] The Hispanic median household income was $13,420, or 77 percent of that for white households. The much lower household income for blacks can be explained in part by the high concentration of black households headed by women. In 1979, about 46 percent of all black households were headed by women, compared with 25 percent for white and Hispanic households. There also is a difference in income among single workers. Single black males had a mean income of $11,320 in 1979, compared with a mean of $15,897 for single white males; single black females had an average income of $8,158, compared with a mean income of $12,095 for single white females. The differences in income can be partly attributed to the greater percentage of blacks in part-time employment. Also, full-time employment is higher for white males than for black males and for white females than for black females. But the median incomes of both white and black male full-time workers are substantially larger than the median incomes of female white and black full-time workers.

Age

There also are differences in the distribution of personal income based on age. Both men's and women's incomes peak between the ages of forty-five to fifty-four.[6] For example, the highest average annual income for males with a college education is reached at age forty-nine,

5. Ibid., p. 4.
6. Ibid., pp. 38–45.

after which it declines. This pattern also applies to college-educated females, to both males and females with high school education, and to all occupational categories except unskilled workers. But this in itself does not prove discrimination, for a number of reasons. Lower incomes at both ends of the age spectrum are related to work experience. In the case of women, a majority have not worked for an extended period of time. Women often leave work to have and to rear children, and often when they return to work, it is at a later age and their lack of work experience results in a lower wage.

Direct Discrimination and Role Differentiation

Differences in the distribution of personal income do not prove discrimination, owing to differences in people's ability, motivation, education, work experience during a given year, and even lifelong work experience. How much income differential, for instance, between men and women, is due to differences in experience or performance on the job, which may be difficult to measure, or is due to discrimination is a hard question to answer. The income differential almost disappears when men's and women's earnings are compared within detailed job classifications and within the same plant. In the very narrow sense of equal pay for the same job in the same plant there may be little difference between men and women. But the focus of the problem is only shifted, not eliminated, for then it is necessary to explain why women have such a different job structure from that of men and why they are employed in different types of establishments. In the professional and managerial occupational categories there is an overwhelming preponderance of men. For example, in 1972 women accounted for 7 percent of the management positions in manufacturing, although women held 41 percent of all editorial positions.[7]

It is difficult to distinguish between the discrimination that bars women from jobs solely because of their sex and the role differentiation that, either by choice or necessity, restricts their careers because of the demands of their households. Some may label the latter as a pervasive societal discrimination that starts in the cradle. But there obviously is prejudice that carries over into the area of work. Employers may discriminate against women by exaggerating the risk of job instability or client acceptance and thereby exclude women from positions that would advance their careers. There are also prejudices that reduce the number of women in given occupations. To some extent this reflects role differentiation: men select an education related

7. C. F. Fretz and Joanne Hayman, "Progress for Women—Men Are Still More Equal," *Harvard Business Review*, 51 (September–October 1973), 134.

to a specific career, whereas women select more humanistic studies, which are more difficult to translate into a career but can be, perhaps, related to the home. There also are men's and women's traditional work roles—the men doing the physical labor in the plant, the women working as its secretaries. Women also are often restricted to specific departments.

In the case of blacks and members of other minority groups, there has been more overt discrimination. Over an extended period of time, blacks have been systematically denied the same educational opportunities as whites have, which is reflected in blacks' occupations. The majority are concentrated in the low-pay, low-skill jobs. Indeed, there has also been discrimination in hiring and promotion policies toward minority groups. Often the discrimination has been indirect, as in testing, which can be a legitimate device to find out something about employees' aptitudes and qualifications. However, testing may be culturally biased in favor of certain types of job applicants and against other applicants from a different social milieu. Many of the differentials in the employment status of blacks and other minorities have been due to their inability to obtain jobs commensurate with their training, and to some degree this inability can be attributed to the restrictive practices of the trade unions, including union referral arrangements, complex seniority systems, and closed shops.

AFFIRMATIVE ACTION

Affirmative action means active efforts by employers to correct any racial, sexual, or other minority imbalances that may exist in a work force. The general principle behind affirmative action is that a court order to cease and desist from some harmful activity may not be sufficient to undo the harm already done or even to prevent additional harm as a result of a pattern of events set in motion by the previous illegality. For example, racial discrimination is one area in which an order to cease and desist may not be enough to prevent continued discrimination. If a firm has engaged in racial discrimination for years and has an all-white work force as a result, then simply to stop explicit discrimination will mean little as long as the firm continues to hire its current employees' friends and relatives through word-of-mouth referral. Clearly, the area of racial discrimination is one in which positive or affirmative steps of some kind appear reasonable—which is not to say that the particular policies actually followed make sense.

Affirmative action is far more comprehensive than simple employment discrimination, which may entail only one person over some issue such as age or sex. It requires any employer with a federal contract to evaluate his or her work force, to analyze his or her employment needs, and to solicit actively to obtain more minority employees. Affirmative action programs must meet certain minimal requirements in which the burden is on the employer. A primary requirement is a written description of the efforts being made to achieve equal employment opportunity. A program must contain certain basic information. For example, the work force must be analyzed to determine where minorities are being underutilized, why they are being underutilized, and how this can be corrected. Goals and timetables must be actual commitments. Additionally, an employer must inform all recruiting sources of this affirmative action policy and of the firm's desire to recruit more minority employees, in keeping with its goals and timetables. There also must be a specific objective with regard to promotions; it is not sufficient for a firm just to state that it will attempt to promote women or blacks to responsible positions.

The Development of Affirmative Action

The principle of affirmative action goes back much further than the civil rights legislation of the 1960s and extends well beyond questions regarding ethnic minorities or women. In 1935 the Wagner Act prescribed affirmative action as well as cease-and-desist remedies against employers whose antiunion activities had violated the law. Thus, in the landmark Jones and Laughlin steel case, which established the constitutionality of the act, the National Labor Relations Board ordered the company not only to stop discriminating against employees who were union members but also to post notices in conspicuous places announcing that they would reinstate back pay to unlawfully discharged workers.[8] Had the company been ordered merely to cease and desist from economic retaliation against union members, the effect of its past intimidation would have continued to inhibit the free-choice election guaranteed by the National Labor Relations Act.

The Civil Rights Act of 1964

The Civil Rights Act of 1964 was an attempt to eliminate all forms of discrimination in employment. Its genesis was in the Civil Rights Acts of 1866 and 1870, both of which were designed to preclude employment discrimination on the basis of race and color.[9] Section 703 of

8. Harry A. Millis and Emily Clark Brown, *From the Wagner Act to Taft-Hartley* (Chicago: University of Chicago Press, 1950), p. 97.
9. U.S. Equal Employment Opportunity Commission, *Laws and Rules You Should Know* (Washington, D.C.: U.S. Government Printing Office, 1975), p. 91.

Title VII of the Civil Rights Act of 1964 obligates employers, labor unions, and government agencies not to discriminate on the basis of race, color, religion, sex, or national origin. Section 704 of Title VII provided for the creation of the Equal Employment Opportunity Commission (EEOC), which consists of a five-member board appointed by the president with the approval of the Senate for a term of five years. Section 701 defines an employer subject to the act as a person engaged in an industry affecting commerce who has fifteen or more employees for each working day in each of ten or more calendar weeks in the current or calendar year. The section also puts employment agencies and labor unions under the jurisdiction of the act. Title VI of the act precludes discrimination on the basis of race, color, sex, or national origin in federally aided employment programs.

The Civil Rights Act of 1964 has been criticized on the grounds that it requires compensatory or preferential treatment of minority groups to compensate for past discrimination. In other words, is anything more than equality of treatment justified under the Fourteenth Amendment's corollary statutes? But the intent of Congress in passing the act was reasonably explicit. Senator Hubert Humphrey of Minnesota, one of the drafters of the legislation, pointed out that it did not force an employer to achieve any kind of racial balance in his or her work force by giving any kind of preferential treatment to any individual or group.[10] He went on to say that there must be an intention to discriminate before an employer can be considered in violation of the law. In fact, Section 703 of the Civil Rights Act states that employers, employment agencies, and labor unions are not required to grant preferential treatment to any individual or any group because of race, color, sex, religion, or national origin on account of any imbalance that may exist with respect to the number or percentage of persons of any race, sex, religion, or national origin.

Executive Orders

Subsequent executive orders declared it a matter of public policy that affirmative action must be taken to rectify the discrimination against minorities. The policy of affirmative action was first proclaimed by President Lyndon Johnson in an executive order in 1965.[11] It states that in all federal contracts or in any employment situation that uses federal funds, employers have to prove they have sought out qualified

10. U.S. Equal Employment Opportunity Commission, *Legislative History of Titles VII and XI of Civil Rights Act of 1964* (Washington, D.C.: U.S. Government Printing Office, 1969), p. 3005.
11. Executive Order *11246*.

applicants from disadvantaged groups, have to provide special training when necessary if qualified applicants cannot be found immediately, and have to hire preferentially from minority group members when their qualifications are roughly equal to those of other applicants. This executive order also applies to women. Another executive order banned discrimination by contractors on the basis of age, and an executive order in 1967 banned discrimination in federal employment on the basis of race, sex, color, and national origin.[12] Directors of federal agencies are required to draw up a positive program of equal employment opportunity for all employees, and to hire more women and minority members at all levels. In the early 1970s, affirmative action was extended to universities, and each school with federal contracts was asked to provide data on the number of women and minority persons in each position, academic and nonacademic, and to set specific goals for increasing the number of women and minority members in each classification.

Executive Order 4   Executive Order 4 of 1971 is the basis of most affirmative action programs. Under this order, affirmative action is required from all employers who hold federal contracts. The type of affirmative action an employer must take is determined by the nature of the federal contract he or she holds. A written affirmative action program, demanded by the Office of Federal Contract Compliance (OFCC) regulations, applies to all nonconstruction contractors and subcontractors of the federal government and to agencies of the federal government that employ fifty or more employees and have a contract in excess of $50,000 a year. All business firms or government agencies that meet these criteria must file a written affirmative action program that contains a statement of good-faith efforts to achieve equal employment opportunity. Such efforts must include an analysis of deficiencies in the use of minorities, a timetable for correcting such deficiencies, and a plan for achieving these goals. In addition, an employer must include an analysis of all major job categories to determine where women and minorities are being underutilized and an explanation of why they are being underutilized.

There are sanctions that can be used to enforce compliance with Executive Order 4. Failure to develop an affirmative action program can lead to possible cancelation of existing contracts and elimination from consideration for future contracts. If a contractor has set up an affirmative action program at each of his or her plants, the OFCC will grant a precontract award conference during which every effort must be made to develop an acceptable affirmative action program. If the contractor has no program at all or one that is not acceptable, the

12. Executive Order *11375*.

agency can issue notice, giving the contractor thirty days to show cause why enforcement proceedings under the executive order should not be instituted. If the situation is not remedied within this period of time, the OFCC will commence formal proceedings leading to the cancelation of all existing contracts or subcontracts the firm may have. It is also possible for the OFCC to initiate a lawsuit against a contractor who fails to live up to his or her affirmative action policies.

Revised Order 14   In July 1974, the Department of Labor gave final approval to its own Revised Order 14 on the procedures that federal agencies must use in evaluating government contractors' affirmative action programs. Among other things, contractors must list each job title as it appears in their union agreements or payroll records, rather than listing only job group, as was formerly required. The job titles must be ranked from the lowest paid to the highest paid within each department or other similar organizational unit. Further, if there are separate work units or lines of progression within a department, separate lists must be provided for each unit or line, including unit supervisors. For lines of progression, the order of jobs in the line through which an employee can move to the job must be indicated. If there are no formal progression lines or usual promotional sequences, job titles must be listed by departments, job families, or disciplines, and in order of wage rates or salary ranges. For each job title, two breakdowns are required, the total number of male and female incumbents and the total number of male and female incumbents in each of the following groups: blacks, Chicanos, American Indians, and Asians.

Other Antidiscrimination Laws

There also are laws that deal with particular forms of discrimination. The Age Discrimination in Employment Act of 1967 forbids any form of discrimination based on age. Particularly mentioned are those workers between the ages of forty and sixty-five. Employers cannot refuse to hire or discharge any person on the basis of age, nor can they segregate or classify persons on the basis of age when this criterion would deprive them of opportunities for promotion. The Equal Pay Act of 1963 precludes differences in wages based on sex and is applicable to employers with public contracts. The Vocational Rehabilitation Act of 1973 requires federal contractors to take affirmative action in hiring the handicapped. The Equal Employment Opportunity Act amended the Civil Rights Act of 1964 to vest more power in the federal enforcement agencies, particularly the Equal Employment Opportunity Commission (EEOC). The EEOC can initiate law suits against employers believed to be guilty of violating the antidiscrimination laws.

Enforcement of Affirmative Action

The enforcement of affirmative action programs is concentrated in a number of federal agencies, including the Office of Federal Contract Compliance, which is responsible for direct government contracts with business firms, and the Equal Employment Opportunity Commission, which was created by the Civil Rights Act of 1964. Jurisdictions overlap among the Department of Labor, the Department of Health and Human Services, the Department of Justice, the EEOC, and the federal courts. There also are regional offices of all these agencies which vary significantly in their practices. Moreover, even though one federal agency approves or requires a given course of action, following such an approved course of action in no way protects the employer from being sued by another federal agency or by private individuals because of these very actions. Indeed, federal agencies have sued one another under the Civil Rights Act.

The Equal Employment Opportunity Commission was created by the Civil Rights Act of 1964 and its enforcement authority was greatly expanded by the Equal Employment Opportunity Act of 1972. The EEOC is empowered to investigate and act on a charge of a pattern or practice of discrimination, whether filed by or on behalf of a person claiming to be aggrieved or by a member of the commission. The commission has the right to initiate civil suits against employers, labor unions, or any group accused of practicing employment discrimination. Private individuals also have the right to sue under Title VII of the Civil Rights Act of 1964. In addition, the commission can investigate company records to see whether there is a pattern of discrimination and to subpoena company records if necessary. Every employer, labor union, or organization subject to the Civil Rights Act and the executive orders must keep records enabling the determination of whether unlawful practices have been committed and must furnish to the commission a detailed description of the manner in which persons are selected to participate in job training programs. Employers and labor unions have to keep posted in conspicuous places on their premises notices approved by the commission setting forth excerpts from or summaries of the pertinent provisions of the Civil Rights Act and information pertinent to the filing of a complaint.

Title VII of the Civil Rights Act of 1964 as amended by the Equal Employment Opportunity Act of 1972 allows a person who thinks that he or she has been discriminated against to file a complaint, called a charge, with the EEOC. The charge has to be filed within 180 days after the alleged discriminatory practice has taken place. The EEOC defers to a state or local agency when such an agency exists. After deferring for the required period of time, or when the state or local agency completes its process, the EEOC assumes jurisdiction of the charge and notifies the employer or labor union accused of discrimination. Because there has been a backlog of approximately sixty thousand charges, it can be a long time before the EEOC begins investigating the charge. The burden of proving no discrimination is on the employer or union. This can be time consuming and costly, as records and witnesses have to be provided. If the EEOC decides that the charge of discrimination is accurate, it can require that corrective measures be taken.

Legal remedies under the Civil Rights Act and related presidential executive orders range from cease-and-desist orders through individual reinstatement and group preferential hiring to the cutting off of all federal contracts to the offending employer. Lawsuits also may be filed under the provisions of the Equal Employment Opportunity Act of 1972. The federal government's most effective means of enforcing compliance with affirmative action goals is the money it spends. One way or another, most business firms derive some part of their revenue from government spending, and the loss of a contract means a loss of revenue. The latter is a virtual sentence of death to a research firm or a university, for they depend on federal money to maintain their competitive standing. Of course, employers also want to avoid lawsuits of the type that led to A.T.& T.'s $75 million settlement in 1973 on employees who had charged that discrimination had deprived them of past promotion and raises. The impact of this lawsuit on all firms, and, for that matter, on unions, has been enormous.

Application of Affirmative Action

From the Civil Rights Act and the executive orders has come the principle of disparate or unequal treatment. There is disparate treatment when members of a minority or sex group have been denied the same employment, promotion, transfer or membership opportunities as have been made available to other employees or applicants. These employees or applicants who have been denied equal treatment because of previous discriminatory practices of policies must at least be afforded the same opportunities as had existed for other employees or applicants during the period of discrimination. The result of the principle of disparate treatment can be a lawsuit like the one that led to A.T. & T.'s settlement. This case illustrates at least two points: first, it is no longer necessary to prove individual discrimination in order to obtain redress, and second, the principle of restitution can be quite costly if applied to a business firm. A.T. & T. had to pay restitution to its women and minority employees on the grounds that this was compensation for lost promotions or raises that they did not receive because of their sex or color.

The A.T. & T. Case

In 1970 the American Telephone and Telegraph Company asked the Federal Communications Commission for a 9 percent rate increase in long-distance telephone rates.[13] Lawyers from the Equal Employment Opportunity Commission persuaded the FCC not to act on the request until the company changed its policies with regard to women and minority employees, as the EEOC regarded these policies as constituting de facto discrimination. The commission took the position that discrimination had been institutionalized in the company's employment policy and moved to change it to provide more jobs at all levels for women and members of minority groups. In addition, the EEOC asked for restitution to compensate workers for past discrimination, according to the principle that payment must be made to certain females and minority group employees, even though they never had applied for better-paying jobs because they knew it was company policy not to give them those jobs.

The results of this case have had far-reaching implications for business. A.T. & T. agreed to promote 50,000 women and 6,600 minority group workers and also to hire 4,000 men to fill such jobs as operators and clerks, jobs traditionally held by females.[14] By 1974 A.T. & T. had also agreed to pay $75 million in compensation to groups that the government said had been victims of discrimination. Some 1,500 female college graduates who held managerial jobs between 1965 and 1971 but who were, according to the government, kept out of certain training programs received $850,000; 500 switchroom helpers at Michigan Bell got $500,000; and 3,000 women in craft jobs received up to $10,000 each.[15] These three groups were awarded back pay not because they had been discriminated against as individuals but because they may have been paid less than men doing equal or comparable work. The fourth group named in the ruling was the women who had been consigned to so-called female jobs and the minority group males employed in menial job categories. This group was so large that it was impossible to indemnify each person, and so the government decreed that the first 10,000 women and minority group males who transferred into craft jobs and held them successfully for six months would receive a lump-sum payment to compensate them for the delay in transferring.

A.T. & T. also agreed to use an elaborate system of goals and timetables to ensure fair representation in the employment of women and

13. See U.S. District Court, Eastern District of Pennsylvania, Civil Action No. 73-149, Consent Decree, 1973.
14. Diane Crothers, "The AT&T Settlement," *Women's Rights Law Reporter*, 1 (Summer 1973), 8-12.
15. Ibid., p. 13.

minority groups in the future. A planned utilization of female and minority groups had to be specified for fifteen affirmative action job classifications covering all of the Bell System's subsidiaries. For example, the Bell System's management development programs should have 25 percent or more females as trainees; otherwise there would be an underutilization of females. In a good-faith effort to meet these goals, each company in the Bell System is supposed to establish intermediate targets for one-, two-, and three-year time periods. At the end of each intermediate three-year time period, the goal for each job classification will be reevaluated to determine whether females and minorities still are underutilized. All goals and all intermediate targets and time frames for each company must be approved individually by the Office of Federal Contract Compliance. Implicit in these goals is the creation of quotas for females and minorities.

The Steel Industry

In April 1974 the Justice Department initiated a complaint against nine steel companies and the United Steelworkers Union on behalf of the Department of Labor and the EEOC.[16] The nine steel companies— Allegheny Ludlum, Armco, Bethlehem, Jones and Laughlin, National, Republic, U.S. Steel, Wheeling Pittsburgh, and Youngstown Sheet and Tube—and the United Steelworkers Union were accused of following a pattern of resistance to the equal employment opportunity provisions of the Civil Rights Act of 1964. The complaint also alleged that the continuation of these practices perpetuated the effects of past practices of discrimination in employment by the companies and the union on the basis of race, color, sex, and national origin. The complaint sought redress, including back pay, for workers who had been affected adversely by the acts and practices attributed to the companies and the union.

The agreement required the companies and the union to pay more than $30 million in back wages to compensate for past racial bias in job assignments. The proportion of the gross amount was to be distributed by each company on the basis of the relationship of the affected number of employees for each company to the total number of affected employees for all companies. The total back pay to females, blacks, and members of other minority groups was to be based on a comparison of pre-1968 wage standards. Average hourly wages of pre-1968 minority employees and nonminority employees of comparable years of plant service within each plant was one standard, and a comparison of the

16. See U.S. District Court, Northern District of Alabama, Civil Act No. 74–128, Consent Decree, April 12, 1974.

average hourly earnings of female employees and male employees of comparable years of plant service was a second standard. For example, if a female worker earned $1.75 an hour and a male worker earned $2.00 an hour at a comparable job, say for a two-year period, the back pay to the female would be the $.25 difference multiplied by the number of hours worked during the two-year period. The United Steelworkers Union was required to contribute to each steel company's payment of back pay to each affected employee, but the extent of the union's contribution was left as a matter to be determined by the union and each of the companies.

The agreement also contained other important provisions:[17]

1. The steel companies were required to try to hire one woman for every four men added to the production and maintenance payroll.

2. In selecting apprentices for craft positions, the firms and the union agreed to allocate two out of every four newly available jobs to minorities and women until they achieved a fair share of higher-paying positions. Although a fair share was not defined, one stated goal was to have women constitute 20 percent of the steel labor force.

3. Twenty-five percent of all employees selected for supervisory and management training positions were to be female, members of minority groups, or both.

4. Fifteen percent of all new jobs in clerical and technical positions were to go to minority group members.

5. In addition to establishing goals and timetables for minority and female representation in each occupational category, each company was required to prepare long-range affirmative action plans for the utilization of females and minorities.

There also are other important points in the agreement. First, it is the first industrywide agreement of this type and could well affect private industries' future personnel practices. Second, in return for signing, the steel firms and the union are entitled to a five-year moratorium on lawsuits filed under the Civil Rights Act seeking back pay for alleged discrimination. This also could set a precedent in future equal employment opportunity bargaining. Third, although the $30 million sum will be paid mainly by the companies, the United Steelworkers Union is also expected to put up part of it, which implies that the impact and cost of equal employment opportunity will be borne by the unions as well as business.

The courts have not gone as far as the federal administrative agencies in forcing numerical goals and timetables on employers. Numerical specifications typically have been invoked by the courts only when there has been demonstrable discrimination by the particular employer

17. U.S. District Court, Northern District of Alabama, Act No. 74-128, pp. 21-28.

in question, not simply when there have been "wrong" racial proportions. In this specific context, numerical goals can be used as a starting point in creating a solution for past discriminatory hiring practices by an employer to whom the court order applies. On the other hand, judging from the EEOC's statements, the only way a company, regardless of whether or not it has discriminated, can completely satisfy the commission is to see that its work force reflects the minority group distribution in the areas where its plants are located.[18] A member of the EEOC has stated that each plant should mirror the percentage of women and minority groups that make up the labor force in its locality. Thus, if a company locates in a city that is 40 percent black, it would be expected to have 40 percent black employees.[19] Discrimination would be inferred if the firm's work force contained a smaller percentage of blacks than resides in the area as a whole.

THE IMPACT OF AFFIRMATIVE ACTION POLICIES ON BUSINESS

As the above cases demonstrate, the impact of the federal government on business firms' personnel practices or, for that matter, on all employers, including educational institutions, is considerable. If equality of opportunity at all levels of business operations is the goal of the federal government, as the A.T. & T. case suggests, there will be repercussions for both business firms and unions. A business firm would have to reorganize according to certain overall criteria, such as the facts that individuals are unequal in many important respects and that a good organization is one that adapts itself to those inequalities to assure equality of result. There is also the issue of meritocracy, as represented by equality of opportunity, versus a communitarian ideal, as represented by equality of result.[20] In the A.T. & T. case the government's action was a direct threat to the contract, which previously had been the device used to resolve inequities in seniority and promotion policies. In fact, the whole system of seniority, so long prized by the unions, is under attack in the interest of achieving social goals.

Thus, federal law is increasing the cost of hiring, maintaining, and promoting the work force required for the private production of goods and services. The point is not that the law is in itself undesirable but

18. Gerald Rosen, "Industry's New Watchdog in Washington," *Dun's Review* (June 1974), 83.
19. Marsha Canfield, "U.S. Minority Hiring Guides Here Called Unfair," *St. Louis Globe-Democrat*, December 1, 1973.
20. John Rawls, *A Theory of Justice* (Cambridge, Mass.: Belknap Press, 1971); and George Lodge, *The New American Ideology* (New York: Knopf, 1975), pp. 279-284.

rather that it does have a significant hidden economic impact, particularly when carried to an extreme in the interest of some social goal. In a very real sense, federally mandated rules governing personnel practices can add to the employer's cost of labor, and this cost is then reflected in the selling price of the goods or services the firm provides or is shifted backward to the employee in the form of lower wages than would otherwise be the case. There is also the matter of employee productivity. For example, the deputy director of the Treasury Department's equal employment opportunity program outlined a ten-point strategy for identifying and correcting equal employment problems. The tenth point was "Refuse promotions or substantial wage increases to those who do not produce satisfactory equal employment opportunity results, no matter what other performance results they achieve."[21]

The Marginal Productivity Theory of Income Distribution

The most basic concept underlying income distribution in a market economy is the marginal productivity concept.[22] This concept can be applied to the distribution of both labor and property incomes. Accordingly, the income received by the owner of a productive resource is determined by supply and demand under competitive conditions, thus equaling the marginal contribution that the resource is able to make to the exchange value of goods and services. With respect to labor income, it is best for employers to hire the number of workers that makes their marginal revenue product equal to their wage. Marginal revenue product, to put it simply, is the revenue added to the total firm revenue by each additional unit of labor, which in turn determines the demand for labor. A firm will hire that number of persons at which the addition made to total revenue by a one-unit increment of labor equals the addition made to total cost by that same increment.

The marginal productivity concept is based on the law of diminishing returns, which holds that an increased amount of a resource applied to a fixed quantity of other resources will yield a diminished marginal product. Thus if employers were to hire so many workers that their marginal revenue product was not worth the wage that had to be paid, they would soon find that number to be excessive. The number of workers that any employer would want to take on is the number that

---

21. Inez S. Lee, "Current EEOC Regulations." (Speech to the Pennsylvania Bankers Association, Philadelphia, February 20-21, 1974), p. 12.
22. See John M. Hicks, *The Theory of Wages* (New York: Peter Smith, 1948), chap. 1.

maximizes profit, and that number is determined by the equality of wages to the marginal revenue of the last worker employed. Below this point an employer would be reducing revenue more than costs and so diminish profits, and above this point profit is not being maximized. Each unit of labor is worth to its employer what the last unit produces.

From the standpoint of the individual business firm, costs are the key determinant of the supply function. The most important cost element in the short run is marginal cost, defined as the cost of producing an additional unit of output. Since marginal cost represents costs associated with changes in output, it is apparent that the behavior of marginal costs is crucial to the understanding of the behavior of prices in response to changes in output. In the short run, with fixed plant capacity, marginal cost is the same thing as a change in variable costs, which are costs that vary directly with changes in output. The most important variable costs are the wages of labor and the cost of materials.

But the marginal productivity theory of income distribution can be debated. It assumes that there is a truly competitive market economy and that all units of an economic resource are basically alike and so may be interchanged in production and may contribute to the output of a number of goods and services with different exchange values. Actually, much of the labor market is characterized by imperfect rather than perfect competition. Thus, labor tends to be relatively immobile, and in some markets there may be one or a few firms, rather than several firms, buying labor inputs. Marginal productivity theory assumes that there is equality of bargaining power between the suppliers and demanders of any productive agent such as labor and that government does not interfere in the distributive process. The presence of unions and government interference in the form of minimum wage laws hinders the smoothly functioning market for labor envisioned in a competitive market situation, in which the price for all the factors of production, including labor, is determined exclusively by the market's supply and demand forces.

Given that the above assumptions may be flawed, it can be argued that there is no close correlation between the income received by resource owners and the value of marginal revenue products of the resources they provide. In a complicated market economy, it is inconceivable that marginal productivity analysis is sufficient in itself to explain the distribution of income. This does not, however, deny the validity of the concept. A business firm has to make some comparison between what a worker contributes to total output and what it costs to employ him or her. An employer will not pay more for a unit of input, regardless of whether it is labor, land, or capital, than it is worth to the firm. He or she will continue to acquire an input as long as each unit purchased adds more to total revenue than it adds to total cost; otherwise the opportunity for profit would not be maximized. In general, a firm's demand for labor is a derived demand based on the productivity of labor, the price of the final product, and the price of labor relative to the prices of other factors.

The marginal productivity principle can be illustrated roughly as follows: assume a minimum wage law requirement of $2.50 an hour for any worker employed in interstate commerce. If the value of a given worker in terms of contribution to firm revenue is more than the $2.50 an hour, the firm will benefit from hiring him or her; if the contribution to revenue is less than the $2.50, the worker should not be hired, for the firm would have to absorb the additional cost. To some extent, this may explain the high rate of unemployment among unskilled workers in the United States. Their contributions to total output and revenue are less than the prevailing minimum wage that would have to be paid to employ them. This may conflict with the idea of social justice in the distribution of income, though our observation of how a market economy does in fact distribute income does not constitute justification or approval of that distribution. Social justice is a normative rather than a positive concept, and its meaning may vary from time to time and from place to place according to a society's customs and beliefs.

Equality of Opportunity Versus Equality of Representation

In aligning the factors of production and allocating the product in a free enterprise market economy, there is implicit in the system an allocation of rewards or income. The innovative company that creates under patent or copyright new products or services that the public demands may, in the short run, realize windfall profits. The individual who learns the skills that are the most in demand will enjoy windfall earnings. On the other hand, the company that does not adapt its products to changing market demands or the individual worker with skills that have become obsolete because of the market's structure will suffer. In both cases, the company or the individual worker has the obligation to move with the times, when it is possible to do so, in order to avoid the penalties incurred from not doing so.

Because of the way a market system works, particularly under competitive conditions, it would be virtually impossible for any company or any individual to realize excessive earnings indefinitely. Even in the case of patented products, the success of one producer would promptly encourage imitation and reduce his or her profit potential to an industry norm. For workers with valuable skills—always excluding the artistic virtuoso in any field—the high income available would lead more people to acquire those skills and thereby reduce the rate of return to a level in keeping with the earnings enjoyed by others, whatever their field, with the same level of skills. The true market system is impersonal, and the race and the rewards go to the swiftest. The impersonal quality of a market system avoids the locking in of products or skills that have become obsolete and therefore nonproductive. Thus, the system has winners and losers, although it has been amended in many ways. Through subsidies and restraints on foreign competition, uneconomical production and job skills have been maintained by government intervention; for example, obsolete job skills have been preserved in the construction industry and elsewhere through federal and local building codes.

Equality of Opportunity

Equality of opportunity is linked to the whole concept of a competitive market economy and marginal productivity analysis. In a truly competitive situation no one buyer or seller is in a position to influence prices or output, and no unions or large firms are capable of circumventing the impersonal market forces of supply and demand. Implicit in the competitive market order is that workers will be rewarded on the basis of their contribution to total output. Provided that there is equality of opportunity, the reward structure is tied to individual output rather than to the precedence of birth, nepotism, patronage, or any other criterion that allocates place in society. Individuals are free to achieve what they can through their own abilities and efforts. This is the basis of the idea of a "just meritocracy,"[23] an ideal derived directly from the Enlightenment as expressed by Immanuel Kant, who codified the principle of individual merit as a categorical imperative. There is a libertarian element in the concept of equality of opportunity, in that everyone supposedly has a roughly equal chance to reach for the "brass ring" in life. Naturally, there will be winners and losers, but this is the inevitable end result in a libertarian society.

Mass education, at least in the United States, always has been held to be the key device through which equality of opportunity would be attained. It has been regarded as the balance wheel in the social machinery that provides the opportunity for everyone to compete for better jobs in society. Differences in status and in income are based on technical skills and higher education, and few high places are open to those without such qualifications. During the 1960s, the Kennedy and Johnson administrations, as a double consequence of the civil rights movement and of the emphasis on higher education as a gateway to a better place in society, made equality of opportunity the central theme of their social policy. This meant that there were many government pro-

23. Bell, "On Meritocracy and Equality," p. 27.

grams designed to remove the barriers of privilege, through legal action
to eliminate racial discrimination and social programs to remedy the
handicaps of the poor. The programs' emphasis was on compensatory
education, Head Start programs, job training to improve skills, school
integration, busing to abolish segregation in schools, open admissions,
and the like.[24]

There are certain conflicts in the concept of equality of opportunity,
for it is very difficult to create a societal situation in which there is
complete equality of opportunity. There is also the question of the relation of intelligence to genetic inheritance. Is intelligence largely inherited? If it is and if all persons are given an equal start and equality
of opportunity is fully realized, then heredity would be the decisive
factor. But it also can be argued that education is not the great social
equalizer that society imagines it to be. In a provocative study called
*Inequality: A Reassessment of the Effect of Family and Schooling in
America*, Christopher Jencks concludes that even if schools could be
reformed to assure that every person received an equally good education, adult society would hardly be more equal than it is now.[25] He
contends that economic success is not due primarily to the kind of
schooling a person has had, but "to luck, or to subtle, unmeasured
differences in personality and on-the-job competence."[26] One cannot
equalize luck and equality of opportunity. The fact remains, nevertheless, that on the job, particularly on the professional level, much talent
and hard work are required if one is to succeed. If a rough equality of
opportunity has allowed one person to go further than another, he or
she has earned the reward—income, status, authority—that goes with
that success.

Equality of Result

In its pristine form, equality of result says social justice should mean
equality, not necessarily at the start of a race, but certainly at its finish,
equality not of opportunity but of result.[27] To some extent, equality
of result is based on group rights rather than individualism, with its emphasis on achievement. Equality of result also involves the principle of
redress, meaning that the use of numerical goals or quotas is considered
a legitimate means to compensate for unjustified disadvantages in the

24. For the results, see James S. Coleman, "The Evaluation of Equality of Educa-
    tional Opportunity," in *On Equality of Educational Opportunity*, ed. Frederick
    Mosteller and Daniel P. Moynihan (New York: Random House, 1972).
25. Christopher Jencks, *Inequality: A Reassessment of the Effect of Family and
    Schooling in America* (New York: Basic Books, 1972), pp. 218-224.
26. Ibid., pp. 227-228.
27. Rawls, *A Theory of Justice*, p. 190.

society and to break a cycle of inequality, as well as to eliminate hiring practices that are seemingly neutral but actually discriminatory. As was pointed out earlier in the chapter, there are income disparities between the sexes and among races. This disparity is attributable in part to the fact that women and minorities are concentrated in the lower-paying occupational groups, whereas white males are dominant in the higher-paying occupational groups. Thus, equality of result or representation may have the effect of reducing the degree of income inequality between the sexes and among the races.

In *The New American Ideology*, George Lodge makes this point with respect to equality of result:

> Blacks, Chicanos and women are now to be employed as a matter of right, according to their numbers and presumed qualifications: that is, if there are a certain number of female college graduates in a corporation or in the community upon which the corporation draws for labor, for example, there must be a comparable representation of women in the corporate hierarchy. Thus what had been an individual opportunity right ten years ago has now become a communitarian principle. A "good" organization must have a specific representational profile. An entirely new definition of equality has developed: equality of result—in income, status, and power for everyone.[28]

In regard to the impact that equality of result will have on employers and unions, Lodge asserts:

> And so it is unjust, today, for a company to employ and promote solely on the basis of potential or ability. It must consider demographics, sexual identity, minority representation, and a host of other political and social factors as well. Equally, a union can no longer count on the traditional contractual notions of seniority. Instead, it must also consider a similar host of political or social factors as they bear upon the organization as a whole. How is a company to weigh all the factors? If it waits for government action, it will sail into a morass of retroactive punishment. How is a union to decide its priorities for pressuring management?[29]

Implicit in the concept of equality of result is a distrust of merit as a basis for reward. Merit may be linked to too many factors that cannot be modified by equality of opportunity—luck, position at birth, and so forth.[30] Therefore, the rules of the game should be changed to reduce

28. George C. Lodge, *The New American Ideology* (New York: Knopf, 1975), p. 178.
29. Ibid., p. 179.
30. Jencks, *Inequality: A Reassessment of the Effect of Family and Schooling in America*, p. 47.

the rewards of competitive success and the costs of failure. Equality always has been taken for granted as a part of the American economic and social rubric. As Thomas Jefferson said, "We hold these truths to be self-evident: that all men are created equal." This statement, when taken out of context, appears patently ridiculous. But Jefferson added to it, "There is a natural aristocracy among men. The grounds of this are virtue and talents. . . . There is also an artificial aristocracy, founded on wealth and birth, without either virtue or talents . . . the natural aristocracy I consider as the most precious gift of nature."[31] To Jefferson, equality meant giving each person an equal opportunity, before the law and under God, on the basis of individual merit.[32]

Among other things, egalitarianism demands equality of result based on ascriptive principles, that is, factors over which the individual has no control, such as race, sex, and so on. This, of course, is diametrically opposed to what Jefferson had in mind. The aristocracy that existed in England was based on the ascriptive principle of lineage. One's economic and social position in England depended on the social class into which he or she was born. But in the United States the reverse was true. Equality came to mean the opportunity to advance regardless of one's origins; no formal barriers or prescribed positions stood in one's way. Discrimination based on race was a barrier; hence, the attack on discrimination consisted of breaking down the ascriptive barrier of race, the denial of opportunity based on a group attribute. But the reverse now holds, namely, that one's place in life must be based on some ascriptive characteristic—sex, race, national origin, and so forth.[33] A person is to be given preference on the basis of membership in a particular group. However, when preference is given on this basis, the inescapable conclusion is that certain groups are less qualified and cannot compete with others, even if given an equal start.

Affirmative Action and the Reagan Administration

Changes in affirmative action policies can be expected from the Reagan administration. It plans to modify the Carter-initiated consent decree under which blacks and Hispanics would be guaranteed federal jobs in proportion to the number of each group being tested for the jobs. Reagan's transition team studying the Equal Employment Opportunity Commission recommended the elimination of quota schemes. Elsewhere

31. Thomas Jefferson, *Notes on the State of Virginia*, ed. Thomas Abernethy (New York: Harper & Row, Pub., 1964), pp. 1–10.
32. Jefferson himself was one of the most versatile and talented individuals that America has ever produced.
33. Bell, *The Cultural Contradictions of Capitalism*, p. 234.

within the executive branch, noticeably at the Office for Civil Rights and the Office of Federal Contract Compliance, the past emphasis on affirmative action goals will probably be either reduced or eliminated. Many people both inside and outside the administration feel that affirmative action goals, quotas, or guidelines just call attention to race, sex, ethnicity, or other ascriptive characteristics, and in the consideration of an individual's qualifications for a job, they make important, if not decisive, the very qualities that the Civil Rights Act said should not matter at all. Indeed, they violate the very principle of nondiscrimination that that legislation was widely understood to have embodied. There is also evidence that goals or quotas have not helped much to increase minority groups' incomes.

The Reagan administration is concentrating on an expanding economy, with tax cuts designed to stimulate business and individual investment. The purpose of the cuts is to increase wealth, rather than to redistribute it. The administration has endorsed the concept of "enterprise zones" in blighted rural and urban areas, with tax incentives providing the stimulus for business investment. It also has cut social programs and has turned to the private sector to create jobs for minorities. But if the economy does not expand in response to the tax stimulus, minorities may legitimately be concerned. Too, it is also the responsibility of business to provide true equality of opportunity for minorities, something it has not done in the past. Failure to do so would be a good way to invite government intervention or social disorder of the type that troubled Great Britain in the summer of 1981.

RECRUITMENT AND SELECTION OF EMPLOYEES

Affirmative action is only a part of equal employment opportunity. Employers also are affected by laws concerning the recruitment and testing of employees. In the area of advertising for workers, it is unlawful for an employer to print or publish an advertisement relating to employment that expresses a preference based on sex, except where sex is a necessary qualification for employment. Somewhat similar requirements have been applied to application forms with respect to race, though it quickly became apparent that if there were no records concerning race, there would be insufficient statistical data on which to prove discrimination or the lack of it. Thus, the EEOC has had to grapple with the fact that the logical time and place to gather certain significant information about a person's qualifications is also the very time when there is the greatest likelihood of discrimination in recruitment and hiring at the preemployment stage. Nevertheless, most of the data that employers requested routinely in the past are now either scrutinized by the EEOC or are denied as permissible questions.

Testing

Certain personnel problems confronting business are quite subtle. The entire area of testing is an excellent example of how genuine efforts at compliance with civil rights laws can still be construed as noncompliance. The courts have held that inquiries into a prospective employee's criminal record would be racially discriminatory unless the inquiry and the answer it was designed to elicit were somehow directly related to the total assessment of the employee. The same is true of all other types of preemployment testing and standards, such as aptitude tests, IQ tests, and educational achievements. It does not matter that there was no intent to discriminate. If the effect is discriminatory, it will be disallowed.

Griggs v. Duke Power

In the landmark Griggs case the plaintiffs attacked the use of the Wonderlic and Bennett tests.[34] The company justified the use of the tests on the basis of increasing business complexity. In the lower court case, it was held that a test developed by professional psychologists need not have a demonstrable relationship between testing and job performance so long as there was no intent to discriminate and there was a genuine business purpose for the test. Finding no intent to discriminate, the court relied on the employer's contention of genuine business purpose. But the Supreme Court reversed the decision on the grounds that there was no satisfactory relationship between the tests and job performance and concluded that if there was no such relationship, then the tests were discriminatory if their effects were discriminatory, regardless of their intent. The Supreme Court included the company's past record of racial discrimination as a reason why it could not use tests that eliminated more black job applicants than white job applicants, tests that had no demonstrated relationship to actual job performance. The decision is particularly noteworthy in view of the findings by the Educational Testing Service, that carefully administered preemployment tests can fairly gauge the ability of prospective employees. These findings came from a six-year study conducted in cooperation with the Civil Service Commission. The study concluded that persons who do poorly on job-related tests, regardless of race, do not do well at work either.

Under the general guidelines of Griggs v. Duke Power, no question that does not have a clear business necessity may be asked either in a preemployment application or of a prospective applicant. It is also forbidden to ask questions that are not related to the job, even without discriminatory intent, when the inquiry might enable discrimination on

34. Griggs v. Duke Power Co., 401 U.S. 424 (1971).

the basis of race, color, sex, age, or national origin. Thus, questions dealing with infant children, number of dependent children, willingness to relocate, and whether or not one is now or plans to become pregnant can get an employer into trouble. Employers also are required to prove that hiring, promotion, or assignment criteria for jobs are job-related. Physical requirements are no exception. If physical strength is required for the performance of a job, all prospective employees must be given an opportunity to prove they have this capability. Educational requirements also are governed by the Griggs case. For example, educational requirements such as the possession of a business or technical degree may discriminate against women or blacks. It is incumbent on the employer to demonstrate the necessity of the requirement, that is, that persons possessing this type of degree are more successful than others in the performance of the job for which it is required.

STATE FAIR EMPLOYMENT LAWS

Federal laws pertaining to employment practices are not the only laws that affect business; there also are state laws. In fact, federal laws are often designed to stimulate activity by the states under their existing laws. The Civil Rights Act of 1964 directs the EEOC to defer to the states for a reasonable time when there is a charge of discrimination. A number of local governments also have antidiscrimination laws. Both state and local laws vary in their impact and enforcement. Most state laws provide for an administrative hearing and the judicial enforcement of orders of an administrative agency or official and carry penalties for violating the laws. Some states do not provide for any type of administrative agency or judicial enforcement of orders but do make discrimination in employment a misdemeanor. Other states have voluntary statutes and no enforcement provisions. State laws are applied to all employers, unions, and employment agencies located within a state without being restricted to those engaged solely in intrastate operations. This application of the state laws to interstate employees has been upheld by the Supreme Court.

State laws vary in their coverage but generally prohibit discrimination on the basis of race, sex, color, and religion, unless this is a necessary occupational requirement.[35] Some states forbid job discrimination based on age, and sex discrimination laws may collide with other state laws prohibiting the employment of women in certain types of work and regulating the hours of work. For example, an employer may reject a qualified applicant for a job that requires overtime solely because a

35. Bureau of National Affairs, *Key Provisions in State Fair Employment Practice Laws*, No. 274, 1975.

state law says that women may not work more than eight hours a day in such jobs. However, the EEOC has ruled that protective laws conflict with Title VII of the Civil Rights Act. Apart from laws governing the employment practices of business firms, many states have separate equal-pay laws requiring equal pay for equal work by male and female employees. These laws are limited to eliminating discrimination in wage differentials and do not touch other forms of job discrimination. In addition to the equal pay laws, discrimination in compensation based on sex also is barred, either specifically or by implication, in states that include sex bias in their employment practice laws.

SUMMARY

In recent years the focus of government regulation has been on social goals. An example is regulation pertaining to the employment of women and members of minority groups. In 1964 the Civil Rights Act was passed, in order to prevent discrimination based on race, color, sex, religion, or national origin. Other acts also were passed to prevent discrimination based on age and to provide equal pay for equal work. Executive orders in 1965 and 1967 introduced the idea of affirmative action, which has come to be identified with the hiring and promotion of certain numbers of women and nonwhites. An affirmative action program now is required of all employers with federal contracts. Thus, even without any complaint of prior discrimination, an employer must analyze the composition of each department and compare it with the relevant available pool of women and designated minority groups. If the department's composition reveals a significant underutilization of the pool of women and minority groups, the employer is required to establish certain goals, usually expressed as statistical changes in the composition of the work force reflecting an increase in the percentage of female or minority employees.

The impact of affirmative action on an employer can be considerable, and noncompliance can lead to severe penalties, including the probable loss of federal contracts, on which many business firms and universities depend. Employers also want to avoid lawsuits that demand payment of restitution to employees who charge that discrimination has deprived them of past promotions and raises. But there also is the problem of paperwork. The sheer volume of resources required to gather and process data, formulate policies, make huge reports, and conduct interminable communications with a variety of federal officials is a large, direct, and unavoidable cost to any employer—whether or not the employer is guilty of anything and whether or not any legal sanction is ever imposed. The hiring has been changed by outside pressures so that it now generates much more paperwork as evidence of "good faith" hiring efforts and in general has become slower, more laborious, more costly, and less certain. It is not that it costs more to hire women or minorities but that it becomes more costly to hire anyone.

One important question raised by affirmative action is whether American society wants equality of opportunity or equality of result. The Civil Rights Act of 1964 was directed toward providing equality of opportunity for all persons, regardless of race, color, or creed. Equality of opportunity always has been based on merit, which means an individual is judged according to his or her qualifications—skills and other personal qualities. But in a society whose members come from a wide variety of backgrounds, some of which have been limited by past discrimination, achieving equality of opportunity can be elusive. Equality of result is very different, as it requires changing the results of a contest, in which equality of opportunity is supposed to give everyone the same position at the start. Equality of result is like a numbers game in which there is supposed to be representation at all levels of a firm on the basis of ascriptive differences—race, sex, national origin, and so forth. The issue of equality of opportunity or equality of result is important to the future pattern of American culture. What value does individual merit have in our culture, and what value do collective group rights have?

QUESTIONS FOR DISCUSSION

1. What is meant by affirmative action?
2. Explain some of the reasons for the differences in income between men and women and between whites and blacks.
3. Distinguish between equality of opportunity and equality of representation.
4. What are the functions of the Equal Employment Opportunity Commission?
5. Discuss the issues in the A.T. & T. case. Why are these issues important to business?
6. When is testing illegal as an employment practice?
7. Genuine equality of opportunity does not exist in American society. Do you agree?
8. Equality of result uses the principle of redress for past injustices. In your opinion, is this a good reason for the use of quotas?
9. What is meant by reverse discrimination?
10. Discuss the *Griggs* v. *Duke Power* case.
11. In what ways do affirmative action policies directly affect business?
12. Equality of result tends to circumvent the operation of the market mechanism. Discuss.

RECOMMENDED READINGS

Bell, Daniel. "On Meritocracy and Equality." *The Public Interest* (Fall 1972), 18–32.

Boyle, Barbara. "Equal Opportunity for Women Is Smart Business." *Harvard Business Review* (March–April), 111–116.

Church, Neil C., and John K. Shank. "Affirmative Action and Guilt-Edged Goals." *Harvard Business Review* (March–April 1976), 111–116.

Dorn, Edward. *Rules and Racial Equality.* New Haven, Conn.: Yale University Press, 1980.

Eastland, Terry. *Counting by Race, Equality from the Founding Fathers to Bakke and Weber.* New York: Basic Books, 1980.

Rawls, John. *A Theory of Social Justice.* Cambridge, Mass.: Belknap Press, 1971.

Sawyer, George C. *Business and Society: Managing Corporate Social Impact.* Boston: Houghton Mifflin, 1979.

Sowell, Thomas. *Affirmative Action Reconsidered.* Washington, D.C.: American Enterprise Institute for Public Policy Research, 1975.

Thurow, Lester C. *The Zero-Sum Society.* New York: Basic Books, 1980, chap. 7.

PART V
DIRECT REGULATION OF BUSINESS

Part V discusses industries that are affected with the public interest, meaning simply that they are too important to the public welfare to be allowed to function without regulation. Coupled with the public interest is a certain absence of competitive conditions in these industries, an example being the electric utility industry which provides a service necessary for society's well-being. Private property rules, which confer on individuals or groups the right and exclusive use and control of acquired economic goods, have been amended in the case of electric utilities and other industries affected with a public interest. These industries have become subject to regulation by regulatory commissions created at both the federal and state levels of government to set rates and prescribe services. These commissions also have judicial powers; that is, they are authorized to implement the law through judicial interpretation. Regulatory agencies, as agents of government, reflect group demands for positive action. Although they are not supposed to be arbiters like the courts, they can initiate policy in accordance with the law.

The regulation of business is economic rather than social, and direct rather than indirect. The current trend is toward less government regulation of business. Under the Carter administration, there was substantial price and service deregulation in the airline, natural gas, trucking, railroad, and banking industries, in order to encourage more competition. Communications may be the next deregulated industry, though the initiative will more likely come from Congress than from the Reagan administration. The Securities and Exchange Commission will probably continue streamlining and simplifying disclosure processes, which is bound to have an enormous impact on business's operating environment. This move toward deregulation reflects a shift in attitudes toward the role of government, a belief that regulation has hampered productivity and job creation and imposes costs that are ultimately absorbed by the consumers in the form of higher prices.

293

Chapter 12
The Regulated Industries

In an important minority of industries—transportation, communications, and electric and gas services—government intervenes actively and regulates business decisions more closely than in most private enterprises. These industries, classified under the general category of public utilities, provide all of us with services that are as essential to today's life-style as, perhaps, food or shelter. Yet, unlike the food or shelter industries, utilities are in a unique business category. From a legal standpoint, utilities are distinguished as a class of business affected with a deep public interest, which therefore makes them subject to regulation. What sets this segment of industry further apart is that in most areas it is considered desirable for a utility to operate as a controlled monopoly. As such, a utility is obligated to charge fair, nondiscriminatory rates and to render on demand satisfactory service to the public. The trade-off is that a utility generally is free from direct competition and is permitted, though not assured of, a fair return on its investment.

The logic behind this kind of operating environment is reasonably straightforward. Utilities operate most efficiently as monopolies, because they usually offer a single service or a quite limited number of services. A utility's operations are localized and limited by the necessary direct connection between the production plant and each piece of customer equipment. To a large degree, a utility plant can be used only for the service for which it is intended. There is concentration within a territory that permits the use of larger and more efficient equipment, hence a lower average expense per unit of output. Direct competition would be uneconomical because it would require duplicate investment and would clutter public property with distribution lines. This could lead to unnecessarily high rates or insufficient earnings, both unacceptable alternatives to the public and to the investor as well. There is some competition, but it is relatively diluted. Thus, a public utility operates under an exclusive franchise granted by a governmental unit.

CHARACTERISTICS OF A PUBLIC UTILITY

There is no set formula that can be used to distinguish a public utility from other business enterprises, no definition that will include all the businesses that have been classed as public utilities and at the same time exclude those that are not generally considered as such. The most general definition of a public utility is that it is a business enterprise affected with a public interest, although there are many companies affected with a public interest that cannot be classified as public utilities. The oil companies are one example. The list of enterprises that have been declared to be public utilities or affected with a public interest is quite extensive. It includes gas companies, electric companies, telephone and telegraph companies, radio and television, railroads, water carriers, pipe lines, air transportation companies, grain elevators, insurance companies, and stock yards. All these enterprises have been declared public utilities by a legislative body without subsequent contradiction by the courts.

The public utilities usually have certain economic and financial characteristics that separate them from other business enterprises. Generally, in order to be classified as a public utility an enterprise must produce commodities or render services of general importance to the public. Furthermore, public utilities usually, but not always, have the important economic characteristic of being natural monopolies. Fire insurance companies have been held to be public utilities, but they are not monopolies. A natural monopoly is a legal monopoly established by the federal or a state government, usually because there can be increasing economies of scale over a wide range of output so that one firm can supply the market more efficiently than several, or because unrestricted competition among firms in the industry is deemed socially undesirable. Such public utilities as telephone companies, gas companies, electric companies, and waterworks are natural monopolies. Of course, it would be possible to duplicate these companies and have two or more of each occupying the same area and competing against each other, but this sort of duplication is not considered economical.

Economic Characteristics

Regulated industries such as public utilities have two economic characteristics. The first is that they generally are very capital intensive, as there is a very high ratio of fixed assets to total assets. A railroad has most of its assets concentrated in rolling stock, terminals, and warehouses; an electric company has most of its assets in power plants and transmission lines. These fixed assets lead to fixed costs that do not vary with output. Examples of these are rental payments, depreciation of plant and equipment, property taxes, wages and salaries of a skeleton staff that a firm would have to employ as long as it stayed in business—even if it produced nothing—and interest payments on debt. The last category is particularly important to a public utility, given the nature of its debt structure. Fixed costs are those costs that a firm would have to bear even if the plant were completely closed down for a period of time. A railroad, for example, has a tremendous investment in land, rolling stock, and repair shops. The expense of maintaining these properties continues regardless of the amount of traffic hauled by the railroad.

Because of certain technical factors, the expenses of many utility companies, particularly those in gas and electric power, decrease as the size of the plant increases. In most market areas the demand for electric power is insufficient to justify the construction of the optimum-sized production and distribution system. A firm considering building a new plant must decide on its size. A relatively small plant would have higher average costs than a larger plant would. For the firm, the average total costs usually drop over a certain range as the scale of operations is increased, then reach a minimum, and then increase when the scale of operations becomes too large. But since the total fixed cost remains the same regardless of output, the fixed costs are spread over more units of output, and consequently, each unit of output bears a smaller share of the fixed costs. Therefore, the average fixed cost curve is downward, sloping to the right throughout its entire length, and so firms with large fixed costs—railroads, for example, with their tremendous fixed costs for roadbeds and rolling stock—can substantially reduce their fixed costs per unit by producing larger outputs.

It is evident that firms operating very small plants are likely to be inefficient, that is, expensive to operate, in almost any line of production. The production unit is too small to take full advantage of the specialized labor and equipment. A good example of inefficient single-plant firms are very small farms. They have proved to be inefficient in comparison with larger farms because they are not large enough to use mechanized equipment efficiently. It would hardly pay a wheat farmer with a ten-acre plot to purchase the combine that the farmer with a thousand-acre plot could use. But it also is true that firms operating very large plants are likely as well to be inefficient in almost any line of production. The production unit simply becomes too large for the job to be done properly. We can conclude, therefore, that the average total costs for the single-plant firm fall as the plant size is increased, reach a minimum, and then begin to increase as the plant grows larger. This is shown in Table 12–1.

Decreasing-cost industries are those for which the demand curve (represented by demand price) lies to the left of the point at which the average total costs are the lowest—that is, in the example, at an output of three thousand units. This means that there is room for only one firm in this hypothetical industry. Under the existing conditions of demand, two or more firms would have such small outputs that their average total costs would be much higher than those of the single firm.

Table 12-1   Cost and Price Figures of a Decreasing-Cost Firm (dollars)

Output (units)	Total Fixed Costs	Total Variable Costs	Total Cost	Average Total Cost	Marginal Cost	Demand Price
0	1,000					
100	1,000	400	1,400	14.00	4.00	9.00
200	1,000	750	1,750	8.75	3.50	8.00
300	1,000	1,050	2,050	6.83	3.00	7.00
400	1,000	1,300	2,300	5.60	2.50	6.00
500	1,000	1,500	2,500	5.00	2.00	5.00
1,000	1,000	2,400	3,400	3.40	1.80	3.00
2,000	1,000	4,000	5,000	2.50	1.60	2.00
3,000	1,000	6,000	7,000	2.33	2.00	1.00
4,000	1,000	9,000	10,000	2.50	3.00	.80
5,000	1,000	13,000	14,000	2.80	4.00	.60

$$\text{Average total cost} = \frac{\text{Total cost}}{\text{Output}} = \frac{\$1,400}{100} = \$14.00$$

$$\text{Marginal cost} = \frac{\text{Increase in total cost}}{\text{Increase in output}} = \frac{\$1,400 - \$1,000}{100} = \$4$$

Hence, they would probably be eliminated in a competitive struggle, until only one firm remained. If, on the other hand, the demand price were larger than the average total cost at three thousand units, there would be room in the industry for a number of competing firms to operate at their lowest average total cost output.

Diagram 12-1 illustrates the points made above. A company considering building a new plant must decide on its size. A relatively small plant, as for example a_1, would have higher average total costs than would a larger plant, a_2. The optimum-sized plant would be a_5, which would produce an output of OL at an average cost per unit of OK. Past this point average total costs will increase. If the market is too small to justify a plant of this size, a smaller one should be constructed. If it is expected that fewer than OX units will be sold per time period, plant a_1 is perferable to plant a_2. If the expected output is OM, that output can be produced by plant a_2 at a lower average cost than by a plant of any other size.

Let us assume that the market is currently being served by a firm with a plant of the a_1 size. If demand is sufficient and a new company builds a plant of a_2 size, it will be able to undersell the first plant. This,

Diagram 12-1 Natural Monopolies and Economies of Scale

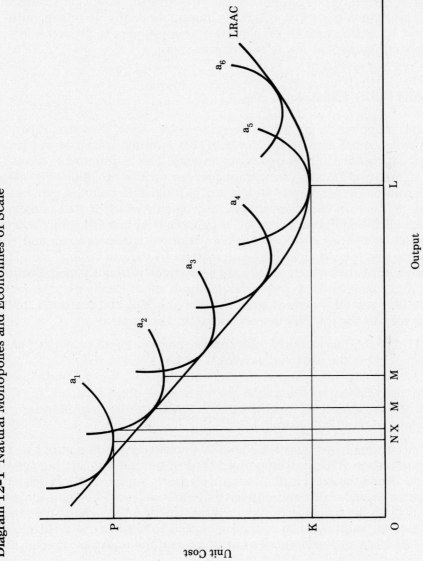

of course, requires a lengthy period in which changes in plant capacities are possible. At any price below OP, the first plant will be selling below cost, whereas the larger plant will be able to sell at a price somewhat below OP and enjoy a considerable profit. If competition is allowed to operate without restriction in this situation, either the first company will be forced out of business or the two companies will get together and agree on a price that will bring monopoly profits to one or both firms. In neither case will the interest of consumers be protected by allowing the market forces to compete freely.

Public Utility Financing

Utility financing is unique in several respects. First, the amount of capital required is much greater than that in other industries and is several times the annual operating revenue. This requirements stems from the need for capital expenditures for various programs. For electric utilities, expenditures are needed to build and maintain generation and distribution facilities to meet projected demand, as well as pollution control equipment. The latter expense is of increasing importance, for public utilities are subject to regulation with respect to air and water quality and related environmental matters by various federal, state, and local authorities, which usually are authorized to require modifications of utility facilities and operations. Second, an unusually high percentage of utility capital is derived from the sale of bonds and preferred stock. The reasons for this reliance on long-term financing are:

1. The relative stability of utility earnings, at least in the past, has made feasible the use of such sources without undue risk.

2. By using bonds and preferred stock whose interest and dividend rates are substantially less than the overall rate on investment, the return on the common stock of a public utility can be magnified to attract common stock capital.

Bonds normally account for about 50 percent of a public utility's capitalization. The most important type of bond is the first mortgage bond. Since the great bulk of a utility's assets are fixed, a mortgage permits the issuance of bonds against physical property. The first mortgage bond gives the owner, who is a creditor, the first lien against the property of the utility and, as such, can be sold to investors to yield a low rate of interest. But because of inflation and the uncertain market that have prevailed in the United States during most of this decade, interest rates on first mortgage bonds have increased precipitously. For example, a first mortgage bond that could have been sold to yield 3 percent on its par value fifteen years ago now would have to yield 8 percent or more. What this means is that the ratio of interest charges to operating revenue and to earnings before interest charges has increased. Interest is a fixed charge that has to be paid out of operating revenue. High interest rates and other increased costs, among other things, have increased the need for rate increases, which in many instances have been subject to regulatory delays and consumer protests.

Preferred stock also is used commonly in public utility financing, particularly by electric and gas utilities. Since preferred stock usually carries no voting rights, the danger of management's losing control of either a public utility operating company or a holding company is reduced to a minimum. Furthermore, the safety of preferred stock, since it has preference over common stock in payment of dividends and prior claim on assets in the event of liquidation, makes it attractive to many investors. Public utility preferred stock is often cumulative; that is, if dividends on preferred stock have not been paid in one year because funds were not available, these back dividends must be paid up before any dividends can be declared on the common stock. But the dividends on preferred stock come out of the public utility's net earnings, which can be burdensome. As a general condition for the issuance of preferred stock, a public utility's net earnings for at least one year must be a minimum of one and one-half times the annual interest requirement on outstanding debt obligations plus annual dividend requirements on preferred stock.

PUBLIC UTILITY REGULATION

Public utility regulation, as we know it, is the consequence of many years of experimentation and change. As mentioned in Chapter 4, American public utilities first were regulated at the state level. In the 1870s the agricultural states of the Middle West began to limit freight rates and curtail railroad rate discrimination in response to political pressures exercised by the Grange. The right of the states to regulate public utilities was made legitimate in 1877 when the United States Supreme Court, in the case of *Munn* v. *Illinois*, declared constitutional a law of the Illinois legislature that regulated the rates and practices of grain elevators. State public utility laws and advisory public utility commissions multiplied rapidly thereafter. But since most commerce was interstate, state legislation and regulation by themselves proved to be ineffective. So in 1887 the federal government created the Interstate Commerce Commission to prevent rate discrimination and various forms of monopoly agreements among railroads engaged in interstate commerce. Since that time regulation has continued to expand with the growth and technological advancements in the utility industry and the American economy.

There are five types of regulation to which public utilities have become subject: regulation by the courts, regulation by state legislatures, regulation by local government units, regulation by state commissions, and regulation by federal commissions. Before the creation of regulatory commissions and in the absence of statutory or legislative control, certain industries were subject to a semblance of regulation by the courts. Under common law they were required to give adequate service to all comers at reasonable rates and without discrimination. Individual grievances were handled by the courts. Then attempts were made to regulate public utilities directly through laws enacted by state legislatures. Rates and service conditions were fixed by law or by charter or franchise provisions. Legislatures, however, did not have the time or ability to handle the specialized problems that were constantly presented for attention. Furthermore, they were too close to the people and too mindful of political pressure from lobbies and the electorate to be able to maintain their objectivity. Today, only general legislation is enacted; administration is delegated to administrative commissions or to local governments as agents of the state. The latter may regulate their own local utilities within the powers granted to them by the state.

Of the several types of utility regulation, regulation by the state and federal commissions is by far the most important. In many cases a public utility is subject to both state and federal regulations. For example, the Southwestern Public Service Company is a utility primarily engaged in the generation, transmission, distribution, and sale of electric energy.[1] Over 99 percent of its operating revenues was derived from these services during fiscal year 1980. The territory served by Southwestern, which covers approximately 45,000 square miles, includes the Texas Panhandle, extends north into the Oklahoma Panhandle and the southern half of Morton County, Kansas, and drops south into Texas over most of the South Plains region, as well as the Pecos Valley region in southeastern New Mexico and a portion of east central New Mexico. Its electric properties are an interconnected system, and approximately 80 percent of the company's operating revenues come from operations in Texas.

Southwestern is subject to the jurisdiction of the New Mexico Public Service Commission, the Corporation Commission of Oklahoma, and the Kansas Corporation Commission for its rates and service and the issuance of some of its securities; and the New Mexico Public Service Commission is empowered to certify the construction of its facilities. The Federal Power Commission governs some of Southwestern's activities, including its rates for reselling electricity, and the FCC's uniform system of accounts is the basis for Southwestern's books. In Texas, the Utility Commission, created by the Public Utility Regulatory Act of

1. Southwestern Public Service, *Annual Report 1980.*

1975, directs Southwestern's books and accounts and its rates and services. However, Southwestern's rates and services in the incorporated cities and towns in which it operates in Texas will continue to be regulated by these municipalities unless a municipality elects to have the Utility Commission assume such jurisdiction. The Utility Act also establishes certain standards for the rates determined by the municipalities. Finally, the Securities and Exchange Commission governs the issuance of Southwestern's securities. The commission is authorized to require the filing of information concerning Southwestern's directors and officers, their remuneration, and the principal holders of Southwestern's securities.

Southwestern is subject to regulation of air and water quality and related environmental matters by various federal, state, and local authorities, which usually are empowered to require modifications of Southwestern's facilities and operations. The Texas Air Control Board and the New Mexico Environmental Improvement Board determine and enforce the permissible level of air contaminant emissions in their respective states. The Texas Water Quality Board and the New Mexico Water Quality Control Commission regulate water discharges and are required to set water quality standards and issue waste control orders covering water discharges that might affect the quality of their states' waters. Diversion of surface waters in Texas for cooling and other purposes is subject to the jurisdiction of the Texas Water Rights Commission, which is empowered to allocate such waters among users.

The Independent Regulatory Commissions

Congress has assigned much of the responsibility for implementing these laws to independent bodies known as regulatory agencies. With few exceptions, they are known as commissions. It is somewhat difficult to define a regulatory agency, because Congress has not distinguished the independent agencies from those in some executive departments. The regulation of stock exchanges, for example, has been delegated to an independent agency known as the Securities and Exchange Commission, whereas until recently the regulation of commodity exchanges had been under the jurisdiction of the executive branch of government. Similarly, the misrepresentation of articles, including drugs, is the concern of an independent agency, whereas the misleading labeling of food, drugs, and insecticides is the concern of an executive department.

In theory, these commissions were established by Congress to regulate and control the economy in accordance with Congress's will. The existence of such agencies is justified on the ground that the complexities of modern society demand regulation in order to avoid economic anarchy, monopoly, and irresponsibility. It has been argued, for example, that the advent of such phenomena as nuclear energy and jet aircraft calls for greater government surveillance in order to allocate these resources appropriately to meet the goals of modern society. From another perspective, the need for many regulatory agencies, such as the Interstate Commerce Commission, is often challenged on the grounds that such regulation hinders free enterprise and encourages waste. These agencies also are criticized because they are somewhat incompatible with the system of separation of powers. Their very existence represents a diffusion of executive power, which the constitution vests in the president. This separate existence, however, is justified because these bodies perform not only executive functions but also legislative and judicial ones.

Their legislative functions principally concern the promulgation of regulations. Within a general policy laid down by Congress, the regulatory agencies issue rules and regulations. Proposals are first published in the Federal Register, and the affected parties are invited to respond to the proposal. There are hearings and studies, usually within a sixty-day period, and a final decision is then made, subject to the president's approval. This the agencies make law, just as Congress makes law, and the rules and regulations they establish can often be changed or reversed only by an act of Congress. The agencies' judicial power may be seen in their power to enforce the laws laid down by Congress and their own regulations through the adjudicatory process. In carrying out the will of Congress to discourage monopolistic enterprises, for example, the Federal Trade Commission has broad powers that affect such activities as mergers between competing corporations. In many instances, conflicts between the regulatory agencies and the private sector are resolved in actual cases before administrative tribunals.

The term *independent* suggests that the president has only limited control over these agencies and no direct responsibility for their decisions or actions. A few such agencies are in the executive department, but most are not. In nearly every independent agency, the governing body contains several persons and is headed by a chairperson. To encourage their independence from both the president and a single political party, Congress has decreed overlapping terms of office so that no one president can pack an agency with his or her followers. This attempt to keep the agencies above politics is further strengthened by congressional limitations as to the number of commissioners who may be appointed from any one political party. In addition, the length of the terms tends to make even a president's own appointees somewhat independent; but despite this and their structural independence from the executive branch, the major regulatory agencies actually are open to a fair amount of executive influence. A member of the presidential staff may attempt directly to persuade a commissioner to adopt the president's position. Executive influence may also be asserted through the budgetary process. Agency requests for funds go through the Bureau of the Budget and as a result are subject to executive surveillance.

To a lesser extent, these regulatory agencies are also subject to Congress and the courts. Congress establishes their jurisdiction and defines their powers but has limited control over their budgets and their personnel and cannot interfere with the agencies' day-to-day operations or attempt to intervene in agency proceedings. Agencies that have been created by Congress can also be terminated by legislative action, though the threat of termination is not taken very seriously. Most of the legislative influence on agencies is the result of the agencies' dependence on Congress for financial support. For example, during the early 1920s, adverse congressional reaction to the Federal Trade Commission's investigation of the meat-packing industry led to a reduction in the funds available to that agency. Personnel had to be discharged; Congress transferred jurisdiction over meat packing to the Department of Agriculture; and the agency was denied appropriations for other investigations that it had planned. As a result of the legislative domination of funds needed by the agencies, agency personnel sometimes are oversolicitous of the opinions of individual legislators who are in a position to block bills that will fund the agency's operations.

The courts do not directly adjudicate the cases brought before the agencies. The cases that are decided by the agencies, however, may be appealed to the federal courts. giving the latter the power of judicial review of agency rulings. When an agency has acted in an adjudicative context, the courts can review its procedures to ensure that they are constitutionally valid, that the agency had proper jurisdiction, and that the statutory rules controlling the procedures have been observed. The courts may also review the agency's interpretation of the law, but they exercise substantial restraint in this area, and their powers are limited. Nevertheless, judicial review of agency actions is a valuable right for the business community to have. Review by the courts of agency decisions provides a safeguard against administrative excesses and the unfair or arbitrary action of overzealous officials. A court is most likely to set aside an agency ruling when an agency has erred in its interpretation of a statute, has acted outside the scope of its authority, or appears to have denied due process because of unfair agency procedures.

There are five federal commissions governing the interstate activities of the natural monopolies and the transportation industry: the Interstate Commerce Commission, Federal Energy Regulatory Commission, Federal Communications Commission, Securities and Exchange Commission, and Civil Aeronautics Board. Each regulates a specific industry —railroads, oil pipelines, television, and so forth. Their powers are broad, and they can make rules that have the force of law. For example, the Securities and Exchange Commission has established many rules designed to protect buyers of securities. One requires broker-dealers, who extend credit to customers buying on margin, to furnish information about credit charges. Both initial and periodic disclosures are necessary. As a result, Congress decided that it would be unnecessary to make the 1968 Truth-in-Lending Act applicable to loans made by brokers to customers buying securities on credit, because the SEC regulation already provided ample legal protection. The Civil Aeronautics Board passed a rule requiring specific sections of commercial aircraft to be designated as smoking areas. Smoking is limited to these areas. In both cases, these actions have the same legal effect as if taken by Congress. Both are the law of the land.

The functions of these commissions and the laws that created them were discussed in Chapters 3 and 4. Table 12-2 presents an encapsula-

Table 12-2 Major Federal Regulatory Commissions

Agency	Date Established	Number of Members	Term (years)	Jurisdiction
Interstate Commerce Commission	1887	11	7	Railroads, motor carriers, shipping by coastal and inland waters, oil pipelines, express companies, freight forwarders
Federal Energy Regulatory Commission*	1920	5	5	Electric power, natural gas and natural gas pipelines, water power sources
Securities and Exchange Commission	1934	5	5	Securities and financial markets, electric and gas utility holding companies
Federal Communications Commission	1934	7	7	Radio, television, telephone, telegraph cables
Civil Aeronautics Board†	1938	5	6	Airlines

*Formerly the Federal Power Commission
†To be phased out by 1985

tion of their basic characteristics. Each commission possesses a somewhat different rationale and mode of regulation. For example, the regulation of radio and television includes licensing and limited control over
service quality, but essentially no control over pricing. The regulation
of electric and gas companies, on the other hand, has considerable control over pricing. The Securities and Exchange Commission is responsible for the securities market. It regulates trading in securities on exchanges and in over-the-counter markets, in order to eliminate abuses,
and prosecutes companies and persons guilty of securities frauds, manip-
ulations, and other violations. But its control over securities pricing is
limited only to the commission rates charged for the purchase and sale
of securities.

State Regulatory Commissions

Federal regulatory commissions are responsible for regulating public
utilities and transportation in interstate commerce, and state commissions regulate intrastate activities. The individual state's authority to
regulate is derived from the state's police power—the authority to
legislate for the protection of the health, safety, morals, and general
welfare of its citizens. The courts have given the states extremely wide
latitude under these powers to regulate all kinds of business activities.
In a 1934 case (*Nebbia* v. *New York*), the Supreme Court asserted that
"a state is free to adopt whatever economic policy may reasonably be
deemed to promote the public welfare and to enforce that policy by
legislation adapted to its purpose."[2] Thus the right of federal and state
governments to regulate economic activity—particularly to set prices or
rates—is clearly established, although the Court recognizes that such
regulation cannot violate individual rights safeguarded by the Constitution and that the activities of all regulatory bodies must be subject to
judicial review. When the police power of the states conflicts with the
power of the federal government, the states must yield.

State regulatory commissions were created to deal with special problems as they have arisen. For example, the development of state regulation of electricity offers interesting parallels to the history of railroad
regulation. As such abuses increased, particularly in the form of high
rates, consumer dissatisfaction laid the groundwork for regulation. As
in the railroad industry, regulation came after the abuses had been dis-
closed and vested interests had become entrenched, and not as a means
of guiding the growth of the industry. As with the railroads, regulation
lagged behind the industry's developing geographic pattern. Statewide
power was not invoked effectively until long after the industry had

2. *Nebbia* v. *New York*, 291 U.S. 502 (1934).

transcended state boundaries. Eventually, state commissions were created to regulate the electric utilities. As in the railroad industry also, regulation remained for a long time negative in character, concerned with discovering and penalizing abuses and checking excessive rates. Again, as with the railroads, regulation has become more positive, concerned with reshaping corporate structures, planning the development of new sources of supply, and controlling and directing marketing policies.

The constitution and laws of each state define more or less specifically the powers and duties of the utility commissions, and consequently, there is great variation in the utility laws of the states and the responsibilities of their commissions. In most states the commissions have the power to regulate the rates charged by privately owned utilities, but the scope of jurisdiction is not the same for all states. In a few, the control is limited to fixing maximum rates only, leaving the companies free to set rates lower than the maximum fixed by the commission. In most states the commissions can regulate the rates that the municipalities pay to privately owned utilities for street lighting, lighting of public buildings, and other public services. They also may regulate the rates that the federal government pays to a privately owned utility. The state commissions' authority to regulate contracts between municipal utilities and ultimate consumers is the same as that governing the private utilities in those states in which the commissions have jurisdiction over the municipal utilities. The power to regulate special contracts between utilities is granted under the commission's authority to regulate rates. Interconnection contracts must be approved by the commissions in many states, though in others such contracts do not require commission approval.

Members of state public utility commissions are either appointed by the governor with the approval of the legislature or elected by direct popular vote. There are defects in both approaches. Often appointments are based on factors that are irrelevant to the qualifications necessary to become a competent public service commissioner. Favoritism and politics are often involved in appointments. To some extent the state commissioners' overlapping terms prevent the appointment of purely political appointees beholden to special interests. Elected officials are presumed to be more responsive to the public will, although this is not necessarily the case. A commissioner who is a good campaigner may not possess the requisites necessary to understand the complex nature of the public utility commissions. In many states, salaries are inadequate to attract and hold the types of persons needed on the commissions. Because a state commissioner has complicated and technical duties, it requires three or four years for the typical appointee or elected official to acquire the experience and information necessary to handle properly the responsibilities of the office.

The main concerns of the state commissions are the intrastate electric, gas, telephone, water, and transit facilities. Their functions are similar to those of the federal regulatory commissions. State commissions act primarily as a legislative agency when they fix rates. When exercising judicial or quasi-judicial functions, commissions sit as a court to hear evidence on both sides of a complaint. They must judge the merits of the arguments presented by their own staffs, representatives of the public, and the utilities. In rate hearings the commissioners find themselves in the conflicting position of being the legislative body whose duty it is to fix rates in the interests of consumers, while at the same time judging the adequacy of such rates to protect the rights of investors. Commissions also have administrative responsibilities, in that they must carry out the acts of the state legislatures pertaining to regulation. A large part of the time of state commissions and their technical staffs is devoted to such duties.

RATE MAKING

The bread-and-butter responsibility of the federal and state regulatory commissions is rate making, establishing prices for the services provided by regulated firms. Public utilities usually are natural monopolies, and their business thus virtually excludes competition. The monopolistic power of a utility would enable it to overcharge unless curbed by public authority. Since it is the natural inclination of monopolies, if left unregulated, to enrich themselves at the expense of their customers, it is essential that the public be provided protection with respect to rates charged and services provided. One of the underlying principles to be kept in mind is that public utilities, since they are deeply affected with a public interest, are not considered legitimate instruments for reaping excessive profits; they should be limited to a fair and reasonable return to the operators and investors. But what a fair and reasonable return is, is debatable. From the consumers' standpoint, no rate is reasonable that yields more than a normal return to the utility or that assesses the costs inequitably among various classes of consumers.

Development of Rate Making

The first efforts to regulate public utility rates were made by the state legislatures. In the case of *Munn* v. *Illinois* (1877), the Supreme Court ruled that rate regulation was a legislative matter not reviewable by the courts.[3] But it became evident that the rapidity of economic change

3. *Munn* v. *Illinois*, 94 U.S. 113 (1877).

required constant, day-to-day regulation, and the legislatures were in session for only a few months of the year, many for only a few weeks. Jurisdiction over rate regulation therefore passed to the courts. In several railroad rate cases the courts decided that the reasonableness of a rate was a matter for judicial investigation. The courts then redefined property as value rather than mere physical assets and extended the due process clause to protect this new concept of property. The courts forbade the confiscation of values and even went one step farther: they asserted their right to determine value, not only as a matter of law, but also as a matter of precedent. But how was fair value to be ascertained?

Smyth v. Ames, 1898

Along with *Munn* v. *Illinois*, *Smyth* v. *Ames* ranks as one of the two most important cases concerning public utility regulation.[4] In *Munn* v. *Illinois* the Supreme Court held that the legislative regulation of grain elevators and railroads did not violate the Fourteenth Amendment. In *Smyth* v. *Ames* the Supreme Court declared that the rate—or price— charged for the product or service of a public utility ought to be calculated to yield "a fair return on the fair value" of the utility's holdings. In the dicta of *Smyth* v. *Ames*, the Court enumerated several factors to be considered in arriving at fair value: original cost of property, less depreciation; the amount spent on current improvements; the amount and market value of a utility's bonds and stocks; reproduction cost of new property, less depreciation; the probable earning capacity of the property under particular rates prescribed by statute; and the sum required to meet operating expenses. But the two most important criteria suggested in *Smyth* v. *Ames* for the determination of fair value were original cost of property, less depreciation, and reproduction cost new, less depreciation. Which should be used? If both are used, should one be favored over another? The Supreme Court did not answer these questions, nor did it define a fair return.

Original Cost Less Depreciation   The original cost method of property valuation can be used as a rate base. This method, which is also called the prudent historical cost method, is easy to determine and administer. The regulatory commission takes from the accounting records of a given utility the figures of the actual money outlay for the original plant and subsequent equipment. After the original cost has been ascertained, the accrued depreciation of the properties from all causes, both physical and functional, must be determined. This accrued depreciation must be deducted from the original cost in order to establish the net cost or

4. *Smyth* v. *Ames*, 169 U.S. 466 (1898).

investment devoted to the public service. From the physical point of view, the property wears out or otherwise deteriorates so that eventually it must be retired from service. This physical decline in service value can be determined by tests and measurements or can be estimated reasonably. When a proper charge has been made for depreciation using the straight-line method and included in the operating expenses, the full original investment is conserved.

Reproduction Cost Less Depreciation The rate base also can de determined by the reproduction cost method: that is, a ten-year-old plant is given a value equal to the cost of replacing it at current prices less depreciation. The utilities generally have favored the reproduction cost method because of rising prices that have inflated the rate base, and the courts generally have favored it because to deny the public utilities the increase in property value owing to rising prices could be said to take property without due process of law. There are some problems with reproduction cost less depreciation. The hypothetical reproduction cost of a new plant that duplicates the old one is not valid even on a competitive basis, because a new plant, if actually built, would use more modern equipment, and the cost might be greater or less, but production would be more efficient. The use of the reproduction cost method when prices are falling would bankrupt many utilities. The service provided would be likely to deteriorate, and although the customers paid lower rates, they would receive less service. Finally, if the rate base determined by the reproduction cost method of valuation is revised by making changes in the price level, valuations become expensive, and the frequent changes in the rate base complicate the work of the regulatory commissions.

In *Smyth* v. *Ames*, as in subsequent decisions, the Supreme Court did not define a fair rate of return. Generally, the fairness of a rate of return on capital depends in large measure on the riskiness of the investment. The riskiness of investment in the public utility field, at least in the past, has been low—at least when the industry is a regulated public utility, because there is no close competition. Because of this, in the past a relatively low rate of return still would have made it possible for the utilities to attract capital as easily as more competitive fields where uncertainty is greater. But this has not been the case in recent years. Utility investors and officials are, of course, anxious to receive the highest possible rate of return on their investment. Administrative commissions and courts have no specific criteria to follow in determining a fair rate of return and most resort to largely arbitrary judgments that often are influenced by the amount of pressure brought to bear by special interest groups. The courts have asserted that no single rate is fair at all times and that regulation does not necessarily guarantee a fair rate of return to a utility. Thus it is still not very clear what a fair rate of return is.

Rates based on the fair return on fair value concept would be calculated by first determining the depreciated value of the physical property in accordance with the fair value rule. To this figure is applied a rate of return that would obtain a return to those who committed capital to the utility, whether bondholders or stockholders. Estimated operating expenses are added to the return, and the total is the amount that the rates should yield. Expressed as a formula:

$$R = E + (V - D)r$$

where:

R is the revenue to be obtained from the rates in question.
E is the operating expense.
V is the value of the physical property new.
D is the depreciation to be deducted.
r is the rate of return expressed as a percentage.

Hope Natural Gas, 1942

The Hope Natural Gas decision is important because in this case the Supreme Court departed from its past procedures in reviewing rates on the basis of a "fair return on the fair value" of property.[5] The Federal Power Commission ordered the Hope Natural Gas Company to reduce its wholesale rates by $3.6 million annually. The commission had valued the property of the company at $33 million after depreciation, on which it allowed a return of 6.5 percent. The company contended that it should be allowed a return of 8 percent on a reproduction cost rate base of $66 million. A lower court set aside the order of the Federal Power Commission because of its failure to give proper consideration to reproduction cost. The commission refused to include well drilling and other investment costs that totaled $17 million, because these investments had been charged to operating expenses as they were made. The net operating income of the company from interstate rates was $5.8 million. Consequently, the reduction required was something over 62 percent.

In ruling against the company, the Supreme Court did not take a stand in favor of any rate base. Rather, it felt that if the end result was a rate that enabled the company to operate successfully, to attract capital, and to compensate its investors for risks assumed, the rate was sufficiently high. The effect of the Hope decision was to absolve the public utility commissions from having to set rates that provided a fair

5. *Federal Power Commission* v. *Hope Natural Gas Co.*, 320 U.S. 591 (1944).

return on the present fair value of the utility property, as required by *Smyth* v. *Ames*. The Court upheld a valuation made substantially on the basis of original cost but stressed that it was not endorsing or requiring any particular method. It stated: "It is the result reached not the method employed which is controlling . . . It is not theory but the impact of the rate order which counts."[6] This decision means that the fairness of rates is to be judged primarily by their effects on the ability of a utility to furnish adequate service and provide needed capital. It also means that the Court will not review a commission's rate orders or allow a utility to obtain a review except under the most extraordinary circumstances.

The Hope case means that a "fair return on the fair value" of property will be used as a criterion for the reasonableness of rates, though the emphasis has shifted from the asset side of a utility's balance sheet to the liability side. Rate proceedings now tend to center more on the ability of rates to maintain the credit of the utility, to ensure fair treatment to its security holders, and to enable it to raise new capital. The rate of return ought to be sufficient to enable a utility to attract the financial capital needed for it to continue to operate. The return should cover interest and preferred stock dividend requirements with enough to spare to yield an attractive but not unnecessarily large return on the common stock. This places a burden on the public utility commissions, for current interest rates must be computed and future ones estimated. Earnings-price and yield-price ratios for the stock of comparable utilities must be computed and compared. A comparability of earnings standard may also be used in rate making. This standard means that the rate of return allowed a utility ought to be comparable to that prevailing in other industries with comparable risks.

Economic Principles of Rate Making

Monopoly is a market situation in which a single firm sells a product for which there are no close substitutes. There are no similar products whose price or sales will influence the monopolist's price or sales, and cross-elasticity of demand between the monopolist's product and other products will be either zero or small enough to be neglected by all firms in the economy. Indeed, the monopoly is the perfect industry from the producing point of view, and the market demand curve for the product is also the demand curve faced by the monopolist. Thus, the monopolist is able to exert some influence on price, output, and demand for the product. It is in a position to ascertain that point on the industry demand curve at which profits will be maximized. This has

6. Ibid.

important implications for resource allocation, because output restriction and higher prices are the end result. There is a possibility of
long-run profits under monopoly because there is little or no entry into
monopolized industries. When there are profits, consumers pay more
for products than is necessary to hold the resources for making those
products.

Diagram 12–2 represents the short-run marginal cost (MC) and the
marginal revenue (MR) curves for a regulated monopoly. If the monopoly is allowed to operate under monopoly market conditions and attempts to maximize profits, it will produce OM units of output and sell
them at a price of MP per unit. To maximize profits the monopoly will
produce at exactly the rate at which marginal cost and marginal revenue
are equal. Up to this point, marginal revenue exceeds marginal cost, and
it would continue to be profitable to produce any unit of output that

Diagram 12–2 Monopoly Price, "Fair" Price, and Socially Optimum
Price for a Public Utility

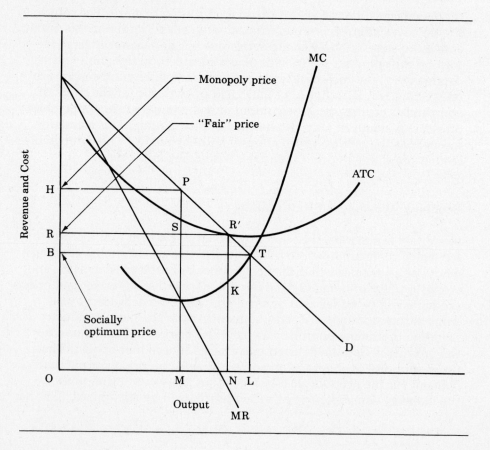

adds more to revenue than it adds to cost, in other words, any unit for which marginal revenue exceeds marginal cost. Beyond this rate, marginal cost exceeds marginal revenue, and it would be pointless to produce additional units of output. At the output OM and the price MP, the monopoly is making a profit per unit of PS and a total profit of HPSR. From an economic and social point of view the result is undesirable, because consumers get less and pay more than would be the case under pure competition. This is so because the price under pure competition tends to equal the marginal cost of production, whereas the price under monopoly exceeds the marginal cost.

A fair rate of return, as allowed by a public utility commission, can be represented by the point OR, since this is the rate at which price equals average total cost (ATC), assuming that average total cost includes a normal or fair rate of return on capital investment. In economic theory, competitive long-run cost is defined to include the opportunity cost of all factors employed—what they could earn in their best alternative employment. In the case of capital supplied to a public utility, this means that the rate of return should be comparable to that which could be earned in alternative investments. In Diagram 12–2, output under government regulation would be MN units greater than that which would exist in an unregulated monopoly situation, and the price would be lower by PS. Although the regulated price, NR', is equal to average total cost, it is greater than marginal cost. The price represents what can be called full cost or average cost pricing, the price at which the utility covers all its costs, both fixed and variable, and earns a normal profit.

The price OR is not the socially optimum price, however, for it is above marginal cost. Marginal cost at output ON is only NK. This indicates that output is still too low in terms of the ideal allocation of resources. This is true because marginal cost represents the amount of additional resources required to put an additional unit of service in the market; price represents the amount that consumers are willing to pay in order to secure the additional unit. As long as price is above marginal cost, more resources should be devoted to producing the service. The price OB illustrates marginal cost pricing, the price at which the utility's marginal cost equals its demand (D), or average revenue. Production is carried to the point at which marginal cost is equal to demand price and there are no customers to which the service is worth more than the additional cost of production. The marginal cost price is therefore the socially optimum price—the price that maximizes society's welfare—because at this price the value of the last unit to the marginal user is equivalent to the value of the resources used to produce that unit.

Under pure competition price equals marginal cost, and the optimum allocation of resources is achieved. But, under pure competition, price is also equal to average cost, and in the long run, firms neither make abnormal profits nor incur losses. Rate regulation for public utilities, therefore, poses a policy dilemma. If prices are set at average total cost levels (OR in the diagram), the output of the utility may be restricted below that which is most desirable socially for consumer sovereignty. But if the price is set at marginal cost levels, the utility company may be unable to cover average costs and thus suffer losses, or it may make monopoly profits. In the diagram, marginal cost pricing would cause the utility company to incur losses, since the price falls below the average cost. If, however, the demand curve were to intersect the marginal cost curve somewhere to the right of the lowest point on the average cost curve, marginal cost pricing would enable the utility to secure an above-normal return.

In actual practice, utility commissions have tried to keep prices at average cost levels, though this can create a problem. Since a utility is legally entitled to a fair return, in other words, a normal profit above costs, there is little incentive for it to cut costs. If, by improving efficiency and curtailing all unnecessary expenses, the utility is able to reduce average costs, the old rates will then provide a surplus above costs, and the utility will enjoy monopoly profits. The utility will be making more than a fair return, and the logic of regulation would require that rates be lowered. But in fact, rates are not adjusted frequently, thus an increase in efficiency may for a time increase the profits of the utility, and this may be sufficient to justify introducing a cost-reducing innovation. However, there are not the same incentives for cost cutting in a regulated monopoly that there are in a highly competitive industry, and sometimes the regulated industries are noticeably inefficient.

Alabama Public Service Commission and Rate Making

The procedure followed by the Alabama Public Service Commission for Alabama Power was to set rates at a level at which they would cover the costs of the utility and also attract enough investment to provide adequate services.[7] The Alabama Power Company prepared and presented its case to the commission using a twelve-month period, ending June 30, 1975, as the test period for the rate proceeding. The data submitted with respect to this period included the rate base, shown in Table 12-3, and operating income, shown in Table 12-4. The rate base is the actual monetary value of the physical assets and working capital of the Alabama Power Company as of June 30, 1975. Original cost less depre-

7. For a concise explanation of electrical utility rate making, see Angela Lancaster, "Electric Utility Rate Making," Economics Division, Library of Congress, March 26, 1976.

Table 12-3 Rate Base of the Alabama Power Company, 1975

	Dollars
Electric plant in service	1,878,683,274
Less accumulated provision for depreciation	461,893,232
Electric plant in service, depreciated	1,416,790,042
Construction work in progress	807,153,929
Electric plant acquisition adjustments	111,200
Electric plant held for future use	2,409,028
Nuclear fuel in process of fabrication	33,972,703
Unamortized leasehold improvements	740,772
Working capital	118,446,873
Less customer advances for construction	945,824
Total original cost, less depreciation	2,378,678,731
New investment to be added during next 12 months:	
Electric construction expenditures	551,316,000
Rate base—Entire electric equipment	2,929,994,731
Rate base applicable to retail electric service	2,718,514,551

Source: Reports of the Alabama Power Company filed with the Alabama Public Service Commission.

ciation was the accounting method used to evaluate the rate base. The commission accepted the statutory rate base at $2.7 billion.

Table 12-4 presents the operating revenue and expenses of the Alabama Power Company for the twelve-month period ending June 30, 1975. The rate of return on the rate base (Table 12-3) must cover all operating costs, depreciation, and taxes, while at the same time providing sufficient revenue to enable the company to meet its capital requirements. Operating revenues and expenses are allocated to retail service, for the Federal Power Commission has jurisdiction over the rates charged by the company for the sale of electric power at wholesale, such as sales to municipal and electric cooperative distribution systems. The operating revenue and expenses were examined by the Alabama Public Service Commission, and certain adjustments were made. For example, the commission disallowed certain advertising costs as an operating expense. The commission ruled that advertising expenses and charitable donations should be charged to the company's stockholders and not to its customers, and it disallowed advertising expenses of $1.5 million.[8]

8. State of Alabama, Alabama Public Service Commission, *Opinion*, Docket No. 17094, July 12, 1976.

Table 12-4 Operating Expenses and Revenues of the Alabama Power Company, 1975

	Dollars
Operating revenues	629,938,239
Operating expenses:	
Operation and maintenance expense	373,360,020
Depreciation expense	50,051,897
Amortization of electric plant acquisition adjust	10,109
Amortization of investment tax credit—credit	(897,567)
Taxes other than income taxes	37,981,825
Income taxes—federal	6,766,928
—state	573,011
Provision for deferred income taxes	41,911,083
Provision for deferred income taxes—credit	(2,674,580)
Provision for investment tax credits	1,762,480
Total operating expenses	508,850,206
Operating income	121,088,033
Portion of above applicable to retail service	
Operating revenues	582,955,010
Operating expenses	467,891,031
Operating income	115,063,979

For testing return on rate base, there is added to the computation above the allowance for funds used during construction account, separated to retail, the amount of $42,491,453.

Source: Reports of the Alabama Power Company filed with the Alabama Public Service Commission.

The rate proceeding centers on the adequacy of rates to maintain the credit of the utility and on the need to ensure fair treatment of its security holders and also to raise new capital. The main objective of the rate determination is to set a return that will cover interest and preferred dividend requirements, with enough to spare to yield an attractive but not necessarily a large return on the common stock. Present interest rates must be computed, and future ones estimated. Future capital needs of the utility must be determined, and future conditions of the capital market estimated. Earnings-price and yield-price ratios for the stock of comparable utilities must be computed and compared. But comparison with other utilities is only of limited value in determining reasonable returns for any one utility, since the relative proportions of capital coming from bonds, preferred stock, and common stock and the percentage of profits paid out as common dividends also affect the market valuation of utility stocks.

Earnings coverage measures the borrower's ability to pay the interest and dividends on its senior securities—bonds and preferred stock. The first mortgage indenture of the Alabama Power Company provides that new bonds cannot be issued unless the annual interest charges to which the company is obligated through its first mortgage bonds are covered at least twice by earnings available before income taxes. The company legally cannot issue additional senior securities until it meets the earnings coverage requirements contained in its indenture and charter. Similarly, the company's charter forbids new preferred stock to be issued unless the actual interest on all debts and dividends on preferred stock are covered at least one and one-half times through earnings available to the company before interest. Such coverage requirements are nearly universal contractual features of electric companies' bond and preferred stock issues. Alabama Power, as an integral part of a public utility holding company, the Southern Company, is under the jurisdiction of the Securities and Exchange Commission, according to the terms of the Public Utility Holding Compact Act of 1935, and is required to conform with the coverage requirements set forth in the act.

The maintenance of fixed charge coverage ratios is essential. An inferior fixed charge coverage is a signal that the return on common stock equity capital is too low, which in turn makes it virtually impossible to raise new equity capital without seriously diluting the equity interest of the current stockholders. A lack of compensation commensurate with the inherent risk associated with common stock ownership discourages the use of this course of financing. Of course, the Alabama Power Company cannot issue new common stock when its rate of earnings has fallen below the specified limits necessary to cover interest on bonds and dividends on preferred stock. The actual ratio of earnings to fixed charges for the calendar year 1974 was 1.62 to 1, below the minimum 2.0 to 1.[9] As was true of other utilities, increasing fuel costs and other costs attributable to a high rate of inflation in the national economy caused the company's earnings to fall, which led to the cancellation of a first mortgage bond sale in November 1974 and the cancellation of first mortgage and preferred stock sales planned for April 1975.

The final step is to compute the rate of return on the rate base, by determining the average total capital invested in net assets devoted to retail electric service. A cost of capital approach is used, which is a percentage figure determined by taking the weighted average of claimed

9. Alabama Power Company, *Direct Testimony and Exhibits*, vol. 1, *Testimony of Walter F. Johnsey*, p. 34, Alabama Public Service Commission, Docket No. 17094, 1976.

return on long-term debt—usually first mortgage bonds—preferred stock, and common stock equity. The cost of debt and the cost of preferred stock are calculated by computing the annual interest or dividend requirements necessary to attract purchasers of bonds or preferred stock. The return on common equity is estimated as the return required to attract additional capital in contemporary capital markets. The costs of the three forms of capital and the capital structure of the utility enable the weighted average calculation to be made, which determines the overall rate of return.

Table 12–5 gives the rate of return on the rate base for Alabama Power. Long-term debt, preferred stock, and common stock are assigned a retail value commensurate with the share of retail electric sales to total sales. The rates are comparable to similar rates, or cost of capital, for comparable utilities capital structures.

SUMMARY

Public utility enterprises are, to some degree, monopolies. For certain industries, operating as a monopoly rather than in open competition seems to be the most feasible way to produce and distribute a commodity or service. Economies of scale may make competition impractical and contrary to the efficient allocation of resources; hence the term *natural monopoly* is often applied to certain types of public utilities. It would be wasteful, particularly in regard to decreasing costs, for two or more firms to serve a given market when a single firm could provide the same service at a lower real cost. Competing electric power companies, for example, would result in unnecessary expense and duplication of services. It would also be wasteful to duplicate railway lines or even some air routes. What happens then is that a public utility usually operates under an exclusive franchise granted by a governmental unit. The utility thus becomes not only a natural monopoly but a legal monopoly as well; there can be no competition from another company for the life of the franchise.

Public utility enterprises are recognized by the courts as being affected with the public interest, as too important to be left exclusively to private enterprise to run as it sees fit. In return for the franchise privilege that allows a utility to provide a service to a particular area, the government establishes operating criteria that the utility must follow. It must render adequate service to all comers and charge reasonable rates. Regulatory agencies are given broad powers to establish prices charged and to control services provided. These agencies are usually referred to as independent regulatory commissions, and they exist at both the federal and state levels. They carry out legislative and judicial functions under a broad grant of power from Congress or from

Table 12-5 Capital Structure, Retail Capital, Cost Rates, and Retail Return Requirements of the Alabama Power Company

	Capital Structure (dollars)	Capitalization (percent)	Retail Capital (dollars)	Cost Rate (percent)	Retail Return Requirement (dollars)
Debt	1,144,748,460	57.47	1,049,728,333	7.75	81,276,446
Preferred Stock	235,860,920	11.84	216,077,189	7.85	16,962,059
Common Equity	611,291,723	30.69	560,017,307	13.10	73,754,279
Total	1,991,901,103	100.00	1,824,822,829	9.42	171,992,784
JDIC*	14,414,256		13,205,206	9.42	1,244,591
Total	2,006,315,959		1,838,028,035		173,237,375

The fair rate of return on the rate base $= \dfrac{\text{return requirement}}{\text{company rate base}} = \dfrac{\$173,237,375}{\$2,718,514,551} = 6.37$

*JDIC is job development investment credit.

Source: Alabama Public Service Commission, Docket No. 17094, vol. 2, p. 103.

a state legislature. Public utility enterprises doing a purely intrastate business are subject to control by the public service or public utility commissions of the states in which they operate. If facilities are used for both intrastate and interstate business, the estimated property and expense devoted to each is calculated. Utility companies engaging in interstate commerce are subject to one of the several federal regulatory commissions or agencies.

Part of the regulation of public utilities is to establish a fair market price for the commodity or service being sold. This market price must allow for an equitable rate of return on the investment of the regulated firm. Since capital is the most important input to a utility, the issue of how to determine its fair value has been a significant one in regulatory proceedings. In the Hope Natural Gas case the Supreme Court asserted that regulatory commissions are not bound to any special theory of valuation to determine the value of the utility's properties to be used to set rates. The original cost less depreciation method of property valuation is used by most commissions to establish the rate base. Once the base has been determined, a commission must decide what return to allow on it. Economic theory suggests that it should be a normal return, what the utility could earn on its capital in a competitive industry in long-run equilibrium.

QUESTIONS FOR DISCUSSION

1. What are some of the economic characteristics of public utilities?
2. Economies of scale accrue to firms operating under conditions of decreasing costs. Discuss.
3. Why are federal regulatory commissions called independent?
4. Discuss the functions of the five major federal regulatory commissions responsible for regulating natural monopolies and transportation.
5. Discuss the importance of the *Smyth* v. *Ames* case.
6. Which method of property valuation, original cost less depreciation or reproduction cost less depreciation, would a public utility prefer to use in a period of rising prices?
7. Distinguish between the concepts of monopoly price, fair price, and socially optimum price as applied to public utility rate making.
8. Distinguish between the concepts of average cost pricing and marginal cost pricing.

RECOMMENDED READINGS

Kahn, Alfred E. *The Economics of Regulation.* 2 vols. New York: John Wiley, 1970.

Lancaster, Angela. "Electric Utility Rate Making." Congressional Research Service, Library of Congress, March 26, 1976.

Phillips, Charles F., Jr. *The Economics of Regulation.* Homewood, Ill.: Richard D. Irwin, 1965.

Posner, Richard. "Theories of Economic Regulation." *Bell Journal of Economics,* 5 (Autumn 1974), 335-357.

Samuels, Warren J. "Regulation and Valuation." *Public Utilities Fortnightly,* 96 (1973), 35-48.

Stigler, George J. "The Theory of Economic Regulation." *Bell Journal of Economics,* 2 (Spring 1971), 3-15.

U.S., Congress, House, Committee on Interstate and Foreign Commerce, *A Short Primer on Rate Making and the Regulatory Process in the Electric Utility Industry: Report for the Energy and Power Subcommittee,* prepared by Douglas N. Jones, 94th Cong., 1st sess., March 18, 1976.

U.S., Congress, Senate, Committee on the Judiciary. *Civil Aeronautics Board Practices and Principles: Report of the Subcommittee on Administrative Practices and Procedure,* 94th Cong., 1st sess., 1976.

Chapter 13
Regulated Markets and Competition

Competition is regarded as a principal desideratum of a market economy. It is thought to maximize productivity, encourage research and development, improve the position of the small businessperson, prevent excessive concentration of economic power, provide for attainment of consumer interests, and eliminate arbitrary barriers to market entry. There is also an interrelationship between competition in a free enterprise market economy and a democratic political structure, in that competition is supposed to prevent the growth of excessively powerful economic units, regardless of whether they are business or labor. This preventive aspect of competition will, it is believed, help maintain basic democratic institutions. In the *Wealth of Nations*, Adam Smith writes that self-interest works not only in the interest of the individual but also in the social interest, that is, it promotes the ends of society as well as those of the individual as long as there is competition in the economic system. When pure competition exists, no one individual or firm can exercise economic control, for economic power comes from the ability to influence or control prices.

As we pointed out in the last chapter, competitive market structures sometimes can cause inefficient resource allocation and a socially undesirable market performance. This can happen when economies of scale are so extensive in relation to the size of the market that only one firm can operate efficiently within that market. It is not feasible to remedy this situation by means of structural modifications intended to create competitive conditions. Instead, direct regulation under the laws governing public utilities is used. Certain industries, including transportation, electricity, gas, telephone service, and the broadcast media, are exempted from the direct application of the antitrust laws on the theory that a regulatory agency protects the public interest and thus there is no rationale for what would be redundant intervention by antitrust enforcement agencies. But regulation differs greatly among the industries in which conditions of natural monopoly may exist, and public utility regulation often has been applied in cases in which a natural monopoly clearly does not exist.

CRITICISMS OF REGULATED MARKETS

Many are discontented with the current system of regulated markets and have called for less government regulation and more competition in the gas, electric, transportation, insurance, securities, and financial industries.[1] This discontent reflects the current general distrust of big government, and regulatory agencies are a part of the big government syndrome. Some critics of regulation feel that the regulatory agencies act more in the interest of the regulated firms than in the public interest. Regulated firms are seen as adapting to regulations in ways that thwart the public benefits intended by regulation. Regulatory agencies also are blamed for "bending with the wind," to change policies and take actions designed to curry favor whenever commissioners see political tides going in a particular direction. There also may be close ties between the agencies and industry because commissioners and others in the agencies frequently receive their appointments because they have worked in the industry and often tend to return to the industry after a period of government service.

But some critics of regulation assert that there is too much regulation by the commissions. The result, they say, is that the individual, the economy, and in fact society as a whole are stifled. Often commissions, which are supposed to be the experts, have made decisions that have hurt both the regulated business and the general public. For example, natural gas producers have been subject to interstate price regulation since 1954. Rate regulation prevented prices from rising in response to growing demand, thereby reducing the incentive to expand supply at the lower prices set to stimulate consumption. The effort to hold prices below a market-clearing level thus created a shortage of natural gas, which has imposed great costs on the economy. The ICC has been accused of following policies detrimental to the interest of the railroads. Even though it was clear in the 1930s that the nineteenth-century concept of the railroads as being responsible for offering complete transportation service to every locality along every mile of track had become obsolete, the ICC only recently and reluctantly allowed the railroads to abandon unprofitable passenger service. But when this policy was in effect, it forced the railroads to continue passenger service, often when it was losing them money, to the detriment of their competitive position.

There are other, more esoteric complaints about the regulatory agencies. In some agencies, the agency personnel not only make the rules and serve as the judges but also decide to bring an action. One

1. There is a useful summary of the reasons favoring regulation and regulatory reform in *The Economic Report of the President* (Washington, D.C.: U.S. Government Printing Office, 1975), chap. 5, pp. 147–159.

highly esteemed American political tradition is the separation of legislative, judicial, and executive power; this tradition would seem to be
violated when the decision to bring an action is not separated from its
adjudication. In other agencies, the commissioners, who make the
ultimate decisions in many cases, are removed from the actual fact
finding. Thus, the commissioners never really know what is going on
because they see only a summary report when they make their decisions. They act only on the basis of facts found by a trial or a hearing
examiner of some kind, but they do not hear the actual testimony.

Finally, critics have decried the effects of economic regulation on
the efficiency of the market economy. There has been a market breakdown in certain regulated industries, the drastic reduction in the quality
and quantity of rail service being one example. The American railroad
system has gained the reputation of being one of the most inefficient
and poorly run systems in the world. It is somewhat ironic that the
British and German railway systems, both of which are state owned and
operated, are more efficient than most of the privately owned railroads
in the United States. In addition, shortages of natural gas and impending shortages of electric power capacity have been widely attributed to
regulation. Governors from fourteen states facing natural gas shortages
accepted the deregulation of gas prices as a long-term solution, even
though then President Gerald Ford assured them that prices would rise
as a result. Their acceptance reflected their awareness that lower regulated prices with no product available are not a preferred solution to
any problem.

DEREGULATION OF AIR TRANSPORTATION

The main issue in the air transportation industry was whether competition or regulation would bring about more socially desirable results.
When commercial aviation in the United States began, there were fears
that ineffectively regulated competition would become cutthroat competition, to the detriment of both safety and the development of a
commercial fleet that might serve as a national defense transport reserve. Originally, it was Congress's intent to place the airline industry
under the jurisdiction of the Interstate Commerce Commission, but
they then decided that the ICC was too close to the railroads and too
judicial and regulatory in its approach to be able to provide the leadership necessary to promote a new means of transportation. In 1938 the
Civil Aeronautics Act was passed, which created the Civil Aeronautics
Board (CAB) and gave it regulatory authority over entry, routes, rates,
airmail payments, and subsidies of common carriers. It was also empowered to grant or withhold the certificates of convenience or necessity needed for operating specific routes, as well as to approve mergers
or pooling arrangements.

Since its inception the CAB has followed a general policy of fostering a mixture of competition and monopoly, mostly the latter. The competition was over service rather than price. As traffic grew on existing routes, the CAB approved applications from existing airlines to extend their routes and add new ones, thereby strengthening the weaker systems and permitting the duplication of service on major routes. The CAB was authorized to regulate domestic air fares and rates and to control entry into the air transportation industry. Its entry policy was restrictive with regard to the entrance of new airlines into the industry, but permissive with respect to entry by existing carriers into specific markets. Thus the regulatory policies of the CAB were somewhat analogous to those that would be followed by a cartel. A cartel is an agreement between legally independent enterprises that restrains competition. Except for self-imposed restraints on output, sales, or prices, the activities of the cartel members remain independent. Entry barriers are created and enforced by legal sanction; the market is divided formally among participants; and internal price competition is discouraged. As in an oligopoly, a cartel heeds other forms of competition. In the airline industry, this competition was primarily service—an excessive number of routes and product differentiation—elaborate cuisines, and attractive attendants.

The greatest criticism of the CAB's regulation of the air transportation industry was that it encouraged inefficient airline operation. In essence the CAB established the fares that could be charged in various markets, and then the airlines tended to compete away the profits they could make through changes in scheduling. The absence of any real form of price competition, coupled with higher than competitive rates, works to the disadvantage of many consumers of air travel. Many passengers would prefer to be able to select airlines on the basis of price as well as type of service. Moreover, comparisons of CAB-regulated airlines with less-regulated intrastate airlines indicated that the latter were generally more efficient and could provide transportation over similar routes at a lower cost. A case in point was the Texas intrastate market, in which Southwest Airlines, a carrier licensed by the Texas Aeronautics Commission, directly competed with Braniff Airways, a CAB-regulated trunk carrier, and Texas International Airways, a CAB-regulated local service carrier. Despite having its service introduction postponed for nearly four years because of judicial challenges by Braniff and Texas International, Southwest Airlines was eventually allowed to serve the so-called golden triangle of Dallas, San Antonio, and Houston, It made a profit, charging fares that ran as much as 50 percent below comparable CAB fares.[2]

2. Few frills are provided, and many flights are scheduled at off-hours.

The Airline Deregulation Act of 1978

This desire to deregulate air transportation and return it to a competitive market resulted in the passage of the Airline Deregulation Act of 1978.[3] One purpose of the act was to eliminate legal barriers to market entry, thus promoting competition. If profits are made in a competitive market, new firms will be attracted into the industry. These new firms will endeavor to obtain a share of the profits by providing the same goods at lower prices, improved goods at the same price, or a combination of the two. Furthermore, should the industry have the productive characteristics that allow a purely competitive market structure to be approximated, the marginal cost of output will eventually equal the price of each good, thereby yielding economic efficiency in production and exchange. Consumers are better served, since they can get the same goods at a lower price, but a firm loses when new firms enter and reduce profits through competition. However, the surviving firms benefit in the long run by earning a market rate of return equal to that which they would get if they were producing their next highest valued alternative product.

The Airline Deregulation Act of 1978 has the following provisions:

1. The Civil Aeronautics Board is to be eliminated by 1985, with economic regulation to be phased out by that time and other CAB functions to be transferred to other federal agencies.

2. The act allows domestic airlines to cut fares in single markets by as much as 50 percent in one year or to raise them by as much as 5 percent for 58 days in one year without CAB approval. If one route is served by two or three airlines, an airline can raise prices by as much as 5 percent for 110 days in one year without CAB approval. If a market is served by four or more airlines, a carrier is allowed to raise rates by as much as 10 percent in one year without CAB approval.

3. Rates must be filed with the CAB, which can hold them unlawful if they are unjustly discriminatory or predatory or represent undue preference.

4. The act allows airlines already in the business as of 1978 to enter one new market a year without CAB approval. In 1982 carriers will be able to add any number of routes.

5. An airline can drop a route on ninety days notice, provided one or more carriers are still serving the route. Any city that had air service before the act was passed is still entitled to a minimum level of service.

6. The deregulation was designed to make it easier for new firms to enter the air transportation industry.

---

3. Public Law 95–504. Another bill, passed in 1977, already provided for the deregulation of the airfreight business.

Results of Air Transportation Deregulation

The deregulation of air transportation may not prove to be the low fare bonanza for which air travelers have been waiting. Transportation costs were considerably higher in 1981 than they were in 1978, and inflation, especially in the cost of energy, was one of the main reasons for the higher air passenger fares. In 1979 there was a rapid increase in jet fuel prices, with a resultant squeeze on the airlines' profit margins. But in 1980 and 1981 many airlines again made profits, especially those that had regional routes. The airlines also have grounded inefficient planes and reduced their flight schedules. The larger carriers have proved to be less efficient, with Braniff and Pan American having particularly severe financial problems. Delta was the exception, making profits when other airlines were losing money. The airlines need to spur labor productivity, and those firms with the lowest cost structures will be the most success-ful. Nonunionized Delta, which controls its own work rules, has already demonstrated this.

The airline industry of the 1980s may turn out to be similar to the railroad industry during the latter part of the last century. Faced with heavy fixed costs and recurring recessions, the railroad industry struggled for survival. There were many bankruptcies or last-ditch mergers. So too, an increase in the number of airline mergers is likely. These mergers will come under the jurisdiction of the antitrust laws rather than the CAB, since the latter is to be phased out. At least in the past, mergers in the airline industry have involved financially weak or poorly run lines, and inefficiencies have been perpetuated. Labor pro-ductivity was not enhanced because usually the entire personnel of both airlines was retained. A merger of a strong airline with a weak air-line is more in keeping with the public interest, and it is conceivable that through bankruptcies and mergers, by the end of the current decade, the airline industry will be dominated by a half-dozen giant air carriers. Total profits may be up for the industry, but some individual airlines will undoubtedly find themselves losing out in the new environ-ment. Deregulation always poses economic losses for someone.

DEREGULATION OF NATURAL GAS

Natural gas is another example of special industry regulation in which competition and monopoly come into intricate interplay. To some ex-tent there is an interrelationship between the natural gas and the oil industries, in that some of the exploration for gas is conducted jointly with the search for crude oil, leading also to joint problems in defining and measuring the cost of exploration for gas. There are also common problems of production and distribution. The natural gas industry, however, differs from oil in that it resembles a public utility. Producers of natural gas search out and develop natural gas reserves and then contract with a pipeline company to deliver gas to them over some time period. Generally the pipeline companies purchase gas in the field, transport it to market and sell it, either to distribution companies for resale or directly to customers. Local distribution is a typical natural monopoly conducted under a public franchise, and facilities for gathering and transporting natural gas also tend to be monopolistic. At the same time, natural gas must compete with alternative energy sources, including oil. Thus the mixture of competition and monopoly in the natural gas industry complicates the establishment of a sound public policy.

The natural gas industry is divided into three broad categories: the field market, the pipelines, and the distribution markets. The field market is the market for gas at the wellhead, and it centers on contracts under which petroleum companies set aside reserves of natural gas to channel into pipelines. The pipeline companies take the gas from the field to wholesale industrial users or retail distributing companies. Generally, the pipeline companies, which link the field and distribution markets, do not act as common carriers. Rather, the distribution companies are usually local public utilities that sell gas to residential, commercial, and industrial customers. Ultimately, more than 45 percent of natural gas production goes to commercial and residential consumers, and the rest is used as energy or process material in industry.

Natural gas was regulated first at the state and local levels of government.[4] As the production and sale of gas was primarily intrastate, the problem of jurisdiction was not a barrier to state control. Markets were local, and gas had little or no commercial value. Eventually there were new industrial uses for natural gas, and through the construction of seamless pipes it became possible to transport gas over long distances. The demand for federal regulation of interstate movements of natural gas came initially from the states and cities, which found that their efforts to control rates were often thwarted by their lack of authority over companies transporting gas from other states or over the basic rates charged for such gas for local distribution. Only the federal government could reach into those interstate transactions, through which companies controlling a large proportion of the country's gas supply escaped regulation. In the absence of federal authority, no regulation was possible, and it was to fill this gap that the Natural Gas Act of 1938 was passed.

4. Robert B. Helms, *Natural Gas Regulation* (Washington, D.C.: American Enterprise Institute for Public Policy Research, 1974), pp. 17-28.

The Natural Gas Act, 1938

The Natural Gas Act gave the Federal Power Commission the same regulatory powers over natural gas in interstate commerce that it already had over interstate movements of electricity. The purpose of the act was to regulate both those companies transporting natural gas in interstate commerce and the sale of such gas for ultimate public consumption for domestic, commercial, industrial, or any other use. This was supposed to prevent the higher consumer prices that would be caused by a natural gas shortage. The act also gave the Federal Power Commission the authority, either on its own motion or on complaint, to determine just and reasonable rates for the transportation and sale of natural gas piped in interstate commerce. To determine the rate base, the FPC is authorized to investigate and ascertain the legitimate cost of the property of natural gas companies and the depreciation methods used in valuing such property. A natural gas company, on request, must give the FPC an inventory of its property and a statement of its original cost. Certificates of convenience and necessity have to be obtained from the commission for all new construction, operation, extensions, and acquisitions of facilities for transporting natural gas.

Phillips Petroleum v. *Wisconsin*, 1954

From the passage of the Natural Gas Act in 1938 until the Phillips decision in 1954, the FPC made no attempt to regulate the sales of natural gas by independent producers to interstate commerce. The Natural Gas Act stipulated that "the provisions of this act . . . shall not apply . . . to the production or gathering of natural gas," and this exemption led the FPC to deny that it had any jurisdiction over producer sales in the field. The Phillips Petroleum case widened the jurisdiction of the FPC over natural gas rates.[5] This case involved an independent producer of natural gas that did not operate interstate pipelines. When Phillips raised its prices for interstate gas, it was challenged by the state of Wisconsin on the grounds that the price increase had resulted in increased charges for consumers. In lower court testimony and briefs, it was argued that the natural gas industry, although regulated at the pipeline level by the FPC and at the retail level by the state regulatory commissions, was unregulated at the wellhead and, indeed, was controlled there by the large field producers. As a result, field price increases could be passed through as "costs" in pipeline wholesale prices and could thereby create higher consumer prices.

5. *Phillips Petroleum Company* v. *Wisconsin*, 347 U.S. 622, 1954.

The Supreme Court ruled that the FPC has a legal responsibility to regulate field market prices, on the grounds that the regulation of pipelines alone does not prevent higher field prices from being passed on to the consumer. Under the Natural Gas Act, it was clear that sales by an interstate pipeline company were under FPC jurisdiction. What was unresolved was whether or not the act governed sales of gas to an interstate pipeline made by a producer or gatherer. In the Phillips case, the Supreme Court decided that the FPC has jurisdiction over the rates of all wholesale sales of natural gas in interstate commerce, whether or not by a pipeline company and whether occurring before, during, or after transmission by an interstate pipeline company. Thus the wholesale prices of natural gas for resale in interstate commerce became subject to FPC regulation, both at the wellhead and at "the city gate"—the final consumer.

Rate Regulation at the Wellhead

In setting rates at the wellhead, the FPC originally tried placing price ceilings on natural gas.[6] The ceiling was based on an estimation of operating costs, allowed rate of return applied to the undepreciated original investment per unit of gas produced under a contract, and depreciation of investment. Then permissible maximums were set equal to the sum of these costs. Eventually this method was discontinued, for standard procedures of price regulation were difficult to apply. The usual standard for finding the proper rate of return—the standard being the average rate of return for public utilities—was difficult to apply to petroleum exploration and development companies. It was also difficult to divide joint costs between oil and gas. A fair return for each individual producer had to be determined, which increased the work of the FPC to the point that it did not have a work force large enough to act on the large volume of rate schedules submitted by producers. A backlog of individual rate cases ensued, and so it became necessary for the FPC to establish a new form of rate regulation, called area rate regulation.

The basic procedure in area rate regulation was to establish a maximum price for gas based on the average cost of production in each of the country's producing areas. The price was to be based on the average historical costs of gas within the area, and in fact, regional production costs, investment outlays, and rate of return averages all were calculated. Hearings were conducted to establish reasonable rates for each area, and price ceilings were set for each, which meant that the FPC had to consider in detail only those interstate contracts above the ceiling. Ceilings

6. The FPC is now a part of the Federal Energy Regulatory Commission (FERC).

were based on estimates of regional costs during a prior base period. It was felt that the best way to protect consumers was to keep current prices in line with past prices. The advantage of area rate regulation was that the FPC had to consider only those interstate contracts above the price ceilings set in each area. These price ceilings, however, were based on the price levels of the late 1950s, and throughout the 1960s the FPC refused to grant any increases in natural gas prices, thus producing a constant price level on new contracts for gas going into the interstate pipelines. This dampened producers' expectations and discouraged them from exploring for and developing natural gas.

In area rate proceedings, the FPC established a two-tiered set of price ceilings—a higher ceiling that applied to "new" gas taken from gas wells and a second, lower, ceiling that applied to "old" gas from gas wells and to all gas from oil wells. The rationale for setting a lower price ceiling for old gas committed to the interstate market was that it would transfer income from the producers to the consumers. In using this approach, the FPC assumed that the natural gas found in conjunction with oil and old gas-well gas cost less to produce than did new gas-well gas. If demand increased and consumers became willing to pay higher prices for gas, the price controls on old gas would prevent field producers from realizing a windfall profit. The FPC also assumed that the lower price for old gas-well gas and gas found in conjunction with oil would not discourage its production, for the supply of it was relatively fixed. On the other hand, higher prices for new gas-well gas would act as an incentive to encourage enough additional gas production to meet consumer demand.

Criticism of FPC Regulation

The main issue in the FPC regulation of natural gas was that rate regulation had prevented prices from rising in response to the growing demand and thereby had prevented producers from responding to this demand.[7] As a result, there was a shortage of natural gas. Since 1967 there had been a declining reserve inventory, a diversion of gas to the intrastate market, increasing curtailments of gas service, and greater use of higher-cost alternative energy sources. Too, the producers of natural gas needed more and more capital to conduct exploration. Apart from the normal cost of capital inflation, there are geological limits that producers have to consider. Since natural gas is a finite resource and the shallowest wells are largely depleted, exploratory probes now have to drill

7. Paul W. MacAvoy and Robert S. Pindyck, *Price Controls and the Natural Gas Shortage* (Washington, D.C.: American Enterprise Institute for Public Policy Research, 1975), pp. 15–16.

deeper into the ground to find new reserves. The biggest risk to a natural gas producer is that it might have to plug up a dry hole. Because the FPC's rate-making procedures did not compensate for drilling risks, gas producers began to commit newly developed reserves to the intrastate market, particularly in Texas where wellhead prices are not regulated by any state agency and are beyond the jurisdiction of the FPC.

Until 1971 the price of Texas intrastate gas was modeled after the interstate rate structure. But with the pace of drilling activity slowing, the developing supply shortage created a seller's market. In the ensuing years, the price of Texas gas increased rather dramatically. In July 1976 new long-term supply contracts called for deliveries at $2.00 per thousand cubic feet ($2.00/Mcf), ten times the going rate in 1971 and far above the interstate ceiling of $.52/Mcf for new gas. The large price disparity between FPC and intrastate price levels effectively excluded the interstate pipelines from competing for Texas reserves of gas. The end result of this interstate lockout meant that regions outside Texas, where much of the nation's gas is produced, were faced with critical gas shortages. This led to curtailments of deliveries by the interstate pipeline companies. Although curtailments fluctuated among particular pipeline companies, the nationwide imbalance between natural gas supply and natural gas demand steadily widened, and it was expected that this trend would not change in the foreseeable future.

Production shortages alone, however, do not accurately describe the gas shortage, because gas is purchased by and sold to pipeline companies before it is actually produced. Producer-pipeline contracts are generally long-term contracts covering the production and delivery of gas from the wellhead for twenty years or more. Gas delivered during a given year is supported by reserves committed in these long-term contracts, thus guaranteeing future supplies. Retail distributors and industrial consumers usually demand that the pipeline companies themselves guarantee a specific rate of delivery and demand reserve backing as security against default on promised deliveries by the pipelines. The inability of pipeline companies to acquire enough gas to meet contract delivery requirements in a given year indicates that there was a deficiency in support reserves before the original production contract was made. In 1974 pipeline curtailments across the United States resulted in an average of about 20 percent below the promised quantities of gas. The shortage of natural gas in the 1970s was prefaced by a deficiency in reserve commitments made in the early and middle 1960s to support future production.

Generally the regulation of prices at the wellhead resulted in lower gas prices to consumers, but it also created a production shortage. The ceilings imposed by the FPC came during a period of rising gas prices, even though it was the buyers who bid up the price of gas in order to obtain a fuel that was cheaper and more convenient than alternative fuels. Logically, price increases should raise production to a point that would clear the market. When there are regulatory price controls, however, the price increase may not be sufficient to clear the market. There is less incentive to explore for new sources of gas, and new discoveries fall short of the reserves demanded by the pipeline companies. The number of actual new field contract commitments falls short of the desired increases of reserve backing. Thus, the pipelines either limit their new delivery commitments to preserve reserve backing for old consumers or make new delivery commitments to draw down previously purchased reserves at a faster rate. Production from reserve commitments fails to meet expanding demand, particularly from industrial consumers, who then have to look for alternative energy sources. Because the 1976 national field price was less than 30 percent of the price of new crude oil on a heating value basis, producers would rather sell oil than gas—a preference that hardly consoles the pipelines.

The Federal Power Commission was in a quandry. On the one hand, the commission had a mandate to regulate field prices. But on the other hand, it was responsible for allocating ample fuel supplies for home and industry. But a principal rule of economics dictates that prices cannot be controlled by the government without sacrificing supply, a rule that frustrated the FPC's effort to satisfy both producer and consumer demand. The commission tried to find a middle ground by gradually raising the ceiling on wellhead prices to encourage new discoveries of natural gas. This created two kinds of problems. First was Congress. It was the original intent of Congress when it passed the Natural Gas Act to control natural gas prices in order to stimulate consumption. Although economic and natural gas reserve conditions had greatly changed in the nearly forty years since the act's passage, Congress had not seen fit to amend the law. Consumer groups, of course, opposed any move toward raising the ceiling on wellhead prices to encourage new gas discoveries and pressured Congress for more regulation of natural gas.

Since 1972, the FPC made several regulatory concessions in attempting to increase the flow of natural gas. In 1974 it established a nationwide price for newly produced gas at $.50/Mcf, with a yearly escalation of $.01/Mcf. The national price replaced the old policy of setting the rates according to the producing area. This uniform rate was far above the average rate for gas that prevailed under older existing contracts but was still well below the price of new crude oil. The field price for newly produced gas sold in Texas in 1974 was between $1.90/Mcf and $2.00/Mcf, compared with the controlled price of $.51/Mcf on the interstate market. The FPC also permitted optional pricing procedures, which allowed interstate pipelines to sign new, limited-term supply contracts at FPC-certified prices above the national ceiling if such agreements would serve the public welfare. Optional pricing, however, gave the producer the right to abandon service at the end of the contract term. Distressed interstate pipelines were allowed to negotiate sixty-day purchase agreements for surplus intrastate gas at free market prices. But none of these FPC policy changes effectively increased the flow of gas to the consumer.

In July 1976 the FPC nearly tripled, from $.52/Mcf to $1.44/Mcf, the price that producers can charge for new gas—supplies from fields discovered or committed to interstate markets after January 1, 1975. The purpose of the increase was to encourage exploration for more natural gas reserves. As an additional incentive, the FPC allowed producers to raise the price of new gas by another $.04 per Mcf each year. The FPC also raised the price of gas in production after January 1, 1973, from $.52/Mcf to $1.01/Mcf. Finally, gas in production prior to 1973 would be allowed to rise from $.295/Mcf to $.52/Mcf when current natural gas contracts expire. These price changes may result in significant amounts of new gas being introduced in the interstate market. In many cases, large reserves of natural gas are thought to exist, but producers will not drill for them because the price has been too low to justify the cost. The Anadarko Basin that runs through Kansas, Oklahoma, and part of Texas, for example, contains an estimated 20 trillion cubic feet of natural gas, which was as much as the total production of gas in the United States in 1975. Much of it lies 15,000 to 30,000 feet under ground, and at the $.52/Mcf price, producers have left it there.

The "Big Freeze" of 1977

The unusually severe winter of 1977 exacerbated the existing shortage of natural gas so much that many factories were closed in major industrial states such as Ohio and Pennsylvania, with a concomitant adverse effect on employment. The dependency of American industry and American homes on natural gas as a major energy source was illustrated graphically during the weather crisis. Transmission companies were faced with insufficient pipeline capacity: they could not fit enough gas into their systems to meet the burgeoning demand. As temperatures dropped, the meters at monitoring stations showed a lowering of pipeline pressure, indicating large surges in demand. At the same time, the gas reserves—stored in underground chambers of porous rock or played-out wells—were being drawn down to dangerously low levels. New supplies of natural gas are now a principal goal of government energy policy.

A major step toward eventual natural gas deregulation was taken when the Natural Gas Policy Act of 1978 was passed. The act had several objectives. The first was to set wellhead prices uniformly by depth without regard to market. Second, the Federal Energy Regulatory Commission was given jurisdiction over the intrastate sales of natural gas. Third, there was a phased decontrol of wellhead prices. The decontrol schedule of the act will allow the price of "new" natural gas to move up gradually to the equivalent of $15.00 for a barrel of oil (in 1978 dollars) by 1985, a level thought at the time to be more than adequate to permit a smooth transition to uncontrolled natural gas prices. Phased decontrol of wellhead prices would provide incentives to producers to explore for more supplies of natural gas. Congress also deregulated the price of natural gas taken from deep wells: specifically, production from any gas reservoir below fifteen thousand feet may command whatever the market will bear. Finally, when the contracts on old gas expire, the new price that can be charged depends on whether the sale is interstate or intrastate. Interstate contracts can rise to $.55/Mcf plus the rate of inflation since April 1977; intrastate contracts can rise to $1.00/Mcf plus the inflation rate since the same date.

There is, of course, a need to protect those directly concerned with deregulation from the transition to market-determined prices. The retail price of natural gas has always been set by state regulatory commissions, which divide customers into several categories—residential, industrial, and commercial—and make accordingly different rate schedules. Industrial users have always absorbed the bulk of natural gas price increases. Moreover, as mentioned above, the Federal Energy Regulatory Commission controls both the intrastate and the interstate sale of natural gas. The Natural Gas Policy Act provides a set of rules under which the interstate pipelines may pass along the more expensive natural gas to industrial consumers. This includes incremental pricing which means that interstate pipelines and gas utilities must pass the costs of selected high-cost gas to large industrial customers that use gas as a boiler fuel to generate steam or electricity. This pricing system will continue until fuel oil becomes competitive in price, at which time, price increases will be spread uniformly over all users of natural gas.

DEREGULATION OF THE RAILROAD AND TRUCKING INDUSTRIES

The air transportation and natural gas industries were not the only industries to be deregulated by the federal government. The trucking and railroad industries now operate under new legislative mandates stressing competition, and more changes can be expected. The Motor Carrier Act of 1980, which was signed into law by President Carter, pared back forty-five years of extensive federal regulation of the trucking industry. It makes it easier for new trucking companies to enter the business and for existing firms to expand their services, and it also gives companies more freedom to raise or lower freight rates without government inter-

vention. The act also gradually will limit the antitrust immunity that
enables competing truckers to agree on the prices they will charge. In
late 1980, the Interstate Commerce Commission adopted final rules re-
laxing much of its traditional trucking regulation; the new policies and
procedures carry out directives in the act as interpreted by the ICC.
One set of rules, which became effective in December 1980, eliminated
the "gateway restrictions" that required truckers to operate through
certain cities, often prohibiting them from using the most direct routes.
The rules also abolished the circuitous routing limitations often imposed in the past on one trucking company to protect the business of
another. Now, a trucker may use any available routing to serve authorized points.

Federal legislation enacted in 1976 gave the railroads increased rate
flexibility.[8] The railroads were permitted to increase or decrease their
rates by as much as 7 percent within a one-year period without seeking
ICC authority. This initial dose of deregulation, however, proved to be
inadequate, and so the Staggers Railroad Act of 1980 brought additional
changes to railroad regulation by giving the railroads significant new
pricing and operating flexibility. The act freed a major part of the rail
rates from ICC regulations altogether and established a zone of flexibility within which railroads can raise, without ICC involvement, the
rates that remain regulated. Railroads are permitted to raise rates by 6
percent per year up to an 18 percent total by 1984 and 4 percent per
year after that. If rates exceed that range, the burden of proof is on the
ICC to declare them excessive, unless a railroad has achieved market
dominance or the rate exceeds 160 percent in 1981 to 180 percent in
1984 of the average variable cost. In addition, the act curtails over time
collective rate-setting practices, authorizes contract rate agreements
with shippers, and eases other regulatory controls. The railroads have
been given significant freedom to alter rates to meet shifting market
conditions, and the rail users have been given some protection against
the abuse of this freedom.

But there has not been complete deregulation of the railroad and
trucking industries. The process is gradual, with a goal of promoting
competition while protecting users of the services against possible
abuses and the pain of withdrawal from regulated rates. The Reagan
administration, with its commitment to a free market philosophy, may
well accelerate the process of deregulation, despite calls for renewed
regulation in the trucking industry by the Teamsters Union and some
trucking firms, neither of which likes the idea of competition. The
Reagan administration may well opt for a smaller ICC whose members
are committed to a free market philosophy.[9] In 1981, the first full year

8. The Railroad Revitalization and Reform Act.
9. Although the ICC can have a maximum of eleven members, its membership as of
   May 1981 was six. President Reagan has no plans to increase the membership.

that the trucking and railroad industries have operated under the legislative mandates stressing competition, change is expected. The ICC plans to move to exempt major commodities from regulation and proposes to exempt from regulation the intermodal service provided when railroads carry trailers or containers on flat cars, the growing "piggyback" service area. How management in the railroad and trucking industries will adjust to deregulation remains to be seen. The railroads, in particular, have big bureaucracies with which to contend.

REGULATION OF ELECTRIC UTILITIES

Electric power companies probably approximate the common concept of natural monopoly as closely as any regulated industry does. Typically, the economies of large-scale production of electricity are so great that, within limits, the larger the plant is, the lower the average costs of production will be. Because returns increase as scale does, a power company using a small plant would not be able to compete with a power company using a larger plant. Electric power companies have very high fixed costs and relatively low variable costs. As a consequence, within very broad limits, the more power an electric utility company generates, the smaller will be the average cost of the service rendered. If four or five electric power companies served the same area, there would be an unnecessary duplication of expensive specialized capital equipment, and it is likely that no one firm would be able to use its facilities at the minimum-cost output. It is concluded, therefore, that in the nature of things, electric power companies must be monopolies; they are "natural" monopolies.

The electric utility industry is a relatively new industry. Though the electric light was invented a century ago, the real development of the industry is a phenomenon of this century. Originally, electric utility companies were almost exclusively local. Then, advances in technology made it possible for larger areas to be served more efficiently by the same operating companies. Entrepreneurs were quick to sense the advantage of consolidation and to capitalize on it. Promoters and banking groups advanced the process for the sake of financial gain. Thus consolidation moved forward in successive stages. At first, two or more local electric utilities would be purchased, and later, more companies would be acquired. Consolidation accelerated in the 1920s, and at the peak of consolidation, before it was reversed by public policy during the 1930s, fifty-seven electric utility systems accounted for 90 percent of the electricity generated by private companies in the United States.[10] The

10. Herman H. Trachsel, *Public Utility Regulation* (Homewood, Ill., Richard D. Irwin, 1947), pp. 394–397.

twelve largest utility systems accounted for half the country's total volume of electrical service.[11] Many of these systems, moreover, were subject to further overall integration and control through investment and financial corporations, banking affiliations, intersystem holdings, and other financial connections. Consequently, management was usually subordinated to financial control groups.

Reasons for Electric Utilities Regulation

The onset of regulation of the electric power industry parallels that in other types of regulated industries. As abuses multiplied, the public demanded some form of local regulation. At first, the responsibility for regulation was given to state commissions, but statewide power was not effective once the industry had transcended local boundaries, and national power was not authorized until after the electrical utilities had outgrown the states' jurisdictional bounds. The balance in regulation favored the electric power companies, for they had the economic power to circumvent the actions of the state commissions. Utility interests limited the scope and effectiveness of regulation by direct pressure on the state legislatures and by the appeals that were taken to the courts when the commissions' decisions on rates and property valuations went against them. Consumers were mollified, for there was a general downward trend in electric rates as costs were reduced through technical advances.

But after the stock market crash of 1929, the control over electrical utilities was increased, particularly at the federal level. The power of control groups was restricted and the interests of consumers and investors protected by the Public Utility Holding Company Act of 1935, which stringently regulated holding company activities. During the 1930s the publicly owned sector of the electric power industry was expanded, both through large federal projects such as the Tennessee Valley Authority and through smaller municipal power plants financed by various federal grants and loans. State regulation was strengthened by the simplification of holding company structures, and pressure on the state public utility commissions to provide more effective control over electric rates also grew. In addition, state commissions were given more power by the legislatures to control rates and services, and they were given greater financial resources in order to function more efficiently.

Electric utilities are probably as much affected with the public interest as any regulated industry, for electric power is one thing few consumers can do without. Air transportation can be dispensed with by

11. Ibid., p. 401.

most consumers, but this is not so for electricity. But there is some competition among similar classes of service. Gas and fuel oil compete with electricity for some uses, particularly heating. For the most part, however, residential and small commercial consumers are so tied to the use of electricity that there are no practical alternatives. If electric rates are high, these groups may attempt to restrict their consumption, but there remains an irreducible minimum below which they cannot go. Large industrial users at least have the option of installing their own generator plants. But although consumers, in general, seek low electricity charges, electrical utilities, particularly in recent years, have been faced with rapidly rising costs. The fuel crisis of 1974 placed an extra burden on their operating costs. In addition, the coverage of interest charges by operating income decreased, which resulted in the lowering of many utility bond ratings which, in turn, meant that the electric utility companies have had to pay a higher interest rate on the issuance of new bonds.

Competition in the Electrical Utility Industry

As mentioned previously, competition among electric utility companies has been held to be undesirable. Apart from the idea that economies of scale accrue to companies with large operating facilities, thus enabling them to produce at lower operating costs than smaller, competitive firms can, there is the aesthetic view that it is unsightly and wasteful to clutter up the environment with power lines. There are external social costs, including visual pollution of the environment, which are not incorporated by private industry into its pricing system but instead are shifted to society. Then, too, electric power is a necessity that supposedly must be shielded from the vagaries of competition in the marketplace. In a freely functioning competitive market, there are winners and losers. The market itself forces financially unstable, poorly managed firms out of business. Failure of an electrical utility company could cause a disruption in the provision of a necessary service. So federal and state regulatory commissions take the position that electrical utility companies have to be shielded from any force that might cause an interruption of a vital service.

But there are possibilities for competition in this industry.[12] In fact, there are today a number of communities in which there is more than one electric utility company, with competing power lines struck on the same utility poles.[13] In some communities a privately owned electric

12. Walter J. Primeaux, "A Reexamination of the Monopoly Market Structure for Electric Utilities," in *Promoting Competition in Regulated Markets*, ed. Almarin Phillips (Washington, D.C.: Brookings Institution, 1975), pp. 175–200.
13. Ibid., pp. 178–180.

firm competes with a municipally owned firm, and the consumer can choose between them. This situation creates what is known as a duopoly market—a condition that exists only when two producers offer identical or nearly identical products. In a duopoly market there are several possible operational outcomes. First, if the products and prices of the two firms are identical, each firm will have an equal chance of selling to any buyer, and the market will be divided equally between them. If both have identical marginal cost curves, each will maximize profits by following the MR = MC rule. They may practice collusion by maintaining a single-price policy. Second, the two firms may have different costs. If one firm is a larger producer than the other because of cost differences, this means that for any given marginal cost it can produce more than its rival can.

This is not to say, however, that competition between firms in a duopoly market situation is impossible. If a smaller firm faces competition from a larger rival, the relative lack of power resulting from its small size can force it to operate more efficiently. But the larger firm's size gives it a relatively secure position compared with its smaller rival, and so it has less incentive to operate efficiently. Thus the duopoly of utilities in certain communities can be compared with the electric utility monopolies operating in other communities. The results indicate that there are some situations in which competition produces better operating results. Competition causes duopoly electric utilities to operate at lower average cost levels than they would otherwise. However, the duopoly utilities apparently have higher marginal costs, and so as output levels increase, a point is reached at which the monopoly utilities have lower costs. Total costs eventually increase with competition because at larger output a competitive utility would probably have higher costs because the effects of economies of scale more than offset the effects of efficiency.

Competition exists and apparently is effective in small market areas, and there may be many more areas in which competition would also be more effective than an existing monopoly. One study indicates that competition would be beneficial in markets in which the aggregate output of electric power is less than 222 million kilowatt hours per year.[14] Past this point, however, a monopoly market structure would yield lower costs than a duopoly market would. Most of the electric utility companies in the United States operate in markets below the above-mentioned level of output, in which economies of scale take hold and make monopolies more efficient. So if viable competition is permitted in more utility markets, a downward pressure on prices could generate favorable results. It is possible that more competition could complement existing rate regulation. But it also is possible that a new firm

14. Ibid., pp. 192–193.

could attempt to compete in a system that is already producing at a level at which economies of scale offset any prospective competitive advantage. In this situation, it would be desirable to prohibit the new firm from entering the market. The study recommends the following minimum policy prescription to cover all market cases: if a monopoly market has annual sales small enough to offset the cost benefits of competition, a potential rival should not be barred from entry merely to protect the monopoly status of the existing firm.[15]

REGULATION AND ANTITRUST

Regulated industries are supposedly exempt from the direct application of the antitrust laws, on the theory that federal and state regulatory agencies protect the public interest and thus there is no rationale for what would be redundant intervention by the antitrust enforcement agencies. In addition, most of these industries are thought to be natural monopolies, thus making competitive considerations irrelevant. The exemptions, however, are not given without question, and the Justice Department has the authority to initiate action in regulated areas once thought immune from antitrust action. For example, although bank mergers were once thought to be immune from the application of Section 7 of the Clayton Act, the Justice Department initiated antitrust action in a proposed merger between the Philadelphia National Bank and the Girard Trust Corn Exchange Bank. At the time of the proposed merger, these were the second and third largest, respectively, of the forty-two commercial banks operating in the Philadelphia metropolitan area.[16] The merger was not allowed on the grounds that Section 7 proscribed anticompetitive mergers, even those limited to a single market area, and since then antitrust enforcement has undoubtedly inhibited increases in market concentration in commercial banking.

Antitrust in the Gas Industry

Antitrust action was also initiated against the electric and gas industries. In the El Paso Natural Gas case of 1962, a civil suit was initiated by the Justice Department charging a violation of Section 7 of the Clayton Act by reason of the acquisition of the stock and assets of Pacific Northwest Pipeline by El Paso Natural Gas. The Federal Power Commission had approved a merger between the two companies, but this action was challenged by the state of California.

15. Ibid., pp. 195–197.
16. *U.S.* v. *Philadelphia National Bank*, 374 U.S. 321 (1963).

Then the Justice Department sued in *U.S.* v. *El Paso Natural Gas*, seeking the divestiture of Pacific Northwest from El Paso on the ground that the acquisition substantially lessened competition in the sale of natural gas in California—a market in which El Paso was the sole out-of-state supplier of gas at the time of the acquisition.[17] Pacific Southwest was a substantial factor in the California market at the time of its acquisition by El Paso. Divestiture took place in 1974, ten years after it was ordered, and Pacific Northwest entered into a contract to supply gas in Southern California, thereby competing with El Paso Natural Gas. As a result of the El Paso Natural Gas decision, the possibility of antitrust action taken against regulated industries was enlarged.

Antitrust in the Electric Industry

In the electric industry there have been several applications of antitrust laws. Market-sharing agreements among bulk-power suppliers were attacked in the Florida Power case.[18] An agreement between Florida Power and Tampa Electric to allocate territories for wholesale power sales, although approved by the Florida Public Service Commission, was challenged by the Justice Department on the grounds that the agreement constituted illegal collusion under Section 1 of the Sherman Act and that approval of sales for resale went beyond the jurisdiction of the state commission. The case was settled by a consent decree requiring the elimination of the market-sharing agreement.

This prohibition of market sharing was then reinforced in the Otter Tail case.[19] This company refused to supply cities with electricity and to transmit over its lines power generated by other cities that had established their own distribution companies instead of renewing their exclusive franchises with Otter Tail. The Justice Department sued Otter Tail, charging that the company's actions amounted to monopolization under Section 2 of the Sherman Act. The Supreme Court affirmed a decision by a district court under which Otter Tail was found guilty of violating the Sherman Act by refusing to sell or transmit power.

SUMMARY

The phased deregulation of certain industries traditionally subject to regulation began during the latter part of the 1970s and has begun to

---

17. *U.S.* v. *El Paso Natural Gas*, 376 U.S. 651 (1964).
18. *U.S.* v. *Florida Power Corporation and Tampa Electric Co.*, U.S.D.C., Middle District of Florida, Tampa Division, Civil No. 68–287–T.
19. *Otter Tail Power Co.* v. *U.S.*, 410 U.S. 366 (1973).

accelerate. Criticism of regulation aided the passage of the Airline Deregulation Act of 1978, the Natural Gas Policy Act of the same year,
and the Motor Carrier Act and the Staggers Railroad Act of 1980. Many
had been discontented with the subordination of competition by the
regulatory process, and others felt there were better substitutes for existing regulations. In the air transportation industry, experience in
Texas and elsewhere suggested that a more flexible control of price and
entry would permit experimentation with price and service, to the ultimate benefit of the consumer. There also were criticisms of the anti-
competitiveness of other regulated industries, and Congress became
more committed to competitive principles and passed acts deregulating
these industries.

The shift from regulation to deregulation has to be gradual because
of the effect of dislocations. The rules of the game cannot be changed
too abruptly, and those directly involved in deregulation—consumers
and workers—must be cushioned against its shock. Requirements for
substitute service, provisions for notice to suspend service, and positions to protect the workers' economic interests have generally been
written into the deregulation legislation. Flexible transition allows industries to weather even large, unexpected shocks by permitting innovation. Deregulation may be instituted even more rapidly under the
Reagan administration, given its predilection for a free enterprise
market economy.

QUESTIONS FOR DISCUSSION

1. What are some of the principal criticisms of regulated markets?
2. Discuss the reasons for deregulating the airline industry.
3. Discuss the issues in the Phillips Petroleum case.
4. What is the purpose of deregulating natural gas?
5. In your opinion, should there be more competition in the electric
   utility industry?
6. Discuss the El Paso Natural Gas and Otter Tail antitrust cases.
7. Service competition rather than price competition long characterized the air transportation industry. Discuss.
8. Complete deregulation of the railroad and trucking industries is a
   desired goal. Do you agree?
9. Why would some groups oppose deregulation of such industries as
   air transportation and natural gas?
10. Do you foresee more deregulation by the Reagan administration?

RECOMMENDED READINGS

Braeutigam, Ronald R. *An Examination of Regulation in the Natural Gas Industry: Study on Federal Regulation.* Appendix to vol. 6. U.S., Congress, Senate, Committee on Government Operations. Washington, D.C.: U.S. Government Printing Office, 1978.

Friedlander, Ann F., and Richard H. Spady. *Freight Transportation Regulation: Equity, Efficiency, and Competition.* Cambridge, Mass.: MIT Press, 1981.

Helms, Robert B. *Natural Gas Regulation, An Evaluation of FPC Price Controls.* Washington, D.C.: American Enterprise Institute for Public Policy Research, 1974.

Keeler, Theodore E., and Michael Abrahams. "Market Structure, Pricing, and Service Quality in the Airline Industry Under Deregulation." Working Paper SL-7902. Berkeley: University of California, November 1979.

MacAvoy, Paul W. *The Regulated Industries and the Economy.* New York: W. W. Norton & Co., Inc., 1979.

——, and John Snow, eds. *Railroad Revitalization and Regulatory Reform.* Washington, D.C.: American Enterprise Institute for Public Policy Research, 1977.

Phillips, Almarin, ed. *Promoting Competition in Regulated Markets.* Washington, D.C.: Brookings Institution, 1975.

Weiss, Leonard W., and Michael W. Klass. *Case Studies in Regulation: Revolution and Reform.* Boston: Little, Brown, 1981.

PART VI
GOVERNMENT AND THE MULTINATIONAL CORPORATION

Multinational corporations transcend national boundaries and are causing an organizational revolution as profound in its impact on world society as were the rise of the nation-state and the Industrial Revolution. These corporations now have the power to act as an agent of change on societies, economies, and cultures; yet they were formed and shaped by those very same forces. Multinational corporations have emerged as the most sophisticated type of organization yet developed to integrate economic activity on an international basis. Some of them have sales volumes larger than the gross national products of many middle-sized European countries. But size is only one component of their power; they also control the means of creating wealth and make decisions that touch hundreds of millions of people. They have contributed to the internationalization of production, and in this process, their investment decisions determine the world's allocation of resources and welfare. Finally, they have an enormous influence on balance of payments and world trade.

Multinational corporations have also expedited the shift from exports and imports of goods and services to direct foreign investment. This shift came about because the products traded in the past—food, cotton, coal, and steel—required no connection between producer and consumer. They could be, and were, shipped and sold through intermediaries; the producer never saw the user. But international trade became more sophisticated as the products became more complex. The marketing of these products required a well-controlled sales organization, as well as instruction, repair, and service units. There also was a need for control over the price of the final product. This meant that the modern industrial corporation had to have some influence and power over its own markets—over prices, costs, and means of consumer persuasion. This could best be achieved by direct foreign investments and subsequent operations in countries that have markets. In addition, with advanced technology, foreign investments can realize economies of scale; the returns on one development cost are realized in several other markets.

The most important issue regarding the multinational corporations is the legal environment in which they operate. This environment varies considerably from country to country, so multinationals play by different game rules. What is illegal action for an American multinational may be entirely legal for a German multinational. For example, bribery is illegal for a U.S. firm, but not for a German firm. There are no international rules of law that govern the actions of multinational corporations; instead, each nation has its own laws. The parent firm is, of course, bound by the laws of its home country. Nonetheless, the legal environment for multinational business operations is a maze of overlapping national legal systems. Perhaps treaties and conventions such as the Treaty of Rome, which laid the antitrust foundation for the Common Market countries, will in the future lead to multinational corporation laws, though this appears unlikely in the immediate future.

Chapter 14
Government and the Multinational Corporation

Most American corporations are not confined solely to domestic operations but participate widely in business beyond the continental limits of the United States, with direct investments in many countries. In 1980 the total amount of direct investments by American firms in foreign plants and equipment was $178.2 billion. As with many aspects of big business, opinions about foreign investments vary. To some, such investments promise progress and prosperity, not only for the United States, but for other countries as well; to others, overseas investments represent jobs lost for American workers. To some, multinational corporations are a worldwide unifying force that will ultimately replace the outmoded interests of existing nation-states; to others, multinational corporations are a sinister force that could lead to world economic and political dominance by a few giant firms. But regardless of the differences of opinion, there is no question that the influence of the multinational corporation on the United States and on foreign economies has become vast. In recent years, over one-fifth of U.S. corporate profits have been earned abroad, and one-fourth of all new corporate investment has been made in foreign countries.

The global influence of business is by no means limited to American corporations. European and Japanese business firms also operate all over the world and have invested in plants and equipment in the United States. These firms operate on an ideological basis quite different from our own. American attitudes toward competition, particularly during the 1980s, will have to be reevaluated in light of increased world competition. Given the dynamic nature of international business, the domestic government regulation of business has become much more complex. In regard to the United States, it is difficult to apply antitrust laws that were written during the last century or the early part of this one to corporations that operate all over the world. Moreover, countries' varying antitrust policies create conflicts of national interest because international commerce is subject to overlapping jurisdictions. Antitrust policy is not the only reason for the conflicts of national laws and interest; tariffs, import and export quotas, balance-of-payments controls, foreign exchange regulations, tax laws, and other national policies present similar problems.

THE MULTINATIONAL CORPORATION

The multinational corporation is defined in many ways. One definition describes it as a company that attempts to carry out its activities on an international scale, as though there were no national barriers, on the basis of a common strategy directed from a corporate nerve center. Another definition holds that a multinational corporation is one that operates in many countries, carries out research and development in these countries, and has a multinational management and multinational stock ownership. A third definition depends on the ratio of foreign sales to total sales; for example, if a company's foreign sales account for 25 percent or more of its total sales, the company qualifies as a multinational. A fourth definition is based on the organization of a company: a company that has global product divisions rather than an international division is considered a multinational.[1]

But despite the lack of agreement on the definition of a multinational corporation, there is no question that American and foreign firms have become more and more global, as shown in a comparison of foreign earnings to total earnings of American corporations. In 1957, for example, foreign earnings amounted to 8.6 percent of American corporations' total earnings.[2] By 1970 the ratio had increased to 12.1 percent, and by 1974 the ratio was 26.9 percent. The ratio remained at around 25 percent through the rest of the decade. In addition, eight of the ten largest firms listed in *Fortune* magazine's Industrial Five Hundred derive over half of their total income from foreign sources. Most of these companies are international oil companies, but the importance of foreign source income is not limited only to them. Such well-known companies as Coca-Cola, Pepsi-Cola, Reynolds Industries, Philip Morris, IBM, and Gillette receive 50 percent or more of their total earnings from their overseas operations.

A Profile of Multinational Corporations

The United States has no monopoly on multinational corporations. In 1979, twenty-two of the world's fifty largest industrial corporations were based in the United States, twenty in Europe, and the remainder in Japan, Brazil, and Venezuela.[3] With few, if any, exceptions, these

1. U.S., Congress, Senate, Committee on Finance, *Implications of Multinational Firms for World Trade and Investment and for U.S. Trade and Labor: Report to the Subcommittee on International Trade on Investigation*, No. 332-69, Under Section 332 of the Tariff Act of 1930, p. 81.
2. C. Fred Bergsten, Thomas Horst, and Theodore Moran, *American Multinationals and American Interests* (Washington, D.C.: Brookings Institution, 1978), p. 10.
3. *Fortune*, "The Fifty Largest Industrial Corporations in the World," August 11, 1980, p. 204.

corporations would be classified as multinationals. In industrial classification, twenty were oil companies, the majority of which were American. More important, seven of the ten largest corporations were oil companies, all of which operated on a global basis. The combined sales of these seven companies amounted to $313 billion. The size of many of these multinationals is considerable. For example, Exxon, the largest of all the industrial multinationals, had in 1979 a total volume of sales of $79.1 billion, a volume larger than the gross national product of Belgium or Denmark. General Motors ranked second to Exxon, with total sales of $66.3 billion, a volume larger than the gross national product of most Latin American countries. IBM, which ranked tenth on the list, had total sales of $22.9 billion, a figure comparable to the gross national product of Portugal. The size of these multinationals certainly affects the international economic system.

Eleven of the fifty largest industrial corporations were auto companies, with a combined sales volume of over $230 billion. Although General Motors and Ford are the world leaders in total sales, the Japanese automakers have shown the greatest gain. In 1970 neither Toyota nor Nissan Motors (Datsun) were in the top fifty, but by 1979 Toyota was thirtieth and Nissan Motors thirty-fifth. Chrysler slipped from being the eighth largest in 1970 to fortieth by 1979. The French company Peugeot-Citroen, the Germany company Volkswagenwerk, and Italy's Fiat were among the twenty largest industrial corporations. Renault, the French state-owned firm, ranked twenty-first and plans to make a large-scale invasion of the U.S. market through its acquisition of American Motors.

In 1979 five of the fifty largest corporations were chemical companies, with a total sales volume of $67 billion. Unlike the oil companies, the chemical companies were not mostly American. The world's three largest chemical companies were German—Hoechst, Bayer, and Badishe-Anilin—all with sales greater than Du Pont, the leading American chemical company. All three German chemical companies operate all over the world, including the United States. The Dutch electrical equipment company, Philips' Gloelampenfabrieken, is larger than any other electrical company in the world except General Electric. Unilever, the British-Dutch multinational, ranked as the world's twelfth largest industrial corporation in 1979 and was first among the food-processing companies. The German steelmaker Thyssen-Huette was the world's largest steel company. The Swiss-based multinational, Nestlé, was the second largest food-processing company on the list, and the British tobacco multinational, B.A.T. Industries, was the world's largest tobacco company in 1979, operating in America through its Brown and Williamson subsidiary.

But firms do not have to be listed in *Fortune*'s fifty largest corporations to qualify as multinationals. There are a number of firms in

Fortune's first and second five hundred largest firms that are bona fide multinationals. Nevertheless, there is a correlation between gross sales and the likelihood that a firm will be a multinational: the larger the sales volume is, the more likely the firm will have multinational operations. Multinationals, whether they be American or foreign, are also likely to represent industries in which there is a considerable degree of industrial concentration. There appears to be a predominance of oligopolistic firms among the multinationals, particularly in the automotive, chemical, electrical, and mining industries, which suggests that oligopoly is part of foreign investment. Also, contrary to popular belief, multinationals, American or otherwise, do not have a predilection for operating in the world's less-developed countries. By far the most direct investments by American multinationals are in Canada, with Western Europe second. Conversely, the United States has become a popular country for direct investment by Canadian and Western European firms. The main attraction here and abroad is the existence of markets; cheap labor is usually not a determinant of location.

Multinational Banks

It would be a mistake to limit our discussion of multinational corporations to industrial corporations. Banks, too, operate on a global basis and, if anything, have more economic power than the industrial corporations do, which depend on them as a prime source of financing. Banks have grown largely because global industries have high cash-flow requirements. Following their clients overseas, the largest banks have established consortia to provide financing, which can include banks of several countries. For example, there is an unusual combination of public, semipublic, and private banking enterprises in an alliance of the state-owned French bank Credit Lyonnais, the 91 percent state-owned Italian bank Banco di Roma, and the privately owned West German bank Commerzbank. This consortium makes large-scale loans all over the world. These banks happen to be among the world's largest banks, and their activities are linked with their governments' economic policies. They also are a major source of loans to the Soviet Union and to the Eastern European countries.

The United States does not have any monopoly on big multinational banks, as Table 14–1 indicates. The banks in this table represent five different countries; some are state owned and some are privately owned. The assets of the tenth largest bank, Barclays, are larger than the assets of Exxon, the world's largest industrial corporation, and for that matter, so are the assets of the world's twentieth largest commercial bank, the Bank of Tokyo. The four French banks are state owned, but all actively compete with each other and with the private French banks for

Table 14-1 The Ten Largest Commercial Banks in the World in 1979 (Assets in billions of dollars)

Bank	Country	Total Assets
Bank America	U.S.	$108.4
Citicorp	U.S.	106.3
Caisse Nationale de Credit Agricole	France	105.1
Banque Nationale de Paris	France	98.9
Deutsche Bank	Germany	92.0
Credit Lyonnais	France	91.1
Societé Generale	France	85.0
Dai-ichi Kangyō Bank	Japan	73.3
Dresdner Bank	Germany	70.3
Barclays Bank	Britain	67.3

Source: *Fortune*, August 11, 1980, p. 202; July 14, 1980, p. 148.

deposits. And all are important to attainment of French economic policy objectives, both at home and abroad.

The Development of the Multinational Corporation

The multinational corporation certainly is not new. In the Italian trading centers of Venice and Genoa, trading firms and banking houses were active in the eastern Mediterranean area as early as the fourteenth century. By the sixteenth century, Holland had become the center of banking activity, with Dutch banks operating branches all over Europe. British trading companies existed during the reign of Queen Elizabeth I. These companies were given charters to promote world trade on a monopolistic basis. The best-known trading company was the British East India Company, which was granted a charter by Queen Elizabeth in 1600. This company, operating primarily in India and the Far East, was the wealthiest and most powerful trading company in the world during the seventeenth and eighteenth centuries. But the trading companies were left behind by the Industrial Revolution, which created a new form of multinational enterprise based on the need for the exploration and development of mineral and oil resources, resulting in the organization and growth of international resource development companies, many of which evolved into the present-day multinational concerns.

The precursors of the existing American multinationals originated as early as in 1850. Anyone familiar with the history of the United States is aware of the operations of the United Fruit Company in Honduras, Nicaragua, and other Central American countries before the turn of the twentieth century. The machinations of the United Fruit Company in the internal affairs of these countries and the direct intervention of the United States government on behalf of the company are a matter of public record. The need to expand into new market areas and to acquire new sources of raw materials facilitated the growth of the American multinational corporation. By 1900 a few manufacturing companies, for example, Eastman Kodak and General Electric, had reached the practical limits of their national markets, which forced them to look beyond domestic boundaries for new markets. Similarly, American-based oil companies, such as Standard Oil, faced with limited domestic resources and an increase in world demand for petroleum, expanded into Mexico and Latin America.

Gunboat diplomacy in support of multinational corporations was practiced by the United States and other industrial countries. Perhaps the best example of this type of diplomacy was the division of China by the major world powers into spheres of commercial and financial influence. China's resentment of this division culminated in the Boxer Rebellion of 1900, which was crushed by an army composed of soldiers from many of the world powers, with the end result that the Chinese were forced to make even more business concessions to these countries' commercial interests. The Boxer Rebellion exacerbated Chinese nationalist feelings and eventually led to friction among the world powers, particularly the Russians and the Japanese in Manchuria. The expansion of business into Asia, Africa, and Latin America was a logical concomitant of the Industrial Revolution. The economic reason for this expansion was business's need to find new markets, new sources of raw materials, and new fields for investment. For the purpose of business, actual political annexation of new areas was unnecessary; economic penetration, often supported by a show of force, was sufficient.

Early Development of the American Multinational

Although the present-day American multinational corporation was born in the last century, it was only after World War I that it came of age.[4] The war stimulated the growth of American industry, in particular, the automotive, chemical, petroleum, and machine tool industries. These and other industries supplied the Allies with the necessary accoutrements of war. Congress also passed measures designed to encourage

4. For a history of U.S. multinationals, see Mira Wilkins, *The Emergence of Multinational Enterprise: American Business Abroad from the Colonial Era to 1914* (Cambridge, Mass.: Harvard University Press, 1970).

American international trade and investment. The Webb-Pomerene Act, which allowed American business firms to join together to export without fear of prosecution under antitrust legislation, was enacted in 1918. Supporters of the act saw it as putting American exporters in a position to compete for European buyers. In 1919 the Edge Act was passed to permit federally chartered corporations to engage in foreign banking or investment banking. Passage of the Webb-Pomerene and Edge acts enabled the federal government to assist American foreign trade and, in many ways, American foreign investment.

The 1920s was generally a period of worldwide economic prosperity, and the participation of American multinational corporations in international commerce increased. There was some shift in the type of American enterprise operating abroad. Although most of the manufacturing firms operating abroad in the 1920s were market oriented, the number of firms dealing in raw material increased as well. Processing certain raw materials required cheap power, for example, the manufacture of electrochemicals and paper and pulp. One result was more investment in Canada by such firms as American Cyanamid and International Paper in order to take advantage of Canadian power resources, including Niagara Falls. Increased investments in meat packing for export led to an expansion of American influence in the Argentine cattle industry. American mining interests broadened their operations in Mexico and Chile, building refineries in both countries for the export of copper, lead, and silver. Petroleum companies also built refineries near foreign sources of supply, from which they could export to other countries.

Recent Development of the American Multinational

The Depression of the 1930s, coupled with the rise of militarism in Germany and Japan, created a world of uncertainty for the American multinationals. Depreciating currencies adversely affected American enterprises abroad, particularly in Latin America and Asia. In general, the 1930s was a decade of retrenchment for American business investments abroad. The 1940s encompassed World War II and a postwar period of reconstruction. But once reconstruction was completed and the European countries had entered a period of prosperity, there was a second stage in the expansion of American multinational corporations, from roughly 1955 to 1970. In 1955 American direct foreign investments amounted to $19.3 billion; by 1970, the value of American investments was $78.2 billion.[5] During the same period, direct invest-

5. *The Multinational Corporation*, "Policy Implications of Foreign Investment by U.S. Multinational Corporations," 1972, vol. 1, p. 11, table 2.

ments in manufacturing alone increased from $6.4 billion to $32.3 billion, and direct investments in petroleum increased from $5.9 billion to $21.7 billion. The bulk of American direct investments were made in Europe and Canada, with Europe receiving the most, particularly in the area of manufacturing. In 1955 American direct investment in manufacturing in Europe amounted to $1.6 billion, and by 1970 such investments had increased to $13.7 billion.[6]

Most of the influx of American capital into Europe was into the Common Market countries. One motive for investment was to get inside the Common Market's tariff barriers and so protect American export markets. But the main reason for American expansion in Europe was the desire for profits, which were expected from the emerging prosperity in Germany, France, and other Common Market countries. In Western Europe there also developed a Eurodollar market for lending and borrowing, mainly dollars but also other currencies; by the late 1960s, it had become one of the world's largest markets for short-term funds. There also developed a Eurodollar bond market. When balance of payments problems motivated the United States government to restrict American direct investments in Western Europe, American business firms operating there were able to continue to grow because they could use European funds.

American business expansion in Europe was a mixed blessing. One concomitant of this expansion was the fear of some Europeans of an impending takeover of the European economy by American multinationals. This fear was epitomized in a book called *The American Challenge*, which was written in 1967 by the French journalist-politician Jean Jacques Servan-Schreiber.[7] Investments by American corporations had produced an economic revolution in European management and technology; stimulated an upsurge in income, employment, and trade; and raised living standards. These facts were acknowledged by Servan-Schreiber; what he objected to was the control of European, but particularly French, industry by American firms. He felt that these firms were acquiring dominant control over the high technology sectors of the European economy on which Europe depended for future growth. Subsequent events, however, have indicated that an American takeover of European industry will not occur; moreover, European firms have expanded into the United States.

American direct investment in the less-developed countries—including those in Latin America, a traditional preserve of American capital—grew much more slowly than did investment in Canada and Europe between 1955 and 1970. Direct investment in manufacturing, for example,

6. Ibid., p. 13, table 3.
7. Jean Jacques Servan-Schreiber, *The American Challenge* (New York: Atheneum, 1968).

increased from $1.4 billion in 1955 to $4.6 billion in 1970 in Latin America; in Asia for the same period the increase was from $100 million to $1.5 billion. The relatively slow growth in Latin America and other less-developed areas was attributed partly to the de-emphasis on investment in the extractive industries that occurred at the same time as the increased emphasis on investment in manufacturing. Mining, petroleum, and agricultural foreign investments, which usually have been concentrated in the less-developed countries, have grown much more slowly than foreign investments in manufacturing industries, which increased from $6.4 billion in 1955 to $32.3 billion in 1970.[8] Thus, both the geographic focus and the investment focus of the American multinational corporation have changed in the last two decades, with Europe supplanting Canada as the favorite site for American direct investment, and manufacturing superseding the extractive industries in investment importance.

The multinational corporation of today differs from the multinational corporation of the past in another respect. There is a conflict between the multinational corporation, with its supranational point of view, and the nation-state, with its national economic concerns and special interest groups. Until fairly recently most countries were too disorganized internally to have much sense of national identity. On occasions—witness the expropriation of American and British oil holdings by Mexico in 1936—a country would express its nationalism rather forcefully. However, this all has changed rather drastically, as the events of recent years have demonstrated. A case in point is the increased influence of the Arab nations in the world. These nations began to articulate national goals and priorities but were confronted by corporate oil entities, which in the past were able to frustrate their efforts toward nationalism. One result has been an increase in the Arabs' involvement in the oil companies' operations.

The 1970s witnessed a decline in the dominance of U.S. multinational corporations in world business. Until 1970 the American multinationals were well ahead of their European competitors in capturing the fragmented overseas markets, but during the 1970s the European multinationals became as tough and competitive as their American counterparts. In Europe, the costs for American firms went up and the profits went down. Chrysler abandoned its operations in Europe; Firestone pulled out of Switzerland; and the French pushed ITT out of the European telephone business. West German business firms, aided in part by favorable government tax policies, accelerated their global expansion. West Germany's position as a world economic superpower was won because it consistently performed better than did its major competitors, includ-

8. *Implications of Multinational Firms for World Trade and Investment and for U.S. Trade and Labor*, p. 97, table 2.

ing the United States. Conversely, during the 1970s, the U.S. record in both economic performance and technological innovation was poor. It was so poor, in fact, that in many aspects of innovation the Japanese and the Europeans have taken the leadership mantle away from the United States. When the United States dominated the world markets, it enjoyed a great reputation as the technological leader. But times have changed, and at present fewer than 60 percent of the world's largest corporations are American, compared with 80 percent in 1970.[9]

Motives for Investing Abroad

Sorting out the motives for investing abroad is complex, for there are a number of factors involved. Probably the most important motive is an obvious one, a search for new sources of profit. A motive can be purely defensive in nature. The location of a plant abroad or the acquisition of a foreign firm may be decided simply to prevent market preemption by a competitor or to keep open market outlets or sources of supply. As foreign markets expand, some economies of scale may be realized by producing abroad. Certain industries are by nature international, and their motives for investing abroad are apparent; the petroleum industry is an example. Its sources of materials are located abroad and exploiting them requires international production and marketing facilities. Some firms may invest abroad to avoid tariff barriers: many American firms located in Western Europe to circumvent tariffs set up by the Common Market. Another motive is to diversify product lines as a hedge against business recessions or strikes. A firm also may attempt to link its technological and managerial capacity to low-cost production inputs in other countries.

There have been several attempts to devise a theory of direct foreign investment, one that would explain the expansion of national firms into international firms. One theory suggests that firms with a monopolistic advantage expand into foreign markets to exploit their advantage abroad. Another theory holds that firms, particularly in oligopolistic industries, encounter limits to increasing the sales of their traditional product in the domestic market. To continue their growth they must choose between expanding across a product boundary in the domestic market or expanding across a national boundary with their traditional product. The latter will be chosen if the economies of scale in domestic production are less than the cost of transportation to and tariffs in the foreign country. A third theory uses the interaction of oligopolistic firms,[10] and a fourth uses the so-called product cycle model, which

9. *Financial Times of London*, "World Business Weekly," April 28, 1980, p. 6.
10. Charles F. Kindleberger, *American Business Abroad, Six Lectures on Direct Investment* (New Haven, Conn.: Yale University Press, 1969), pp. 1–18.

traces the maturation of a product from its development and domestic sale to its export and, finally, to its production by a subsidiary abroad.[11] These last two theories are explained below.

Oligopolistic Factors

Most American direct investments abroad are concentrated within a few industries, and the market structure of these industries is generally dominated by a few firms; thus, oligopolistic conditions are present. One essential characteristic of oligopoly industries is the interdependence of firms in making decisions. In contemplating a new product, a price change, or an investment, each firm must speculate on the reactions of the other firms in the industry. Investment moves by one firm are followed by similar moves by other leading firms in the industry. No follower wants to risk the possibility of a rival firm's gaining an advantage from a profitable foreign investment that could later be used against it in the domestic market. So when one business firm establishes a branch plant in the Common Market, other firms feel they have to do the same thing, for fear they might lose their overall market position in the industry. The firms use a "follow-the-leader" or defensive strategy, which may well be the reason for certain direct investments by U.S. firms, particularly in chemicals and drugs, in other countries.

The Product Cycle Model

The product cycle model also attempts to explain why firms invest abroad. According to this theory, a product goes through several stages of development. The first stage is the creation of the product, and the second stage is its introduction into the domestic market. The next stage is the export of the product. As the product matures, it becomes more standardized, and the possibility of its being imitated and produced overseas by a foreign firm increases. If the product has a high income elasticity of demand or if it is a satisfactory substitute for high-cost labor, the demand for it, particularly in the more advanced countries, may grow rapidly. Then the firm has to decide whether or not to invest in a foreign subsidiary. As long as the marginal production cost of the product plus the cost to transport it abroad is lower than the average cost of having a subsidiary produce it in the export market, the firm would probably avoid investment in a subsidiary. But if foreign manufacturers begin to put out the product, the firm is likely to set up

11. Raymond Vernon, "International Investment and International Trade in the Product Life Cycle," *Quarterly Journal of Economics*, 80 (1966), 190–207.

a foreign subsidiary in order to maintain its market share abroad and to recapture the remaining rent from the product's development. The local market then will be filled by production units from the subsidiary.

Eventually the subsidiary, located, for instance, in France, may serve third-country markets so as to exploit economies of scale. If cost differences are large enough to offset transportation costs, then the subsidiary may even export back to the United States. Once one firm undertakes an investment in a foreign country, competing firms may then be galvanized into action to do the same thing, in order to maintain the status quo. Their share of the market, viewed in global terms, may be threatened, and their ability to estimate the production cost of their competitor, operating in a foreign market area, is impaired by their inability to assess foreign conditions. Any uncertainty can be reduced by imitating the original investing company and investing in the same geographic area. In the final stages of the product cycle, new competitors arise to challenge the position of the original firms. These competitors are often European and Japanese corporations, and the focus of their challenge is not only the subsidiaries of U.S. firms in Western Europe and elsewhere, but the U.S. market itself. In some cases, foreign competitors, notably the Japanese, have been helped through licensing agreements by the very U.S. firms they are challenging.

Although investment decisions are usually based on several factors, there is some evidence to support both the oligopoly and the product cycle theories. Modern multinational corporations, regardless of whether they are American, German, or Japanese, usually represent industries that are oligopolies. Defensive considerations are often responsible for locating a plant in another country. Once one firm makes a move, others follow suit, and the structure of the oligopoly remains undisturbed. If no move is made by the other firms, the balance of power within the oligopoly may well shift to the firm that did move. Sometimes a defensive move is motivated by the need to imitate competitors in the areas of technology and marketing. For example, Olivetti, the Italian manufacturer of typewriters, acquired the American firm, Underwood, in order to share with its U.S. competitors the challenges of operating in the American market. The rationale for the acquisition was in large part defensive—if U.S. firms were stimulated by their home environment to innovate, then Olivetti could best protect itself from the rivalry of these firms by being exposed to the same conditions.

The U.S. television industry conforms to the product cycle model.[12] In the first stage of the industry, television sets were developed and then manufactured exclusively in the United States. As mass-production and mass-marketing techniques were perfected, costs were reduced and

12. Richard J. Barnett and Ronald E. Muller, *Global Reach: The Power of the Multinational Corporation* (New York: Simon & Schuster, 1974), pp. 129–133.

prices dropped. Eventually, a saturation of the U.S. market appeared imminent, and the second stage began. It was necessary to look for new markets; Europe appeared to be a logical choice, and the export of television sets commenced. For a while, American firms dominated the European market, but then European firms themselves began producing television sets and recaptured a part of the market. This marked the beginning of the third stage. At this point, U.S. firms decided to build plants in Europe to produce sets for local markets. Often, American companies bought up European competitors, and some began to use their European plants to export to other countries. In the fourth, or present, stage of the cycle, European and Japanese firms challenged the U.S. firms' position in the world markets, though the locus of the challenge was the U.S. market. In particular, Japanese firms were able to undersell U.S. firms in their home market. In response to the Japanese challenge, U.S. firms then attempted to cut their production costs by setting up plants in low-wage countries and exporting back into the United States.

Explanations of the motives for U.S. direct investments abroad are not necessarily applicable to the reverse situation, foreign direct investment in the United States. The influence of oligopoly factors may be relevant to European firms, since the creation of the Common Market permitted firms to expand enough to achieve the economies of large-scale production. Average firm size has increased in Europe, enhanced in part by a generally permissive attitude toward mergers. The forces favoring oligopoly were largely absent in Europe until recent years. In most European countries in the past, one firm would comfortably supply the whole market for a product. As will be pointed out in Chapter 15, rather mundane forces have been responsible for the expansion of European and Japanese firms into the United States, not the least of which have been the devaluation of the dollar and rising labor costs in Europe and Japan.

ISSUES INVOLVING THE MULTINATIONAL CORPORATION

There is much ambivalence about the role of the multinational corporation in the world economic order. On one hand, it can be argued that multinational corporations have broken down regional barriers and have created a wider distribution of economic benefits. They have increased employment in the less-developed countries and have contributed to their welfare. On the other hand, multinational corporations have been accused of taking advantage of the less-developed countries' cheap labor and causing the loss of domestic jobs to foreign workers. They have also been blamed for making decisions inimical to the national interests of the countries in which they operate, decisions that often have led to an antiforeign investment bias. Finally, in some countries, notably Canada, foreign investments, principally from U.S. companies, control as much as half of the country's manufacturing. But what is most striking about the debate on multinationals is the complete lack of agreement.

We shall examine some of the more controversial issues regarding multinationals: their effect on employment, political interference in the internal affairs of host countries, impact on the balance of payments, and restraint of trade. The frame of reference will be the American multinational corporation, though these problems apply to all multinationals, regardless of their base of operations. We should emphasize that there are no set answers to these problems. No two multinationals are exactly alike in their operations and their economic and political impact. Moreover, these issues have to be considered within the framework of the 1980s, a decade that may well see the reshaping of the United States' domestic economy and the competitive atmosphere of world business. What counts in the 1980s is the trend and momentum of foreign investment, and by those standards, the Japanese are on a very fast track and are likely to accelerate. American economic policy may well turn on what can be done to make the American multinationals more competitive in world markets.

Effect on Employment

Labor unions, American or otherwise, have not looked with fondness on the multinational corporations, taking the position that a job created abroad is a job lost at home. International shifts in production within an existing family of plants is, by definition, unique to multinationals. In labor's view, American firms locate in Mexico or Taiwan to take advantage of lower labor costs. It believes that production in the United States would continue if foreign direct investments were not made. But this is not necessarily the case—plants may close anyway. There also is quite a difference between low unit-labor costs and low labor costs, for productivity is the prime desideratum, not just cheap labor. The bulk of the multinational corporations' investments have been made in the relatively high wage areas of Canada and Western Europe. The less-developed countries are more likely to be attractive to multinationals because of their supplies of raw material than because of their cheap labor. Usually, the effect of multinationals has been to raise wages in the less-developed countries.

Labor's attitude toward American multinationals shifted during the latter part of the 1970s. There are two reasons for this shift, the massive influx of foreign direct investment into the United States and the Japanese challenge to the U.S. auto industry. The influx of foreign investment into the United States has created thousands of jobs for American workers, but the Japanese incursion into the U.S. auto market has terrified both the United Auto Workers (UAW) and the U.S. auto companies. In 1970 the Japanese carmakers had 3 percent of the U.S. domestic market; by 1980 their share increased to 21 percent. The giant Chrysler company totters on the edge of bankruptcy, in part because of the Japanese imports. Both labor and management have petitioned Congress to do something about the Japanese car industry, to use import quotas to restrict the sale of the Japanese cars in the United States or to compel them to build Toyotas and Datsuns here, thus creating jobs for unemployed UAW workers. The success during the 1970s of the Japanese and German multinationals in capturing world markets has made the American labor unions realize that U.S. firms have to be more viable in international competition.

Political Interference

History is replete with instances of political meddling by American and other multinational corporations in the internal affairs of the countries in which they operated. Two examples appear at the end of the chapter. But this meddling is far more subtle today than it was in the past, probably because it is no longer fashionable for a country to send in its marines and gunboats to shoot up a banana republic in order to protect its business interests. For the most part, multinationals have come to learn that their own economic survival in a given country depends on their willingness to operate within the existing conditions of that country, though many countries still suspect that the presence of foreign capital eventually will lead to internal political machinations by the companies owning the capital. The ITT involvement in Chile reinforced this suspicion. The mere presence of foreign capital can often stir up xenophobia and nationalism, as has been evident in Latin America and the Middle East. Xenophobia is by no means limited to U.S. multinationals; the Japanese also have been included in the criticism.[13]

Impact on the Balance of Payments

A balance of payments is simply an account of the value of goods and services, capital loans, gold, and other items coming in and out of a country. This account can be divided into several subcategories: current

13. Resentment of the Japanese was expressed in Malaysia and Indonesia in the rioting and loss of lives during the visit of then Prime Minister Kakuei Tanaka in 1974.

accounts, capital accounts, unilateral transfers, and net gold exports or imports. The current accounts summarize the difference between total exports of goods and services and total imports of goods and services. It is the "stuff" of which international economic relations are composed. A country can have either a surplus or deficit in its current accounts. Capital accounts refer to long- and short-term movements of capital into and out of a country. A country also can have a surplus or deficit in its capital accounts—the former occurring when capital outflows to other countries exceed capital inflows from these countries, and the latter occurring when capital outflows are exceeded by capital inflows. Unilateral transfers are capital movements and gifts for which there are no return commitments or claims. Gold exports or imports reflect the position of current and capital accounts. As an international medium of exchange, gold is used to compensate for deficits in the balance of payments. A deficit is accompanied by an outflow of gold; a surplus by an inflow.

Multinational corporations are linked to the United States' balance of payments position through both capital and current accounts. The United States has sustained on numerous occasions deficits in its balance of payments, and a contributor to these deficits has been the outflows in the capital accounts. The bulk of U.S. direct investment abroad is made by multinational firms, and so it is natural to want to examine the extent to which these firms contribute to the balance of payments problem. Capital accounts also are linked to current accounts, in that direct investment by American firms in other countries results in an inflow of income to this country in the form of dividends or remitted earnings. There also may be other types of income payments, such as fees and royalties, from the foreign investment.

Multinationals and the U.S. Balance of Payments

There has been some deficit in the U.S. balance of payments in almost every year since 1965. The balance on current accounts and long-term capital has shown a continuous deficit for each year since 1965.[14] Capital outflows in general and U.S. direct investment abroad in particular, which are debit or negative items in the balance of payments accounts, have come under scrutiny. Direct investment abroad increased from $51.8 billion in 1965 to $168.1 billion in 1978.[15] The great bulk of this increase of $116.3 billion was concentrated in the industrially advanced countries of Canada and Western Europe, and the increase was financed

14. U.S. Department of Commerce, *Survey of Current Business*, August 1979, pp. 24–25.
15. Ibid., p. 26.

by $41.2 billion from U.S. subsidiaries' retained foreign earnings and $75.2 billion from U.S. firms' direct investment capital outflows. The latter figure is significant in its effect on the balance of payments.

The impact of the U.S. multinationals on the balance of payments comes primarily from the direct foreign investments made by these firms. This is true because these investments represent an outflow of capital from the United States. Other items in the balance of payments may also be affected by foreign investments, including travel, transportation, and payment of interest on foreign borrowing. But direct foreign investments eventually generate earnings that are brought back, at least in part, to the United States in the form of dividends, interest, and branch profits. All are credit items in the balance of payments accounts. Royalties and fees from patents may be remitted to the United States as well.

There are also other factors in the relationship between the multinational corporation and the balance of payments. Foreign direct investment by U.S.-based multinationals can stimulate demand for U.S. exports by increasing aggregate demand in the host countries. But U.S. exports also can be displaced by the production and sale of goods from foreign subsidiaries that otherwise would have come from the United States. A second factor is the extent to which foreign investment by U.S. multinationals supplements or substitutes for the investment by firms already in those countries. Would similar investments have been made by these firms in the absence of U.S. investments? Third, other countries' multinational corporations invest in the United States, resulting in a capital inflow into the United States, with a more or less opposite effect on the capital outflows in the home base of these foreign multinationals. Foreign direct investments also may have an impact on American imports, as goods formerly manufactured at home by the parent multinational are produced by subsidiaries abroad at lower cost and shipped back to the United States.

Table 14–2 compares for selected years private capital outflows for direct U.S. investments in other countries and receipts of income from direct investment. Capital outflows are a negative item in the balance of payments, and income received from foreign investment is a positive item. Most income received from foreign direct investment comes from investments made in an earlier time period, whereas direct investments are for a specific or current year. Income received in 1974 could have been from investments made in, say, 1947 or 1955. The results of 1974 direct investment may not be felt for ten years, depending on the nature and location of the investment, its profitability, and the remissions policy of the company doing the investing.

As Table 14–2 indicates, the return flow of income to the United States in the form of dividends, remitted earnings, royalties, and other forms of payment more than offset capital outflows. In 1978 capital

Table 14-2 U.S. Private Direct Investment Abroad and Receipts of Income from U.S. Direct Investment Abroad (millions of dollars)

Year	Direct Investment Outflows	Fees and Royalties	Interest, Dividends, and Other Earnings	Inflows
1970	4,413	1,758	4,992	6,750
1971	4,441	1,927	5,983	7,910
1972	3,214	2,115	6,416	8,531
1973	3,195	2,513	8,384	10,897
1974	1,275	3,070	11,379	14,449
1975	6,196	3,543	8,547	12,090
1976	4,253	3,530	11,303	14,833
1977	5,612	3,793	12,795	16,588
1978	4,606	4,806	13,593	18,399

Source: U.S. Department of Commerce, "Survey of Current Business," August 1979, pp. 24–25.

inflows exceeded outflows by some $2.3 billion; from 1972 to 1978 capital inflows exceeded outflows by $75 billion. Thus, direct U.S. investments abroad, the bulk of which are made by multinationals, even if they are a negative factor in the balance of trade accounts, may be a positive factor in the balance of payments, as earnings from abroad are repatriated. In the short run, direct foreign investment is a negative factor in the balance of payments. In the long run, direct foreign investment will have a positive effect on the balance of payments. It has been estimated that the receipts of multinational corporations normally pay for the initial outflows in the balance of payments in about two years. Perhaps the central point here is that there is a dynamic process in foreign investment and that time must be considered in assessing its effect on the balance of payments.

The balance of payments is a residual, and it cannot be treated as an end in itself. Because inward or outward investment affects the balance of payments, it must be interpreted within the framework of the economic policy adjustments necessary to achieve basic objectives of employment, prices, economic growth, social equity in income distribution, and so forth. An outflow of investment has repercussions for domestic incomes and employment. If there is a displacement effect, in that the outflow results in less investment at home, the initial effect is a decline in the flow of expected incomes, unless full employment existed already, in which case it would help to maintain an acceptable level of aggregate demand. Then the displacement has the same effect as would a disinflationary policy of increased taxation or tighter credit. The eventual inflow of income from dividends and remitted earnings accrues to American onwers of domestic factors of production, and the incomes generated can lead to increased imports or higher domestic output and employment.

Balance of Payment Effects on the Less-Developed Countries

Multinational corporations make transactions across national frontiers, and this influences foreign receipts and payments in all the countries in which they operate. These transactions have varying effects. A U.S. multinational operating in a highly developed country such as West Germany will have an impact on the economy different from that if it were operating in Malaysia. West German multinationals also operate in the United States, and so capital outflows and inflows will be somewhat balanced. But for less-developed countries the balance of payments effect of direct investments by multinationals can be crucial. In the short run, a capital inflow brings net benefit to the balance of payments. But in the longer run, as outflows of earnings to the parent company increase, this situation changes. The balance of payments of the less-developed country continues to benefit as long as the remittance of earnings to the American, Japanese, or German parent company and the value of any imported items are less than the increased exports from the new plant, plus any import savings that result from the creation of the new plant.

The less-developed countries are more vulnerable to shifts in world prices than are the developed countries. One characteristic of the less-developed countries is a lack of foreign exchange. Typically, they are dependent on the export of an agricultural product or products, for which prices fluctuate almost at random in the world markets. Imports, on the other hand, are usually capital or consumer goods, which have gone up in price. Multinationals locating in these countries will eventually generate an outflow of income from their investments, and this may cause a transfer problem for a poor country, which is already faced with a shortage of foreign exchange. There is also the problem of transfer pricing. It is possible for a multinational to fix the value attached to a service or product transferred between subsidiaries to suit its own ends. Such transfer prices deviate from the market price of the service or product for business reasons. For example, a parent company can direct a manufacturing subsidiary in one country to undervalue its exports to a distribution subsidiary in another country. The purpose is to save on taxes if the taxes in the manufacturing country are higher than the taxes in the distributing country, but the result is the loss of foreign exchange and tax revenues for the manufacturing country.

Taxation

American taxation of foreign direct investment by U.S. multinationals and other entities has two main features: the foreign tax credit on which income, withholding, and certain other taxes paid in foreign countries are credited against U.S. tax liabilities; and tax deferrals, by means of which no U.S. tax is levied on the income of subsidiaries incorporated in other countries until that income is repatriated to the United States. The rationale for the foreign tax credit is the avoidance of double taxation of foreign-source income earned by American corporations, which must pay taxes on income earned in the countries in which they operate. Double taxation is the imposition of comparable taxes on the same income on the same taxpayer by two or more countries. The foreign tax credit is supposed to reduce the effective combined rates on foreign-source income. Only one tax is paid at the higher of two rates, provided that the tax bases are comparable in the countries concerned. To some extent, the foreign tax credit can be regarded as a tax inducement that has the effect of stimulating American capital formation in other countries. It also can be considered a compensation for the risks in investing abroad.

There is probably less of a rationale for the tax deferral than for the foreign tax credit. Deferral was put into U.S. tax law to help American firms compete with foreign firms whose home countries permit deferral. Thus, the retained earnings of a foreign subsidiary can be reinvested abroad without being subject to the U.S. corporate income tax. The American corporation that invests in a country with low taxes is privileged in that it has more income available for reinvestment purposes. The deferral essentially amounts to an interest-free government loan that, because profits are not repatriated to the United States, is tax exempt. The tax deferral arrangement has two possible drawbacks. First, it subsidizes investment by U.S. multinationals in foreign operations and therefore misallocates U.S. capital between U.S. and foreign site uses. Second, tax provisions such as deferral transfer specialized U.S. technology to the economies of other nations, thereby increasing foreign productivity at the expense of U.S. productivity and, as a result, impairing the U.S. balance of payments. The deferral method of treating foreign-source income allegedly violates the principles of both tax neutrality and tax equity.

Multinationals are supposed to have certain tax advantages not available to purely domestic firms. The foreign tax credit enables them to reduce their tax liability at home, and the tax deferral should encourage them to invest abroad at the expense of domestic investment. But the impact of these advantages varies widely among firms and industries. For the major U.S. international oil companies, the foreign tax credit is the single most important item reducing tax liability to the U.S.

Treasury. Companies such as Exxon and Texaco are able to lower their U.S. income tax rate to less than 10 percent, compared with the maximum rate of 48 percent. In 1972, for example, the nineteen leading oil companies paid $700 million in federal income taxes on a net income of $11.5 billion, for an overall effective U.S. tax rate of 6 percent. These companies, however, paid $5.1 billion in taxes to foreign governments, for an overall effective tax rate of 44 percent.[16] When multinationals earn most of their income from foreign sources, it follows that their U.S. income tax will be reduced by the credit, and this is true for any type of multinational, oil or otherwise.

The taxation of foreign-source income must be considered within the frame of reference of the 1980s. American multinationals will have to compete in an increasingly competitive world environment. All industrial countries have tax credits to avoid the double taxation of their companies' foreign earnings. In fact, a majority of the countries, including Japan and West Germany, do not tax the foreign earnings of their corporations at all. The Japanese aid their foreign trade industries through tax breaks and low-interest loans, and the French exempt all their exports from their main tax, the value-added tax. In all cases, the American method of taxing foreign-source income is regarded as consistent with international tax law. The basic foundations of U.S. tax policy, the foreign tax credit and deferral, were laid down sixty years ago and, although modified several times, have remained more or less intact ever since.[17] It would appear that the U.S. tax system does not provide any overall net incentive to invest abroad rather than at home. The current policy is roughly neutral toward foreign direct investment by multinationals.[18]

Restraint of Trade

Multinational corporations operate in many countries and are difficult to regulate under American antitrust laws. The end result of attempting to do so may well be restraint of trade, which has an adverse effect not

16. The Tax Reduction Act of 1975 tightened the tax treatment of foreign income earned by U.S. multinational oil companies. To force these companies to pay higher U.S. taxes, Congress modified their foreign tax credit in two ways. First, a separate limitation was placed on the foreign tax credit derived from the extraction of oil. Second, the per-country method can no longer be used for any oil-related income.

17. U.S. tax treatment of foreign-source income goes back to the Revenue Act of 1918, long before multinationals became a controversial subject.

18. See C. Fred Bergsten, Thomas Horst, and Theodore H. Moran, *American Multinationals and American Interests* (Washington, D.C.: Brookings Institution, 1978), pp. 165–212; and Gary C. Hufbauer, "The Taxation of Export Profits," *National Tax Journal*, 28 (March 1975), 43–59.

only on the economy of the United States but also on the economies of other countries. The international oil companies are an example. In 1922 the Justice Department's antitrust division alleged that decisions made by the major American international oil companies—some dating back to the 1920s—intentionally limited world oil supplies and paved the way for an energy crisis fifty years later. The division explained how a series of secret agreements led to a cartel-like domination of world oil supplies and prices by a handful of major oil companies. The whole purpose of this cartel was to maintain a monopoly in which each participant would be protected in its part of the market, competition would be eliminated, and the price of oil could be maintained for the benefit of the cartel's members. Moreover, Presidents Harry Truman and Dwight Eisenhower, acting in the interest of the national security, were supposed to have thwarted the Justice Department's attempts to initiate antitrust action.

The Achnacarry Agreement

In the 1920s, because they wanted to get in on the new discoveries of oil in the Middle East, the Justice Department contended that several American oil companies pressured the State Department to negotiate with European countries for a share of the new oil. These negotiations were successful, and the American companies were able to penetrate an existing British-Dutch monopoly of oil. At first, an "open door" policy was adopted in the Middle East, and competition was promoted among all the oil companies for concessions to drill for oil. But by 1927 there was a worldwide surplus in the production of oil, and the oil companies became much less interested in competing and more interested in regulating supply. In the Middle East, four major oil companies, British Petroleum, Royal Dutch Shell, Esso, and Mobil agreed to a joint venture to control a major source of crude oil. The venture, called the Red Line Agreement, was signed by these companies, in which they agreed to share equally all oil discoveries in the Middle East.[19]

The Achnacarry Agreement itself was a consequence of a price war between Shell and Mobil. This war began in India and then spread to other countries, including the United States. British Petroleum and Esso were concerned that the price war would jeopardize the interests of all the major international oil companies in the consuming countries. A conference was then called to work out an agreement among the oil companies. This agreement was made in 1928, later becoming known as

19. U.S., Congress, Senate, Committee on Foreign Relations, *Multinational Corporations and United States Foreign Policy: Hearings Before the Subcommittee on Multinational Corporations*, 93rd Cong., 2d sess., 1974, pt. 7, p. 46.

the Achnacarry Agreement. Its purpose was to cease the overproduction of oil and prevent excessive and destructive competition among the companies. This agreement was the first of a series, the last signed as late as 1948, in which four companies, British Petroleum, Royal Dutch Shell, Esso, and Mobil, and, later, other companies, agreed to eliminate competition and to limit supply among themselves.

The Achnacarry Agreement, or the As Is Agreement, still another name, set forth a number of principles for the oil companies to follow, the foremost of which was a call for the companies to accept and maintain their relative shares of the world petroleum market as of 1928.[20] The companies also agreed to share among themselves on a preferential cost basis their existing facilities, to avoid unnecessary duplication of new facilities, to avoid using surplus crude oil production from any geographic area to upset the price structure of any other area, to draw supplies for a given market from the nearest producing area, and not to do anything that would materially increase costs and prices. In addition to these principles, a series of policy and procedural provisions were adopted, including product standardization, uniform freight rates, and the pooling of shipping charges. One provision was the reciprocal exchange of oil among the cartel participants. By 1934 the companies had sealed their arrangements through several other pacts, and these formed a rigid code of rules, designed to implement the Achnacarry Agreement, that was the basis of their control over world oil production for the next thirty years.

The most significant aspect of the Achnacarry Agreement was the development of an international pricing system, implemented by a code of rules. A two-price system was used—an internal one favoring the cartel and a second, higher one for the world market. For oil supplies shipped among cartel members, each origin point of supply was used as a base point, but for oil supplied to noncartel members, a uniform delivered price was used based on a single base point, the U.S. Gulf Coast, to which was added freight costs from the Gulf Coast to the point of destination, regardless of the origin of the shipment.[21] Thus, phantom freight charges were added to the costs that outsiders paid to the cartel. A basing point system also was used for all overseas prices of oil. The price was ultimately based on U.S. crude prices at the U.S. Gulf Coast, though that price bore no relationship to the actual cost of the oil from the foreign sources, and its purpose was to maintain the world price at an artificially high level.

20. Ibid., pt. 7, p. 48.
21. Ibid., pt. 7, p. 50.

Postwar Arrangements

After World War II, the character of the international oil cartel changed, even though its objective remained the same. The cartel's emphasis turned to developing a more efficient supply system, as distribution depended on controlling a few strategically located sources. In pursuit of supply sources, the cartel invoked the Achnacarry Agreement to gain centralized control over the Middle East's crude oil. First, the companies expanded the number of interlocking, jointly owned production companies so as to unify control of concessions and crude oil output as its Middle East source. Second, they created a system of long-term mutual supply contracts, under which enormous quantities (more than a billion barrels) of crude oil were sold or exchanged among themselves at mutual savings. At the same time, the surpluses and deficits of crude oil were quantitatively and geographically balanced in order to avoid competitive disruption of world market prices.

The original four members of the cartel, Esso, Mobil, British Petroleum, and Royal Dutch Shell, were joined by Standard Oil of California, Texaco, and Gulf. Standard Oil of California (SoCal) and Texaco were joint owners of the Saudi Arabian Company, Aramco. They had enormous reserves of oil, particularly in Kuwait, but lacked established market outlets. The companies were faced with two alternatives: either to force their way, by competition, into the world markets dominated by the cartel or to join the cartel and thus secure the established market outlets. Competition did not appeal to the cartel, because it would disrupt world market prices and affect the stability of oil output from other Middle East areas. So the cartel allowed SoCal and Texaco to join them in return for shared interests in Aramco. The cartel was then able to fit Aramco production into world markets without disruptive price competition. Esso and Mobil were given, respectively, 30 percent and 10 percent interest in Aramco and were able to continue the cartel's control over crude oil supplies and world markets.[22]

During the 1960s the oil companies are alleged to have limited petroleum production in order to avoid overproduction. To underscore this allegation, the Senate Foreign Relations Subcommittee on Multinationals released three private documents concerning their attempts to limit oil production.[23] One document, from SoCal's files, warned of a large potential surplus of oil in the world between 1968 and 1973 and suggested limiting production in the Middle East to avoid this surplus. A second document, also from SoCal's files, called for a reduction of domestic production in California and a cutback in the import of oil

22. Ibid., pt. 7, p. 53.
23. Ibid., pt. 8, pp. 1–35.

from Canada to counteract new oil discovered on Alaska's North Slope. A federal government document recommended an investigation into the way oil companies joined the Iranian consortium and stated that potential members were screened and certified by the Price Waterhouse Company, a private auditing firm, before being selected as participants in the overseas venture. A fourth, and unreleased, document alleged that the oil companies drilled wells at the wrong depths in Iraq and plugged up others to confuse the Iraqi government regarding the group's actual oil production.

The allegations concerning the oil companies demonstrates that price fixing and other forms of trade restraint can cut across national boundaries and can involve various countries' multinational firms in a cartel arrangement. Remedies, which will be discussed in Chapter 15, include the application of antitrust laws to monopoly and oligopoly arrangements that restrain trade. Antitrust laws vary in intensity and application among countries. American efforts to regulate the conduct of multinational firms through the application of its antitrust laws outside the United States have in the past engendered conflicts with the laws of other nations. Moreover, combinations and cartel arrangements are regarded differently by other countries. What is needed is some form of international standard for the enforcement of antitrust laws against companies that conspire to restrain trade in international commerce.

SUMMARY

The role of multinational corporations in the world's economy is increasing in importance as the processes of production and distribution transcend national boundaries. More and more of the world's gross national product is being produced by large firms that operate all over the world. Their impact is enormous. It is estimated, for example, that by 1985, two hundred to three hundred multinational corporations will control 80 percent of all the productive assets of the non-Communist world and will produce half the world's gross national product.[24] Another estimate places the productive assets of several hundred multinationals at more than $4 trillion by the end of the century.[25] Some of the current multinationals have a volume of sales larger than the gross national product of many middle-sized European countries, let alone many of the less-developed African or Asian countries. But size is only one component of the multinationals' power; they also control the

24. Howard Perlmutter, "Super-Giant Firms in the Future," *Wharton Quarterly* (Winter, 1968), 1-8.
25. U.S. Chamber of Commerce, "International Trade and Investment: A New Challenge for Management and Labor," undated.

means of creating wealth and make decisions that affect millions of persons.

Whether multinational corporations are good or bad is largely a matter of opinion. The leading multinationals are very large in relation to most national economies outside the United States. Some people worry that a country could become economically and politically subservient to the power of giant multinationals. With their size and the flexibility that arises from being able to operate in many places at one time, multinationals may not be responsive to the dictates of the countries in which they are legally domiciled. Some people also believe that multinationals create unemployment in their home countries as they move to countries with a large supply of cheap labor, and they are concerned that multinationals have increased the possibility of monopolies and cartels forming on a worldwide scale, thus placing them in direct conflict with antitrust laws. Multinational corporations also may create balance of payments problems, particularly for the less-developed countries.

But proponents of the multinationals argue that the fastest way of reducing the technological disparities among countries is to use the multinational enterprise to bridge the gap. Also, the economic benefits to a given company from worldwide operation may result in greater output and lower unit costs. These benefits can accrue from production, research, finance, and growth, through geographic and product diversification. Multinationals also contribute to the level of employment and the economic growth of the countries in which they operate. Many observers also allege that the multinationals are a world force leading to cooperation among countries and breaking down nationalistic barriers. The consequence could be the transformation of single-economy nation-states into a true world economy.

This ambivalence toward the role of multinationals creates problems for public policy. There is no clear consensus as to the appropriate policies to be followed. The influence of the multinationals is so pervasive that public policy would have to include antitrust laws, capital constraints, international tax laws, national sovereignty, and many other areas. Differing national attitudes toward the multinationals also present a problem. Countries often compete with others for the investments of multinationals. For them, all facets of economic policy making are subservient to this aim. Finally, many feel that the whole area of investment decision making is the private sector's prerogative. Government intervention, particularly piecemeal, will only disrupt a complex system of relationships that has had some benefits for the public welfare.

APPENDIX

STANDARD OIL AND ITT—A TALE OF TWO MULTINATIONALS

Political interference by the government in support of its business interests is not new. The two following cases compare Standard Oil's
involvement in Mexico in the early part of the century and ITT's involvement in Chile in the 1970s. In the Standard Oil case, U.S. government support was clear, taking the form of political assassinations, the
dispatchment of the marines into Mexico to seize the customs house at
Vera Cruz, and the support of the right general or bandit. In the ITT
case, gunboat diplomacy was not used, and any government support
there might have been was covert.

STANDARD OIL AND MEXICO

The Standard Oil Company was created by John D. Rockefeller in
1879. By 1884 it was selling more than 80 percent of all the oil that
flowed from domestic wells, and by 1890 it was the largest corporation
in America. In 1906 the U.S. Bureau of Corporations reported that
about 91 percent of the refining industry was either directly or indirectly under the control of Standard Oil. In the same year, the total
production of refined oil in the United States was 27.1 million barrels,
or about 86 percent of the entire domestic output. Given its control
over the domestic market, it was logical for Standard Oil to look for
new sources of oil. One such source was Mexico, where the first effort
to develop oil on a commercial basis had begun shortly after the middle
of the nineteenth century. The British had become interested in the
possibility of commencing production on a commercial scale in Mexico
and therefore formed the London Oil Trust. The British were given desirable oil concessions virtually free by the Mexican dictator Porfirio
Diaz, who wished to attract foreign capital into Mexico. These concessions, however, were not limited to oil resources but applied to other
resources as well.

Standard Oil obtained concessions from the Mexican government on
properties in the Tampico area. Drilling began in 1901, but for several
years thereafter production was small. Then in 1908 the first of the
great gushers was drilled in northern Vera Cruz, near the Laguna de
Tamiahua. In 1910 the oil pools of Pánuco and Topila were discovered
in the basin of the Rio Pánuco, near Tampico, and the gushers at Juan
Casiano and Portrero del Llano came in near Tuxpan. These wells
around Tuxpan were the beginning of the Faja de Oro (the Golden Belt)

that was for many years the principal source of Mexican oil. This belt was controlled by the British through British Petroleum and the Americans through Standard Oil, with the British favored by the dictator Diaz, who once lamented, "Poor Mexico, so far from God and so close to the United States." A law giving foreign investors ownership rights to any resources found in the subsoil of properties was passed during the Diaz dictatorship and was the basic bone of contention between the British and U.S. oil companies and the Mexican government until 1936, when the oil fields were nationalized.

The Standard Oil interest in Mexico was expanded through land purchases and leases from property owners, which gave Standard Oil the title to the subsoil as far as oil was concerned, or at the very least the right to exploit the oil under their lands. Many Mexicans hold that the property owners were robbed of their lands. Many titles were invalid, and many others could not be traced. Government control of title determination was nonexistent, and the government officials were amenable to graft. Standard Oil and other companies paid prices that were far lower than they would have had to pay in the United States, but prices that, at least in some cases, were higher than their Mexican lawyers advised them to pay. In its 1913 annual report, Standard Oil stated, "Every landowner who sold us land during the early years of our operation was the envy of his neighbors and was convinced that he had made a good bargain." But regardless of who exploited whom, the oil fields of Mexico proved a bonanza to British and U.S. oil interests. In 1901 Mexico produced 10,000 barrels of oil; by 1915 its output had increased to 32.9 million barrels, and by 1921 Mexican output had increased to 193.4 million barrels.

Standard Oil and other oil companies took an active interest in Mexican politics, particularly during the Mexican Revolution which began in 1910. One of their objectives was to back the right general, the one who would safeguard their oil interests. Since Diaz had favored the British, it was natural for Standard Oil to back Francisco Madero, who led the revolution that toppled Diaz. But then Madero was assassinated, and the actors changed rapidly, with Huerta, Villa, and Zapata all running Mexico during a period of only fifteen months. The British would support the general who favored their oil interests, and the Americans would do the same. Standard Oil supplied guns to Villa and financed local generals and politicians to keep peace in the oil fields. This was done with the approval of the U.S. State Department, just as the actions of the British oil companies had the approval of the British Foreign Office. World War I provided an excuse for intervening, because oil itself was becoming more important. Consumption by the belligerents in Europe and the development of oil-burning ships brought about a tremendous increase in demand.

The Mexican Constitution of 1917 in principle nationalized oil holdings by stating that all subsoil rights belonged to the state. Although the policy of nationalization was not implemented, tax and registration requirements were imposed on the oil companies. But they were not enforced, as both British and American oil interests supported enclaves of local power—generals, politicians, and bandits—in return for protection. By 1921 Mexico produced one-fourth of the world's oil, with American and British companies controlling 98 percent of Mexico's output. Standard Oil was the single largest producer of Mexican oil, producing 35 percent of the total. Gulf and Texaco also were large producers. After 1921, however, Mexican oil production began to decline, for several reasons. First new sources of oil were discovered in Colombia, Venezuela, and the Persian Gulf region. Second, there was the possibility of nationalization. Third, a policy of new and increased taxation took effect during the 1920s. Although Mexican taxes were not particularly excessive, Colombia and Venezuela gave special tax breaks to encourage oil exploration. And so Mexican oil production slumped from a high of 193.4 million barrels in 1921 to 44.7 million barrels in 1929.

In 1937 foreign oil interests were nationalized by the Mexican government, the two largest being owned by Royal Dutch Shell and Standard Oil. Although the oil companies were partly to blame, for meddling in Mexican politics, probably the main reason was the anti-American sentiment in Mexico that dated from the Mexican War of 1847–1848, when Mexico lost half its territory to the United States and had to pay an indemnity of $15 million to boot. Then the dictator Porfirio Diaz attempted to encourage the nation's economic progress by granting favorable mineral concessions to foreign business firms. By the end of the Diaz regime, these firms had become the real masters of Mexico. The Mexican Revolution was, to some extent, a protest against the church and the foreign domination of Mexico and, to some extent, a vehicle for the many political opportunists to gain control of the country. But the revolution did foster the idea that Mexico was for the Mexicans, and a general animus toward the United States, "the Colossus of the North," remains to this day.

ITT AND CHILE

When the president of Chile, Salvador Allende, was deposed by a military coup in September 1973, a multinational corporation, ITT, and the Central Intelligence Agency (CIA) were alleged to be involved. There is some evidence of ITT's involvement in Chilean internal affairs, although its culpability in the coup has not been proved. In 1970 Salvador Allende, an avowed Marxist and the candidate of a coalition of minority parties, including the Communist Party, received 36 percent of the popular vote in a three-way race in the presidential election. Although Allende's vote was far short of a majority, Chilean law requires only a plurality for victory, and so there was no run-off with the second candidate, who had received 35 percent of the popular vote. Allende had campaigned for a program of extensive land reform and the rapid nationalization of basic industries, banks, and communication systems, many of which were controlled by American and other foreign interests. Needless to say, there was some reason for concern by American business firms with direct investments in Chile.

ITT was one such American firm. Its primary investment in Chile was a 70 percent interest in the Chilean Telephone Company, Chiltelco. The book value of ITT's investment in Chiltelco was estimated to be $153 million, $92.5 million of which was covered by an investment guaranty made by the Overseas Private Investment Corporation (OPIC), which was set up to insure against, among other things, the possibility of expropriation, a possibility mentioned by Allende himself in a campaign speech just before the election. ITT pressured the American government to intervene in the Chilean elections so as to preserve its property interests, and the company offered money to the CIA to support the conservative candidate in the presidential election. The CIA refused this offer. When Allende turned out to be the leader in the three-way race, ITT offered the CIA $1 million to support any means of forming a coalition in the Chilean Congress to prevent Allende from becoming president. This offer gained some support in Washington and was transmitted to the State Department, but no action was taken. In late September of 1970 the CIA initiated tentative discussions with ITT concerning a plan to create economic chaos in Chile. The American banks operating in Chile felt that the plan would be counterproductive.

Allende was elected president by the Chilean Congress in October 1970.[26] In early 1971 an ad hoc committee on Chile was formed by several American companies, including ITT, that had investments in the country. The purpose of the committee was to pressure the White House and the State Department to make it clear to Chile that the nationalization of American firms would not be tolerated. The committee recommended that loans to Chile be blocked. We should emphasize, however, that not all American firms operating in Chile joined the ad hoc committee. In 1971 the properties of Anaconda and Kennecott copper companies were nationalized, and in the same year the Chilean government also took over the operation of Chiltelco, the ITT subsidiary. Following the expropriation of Chiltelco, ITT devised a plan to

26. For background on Allende's election, see U.S., Congress, Senate, Committee on Foreign Relations, *The ITT in Chile: Staff Report of the Subcommittee on Multinational Corporations*, 94th Cong., 2d. sess., 1974, pt. 1, pp. 2-7.

aggravate the Chilean economic situation. Among other things, the plan proposed that the U.S. government and U.S. banks apply loan restrictions to Chile and also postpone buying copper and other Chilean products.[27] But the plan was rejected by elements of the U.S. business community and by the State Department as not feasible.

But attitudes toward Chile hardened after the nationalization of the Anaconda and Kennecott copper mines in 1971, and so parts of the ITT plan were implemented. Export-Import Bank credits, on which Chile's imports from the United States depended, were cut off,[28] and private American banks also were encouraged to stop short-term credit. The United States' Agency for International Development program was terminated, and the multilateral institutions, such as the World Bank and the Inter-American Development Bank, were urged not to approve further loans to Chile. The process of economically isolating Chile was under way. Some American firms refused to sell Chile spare parts for trucks and machinery, even for cash. Kennecott conducted a worldwide legal battle to keep Chile's expropriated copper off the market. But again, not all American firms operating in Chile took part in the boycott, and the State Department was not necessarily a willing accomplice. There is no question that there was a relationship between ITT and the CIA, in which ITT attempted to equate national interests with corporate interest. There was also some carry-over into the White House, with Harold Geneen, the president of ITT, having lunch with Major General Alexander Haig, at that time a deputy to then Secretary of State Henry Kissinger, to discuss Chile.[29]

In September 1973 the Allende Government was overthrown by a military coup, and Allende lost his life. There is no tangible evidence that either the CIA or ITT was connected with the military coup. The Chilean economy was in a state of chaos, and Allende's internal problems were so great that it is likely that he eventually would have been deposed anyway, with or without the machinations of the CIA and ITT. Nonetheless, loans to the Chilean military establishment had been made by U.S. banks at the same time than loans to the Allende government were being curtailed. Rightly or wrongly, ITT was blamed for encouraging the coup, and its world image, which was not too good to begin with, was further tarnished. Its long, deep involvement in the affairs of foreign governments is a matter of record, and it, more than any other American firm, has come to be a symbol of the wicked multinational firm acting in the interests of international capitalism.

27. Committee on Foreign Relations, *Multinational Corporations and United States Foreign Policy*, pt. 1, pp. 27–37.
28. Anthony Sampson, *The Sovereign State of ITT* (Briarcliff Manor, N.Y.: Stein & Day, 1974), pp. 279–283.
29. Alexander Haig was questioned about his involvement in the ITT–Chile arrangement during his confirmation hearings for secretary of state.

QUESTIONS FOR DISCUSSION

1. What is a multinational corporation? Are multinationals solely an American phenomenon?
2. What is the relationship of large international banks to multinational corporations?
3. Discuss the produce cycle model as an explanation of why firms invest abroad.
4. One of the major criticisms of U.S. multinationals is that they exploit cheap labor and cause the loss of domestic jobs to workers in foreign countries. Is this criticism valid?
5. National sovereignty and the multinationals' objectives may often conflict. Discuss.
6. Multinationals may adversely affect the balance of payments of less-developed countries. Discuss.
7. What is the rationale of the foreign tax credit?
8. What are tax deferrals, and what advantages do they offer to U.S. firms operating abroad?
9. What was the Achnacarry Agreement?
10. On balance, are multinationals a positive or a negative influence on world society?

RECOMMENDED READINGS

Barnet, Richard J., and Ronald E. Muller. *Global Reach: The Power of the Multinational Corporations.* New York: Simon & Schuster, 1974.

Bergsten, C. Fred, Thomas Horst, and Theodore H. Moran. *American Multinationals and American Interests.* Washington, D.C.: Brookings Institution, 1978.

Dunning, John H., ed. *Economic Analysis and the Multinational Enterprise.* New York: Praeger, 1975.

Feld, Werner J. *Multinational Corporations and U.N. Politics.* Elmsford, N.Y.: Pergamon Press, 1980.

Hymer, Stephen. *The Multinational Corporation: A Radical Approach.* Cambridge, England: Cambridge University Press, 1979.

Kindleberger, Charles P. *American Business Abroad: Six Lectures on Direct Investment.* New Haven, Conn.: Yale University Press, 1969.

Madden, Carl H., ed. *The Case for the Multinational Corporation.* New York: Praeger, 1977.

Parry, Thomas G. *The Multinational Enterprise.* Greenwich, Conn.: JAI Press, 1980.

Sampson, Anthony. *The Seven Sisters.* New York: Viking, 1975.

Solomon, Lewis D. *Multinational Corporations and the Emerging World Order.* Port Washington, N.Y.: National University Publishers, 1978.

Wilkins, Mira. *The Emergence of Multinational Enterprise: American Business Abroad from the Colonial Era to 1914.* Cambridge, Mass.: Harvard University Press, 1974.

——. *The Maturing of Multinational Enterprise: American Business Abroad from 1914 to 1970.* Cambridge, Mass.: Harvard University Press, 1974.

Chapter 15
Further Issues Involving Multinational Corporations

Chapter 14 focused on the development of the multinational corporation and its increased impact on the world's economies. The multinational corporation transcends economic and political barriers and is limited to no one country or political ideology. In fact, the centrally planned socialist economies have their own multinationals, which often operate in conjunction with capitalist multinationals in joint exploration and trading ventures. Chapter 14 also discussed some of the more controversial issues involving the multinationals, especially the U.S. multinationals. But these issues are by no means limited to American multinationals; they apply to any multinational. Probably the most important issue is the multinationals' ability to engage in restrictive trade practices through the formation of cartels and other types of combinations, and because multinationals operate all over the world, policing and regulating these unfair business practices have become more difficult.

Chapter 15 will examine the legal implications of multinationals, with emphasis on American and foreign antitrust regulation and practices, as well as bribery as a way of doing business. There is some conflict in the attitudes of the United States and other countries toward the appropriate application of antitrust in controlling the multinationals. This conflict can be attributed partly to the differing opinions of the merits of a freely competitive economic system. American efforts to regulate the conduct of multinationals through the application of U.S. antitrust laws both internally and externally have sometimes conflicted with the laws of other countries. Moreover, in recent years, Congress passed a law designed to boost the moral image of U.S. multinationals abroad. This law, the Foreign Corrupt Practices Act, makes it a criminal offense for any corporation, its employees, or agents to make improper payments to foreigners to win business or influence foreign legislation. Critics argue that this law makes it difficult, if not impossible, for U.S. companies to do business in those parts of the world in which bribery is acceptable and expected.

We also shall discuss the increasing importance of foreign investments in the United States. From after World War II up to 1970, the United States was a huge exporter of capital. But now that is changing, and recent events have dramatized the fact that both direct and indirect foreign investment have accelerated. In 1979 the book value of foreign direct investment was $55.5 billion and of indirect, or portfolio, investment, $177.1 billion. Foreign investment affects the American economy in that it creates jobs, brings in new technology, provides a new source of competition, and, at least in the short run, has a positive effect on the balance of payments. There is some concern that foreign investors eventually may control a significant segment of U.S. agriculture and industry, but this concern appears to be unwarranted. Foreign investment in the United States also means that the antitrust laws must be applied as well to foreign corporations, as jurisdiction is based on the corporation's legal site, not on its parentage. Each country, including the United States, has certain categories of restrictions; for example, foreigners may not own certain real estate judged to be strategic, nor may they control communications companies. But this is an illustration of, rather than an exception to, the principle that a corporation is subject to the law of the place in which it does business.

CONTROLLING THE MULTINATIONALS — ANTITRUST LAWS

It is somewhat difficult for the government to control the multinational corporations' operations. The multinationals are active in a number of different countries, often under the cover of a closed local corporation. The laws relating to the public disclosure of financial results are generally designed for large, publicly held domestic corporations, and thus the multinational corporation can escape the more stringent of these laws. Too, the United States is not the sole base of the multinational corporations. On the contrary, foreign multinational corporations are rapidly multiplying their bases of operations, and some are merging with American companies. It is clear that American-based multinational firms have to expect increasingly tough competition from foreign multinationals, at home as well as abroad.

U.S. antitrust laws were enacted in part because of the belief that competition would best ensure a prosperous economy and in part because of the political conviction that a competitive economy would best promote the interests of society. Congress supported these laws, not only because it believed that a competitive economy would encourage material prosperity, but also because it believed that such competition would preserve the Jeffersonian society of many independent small businesspersons. Thus, the operation of the economy would be determined by the impersonal judgment of the marketplace, rather than by combinations of business firms or by central planners. The framers of the antitrust laws insisted that commerce in goods and services stand the cold test of competition and thereby avoid controlling prices, restricting production, and other evils arising from undue limitation of competition.

The American view that a freely competitive economic system is the most efficient and most desirable form of society is not necessarily held by the other major industrial powers, including the Soviet Union. On the contrary, their premise is that restrictive business practices are often beneficial to their national interests, particularly in the international business arena. The Western European countries and Japan favor the use of combinations and cartels of domestic enterprises in order to compete more effectively with the powerful American-based multinationals. Too, the creation of new markets in the Soviet Union and Eastern Europe favors combinations and cartels to some extent, for the Russians and the Eastern Europeans favor package deals of a magnitude that cannot be handled by the typical multinational firm. As the multinational industries form more and more international cartels, domestic laws alone will no longer be able to control them.

Application of U.S. Antitrust Laws to Multinationals

American antitrust policy is applicable to any U.S. firm engaged in international business. In regard to foreign commerce in general, U.S. antitrust policy has three separate objectives: to eliminate unreasonable restraints on American exports and imports, to encourage foreign firms to enter the American market, and to prevent American or foreign firms from restraining commerce in the United States through their foreign operations. These objectives are governed primarily by four laws: the Sherman Antitrust Act, the Clayton Antitrust Act, the Federal Trade Commission Act, and the Webb-Pomerene Act. Of these, the Sherman and Clayton acts have had the greatest impact on the multinationals' operations. The Sherman Act has been extended through judicial interpretation to apply to both American and foreign firms operating in the United States, which permits American courts to govern parties and acts both inside and outside the United States.

There are two important concepts that pertain to the application of U.S. antitrust laws. One is extraterritorial reach, which is defined as the employment of U.S. domestic antitrust statutes in considering business operations outside American territorial limits. Extraterritorial reach is also the legal basis for controlling the actions of corporations operating outside the United States, thus subjecting worldwide actions to national control. The second concept is the effects test, which means that any action, no matter when or where committed, is subject to U.S. antitrust law if it affects American commerce. This gives the U.S. courts a potentially limitless charter of jurisdiction, because an act committed anywhere in the world conceivably can affect U.S. commerce.

The Sherman Act

The Sherman Act aims primarily at maintaining and promoting interstate and foreign trade or commerce. Both Sections 1 and 2 are applicable to American corporations operating in other countries. Section 1
provides that any contract or combination in the form of a trust or
otherwise, or any conspiracy in restraint of trade or commerce among
states or with foreign nations, is illegal. Section 2 makes it a crime to
monopolize or attempt to monopolize, or combine or conspire with
anyone to monopolize, any part of trade or commerce among the states
or with foreign nations. To invoke the Sherman Act, involvement in
either interstate or foreign commerce is enough. Foreign commerce
normally refers to U.S. exports and imports, but the act may also apply
to transactions whose impact is entirely outside the limits of the United
States if American interests are involved. In the 1968 Pacific Seafarers
case, the act set up restraints used solely in shipping between foreign
ports, in which any shipments financed by the U.S. government were
limited by law to transportation in U.S. ships.[1]

The first major international application of the Sherman Act came in
the landmark American Tobacco case of 1911.[2] The American Tobacco
Company and the Imperial Tobacco Company of Great Britain had
agreed to divide markets, with Imperial agreeing not to sell tobacco in
the United States except through the American Tobacco Company.[3]
The two companies then formed a third corporation, the British-American Tobacco Company, which took over all the foreign business of
American and Imperial, though British-American Tobacco could not
export to the United States. As a part of its overall decision with regard
to the American Tobacco Company, the Supreme Court ruled that this
allocation of markets illegally restrained trade under the provisions of
the Sherman Act. All parties to the agreement, including Imperial Tobacco, were held to have violated the act. The pooling agreement under
which the American Tobacco Company and the Imperial Tobacco Company had combined to form the British-American Company was canceled. The Court held that the Sherman Act applied to restraints, including contracts or combinations, that operated to the prejudice of the
public by unduly restricting competition.

The Sherman Act has been applied outside the United States by reasons of market power, intent, and effect, although until World War II,
the courts required that for an act to be considered a violation of the
Sherman Act, it had to be committed within the United States.

1. *Pacific Seafarers, Inc.* v. *Pacific Far East Lines, Inc.*. 404 F.2d 804 (D.D.C.
   1968).
2. *U.S.* v. *American Tobacco Co.*, 221 U.S. 10C, 31 Sup. Ct. 632 (1911).
3. This was only a part of the American Tobacco Case.

In 1927, in a case involving the Sisal Sales Corporation, the Supreme Court declared a conspiracy to monopolize United States foreign commerce to be illegal.[4] The Court emphasized the aspect of unlawful results within the United States and asserted that for an act to be illegal it had to be committed by both domestic and foreign firms within the country. After World War II, however, the courts shifted their position to include acts committed outside the United States. The landmark Alcoa case of 1945 established the principle that the U.S. courts could regulate actions conducted outside the United States that have direct and foreseeable economic consequences inside the United States.[5] In the National Lead case of 1947, American and foreign companies were found to have participated in an international restraint of trade in the production of titanium pigments.[6] A majority of the Supreme Court ruled that the Sherman Act was applicable because the restraint affected American commerce. In the Timken Roller Bearing case of 1951, the Supreme Court ruled that a joint venture between Timken and British and French roller-bearing firms created a cartel arrangement to allocate world markets and restrict imports to the United States.[7] In addition, Timken held 30 percent of the British company's common stock and 50 percent of the French company's common stock.

The test of the applicability of the Sherman Act in both the National Lead and Timken cases came to be known as the effects test and enabled an almost unlimited extraterritorial application of the Sherman Act, for almost any commercial enterprise anywhere in the world conceivably could have an effect on U.S. domestic commerce. Agreements made on foreign soil do not relieve an American defendant from the responsibility for restraint of trade. So, at present, proven effects on American commerce may bring totally foreign conduct under the purview of the Sherman Act. It is no longer the place where the act occurs that is the key; rather, when an act or agreement can be shown to have a direct effect on markets within the United States, the Sherman Act will cover it. Of course, it is necessary to have jurisdiction over the party or parties committing the act for this to have any effect. This normally presents no problem with a subsidiary of an American corporation, let alone with the corporation itself.

4. *U.S.* v. *Sisal Sales Corporation*, 247 U.S. 268 (1927).
5. The Alcoa case was discussed in Chapter 6.
6. *U.S.* v. *National Lead Co.*, 63F, Supp. 513 (S.D.N.Y. 1945) modified 332 U.S. 319 (1947).
7. *U.S.* v. *Timken Roller Bearing Co.*, 83F, Supp. 284 (N.D. Ohio 1949) modified 341 U.S. 593 (1951).

The Clayton Act

The Clayton Act, particularly Sections 1 and 7, also can be applied to American firms operating abroad. Section 1 includes trade with other nations in its definition of commerce, and Section 7 prohibits one firm from acquiring the stock or assets of another firm when the result may substantially lessen competition or create a monopoly. Section 7 applies to the acquisition of foreign firms by U.S. firms only if the latter are engaged in the foreign commerce of the United States and if the acquisition lessens competition in any part of the country. A transaction that reduces competition does not have to occur within the continental limits of the United States. For example, an American firm could acquire a foreign firm in Argentina that resulted in its controlling the market for a given product in that country. If this restricted American exports to this market, with adverse effects being felt by a particular part of the United States, then Section 7 would apply. The key is whether or not the acquisition will lessen competition in U.S. markets or among U.S. firms engaged in foreign commerce. Thus, the Clayton Act could be used to promote greater competition in a foreign market if the business activities in some way reduced competition in the United States.

A merger between an American firm and a foreign firm not operating in the United States can be challenged by Section 7 of the Clayton Act when the consequence is to reduce competition. In fact, foreign acquisitions can also be challenged under the doctrine of potential competition. In *U.S.* v. *Joseph Schlitz Brewing Company*, Schlitz's proposed acquisition of John Labatt, Ltd., a Canadian brewery, was challenged on the grounds that a small California brewer owned by Labatt was a competitor of Schlitz and that Labatt was a potential entrant on a larger scale in the U.S. market.[8] This doctrine was also applied to the Gillette case.

In this case resolved in December 1975 involving Gillette, the leading American manufacturer of razors, and Braun, a major European electric razor firm, the acquisition of Braun by Gillette was challenged on the grounds that potential competition would be eliminated.[9] The rationale behind this challenge was that a potential entrant, while standing at the periphery of the market, may significantly affect the performance of an oligopolistic industry.[10] This is true whether the potential entrant is domestic or foreign. Gillette, given the nature of its product, does operate in an oligopolistic industry and probably dominates it. The fact that Braun had not entered the U.S. market was not a deterrent to the merger challenge, as the company had the ability to enter the market and

8. *U.S.* v. *Joseph Schlitz Brewing Company*, 253F, Supp. 129 (1966) and 385 U.S. 37 (1966).
9. *U.S.* v. *Gillette Co.*, Civ. No. 68-141 (D.C. Mass., 1975).
10. Trade Reg. Rep. 4.345.19.

provide competition. Thus, the merger was not allowed, and Gillette was ordered to create a new company to market Braun's products in the United States.

The Clayton Act requires only that anticompetitive effects be felt in any line of commerce in any section of the United States. The transaction that causes the effects does not have to occur within the geographical limits of the United States, nor do transgressors have to be American firms. Thus, the Justice Department challenged a merger between two foreign firms that would have the effect of merging their two American subsidiaries, which were important direct competitors in the same market.[11] The outcome of this case was to force divestiture of one of the subsidiaries so that preexisting competition could prevail in the American market. The wording of Section 7, restricting its application to combinations of corporations engaged in commerce, does not exclude foreign mergers. Even potential competition with an American firm, as shown above, may fall within the purview of the Clayton Act.

The Federal Trade Commission and Webb-Pomerene Acts

The Federal Trade Commission Act and the Webb-Pomerene Act also can be applied to multinational corporations. The Federal Trade Commission has concurrent jurisdiction with the Justice Department in dealing with acts that are illegal under antitrust laws. Moreover, Section 5 of the Federal Trade Commission Act supplements the power of Section 7 of the Clayton Act. The Webb-Pomerene Act exempts American firms from the antitrust laws for cooperative participation in export associations. Its purpose is to ensure free access to foreign markets for domestic exports on a basis that will be competitive with foreign exporters. But the act does prohibit the formation of associations when the result is to restrain trade in the United States or to restrain exports of domestic competitors. Section 4 of the Webb-Pomerene Act expands the jurisdiction of the Federal Trade Commission to include unfair methods of competition outside the United States, and Section 5 provides for the registration of all export associations with the Federal Trade Commission.

The Webb-Pomerene Act does not automatically immunize every type of joint export venture from the Sherman Act. There are prohibitions against acts in foreign trade that substantially reduce competition in the United States. In the Minnesota Mining and Manufacturing case of 1950, which involved a joint venture by nine American abrasive manufacturers to establish an export association and create a joint subsidiary in Europe, the Supreme Court ruled that the move would

11. *U.S.* v. *Ciba Corporation*, 1970 Trade Case (S.D.N.Y. 1970) consent decree.

restrict exports from the United States.[12] The Court reasoned that the association would reduce the firms' zeal for competition in the American market. In general, then, the rule for applying Webb-Pomerene is that participating companies in an export association may agree among themselves on prices and allocate world markets for exports, as long as competition within the United States is not affected. In practice, Webb-Pomerene has proved to be of little practical importance because most joint export arrangements may be carried on under the Sherman Act and because American firms selling highly differentiated products have generally not wanted to merge with their competitors.

Criticism of U.S. Antitrust Laws

Many business firms insist that U.S. antitrust laws place them at a disadvantage in competing with firms abroad. They argue that investment opportunities are often avoided in the world marketplace for fear they would attract the attention of the Justice Department or the Federal Trade Commission. In some cases, American firms feel that they have lost business to foreign competitors because the latter have been able to form consortia and offer package deals, whereas the American firms have had to bid independently. Moreover, a study published by an antitrust task force of the U.S. Chamber of Commerce concluded that American exporters and overseas contractors are restricted by U.S. antitrust laws.[13] Foreign countries, including Japan and the leading industrial countries of Western Europe, do not impose their antitrust laws on export trade and, indeed, often encourage their exporters and contractors to combine in the national interest. Thus U.S. business firms see their foreign competition playing the international trade game under different, more lenient ground rules, with a deleterious effect on the U.S. balance of payments.

U.S. antitrust laws to control unfair business practices have long been considered the most stringent in the world. But the American firms' contention that U.S. antitrust laws place them at a competitive disadvantage with European and Japanese business firms is difficult to prove. The Justice Department argues that American firms have failed to deliver any conclusive evidence that U.S. foreign trade is hampered by the antitrust laws. The business firms retort that the laws have an inhibiting effect on investments; the laws exist, and the firms are never sure of what constitutes a violation. The firms also argue that joint ventures or consortia often are needed to do business with state trading companies

12. *U.S.* v. *Minnesota Mining and Mfg. Co.*, 92 F. Supp. 947, 1958 (D. Mass. 1950).
13. U.S. Chamber of Commerce, Antitrust Task Force on International Trade and Investment, *Final Report on U.S. Antitrust and American Exports*, 1974.

in the socialist countries. But the Justice Department emphasizes that when the size of a project or the risks involved are so great that one company cannot undertake it alone, it will be held to be legal under U.S. antitrust law. It is when the joint venture is proved to have been a device for suppressing individual competition that could or would have occurred that the transaction will raise antitrust problems.

Foreign Antitrust Laws and the Multinationals

The attitudes of the United States and of other countries toward the role of antitrust laws in regulating various forms of industrial concentration differ. U.S. antitrust law is based on the principle that competition per se is good. The Western European and Japanese governments do not agree, particularly with respect to foreign trade, feeling that industrial concentration and anticompetitive agreements are beneficial, as long as they lead to increased productivity, economic growth, and the advance of technology. European and Japanese antitrust laws are not directed toward breaking up cartels and combinations, but toward regulating and guiding them in the national interest. This is to be expected, since government is more directive in most European countries and in Japan than in the United States. Several European countries not only permit but encourage agreements, combinations, and mergers among companies for the purpose of rationalizing production. They have encouraged joint research and joint marketing, have permitted pricing agreements, and also have allowed the formation of export cartels.

One example of this point of view has been the French government's policy with respect to large-scale enterprises. In January 1972 the largest French industrial combine of all, with $2.7 billion in annual sales, was formed when a new stock issue united two companies, Pechiney and Ugine Kuhlmann, which dominate Europe in the production of aluminum, stainless steel, specialty steels, and nonferrous metals such as titanium and zirconium. The main reason for the formation of the combine was to take advantage of a worldwide marketing network set up by Pechiney. In 1973, Pechiney acquired the United States' Howmet Corporation, an aluminum maker and fabricator that had sales of $300 million. The Pechiney–Ugine Kuhlmann combine also concluded joint negotiations with the Soviet Union to help design and build a $500 million aluminum complex in Siberia which has an output equal to nearly half of Pechiney's worldwide capacity.

Antitrust Laws in Japan

The cartel arrangement has been synonymous with the growth of the modern Japanese economy. In 1880 the first Japanese combines, called *zaibatsu*, were formed. These combines dominated the economy to the point that by the beginning of World War II five family-owned *zaibatsu* produced over one-half of the Japanese gross national product and controlled 80 percent of the total private overseas investment.[14] After the end of the war, American occupation authorities passed an antimonopoly act to dissolve the *zaibatsu* and to create a free market economy. Later, however, the Japanese government enacted various laws to exempt certain industries from the antimonopoly act. Generally, these laws permitted exemptions for three types of cartels—cartels to prevent excessive competition among smaller enterprises, cartels for export and import industries, and cartels for special rationalization in which economies of scale are involved. These exemptions were designed to improve Japan's position as a world exporter, to stimulate its rate of economic growth, and to enable it to compete effectively with American multinationals. Indeed, the present Japanese antimonopoly legislation permits the development of cartels and other forms of combinations to a far greater extent than is permitted by U.S. antitrust laws.

Japanese government policy, however, has stressed consumer protection against such practices as price fixing. The Japanese Fair Trade Commission has taken action against internal price-fixing agreements in such areas as automobile tires, synthetic fibers, petroleum, and household electrical appliances. The commission also has initiated action against false or misleading advertising. With regard to unfair business practices, Japanese antitrust law is as stringent as American law, but with regard to mergers, corporate interlocking directorates, and stockholdings, Japanese law is far more lenient, particularly when international trade is involved, than American law. In one merger case, the merger of three firms, each dominant in its field, was allowed on the grounds that it was necessary to meet international competition. But mergers that account for over 30 percent of a given market may be challenged unless it can be demonstrated that foreign competition must be met or that a company is failing. Most mergers in Japan have been between competing enterprises; that is, they have been of the horizontal type.

14. Corwin Edwards, "The Dissolution of Zaibatsu Continues," *Pacific Affairs* (September 1946), 8–24.

Antitrust Laws in West Germany

West German multinationals also compete with U.S. corporations. In the area of antimonopoly legislation, West Germany passed a law called the "Law Against Restraints of Competition."[15] The law did several things with respect to cartels and combinations. It prohibited horizontal and vertical restrictive agreements among groups, including price fixing and market sharing. The law also created a Federal Cartel Authority. One function of the authority is the supervision of cartels, all of which have to register with it. For individual enterprises that have no competition or have no substantial competition for a particular category of goods, the authority can initiate court action if an enterprise abuses its position. In addition, all mergers in which the participating firms employed ten thousand or more persons at any time during the previous year, had a turnover of DM 500 million and over, or maintained a balance of DM 2 billion or over in the last completed business year have to register with the authority. Details of horizontal and vertical mergers of business firms also have to be filed with the authority.

The stated purpose of the West German antimonopoly legislation is to improve the functioning of a competitive market system—something to which the Germans historically have been unaccustomed. The government is somewhat ambivalent toward the legislation. For example, mergers are allowed if they are deemed good for the economy as a whole or if they promote the public welfare. The same holds true for cartels. There are exceptions to the prohibition of vertical agreements, particularly with respect to resale price maintenance for branded goods, as long as the products concerned are open to some form of price competition. The German position is that it would be disadvantageous to control unilaterally mergers and concentrations as well as restrictive practices if elsewhere in the same economic area other governments are encouraging them. Indeed, to prevent concentration in certain areas may be to preclude the economies of scale that is one of the chief advantages of the Common Market.

International Antitrust Laws

The antitrust laws of the United States, Japan, and West Germany are national laws that reflect differences in attitudes toward cartels and combinations. In the United States business practices are illegal if they are prohibited by any of the antitrust laws. In Japan and West Germany there is an attempt to differentiate between those restrictive practices that may have a harmful effect on a given market situation and those

15. Gesetz gegen Wettbewerbsbeschränkungen.

practices that, although restrictive, may benefit the economy as a whole. But it should not be assumed that foreign countries are always more lenient in their application of antitrust laws than is the United States. National policies are similar in their commitment to certain goals. These policies attempt to prevent any private action that may impair business access to markets, and they attempt to keep prices low and supplies of goods adequate to the needs of the consumers. The difference among national antitrust policies lies in attitude. To the Europeans and Japanese, national economic well-being is the prime desideratum, and restrictive practices that are felt to be in the national interest may be promoted actively.

There are bound to be conflicts with the various antitrust laws of different countries. One such conflict arises from the cartelization of domestic enterprises in Germany, Japan, and other countries for the purpose of competing with U.S.-based multinationals. In fact, the Commission of the European Economic Community, which is the antitrust governing body of the Common Market, issued a memorandum in 1966 stating that an increase in combinations of European firms in the Common Market was necessary to allow European business firms to meet the competition of American and Japanese multinationals.[16] Another source of conflict is the jurisdiction of antitrust laws. There may be conflicts in the sovereignty inherent in the extraterritorial application of antitrust laws. An example of this is the Imperial Chemical Industries of Great Britain (ICI) case, in which a U.S. federal court ordered ICI, which had entered into a licensing agreement with Du Pont, to retransfer British patents to Du Pont for licensing.[17] A British court refused to carry out this order because an American court had ordered an act on British soil that conflicted with British law and this could not be enforced.

Because national attitudes toward the enforcement of antitrust laws vary, standard international antitrust laws would be difficult to design. About the only thing that resembles an antitrust policy cutting across national boundaries is the antitrust laws written by the European Economic Community. At present there is a dual system of national and community antitrust laws, with each member country maintaining its own set of domestic antitrust laws, and there is a different tier of antitrust laws governing actions within the Common Market itself. These laws are spelled out in the Rome Treaty of 1957, which created the Common Market.[18] Article 85 prohibits restrictive practices by business

16. Unpublished memorandum of the Commission of the European Economic Community, 1966, p. 1251.
17. *U.S.* v. *Imperial Chemical Industries, Ltd.*, 100 F. Supp. 504 (S.D.N.Y. 1951).
18. The European Economic Community has merged with the European Coal and Steel Community and Euratom and is now referred to as the European Communities.

firms operating within the Common Market. A practice is restrictive if it affects trade among member countries or has as its objective the prevention, restriction, or distortion of trade in the Common Market. However, certain transactions are exempt from Article 85 sanctions if they are found to stimulate the general economy and strengthen the position of member states. Article 86 prohibits the abuse of a dominant position within the Common Market or a part of it. The Rome Treaty also created the European Economic Community Commission (Article 60) as the antitrust governing body of the Common Market. Articles 85 and 86 are directed, respectively, at agreements in restraint of trade and abuses of dominant market position, but they contain no provision that deals expressly with mergers and acquisitions.

Significance for American Multinationals

As mentioned earlier, Europe is one of the main areas for investment by U.S. multinationals, and much of the expansion in the Common Market has been through mergers or acquisitions. Both American and European multinationals are free from antimerger prohibitions, for the policy of the Economic Communities has been to promote the integration of firms in the Common Market in order to achieve enterprises of larger scale, and national governments have encouraged economic integration in order to forestall a supposed American takeover of European business enterprises.[19] But it is possible to apply Article 86 to mergers in that it prohibits abuses of a dominant position in the Common Market. The focus is not on the acquisition of one firm by another, but on an abuse that may result from a dominant position achieved by a firm either before or after the merger.

The Continental Can Case

The Continental Can case of 1971 illustrates the application of Article 86 to the abuse of a dominant market position.[20] Continental Can, an American manufacturer of metal containers and paper and plastic packaging materials, acquired through its European subsidiary, Europenballage Corporation, a controlling interest in German and Dutch con-

19. Howard Adler and Murray J. Belman, "Antitrust Enforcement in Europe—Trends and Prospects," *Journal of International Law and Economics*, 17 (1974), 31–41.
20. U.S., Congress, Senate, Committee on Foreign Relations, *Multinational Corporations and United States Foreign Policy: Hearings Before the Subcommittee on Multinational Corporations* (Washington, D.C.: U.S. Government Printing Office, 1975), pt. 10.

tainer companies. The European Economic Community Commission initiated action against Continental Can, contending that its acquisitions virtually eliminated competition in light metal containers for canned meats, metal lids, and so on, for a substantial part of the Common Market.

Continental Can appealed to the Court of Justice of the Economic Community, which overruled the commission on the grounds that Article 86 was applicable only to an abuse of a dominant position in a market. It also ruled that an increase in market dominance at the expense of competition could be an abuse but that the ultimate test was whether competition was affected so substantially that any remaining competitors no longer could provide sufficient counterbalance. In this respect, the court found the commission's decision wanting.

CORRUPT PRACTICES

Bribery is an accepted way of life in many countries, a way to get things done. In fact, there are special words for bribery: in the Latin countries it is called *mordita*, which literally means "bite"; in the Arab countries it is called *baksheesh*, which can be translated as "rake-off"; and in the Soviet Union it is called *blat*, which means "under the table." The moral implications of bribery are irrelevant in these countries, if, indeed, moral considerations are even considered. To customs officials in a Latin American country, a bribe is regarded as a way to supplement an income that is typically low. Foreigners, then, are often faced with a dilemma—do they play by the rules of the game, give the bribe, and get what they want done; or do they stand on their own principles and refuse to play by the rules of the game? Noble sentiments can be costly in societies that are conditioned to accepting various forms of bribery. One person may be delayed in customs for several days for failing to get a needed appointment, whereas another person, who has played the local game, is immediately cleared through customs and obtains the needed appointment.

The Foreign Corrupt Practices Act

The Foreign Corrupt Practices Act (FCPA) was passed in 1977 in response to scandals arising from the revelation of large payments that U.S. corporations had made to foreign government officials. Although this was hardly a new phenomenon, it did not become a public issue in the United States until the Watergate investigations revealed corporate slush funds through which contributions had been made to President Richard Nixon's campaign fund. The Securities and Exchange Commission found that the slush funds were also being used for contributions to foreign political parties and for bribery of foreign officials.[21] The SEC then began to bring suits against some companies under the disclosure of the material information requirement of the 1933 and 1934 securities acts. When the pervasiveness of the problem was recognized, the commission began a voluntary disclosure program that, to a certain extent, insulated companies from litigation. In all, about four hundred American companies admitted making payments to officials in various countries. The amounts ranged from a few thousand dollars to over $250 million for Lockheed.

Why Payments Are Made

There are four major categories of payments to foreign countries:

1. Those made to obtain or keep business. Many companies have argued that not making payments puts them at a competitive disadvantage in markets in which payments are a routine part of doing business. For example, Lockheed claimed that any prohibition against payments would cripple its position vis-à-vis Japanese and European firms, affecting not only Lockheed's potential sales but also its backlog orders.[22]

2. Preventive maintenance. This includes averting undesirable events such as the expropriation or nationalization of assets, the expulsion of a company from a country, and the cancellation of existing rights such as drilling concessions. This kind of payment is especially important to oil companies.

3. Establishing or preserving a favorable business climate. This means influencing foreign administrative or legislative action in such areas as taxes, price controls, and the extent of government regulation of business. More concrete examples are payments to high-level bureaucrats to obtain product registration, import permits, and construction permits.

4. "Grease." This is a term for payments to low-level officials to expedite performance of routine public services. In less-developed countries, bureaucrats are often paid low salaries, and so many augment their incomes by doing favors for businesspersons and individuals. In countries where this is a common practice, it is an accepted, although technically illegal, way for bureaucrats to act and for business to be conducted.

21. U.S. Advisory Committee on Corporate Disclosure, *Report on Corporate Disclosure to Securities and Exchange Commission*, November 3, 1977.
22. *Wall Street Journal*, "Damage to Governments Friendly to U.S. Is Seen in Disclosure of Lockheed Bribes," February 9, 1976, p. 7.

Types of Industries

Certain industries are more prone to offer bribes than others are.[23]
Huge government contracts are often written in heavy capital goods
industries such as aerospace. Because any one contract is important to a
company and bids tend to be close, companies may be tempted to try
to improve their chances of winning a given contract by bribing the decision makers. Similarly, companies selling arms to foreign governments
are more likely to make payments. The arms are paid for with public
money, and in the absence of a profit motive, the only risk to the
bureaucrat is disclosure. In addition, industries closely regulated by
foreign government agencies are apt to take payments for such purposes
as obtaining product registration. For example, American drug companies were among the top spenders in regard to foreign payments.
Finally, the oil industry made foreign payments to avert the possibility
of oil expropriation, among other things.

Provisions of the Foreign Corrupt Practices Act

The Foreign Corrupt Practices Act does three things:

1. It sets accounting standards by requiring business firms to keep
accurate books and records and to devise and maintain a system of
internal accounting controls.

2. It prohibits the corrupt use of the mails or any means of commerce to offer, pay, or promise to pay an authorized payment or gift
to any foreign official, foreign political party, officer, candidate, or
third party who might have influence with foreign officials or politicians, when the objective is to influence an act or decision favorable
to the business firm giving the payment.

3. It provides sanctions for violation: fines of up to $1 million for
companies and fines of up to $10,000 and imprisonment for up to five
years for individuals.

Attitudes Toward Bribery in Other Countries

Bribery and other forms of payments are by no means the sole preserve
of American firms; European and Japanese firms have also made their
share of bribes. Siemens, the giant West German electrical equipment

---

23. Edward D. Herlihy and Theodore A. Levine, "Corporate Crisis: The Overseas
Payment Problem," *Law and Policy in International Business*, 8 (March 1976),
547–629.

multinational, has been accused of making payoffs in several countries to obtain lucrative contracts.[24] The Austrian government has charged that Siemens used bribes to win a contract to build a hospital in Vienna. In Indonesia, the state company Pertamina has alleged that Siemens paid out millions of dollars in illicit payments to a former official of the company. Siemens supposedly made the payments to win contracts to build power facilities at a large Indonesian steel plant. A scandal in Italy resulted in the suspension of Giorgio Mazzanti, the president of ENI, Italy's state-owned oil company, for making payments of $130 million to a go-between in negotiations for a large oil contract in Saudi Arabia. Another European scandal emerged when a Belgian firm, Euro-systems Hospitalies, went bankrupt in 1979. The company had won a bid to build a five-hundred-bed hospital in Saudi Arabia by promising a commission of 30 percent of the original price to influential Saudis. Prince Albert, a brother of the Belgian king, was implicated in the scandal.

More important than the actual bribes are the attitudes of foreign governments toward payoffs made by their multinationals. Companies based in West Germany have something extra going for them when it comes to payoffs. If a payoff is made outside Germany, the German company can consider it a legal and tax-deductible business expense. The same holds true for the United Kingdom. British firms resorting to bribery in overseas business need only to report the bribe to Inland Revenue as a cost of doing business. The main competitor of the United States, Japan, also has no legal proscriptions against bribery, and Japanese firms have been involved in payoffs to government officials in Indonesia and the Malay States. French firms, too, are not bothered by antibribery laws. The consequence is that multinationals of other countries play by different game rules, with a resultant loss of business to U.S. multinationals. The best solution to the bribery problem would be an enforceable international agreement. According to such an agreement, the firms of all countries would be forced to compete on equal grounds, and the United States would avoid the appearance of trying to export its morality.

FOREIGN BUSINESS INVESTMENT IN THE UNITED STATES

Much has happened since Servan-Schreiber wrote *The American Challenge*.[25] Today, the shoe appears to be on the other foot, for there has

24. *Wall Street Journal*, "West German Concern Faces Bribery Charges in Contracting Abroad," February 17, 1981, p. 1.
25. Jean Jacques Servan-Schreiber, *The American Challenge* (New York: Atheneum, 1968), p. 205.

been a complete turnabout. Now Americans are concerned that foreigners will take over their country and that Arab sheiks and Japanese businessmen will impose their values on them. Somewhat reinforcing this view, *Newsweek* magazine published an article called "The Buying of America."[26] Although the title was rather sensational, the claim does have at least some validity. Foreigners invest in American real estate and securities, purchase American companies, and produce a variety of items in the factories they build. The Germans make Volkwagen Rabbits in a factory that Chrysler had to abandon. The Japanese bottle Coca-Cola in New Hampshire, raise cattle in Utah, and make soy sauce in rural Wisconsin. Through the acquisition of American firms, foreign companies now control such standard American products as Peter Paul candy bars, Pepsodent toothpaste, Hardee's hamburgers, Baskin-Robbins multi-flavored ice cream, A & P groceries, Howard Johnson motels and restaurants, and the upset-stomach nostrum, Alka-Seltzer. And foreigners now lease 60 percent of the shops along the carriage-trade mile of New York's Fifth Avenue.

There are several reasons why the United States has become such a popular place for foreign investment. Probably the most important reason is the devaluation of the dollar relative to foreign currencies, making the lower U.S. prices attractive to foreign investment.[27] Land, energy, transportation, and work space are often cheaper in the United States. Another reason is America's political stability, with foreign investors seeing the United States as a pillar of free market capitalism in a world sliding toward socialism and political and social unrest. There are no Red Brigade terrorists running around, as in Italy, shooting political leaders and businesspeople. A third reason is America's lower labor costs. Worker compensation in the United States translated into other currencies is lower today than in many European countries: Europe is no longer a cheap place in which to invest or employ labor. Finally, the United States has the largest single market in the world.

Types of Foreign Investment in the United States

There are two types of foreign investment: direct investment and portfolio investment. Direct investment means both ownership and control of assets, and portfolio investment means ownership only of assets. For statistical purposes, the U.S. government considers an investment to be direct rather than portfolio when 25 percent or more of the voting stock of a U.S. firm is owned by a foreign firm or person. Direct investment also may include those foreign concerns not incorporated in the

26. *Newsweek*, November 27, 1978, pp. 78–90.
27. This trend may reverse, as the dollar appears to be gaining strength relative to other currencies.

United States that control branches and subsidiaries producing goods and services. In contrast, portfolio investment includes nonvoting securities, such as bonds or warrants, or investment in voting stock whose foreign interest is less than 25 percent of the total. A large portion of current foreign portfolio investment is in U.S. Treasury securities. These represent, in part, America's past balance of payments deficits, as well as the desire of foreign investors for liquid, easily marketable securities. The preference for U.S. Treasury securities may also be due to the size and relative stability of the U.S. capital market.

Historically, foreign investors have preferred portfolio investment to direct investment. Foreign portfolio investment currently comprises 65 percent of total investment inflows into the United States, compared with 35 percent for direct investment. This is in contrast to American investment abroad, of which more than 80 percent of the investment is direct and the remainder portfolio.[28] This conforms to a pattern that has been maintained for almost a century, when foreign investors provided the finance capital necessary to build the United States' railroads and steel mills. The preference of U.S. investors for direct investment over portfolio is, in part, due to the special advantages that American industry has developed over a period of time, advantages that, however, it may be losing. In the past, industry was able to grow and achieve economies of scale in the large American market. The size and wealth of the market enabled competition to thrive and spurred business firms to make innovations. Managerial skills in marketing and distribution advanced, giving American firms an advantage over foreign competitors, and so the expected profits from establishing a subsidiary were greater than the expected return from portfolio investment. Conversely, foreign investors' preference for portfolio investment in the United States can be attributed to the country's highly developed capital markets and generally stable rates of return on investments.

Foreign Direct Investment in the United States

In 1978 foreign direct investment in the United States amounted to $40.8 billion, and by 1979 it had increased to $55.5 billion.[29] These investments were of three types: the creation of branch plants in the United States, joint ventures with U.S. firms, and outright acquisitions of American firms. The last approach became more popular as the dollar declined in value relative to other currencies. Such takeovers, that is, the outright purchase of a majority interest or the complete

28. U.S. Department of Commerce, Bureau of International Commerce, "Foreign Investment in the United States," January 1980, p. 1.
29. Ibid., p. 15.

control of ownership, enable some foreign firms to gain immediate access to American business-management talent, mass-production techniques, and technological know-how, as well as the marketing skills and network distribution developed by U.S. companies. These acquisitions provide a means of surmounting the various problems associated with entering the U.S. market, with the result that European and Canadian firms have acquired many U.S. firms. The $630 million acquisition of Howard Johnson, an American hotel and restaurant chain, by Imperial Group, Ltd., a British conglomerate, is an example. Foreign banks have also come to occupy an important position in the U.S. banking sector through the acquisition of American banks. In 1979 the National Bank of North America was acquired by a British bank for $429 million.

Issues Involved in Foreign Direct Investment

There is some concern that foreign investment in the United States may mean eventual dominance of certain sectors of the economy by other countries. Television shows and feature articles on Japan's growing investment have led many persons to conclude that the United States is facing a new kind of Japanese invasion.[30] The huge potential revenues of the oil-producing nations have also created fears of takeovers of critical sectors of the U.S. economy. However, this concern, at least for the present, is largely unwarranted. Foreign direct investment is so small in relation to the size of the U.S. economy that it has no significant effect on such factors as aggregate demand. For example, estimated foreign direct investment for 1979 was only 3 percent of the amount spent in the United States on business plants and equipment. Foreign direct investment in the United States was also very small when compared with similar investment abroad by U.S. firms. In 1978 foreign direct investment in the United States amounted to $40.8 billion compared with U.S. direct investments abroad of $168.1 billion. U.S. direct investment abroad is, nonetheless, beginning to decrease at a rate less rapid than foreign direct investment in the United States. In 1960 the ratio of U.S. direct investment abroad to foreign direct investment in the United States was 4.6 to 1; in 1972 the ratio had increased to 6.5 to 1;[31] but in 1978, the ratio had decreased to 4.2 to 1.

Measuring the economic impact of foreign direct investment on the U.S. economy is difficult, since it entails some offsetting factors. For example, direct inflows of foreign capital are an immediate benefit to

30. To the contrary, Japan in 1980 ranked seventh in direct investment in the United States. The Dutch ranked first and the British second.
31. U.S. Department of Commerce, Bureau of Economic Analysis, "Survey of Current Business," August 1979, pp. 2, 15, 38.

the U.S. balance of payments. But, as in the case of U.S. investments abroad, the initial inflow ultimately causes outflows of dividends, interest, and royalties, as foreign investors receive returns on their investment. These direct flows are only a starting point for assessing the balance cf payments effect. Much of the foreign direct investment is in the form of reinvested earnings, which do not represent a capital inflow. In addition to the capital-related impact, foreign direct investment has secondary and even tertiary effects on the U.S. trade account. It may cause import substitution by replacing imports with products manufactured in the United States, or it may generate new exports by sales to third-country or home-country markets. It also may lead to increased imports of capital equipment for construction, raw materials or parts, or semifinished goods for final assembly in the United States.

On balance, the United States should benefit from foreign direct investment. First, there is the effect on employment that has already been mentioned. This employment usually has been concentrated in industries, such as chemicals, electrical equipment, and scientific machinery, in which wages are above the national average. Second, there is an import of foreign technology, which is often superior to that of the United States. Such technological innovations as the radial tire, the Wankel engine, and prestressed concrete all have come from foreign research and development efforts. At a minimum, these factors taken by themselves increase the competitive forces in the U.S. market. Third, new management techniques are introduced into the U.S. market. Japanese management apparently relies on techniques to motivate workers that are different from those used by their American counterpart. The Japanese techniques are directed toward making workers feel like part of a team instead of just a cog in the organization. Finally, there is the increase in tax revenues that comes from direct foreign investment.

Foreign corporations operating in the United States are subject to the same laws that govern American corporations. The United States taxes foreign corporations only on that income earned within the country and at the same rates as apply to domestic corporations. There are certain government restrictions on the operation of foreign banks; for example, they cannot accept deposits. Some states have laws restricting foreign ownership of land. The two areas that would be the most likely to impinge on the operations of foreign corporations in the United States are the antitrust laws and the regulation of securities by the Securities and Exchange Commission. State and local government securities laws also may affect foreign corporations, though these laws vary from state to state.

Application of U.S. Antitrust Laws to Foreign Multinationals

Antitrust laws are applied equally to U.S. and foreign corporations in order to preserve competitive market structures and to forbid specific anticompetitive business practices. It is argued that by maintaining a competitive market, such laws do not discourage foreign investment in the United States, but rather make it more attractive than other countries to the foreign investor. In fact, foreign competition has proved to be particularly important to American consumers in two situations. The first is when most or all of the goods originate abroad, and the second is an oligopoly situation in which outside competition is needed. As a result, such products as small cars and stainless steel razor blades have become available in the United States largely because of the pressure of the foreign firms selling them here. It is an important goal of antitrust policy to preserve this kind of foreign competition in the American market.

Section 7 of the Clayton Act is the principal statute safeguarding against further industrial concentration in the United States. It prohibits any merger or acquisition that may substantially reduce competition or create a monopoly in any line of commerce in any section of the United States. Foreign direct investment is subject to antitrust scrutiny when such investment involves a purchase, merger, or joint venture with an existing American firm. The antitrust laws are applicable in the following situations: the merger of actual competitors in the American market, the merger of potential competitors in the American market, and joint ventures between potential competitors in the American market. The acquisition of an American company may be the easiest way to enter the U.S. market, but the antitrust laws may prevent the particular acquisition because of its effect on actual or potential competition. A merger between an important exporter to the United States and a significant domestic company will be treated in much the same way as would the merger of two U.S. companies with corresponding shares of the market.

In one such case, British Petroleum (BP), already a major petroleum distributor on the East Coast, in 1968 acquired Standard Oil of Ohio (Sohio), which controlled about 30 percent of the Ohio market.[32] The Justice Department objected to the merger on the grounds that BP was a potential entrant into Ohio, Sohio's primary market, and that the merger would foreclose an independent entry into that market. The case was settled by a consent decree under which the merger was allowed to proceed, provided that Sohio divested itself, by sale or

32. *U.S.* v. *British Petroleum Co.*, Civ. No. 69-954 (N.O. Ohio, 1969), settled by consent decree, 1970 Trade Cases Par. 72, 988.

exchange for stations in other parts of the country, of stations handling a total of 400 million gallons of fuel per year in the Ohio market. This case is important in that it indicates that the Justice Department will challenge acquisitions when a major foreign firm, an actual or potential competitor in the U.S. market, merges or enters into a joint venture with a major U.S. firm in a concentrated market and the effect is to foreclose independent entry or expansion of the foreign firm.

Securities Regulation

U.S. securities laws are generally more stringent than those of most foreign countries. Foreign companies dependent on U.S. sources of financing have to comply with the Securities Exchange Act of 1934 and the Securities Act of 1933. If a foreign corporation wishes to raise funds through the sale of securities to the general public, it must register the issue as required by the Securities Act. The act also requires disclosure of the company's financial operations, disclosure to which the company may not be accustomed. The company also is subject to the reporting requirements of the Securities Exchange Act. Section 13(d) of the act requires an investor acquiring more than 5 percent of the ownership of a class of securities to file with the Securities and Exchange Commission the name and occupation of the purchaser, the source of the funds employed, and the purpose of the transaction. Section 14 requires an investor intending to make a tender offer or takeover bid for more than 5 percent of a company's shares to file the information called for in Section 13(d). Section 16 calls for investors owning more than 10 percent of a public company, and its corporate directors or officers, to file with the SEC a statement of the amount of securities owned.

SUMMARY

American antitrust laws cover much ground. Multinational companies seeking to expand through foreign mergers or acquisitions must be increasingly wary of possible antimerger enforcement. For example, if an American company acquires abroad, or if a foreign company acquires a U.S. competitor, Section 7 of the Clayton Act may be applied. The scope of Section 7 is broad and has been extended to include acquisitions that eliminate potential competition in U.S. markets. Section 1 of the Sherman Act also has widened its application to multinationals. It declares illegal every contract, combination, or conspiracy in restraint of interstate or foreign commerce. The act has been expanded through judicial interpretation to cover parties and acts outside the confines of the United States, which has permitted domestic courts to exercise jurisdiction over foreign nationals and corporations and over U.S. corporations domiciled overseas. The Supreme Court has broadened the interpretation of the Sherman Act to include certain types of conduct that are regarded as illegal per se. Included are price-fixing agreements, agreements among competitors dividing geographic markets or classes of customers, tying agreements, concerted refusals to deal, and certain kinds of reciprocity agreements.

A new dimension has been added to the scope of the multinational corporations. In recent years, the United States has become more attractive as a repository for foreign investment, both direct and portfolio. Both European and Japanese multinationals have acquired American firms and have established branch plants in this country. The impact on the U.S. economy can be regarded as favorable, at least in the short run, as jobs are created and the tax base is expanded. These multinationals also are subject to American antitrust laws. In general, foreign firms will be welcomed as long as they provide competition for American firms. But a merger between a foreign and an American firm would be treated the same way as a merger between two U.S. firms would. If competition is reduced, then the Clayton Act is applicable. If the foreign corporation restrains trade in interstate or foreign commerce, then the Sherman Act can be applied.

QUESTIONS FOR DISCUSSION

1. Discuss the international application of the Sherman Act in the American Tobacco case of 1911.
2. What is the effects test? Discuss its application to the Timken Roller Bearing case.
3. What is meant by the concept of extraterritorial reach?
4. What is the significance of the Gillette case?
5. In your opinion, should the Foreign Corrupt Practices Act be replaced?
6. Can it be demonstrated that U.S. antitrust laws hinder American firms in their competition with firms from other countries?
7. What are the ways in which Section 7 of the Clayton Act can be applied to mergers of American and foreign firms?
8. There are differences between the United States' antitrust laws and other countries' antitrust laws with regard to industrial concentration. Discuss.
9. Discuss the factors responsible for increased foreign investment in the United States.
10. What is the relationship between U.S. antitrust laws and mergers consummated in the United States by foreign firms?

RECOMMENDED READINGS

Baruch, Hurd. "The Foreign Corrupt Practices Act." *Harvard Business Review*, 57 (January–February 1979), 32–51.

Bengsten, Fred C., Thomas Horst, and Theodore Moran. *American Multinationals and American Interests*. Washington, D.C.: Brookings Institution, 1978.

Fouch, Gregory G., and L. A. Lupo. "Foreign Direct Investment in the United States in 1978." U.S. Department of Commerce, Bureau of Economic Analysis, August 1979, pp. 38–41.

Fugate, Wilbur L. *Foreign Commerce and the Antitrust Laws*. Boston: Little, Brown, 1973.

Jacoby, Neal H., Peter Nehemkis, and Richard Eells. *Bribery and Extortion in World Business*. New York: Macmillan, 1977.

Kugel, Yerachmiel, and Gladys W. Gruenberg. *International Payoffs*. Lexington, Mass.: Lexington Books, 1977.

Neale, A. D., and D. G. Goyder. *The Antitrust Laws of the U.S.A.* 3rd ed. Cambridge, England: Cambridge University Press, 1980.

Plaine, Daniel J. "The OECD Guidelines for Multinational Enterprises." *International Law*, 11 (Spring 1977), 339–346.

Rahl, James A. "American Antitrust Policy and Foreign Operations: What Is Covered?" *Cornell International Law Journal*, 8 (December 1974), 1–15.

Townsend, James B. *Extraterritorial Antitrust: The Sherman Antitrust Act and U.S. Business Abroad*. Boulder, Colo.: Westview Press, 1980.

U.S. General Accounting Office. *Impact of Foreign Corrupt Practices Act on U.S. Business*. Washington, D.C.: March 4, 1981.

PART VII
GOVERNMENT AS A
PROMOTER OF BUSINESS

The federal government runs a number of programs that offer financial assistance to private enterprise. Some of these programs are of a permanent nature, whereas others are of limited duration and are intended to help a firm or industry through a temporary crisis. The permanent programs give assistance to agriculture, housing, transportation, small business, and banks, among others. Many federal programs are an important source of credit for certain sectors of the economy. For example, the housing industry relies on the various federal mortgage credit programs and the Federal Home Loan Board for a good portion of its funds, particularly when money is tight. Agriculture receives credit assistance from the Farmers Home Administration and government-sponsored credit corporations such as the Federal Land Banks and Federal Intermediate Credit Banks. Exporters also can obtain financial assistance from the Export-Import Bank. Many of these programs were created during the 1930s to help various sectors of the economy through the Depression. Instead of being abolished after this economic crisis, they have continued to operate and have become an important part of the nation's credit structure. The temporary programs, though, have not become an institutionalized source of funds and, with the ending of a particular financial crisis, have lapsed.

Taxation is another area in which government affects business. It can be used as a stimulus or a deterrent to methods of doing business or to the kind of business being done. A tax can be used as a subsidy or a negative tax to encourage a specific course of action. The agricultural price-support program is a large-scale example of this. Other examples are subsidies to airlines and to the merchant marine. Then there are tariffs that protect domestic industries from foreign competition, though this goes against the grain of competition. The consumer pays higher prices for protected goods, and efficiency may suffer because the producer is spared the necessity of striving to reduce his or her costs. There is much public support for protection, however, because many individuals regard themselves as having primarily a producer's rather than a consumer's interest. They are, therefore, more concerned about the possibility of losing profits or becoming unemployed because of foreign competition than they are about being able to buy the imported commodity at a lower price.

407

Tax incentives are used to stimulate many activities. At the federal level, tax credits and accelerated depreciation are used to encourage business investment. Depletion allowances are used to encourage oil and mining companies to explore for new sources of energy. The foreign tax credit is said to be an incentive for American firms to invest abroad. At the state and local level, there are also a variety of tax incentives, the most common being an exemption from the property tax as an inducement to encourage the location of industry. In fact, states use this device to compete against each other in attracting industry. The exemption of interest on state and local bonds for federal income tax purposes also has been used to stimulate industrial development, with states or localities using the proceeds from tax-exempt bonds to build a plant to be leased to industry. Both the federal and state governments grant special tax concessions to firms that comply with environmental protection laws by acquiring pollution control equipment. Some states permit the deduction of pollution control costs as a credit against state income taxes.

Chapters 16 and 17 examine several areas of government support of business. In Chapter 16 we shall discuss direct loans and loan guarantees. Federal credit programs are an important, but neglected, area of government and business relations and are influential in allocating capital in domestic credit markets. Of the $348 billion advanced in U.S. credit markets in 1980, $56.7 billion, or 16.3 percent of the total, was advanced under federal auspices. This has an impact on resource allocation because there is some transfer of resources from the private to the public sector. Credit extended by the federal government may also serve to raise interest rates and add to inflationary pressures. Taxes are a second area that we shall study. Income and sales taxes also influence resource allocation by transferring resources from the private to the public sector. Savings and capital formation are affected by taxation as well. Another area of government support of business is protection against foreign competition, import quotas being an example. The government protects the steel industry against foreign steel competitors, and the automobile industry has lobbied for import quotas on Japanese car imports. In Chapter 17, we shall consider taxes and import quotas.

Chapter 16

Government as a Promoter of Business

The public, if it thinks about government and business relations at all, conceives of the government as the tax collector, trust buster, consumer advocate, and protector of the environment, all of which place business on the receiving end of a number of requirements that generally do not have pleasant connotations. There is, however, another area in which government influences business, and this is in the area of direct and indirect financial aid. This aid dates back to the time of Alexander Hamilton, who identified the prosperity of the nation with the prosperity of the business class. It was government's duty to dispense privileges to business; the resulting economic benefits would percolate throughout the whole economy. Hamilton wished to establish a strong central government that would dedicate its energies to promoting business enterprise. To do this, he set up a program that was enacted, in the main, during President George Washington's first term in office. This program provided for the assumption of federal and state debts by the federal government, the creation of a national bank that would make loans to business, and the passage of a protective tariff that would shield business from foreign competition.

Government aid to business came in a number of forms in the nineteenth century. The tariff was one that proved highly effective in stimulating the development of business, because it essentially guaranteed a domestic market free from foreign competition. Tariffs are, in effect, taxes that raise consumer prices. The subsidy was another form of direct government aid to business, particularly in the field of transportation. In 1845 Congress authorized subsidies for ships carrying mail, with preference given to steamships, which could be converted into warships. Various other forms of subsidies have been used for ocean transportation, right up to the present time. Grants also were used as an aid to business, particularly to the railroads. Between 1862 and 1866 Congress gave over 100 million acres of public lands to the railroads. This was the period of the Pacific railway charters, when the rush to span the continent was in full swing. Loans to business were a fourth source of government aid and were first used to encourage the construction of inland waterways, a branch of commerce in which private enterprise depended completely on government support.

In addition to these forms of government aid, a number of federal agencies have been created to assist business. Most of this assistance is provided by the Department of Commerce, which was established in 1903 and has become a general service agency for American business. Its subordinate units include the Bureau of the Census, the Office of Business Economics, the Patent Office, and the Bureau of Foreign Commerce. A second agency is the Small Business Administration, which makes loans to small business firms and offers various consulting services. In foreign trade, the Export-Import Bank has been an important source of credit since its creation in 1934. Its functions have been expanded to include the financing of general foreign trade to exporters and their foreign customers when private funds are not available on reasonable terms. Other agencies, such as the Federal National Mortgage Association and the Public Housing Administration, offer credit, which, directly or indirectly, aids business. The overwhelming majority of the guaranteed and insured loans of these two agencies benefit the housing sector. There also are other federal agencies that offer services to business.

We shall explore in detail some of the more important areas of government assistance to business. One area is credit, which can be divided into two categories—direct federal loan programs and loan insurance. Of course, the credit extended in the federal credit programs goes into several economic activities. Business is the direct beneficiary of a few of these loans, though the sheer volume of federal loans has an impact on business through the loans' effect on the total volume of spending in the economy and on the interest rate. A second area is subsidies, which also are of two types—direct subsidies to business that come out of the federal budget and subsidies that do not involve direct payments. Many credit programs offer loans or insurance at rates below those that would be charged by a private firm for comparable services and at rates below those at which the government itself borrows money. If a business firm can borrow from a federal agency at 6 percent interest, but the Treasury is paying 8 percent on the money it borrows, this, in effect, is a subsidy. This is not necessarily bad, for the end result of the subsidy may be the promotion of some socially useful activity.

FEDERAL LOAN PROGRAMS

Federal loan programs exist to erase imperfections from the direct market, to provide subsidies for socially desirable activities, and to stimulate the economy when there are idle resources. Imperfections in the credit market occur because borrowers differ in size, geographic location, and types of activity. Federal loans are designed to fill certain gaps in the private lending market. In addition, many economic transactions benefit not only the principal participants in the transaction but other members of society as well. Home ownership, which increases social stability, and education, which increases productivity and economic growth, are two examples of activities with external benefits. When there is a difference between the total costs and benefits and the private costs and benefits, federal loan programs can supply credit for socially desirable purposes at less than the market interest rates. This has a subsidy effect, in that subsidies reduce the private cost of a particular transaction. By setting the subsidy at an appropriate level, the government can induce the level of activity that would prevail if social benefits were taken into consideration by the market process.

Direct Loans

Direct federal loans have several characteristics. First, they are designed to promote socially useful activities rather than to remove imperfections in the credit market. Second, they contain a subsidy element. For example, loan programs of the Rural Electrification Administration and loans for the construction of higher-education facilities and college housing offer borrowers subsidies at around 50 percent of the total value of the loan. Third, direct loans are financed directly out of the federal budget. Through the tax-transfer mechanism of the federal budget, the government can influence the amount—and presumably the allocation—of credit extended in the private market. Fourth, foreign loans are by far the largest single component of direct loans, accounting for more than 40 percent of the total loans outstanding in 1980. In quantity, the most important types of outstanding foreign loans are development loans and loans of the Export-Import Bank. Both types create a foreign demand for the products of American business. An example of a foreign loan that benefits business is the military sales credit extended to countries to assist them in purchasing military equipment from the United States, which benefits firms making aircraft, tanks, and so forth.

Table 16-1 presents the amount of new direct federal loans made by major government agencies in 1980. There are two categories of loans or credits, those financed out of the federal budget through various federal agencies and those financed by the off-budget federal agencies. Excluded from the table are the loans of the federally sponsored agencies that are also not included in the federal budget. Government-sponsored agencies were originally financed by subscriptions of government capital, but this capital now has been retired and the agencies are entirely privately owned. Direct loans financed out of the federal budget include business loans made by the Small Business Administration, loans made by the Economic Development Administration of the

Table 16-1 New Direct Loan Obligations by Agency
(millions of dollars)

Out-of-Budget	
Agriculture	21,537
Commerce	161
Education	689
Housing and Urban Development	4,967
Veterans' Administration	626
Other Agencies	
Export-Import Bank	4,365
Small Business Administration	1,998
All other agencies	3,433
Subtotal	37,776
Off-Budget	
Rural Electrification Administration	1,175
Federal Financing Bank	22,188
Other	219
Subtotal	23,583
Total direct loans	61,359

Source: Executive Office of the President, Office of Management and Budget, *Budget of the U.S. Government, Fiscal Year 1982* (Washington, D.C.: U.S. Government Printing Office, 1981), p. 594.

Department of Commerce, and loans made for ship construction by the Maritime Administration. In addition, the Export-Import Bank, a federally owned enterprise, lends directly to exporters and importers and insures and guarantees loans extended by private lenders.

Since direct loans are included in the federal budget, we shall examine their possible economic impact. The method of financing used in the budget is important. If there is a deficit in the budget, the whole process, including the loans, can have an income-generating effect, particularly if new money is created to finance the deficit. This would affect both consumption and investment. The impact on consumption may be divided into income and wealth effects. The income effect comes about because the government spends and consumers receive income. The wealth effect comes about because savings accumulate as income increases. Assuming that income and consumption continue to expand for a long enough period, consumption increases also will produce increases in investment. And because the deficit was created by means of new money, interest rates will remain low, which also should encourage an increase in investment spending unless, of course, the investment schedule is interest inelastic.

There would be a similar effect if the federal government borrowed directly from the Federal Reserve or from the excess reserves of the commercial banks to finance the deficit. In all three cases, the money supply is increased, the income and wealth effects operate on both consumption and investment, and there should be little or no pressure exerted on interest rates. Thus, federal lending conceivably could have a double-barreled effect with respect to stimulating gross national product. The deficit incurred in the budget, financed by any of the three methods referred to above, would provide one stimulus to the economy, and the loans supported by the budget from deficit financing would provide the other stimulus.

On the other hand, increases in taxes to finance budgetary outlays, including loan programs, would reduce directly disposable income and the level of consumer spending. The effect of loans could be counterbalanced by the effect of decreased spending. Federal borrowing through the sale of bonds to the nonbank public also could reduce the expansionary effect of federal loans if interest rates were raised and cash balances reduced, both of which tend to discourage private spending. Then, of course, loans could also generate a reverse flow of income to the government. It is possible for the expansionary effect of loan disbursements to be equaled by the contractionary effects of loan repayment. This would require comparison of the reduction in spending associated with a decrease in disposable income resulting from loan repayments, with the increase in spending associated with an increase in disposable income resulting from loan disbursements. But in some cases the reduction in spending associated with loan repayments may be nil. For example, a loan is used to finance the construction of a building. In later years, during the life of the loan, the building yields a return sufficient for the borrower to repay the loan. Society thus has an asset it otherwise would not have had, but the loan repayments, being in a sense self-financed, do not have any contractionary influence on the gross national product.

We also should consider the case of the borrower who, in the abscence of the federal loan, presumably would have been able and willing to obtain funds from private lenders. But we can assume that the borrower would not borrow as much from the private lender, since the interest rates on federal loans are typically lower than those on private loans. In this case, it would no longer be possible to equate the effects of the loan with the entire amount of the increase in gross national product that may be attributable to the loan. To determine the net increase in gross national product that may be attributable to the federal loan, one first would have to subtract the increase that would have occurred if a private loan had been made instead of the government loan. And second, one would have to add the effect of the increased funds available to private lenders.

One issue in the federal credit programs is the existence of subsidies. Many of these credit programs offer loans or insurance at rates below those that would be charged by a private firm for such services and at rates below those that the government itself would have to pay to borrow money. The subsidy can be defined as the difference between the amount the borrower has to pay for a government loan and the price he or she would have to pay for a similar loan from a competitive private lender. In essence, the subsidy circumvents the forces of the free market. In the market for loanable funds, the interest rate is supposedly determined by the interaction of the supply of funds with the demand for the funds. An equilibrium point is reached when supply and demand are in balance at a given rate of interest. In a competitive market economy, borrowers are free to obtain loans at the going interest rate. If this market rate is 6 percent and the government charges 2 percent to a specific set of borrowers, then there is a subsidy that, in the final analysis, is paid by the taxpayers. The effectiveness of the market as an allocator of loanable funds is circumvented.

Two agencies—the Small Business Administration and the Export-Import Bank—are examples of agencies that make direct loans to business. In 1980 the total loans of the Small Business Administration (SBA) amounted to $2.0 billion, and the loans of the Export-Import Bank (Eximbank) amounted to $4.4 billion.[1] Both agencies were created to achieve specific economic objectives, the SBA to offer loans and assistance to small business firms and the Eximbank to stimulate business involvement in foreign trade.

The Small Business Administration — SBA

The principal governmental agency concerned with the problems of small business is the Small Business Administration (SBA). The SBA was created by the Small Business Act of 1953, which had as its objective the assistance of small business firms in order to ensure fair competition. The common problem of small business firms is securing capital, and so the act authorized the SBA to provide two types of financial assistance to small firms—loans for plant construction and the acquisi-

1. Executive Office of the President, Office of Manpower and Budget, *Budget of the U.S. Government, Fiscal Year 1982* (Washington, D.C.: U.S. Government Printing Office, 1981), p. 594.

tion of land, equipment, and materials, and disaster loans to business concerns that suffer financial loss from floods, hurricanes, drought, or other natural catastrophes. In addition, the SBA was responsible for helping small business firms secure a larger share of government contracts for materials, construction, and research and development, as during World War II the great bulk of government procurement contracts went to large corporations. The SBA was also supposed to provide counseling for small firms. In applying for a loan, a small business concern must submit credit data, and in evaluating these data, SBA officials often are able to advise on alternative ways of solving a problem.

In 1958 the Small Business Investment Act was passed by Congress to help small businesses secure additional equity capital and long-term loan capital. This law, which is administered by the SBA, provides equity capital and long-term capital through privately owned and operated small business investment companies and state and local development corporations. Small business investment companies operate by supplying equity capital in exchange for convertible debentures under conditions approved by the SBA. These securities give the investment company the privilege of converting such debentures into the small business firm's common stock. The investment company also may make long-term loans to small business concerns for up to twenty years, with provision for an additional ten years for repayment. State and local development corporations have been formed to assist the development of small business, and loans made to them by the SBA are used to make loans to small business firms. In its community development work, the SBA works closely with the Department of Commerce's Economic Development Administration to establish, expand, and assist in financing local industries in areas designated for redevelopment.

The Export-Import Bank—Eximbank

Eximbank is a wholly federally owned enterprise, and its mission is to promote U.S. exports. It does this by making direct loans to exporters and importers and by insuring and guaranteeing loans extended by private lenders. Through the Export Expansion Act of 1971, the Eximbank is excluded from the budget. The principal reason given for its exclusion is that the bank's disbursements exceed its repayments, and therefore the bank appears to be operating at a loss. This, of course, is not the case, for the bank actually operates at a profit. It is argued that since the budget takes account only of disbursements and receipts, if the bank were kept in the budget, it would give a misleading impression of the bank's condition. The budget is not, however, a financial report on each of the myriad federal enterprises; rather, it should show how funds are being allocated among different programs and agencies, what the fiscal policy of the government is, and how deeply the government is involved in the economy. Excluding the Eximbank from the budget frustrates the accomplishment of all of these goals.

Direct loans extended by Eximbank are dollar credits made to borrowers outside the United States for the purchase of U.S. goods and services. Disbursements under the loan agreements are made in the United States to the suppliers of the goods and services, and the loans plus interest must be repaid in dollars by the borrowers. The purposes for which the loans can be used are:[2]

1. To supplement private sources of financing when the private financial source is unwilling or unable to assume the political and commercial risks under current conditions
2. To extend credit on terms longer than those private lenders can provide
3. To enable U.S. suppliers to provide terms on major projects that are competitive with those offered by government-sponsored export financing institutions in other exporting countries

In addition, Eximbank has financial guarantee programs under which it can guarantee, backed by the full faith and credit of the United States, the repayment of credits extended by private lenders to foreign purchasers of U.S. goods and services. In this respect, the bank's role is comparable to that of the many foreign institutions that provide guarantees and insurance to aid their countries' exporters and safeguard them from undue risk from overseas sales. Under the financial guarantee loan authority, the Eximbank will unconditionally guarantee repayment by a borrower of up to 100 percent of the outstanding principal due on such loans, plus interest equal to the U.S. Treasury rate for similar maturities, plus 1 percent per annum, on the outstanding balances of any loan made by an American financial institution to a buyer in another country for the purchase of U.S. goods and services.

Insured Loans

From the standpoint of the amount of money involved, insured loans are by far the most important segment of federal government credit. In 1980, for example, insured loans by the federal government amounted to $404 billion, compared with $109 billion for direct federal loans.[3] The government may either insure or guarantee loans made by private

2. Export-Import Bank, *Description of Eximbank Export Financing Programs and Services*, 1975, pp. 5-8.
3. *Budget of the U.S. Government, Fiscal Year 1982*, p. 90.

lenders. The best-known example of the former is Federal Housing
Administration mortgage insurance, in particular, the Veterans Administration's mortgage guarantee program. The major difference between
loan insurance and loan guarantees is that a fee generally is charged for
insurance.

Loan insurance is of particular importance in the housing market. In
fact, when FHA mortgage insurance was introduced, it led to a revolution in home mortgages and home ownership. Before its introduction,
home mortgages for the average family were difficult to obtain. The
typical home mortgage was a medium-term loan—on the average of
three to five years—and covered only a relatively small portion of the
price of the house. In addition, these mortgages were typically non-
amortizable; that is, the monthly mortgage payments covered only
interest on the loan, and these payments did not reduce the principal
of the loan. The FHA insurance permitted private lenders to extend
mortgages with much higher loan-to-value ratios than before, without
incurring any more risk than they assumed by making uninsured mortgage loans of considerably less value. The higher loan-to-value ratio
associated with the FHA mortgages implied that a correspondingly
lower down payment would be required to take possession of a house,
and the mortgages thus undoubtedly stimulated the demand for, and
the construction of, private housing.

Federal loan insurance is subject to fiscal offsets, just as direct federal
loans are. For those types of insurance that carry a premium and are
just self-supporting, the premium itself is not an offset. Funds collected
as premiums are used to cover administrative costs and to settle claims.
The settlement of claims does not offset the income and loan-generating
effects of loan insurance; it redirects these effects. Premiums are collected from one group of lenders and distributed to another group of
lenders. It is in the case of loan guarantees, in which no premiums are
charged and losses are financed out of general revenues, and in the case
of loan insurance programs that do not break even, that the possibility
of fiscal offsets arises. The analysis of offsets to insured loans is identical with that made for direct loans.

Federal loan insurance and guarantees generally are intended to
promote a particular purpose, such as economic development or agricultural production, not to help a particular business firm. But in 1971
the Emergency Loan Guarantee Act was passed to provide federal loan
guarantees to large business enterprises whose failure would seriously
affect the nation's economy and the level of employment. The program is administered by the Emergency Loan Guarantee Board, which
was created by the same legislation. The board was given the power to
decide whether a firm is eligible to receive a guarantee. Eligible firms
can have loans made to them guaranteed against loss of principal and
interest. To be eligible, firms have to meet three qualifications. First,

the loan is required to permit the firm to furnish goods or services when the failure to do this would seriously affect the economy or employment. Second, credit cannot be obtained without a guarantee, and third, it must be reasonably certain that the firm can repay the loan. The maximum amount of guaranteed money to be made available to a firm was set at $250 million.

Aid to Railroads

Federal assistance to the financially troubled railroads has been of concern to Congress for years. Since 1970 several acts have been passed to administer various subsidies to the railroad industry. In 1970 the Emergency Rail Services Act was passed to provide for loans to the railroads. Under this act, the Penn Central was guaranteed and received $100 million in loans, at an interest rate of three-eighths of 1 percent. In 1972 the Emergency Facilities Restoration Act was passed to aid in the rebuilding of track and roadbeds that were damaged by Hurricane Agnes. This assistance to the railroads took the form of loan guarantees. The Regional Rail Reorganization Act of 1973 established the United States Railway Association, a nonprofit, off-budget, government-sponsored railroad system formed from the bankrupt railroads of the northeastern United States. The association was given the right to issue $1.5 billion in bonds, debentures, trust certificates and other obligations that would be sold to the public. The proceeds from the sale were to be used to make loans to the Consolidated Rail Corporation (Conrail), a nonprofit government corporation created by the Railroad Reorganization Act to run the restructured railroad system. Loans can be made to upgrade the new rail system, to help railroads that connect with the restructured system if they are in financial trouble, and for further implementation of improved high-speed rail passenger service in the so-called Northeast Corridor—the existing roadway and track of the Penn Central between Boston and Washington, D.C.

In February 1976 the Railroad Revitalization and Reform Act was passed, taking the federal government an irreversible step farther into the sponsorship and subsidization of the railroad system, as the act committed the federal government to putting $6.4 billion into the railroads.[4] Included in this money authorization was $1.6 billion in grants to finance improvements in the Northeast Corridor. Also under the new law, a $600 million rail fund was to be established within the Treasury Department. The rail fund, to be administered by the secretary of transportation, is intended to help finance facilities, maintenance costs,

4. *New York Times*, "New Railroad Aid Law: A Giant Step," February 5, 1976, pp. 44–45.

rehabilitation, and improvement expenditures for all the nation's railroads. There also was an authorization of $1 billion for loan guarantees to cover facility acquisitions by railroads and $360 million to assist the states in rail freight improvements on light-density branch lines. The law authorized the United States Railway Association to purchase up to $2.1 billion of Conrail debentures and preferred stock. The proceeds are to be used to modernize and rehabilitate bankrupt railroad lines.

In 1975 the Regional Rail Reorganization Act was amended to offer increased financial assistance to railroads in the Northeast and Midwest. The amendment sprang from Penn Central's warning that it would be forced to shut down unless it received some form of federal assistance. The amendment authorized operating funds for Penn Central and other railroads to continue transportation services until Conrail could develop a new plan for a railroad system for the Northeast and Midwest. In addition, there was a supplementary appropriation, making a total of $143 million for emergency railroad aid. The operating funds amounted to $347 million, $150 million in loan guarantees and $197 million in grants. However, these measures proved to be insufficient to halt the decline of Penn Central and other railroads.

Most federal credit assistance programs, direct or indirect, offer credit to recipients at or near the federal borrowing rate. For most borrowers, this is a substantial subsidy that is never explicitly dealt with in the budgetary process. In contrast, if the federal government were to make payments to a private lender to induce it to lend at comparably low rates, the expenditure would be explicitly recognized and closely examined. Some have argued that the effect of much of the federal credit assistance is to provide a subsidy with little control or review, rather than to provide credit to those lacking access to it at a reasonable cost. Explicit subsidies come from programs lending at interest rates below the Treasury's cost of funds. These also are not adequately reflected in the federal budget. It is estimated that $20.2 billion in interest subsidies assistance will be paid by federal credit programs in 1982.[5]

The Reagan administration plans to cut back on some of the federal credit programs, to reduce the credit assistance programs of the Small Business Administration by 25 percent in 1982 and to increase the interest rate charged on direct loans to market levels. The Export-Import Bank also faces cuts in its lending programs. The Economic Development Administration, which makes loans to business firms in depressed areas, has been eliminated. Most federal loan programs, however, are built into the system as a form of entitlement and are difficult to eliminate.

5. *Budget of the U.S. Government, Fiscal Year 1982*, p. 55.

APPENDIX

LOCKHEED AND CHRYSLER—A TALE OF TWO BAIL OUTS

We have made the point repeatedly that in a free enterprise market, economy competition is regarded as a virtue rather than a vice, particularly if businesses are involved. A free enterprise system is a profit-and-loss system, in which the efficient firms make profits and the inefficient firms incur losses. The proper use of resources in a free enterprise system is assured by the fact that if a firm does not use resources properly, it will go broke. In fact, the doctrine of failure is at the heart of competition and free enterprise. The inefficient are driven out of business by the efficient. The market is a hard taskmaster: those firms that lose are forced out. If the rules of the game are to be followed, there can be no protection for the losers, whether they be Chrysler or the corner grocery store. To help one and not the other further alters the rules of the game, and then there are selective winners and losers and a double standard is created. To support the U.S. automobile industry against Japanese competition by imposing import quotas on Japanese cars is an admission that somehow the U.S. auto industry has lost its competitive edge and must be protected from a younger and more viable competitor.

It is argued that no government can tolerate the failure of any large economic unit, be it Lockheed, Chrysler, or New York City, because the disruption to its economy would be too great to sustain. In the case of Chrysler, needed military goods would not be delivered, workers would lose their jobs, dealers would go out of business, bondholders and stockholders would lose their money, and the economy of the state of Michigan would be damaged. In addition, there would be a ripple effect, for Chrysler's suppliers also would be affected. The steel and rubber industries are two such suppliers, and their workers as well could lose their jobs. But one also can argue that a competitive market system allows the price mechanism to reflect actual demand and cost and thus maximize efficiency in the use of capital and other resources. Loans diverted to support Chrysler could be put to better use by supporting more viable business firms. A diversion of credit away from market determined use occurs when the government intervenes to support Chrysler. The key issue is whether or not the federal government should support a poorly managed company at the expense of its more efficient competitors.

The Lockheed loan guarantee, which amounted to $250 million, raises the question of the relationship of government and business in an economy in which business has been continually involved in functions that have been thought of as wholly governmental, such as national defense, space exploration, and education. Because some firms, such as Lockheed, have a large percentage of their business locked into programs that are paid for by the federal government, one wonders how private these private firms really are and how much they are in fact a part of the federal government. How much responsibility does the federal government have for the continued survival of these firms when they do not meet contract requirements or are hurt by changes in federal spending? Is it a proper function of the federal government to give emergency financial assistance to private enterprise, or is it something that commercial banks and other financial institutions should do without a federal guarantee? The rationale for the Lockheed loan was that the company's failure would seriously affect the nation's economy and the level of employment.

LOCKHEED AIRCRAFT

The Lockheed Aircraft Corporation is one of the country's largest defense contractors.[6] Despite the economic, political, and technological risks unique to the defense weapon systems industry, Lockheed was able to grow and prosper until the late 1960s. Much of Lockheed's success was the result of its government contracts for military aircraft. Recognizing its dependence on the military market, Lockheed made strong efforts to enter the commercial market. During the late 1950s it created the Turboprop Electra in the hope that the commercial airlines were not yet ready to plunge into straight jet aircraft. The company guessed wrong and the airlines ordered the straight jet 707s from Boeing and DC8s from Douglas. In 1962 the military devised a cargo plane that would give the United States the ability to deploy fully equipped forces worldwide on little notice, thereby reducing the necessity for maintaining so many overseas bases. In December 1964 the Air Force issued a detailed request for bids on the aircraft, which was called the C-5A. In April 1965 the final bids were submitted for the 115-plane contract, plus 5 experimental models. Lockheed submitted a low bid of $1.9 billion; however, price was only one factor in determining acceptance, and flaws were found in Lockheed's designs. So the company changed its designs and made the plane larger but did not change its price.

6. The following sources were used for the Lockheed case: U.S., Congress, House, Committee on Armed Forces, *Hearings on Military Posture*, 91st Cong., 1st sess., 1969; *Business Week*, "Lockheed's Ledger on the C-5A," June 7, 1969, pp. 35–38; Berkeley Rice, *The C-5A Scandal* (Boston: Houghton Mifflin, 1971); and Arthur E. Fitzgerald, *The High Priest of Waste* (New York: W. W. Norton & Co., Inc., 1972).

Lockheed was awarded the contract because of its previous excellent record in producing military cargo aircraft and the substantial savings to the government promised by the bid. The bid represented the target price, which included profit, research and development, testing, evaluation of five prototype plans, and two production runs of fifty-three and fifty-seven planes. The bid covered the airplane frames, but not the engines, which were to be built by General Electric. There was also a ceiling price of $2.3 billion on the airplane frame, with the government to pay 70 percent and Lockheed 30 percent of the cost between the target and ceiling prices. In addition, the contract also set a separate price for the second run, called Run B, along with a formula for adjusting the overall price of the contract, should actual costs in the first run, or Run A, exceed 130 percent of the Run A target cost. The adjusted contract price had no provision for profit, which, under the cost-sharing features, would have been eaten up in offsetting the costs of Run A.

Soon after work had begun on the C-5A in 1965, unexpectedly severe inflation and various technical problems, coupled with shortages of skilled workers and essential materials, upset cost and schedule estimates. Instead of the $177 million the company expected to make on the $1.9 billion contract, Lockheed projected a cost to the government of $3.2 billion for the airplane frames through Run B, with the company absorbing a loss of some $13 million. The overrun of $1.3 billion was about 68 percent of Lockheed's original target cost. The cost overruns continued, and from time to time Lockheed requested additional funding from the Air Force, and the latter revised the C-5A budget. Problems continued with the C-5A program on into 1969, with the estimated cost increasing to around $5 billion, $3.1 billion above the original bid. The number of planes ordered was cut back from 115 to 81. When these were delivered, they developed certain structural flaws, including cracks in the wings, that necessitated corrections by Lockheed. Because of these and other problems, by 1971 the overall cost of each plane had increased from $23 million to around $60 million. The C-5A continued to incur losses, reaching an estimated $400 million by 1971, and the Defense Department claimed that the C-5A's collapse would cause Lockheed's financial collapse, which, in turn, would weaken the nation's defense.

Because of this, Congress approved a contingency fund of $200 million. After the loan from Congress, the commercial banks agreed to lend Lockheed $150 million more. But there were other problems. Lockheed for some time had wanted to return to the commercial aviation market. With this in mind, the company had utilized the technology and production techniques developed for the C-5A to begin planning the L-1011, a wide-bodied, medium-range, trijet passenger liner. The market for such a plane was estimated to be enormous. For the planes' engines, Lockheed accepted a bid from Rolls-Royce because of its low cost and superior design. But orders for the L-1011 did not come in early enough or fast enough to cover Lockheed's development costs of about $500 million. As a result of this and the C-5A's cost problems, the company ran short of cash. Rolls-Royce also had its own problems. During the first half of 1970 Rolls reported a $115 million loss, which was in part attributable to technical problems in the development of the engine for the L-1011. In 1971 Rolls filed for bankruptcy, despite earlier loans from the British government. This placed additional pressures on Lockheed. It calculated that, regardless of whether the engines were British or American, it would require another $350 million of outside financing to put the L-1011 into full production.

The British government decided to grant the funds to save Rolls, contingent on some form of guarantee from the U.S. government. The core requirement had to be a U.S. government guarantee of loans. Eventually, an agreement between Lockheed and Rolls calling for the construction of 555 engines was signed, with the British government agreeing to pay all further development costs for Rolls and to subsidize its production costs if necessary. Lockheed approached the secretary of the treasury, John Connally, to arrange U.S. government backing for an additional $250 million in bank loans. Loan guarantee legislation was then sent to Congress, backed up by Lockheed's contention that its bankruptcy would be detrimental to the national interest and that thousands of jobs would be lost. When asked if such aid to Lockheed would establish a precedent or if the government had done such a thing before, Secretary Connally replied:

> Sure the government has done it before . . . they did it in the days of the Reconstruction Finance Corporation; in defense contracts now. We do it through the FDIC, we guarantee bank deposits and savings and loan deposits and export-import loans. We are now guaranteeing investment in the market. We guarantee a lot of things.[7]

The main argument against the loan legislation was that the federal government would set the precedent of supporting a poorly managed company at the expense of its more efficient rivals, giving Lockheed and Rolls-Royce special and competitive privileges in markets that may be better and more cheaply served by McDonnell-Douglas, Boeing, General Electric, and Pratt and Whitney. From the standpoint of the market system, the loan was logically indefensible. As *Fortune* magazine commented: "Any company that can lose huge sums on four

---

7. *U.S. News and World Report*, "Why the Drive to Bail Out Businesses in Trouble?" May 24, 1971, p. 41.

defense contracts at the same time must be doing something wrong."[8] However, by a one-vote margin, the Senate passed and sent to the White House a bill authorizing up to $250 million in federal loan guarantees for Lockheed. The bill created an emergency loan guarantee board headed by the Secretary of the Treasury. All of the guaranteed loan had to be repaid before the $400 million in earlier loans advanced by the banks and before the resumption of dividend payments by Lockheed. In the event of bankruptcy, the government's claims would have precedence over those of other creditors.

CHRYSLER

The Chrysler Corporation was formed in 1925 with the acquisition of Maxwell Motors by Walter Chrysler.[9] In 1928 Chrysler acquired Dodge Brothers, and by the end of the decade, the domestic automobile industry was dominated by three firms—General Motors, Ford, and Chrysler. During the 1920s the automobile companies began to emphasize a range of vehicles rather than a single car line. There were rapid styling changes and engineering advances, with General Motors in the lead. Ford, the original pioneer of mass production, began to lose ground, as Henry Ford relied on the Model T as his main car. Ford had a rather utilitarian approach to production and marketing, maintaining that price, not style, was important. The American public could have any car it wanted, as long as it was black. Unfortunately for Ford, the American public wanted other colors and styles. Both Ford and General Motors expanded abroad in the 1920s, a move the benefited both companies in later years when domestic earnings began to fall.[10] Chrysler's expansion into foreign markets was much more limited, particularly before World War II. By the time Chrysler went overseas, General Motors and Ford had already acquired the best markets.

Nevertheless Chrysler supplanted Ford in the number two position by the late 1930s, a position it held, allowing for the interruption of

8. Harold B. Meyers, "The Salvage of the Lockheed 1011," *Fortune*, June 1971, p. 69.
9. The following sources were used in the Chrysler case: U.S., Congress, House, Committee on Banking, Finance and Urban Affairs, *The Chrysler Corporation Financial Situation: Hearings on the Chrysler Corporation Loan Guarantee Act*, 96th Cong., 1st sess., 1979, pts. 1, 2; U.S., Congress, Senate, Committee on Banking, Housing and Urban Affairs, *Chrysler Corporation Loan Guarantee Act of 1979*, 96th Cong., 1st sess., 1979, pts. 1, 2; and Paul Meising, "The Chrysler Corporation Loan Guarantee Act of 1979," Cleveland, Ohio: Case Research Association, 1981.
10. In 1980 Ford derived 50.3 percent of its total revenue from foreign sales. Its foreign operating profit was $475 million, but its total operating loss was $1.5 billion. Were it not for its foreign operating profits, Ford would have lost more money in 1980 than Chrysler did.

World War II, until 1950. In part, Chrysler reached this position because Ford had managerial problems after Henry Ford's death, though the company did have a good reputation for engineering quality. In 1946 Chrysler had 25 percent of the automobile market, a share it maintained until 1950. But from then on it has been mostly downhill for Chrysler. By the middle 1950s Chrysler's market share had fallen to 13 percent, but by the end of the decade Chrysler bounced back to 19 percent of the market when it introduced large cars. The problem with Chrysler during the 1950s was that Ford and General Motors capitalized on the "bigness is better" mentality of the American driving public. Cars symbolized mobility, freedom, and above all, status and self-expression. Chrysler's cars, which resembled Sherman tanks, did not allow for much self-expression, although they continued to enjoy a reputation for engineering quality. Chrysler's pitch for its 1954 Plymouth and Dodge cars was that they were "smaller on the outside, but bigger on the inside," the wrong pitch at the wrong time.

Most of Chrysler's problems were already present in the 1960s. It had allowed Ford and General Motors to preempt the more lucrative foreign markets; it lagged behind Ford and General Motors in expenditures on research and development; it lost many of its better engineers and managers to Ford and General Motors; and its factories were becoming obsolete. Chrysler's financial policies also were questionable. Its dividend pay-out ratio was much more generous than those of Ford and General Motors. This may have made its stockholders happy, but the company would probably have been wiser to put more of its earnings into research and development and plant modernization. By 1959 new management turned Chrysler to produce massive, finned cars and saved the corporation but regained only a fraction of its lost market share. Smaller dealer margins and poor dealer-manufacturer relations also were problems.

During the 1960s Chrysler attempted to expand its overseas operations by acquiring interests in foreign auto firms. In 1957 it acquired a substantial interest in the French automotive firm Simca. In 1963 it purchased an additional interest in Simca, and in 1964 it bought two-thirds of the stock in Rootes, an English auto firm that had already required financial support from the British government. But Chrysler found it hard to sell the Hillman Minx, Simca, and like products to English and French consumers, much less to Americans. Chrysler again was in the wrong place with the wrong cars. But it did make one right decision when it made a link with Japan. The Japanese government permitted the company to buy a minority share of Mitsubishi, whose products sold well under the Dodge and Plymouth labels. Too, whereas Ford responded to a shift in consumer demand for smaller cars by bringing out the successful Falcon and Mustang cars in the early and middle 1960s, Chrysler continued to go with its higher-priced, large cars. The 1960s also was a period of social change that had a far-reaching impact on the U.S. automobile industry.

The 1970s proved to be mostly an unmitigated disaster for Chrysler.[11] Again, its main problem was poor timing of product introduction. In the early 1970s Chrysler's market position suffered from three ill-timed new model introductions. It restyled its 1971 intermediate models when demand was swinging back toward full-sized models. It introduced its new full-sized models when demand shifted to small cars following the Arab oil embargo and subsequent oil crisis. Only its strong truck sales, which were not yet subject to federal fuel requirements, prevented a cash crisis in 1975. Chrysler addressed its financial problems by firing numerous engineers, designers, and sales personnel to cut its overhead costs and reduce its break-even point. Imports of Japanese cars also contributed to Chrysler's problems. Chrysler did manage to introduce its smaller and successful Volare and Aspen in 1976, but it also stayed with its full-sized cars. By 1978 buyers were demanding fuel-efficient cars, but Chrysler's habit of shipping cars to dealers before they were ordered had created an inventory of large cars valued at $700 million. The glut of cars cost money in handling and interest charges and interfered with the introduction of new car models.

In asking for government support Chrysler claimed that government regulation was responsible for most of its problems. Regulations require large compliance costs for all auto companies, but the large ones can spread their costs over a higher production volume. Chrysler argued that it cost Chrysler twice as much as General Motors to comply with pollution control requirements, an estimated $600 per car, compared with $300 for General Motors. Regulations also require huge capital outlays, and smaller companies, with fewer resources and less access to lower-cost capital, are further penalized. Regulation came at a time when Chrysler was generally short on capital, and as a smaller company it had to devote a greater part of its more limited personnel and technical resources to meeting regulatory requirements, thus diverting these resources away from research and development. There is no question that regulations do have an impact on investments, profitability, prices, and sales, but regulation was only a secondary source of Chrysler's problems. These problems went back long before regulation and can be summarized as follows:

1. A lack of continuity in its image and an inconsistent long-run strategy
2. A failure to modernize its plants and equipment and also a loss of skilled personnel at inappropriate times
3. A weak overseas market

11. Chrysler lost money for five years during the decade. In 1978 and 1979 it was the biggest money loser in the United States.

4. A heavy reliance on outside suppliers that reduced control over costs
5. A concentration of marketing efforts on blue-collar consumers who, unfortunately for Chrysler, do not buy high-margin options, keep their cars longer, and are the first to be hurt by a recession
6. A reliance on debt that limited its financial flexibility by locking it into fixed capital charges
7. A general unawareness of the sociopolitical realities of the times, particularly during the late 1960s and early 1970s when the auto industry fell victim to government regulation

Back-to-back financial losses in 1978 and 1979 brought an appeal to the federal government for support. Chrysler had several arguments. First, its problems were in large part due to government regulation. Second, a Chrysler failure would cause numerous dislocations in the U.S. economy. Thousands of jobs would be lost; both state and federal tax revenues would decline; and there would have to be a corresponding increase in other tax revenues to offset the revenue loss. There would also be a deleterious impact on the U.S. balance of payments because the imports from Japan would increase. Third, rigorous competition, and the corresponding benefits of lower prices, product innovation, and efficiency that come with it, requires three significant automobile makers. With only two major domestic corporations left, the automobile industry would become even more concentrated. Saving Chrysler would provide more viable competition in the future and negate the possibility of antitrust threats to the industry, threats that make lawyers rich but that are costly to both business and government.

Opponents of the Chrysler bail out claimed that interest rates for more viable companies would be raised and that credit would be directed away from more important and reliable uses. They also contended that subsidizing inefficient companies would create perverse incentives to produce undesirable products and contribute to waste and mismanagement in corporate boardrooms. David Stockman, a former Michigan congressman and now the director of the Office of Management and the Budget, used a Social Darwinist position, contending that if the Japanese can produce a better car than the American auto industry can, then the whole (American) industry should go down the drain.[12] Simply translated, this means compete or die. But perhaps Senator William Proxmire of Wisconsin best summed up the rationale for opposing aid to Chrysler when he stated that a free enterprise economy means the freedom to fail as well as to profit. If we bail out Chrysler, where do we draw the line? On what basis do we say that some firms

12. Stockman was the only Michigan congressman to oppose the Chrysler loan guarantee. His views on competition and the U.S. auto industry were expressed to the author.

but not others are worthy of government support? Why is Chrysler more deserving than the more than six thousand firms that failed in 1979? Proxmire answered the last question by stating that, indeed, Chrysler was able to employ the lobbyists and public relations specialists that most firms could not afford.[13]

On September 19, 1979, the Senate Banking Committee approved a $4 billion package consisting of $1.25 billion in loan guarantees and $2.75 billion in outside financing. The latter was obtained from a variety of sources. Wage concessions were also made by the UAW,[14] but in return, Douglas Fraser, the president of the United Auto Workers' Union, was made a member of Chrysler's board of directors. Chrysler lost close to $2 billion in 1980, again achieving the distinction of being the biggest money loser for the year and setting an all-time record in the process. Chrysler, however, did make a profit of $11.6 million for the second quarter of 1981, though this profit may well be temporary. If losses continue and Chrysler fails, taxpayers will have to shell out $1.25 billion to cover the federal loan guarantees. The Pension Benefit Guaranty Corporation also would be liable for $1.4 billion in Chrysler's unfunded pension obligations, which would also affect taxpayers because the corporation's assets as of July 1981 were only $332 million. There is also the possibility that Chrysler and Ford will merge (Chrysler wants Ford, but Ford does not want Chrysler). This would result in more concentration in the U.S. auto industry, but the frame of reference is now global, particularly with the Japanese claiming around a fourth of the U.S. auto market.

QUESTIONS FOR DISCUSSION

1. Federal loans to business often contain a subsidy element. Discuss.
2. Distinguish between the objectives of direct loans and those of insured loans.
3. What types of risks are covered by federal loan insurance?
4. In your opinion, should Lockheed have been given emergency financial assistance by the federal government?
5. Compare the Lockheed and Chrysler cases.
6. From the standpoint of a free enterprise market economy, the Chrysler loan is indefensible. Do you agree?

13. Large firms can afford to hire lobbyists. The importance of lobbying is discussed in Harrison W. Fox and Martin C. Schnitzer, *Doing Business in Washington* (New York: Free Press, 1981).
14. Chrysler received $1.07 billion in UAW wage and benefit concessions, of the sort that Ford and General Motors may well need if they are to compete more successfully against the Japanese. Ford has also estimated that Chrysler has ended up with a per-car labor-cost advantage of $200.

7. How should Chrysler gain the confidence of the market and the public?
8. Under what circumstances is it in the public interest to avoid bankruptcies?
9. Trace the success of Lockheed since its bail out. Can its success be attributed to the bail out?
10. Have the interests of the general public been served in the Chrysler bail out?

RECOMMENDED READINGS

Fox, Harrison W., and Martin C. Schnitzer. *Doing Business in Washington.* New York: Free Press, 1981, chap. 13.

Holtzman, Abraham. *Interest Groups and Lobbying.* New York: Macmillan, 1968.

Kraar, Louis. "Japan's Automakers Shift Strategies." *Fortune*, August 11, 1980, pp. 106–113.

Meising, Paul. "The Chrysler Corporation Loan Guarantee Act of 1979." Cleveland, Ohio: Case Research Association, 1981.

Tsurumi, Yoshi. "How to Handle the Next Chrysler." *Fortune*, June 16, 1980, pp. 87–88.

U.S. Congress, Joint Economic Committee. *Federal Subsidy Programs: Staff Study Prepared for Subcommittee on Priorities and Economy in Government*, 93rd Cong., 2d sess., 1974.

U.S. Congress, Senate, Committee on Banking, Housing and Urban Affairs. *Chrysler Corporation Loan Guarantee Act of 1979*, 96th Cong., 1st sess., 1979, pts. 1, 2.

U.S. Executive Office of the President, Office of Manpower and Budget. *Budget of the United States Government, Fiscal Year 1982.* Washington, D.C.: U.S. Government Printing Office, 1981.

Chapter 17

Government Aid to Business: Taxation and Import Policies

Government aid to business extends far beyond the credit subsidies discussed in the last chapter. There also are direct cash benefits that the federal government pays to a particular firm or industry to accomplish a particular objective. For example, the government pays the sugar beet and sugar cane growers to protect the sugar industry against world competition. Cash payments also are used to help support the privately owned U.S. merchant marine. For financial and security reasons the federal government has determined that it is necessary to have a domestic merchant marine capable of carrying a part of the United States' ocean-going trade, though there are few industries in whose affairs the federal government is so active.[1] Nearly every aspect of the merchant marine industry is affected by a public measure or action intended to promote the U.S. fleet. Without the subsidies, there probably would be no U.S. fleet and no U.S. shipbuilding industry; with the subsidies, the cost of U.S. ships is more than double the price of those built in foreign shipyards. The maritime unions also are beneficiaries of the subsidies.

Tax incentives are also given to business to encourage specific economic or social objectives, for example, to encourage oil exploration and production and to hire and train minorities. The U.S. tax laws and, for that matter, the tax laws of other countries, reflect economic and social policy. They create incentives and disincentives for the use of capital and for the allocation of wealth between consumption and investment. The federal government also sets tariffs on imports that allow domestic producers to earn higher prices than free markets would allow. Import quotas are used to protect U.S. business firms from foreign competition. Other countries do the same. Because of restrictions on American sales abroad and tougher competition from foreign products inside the United States (Japanese automobiles are a good example), protectionist sentiment has been revived. One has only to look at the U.S. automobile industry importuning both the Carter and Reagan administrations to use import quotas to reduce the number of Japanese automobiles that can be sold in the United States. Conversely, American business firms are finding it more difficult to compete in certain

1. Gerald R. Jantscher, *Bread upon the Waters: Federal Aid to the Maritime Industries* (Washington, D.C.: Brookings Institution, 1975).

markets, especially in Japan and the Common Market, because there is protectionist sentiment in both places.

The remainder of this chapter will be devoted to two areas in which the government offers support to business. The first is tax policy, particularly the use of tax incentives. This area has become even more important as a result of the Reagan tax cut program that was passed in 1981. One aspect of the tax cut is the provision of incentives to stimulate savings and investment. The success or lack of success of the Reagan tax cut will depend to a considerable degree on business reaction. The second area is also attuned to the 1980s. As the rest of the world, but particularly Japan, becomes more competitive, how should the U.S. policy toward free trade be modified? Is it desirable to protect U.S. industry from foreign competition? This is what is being done in a number of industries; for example, the textile industry is protected by the Multi-Fiber Agreement, which allows a 6 percent annual growth in textile imports.[2] But U.S. textile interests are trying to reduce the quotas allowed the three big Asian suppliers—Hong Kong, Taiwan, and Korea—to take care of the proposed boosts in imports from China and other less-developed countries.

TAXATION AND THE CONTROL OF BUSINESS

Taxation is often used as an instrument of regulation to supplement the states's police power. Every tax necessarily exerts some kind of effect on the ability or willingness of an individual or a business firm to undertake an economic act. If an individual or firm pays the tax, there is less purchasing power to use for other things. If the tax is avoided by a decision not to perform a taxable action, then the tax has conditioned the action of the individual or firm. Usually a tax is used to combine revenue and regulation. In some cases, however, the revenue and regulatory aspects of a tax can conflict. An example of this would be a moderate tax on the undistributed profits of corporations. The effect of such a tax might be to increase dividends, but not to eliminate undistributed profits altogether. Therefore, some revenue would be collected, but at the same time, revenues would be sacrificed if the firms responded to the tax by declaring dividends.

The tax instrument is used extensively to control business and commerce. Taxes are imposed to affect the form of business enterprise, as well as the methods of doing business and the kind of business done. For example, in an attempt to protect the dairy industry, discriminatory taxes have been levied on oleomargarine, and in order to protect the independent grocer, special taxes have been imposed on chain stores. Moreover, a tax can often become a subsidy when the explicit intention

2. The Multi-Fiber Agreement expired at the end of 1981.

is to encourage a specific course of action. One example of this is a tax reduction for a particular type of business firm. An exemption of a few thousand dollars of corporate income from the corporate income tax may be granted in an effort to encourage the growth of small business firms. Firms engaged in favored forms of output may be allowed to reduce their income tax liability for a few years by taking accelerated depreciation of plant and equipment for tax purposes. Oil and mineral producers are permitted deductions, called depletion allowances, from taxable profits, presumably in order to encourage the opening up of new sources. Firms having good employment records also are granted lower payroll tax rates under state unemployment insurance systems.

Taxes can be used to effect new methods of achieving worthy social ends. In the environmental area, for example, tax incentives could be used to replace many of the present direct controls. Sumptuary excise taxation—to which consumers have grown accustomed for tobacco products and alcoholic beverages—could be used to alter basic production and consumption patterns. The desired results would no longer be accomplished by fiat, but by making the high-pollutant product or service more expensive than the low-pollutant product or service. The guiding principle would be that people and institutions pollute because it is easier, cheaper, or more profitable to do so, and not because they enjoy messing up the environment. In lieu of a corps of inspectors or regulators, it would then be possible to use the price system to make pollution harder to accomplish, more expensive, and less profitable. The growing scarcity of energy sources provides another opportunity for choosing between greater government control of industry and the use of markets to achieve the same results. This could be achieved by imposing heavier taxes on the use of energy and thereby reducing the demand for it.

Antimonopoly feeling in the United States has resulted in a number of modest attempts to supplement monopoly control as exercised through antitrust legislation with a tax discouragement for monopoly. Taxes on intercorporate dividends and consolidated returns have been enacted by the federal government to discourage concentration of ownership. The undistributed profits tax of 1936 was in part intended to reduce monopoly power by forcing profitable coporations to distribute dividends; they would thus have to compete in the private investment market on even terms with the others. Then, of course, there is a special form of corporate profits tax that is a levy on excess profits. The assumption behind an excess profits tax is that some form of monopoly power exists and that the tax will keep the monopoly from retaining its excess profits. The taxation of excess corporate profits traditionally has been restricted to wartime. Public opinion always has favored special war-profits taxation of firms that benefit from military spending. A large production of war profits is, in effect, a windfall, and therefore it is believed that there is a special obligation to pay. Advocates of a peacetime excess-profits tax justify its use on the grounds that it can discourage monopoly by reducing the economic power of the profitable enterprise.

In addition, changes in tax rates are one of the instruments a central government can use to influence the level of national income and employment. The effects of the rate variations are twofold. On the one hand, the manipulation of tax rates brings about changes in the disposable income remaining in the hands of individuals and business firms. On the other, pressure can be exerted on individuals and business firms to consume and invest. Certainly the latter is of paramount importance to business. Such tax changes come under the general heading of fiscal policy, and a full discussion of the use of fiscal policy to encourage full employment and economic growth is reserved for a later chapter.

Federal Income Taxation

Although all levels of government—federal, state, and local—use various forms of direct and indirect business taxes, it is the federal government that has the most impact on business. One of the most important federal taxes is the corporate income tax. In 1981 corporate income taxes amounted to $66.0 billion—about 11 percent of the total federal budget receipts from taxes. The corporate income tax is considered a highly lucrative tax, and now that it has been accepted, it is hard to do without it. It is sometimes rationalized on the grounds that it can be used as an antimonopoly weapon, in that it reduces the net profits of monopolistic firms that enjoy the advantages from restricting market entry. Its effect here is to make it more difficult for profitable corporations to strengthen their monopoly position. Not all firms subject to the corporate income tax, however, are monopolies. The definition of income that is subject to the federal income tax is not identical with the definition of monopoly profits. Indeed, no legislature can define taxable profits as precisely as the economist can define monopoly profits. Even competitive firms make proftis that are normal for the industry. Again, dynamic changes in the level and distribution of national income cause profits and losses in competitive industry. Finally, a corporate income tax may hinder new rivals from financing expansion out of undistributed earnings.

For business, it is not the corporate income tax as a revenue source for the federal government that is important, but the structure of the tax—exclusions, exemptions, deductions, credits, preferential rates, and deferrals. This is true because there is a major link between the corporate income tax and the business firms' investment. Investment is one of the key components of national income. Among other things, investment includes all purchases by business firms of new construction and durable equipment, additions to the economy's stock of productive instruments. Investment is a fundamental determinant of economic growth, in that it defines the potential for production in any economy. Among the top twenty industrialized nations, however, the United States has failed badly in terms of new industrialized investment; only the United Kingdom, which is well on its way to becoming a third-rate industrial power, ranks lower in per capita investment. As a result, the United States may have become enmeshed in an economic dilemma in which the nation's private employers no longer create enough new jobs to absorb new workers into the labor force.

Probably the most important influence the federal government has on private investment expenditures is that effected through taxes and tax laws. The marginal efficiency, or rate of return, of capital is concerned with the profitability that additional amounts of capital will bring to the business enterprise, and so the businessperson or entrepreneur will be acutely aware of the influence of anything as direct as taxation on the expected rate of return on capital assets. Investment expenditures depend on the expected rate of return over cost, and thus presumably taxes, because they lower the expected returns, will lower investment expenditures. High taxes, to put it another way, impinge on incentives and therefore tend to affect adversely the investment decision. Nonetheless, nontax considerations also are very important to business firms' investment decisions. With respect to incentives, tax considerations may determine how a thing is to be done rather than whether it is to be done. High personal and corporate income taxes also may reduce saving and thereby dry up many important sources of finance for investment expenditure.

Federal Tax Incentives and Investment

It has been estimated that the United States will need up to $4 trillion in capital investment during the decade of the 1980s to create an economy with full employment. Despite the general agreement about the need for massive amounts of new capital, there is no general consensus about how the money can be raised. Federal tax policies certainly will be important, for taxes can be used to promote capital accumulation, as they have in all industrial countries, particularly in the German and Japanese economies. Generally, tax policies enable companies to keep more of their earnings, either through higher depreciation allowances for acquiring new equipment, tax credits for the same purpose, or a lowering of the corporate income tax rate. The last approach increases retained earnings, which are important for investing in new plants and machinery, which then raise production, improve product quality, and create jobs.

Liberal depreciation policies are one example of a federal tax policy that can have a direct impact on private capital investment. Without a tax on business income, the rate at which a firm chooses to charge off the depreciation of its capital goods is purely a matter of statistical information; the enterprise generally tries to obtain as realistic a picture of costs and current net income as possible. On the other hand, when business income is taxed, there are certain advantages for the firm to depreciate its capital goods over a shorter period of time than it would normally. The rate at which depreciation can be charged in computing business income is regulated by the tax statutes. Liberal or accelerated depreciation policies can affect investment demand. The key to the link between accelerated depreciation and investment is simply that accelerated depreciation reduces the impact of the corporate income tax, and therefore, it reduces whatever curtailing effect the income tax may have on investment.

Accelerated depreciation is only one of several tax policies that influence investment. For example, there is the tax offset of business losses. Investment typically involves some degree of risk and thus is a gamble in which the investor bets some amount, which may be lost, on the chance of winning some return. If a tax reduces the potential winnings, certain bets will no longer look attractive. But that conclusion can be changed by setting off a loss against other income. Thus, if income on an investment is taxed at 50 percent, but any loss can be used as a deduction against other income so that the possible loss is also cut by 50 percent, both the amount bet and the potential winnings are reduced proportionally. If there is a full offset of losses, the corporate income tax will not change the relationship between the investment risk and the rate of payment for taking the risk. If only a partial offset of losses is possible, the payment is reduced relative to the risk, and the investment may be reduced by the tax.

The tax credit for investment in business equipment is the largest item in the business investment category included in the 1981 federal budget. Although budget outlays are the most obvious method by which the federal government allocates resources, its other fiscal activities also influence resource allocation. Tax expenditures are an example of such activity, as they are instruments of public policy and generally can be viewed as alternatives to other government fiscal action, such as direct outlays and credit programs. Consequently, the Congressional Budget Act of 1974 requires that they now be included in the federal budget. Almost all tax expenditures serve either to encourage particular economic activities or to reduce the taxes of persons considered to be in adverse circumstances. One of the largest tax expenditures is classified as a business investment, the investment credit and accelerated depreciation being examples.

The investment credit is one type of investment incentive offered to business. It is a relatively new concept in the United States, although it has been used with varying degrees of success in West Germany, Japan, and other major industrial countries. The investment credit is a credit against the income tax liability of an individual or corporation that is allowed by the government for amounts invested in particular assets that meet specific requirements. It can be thought of as a negative tax in that it provides, through the reduction of income taxes, a direct increase in after-tax profits to a business firm investing in new plants and equipment that fall within the law's guidelines. It ordinarily comes about, as the one now in use in the United States did, through the desire of the government to stimulate economic growth. The investment credit, along with accelerated depreciation, can be used as an instrument of countercyclical fiscal policy and will be discussed in this connection in Chapter 18.

Changes in the corporate income tax rate also affect investment. In 1975 there were temporary provisions to reduce rates on the first $50,000 of corporate profits to less than one-half of the rate that applies to profits in general. Although these lower rates aid all businesses, they especially help small businesses, because the first $50,000 of profits is of relatively greater importance to them. The total tax expenditure resulting from favorable tax rates on the first $50,000 of profits was about $6.2 billion in 1977. Favorable treatment of capital gains also encourages investment in general and the retention of earnings by corporations in particular. The difference between the original purchase price and the sales price of an asset held more than six months is not treated as ordinary income: only one-half of this gain need be reported as income, and this is taxed at a preferential rate. This provides a tremendous incentive for ordinary income to be converted into capital gains in order to secure this favorable tax treatment. One of the ways in which this may be done is for a corporation to plow back its earnings into investment rather than paying them out to stockholders as dividends.

Tax Policies and Foreign Trade

A device used rather frequently by American policymakers in an effort to restrict the free flow of goods into the country is the protective tariff. By levying a tax on goods coming into the country, the government can make imported goods more expensive than comparable domestic goods, which, of course, are not subject to the tariff. If the tariff is sufficiently high, American consumers will find the imported goods too expensive to buy; if they consume the commodity at all they will probably buy the domestic good. This raises the prices of the commodities protected by it; if it did not raise prices, it would afford no protection. The increase in prices represents a gain to domestic producers, at least in the short run, and a loss to consumers. The reduction, or perhaps the elimination, of foreign competition secures the domestic market for domestic producers who usually favor such a tariff when the threat of foreign competition is significant. But the tariff counteracts the effectiveness of a competitive market in that it protects the potential losers. And the consumers are also losers in that they have to pay higher prices for the protected goods.

Yet tax policies are used by all industrial countries as a device to stimulate exports. One very common export incentive used by the Common Market countries is an exemption of exports from the value-added tax. The value-added tax, which is a tax levied on the increment in value at each stage in the production process of a good, is the single most important tax in such countries as France and West Germany. The West German value-added tax rate of 13 percent does not apply to exports. Some countries, notably Japan, exempt the income of foreign subsidiaries from taxation. Foreign source dividends also may be excluded from taxation. Most countries, including the United States, permit the deduction of foreign losses from domestic income for tax purposes. Some countries grant special depreciation allowances and tax credits to industries that produce specifically for export markets. The purpose of all these incentives is to enable the firms of one country to gain a competitive advantage or at least compete on a par with firms in other countries.

Some economists claim that the foreign tax credit is, in effect, a subsidy for the investment of U.S. private capital overseas.[3] The existing law permits corporations subject to U.S. taxes on foreign-source income to take a foreign tax credit for the amount of foreign taxes paid on income from sources outside the United States. The credit is provided only for the amount of income taxes paid or accrued during the taxable year to any foreign country. The purpose of the foreign tax credit is to prevent double taxation of income from the same source. Some countries avoid double taxation by exempting foreign-source income from domestic income taxes altogether. For U.S. taxpayers, however, the foreign tax credit system, providing a dollar-for-dollar credit against U.S. tax liability for income taxes paid to a foreign country, is the mechanism by which double taxation is avoided. The foreign tax credit essentially cedes to the host country the first slice of tax jurisdiction, and hence most of the revenue.

The idea that this is a subsidy is because the U.S. government gives up a part of its tax revenue to a foreign government through the credit. For example, assume, for computational simplicity, a U.S. corporate income tax rate of 50 percent, and assume a foreign income tax rate of 30 percent. Suppose a U.S. corporation operating abroad earns $100 before any foreign or U.S. income taxes. It can remit $70 ($100 minus $30) to this country. U.S. tax law, for the purpose of calculating taxes due the Internal Revenue Service, requires the corporation first to calculate the U.S. tax liability, assuming there was no foreign income tax.

3. Peggy Musgrave, "Tax Preference to Foreign Investment," in *The Economics of Federal Subsidy Programs*, International Subsidies, U.S., Congress, Joint Economic Committee, 92nd Cong., 2nd sess., 1972, pt. 2, pp. 196–219.

The tax due the Internal Revenue Service before the tax credit would be $50, but the credit of $30 paid to the foreign government is deducted from this amount, leaving a tax of $20 payable to the IRS. A corporation operating in the United States would have paid the full $50 tax on earnings of $100. The returns to both companies are the same, but the domestic operation provides $50 of tax revenue to the U. S. government, compared with the $20 provided by the foreign operation. Supposedly the credit causes the U.S. taxes paid by all Americans to be higher than they would be otherwise for any given level of income in the private sector of the economy, hence the subsidy effect.

But we should point out that no other country imposes its full corporate tax rates on income from direct investment abroad. Other countries either use tax credits similar to ours or give full or almost full exemptions to such income. Taxation by the United States without giving credit for foreign taxes paid would cut net foreign-source income in half. U.S. foreign subsidiaries would be forced into an unfavorable competitive position abroad, both with local companies and with international companies based in countries other than the United States. With U.S. taxation at about double the rates existing elsewhere, the source of the income—as well as the revenue from taxes on the income—would dwindle away.

The Reagan Administration and Tax Incentives for Business

In July 1981 Congress passed massive tax cuts for both individuals and business. The rationale of the tax cuts is to generate a wave of saving and investment that will carry the country to economic prosperity. A premise of the tax cut is that excessive tax rates retard business investment and entrepreneurship. Specifically, business is to benefit by more liberal depreciation allowances which are supposed to help redress the nation's lagging rate of corporate investment. The new allowance plan would replace the old depreciation plan that categorized various forms of investments according to estimates of the useful life of each asset. Instead, there are now four basic depreciation categories: three years for autos, light trucks, machinery and equipment used in research and development, and some special tools; five years for all other machinery and equipment; and ten years for certain public utility properties. For investments in the three-year category, business firms would also receive a 6 percent tax credit in the year the asset is placed in service. Five-year equipment would get a 10 percent tax credit, as would public utility equipment.[4]

---

4. There are other tax breaks for business; for example, oil companies are exempt from the oil profits tax.

Table 17-1 Costs of Tax Breaks to Business in 1981

Tax Break	Estimated tax loss (billions of dollars)
Investment tax credit	$16.4
Reduced tax rates on first $100,00 of income	7.4
Exemption of interest on state and local bonds and debt	5.9
Depreciation deduction	3.9
Special treatment for corporations in world trade	2.1
Research and development deductions	2.0
Deduction of energy-exploration costs	1.9
Special treatment of capital gains	1.4
Excess energy-depletion allowance	1.1
Credits for firms doing business in U.S. possessions	1.0
Deductions for charity	.9
Other tax breaks	5.0
Estimated total	$49.0

Source: *U.S. News and World Report*, March 16, 1981, p. 67.

Benefits and Costs of Tax Incentives for Business

All too often the cost of government action is ignored, and attention is focused on the action's benefits. Tax breaks to oil companies do encourage oil exploration, but there is a cost to the U.S. Treasury in revenues lost. Table 17-1 shows the loss in revenue resulting from tax breaks to business. These lost revenues have to made up from other tax sources, usually the general body of taxpayers. The benefits gained by society from, for instance, the provision of more energy, can more than offset the loss in tax revenue to the Treasury and the cost of the subsidy to the taxpayer, but then again, they may not. Any subsidy, regardless of the type, has an income redistribution effect, and tax breaks for business serve to redistribute income to business. This is not necessarily bad because there are times when it is in the national interest to stimulate the rate of capital formation. The Depression of the 1930s was a time when it was necessary to stimulate consumption; the 1980s are a time when U.S. capital formation is lagging relative to world competitors, who also offer tax incentives to their business firms.

INTERNATIONAL COMMERCIAL POLICY

If there were no restraints on the free movement of productive factors from one region to another or from one nation to another, the total world production of goods and services would be maximized when the marginal products of similar units of each productive factor were equal in all uses and all places. Resources are attracted to those areas in which they are the most productive, and the total output of goods and services is maximized when similar units of resources produce marginal products of equal value in all regions. From this it is easy to see that if the whole world were one economic unit and the maximization of world production were accepted as the appropriate policy goal, the same principles would apply. This suggests that from the consumers' standpoint, free international trade is beneficial, contributing to higher living standards. The interests of the consumers and the general welfare would be identical if there were free mobility of resources from one area to another.

Of course, in the real world, productive resources do not readily move across international boundaries in response to economic regards; rather, the impetus for trade across national boundaries is increased. This is because differences in the efficiency and proportion of labor and capital make it profitable for nations and regions to specialize in the production of those goods and services for which the resource situation is the most advantageous. From this, the law of absolute advantage states that there is a basis for trade when one nation can produce a good or service more cheaply than another nation can.[5] The latter should buy from the former. To put it simply, if the Japanese can produce automobiles more cheaply than the United States can, then we should buy Japanese autos; conversely, if the United States can produce computers more cheaply than the Japanese can, then they should buy our computers. Consumers in both countries stand to gain from the specialization of trade, though the American auto producers and Japanese computer firms do not. Each country gains by concentrating on that one thing it does best. Resources are allocated to those areas in which they can be used most efficiently.

Restraints on Trade

In the real world, however, American auto companies and Japanese computer firms are not going to stand by idly while the other side wins.

---

5. The law of absolute advantage is not to be confused with the law of comparative advantage. The latter holds that if one country enjoys an advantage over another country in the production of several goods, it should produce the good in which it has the greatest advantage and buy the good in which it has the least advantage from the other country.

Each will ask its government for some assistance, and this is exactly what has happened in the case of the U.S. automobile industry, which has lobbied intensively for protection against Japanese auto imports. All too often, American business firms praise the virtue of free competition in their annual reports to their stockholders and in their pronouncements to the general public—but lobby in Washington for government import controls on foreign competitors. Competition thus has a double standard: it is fine if we win, but wrong if foreigners win. The rules of competition, which include the right to fail as well as the right to succeed, are altered to suit the home team. But trade restrictions to help the home industries is by no means an exclusive prerogative of the United States; other countries, including Japan, also have their own trade restrictions.

Protective Tariffs

The tariff is probably the most common device used by the United States and other countries to restrict foreign trade. It is simply a tax levied on foreign goods coming into the country. The result is to make imported goods more expensive than comparable domestic goods, which, of course, are not subject to the tax. If the tariff is sufficiently high, American consumers will find imported goods too expensive to buy; if they buy at all, they will probably buy the domestic goods. The main effect of a tariff is that it raises the prices of the commodities protected by it; if it did not raise prices, it would afford no protection. The increase in prices represents a gain to domestic producers, at least in the short run, and a loss to consumers. The higher price for the product is likely to mean a greater income for producers and a reduction in living standards for consumers, for consumers are denied the opportunity of buying foreign goods, which could come into this country at a lower cost and with greater quality than comparable American goods.

Import Quotas

Import quotas are relatively new, compared with tariffs which have been used by countries since the days of mercantilism. The import quota was introduced in France in the 1930s as an antidepression measure, and it has become a significant part of most countries' international commercial policy. As the name implies, a quota places limits, numerical or otherwise, on the amount of a product that can be imported. For example, one country decides to restrict its auto imports from another country to two million cars a year. An import quota is generally considered to be more restrictive than a tariff. With a tariff, there is still the option of buying the foreign product, albeit at a higher price, but the import quota limits even this option. Prices cannot be forced by a tariff to rise by more than the amount of the tariff, but there is no upper limit to the price increase that can result from a quota. The prices to consumers are raised, and the restrictions placed on imports takes away the incentive of domestic producers to innovate and promote efficiency.

U.S. Protection of the Auto and Steel Industries

Since its inception, the United States has followed a protective tariff policy designed to aid producers. In this respect it is no different from other countries. Trade protection reached its peak during the Depression of the 1930s when all the major industrial countries used tariffs and other restrictive devices to restrict imports. To a considerable degree this was self-defeating, for as soon as one country placed restrictions on imports from another country, the other country would retaliate. The rationale of protection was to protect home industries and workers from the impact of the worldwide Depression, but the benefits of trade protection on unemployment were short lived because of the retaliatory protection measures that offset any short-run gain. The Depression also brought about the use of many different kinds of trade restrictions, including exchange controls, which limited the amount of foreign exchange that could be allocated to specific imports and import quotas. But these restrictions probably did more to exacerbate world economic problems than to solve them.

Economic problems in several U.S. industries during the 1970s and early 1980s have led to renewed demands for protection against foreign competition. The U.S. auto industry is an example. Once considered the industry synonymous with America's success as the leading world economic power, the U.S. automobile industry has fallen on hard times. In 1970, the U.S. automobile industry produced five million more cars than the Japanese automobile industry did, but in 1980 the Japanese auto industry produced three million more cars than the American auto industry did. In 1980, two of the big three auto companies, Chrysler and Ford, lost more than $3 billion between them. Chrysler was close to financial collapse, and only Ford's foreign sales kept it from collapse as well. Japan's penetration of the U.S. auto market was a prime contribution to the U.S. auto industry's problems. In 1970 Japanese imports represented less than 8 percent of the total U.S. purchases of all cars, but by 1980 one out of every four cars purchased by American consumers was Japanese. Foreign imports accounted for 30 percent of all cars sold in the United States.

U.S. automakers have been quick to blame their problems on the Japanese. They blame Japan's tariff policies that limit the number of American autos sold in Japan, failing to mention that the Japanese usually do not buy large American cars anyway. They cite favorable business and government relations in Japan, with the government aiding and supporting business. But, the extent of government aid and support is probably overrated. The fact is that Japanese automobile plants are more modern and more automated than their American counterparts. Some argue that American managers, including those in the auto industry, are managing the U.S. economy into a state of decline[6] and pay too much attention to short-term objectives. Furthermore, the Japanese have proved themselves increasingly adroit at organizing and running manufacturing operations. Others claim that Japanese automobile workers are more productive than American auto workers; that somehow Americans have lost the desire to excel.[7] But regardless of the reasons for the success of the Japanese auto industry, the fact remains that Japan is an extremely viable world competitor in the production of automobiles.

In a free market, prices allocate resources to the areas in which they can be used the most efficiently. Competition regulates economic activity, whereby the production of individual firms is correlated with the desires of consumers as expressed in the marketplace. If the world were a free market, the same principles would apply. Thus, if Japanese auto companies can produce autos, pay to export them to the United States, pay taxes and tariffs, and still make a profit, and American auto firms are losing money, perhaps from the standpoint of resource allocation, American consumers would be better off purchasing Japanese cars. In world competition the Japanese are apparently using scarce resources more efficiently than the U.S. auto firms are. Japan is enjoying an absolute advantage, at least for the present, in the production of automobiles. So the question is, "should the U.S. government aid the ailing U.S. automobile industry through the use of some form of trade protection, or should the industry be left to sink or swim against the Japanese competition?" To a considerable degree the latter approach would be Social Darwinism applied to the international marketplace.

The Automobile Industry and Import Quotas

Competition is a hard taskmaster, for there are losers as well as winners. What has happened over time is that individuals and groups have altered the rules of the competitive marketplace when they do not like the results. Chrysler is an example, but it is not the only one. Farmers want subsidies, individuals join unions, and people turn to the government to provide security. Thus, with considerable precedent, the U.S. auto

6. Robert H. Hayes and William J. Abernathy, "Managing Our Way to Economic Decline," *Harvard Business Review*, 58 (July –August 1980), 67–77
7. University of Virginia, Charlottesville, "Conference on Productivity," April 1981.

companies asked Congress and the Reagan administration for import quotas against Japanese automobiles. At stake, the auto companies claimed, was the survival of the U.S. auto industry. Import quotas would provide a time out or a respite, so to speak, while the automobile industry could recuperate, retool, and come out with new cars that could compete successfully against Japanese cars. The alternative to import quotas would be the possible ruination of the U.S. auto industry. Even mighty General Motors would not be above the possibility of a collapse if Japanese imports were not curtailed. Unemployment was also a factor, for during the 1970s alone, 200,000 jobs were lost in the industry. Needless to say, the UAW also supported the idea of import quotas. Another factor was the impact of Japanese imports on the U.S. balance of payments: in 1980 the U.S. trade deficit with Japan was $8 billion.

On balance, the Reagan administration is committed to reducing trade restrictions, though it is also pragmatic and realizes that public opinion is more concerned about jobs and income than the purity of the competitive market system. Generally, business firms and their employees are prepared to accept only favorable market verdicts. Competition is fine as long as someone else loses. In practice, the national doctrine of tooth-and-claw competition applies only to the small retailers. For groups that can organize, protection is in order. The list is long: beef quotas assist cattle raisers; sugar quotas keep in business high-cost domestic sugar cane and sugar beet growers; and trigger prices prevent the domestic steel producers from further losses to Asian and European steel producers. Thus the Reagan administration made a compromise. Though not exactly imposing hard and fast quotas on Japanese auto imports, the administration reached an agreement with Japan whereby Japanese automakers would voluntarily limit their exports to 1.6 million cars a year for three years. This agreement represents a divergence between theory and reality. In theory free trade is fine, but in reality protection can be arranged through political forces that theory never seems to consider.

The import quota placed on Japanese cars may give the U.S. automobile industry some breathing space in which to recuperate, but there are other factors to consider. The car deal with Japan has forced the Japanese auto companies to concentrate on the one market with enormous growth possibilities—the more advanced developing countries. Thus, protection at home may have been bought at the cost of considerable loss in the United States' potential market shares abroad.[8] The quota also adversely affects the consumers in that it takes away their freedom of choice after the limits of the quota have been exceeded. And with less foreign competition, the U.S. automakers may be less restrained when it comes to price increases. In addition, since many of

8. *Washington Post*, July 30, 1981, p. 1.

the problems confronting the automobile industry are self-made, where is the incentive for correction when errors can be canceled out by government protection?

The Steel Industry and Trigger Prices

The U.S. steel industry also is in trouble. Its plants are old, its profits low, and its prospects uncertain. It has taken a beating in world competition from the Germans and Japanese, particularly the latter. In the past thirty years, the Japanese steel industry has become the world's largest and most sophisticated. The Japanese refer to steel as the mother of industry, and Japan's steelmakers occupy an honored place in its society. The Japanese steel industry possesses two characteristics that have been absent in the American steel industry—a devotion to quality and a willingness to invest a large amount of money in projects that might not show profits for years.[9] The most modern Japanese steel mills are models of efficiency. High-pressure gases leaving the blast furnaces turn electrical generators. A computer may regulate the flow of energy to every part of a plant. Computer-controlled cranes automatically lift and store bars and sheets of steel. And the steel itself meets the highest standards of purity and tight specifications.

The United States' share of world steel production slipped from 26 percent in 1960 to 14 percent in 1980; conversely, Japan's share of world steel production increased from 6 percent to 16 percent over the same period. There are several factors responsible for America's decline.[10] First, governmental regulations, such as those pertaining to environmental protection, have required significant capital expenditures by the industry. At the same time, the government has not attempted to offset such expenditures—as do the Japanese and other countries with similar regulations—so that the industry could update its plants and equipment. This is one reason why most of the productivity growth in the American steel industry has come piecemeal through improvements to existing facilities. A second reason for the decline of the U.S. steel industry is an increase in wages exceeding its productivity. As well, the industry's plants and equipment have not been modernized rapidly enough to give efficiency improvements that would keep pace with rising wages. A third reason is the feeling that the managers of the U.S. steel industry are just not as good as the managers of the foreign com-

9. *Wall Street Journal*, April 15, 1981, p. 2.
10. U.S., Congress, Office of Technology Assessment, *Technology and Steel Industry Competitiveness* (Washington, D.C.: U.S. Government Printing Office, 1980).

petitors.[11] The American steel managers have simply failed to keep their companies technologically competitive over the long run.

The trigger price mechanism was adopted in 1977 to protect the U.S. steel industry against a possible collapse. Two major steel firms had announced plant closings, and a third firm had suspended production altogether. Foreign import competition, particularly from the Japanese, was fierce. Japanese steel firms enjoyed a cost advantage over their U.S. steel competitors. The Carter administration was pressured by both the steel companies and the United Steel Workers to place some restrictions on the imports of steel to the United States. The American steel companies also accused European and Japanese firms of dumping, that is, selling their steel in the United States at a price below the cost of production.[12] The Carter administration was faced with a dilemma: if it supported the claims against European and Japanese steel firms, it would hurt European steel exports to the United States, but not Japanese exports, for Japan had an absolute advantage over both Europe and the United States in the production of steel. Japanese exports then could easily supplant Euopean steel exports to the United States. Too, it was necessary for the United States not to alienate the European steelmaking countries, for to do so would damage American-European trade relations. But it was also necessary to keep the Japanese from taking over too much of the U.S. steel market.

The Carter administration established a set of reference, or trigger, prices based on the cost of production in the world's most efficient steel industry—the Japanese steel industry. The Japanese cost of production was calculated at a five-year average rate of capacity utilization, 85 percent.[13] Prices could be set at or above this reference price, based on the Japanese unit cost of production plus freight from Japan. Any steel shipped to the United States below the reference price was monitored to determine if there was prima facie evidence of dumping. What the reference price did was to establish a price below which steel imports were restricted into the United States. European steel producers, which had higher production costs than the Japanese did, could sell in the United States. The Japanese were prohibited from competing in terms of market-determined price. They could sell at the U.S. determined price, but sales below the price would trigger import controls. Thus Japanese exports to the United States were kept down to around 6 million tons a year. The European steel firms were thus given some opportunity to sell in the United States, and the U.S. steel firms were pro-

11. William J. Abernathy, *The Productivity Dilemma: Roadblock to Innovation in the Automobile Industry* (Baltimore: Johns Hopkins University Press, 1978).
12. Robert W. Crandall, *The Steel Industry in Recurrent Crisis* (Washington, D.C.: Brookings Institution, 1981).
13. Ibid., p. 43.

tected against Japanese steel exports. The cost of steel to the U.S. consumer was raised.

The trigger price mechanism was adopted as the latest in a series of temporary policy measures designed to protect the U.S. steel industry, which has deteriorated since World War II. The mechanism was a short-run palliative that was withdrawn in March 1980 when U.S. Steel filed a dumping complaint against the European steel producers. In addition, the U.S. steel industry found it difficult to compete with imports of steel from Japan and the less-developed world. As a result, capacity has not increased, and existing capacity was underutilized during most of the 1960s and 1970s. Only two new integrated steel plants have been constructed in the United States since World War II. Imports expanded to 20 percent of the domestic market, and the European and Japanese steel industries agreed to voluntary quotas at the request of the U.S. government.[14] The voluntary quotas lasted from 1969 to 1974. The Trade Act of 1974 contained provisions restricting the dumping of steel in the United States, particularly by Japan and the Third World. The act also extended the definition of dumping to include substantial sales below the average cost of production over an extended period of time, even when exports to the United States were not below the exporter's domestic price.

The decline in the world position of both the American and Western European steel industries is real. In 1980 the United States and Western Europe accounted for 32 percent of world steel production, compared with 54 percent in 1960; conversely, Japan and the rest of the world accounted for 68 percent of world steel production in 1980, compared with 46 percent in 1960.[15] The decline in the position of the American and European steel industries can be attributed to the fact that the economic forces of world competition favor the Japanese, South Koreans, and other steelmakers offering lower costs than their American and European competitors. The European response has been to form a cartel to restrict Japanese imports and to preserve Europeans markets for their own steelmakers. The American response has been cosmetic in its approach. Steel firms have sought from the U.S. government policies and regulations that will help them gain an advantage over their foreign competitors. Torn between a desire for free trade and a political response to a special interest group, the government has compromised by coming up with a temporary palliative, that is, the voluntary import quota. International competitiveness has seldom been treated as a major policy goal by the U.S. government; rather, shifts in international competitiveness are influenced by public policies. But the United States has no policies; Japan does.

14. These arrangements were called Voluntary Restraint Agreements.
15. Office of Technology Assessment, *Technology and Steel Industry Competitiveness.*

SUMMARY

Tax incentives to accomplish certain economic and social objectives and to restrict imports are two important areas in which any government helps business. The first is an important part of Reagan's economic program. Business firms have been given more liberalized depreciation schedules and other incentives designed to stimulate saving and investment. But there are gains and losses that have to be considered. The U.S. position in a competitive world economy has declined in many areas, and its rate of savings and investments is low in comparison with that of other countries. Productivity is also low by comparison. If plant modernization and productivity are stimulated by the tax incentives, there is a gain to the economy. But counterbalanced against this gain is a loss of tax revenue to the U.S. Treasury, which then has to find alternative sources of income. There is also a transfer of resources from consumption to production, which is not necessarily bad.

The automobile, steel and other American industries all are increasingly pressed by foreign competition, which has led to demands for some form of government protection. The government has responded by imposing voluntary import quotas on the Japanese auto industry and creating a wide variety of policies intended to insulate American steel firms from foreign competition. At best, these policies have had or will have limited success, with consumers paying higher prices for the protected products. Moreover, the incentive to solve some of the problems responsible for the decline in U.S. competitiveness would be discouraged by protection against foreign competition. Trade restrictions are at best an ad hoc approach to the problems of specific industries. The government intervenes in many ways in the activities of industry and will continue to do so. But what is needed is an integrated and consistent U.S. industrial policy to reduce the risks of capture by firms or industries in temporary distress or in long-term decline.

QUESTIONS FOR DISCUSSION

1. What is an import quota?
2. Distinguish between an import quota and a tariff. Which is more effective in restraining trade?
3. The Reagan administration is emphasizing tax incentives to stimulate business investment. Discuss.
4. There are costs as well as benefits when government offers tax breaks to business. Discuss.
5. What is the principle of absolute advantage? How would it apply to the American and Japanese auto industries?

6. Should the U.S. automobile industry be protected by an import quota on Japanese autos?
7. What are some of the reasons for the decline in the international competitiveness of the U.S. steel industry?
8. How can government policy improve the competitive position of the auto and steel industries?
9. Discuss the effect of accelerated depredication on business investment.
10. The foreign tax credit is considered to be a subsidy for U.S. investments overseas. Do you agree?

RECOMMENDED READINGS

Abernathy, William J. *The Productivity Dilemma: Roadblock to Innovation in the Automobile Industry*. Baltimore: Johns Hopkins University Press, 1978.

Bauer, Raymond A. *American Business and the Politics of Foreign Trade*. Chicago: Aldine, 1979.

Crandall, Robert W. *The U.S. Steel Industry in Recurrent Crisis*. Washington, D.C.: Brookings Institution, 1981.

Hayes, Robert H. "Why Japanese Factories Work." *Harvard Business Review*, 59 (July–August 1981), 56–66.

————, and William Abernathy. "Managing Our Way to Economic Decline." *Harvard Business Review*, 58 (July–August 1980), 67–77.

Ornstein, Norman J., and Shirley Elder. *Interest Groups, Lobbying and Policy Making*. Washington, D.C.: Congressional Quarterly Service, 1978.

Surrey, Stanley. "Tax Incentives as a Device for Implementing Government Policy: A Comparison with Direct Government Expenditures." *Harvard Law Review* (December 1970).

U.S., Congress, Office of Technology Assessment. *U.S. Industrial Competitiveness: A Comparison of Steel, Electronics, and Automobiles*. Washington, D.C.: U.S. Government Printing Office, 1981.

————. *Technology and Steel Industry Competitiveness*. Washington, D.C.: U.S. Government Printing Office, 1980.

PART VIII
GOVERNMENT AND BUSINESS: OTHER ISSUES

Much has happened to the United States during the twentieth century: involvement in two global wars, the Great Depression of the 1930s, and now an inflation that is the most virulent in the nation's history. As the United States enters the 1980s, it has reached a crossroad in its development as the world's leading economic power. There has been an erosion of U.S. industrial strength in the world, particularly during the 1970s. In this decade, the United States lost 23 percent of its share of the world market, compared to a 16 percent decline during the 1960s. The losses in the 1970s were particularly telling, because they came in the wake of a 40 percent decline in the value of the dollar, which made U.S. exports cheaper and foreign imports more expensive. There is also evidence that the ability of U.S. industry to innovate—to convert ideas into commercial products and processes—is slipping. Declining investment has helped to reduce U.S. productivity; this has become serious in the industrial sector where the United States once reigned supreme. The rest of the industrial world, especially Germany and Japan, is rapidly closing the gap. The lack of a coherent U.S. government economic policy is responsible for a major part of the national decline in world competitiveness.

The election results of 1980 may prove to be significant as far as economic policy is concerned. Various policy changes are bound to have an impact upon business. The Reagan administration, armed with a mandate to curtail the federal regulatory burden on business, has attempted to make a potentially lasting imprint on the activities of government agencies. The implementation of supply-side economics favors measures designed to increase the total output of goods and services. Taxes have been lowered to stimulate savings and the rate of capital formation, and various tax incentives to stimulate investment have been introduced into the tax system. The Reagan administration has made rather drastic cuts in government spending as a major part of its anti-inflation program, cuts that have been resisted by a wide variety of special interest groups. However, it is difficult, at least for now, to forecast what will happen to the U.S. economy in the 1980s. It remains to be seen whether or not the Reagan policies are successful.

Chapter 18
Government Stabilization
Policies

Probably the most important development in the role of the federal
government, at least in the last thirty years, has been its explicit assumption of responsibility for the nation's general economic health. A high
level of employment, price stability, and an adequate rate of economic
growth are accepted as goals that the government must attempt to fulfill. To these goals, a fourth, a more equitable distribution of income,
may be added. Each goal in itself has proved to be somewhat difficult
to attain. Moreover, the attainment of one may not necessarily assist in
the achievement of the others. For example, efforts to achieve full employment and price stability often are at cross-purposes with each other:
achieving one goal usually has meant sacrificing the other.

Government responsibility for economic stability is a relatively recent phenomenon, dating from the end of World War II when the Employment Act of 1946 was passed. The Depression of the 1930s was the
catalyst for the government to change from being passive to being active
in using economic policy measures to achieve prosperity. Before and
even during the Depression, the government was expected to maintain a neutral or laissez faire attitude toward the general working of
the American economy. The Depression, however, was unprecedented
in both size and duration. Almost one-fourth of the labor force was
unemployed in 1932, and throughout the decade unemployment remained higher than ever before in this century. The feeling grew that
something was inherently amiss in the market system and that the
country might be facing permanent economic stagnation. It was thus
only a short step to formally accepting the government's responsibility
for overall economic growth and stability, a step symbolized by the
Employment Act of 1946.

Taxes and transfer payments and in some cases government purchases of goods and services serve as incentives or disincentives to the
private sector of the economy. Changes in existing rules and norms
for taxation and transfer payments may thus have, in a broad sense,
incentive, or substitution, effects. An increase in the progression of
the personal income tax may, for instance, lead to the substitution of
leisure for work. An increase in the rate of payroll taxes may lead to
the substitution of resources in production, and a change in depreciation allowances may affect the expected rate of return on investment.

Moreover, any payment between the federal budget and the private sector will correspondingly change the wealth and liquidity position of the private sector's assets and may thus affect private spending with regard to liquidity or assets, either directly or via the reactions of the credit market.

As mentioned earlier, monetary and fiscal policies are the instruments for controlling or influencing economic activity. The most pervasive instruments are a part of monetary policy. Changes in the legal reserve requirements of member banks in the Federal Reserve System can be made by its board of governors to influence the supply and cost of loanable funds. Most of the contraction or expansion in the nation's supply of money occurs as a result of changes in the volume of bank credit. Commercial banks expand the money supply by making loans and creating new deposits, though legal reserves must be held against deposits. When reserve requirements are raised, there is a contraction in the amount of funds that banks can make available for loans; the reverse holds true for a lowering of legal reserve requirements. The Federal Reserve Banks' open-market operations also expand or contract the money supply. When a Federal Reserve Bank buys government securities from a commercial bank, the payment increases the latter's deposits and enhances its lending capabilities. And when a Federal Reserve Bank sells government securities to a commercial bank, it has the reverse effect. Changes in the rediscount rate by the board of governors influence the level of interest rates. Since the interest rate is the price paid for borrowed capital, its level in turn affects the volume of business investment.

Fiscal policy measures—changes in government expenditures and taxes—directly change aggregate demand by altering income and expenditures flows, whereas monetary policy measures indirectly change aggregate demand by altering prices and the absolute and relative supplies of different kinds of financial assets. Fiscal policy makes deliberate changes in government expenditures and taxes as a means of controlling economic activity. The budget of the federal government is the key instrument through which fiscal policy is effected, and it can be used as a flywheel to change the level of economic activity. Taxes are a withdrawal of income from the income stream, and government expenditures are an injection of income into it. When a government's income, as represented by taxes and other revenues, exceeds its expenditures, the net effect is to damp down the level of economic activity. But when government expenditures exceed revenues, the net effect is economic stimulation. Budgetary surpluses or deficits, then, can be used to effect changes in the level of economic activity. Fiscal policy controls the provision of public goods and services through expenditures, and income redistribution through taxes and transfer payments.

Government stabilization policies have an important impact on the operations of business firms. Monetary policy influences the rate of interest and the supply of loanable funds. When interest rates are high and loanable funds are scarce, business firms will be forced to postpone certain types of investments that would have been profitable during a period of lower interest rates and easy credit. Fiscal policy relies on changes in taxation and expenditures to effect changes in the level of economic activity. Changes in taxation will touch any business firm; for example, a reduction in the rate of the corporate income tax would give business firms more funds to invest or pay out to stockholders.

THE IMPACT OF THE DEPRESSION ON ECONOMIC POLICY

The Depression did more to reshape the American economy than any other event has since the nation was created. As mentioned in an earlier chapter, there was massive government intervention in a number of areas affecting business. Banks were made subject to closer regulation and supervision. The program of government support for prices of agricultural products was greatly enlarged to prevent losses and bankruptcy for farmers already hurt by market forces in the form of falling prices. Labor unions were encouraged by new legislation so that workers would no longer have to bargain individually in the market for labor. For a time, through the National Industrial Recovery Act, business firms were encouraged to join together to plan how to avoid subjecting their products to the vagaries of supply and demand. Legislation was passed requiring compulsory contributions to retirement funds through a government-operated social security system, which had the effect of partly replacing individuals' voluntary savings, in response to market forces such as the level of interest rates. Legislation also was passed imposing compulsory costs on business to finance automatic payments to unemployed workers.

Perhaps the most important, however, the Depression persuaded the United States and most other Western democratic governments to commit themselves to the goal of full employment. This was in response to the Depression's perhaps most memorable feature, mass unemployment, both at home and abroad. In 1933, for example, 24.9 percent of the American civilian labor force was unemployed; one out of every four workers was out of work. Even as late as 1939, ten years after the onset of the Depression, unemployment was still at the high figure of 17.2 percent of the labor force. To many it appeared that the capitalistic system was in a state of collapse and that the Marxist predictions of capitalism's demise were about to come true.[1] Unemployment had also contributed to social upheaval in other countries. In Germany, the main reason for the rise of Adolph Hitler was social discontent caused by an

1. Karl Marx, *Das Kapital* (New York: Modern Library, 1949), pt. VII, pp. 671—688.

unemployment rate of over one-fourth of the labor force. The choice for many Germans was Hitler's National Socialism, or communism. The result was that fascism replaced parliamentary democracy in Germany.[2]

Classical Economic Theory and Unemployment

Until the 1930s, the American economy had never experienced a deep and prolonged depression. Everything about the past supported the view of classical economic theory that full employment of labor and other resources could be accepted as the norm.[3] There could be lapses from full employment, but self-correcting market forces would pull the economy back to the normal state. Classical economic theory was based on many assumptions. First, there was a competetive market system, in which resources were mobile. There were many buyers and sellers in both the product and resource markets, and prices were free to move either upward or downward. Second, income was spent automatically at a rate always consistent with full employment. There could not be too much saving, for saving was channeled into investment through the mechanism of the interest rate. If there was excessive saving, the interest rate would fall and investment would increase. Conversely, if there was too little saving, the interest rate would rise and investment would decrease. An equilibrium point would always be reached at full employment. Both saving and investment were functions of the interest rate. Since saving was just another form of spending, according to classical theory, all income was spent on either consumption or investment.[4]

Say's Law of Markets

The catalyst, so to speak, in classical economic theory was Say's Law of Markets.[5] Say's Law states, in effect, that supply creates its own demand. Whatever is produced represents the demand for another product.

2. William L. Shirer, *The Rise and Fall of the Third Reich* (Greenwich, Conn.: Fawcett Publishers, 1973), p. 215.
3. The term *classical economics* was invented by Karl Marx to refer to the writings of David Ricardo and his predecessors, including Adam Smith. Later the term was applied to the writings of John Stuart Mill, Alfred Marshall, and A. C. Pigou.
4. For a good description of classical economics, see Dudley Dillard, *The Economics of John Maynard Keynes* (Englewood Cliffs, N.J.: Prentice-Hall, 1960), chap. 2.
5. Jean Baptiste Say was a French economist who lived during the time of Adam Smith. His major work, entitled *Treatise on Political Economy,* was the first popular book on economics published on the European continent.

Additional supply creates additional demand; hence, any increase in production is an increase in demand, and any general overproduction is impossible. This assertion is supported by the argument that goods really exchange for goods, money being merely a medium of exchange. Say reasoned that whenever workers and other resources are hired to create goods and services, a demand equal in value to the incomes paid to the factors of production is created automatically. Since the purpose of earning income is to spend it on output, income will automatically equal that output. In an exchange economy, Say's Law means that there will always be a rate of spending sufficient to maintain full employment.

The crucial assumption underlying Say's Law is that free competition and flexible prices, wages, and interest rates are part of the economic system. For example, all income received by labor may not necessarily be spent on consumption. Overproduction is possible, with the result that incomes decline and unemployment occurs. But the nonexpenditure, or saving, of income creates no problem, for all saving is transformed into investment spending through the mechanism of the interest rate. The increased saving will cause interest rates to decline, which will encourage business firms to invest. This in turn will cause the demand for goods and services to grow, which will counterbalance the decline in demand caused by consumer saving. Thus, the act of saving cannot lead to a deficiency of total demand or an interruption in the flow of income and expenditure.

The classical assumption of full employment was made easier to accept by making the concept consistent with voluntary unemployment. In classical economic theory, involuntary unemployment did not exist. Voluntary unemployment existed when workers were unwilling to accept the going wage. If there was competition and the market system was allowed to function, supply and demand would eventually drive wages down to a point at which unemployed workers could find employment. If they did not accept the wage, they were unemployed by choice and were not to be counted in the unemployment statistics. But this was obviously inconsistent with the facts. In 1932, there were fifteen million unemployed workers; most were hardly unemployed as a matter of choice. The classical rationale for this situtiation was that labor markets had been made imperfect by union and government intervention in supply and demand. Wage rates were therefore not free to fall to a competitive level, at which point all who were willing to work could find employment.

Policy Implications for Government

The classical theory of employment has a predilection for laissez faire, the policy that minimizes the extent of government intervention in the economy's operation. The reason is readily apparent. Classical economic theory asserted that the normal market situation is one of full employment of all resources. If there was a departure from full employment, self-adjusting market forces would move the economy to the full employment level. Given the classical assumption of a competitive market economy, with a flexible system of prices and free mobility of resources, no depression could be prolonged. Interest rates would decline to a point at which business firms would be encouraged to borrow and spend on capital goods to expand productive capacity. Savers, in response to declining interest rates, would save less and spend more. With these market adjustments freely functioning, mass unemployment could not be sustained. Through price flexibility and the free play of market forces, there eventually would be an automatic adjustment to a level of full employment.

Keynesian Economic Theory

An economic theory is valid until events prove otherwise, and the facts of economic life simply did not correspond to the way the economy was supposed to act in the classical system. The automatic adjustment toward a level of full employment did not occur; on the contrary, as the Depression of the 1930s continued, serious and prolonged unemployment became the normal condition of the economy. Under these conditions not even the staunchest defenders of classical theory could maintain seriously that there existed within the economy forces that automatically would generate continuous full employment. The classical theory offered little help to policymakers who were responsible for devising measures to combat unemployment, and it was no consolation to those who were unemployed to be told that unemployment was temporary and that eventually market forces would effect the conditions necessary for full employment. What was needed was a new theory that would explain the causes of unemployment and offer solutions for the policymakers to follow.

In 1936 the British economist John Maynard Keynes published the *General Theory of Employment, Interest, and Money*.[6] Only Adam Smith's *Wealth of Nations* and Karl Marx's *Das Kapital* have had as much impact on economic and political thinking as the *General Theory* did, but it was some years before its analysis was accepted by economists and its prescriptions for unemployment accepted by policymakers both in the United States and in other countries. The purpose of the *General Theory* was twofold. First, Keynes explained why classical economic theory was wrong to assume there would be full employment of

6. John Maynard Keynes,*The General Theory of Employment, Interest, and Money* (New York: Harcourt, Brace & Co., Inc., 1936).

labor and capital. Second, and much more important for government policy purposes, Keynes constructed an alternative theory of how employment is determined in a complex industrial society. Keynes took the position that there was nothing inherent in the market system that would assure an equilibrium of resources at a level of full employment. In fact, an equilibrium position could be attained at a high level of unemployment. Moreover, as the Depression demonstrated, this position could remain relatively unchanged for a long period of time.

In classical economic theory, it was the flexibility of wages and the rate of interest that could be counted on to keep an economy in balance at a high level of employment. The classical economists reasoned that unemployment would eventually disappear because the workers' competition for jobs would drive wages down to the point at which it would be profitable for employers to hire them. But Keynes contended that the volume of employment depended on aggregate demand, not flexible wages. Obviously, a drop in wages meant a drop in aggregate demand. In classical rubric, the flexibility of interest prevented a glut of savings. An oversupply of savings could reduce consumption and the level of demand, but the increase in saving would lower the interest rate and thus stimulate investment. The increase in investment would counterbalance the decrease in consumption. But Keynes claimed that the rate of saving bore little relation to the interest rate.

In Keynesian economic theory, the level of employment is linked to the business firms' volume of output of goods and services. The volume of output, in turn, depends on the level of income and aggregate demand. The catalyst in the Keynesian analytical framework is aggregate demand, for it determines, at least in the short run, the extent to whcih an economy's productive capacity will be used. It is at one and the same time the source of total income and the basis on which the level of employment is determined. If demand is not sufficient to employ all available resources, income will be lower than it need be. As demand falls, so will income, and as income falls, so will output and employment. The key to economic stability is to maintain income at a level consistent with high employment of labor and other resources.

Since income is derived from demand, we shall consider the components of aggregate demand. The two main components in Keynesian analysis are the consumers' demand for goods and services and the private business firms' investment demand for capital goods. To these parts, a third component, the government's demand for goods and services, may be added. Both the consumer and investment demands are based on certain determinants. Income is the prime determinant of consumption expenditures. Income, for practical purposes, is disposable income, or income after taxes. As disposible income increases, so will consumption, but not at the same rate. This functional relationship between income and consumption has been formalized in the concept of the consumption function, or the propensity to consume, which has become one of the key analytical tools of modern income and employ-ment theory. A high propensity to consume is favorable to employ-ment.

Investment expenditures have complex determinants. Investment is the application of productive resources to the manufacture of capital goods. Capital goods are valuable because of the services they are ex-pected to yield in the future. The efficiency of a capital good, or the rate of return over cost, is the captial good's rate of yield. This rate of yield is called the marginal efficiency of capital, a term denoting the discount necessary to equate the expected future earnings derived from the most profitable capital asset that can be added to an existing stock of capital goods with the cost of reproducing that added capital asset. The marginal efficiency of capital in conjunction with the interest rate determines the level of investment. The interest rate is the cost of borrowing money. There is a relationship between the marginal effi-ciency of capital and the interest rate—one is the rate of return on a capital asset, and the other is the cost of borrowing to acquire the asset. A functional relationship can be expressed as follows: Investment, $I = f(n, i)$, where n = marginal efficiency of capital, and i = rate of interest.

Consider, for example, a simple situation in which a business firm is considering an investment that has an initial cost of $1,000 and an estimated length of life of only one year. Assume that the proceeds expected from the investment are $1,200 and the rate of interest is 5 percent. The business firm compares the expected rate of return, or the marginal efficiency of capital, with the cost of borrowing to acquire the asset or, if it chooses to use its own money, the interest it could re-ceive. The marginal efficiency of capital is 20 percent, which is much greater than the rate of interest. As long as the marginal efficiency of capital is greater than the rate of interest, or $n > i$, the investment pro-ject is worthwhile to the business firm, for it will yields a rate of return greater than the cost of borrowing $1,000 to acquire the asset, or the interest forgone if it uses its own money. On the other hand, if the marginal efficiency of capital is less than the rate of interest, or $n < i$, the project will be rejected.

Keynes's Basic Thesis

The basic thesis of Keynes's General Theory, then, is that in the short run, both the level of income and employment are determined by ag-gregate demand, which in turn, depends of the propensity to consume and the amount of investment. This relationship can be expressed by the equation $Y = C + I$, where Y = total output, C = consumption ex-penditures, and I = investment expenditures. Y is referred to as the ag-gregate supply determined by the income that business firms receive from consumption and investment expenditures. In the short run, such fundamental conditions of supply as capital accumulation and population growth remain stable enough to permit the assumption that aggregate supply is determined mainly by aggregate demand. Aggregate supply and aggregate demand interact with each other to determine an equilibrium level of income and employment. They are made equal when expenditure or demand equals income or supply.

This most basic Keynesian macroeconomic model is illustrated in Diagram 18-1. The vertical axis measures aggregate demand, or consumption and investment expenditures, and the horizontal axis measures output, or real gross national product. The forty-five-degree line is the aggregate supply schedule, which shows, in effect, that the total

Diagram 18-1 Aggregate Demand and Aggregate Supply

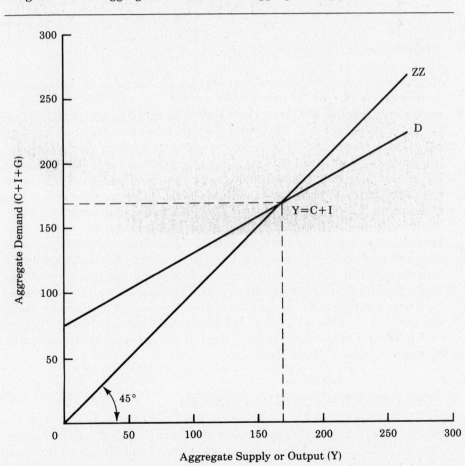

cost of national output must be matched by an equivalent amount of sale proceeds if producers as a whole are to justify total output. The line implies that there always must be an equal vertical amount of expenditure for each horizontal cost of national output. The aggregate demand line is a schedule associating spending decisions with different levels of real income. It shows, in other words, the amounts that will be spent for output at each and every possible level of income. Given the aggregate supply and aggregate demand schedules for the economy, the equilibrium level of income and employment will be determined by the intersection of the two schedules. This equilibrium is represented by the fundamental identity equation, $Y = C + I$. At any point below the equilibrium point, aggregate demand exceeds aggregate supply, and so business firms in total would be induced to increase the level of output. At any point above the equilibrium point, aggregate supply exceeds aggregate demand, and the revenue that business firms receive does not cover the cost of total output.

Implications for Government Policy

Keynesian economic theory repudiates laissez faire and accepts government intervention as the prime requisite for economic stability. The policy implications are clear: there has to be more government participation in economic life. This participation, however, does not have to be a total reconstruction of society along socialist lines. On the contrary, Keynesian economics tries to create a better economic and social milieu in which industrial capitalism can survive. The first desideratum of such a better environment is the abolition of unemployment, through government fiscal and monetary policies that stimulate consumption and investment expenditures. The second desideratum of a better system is a more equitable and less arbitrary distribution of income, through progressive income taxation and various social welfare measures designed to increase consumption. Prosperity can be achieved more easily by stimulating the consumers' purchasing power. The Keynesian view that inequality of income is a barrier to the creation of new wealth reversed the traditional notion that the accumulation of wealth depends on the savings of the rich. In fact, Keynes advocated what he called the euthanasia of the rentier class.[7]

WORLD WAR II AND ITS AFTERMATH

World War II had a rather salubrious effect on the American economy. For one thing, it cured unemployment. Despite the efforts of President

7. Keynes, *The General Theory of Employment, Interest, and Money*, p. 376.

Franklin D. Roosevelt's New Deal, unemployment continued at a high level, although well below the peak unemployment rate of 24.9 percent in 1933. By 1937 the unemployment rate had declined to 14.3 percent; however, in 1938 the rate increased to 19.0 percent, and in 1939, the year Hitler marched into Poland, the rate was 17.2 percent.[8] In 1940, even with Lend-Lease and the eventual realization that in one way or another, the United States would be drawn into the war, the unemployment rate was 14.0 percent. In 1941, the year of Pearl Harbor, the rate was 9.9 percent, but in 1942 the rate declined to 4.7 percent and in 1943, to 1.9 percent. The war also cured unemployment in Great Britain and Germany.

After the war was over, the governments in this and other countries were less than sanguine about the future, as they realized that the problems created by the Depression, particularly unemployment, had not been solved. In the United States there was no reason to doubt that the unemployment ratio of the 1930s would return. Demobilization itself would create an enormous readjustment. How would the vast majority of the veterans be assimilated into the labor market? History offered horrible examples. In the United States in the immediate post–World War I period, there was a recession and a high rate of unemployment. In the United Kingdom between 1919 and 1939 the average annual rate of unemployment was over 10 percent. Germany after World War I was in a state of chaos, as unemployed war veterans joined various private armies to fight anyone.[9] The authority of the state was subverted, and eventually mass unemployment led to the rise of Hitler.

The Employment Act of 1946

The Employment Act of 1946 is a landmark act in that it gave legislative sanction to the view that the federal government has a direct responsibility for the level of employment and income prevailing in the economy. This marked a complete departure from the government's laissez faire idea that broad segments of American society had supported as late as 1929. Before the onset of the Depression, the major explicit goal of American public economic policy was to maintain price stability. Little intervention by the federal government was needed to achieve this goal. If this goal was achieved, it was credited to the natural forces operating in the economy that would assure expanding employment and economic growth. But the Depression was a trauma without

8. *Economic Report of the President, 1975* (Washington, D.C.: U.S. Government Printing Office, February 1975), p. 276.
9. John Maynard Keynes, *The Economic Consequences of the Peace* (New York: Harcourt, Brace & Co., Inc., 1920). This book lists the mistakes the Allies made in the Treaty of Versailles, which led to disruption and eventually chaos in the German economy.

a parallel in American history, and the old order broke down. The act reflected the hope, derived from the war experience, that the proper use of fiscal and monetary policies could help stabilize the economy at a level above that of the Depression years.

The significance of the act is in the general direction it gives to economic policy and the machinery it established to enable both the executive and legislative branches of the federal government to assume responsibility for the overall functioning of the American economy. The act makes maximum employment only one of three public policy objectives.[10] The other two are maximum production and purchasing power, which are to be advanced conjointly with maximum employment.[11] To facilitate the pursuit of these objectives, the act created a Council of Economic Advisers to the president, consisting of three members charged with the responsibility of gathering and analyzing information on current and prospective economic trends and of formulating and recommending national economic policy. The president, with the assistance of the Council of Economic Advisers, is required to transmit annually an economic report, which analyzes current economic conditions and presents a program for carrying out the public policy objectives expressed in the act. On the legislative side, the act created the Joint Economic Committee, composed of eight members of the Senate and eight members of the House of Representatives. Its task is to advise Congress on the president's recommendations.

The effectiveness of the Employment Act of 1946 was never tested. Contrary to expectations, the economy did not revert back to Depression conditions. First, the period between 1942 and 1945 had been one of austerity for American consumers. Although money was fairly abundant, consumer goods were either rationed or not produced at all. There were also forced savings, which took the form of compulsory war bond purchases. After the war was over, there was a massive accumulation of savings and a pent-up demand for consumer goods, which were in short supply. Many veterans were absorbed into the defense industries, which were reconverted into capital and consumer goods industries to satisfy the demand for goods and services. Other veterans enrolled in schools under the G. I. Bill and did not become a part of the labor force. The Marshall Plan stimulated exports to Europe. The period of détente with the Soviet Union came to an abrupt end with the Berlin Blockade, and the renewed fear of war stimulated defense spending. The federal government's expenditures on goods and services had declined from a 1944 high of $165.4 billion to $19.1 billion in 1947, but by 1952 these expenditures had increased to $63.8 billion.[12]

10. Section 2 of Public Law 304, 79th Cong., 1st sess.
11. Section 2 of Public Law 304, p. 1.
12. *Economic Report of the President, 1976*, p. 245.

Acceptance of Keynesian Economics in the United States

It is commonly believed that Keynesian economics, or the new economics, as it came to be called by many, was introduced into the Unied States during the Kennedy administration. There was an intellectual revolution in policymaking at that time, based on the belief that a steadily growing, fully employed economy was both desirable and attainable; that fiscal and monetary policies could contribute greatly to full employment and economic growth; and that these policies should be dedicated to economic objectives rather than to other ends.[13] Fiscal policy measures, as practiced by the Kennedy and Johnson administrations, were directed largely toward influencing the level of aggregate demand so as to bring it into line with the economy's changing productive capacity. One requirement of this approach was a massive reduction in both personal and corporate income taxes. It was expected that these tax cuts would stimulate both consumption and investment spending, thus increasing output and the level of employment.

Reasons for the Acceptance of the New Economics

There were two economic factors that contributed to the election of John F. Kennedy as president. One was the United States' low rate of economic growth in comparison with that of the Soviet Union, Japan, and most of the Western European countries. It was little consolation that only the United Kingdom, among the major industrial countries, had a lower rate of economic growth. Much more serious was that the growth rate of the United States was lower than that of the Soviet Union. In 1958, the Soviet Union sent Sputnik into orbit, to the horrified disbelief of the United States. The lower growth rate seemed to confirm Nikita Khrushchev's statement that the Soviet Union would bury the United States: he must have been referring to economic competition. The growth rate was an issue in the 1960 campaign, and the Democratic Party's national platform promised to raise it to 5 percent a year.

The second factor was unemployment. Although the rate of unemployment during the post–World War II period had never reached the unemployment rates of the 1930s, there had been several business recessions. The peak unemployment rate in the 1949 recession was 8.1

13. James Tobin, "The Intellectual Revolution in U.S. Economic Policy-Making," Noel Buxton Lecture at the University of Essex, England January 18, 1966, published in *Public Finance and Public Policy Issues*, ed. Martin Schnitzer and Yung-Ping Chen (Scranton, Pa.: International Textbook Company, 1972), pp. 72–91.

percent, but it was of short duration and recovery was rapid. During the
1953–1954 recession, the peak was not as high but was of longer duration. Further, the level of unemployment during the following recovery
period was substantially higher than during the previous recovery
period. The unemployment rate during the 1957–58 recession was significantly higher than during the previous recession. In addition, the
rate during and after recovery was again much higher than during the
same period following the 1953–1954 recession. The rates during 1959
and 1960 averaged 5.5 and 5.6 percent, respectively. The average rate
of unemployment was higher after each of the postwar recessions, and
thus, the unemployment situation became progressively worse after
each recession. Moreover, a balance of payments problem constituted
an important new policy constraint not noticeably present in the
earlier postwar recessions.

There was a fourth recession in the 1960–1961 period, which over-
lapped the Eisenhower and Kennedy administrations. The average unemployment of 5.6 percent in 1960 increased to an average rate of 6.8
percent in 1961. Kennedy took office confronted by a stagnant economy and a rising rate of unemployment. As well, there were policy constraints imposed by more than a century of tradition. One constraint
was the strong instinctive American opposition to government spending, especially deficit spending. It was an article of faith, a matter of
fiscal rectitude, among most Republicans and some Democrats that
the federal budget should be balanced. A second constraint was the
general disagreement over the causes of unemployment. Some people
felt that unemployment could be attributed to structural changes in
the economy. Automation was alleged to be rapidly eliminating old
jobs while creating new ones for which neither the displaced workers
nor the new entrants to the labor markets were qualified by skill, experience, or location. But other people believed that unemployment
was due to a lack of aggregate demand. Moreover, the national unemployment rate was not widely regarded as a politically urgent problem.

During the Kennedy administration, the traditional concepts of public finance underwent a major change: government fiscal policies came
to be viewed as instruments for influencing the magnitude and direction of income flows throughout the economy. The impact of these
policies on business was considerable. The acceleration of the economy's rate of growth was a prominent national objective, and the key
to stimulating economic growth was to increase investment, both public and private. But to increase private investment during a period of
unemployment and underutilization of productive capacity required
an increase in profits and an upward revision of business expectations.
Policy measures were needed to stimulate investment, and some, in
fact, were adopted: a tax credit for investment and a liberalization of
depreciation rules.

The Investment Credit

In 1962 the investment tax credit was passed in order to stimulate new investment and thus encourage a more rapid rate of economic growth. The investment credit is a credit against the income tax liability of an individual or corporation, allowed for amounts invested in particular assets that meet specific requirements, namely, that they improve productivity and create employment.[14] Through the modernization of plants and equipment, it was hoped that the United States' competitive position would be improved and, in turn, that pressure on the balance of payments would be decreased, thereby aiding in the stabilization of the dollar. The investment credit can be thought of as a negative income tax in that it lowers taxes and increases the rate of return on new capital investment.

Under the terms of the Revenue Act of 1962, a business firm was able to receive a credit against income taxes of up to 7 percent of the cost of new machinery and equipment and up to $50,000 for purchase of used machinery and equipment. Buildings were excluded, and the property had to be depreciable and also be used in trade or business to produce income. To secure the 7 percent credit against cost, the asset had to have a life of at least eight years. If the life of the asset was from six to eight years, the credit was 7 percent of two-thirds of the cost of the property. If the life was four to six years, the credit was 7 percent of one-third of the cost of the asset. For an asset with a life of less than four years, there was no tax credit. In addition, the investment credit was against the first $25,000 of income tax and also against 25 percent of income taxes in excess of $25,000. This was the maximum for any one year.

The following example is designed to illustrate the investment credit. The provisions of the 1962 credit, which have been modified from time to time, are used. Assume that a firm earns $1 million after expenses, but before income taxes. Given the rate of the corporation income tax as 48 percent, the firm would pay around $480,000 in federal income taxes. The limit of the investment credit for the year is $25,000 plus 25 percent of the income tax in excess of $25,000, or $25,000 + $.25 ($480,000 − $25,000) = $25,000 + $113,750 = $138,750. If a firm purchases $2 million in new equipment having a useful life of eight years or longer, it is entitled to a credit of 7 percent of the amount and arrives at a figure of $140,000. This is almost completely within the allowable limits. It subtracts the $138,750 from the $480,000 that it would have had to pay in the absence of the credit to arrive at a tax bill that it must pay of $341,250. The merit of the tax credit is that it raises the rate of return on capital, increases the cash flow of a firm, and rewards new investments.

14. Ibid., p. 90.

Accelerated Depreciation

In July 1962 liberalized depreciation guidelines were written to stimulate corporate investment. These guidelines allowed a faster rate of write-off of costs for investment outlays and shortened the useful length of life of equipment for the purpose of computing investment. By increasing the depreciation allowance, a firm's tax burden is reduced and cash flow is increased. Accelerated depreciation means that for tax purposes a firm charges off higher costs, which results in a lower tax base and a lower tax burden for the present period. Thus depreciation allowances are concentrated in the early years of an asset's life. If accelerated depreciation is to apply only to investments as of a current date, the effect should be to stimulate new investment. But accelerated depreciation may not reduce a firm's long-run tax burden; it may merely postpone it. It does result in an interest-free loan; that is, since the firm does not pay the tax in the immediate period, it has the use of an additional supply of funds interest-free, which it would not have without accelerated depreciation.

Both the investment credit and accelerated depreciation show the impact that government can have on business simply through changes in taxes that affect investment. There are certain variables in arriving at an investment decision. The businessperson, in one manner or another, attempts to estimate the present value of a stream of net receipts from an investment project. If the present value exceeds the cost of the capital asset, after allowances for risk, taxes, interest, and operating charges are calculated, the investment should be made. A reduction in taxes, which both the investment credit and accelerated depreciation are designed to accomplish, will raise the present value of a capital asset above its purchase price and stimulate investment. Cash flow will be increased and thus make more funds available for investment. The elimination of the investment credit and accelerated depreciation will have the reverse effect. Present value and cash flow will be reduced, fewer funds will be available for investment, and an investment project will become less profitable.

The Revenue Act of 1964

The Revenue Act of 1964 is a classic example of the application of Keynesian economic policy. The purpose of the act was to provide a stimulus to the American economy through the use of tax cuts. Income tax rates were reduced for all individual and corporate taxpayers. Personal income taxes were cut by more than 20 percent and corporate income taxes by about 8 percent. Before the cut, the marginal personal tax rates ranged from 20 to 91 percent; afterwards the range was 14 to 70 percent. For most corporations, the rates fell from 52 to 48 percent. For calendar-year liabilities, tax rates were cut in two stages, with part of the cut postponed until 1965. Personal witholding rates were reduced by the full amount by as early as March 1964. The Revenue Act was aimed at the demand side rather than the supply side of the nation's economy, and its main objective and achievement were to put productive capacity to work by raising the level of private aggregate demand. Effects on the productive capability of the country were largely incidental, but nonetheless important.

The tax cuts proved to be succesful in terms of their impact on the economy.[15] They created business incentives for growth-oriented activities, which were apparent in the subsequent investment boom, with its widening and updating of capital equipment, particularly in such areas as transportation, and in heavy industry, such as steel. The tax cuts also enabled the fuller employment of labor, which can be attributed to increases in both consumption and investment expenditures. It is estimated that personal income taxes were cut by $10 billion and corporate income taxes by $3 billion.[16] The overall gain in gross national product as a result of the cuts was $36.2 billion—$28.4 billion in consumption and $7.8 billion in business fixed investments. Of this $36.2 billion gain in gross national product, $25.9 billion came from the personal income tax reduction and $10.3 billion from the corporate tax cut. The estimated multiplier for the personal tax cut was 2.59, and the estimated multiplier for the corporate tax cut was 3.4.[17] The stimulus of the cut lasted through 1964 and 1965 and into 1966. Of course, the overall stimulus to economic expansion in this period was not limited to the cut in income taxes; it also included the delayed effects of the investment credit and liberalized depreciation allowances.

The Excise Tax Reduction Act was passed in 1965 to provide a further stimulus to the economy. The act repealed federal excise taxes on appliances, radios, television sets, jewelry, furs, toilet preparations, luggage and other items, and made systematic reductions in rates on passenger automobiles and parts and on telephone and other communication services. A multiple-stage cut in excise taxes was enacted in the spring of 1965. The first stage—amounting to a $1.7 billion tax cut—became effective in mid-June 1965; the second stage, of an equal amount, was scheduled to become effective at the start of 1966. But by that time U.S. participation in the Vietnam War had accelerated, and there were inflationary pressures in the economy. In early 1966, the Johnson administration recommended several compensatory fiscal actions designed to increase revenues, and excise taxes on automobile and telephone services were restored to the levels preceding the second-stage reduction in January 1966.

15. Arthur M. Okun, "Measuring the Impact of the 1964 Tax Reduction," in *Perspectives on Economic Growth*, ed. Walter Heller (New York: Random House, 1966), pp. 27—49.
16. Ibid., p. 34.
17. Ibid., p. 45.

Subsequent Economic Policy Measures

The above-mentioned policy measures were fiscal in nature. Both Kennedy's and Johnson's Councils of Economic Advisers gave priority to fiscal policy over monetary policy, as they felt that it was possible to subject the economy to "fine tuning" through changes in taxation and expenditures. In essence, fine tuning meant that the economy could be nudged in a desired direction, just as the temperature in a room can be changed by regulating the thermostat. Monetary policy was important, although secondary, to fiscal policy. To a considerable extent, the 1960s was a period in which the federal government actively used fiscal policy measures to stimulate or restrain the economy.

During the second half of the 1960s the problem in the United States was inflation, and changes were made in both fiscal and monetary policy. In 1966 the investment credit, along with accelerated depreciation options as they applied to buildings, were suspended so as to reduce the volume of capital investment. In 1968 a 10 percent surcharge was levied on individual and corporate income taxes, which was later used in 1971 by the Nixon administration. Legislative constraints were placed on spending, and excise tax rates on automobiles and television sets were retained, with a cut previously scheduled for April 1968 postponed until 1970. The ceiling in the social security payroll tax was increased from $6,600 to $7,800, and the payroll tax itself was increased. Although changes in the payroll tax were not used in a conscious effort to regulate spending, the impact of the 1968 increase was to reduce consumer spending.

When Richard Nixon assumed office in early 1969, his first priority for the domestic economy was to bring inflation under control. Ever since the escalation of the Vietnam War in 1966, the price indices had risen at an increasing rate. Nixon's approach to inflation was to slow down the rate of growth in federal expenditures for goods and services and in the money supply. In both cases the approach was successful; federal government expenditures for goods and services dropped from an annual rate of increase of 9.7 percent in 1968 to only 1.8 percent in 1969, and the rate of growth in the money supply (currency plus demand deposits) slowed from an annual rate of 7.8 percent in 1968 to 3.1 percent in 1969. This gradualist approach of the Nixon administration lasted for several years.

THE 1970s—A DECADE OF TURBULENCE

The Golden Age of the Consumer Ends

The 1970s will not be remembered as one of the better decades of this century, particularly in comparison with the three preceding ones. The golden age of ever-increasing living standards came to an end, with rising prices offsetting increases in income. Between 1967 and 1973, real disposable income per person increased by 17.5 percent, but over the next six years, the gain fell to 5.5 percent.[18] In 1979, median family income rose by 11.6 percent over 1978, but the rate of inflation increased by 11.3 percent.[19] The purchasing power of the median family rose at an average annual rate of 3.3 percent in the 1950s, by 3 percent in the 1960s, and by only 0.7 percent in the 1970s.[20] What all of this means is that the standard of living began to shrink in the 1970s after more than a quarter century of unprecedented economic growth. This goes against the American grain of always "more." The political slogan "a chicken in every pot, a car in every garage," which was fine for 1928, would be ineffective in more recent years as rising living standards demanded Cornish hens in every pot, two cars in every garage, and two houses. But the golden age of the consumer may be gone forever—a victim of such economic problems as inflation, a low growth rate, and rising unemployment in 1982.

The 1970s also witnessed the worst combination of unemployment and inflation in modern U.S. experience. The average rate of unemployment ranged from a high of 8.5 percent in 1975 to a low of 5.3 percent in 1973.[21] The unemployment rate for the decade, however, was over 6 percent—the highest rate for any decade since the 1930s. During the same decade, the inflation rate was the worst for any decade in this century. In fact, the rate of inflation was 12 percent in 1974, the highest peacetime rate since the Civil War. The rate of inflation decreased to less than 6 percent by 1976, but was back to double-digit levels by 1978. By 1980, the misery index, a term coined by former President Carter during the 1976 presidential campaign, was over 20 percent—an unemployment rate of 7.8 percent plus an inflation rate of 12.4 percent. Both unemployment and inflation have deleterious effects on the American economy—unemployment because of the loss of income that can never be regained, and inflation because of the impact it has on consumer purchasing power and business investment.

18. *Economic Report of the President, 1981*, p. 198.
19. Ibid., p. 202.
20. The Bureau of the Census reported that although money median income doubled during the 1970s, there was no gain in real income. "ABC Nightly News Report," April 19, 1982.
21. U.S., Congress, House, Committee on the Budget, *Economic Policies: The Historical Record, 1962—76* (Washington, D.C.: U.S. Government Printing Office, 1978) p. 15.

Government Economic Policy: Supply-Side Economics

Supply-side economics has received considerable attention in the early 1980s. The term *supply-side economics* represents a reaction against the demand-side economics of John Maynard Keynes, which has guided government stabilization policies in most countries since the end of World War II. The Keynesian prescriptions—tax tinkering and government spending to stimulate aggregate demand—became an article of faith in the Western world. Everything worked fine when demand was slack and unemployment was on the increase. But times have changed, and inflation, not unemployment, has become the bête noire of Western society. The economic pendulum has swung from underutilization of capacity to an overstraining of resources, and policies designed to stimulate demand simply fire up inflation. Economies have become more complex, and techniques have to be adapted to provide solutions to "stagflation"—low growth and high inflation. One thing that is necessary is an increase in investment in the United States. Investment spending that results in expansion of capital and in increases in productivity will result in increases in the nation's productive capacity.

There is nothing new about supply-side economics. Supply was an important component of nineteenth-century classical economics with an emphasis on increasing total output by concentrating on the quantity and quality of such productive elements as labor, natural resources, physical plant and equipment, and financial capital. This emphasis has been updated, and today supply-side economics is proposed as a solution to the problem of stagflation. Attention is placed on the supply side of the economy, where certain impediments to economic growth have developed. Foremost among them is a low rate of saving and investment, which has retarded capital formation and reduced the growth rate of productivity. The solution, according to the supply-side economists, is to reduce taxes, particularly those that impinge upon saving and investment. Incentive and response logic is at work: cut taxes, and saving and investment will increase. Given the right incentives, the free market is better equipped than the government to bring about lower prices and more supplies of what people want and need. Output and productivity will go up, and inflation will go down.

The Reagan tax cuts reflect the administration's belief in the efficacy of supply-side economics. The cuts are designed to favor those persons with an income of $50,000 or more, for they do the bulk of saving in U.S. society. Saving is supposed to increase and to be channeled into investment. The flow is tax cut to saving to investment, but if the flow is interrupted, meaning if saving does not occur, then the logic of the cut is defeated. Unquestionably, low productivity, saving, and capital formation are major reasons for the poor performance of the U.S. economy. Measures designed to increase productive capacity and productivity are necessary. Increases in consumption spending, a mainstay of Keynesian economic policy, do not increase productivity unless the increased consumption spending is a catalyst to more investment spending.

Supply-side economics, however, is not limited to tax cuts. The Reagan administration is continuing a process begun by the Carter administration, namely, the dismantling of a plethora of government regulations that generated costs and lowered productivity. Too much attention had been placed on benefits, but none on costs.

SUMMARY

Momentous turning points in economic and social history can occur with amazing speed. The last great upheaval in peacetime Western society occupied a single decade, the thirties, and it put its lasting imprint on the political, economic, and social trends of the succeeding decades. Whatever might be said about the continuity of historical forces, the Depression caused a radical change in a number of areas of Western society. Bad times spread throughout the world, and societies most akin to our own were coping poorly. The strain proved to be too strong in Germany, and democracy was replaced by a totalitarian state. Unemployment was proving to be an intractable problem in the United States, as well as elsewhere. Existing policies appeared to be incapable of lifting the Western economies out of the unemployment rut, for classical economic theory and nineteenth-century laissez-faire ideology allowed government only a limited role in shaping economic policy. Classical theory maintained that full employment was normal; lapses were due to wage rates that were too high, to monopoly, or to similar causes. Laissez-faire ideology taught that the least government is the best government; the government's budget always should be balanced; the lowest levels of taxes and expenditures are the best level; and the self-regulating free market is the best guide to the efficient allocation of a country's resources.

What was needed was a new theory upon which a set of economic policies could be based. This theory was presented by John Maynard Keynes in 1936, when his book, *The General Theory of Employment, Interest, and Money*, was published. Before his theory could be digested adequately and new economic policy measures tried, World War II intervened. However, after the war, the theory was generally accepted as the framework for economic policy in the major Western industrial countries. The central objective of this policy was the maintenance of a high level of employment. The basic premise of Keynes was that unemployment is caused by an insufficiency of aggregate demand. Therefore, to increase the level of demand consistent with the level of full employment, it was necessary to increase the role of the public sector. Both fiscal and monetary policy measures could be used to stimulate demand. But Keynesian economics, by premise, required increased intervention by the state into economic affairs, which meant that laissez-faire ideology was obsolete.

In the American economy, Keynesian economics was accepted as a foundation of economic policy during the Kennedy administration. Kennedy surrounded himself with economists who favored an active, expansionary fiscal policy to stimulate the rate of economic growth and to reduce the level of unemployment. Fiscal policy measures were used to increase the level of spending. In 1961 there was an increase in the volume of government spending. In 1962 the investment tax credit was instituted to stimulate investment and thus promote a more rapid rate of economic growth. In 1964 personal and corporate income tax rates were reduced for the purpose of stimulating aggregate demand. The Kennedy period produced a greater than ever consensus that a steadily growing, fully employed economy is both desirable and attainable; that the government's fiscal and monetary policies can contribute greatly to achieving full employment, steady growth, and price stability; and that these policies should be dedicated to economic objectives. The shibboleth that the federal budget was like a household budget that must be balanced year in and year out was discarded. Budget deficits to stimulate the economy were accepted as a matter of course.

Nobody is going to look back on the 1970s with nostalgia. The economy's most disruptive decade since the Depression of the 1930s witnessed the contradiction of no growth plus inflation, a condition called stagflation by economists. Stagflation was accompanied by the depreciation of the dollar, a decline in productivity, and an energy shortage in the land of supposedly limitless resources. Keynesian economic prescriptions, which had once worked when demand was slack, did not seem to work anymore. A new group of economists, eclectic in their views, provided new prescriptions for how to fix the economy. Their approach has come to be known as supply-side economics because they believe that increasing supply is the only long-range antidote for rising prices. Total output and productivity is to be stimulated by measures designed to increase the rates of saving and investment. Translated into government policy terms, this means that taxes should be lowered on capital, profits, and personal income. Government regulations and programs that aggravate inflation and reduce productivity should be eliminated. Supply-side economics was adopted by the Reagan administration, but it remains to be seen if it is successful.

QUESTIONS FOR DISCUSSION

1. What is meant by the term *classical economics*, and why was the full employment of resources automatically assumed?
2. Distinguish between monetary and fiscal policy.
3. Present a good case against Keynesian economic policy.
4. What is supply-side economics?
5. Why is the Employment Act of 1946 considered to be an important act?
6. What is the purpose of the Reagan tax cuts?
7. What is the causal relationship between the Depression of the 1930s and the kind of economic system the American nation found itself with several decades later?
8. Why is Keynesian economics called demand-side economics?

RECOMMENDED READINGS

Aaron, Henry J., and Michael J. Boskin. *The Economics of Taxation*. Washington, D.C.: Brookings Institution, 1980.

Chase Manhattan Bank. "Getting Serious About Supply." *Business in Brief*, No. 150 (March–April 1980). A good discussion of supply-side economics.

Committee for Economic Development. *Fighting Inflation and Promoting Growth*. New York: Committee for Economic Development, 1976.

Dornbusch, Rudiger, and Stanley Fischer. *Macroeconomics*. New York: McGraw-Hill, 1978.

Economic Report of the President, 1981. Washington, D.C.: U.S. Government Printing Office, February 1981.

Feldstein, Martin S., ed. *The American Economy in Transition*. Chicago: University of Chicago Press, 1980.

Hansen, Alvin. *A Guide to Keynes*. New York: McGraw-Hill, 1953.

Keynes, John M. *The General Theory of Employment, Interest, and Money*. New York: Harcourt, Brace & Co., 1936.

Pechman, Joseph, ed. *Setting National Priorities: Agenda for the 1980's*. Washington, D.C.: Brookings Institution, 1980.

U.S., Congress, House of Representatives, Committee on the Budget. *Economic Stabilization Policies: The Historical Record, 1962-76*. 95th Cong., 2nd sess., November 1978.

Chapter 19

Business and Government
Relations in the 1980s

"Optimism," says a character in one of Voltaire's plays, "is a mania for maintaining that all is well when things are going badly."[1] There does not appear to be much room for optimism, at least as far as the immediate future is concerned. The period of U.S. supremacy that began after World War II has now come to an abrupt end. The turn came in the 1970s when the United States failed to keep pace with development in key countries in Europe and East Asia. By the end of 1980, the Japanese had become the world's largest producer of automobiles, the first time that any country replaced the United States at the top in fifty-six years. The financial problems of Chrysler and Ford became acute, leading the Reagan administration to impose voluntary import quotas on Japanese cars in April 1981. The opening words of an International Workers of the World (IWW) song of the early 1900s, "Times are getting hard, boys; money is getting scarce," are as relevant to the United States in the early 1980s as they were then. By almost any standard, the United States has entered the 1980s, faltering in its stride both at home and abroad.

Economic performance is not a straightforward concept. Any number of standards can be used to define and measure it. There are several standard measures that are acceptable—real economic growth, inflation, unemployment—and all are interrelated. What is crystal clear is that the performance of the U.S. economy, particularly during the 1970s, has not been good. The U.S. economy has to undergo a fundamental change if it is to retain a measure of economic viability, let alone leadership, in the remainder of this century. U.S. industry will need large amounts of new capital to increase primary processing capacity, and the problem of a capital shortage—because of a low rate of household savings and a declining profit margin for many U.S. firms—is a real one. The rest of the world either is catching up or has caught up with the United States.

ECONOMIC GROWTH

A high level of living in the present is made possible by the economic growth of the past. A rising level of living is made possible by continued

1. *Candide*, Chap. 1.

economic growth in the present. The same holds true for a rising level of employment. In the United States, the rate of unemployment has been high for several years. This problem has been compounded by the fact that the size of the labor force is constantly expanding. If the economy does not grow, there is no way in which the rate of unemployment can be reduced and new job seekers can be absorbed into the labor force. Further, the nation will not be able to obtain the resources to solve its social problems—to provide the schools, medical care, hospitals, and other things it needs.

Table 19-1 presents U.S. real gross national product in 1972 dollars. A measure of economic growth is the rate of change of real gross national product, either total or per capita, over time. The total real gross

Table 19-1 Real Gross National Product, United States, 1960–1980

Year	Total Real GNP	
	Billions of Dollars of 1972 Purchasing Power	Percentage Change from Previous Year
1960	737	2.2
1961	757	2.6
1962	800	5.8
1963	832	4.0
1964	876	5.3
1965	929	6.0
1966	985	6.0
1967	1,011	2.7
1968	1,058	4.6
1969	1,088	2.8
1970	1,086	−0.2
1971	1,122	3.4
1972	1,186	5.7
1973	1,255	5.8
1974	1,248	−0.6
1975	1,234	−1.1
1976	1,300	5.4
1977	1,372	5.5
1978	1,437	4.8
1979	1,483	3.2
1980	1,481	−0.2

Source: *Economic Report of the President* (February 1981), pp. 234–235.

national product of the United States measured in dollars of 1972 purchasing power rose from $1.1 trillion in 1970 to $1.5 trillion in 1980. The rate of change from year to year during the 1970s was the lowest for any decade since the Depression of the 1930s. The end result was a slippage in living standards relative to other countries. By 1981 the United States ranked tenth among the nations of the world in per capita gross national product.[2] West Germany and France, two major world competitors, had higher per capita incomes than the United States.

Productivity

Productivity is linked to economic growth. A nation's ability to consume ultimately depends upon its ability to produce. Productivity growth has long been recognized as one of the most important determinants of national economic growth and stability. Money incomes may rise, but if productivity does not rise, it is not possible to have more real purchasing power. Increased productivity will help reduce inflation by tempering the growth of unit labor costs. Unfortunately, the productivity of the United States has fallen to the point where eventually we may be replaced by the Japanese as the world's number one economic power. During the period 1972–1978, for example, industrial productivity rose 1 percent per year in the United States and over 5 percent in Japan.[3] U.S. productivity has shown a steady decline over the last three decades. As measured by the growth in output per worker —the most widely used measure of productivity—the average annual rate of increase declined from 3.0 percent during the period 1950–1965 to 2.4 percent during 1965–1973 and to only 0.6 percent during 1973–1980 with actual declines in 1978, 1979, and 1980. In the absence of productivity gains, there can be no general improvement in real U.S. living standards.

Table 19-2 presents U.S. productivity performance during the period 1970–1980, with 1977 used as the base year. Average real output per hour is used as the measure of productivity. The productivity slowdown during the 1970s contributed to a deterioration in the ability of American industry to compete in the world economy. All the industrialized Western countries experienced a marked decline in productivity, particularly after 1973. But the reduction experienced by the U.S. economy exceeded the decline in every other country except the United Kingdom and Sweden. Thus, a primary goal of U.S. economic policy during

2. The World Bank, "Summary of International Statistics," April 1982, p. 1.
3. U.S., Congress, Joint Economic Committee, *The 1981 Midyear Report: Productivity* (Washington, D.C.: U.S. Government Printing Office, 1981), pp. 2-3.

Table 19-2 Annual Indexes of Productivity in the United States, 1970–1980 (1977 = 100)

Year	Real Output Per Worker
1970	86.1
1971	89.3
1972	91.4
1973	94.8
1974	92.7
1975	94.8
1976	97.9
1977	100.0
1978	99.8
1979	99.4
1980	99.0

Source: U.S., Congress, Joint Economic Committee, *The 1981 Midyear Report: Productivity* (Washington, D.C.: U.S. Government Printing Office, 1981), p. 3.

the 1980s must be to restore healthy productivity growth. To do this, it is necessary to pursue macroeconomic policies designed to reduce inflation and achieve high economic growth, as well as microeconomic policies designed to enhance productivity directly.

Economic Growth and Productivity: International Comparisons

The performance of the United States must be placed in a global perspective. No longer is it possible for the United States to exist in splendid isolation and ignore the rest of the world. The Japanese have already surpassed the United States as the world's leading producer of automobiles and steel products. In many industries, the United States lags behind other countries in the introduction of new technology. In an increasingly interdependent world, no economy operates in a vacuum. All the world's industrial countries have fallen victim to a hydra-headed economic monster of slower growth, higher inflation, and higher unemployment. However, there has been wide variation among industrial countries in economic performance levels. Real economic growth and productivity is one basic measure of economic performance. Another measure is the rate of employment and unemployment, and a third is the keeping of purchasing power of earnings as stable as possible.

Table 19-3 presents an economic performance index for eight major industrial countries, including the United States, for the two time periods, 1960–1973 and 1974–1980. The economic performance index was arrived at by dividing the real economic growth rate for each country by its unemployment and inflation rates. All else being equal, the higher the rate of economic growth, the higher the index; the higher the rate of inflation or unemployment, the lower the index. The higher the index, the better the economic performance. The table indicates that for both periods, Japan's economy performed best with West Germany second. However, there was a marked deterioration in the performance of each country during the 1974–1980 period. Though Japan ranked first in both periods, its economic performance index for the 1974–1980 period (37.8) was but one quarter of the 145.9 registered for the 1960–1973 period. The performance of the United States was poor for both time periods. All countries showed a decline in economic performance for the 1974–1980 period.

Table 19-3 Economic Performance Index for Eight Major Industrial Countries, 1960–1973 and 1974–1980

Country	1960–1973	Country	1974–1980
Japan	145.9	Japan	37.8
West Germany	123.9	West Germany	29.0
France	85.5	France	18.0
Italy	67.7	Canada	16.5
Canada	64.2	Sweden	15.3
Sweden	55.6	United States	15.2
United States	50.4	Italy	13.4
United Kingdom	43.1	United Kingdom	2.2

Source: New York Stock Exchange, Office of Economic Research, *U.S. Economic Performance in a Global Perspective*, February 1981, p. 11.

Table 19-4 compares the average annual compound rates of real economic growth for the same countries during the time periods, 1960–1973 and 1973–1979. Gross domestic product is used as the measurement of economic growth.[4] The table indicates that the performance of the United States relative to the other countries is somewhat mixed. For the period 1960–1973, the performance of the U.S. growth rate

4. Gross domestic product is the value of all output produced within the geographic confines of a country.

Table 19-4 Real Economic Growth Rates for Eight Major Industrial Countries, 1960–1973 and 1973–1979

Country	1960–1973	Country	1973–1979
Japan	10.5	Japan	4.0
France	5.6	Canada	3.2
Canada	5.6	France	2.9
Italy	5.3	United States	2.7
West Germany	4.5	Italy	2.4
United States	4.1	West Germany	2.4
Sweden	3.9	Sweden	1.7
United Kingdom	3.2	United Kingdom	0.8

Source: New York Stock Exchange, Office of Economic Research, *U.S. Economic Performance in a Global Perspective*, February 1981, p. 17.

ranked fifth among the eight countries. The growth rate was less than half of Japan's. However, the U.S. growth rate for the 1973–1979 period, although low compared to the previous time period, actually was relatively better than the other countries in that there was less of a decline—4.1 percent in 1960–1973 to 2.7 percent in 1973–1979—compared to a drop in the Japanese growth rate from 10.5 percent to 4.0 percent. Only three countries—Japan, Canada, and France—had growth rates during the second period that were higher than the United States. The growth rates of all countries deteriorated during the 1973–1979 period. Moreover, the deterioration continued in 1980 and 1981, with the United Kingdom showing a negative rate of economic growth for both years, and the United States for 1980.[5]

Table 19-5 compares productivity in the United States and other countries for two periods, 1960–1973 and 1973–1979. Productivity is measured in average annual compound rate of change of real output per man-hour. Again the performance of the United States has been poor, particularly during the second period. This has contributed to a deterioration in the ability of U.S. industry to compete in a world economy. All major industrial countries showed a decline in productivity growth after 1973, but the decline experienced by the U.S. economy exceeded the decline in every other country except the United Kingdom and Sweden. Overall, when the 1973–1979 period is compared with the 1960–1973 period, productivity growth declined twice as sharply in the United States as it did elsewhere, and the rate of increase in unit labor costs accelerated four times as rapidly here as abroad.

5. *Washington Post*, Section F5, September 20, 1981.

Table 19-5 Annual Percent Change in Manufacturing Productivity for Eight Major Industrial Countries, 1960–1973 and 1973–1979

Country	1960–1973	1973–1979	Percent Decline
Japan	10.3	6.9	33.0
Italy	7.2	3.7	48.6
Sweden	6.7	2.4	64.2
France	5.8	4.8	17.2
West Germany	5.5	5.3	3.6
Canada	4.6	2.2	52.2
United Kingdom	4.0	0.5	87.5
United States	3.1	1.4	54.8

Source: U.S., Congress, Joint Economic Committee, *The 1981 Midyear Report: Productivity* (Washington, D.C.: U.S. Government Printing Office, 1981), p. 4.

The famous baseball pitcher, "Satchel" Paige, once made the statement, "Never look back, for you don't know who is gaining on you." Perhaps this advice is good for the United States, for the rest of the world is indeed gaining on us, as Table 19-6 indicates. The United States still remains first in the world in terms of productivity as measured by real output per worker. However, if current trends continue, it will not be very long before other industrial countries match or exceed U.S. productivity levels. The productivity slowdown hits particularly hard at U.S. industrial firms that compete head-on in the world market

Table 19-6 Real Gross Domestic Product per Worker for Eight Major Industrial Countries, 1950–1979 (United States = 100)

Country	1950	1960	1970	1979
Belgium	55.6	59.7	73.7	90.7
Canada	84.5	89.5	92.6	94.8
France	42.4	53.7	71.0	88.8
West Germany	37.3	56.0	71.3	87.9
Italy	25.5	34.9	53.4	59.5
Japan	15.5	23.8	48.7	66.4
United Kingdom	53.4	53.7	57.6	59.5
United States	100.0	100.0	100.0	100.0

Source: U.S., Congress, Joint Economic Committee, *The 1981 Midyear Report: Productivity* (Washington, D.C.: U.S. Government Printing Office, 1981), p. 5.

with highly productive foreign firms. The U.S. auto industry is a case in point, with Japan's automated factories outproducing older U.S. auto plants. Consistently, the U.S. automobile industry has found that there is as much as a 50 percent differential in labor productivity in favor of the Japanese auto industry.[6] In 1955, there were 150 television set manufacturers in the United States. In 1980, the only television sets that were produced in the United States were produced by Japanese firms.

INFLATION

As was discussed earlier in Chapter 18, the decade of the 1970s produced the worst combination of unemployment and inflation in modern U.S. history. The figures given there bear repeating: an average rate of unemployment ranging from a high of 8.5 percent in 1975 to a low of 5.3 percent in 1973;[7] an unemployment rate for the decade in excess of 6 percent, the highest rate for any decade since the 1930s; an inflation rate for the decade that was the worst for any decade in this century; a rate of inflation in 1974 of 12 percent, the highest peacetime rate since the Civil War; and an inflation rate that, though it decreased to less than 6 percent by 1976, was back to double-digit levels by 1978. In 1979, although median family income rose by 11.6 percent over 1978, the rate of inflation increased by 11.3 percent.[8] The purchasing power of the median family rose at an annual average rate of only 0.7 percent in the 1970s.[9]

OPEC: A Scapegoat for Inflation

It is convenient to find scapegoats for problems, and the Organization of Petroleum Exporting Countries (OPEC), by quadrupling oil prices in 1974, provided and continues to provide the scapegoat for American politicians and the general public. There is no question that OPEC pricing policies have contributed to inflation, but it might be added that inflation in the United States and other industrial countries caused OPEC to raise its prices originally. So a vicious cycle developed—inflation, oil price increases, more inflation, more price increases. However,

6. U.S., Congress, Office of Technology Assessment, *U.S. Industrial Competitiveness: A Comparison of Steel, Electronics, and Automobiles* (Washington, D.C.: U.S. Government Printing Office, 1981), p. 47.
7. *Economic Report of the President* (Washington, D.C.: U.S. Government Printing Office, February 1981), p. 244.
8. Ibid., p. 198.
9. Ibid., p. 202.

OPEC is only a partial explanation of the problem. West Germany, which is far more dependent on OPEC oil than the United States, had a much lower rate of inflation, a higher rate of economic growth, and a lower rate of unemployment than the United States during the 1970s. Evidently there must be other causes of inflation.

Government's Role in Inflation

One of the prime causes of inflation has been the rather inept record of the federal government in controlling spending. As Table 19-7 indicates, a deficit has existed in the federal budget for every year during the 1970s and has continued in 1980 and 1981. The largest deficits were incurred during the 1975–1979 period, as both the Ford and Carter administrations stimulated the economy after the 1975 recession to reduce the rate of unemployment.

Table 19-7 does not reflect the impact these deficits have had on the American economy. The federal government, by borrowing to finance social welfare and defense programs, has increased the money supply, particularly since most of the borrowing is from banks and other financial institutions. Government competes with private industry for the supply of loanable funds. There is a constant roll-over of the federal debt as it becomes due; thus the government is always in the money market, bidding for loanable funds. This results in a diversion of credit from the private to the public sector. It is easier to borrow than to raise

Table 19-7 Federal Budget Recipts and Outlays: Fiscal Years 1970–1980 (billions of dollars)

Fiscal Year	Receipts	Outlays	Deficit
1970	193.7	196.6	− 2.8
1971	188.4	211.4	− 23.0
1972	208.6	232.0	− 23.4
1973	232.2	247.1	− 14.8
1974	264.9	269.6	− 4.7
1975	281.0	326.2	− 45.2
1976	300.0	366.4	− 66.4
1977	357.8	402.7	− 45.0
1978	402.0	450.8	− 48.8
1979	466.0	493.6	− 27.7
1980 (preliminary)	520.0	579.0	− 59.0

Source: U.S. Office of Management and Budget, Annual Report for 1980, p. 4.

taxes, but borrowing creates the inflationary bias in the economy. As the rate of inflation increases, however, the normal response of the Federal Reserve is to reduce the money supply. Interest rates rise as a result of competition for loanable funds. Rising interest rates tend to hurt such crucial sectors as construction and home building. Continuation of deficits in the federal budget simply fuel inflation and do nothing to dampen the expectation of society that prices will continue to rise in the future.

The cartoon character Pogo once said, "We have met the enemy and he is us." Government is supposedly us, giving us what we want or what it thinks we want. Often, however, the public is ambivalent about what it wants—lower taxes *and* better social services. The idea that solutions for any problem can be bought has encouraged overpromising by government and has inflated the expectations of the governed. A "revolution of rising entitlement" developed in the United States during the last decade, which was reflected in an enormous increase in spending on social welfare programs. Experience showed that some of these programs were expensive exercises in futility, whereas others did some good. Spawned in the process were vast new constituencies of government bureaucrats and public beneficiaries whose political clout will make it very difficult to kill programs off even though they are abject failures.

A Service Economy and Inflation

Another contributing factor to inflation has been the growth of a service economy. An imbalance has developed between the industrial and scientific sectors on one hand, and the human and government services sectors on the other, in relation to productivity, wage increases, unit costs, and inflation. Wage increases in the industrial and scientific sectors are easier for the economy to absorb because there may be at least some gain in productivity. If wages go up in the automobile industry by 10 percent, unit costs will rise. But labor costs are only a part of the total costs of producing an automobile and can be offset by increases in productivity. The service industry, which has replaced manufacturing as the main employer in the United States, offers no such hope. Labor is the major cost in the service industry, amounting to around 70 percent of total costs. If wages go up 10 percent in a given year, this is translated into a 7 percent gain in unit costs. If productivity increases by 2 percent, there is a 5 percent inflationary gap as a result of the wage increase.[10]

10. U.S., Congress, Joint Economic Committee, *Productivity: The Foundation of Growth*, Staff Study, November 1980.

EMPLOYMENT AND UNEMPLOYMENT

A low rate of unemployment is another desirable goal of any economy. In fact, government economic policy in most of the advanced industrial countries of the Western world has been to prevent mass unemployment of the type that occurred during the 1930s. Keynesian economic policies that stressed the stimulation of aggregate demand were accepted as an integral part of government policy. To a considerable extent, liberal social policy was associated with the rise of Keynesian economics. Economic growth became tied to various social objectives, the chief of which has become full employment and a steady increase in consumption. What this has meant is that the United States and other Western governments have increased spending and run larger budget deficits when unemployment rises; equally, governments have been called upon to increase social expenditures. Where workers once feared losing a job, which was a common experience during the Depression, they now expect a job and an ever-rising standard of living, and this puts pressure on governments to deliver. Some inflation becomes an inevitable concomitant of government full-employment policies.

The inflation-unemployment dilemma began in the United States around the latter part of the 1960s. As inflation increased, so did unemployment. A goal of full employment with price stability was becoming more difficult to achieve. This fact was reflected in the attitudes of various administrations as revealed in various economic reports of the president.[11] In the Kennedy administration, 4 percent unemployment was set as the goal consistent with full employment. There was recognition of the fact that a certain amount of unemployment would always occur for one reason or another.[12] By the time of the Johnson administration, an unemployment rate of 4.5 percent was accepted as a norm for full employment and price stability. By the end of the Ford administration, the Economic Report of the President was listing a goal of 5 percent unemployment as being consistent with full employment, and during the Carter administration, 6 percent became the implied target. These changing goals indicate that it has become more difficult to achieve a low level of unemployment and price stability. The trade-off has become higher and higher as the years have passed.

11. Lester C. Thurow, *The Zero-Sum Society* (New York: Basic Books, 1980), p. 73.
12. There is *frictional* unemployment that occurs when workers are between jobs, and *structural* unemployment that occurs when industries decline or become automated. Coal mining is an example of the latter.

Unemployment Rates for the United States

Table 19-8 presents the average percentage annual rate of unemployment in the United States for the period 1970–1980. These rates, although by no means comparable to the very high unemployment rates that existed during the Depression, are nevertheless higher than those prevailing during the 1950s and 1960s. Moreover, there are differences in the rates of unemployment among such ascriptive characteristics as race and sex. Unemployment rates are higher for blacks than for whites. The rate of unemployment is highest for teen-agers sixteen to nineteen, with black teen-agers more than twice as likely to be unemployed as white teen-agers. There are less differences based on sex, with the unemployment rates for males and females, white or black, somewhat similar.

In April 1982, the unemployment rate in the United States reached 9 percent. At the same time, the rate of inflation slowed to an annual rate of less than 6 percent. Unemployment and inflation typically have shown an inverse relationship. In general, the lower the unemployment rate, the higher has been the rate of inflation of both wages and prices. Higher unemployment, conversely, normally has been associated with a reduced rate of inflation. This relationship is by no means unvarying or very precise.

To the extent that it exists, however, it appears to be closely related to the influence of aggregate demand, since this tends to exert a simultaneous impact on both prices and employment. The unemployment-

Table 19-8 Unemployment Rates in the United States by Demographic Characteristics, 1970–1980

Year	Total All Workers	White		Black	
		Male	Female	Male	Female
1970	4.9	4.5	5.4	7.3	9.3
1971	5.9	5.4	6.3	9.1	10.8
1972	5.6	5.0	5.9	8.9	11.3
1973	4.9	4.3	5.3	7.6	10.5
1974	5.6	5.0	6.1	9.1	10.7
1975	8.5	7.8	8.6	13.7	14.0
1976	7.7	7.0	7.9	12.7	13.6
1977	7.0	6.2	7.3	12.4	14.0
1978	6.0	5.2	6.2	10.9	13.1
1979	5.8	5.1	5.9	10.3	12.3
1980	7.1	6.3	6.5	13.3	13.1

Source: *Economic Report of the President* (February 1981), p. 269.

inflation link would pose no particular problem if it pointed to the existence of some level of aggregate demand at which neither the rate of price increases nor the level of unemployment exceeded socially acceptable limits. But it doesn't. Moreover, the economic situation for much of the last decade and extending to 1982 has been the existence of unemployment and inflation at the same time. This has increased the problems for economic policy, for measures designed to reduce inflation (high interest rates) can push up the rate of unemployment, and measures designed to reduce unemployment (low interest rates and increases in the money supply) can also push up inflation.

SAVING AND INVESTMENT

Saving is a precondition for investment; without it, investment could not take place. There is a direct relationship between saving, investment, productivity, and economic growth. By any measure, the United States lags behind the rest of the industrial world in its ability to make resources available for investment through saving. Gross saving by both the private and public sectors of the U.S. economy is a smaller percentage of gross domestic product than it is for any other major industrial country. The Japanese gross saving rate is more than twice that of the United States, and the personal household saving rate by Japanese households is usually three to four times our own. But as Table 19-9 indicates, Japan is not alone in saving more than the United States does. The table presents household saving ratios expressed as a percentage of disposable income for the United States and other major industrial countries for the two periods, 1965-1969 and 1970-1976. The table also presents the ratio of total private saving (corporate and household) to gross domestic product, and the ratio of total saving (private and public) to gross domestic product, for the same periods.

There are a number of explanations for the low rate of saving in the United States relative to other countries. The United States is a consumer-oriented society in which instant gratification is the norm. U.S. tax laws favor consumption at the expense of saving. For example, the United States does not use the value-added tax, which is a major source of government revenue in France, Italy, the United Kingdom, and West Germany. The value-added tax, like any sales tax, tends to inhibit consumption. The taxpayer burden on investment income is higher in the United States than it is in any of the other countries in Table 19-9. In 1980, the average tax on investment income in the United States was 33.5 cents per dollar compared to an average tax on investment income of 14.4 cents per dollar in Japan and 11.8 cents per

Table 19-9 Selected Saving Ratios, United States and Other Countries, 1965-1969 and 1970-1976

Country	Gross Private Saving Ratio	Gross Saving Ratio	Household Saving Ratio
Japan			
1965-1969	29.6	36.6	18.6
1970-1976	31.7	37.0	22.0
West Germany			
1965-1969	21.6	26.4	12.1
1970-1976	21.2	25.4	15.8
United Kingdom			
1965-1969	14.5	19.6	5.9
1970-1976	14.6	18.5	8.1
France			
1965-1969	N.A.	25.2	N.A.
1970-1976	20.5	23.5	13.6
Italy			
1965-1969	22.1	23.5	15.7
1970-1976	24.3	22.5	21.0
United States			
1965-1969	16.9	19.7	7.4
1970-1976	15.8	17.8	7.8

Source: Board of Governors of the Federal Reserve System, "Public Policy and Capital Formation," April 1980, p. 67.

dollar in West Germany.[13] Cultural differences may also explain variations in saving rates among the countries. The Japanese traditionally have been thrifty. Government policies after World War II and extending up to the present have been designed to encourage saving. The same holds true for West Germany.

DEFICIENCIES IN U.S. BUSINESS MANAGEMENT

An article appeared in the *Harvard Business Review* called "Managing Our Way to Economic Decline."[14] The premise of the article is that

13. New York Stock Exchange, Office of Economic Research, *U.S. Economic Performance in a Global Perspective*, February 1981, p. 27. Investment income consists of capital gains, dividends, and interest.
14. Robert H. Hayes and William Abernathy, "Managing Our Way to Economic Decline," *Harvard Business Review* (July-August 1980), 67-77.

U.S. business managers are at least in part responsible for the poor performance of the U.S. economy. Too many managers are more interested in short-run profit than in long-term growth. Partly to please stockholders, managers feel it necessary to show continually growing profits, quarter to quarter, at the expense of research and development programs that may not pay off for eight to ten years. Many executive compensation plans tie bonuses to year-to-year returns. U.S. managers are also accused of not being innovative. For example, U.S. auto firms have not had a major innovation since the development of the automatic transmission during the 1930s and wouldn't significantly reduce the size of their cars until after the 1973 oil embargo, which opened up our domestic market to small, fuel-efficient cars from Japan. Criticism of inefficient government bureaucracies has also been extended to business bureaucracy. The bigger the firm, the bigger the bureaucracy: excessive paperwork, committees reviewing committees, institutional caution and delay, and the Parkinson's Law effect of superiors creating more subordinates. Some corporate mergers, particularly those of the conglomerate type, may also inhibit innovation.

INTEREST GROUP PLURALISM

The foundation of any liberal society, as Daniel Bell points out, is a willingness on the part of all groups to compromise private ends for the public interest.[15] There has to be a set of reciprocal obligations between individuals in a group situation to hold the institutions of a society together. In the United States, there has been a loss of cohesiveness, resulting from the fragmentation of society into a congeries of special interest groups ranging from environmentalists to the National Rifle Association. There has been a shift from market to political decisions. Everybody organizes and goes out to fight. The result is an increase in conflict and in the politics of confrontation. There is the loss of civitas, a spontaneous willingness to obey the law and to respect the rights of others. Each group goes its own way and pursues its own goals, but the interests of society count for little. Paralysis or lack of nerve can result on the part of the national leadership. When it becomes necessary to take an action that requires a sacrifice, each interest group expects someone else to make it. It is becoming more difficult to live by consensus. Presidents are now measured on the basis of immediate performance, reflecting the immediate-gratification syndrome that

15. Daniel Bell, *The Cultural Contractions of Capitalism* (New York: Basic Books, 1978).

pervades U.S. society. One-term presidents have become the norm for the times.[16]

BUSINESS AND GOVERNMENT COOPERATION IN AN ERA OF LIMITS

Effective collaboration between business and government is a sine qua non for dealing with most of the major problems facing American society today. Many unresolved issues are a consequence of the failure of business and government, the two primary institutions in American society, to function effectively, both individually and in relation to each other. At best, the relationship between business and government is comparable to the joke about how porcupines make love—very carefully; at worst, the relationship has been tantamount to border warfare. But societies survive because crises that need to be resolved are eventually resolved, and with luck, the forces making for social maturity will overbalance the forces making for disintegration. The business-government relationship can improve because by nature, business firms are adaptable; they have to be in order to survive. In adapting, they may have to alter the utilitarian business ethic, but perhaps not by much.

Problems of Business-Government Relations

The Conference on U.S. Competitiveness, which was held at Harvard University in 1980, listed five problems of business-government relations. These problems are as follows:

1. A distrust between business and government has led to an excessively adversarial relationship which discourages serious efforts to solve problems.

2. Government decisions are difficult to predict reliably and suffer from "hyperlexis"—an excessive complexity of the legal process of U.S. decision-making that amounts to one-person-one-veto policy-making.

3. Public policy development lacks the capacity for strategic coherence—a lack of political or bureaucratic capacity to develop and implement an industrialization policy.

4. A trend toward conservative protection against the discipline of the market. The Chrysler "bail out" is a prime example.

16. In April 1982, President Reagan's approval rating was at the lowest level for any president since Harry Truman in 1948.

5. The growth of bureaucratization of the private sector in response to filling out government forms and also reducing risks from government regulations. This bureaucratization delays effective business decision-making.[17]

Like it or not, and most business firms don't, government has become a major determinant, often *the* major determinant, of the business environment. Too often, business and government find themselves in excessively polarized positions. In part, this is the fault of business, for it has maintained a stance of aloofness that inhibits cooperation with government on national policy issues. The views of business that do receive public attention often seem extreme and antisocial. This has contributed to the generally low esteem in which business is held by the public. However, this low esteem is not new, for big business in particular has been consistently unpopular over the years. The animus began in the last century, when the large corporations first began to replace small shopkeepers and artisans, and then grew stronger during the period of robber-baron exploitation and labor wars. More of this animus was directed against individuals—Rockefeller, Vanderbilt—than against business itself,[18] although the development of the trust redirected some of the public's discontent toward impersonal big business. During the 1920s, business improved its public image considerably, not so much because of its own efforts, but because the time was one of unprecedented prosperity.[19] The economic collapse of the 1930s had an adverse impact upon the business image.

Improving Business-Government Relations

It is an ineluctable part of business life that government is here to stay, regardless of whether business likes it. Almost every business decision is affected by the laws, regulations, or guidelines of some level of government. Governments—federal, state, and local—are purchasers of more than one-fifth of the goods and services produced in our economy. Its impact on resource allocations is substantial. Market responses are altered by government through subsidies, grants, investment credits, and depreciation allowances. Government holds itself responsible, rightly or wrongly, for leveling the ups and downs of the economy, for maintain-

17. "Summary of the Proceedings" (Conference on U.S. Competitiveness, Harvard University, Cambridge, Mass., April 26, 1980), pp. 2–3.
18. John T. Dunlop, Alfred D. Chandler, Jr., George P. Shultz, and Irving S. Shapiro, "Business and Public Policy," *Harvard Business Review* (November-December 1979), 88–89.
19. President Calvin Coolidge said, "The business of America is business."

ing a high level of employment, for fostering a satisfactory rate of economic growth, and for sustaining a sound dollar. Little of this will simply dry up and go away during the Reagan administration because, primarily, it has been American public demands, legitimate or imagined, that has pushed government into an ever larger role. These demands are often hard to reconcile: curb inflation by cutting back government spending as long as the cuts are not made in our favorite programs.

The business and government sectors have one important interest in common, the condition of the U.S. economy in the 1980s. *Newsweek*, in a 1981 feature article called "The Economy in Crisis," placed the U.S. economy in a position similar to that existing in late 1932, at a crisis point that needed immediate action. The Reagan administration, through the Economic Recovery Tax Act of 1981, has undertaken measures designed to increase the rate of savings and capital formation and has cut back government expenditures, particularly in many entitlement programs. As of April 1982, the rate of inflation was down considerably to an annual level of less than 6 percent, but the unemployment rate was up to 9 percent and the rate of business bankruptcies was the highest in thirty years.[20] The inflation-unemployment dilemma has not been solved.

Government is not very efficient at delivering goods and services, but business is. It has to be if it expects to survive. Business, on the other hand, is not effective in identifying social problems and mobilizing corrective action, whereas government is. The problem is to reconcile the interests of the two groups so that each is able to do what it does best. The government's role is to identify areas where the market mechanism has failed and to motivate business to take corrective action. This perhaps can be done through tax policy, which is important to business because many business decisions are heavily based on their tax consequences. Improvement is needed in regulatory policy because too many government agencies, with their often overlapping, cumbersome, and even contradictory or biased regulations, make business planning and decision making unduly difficult. If tax laws and regulations were simplified and neutralized to permit decisions to be made primarily on the basis of productivity, the economy would benefit. Business-govern-

20. Times are bad all over. The unemployment rate in the United Kingdom reached a high of 12.2 percent in January 1982, the highest since the 1930s. In France, under a socialist government, the unemployment rate is around 8 percent and inflation is 14 percent. The People's Republic of China has unemployment rates of 10 to 20 percent among urban youths. Poland is in danger of going broke, and the growth rate of the Soviet Union is at its lowest point in forty years. To some extent, there is an interrelationship of these problems in that limits have probably been reached in terms of resource allocation and consumer expectations.

ment friction will never be completely eliminated, but compromises can be reached on common goals.

However, the business-government relationship should be seen as a rather small subset in the total set of relationships in U.S. society. To talk about a new partnership between business and government would be meaningless unless labor is considered as an equal, in every sense of the word, in any dialogue undertaken. The relations between business and government depend more on the total matrix of U.S. society than upon any interaction between the two institutions. During the last three decades, the social dynamics of the United States—the dynamics of a national society, entitlements, and a public ethos concerned with the quality of life—have changed. There has been a shift from market to political decision making, as various groups have used political power to change unpopular market decisions. There have been societal shifts in the legitimacy of such concepts as economic inequality, profits, and the work ethic that touch on both business and government. For example, a demand for greater income equality can be met only by a public transfer economy, which necessitates a favorable attitude toward the legitimacy of government.

SUMMARY

The relationship between business and government—especially between large corporations and the federal government—has traditionally been that of adversary. To some extent, this adversarial relationship was inevitable, given the nature of the two institutions—one private and the other public, each with different goals. However, the economic problems of the United States in the 1980s—inflation, a low rate of economic growth, and a decline in the U.S. competitive position in international markets—make the adversarial relationship seem counterproductive. The tasks of the 1980s are monumental at both the domestic and international levels. At the domestic level, it is necessary to find new sources of energy, and the social infrastructure needs to be improved. We need, for example, to bring private employment to the inner-city ghetto. A more viable railroad system may be desirable. At the international level, American firms must become more competitive in order to create a healthier economy at home. None of these goals can be achieved without at least some cooperation between business and government. Skillful and creative leadership will be needed to provide solutions to the economic and social problems of this decade.

APPENDIX

BUSINESS AND GOVERNMENT IN JAPAN

International economic experts feel that the United States is in the process of being replaced by Japan as the world's leading industrial power.[21] This feeling was substantiated by motor vehicle production statistics for 1980. The United States was the leading producer of motor vehicles from 1908 to 1979, but in 1980, Japan assumed world leadership. In 1979, the United States produced 11,475,107 vehicles; in 1980, its production dropped to 8,011,740 vehicles, a drop of 30 percent in one year. In 1979, Japan produced 9,635,546 vehicles; in 1980, 11,042,884 vehicles.[22] American television was the world leader in the 1960s, but this field is now dominated by the Japanese. Japan's steel plants have a capacity roughly the same as that of the United States, or almost as much as the entire European Economic Community, but their capacity is the most modern and sophisticated in the world. In shipbuilding, Japan produces shipping tonnage equivalent to that of all of Europe and the United States combined, and in pianos, hardly a traditional Japanese musical instrument, Japan is competitive in the U.S. market. The Japanese have taken over world leadership from the Swiss in the production of watches, and from the Germans, in the production of cameras. In the manufacture of industrial robots, which facilitate mass production, Japan is the world's leader.

One of the three major U.S. television networks ran a two-hour program entitled, "If the Japanese Can Do It, Why Can't We?" That is a good question for which there are many possible answers. Japan has a more disciplined work force than the United States does, with fewer unpredictable work stoppages. Moreover, the Japanese work force is better educated, particularly in science and mathematics. The personal savings rate in Japan is higher than in the U.S., averaging 20 percent of personal income compared to less than 6 percent for the United States. These savings result in investment in new plants and equipment. The proportion of GNP going into research and development (R&D) has been falling in the United States but rising in Japan. Japanese R&D is concentrated in areas likely to have a high payoff in industrial competitiveness. Japanese businessmen are usually better informed than their U.S. counterparts about world developments. Finally, the absence of a wide variety of social welfare benefits help create a "root hog or die" work environment. For example, unemployment compensation in Japan is

21. Ezra F. Vogel, "The Challenge from Japan" (paper presented at the Conference on U.S. Competitiveness, Harvard University, Cambridge, Mass., April 25, 1980).
22. *Wall Street Journal*, January 26, 1981.

low, and the differential between it and wages is great enough that workers are anxious to retain their jobs.

There is also closer cooperation between business and government in Japan than in the United States, a combination of free enterprise and government control dating back to the Meiji Restoration of 1868. The government was active during the Meiji era in introducing Western industrial methods into Japan, and it also took the lead in promoting the development of industries of strategic importance. From the Russo-Japanese War of 1904 to World War II, responsibility for development and innovation was shared between the government and the giant business combines called *zaitatsus*. After World War II, the American Occupation authorities attempted to break up the combines by imposing antitrust laws to lessen the concentration of economic power. However, Japanese government policies after the Occupation and up to the present have been directed toward the promotion of Japanese business interests, particularly in foreign trade. Antitrust policies have been amended to favor mergers that result in large-scale business operations and strengthen Japan's international competitiveness. The government has favored certain industries, certain types of economic activity, and certain groups of firms through such measures as special tax policies promoting investment and corporate saving.

It is really more in the international area that business and government combine to penetrate the world markets. This is done under the guidance of the Ministry of International Trade and Industry (MITI). Japanese multinationals enjoy certain privileges. They can create export cartels, they are exempt from Japanese taxation on income earned abroad, they are permitted special depreciation allowances, and they can obtain low-cost loans from the banks. MITI has published a report called "Industrial Policy Vision of the 1980's,"[23] which is given to Japanese business firms as an investment guide. The report pinpoints the industries that are supposed to have the best growth potential during the 1980s. It provides the framework for Japanese industrial strategy for that decade and indicates which industries and types of investments are likely to receive official financial assistance and incentives. The knowledge-intensive industries are to be encouraged, and financing for investments in these industries will be provided by MITI, the government's Japan Development Bank, and private banks. In R&D, MITI is wholly or partially funding nine projects by Japanese companies working in teams to develop technologies ranging from steel production and jet engines to automated factories and alternative energy sources.

In comparing policy attitudes of Japanese and U.S. business firms, the Japanese are more likely to take into consideration the national

23. *Business Week*, June 30, 1980, p. 140.

interest.[24] They are expected to start off with the question, "What is good for the country?" when considering various policy alternatives. This attitude dates back to the beginning of industrial development in Japan, and it facilitates a national consensus, something that is rather difficult to achieve in the United States, given the general fragmentation of society which leads to fragmented politics, often dominated by small groups of single-issue zealots. U.S. business firms are usually preoccupied with their own needs, as is true of other groups. They themselves rarely propose, but often oppose what others propose. The "self-interest first" approach, which ignores the national interest, is relevant to a society that has prized individualism that carries with it a sense of independence, personal initiative, and self-responsibility. This has resulted in a pluralistic society in which individuals have coalesced into special interest groups. In Japan, both leaders and special interest groups derive their legitimacy from their stewardship of the national interest; in the United States, the reverse is true.[25]

QUESTIONS FOR DISCUSSION

1. In what ways might the government of the United States have an impact on business during the remainder of this century?
2. Business and government in the United States are often cast in the role of adversaries. What should be done to improve business-government relations?
3. Why is it difficult to reduce federal government spending?
4. Big government in itself has created a number of problems. Discuss.
5. What are some of the factors that have led to a decline in the U.S. competitive position in the world economy?
6. Compare business-government relations in the United States and in Japan.
7. What are some of the factors that have contributed to the rise of Japan as a world economic power?
8. How can U.S. business firms contribute to the solution of the economic and social problems of the United States during this decade?

24. Peter F. Drucker, "Behind Japan's Success," *Harvard Business Review*, January-February 1981, pp. 83-90.
25. Ibid., p. 87.

RECOMMENDED READINGS

Business Week Team. *The Decline of U.S. Power*. Boston: Houghton Mifflin Co., 1980.

Dodge, Kirsten, ed. *Government and Business: Prospects for Partnership*. Austin: University of Texas, Lyndon B. Johnson School of Public Affairs, 1980.

Drucker, Peter F. *Managing in Turbulent Times*. New York: Harper and Row, 1980.

Dunlop, John T., ed. *Business and Public Policy*. Cambridge, Mass.: Harvard University Press, 1980.

Fox, Harrison W., and Martin C. Schnitzer. *Doing Business in Washington: How to Win Friends and Influence Government*. New York: Macmillan, 1981.

Friedman, Milton, and Rose Friedman. *Free to Choose*. New York: Harcourt Brace Jovanovich, Inc., 1980.

Hall, William K. "Survival Strategies in a Hostile Environment." *Harvard Business Review* (September-October 1980), 75–85.

Hayes, Robert H., and William Abernathy. "Managing Our Way to Economic Decline." *Harvard Business Review* (July-August 1980), 67–77.

Kristol, Irving. *Two Cheers for Capitalism*. New York: Basic Books, 1978.

"Revitalizing the U.S. Economy." *Business Week*, June 30, 1980, pp. 56–142.

Thurow, Lester C. *The Zero-Sum Society*. New York: Basic Books, 1980.

Winter, Ralph. *Government and the Corporation*. Washington, D.C.: American Enterprise Institute, 1978.

Appendix A
Federal
Regulatory Commissions

Table A-1 Regulation of Banking and Finance

Organization	Year Established	Primary Regulatory Functions
Office of the Comptroller of the Currency	1863	Licenses and regulates national banks
Board of Governors of the Federal Reserve System	1913	Determines monetary and credit policy for the system and regulates member commercial banks
Federal Home Loan Bank Board	1932	Provides credit reserves for and regulates federally chartered savings and home-financing institutions
Federal Deposit Insurance Corporation	1933	Insures deposits of eligible banks and supervises certain insured banks
Federal Savings and Loan Insurance Corporation	1934	Insures savings in thrift and home-financing institutions
Securities and Exchange Commission	1934	Requires financial disclosure by publicly held companies; regulates practices of stock exchanges, brokers, and dealers; regulates certain practices of mutual funds, investment advisers, and public utility holding companies
National Credit Union Administration	1970	Charters, supervises, and examines all federal credit unions
Farm Credit Administration	1971	Supervises and regulates all activities of credit disbursed through the Farm Credit System

Table A-1 (continued)

Organization	Year Established	Primary Regulatory Functions
Commodity Futures Trading Commission	1975	Licenses all futures contracts and the brokers, dealers, and exchanges trading them
International Trade Commission (formerly U.S. Tariff Commission, established in 1916)	1975	Investigates and rules on tariff and certain other foreign trade regulations

Table A-2 Regulation of Energy and Environmental Matters

Organization	Year Established	Primary Regulatory Functions
Army Corps of Engineers	1824	Issues permits for all construction in navigable waterways; constructs and maintains rivers and harbor improvements
Mississippi River Commission	1879	Approves plans for and constructs flood control projects in lower Mississippi River Basin
Bureau of Reclamation	1902	Establishes criteria for use, development, and pricing of resources obtained from reclamation projects
Forest Service	1905	Manages U.S. forest preserves by determining amounts of land eligible for harvest, conditions of cutting, need for reforestation, etc.
National Forest Reservation Commission	1911	Rules on requests from Secretary of Agriculture for authority to acquire or exchange national forests
Federal Power Commission	1930	Regulates wholesale rates and practices in interstate transmission of electric energy and regulates transportation and sale of natural gas

Table A-2 (continued)

Organization	Year Established	Primary Regulatory Functions
Tennessee Valley Authority	1933	Operates river control systems and sets rates for power generated from TVA hydroelectric projects
Bonneville, Alaska, Southeastern, and Southwestern	1937 (abolished 1967)	Sets prices and markets federally generated hydroelectric power
Bureau of Land Management	1946	Classifies, manages use of, and disposes of all federal lands
Delaware River Basin Commission	1961	Develops and/or approves all plans for control and utilization of water resources in Delaware River Basin
Environmental Protection Agency	1970	Develops environmental quality standards, approves state abatement plans, and rules on acceptability of environmental impact statements
Susquehanna River Basin Commission	1970	Develops and/or approves all plans for utilization and control of watershed resources in Susquehanna River Basin
Federal Energy Administration	1973	Regulates price and allocation of certain petroleum products under emergency energy legislation
Mining Enforcement and Safety Administration	1973	Sets and enforces mine safety standards
Nuclear Regulatory Commission (formerly Atomic Energy Commission, established in 1946)	1975	Promotes and regulates civilian use of atomic energy
Ocean Mining Administration	1975	Supervises leasing of ocean resources and regulates ocean mining

Table A-3 Regulation of Commerce, Transportation, and Communications

Organization	Year Established	Primary Regulatory Functions
Patent and Trademark Office	1836	Administers patent and trademark laws
Interstate Commerce Commission	1887	Regulates rates, routes, and practices of railroads, trucks, bus lines, oil pipelines, domestic water carriers, and freight forwarders
National Bureau of Standards	1901	Establishes standards of measurement in trade, public safety, technical, and scientific performance
Coast Guard	1915	Sets and enforces safety standards for merchant vessels and navigable waterways
Federal Communications Commission	1934	Licenses civilian radio and television communication, and licenses and sets rates for interstate and international communication by wire, cable, and radio
Foreign Trade Zones Board	1934	Grants authority to public or private corporations to establish and/or utilize foreign trade zones within United States
Federal Maritime Commission	1936	Regulates fares, rates, and practices of steamship companies engaged in U.S. foreign commerce
Maritime Administration	1936	Determines eligibility for merchant marine subsidies, and regulates construction and operation of certain merchant ships
Civil Aeronautics Board	1938	Promotes and subsidizes air transportation, and regulates airline routes, passenger fares, and freight rates

Table A-3 (continued)

Organization	Year Established	Primary Regulatory Functions
Appalachian Regional Commission	1965	Approves state plans for projects in Appalachian area before requests for funds can be considered by federal departments
Federal Highway Administration	1966	Determines highway safety standards and administers federally funded highway construction programs
Federal Railroad Administration	1966	Administers high-speed railroad development program and the railroad and oil pipeline safety programs formerly administered by the ICC
Office of Telecommunications Policy	1970	Sets standards for broadcast technology and performance and assigns federal telecommunication frequencies

Table A-4 Regulation of Food, Health, and Safety, and Unfair or Deceptive Trade Practices

Organization	Year Established	Primary Regulatory Functions
Federal Trade Commission	1914	Administers some antitrust statutes, and laws concerning advertising misrepresentation, flammable fabrics, packaging, and labeling of certain products
Packers and Stockyards Administration	1916	Regulates fair business practices in livestock and processed meat marketing
Food and Drug Administration	1931	Administers laws concerning purity, safety, and labeling accuracy of certain foods and drugs

Table A-4 (continued)

Organization	Year Established	Primary Regulatory Functions
Commodity Credit Corporation	1933	Finances and determines farm price supports and administers production stabilization programs
Social Security Administration	1933	Determines eligible medical expenses under Medicare/Medicaid
Agriculture Marketing Service	1937	Sets grades and standards for most farm commodities, inspects egg production, administers product and process safety acts, licenses and bonds warehouses
Agricultural Stabilization and Conservation Service	1953	Administers commodity stabilization programs, and rules on eligibility of participants
Animal and Plant Health Inspection Service	1953	Sets standards, inspects and enforces laws relating to meat, poultry, and plant safety
Federal Aviation Administration	1958	Certifies airworthiness of aircraft, licenses pilots, and operates air traffic control system
Federal Insurance Administration	1968	Sets standards for all insurance programs related to natural disasters and similar occurrences
Office of Interstate Land Sales Registration	1968	Requires disclosure and regulation for interstate sales of land in quantities of over fifty lots
Interim Compliance Panel	1969	Grants permits for noncompliance with health standards in underground coal mines
National Highway Traffic Safety Administration	1970	Establishes safety standards for trucks and automobiles and certifies compliance with emission standards for pollution control

Table A-4 (continued)

Organization	Year Established	Primary Regulatory Functions
Occupational Safety and Health Review Commission	1970	Adjudicates all enforcement actions when OSHA rulings are contested
Consumer Product Safety Commission	1972	Establishes mandatory product safety standards and bans sale of products that do not comply
Occupational Safety and Health Administration	1973	Develops and enforces worker safety and health regulations
Professional Standards Review Organization	1973	Reviews and sets private medical practice and health care standards
Foreign Agricultural Service (absorbed Export Marketing Service, established in 1969)	1974	Determines eligibility price and terms of payment for commodities allocated to export market
National Transportation Safety Board	1974	Investigates transportation accidents, and rules on needed improvements in airline, rail, and highway safety

Table A-5 Regulation of Labor, Housing, and Small Business

Organization	Year Established	Primary Regulatory Functions
Civil Service Commission	1833	Sets job standards and classifications for most federal employees and enforces Equal Employment Opportunity Act within federal government
National Mediation Board	1926	Conducts union representation elections and mediates labor-management disputes in the railroad and airline industries

Table A-5 (continued)

Organization	Year Established	Primary Regulatory Functions
Employment Standards Administration	1933	Sets and administers standards under laws relating to minimum wages, overtime, nondiscrimination, etc.
Unemployment Insurance Service	1933	Reviews state unemployment insurance laws to ensure compliance with federal standards
Federal Housing Authority	1934	Sets and enforces standards for federally insured residential and commercial properties
National Labor Relations Board	1935	Conducts union representation elections and regulates labor practices of employers and unions
Railroad Retirement Board	1935	Administers retirement and insurance acts for railroads, and rules on eligibility of retiring or disabled workers
General Services Administration	1949	Establishes critical needs for national stockpile and regulates purchase/sale of required/surplus materials
Renegotiation Board	1951	Sets standards for private contracts with federal government and rules on contractors' liabilities
Small Business Administration	1953	Makes loans and gives advice to small businesses
Labor-Management Services Administration	1963	Determines (with Treasury) eligibility of employee welfare and pension plans and sets standards for financial disclosure
Equal Employment Opportunity Commission	1964	Investigates and rules on charges of racial and other discrimination by employers and labor unions

Table A-5 (continued)

Organization	Year Established	Primary Regulatory Functions
Federal Labor Relations Council	1969	Oversees and prescribes regulations pertaining to labor-management relations programs in federal government
Cost Accounting Standards Board	1970	Promulgates rules and regulations for implementation of cost accounting standards to be included in federal defense contracts and subcontracts

Appendix B
Competition, Monopoly, and Oligopoly

In a market economy, business firms are supposed to make most of their economic decisions on the basis of prices, price changes, and price relationships. Demand and supply forces acting in several separate market situations are supposed to determine prices. In any given market situation, some degree of competition is assumed to exist. The degree of competition varies considerably from one market situation to another. In one situation there may be a large number of sellers and buyers of a given product; in another situation there may be a few sellers and a number of buyers; and in a third situation there may be one seller and a number of buyers. In price theory, pure competition and monopoly can be considered as opposite points on the competitive spectrum. The essential feature of competition is that there are so many sellers and buyers of a good that no one seller or buyer is able to influence prices in the marketplace; the essential feature of monopoly is control over supply by a single seller. This control can be translated into control over the price of a good in the marketplace.

COMPETITION

Clearly, competition in the economic sense is not a natural thing, but is a social pattern produced by the operation of various supporting institutions, including private property ownership and freedom of enterprise. Its justification, like that of the other capitalistic institutions, is that it contributes to the social welfare. When the industries and markets of an economy are organized competitively, certain supposedly desirable results will ensue.

First, competition should bring about efficiency in the operation of industry and business by granting economic success to those firms that are efficiently operated and by relentlessly eliminating those that are inefficiently and wastefully operated. Thus, to survive, each enterprise must use the best machines and productive methods available and eliminate waste at all points in its organization. The removal of inefficient producers from the market is meant to leave the productive factors in the hands of those firms that use them most effectively.

Second, competition should lead to innovation and technological progress. Better productive methods, machines that increase efficiency or lower cost, or a product that appears to satisfy a human want more effectively than similar products from other business firms give certain firms a greatly prized advantage over the others with respect to income. But such advantages tend to be lost sooner or later in a competitive industry, and the continuing result should be the consumers' ability to obtain better and better products at lower and lower prices.

Finally, competition is said to be a regulator of economic activity, a means by which the productive efforts of numerous business firms are correlated through prices with the desires of consumers as expressed in the market. Success in competition depends on the ability to give consumers the right amount, quality, and kinds of goods, at the right price. Firms that supply goods not suited to consumers' desires or that cost more than similar products of other firms, usually fall by the wayside. If the total output of a good is small in relation to the demand for it, the possibility of making a profit will stimulate a competitive industry to expand production and, if necessary, its plant facilities. But if competitive producers turn out far more goods than are demanded, the lack of profits will force some firms from the industry and adjust output to demand.

Economic Concepts of Competition

Competition as an economic concept can mean a number of things, the most common of which is pure competition. Certain elements must be present in order for pure competition to exist in a market. First, there must be a large number of buyers and sellers of a standardized product. Second, there must be complete freedom of entry and exit into and out of the market. Third, no one buyer or no one seller can influence the price of the product sold. Fourth, there must be no collusion of any form between the buyers and the sellers. Finally, there can be no interference in the market from outside forces—government, labor unions, and so forth.

Pure competition is a theoretical concept. It can be used to define a desirable market situation, which, if it existed, would redound to the advantage of the consumer for the simple reason that supply and demand forces acting in a given market would determine the price and output of a product. No single seller or buyer could affect the market in any way. The hallmark of competition is the existence of many producers, each of which contributes only a small part of the output traded in the market. A competitive market price is decided by an equilibrium of supply and demand, which is determined independently of the actions of any single seller or buyer. Sellers may sell all they

please, and buyers may buy all they please, but only at the price set in
the market by supply and demand.

Diagram B-1 illustrates price and output determination under conditions of pure competition. The supply curve, labeled S, indicates the
quantity that sellers are willing to provide at each price. There is a direct relationship between the amount supplied and the price: the higher
the price, the greater the amount supplied. The demand curve, labeled
D, indicates the quantity that buyers are willing to purchase at each
price. The relationship between the amount demanded and the price is
inverse: the higher the price, the lower the amount demanded. Equilibrium is reached when the quantity that sellers are willing to sell is equal
to the quantity that buyers are willing to buy. The market price is set
by this equilibrium point. At any point above the equilibrium point,
supply exceeds demand; at any point below the equilibrium point, demand exceeds supply. In the diagram, the price OP is the market price,
and the quantity OA is what is sold.

Diagram B-1 Supply and Demand Analysis

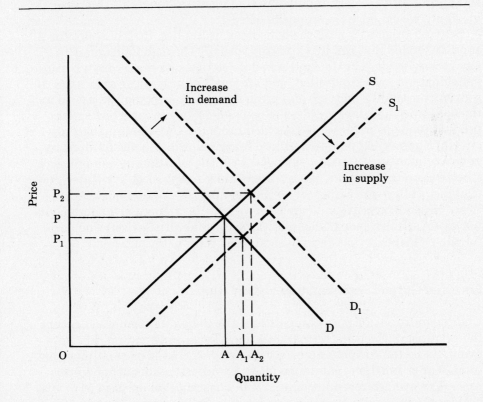

Competitive prices are explained mainly as the supply and demand for two different time periods: first, a short-run period during which sellers can vary supply only as is possible using existing production facilities and, second, a long-run period during which sellers can freely vary their actual production capacity. In the short run, sellers can sell all they please, but only at the equilibrium price that clears the market. This equilibrium price bears no relation to the cost of production for an individual seller, which may be higher or lower than the price. In the short run, some firms can make profits, and others can sustain losses.

Demand, supply, or both can change in the short run. For instance, an increase in demand means that buyers are willing to purchase more at each of a series of prices than they were formerly. In the diagram, the demand line would shift to the right, as indicated by the curve D_1. A decrease in demand means just the opposite. An increase in demand, with supply remaining constant, would result in an increase in both price and quantity; a decrease in demand would have the opposite effect. An increase in supply means that sellers are willing to offer more at each of a series of prices than formerly. In the diagram, the supply curve would shift to the right. The result would be a decrease in the equilibrium price and an increase in the quantity bought. A decrease in supply would have the opposite effect.

Demand originates with the consumer. It implies, first, a desire for a good or service that can be expressed, usually through willingness to pay money for it. The demand schedule assumes its shape, first, because individual incomes are limited, and second, because as the quantities of a given commodity increase at a given time, they become less useful to the consumer. In other words, the consumers' desire for a particular product tends to diminish as they acquire more of it. This is the principle of diminishing marginal utility. Marginal utility is the amount by which total utility would be changed with the addition of one unit to a stock of goods. The principle of diminishing marginal utility states that marginal utility varies inversely with the number of units acquired. When expenditures are increased for a given item, successive increments will make smaller and smaller additions to total satisfaction. The basis for the principle is that any physical want is probably satiable.

Price and Output Determination—Short Run

Under conditions of pure competition, the individual firm must accept the price established in the market by market supply and market demand. Since the firm has no effect on or control over price, it must try to maximize profits or minimize losses by adjusting its output to this price. The average revenue curve, AR in Diagram B-2 on page 516, is a horizontal line, indicating that the firm can sell varying amounts of output at the established price. Average revenue is the total revenue divided by the number of units of output and is synonymous with the price per unit. For a competitive firm, average revenue and price are the same. Since the price remains unchanged as more units are sold, each additional unit sold increases the total revenue by an amount equal to the price. This is illustrated in the example below. There is also the economic concept of marginal revenue. Marginal revenue is the amount by which the total revenue is increased by the sale of one more unit of product. As shown in the example, marginal revenue, average revenue, and selling price are the same.

Output	Selling Price ($)	Average Revenue ($)	Total Revenue ($)	Marginal Revenue ($)
1	20	20	20	20
2	20	20	40	20
3	20	20	60	20
4	20	20	80	20
5	20	20	100	20
6	20	20	120	20

The firm can sell all it can produce at the selling price of $20, and so we shall figure how much it will produce under conditions of pure competition in the short run. Output is based on the cost of production. In the short run, there are both fixed and variable costs. Fixed costs are those that remain constant regardless of the amount of output. Variable costs are those that vary in amount in accordance with changes in the volume of output. From the standpoint of cost, the firm can adjust its output by changes in variable factors, such as labor, but cannot change its fixed physical factors. The key cost concept, however, is marginal cost, which is the amount by which the total cost is increased when an additional unit of output is produced. Given these cost concepts, the basic economic principle governing the behavior of the firm in the short run is that output will be adjusted to the point at which marginal cost and marginal revenue are equal. The firm must do this to maximize its profits or, for that matter, to minimize its losses. Whenever marginal revenue is greater than marginal cost, total profit can be increased by expanding production, but whenever marginal cost exceeds marginal revenue, total profit is increased by reducing production.

The following example shows the principle of profit maximization in the short run under conditions of pure competition. The price, as determined in the marketplace by supply and demand, is assumed to be $20, and total fixed costs are assumed to be $10, regardless of the number of

514   APPENDIX B: COMPETITION, MONOPOLY, AND OLIGOPOLY

units of output produced. Profit maximization occurs at ten units of output. If a firm stopped producing before this point, it could still add more to unit revenue than to unit cost; if it went beyond this point, the cost of producing an additional unit of output would more than offset the addition to revenue.

Output	Fixed Cost ($)	Variable Cost ($)	Total Cost ($)	Marginal Cost ($)	Price ($)	Total Revenue ($)	Marginal Revenue ($)
1	10	15	25	15	20	20	20
2	10	28	38	13	20	40	20
3	10	39	49	11	20	60	20
4	10	50	60	11	20	80	20
5	10	59	69	9	20	100	20
6	10	67	77	8	20	120	20
7	10	81	91	14	20	140	20
8	10	97	107	16	20	160	20
9	10	115	125	18	20	180	20
10	10	135	145	*20*	20	200	*20*
11	10	160	170	25	20	220	20

Reaching the point of equality of marginal cost and marginal revenue does not imply that a firm always makes a profit. Whether or not it does make a profit depends on the relation between total cost and total revenue, or average cost and price. The equality between price and marginal cost guarantees that a position of maximum profit or minimum loss has been attained, but it does not offer any information about the absolute profit or loss position. If a firm has decided what to produce and has constructed a single plant to house a certain quantity of physical resources, its ability to change output is limited. It can change the inputs of its variable factors and thus adjust output somewhat, but it cannot change its overall scale of operations, since that would require changing fixed as well as variable factors. The marginal cost function represents the rate of change in total cost as output is changed within a given plant. Since for the individual seller in a purely competitive market, price does not vary as output varies, the marginal cost function becomes, in the short run, the supply function for the competitive firm, that is, the quantities that will be supplied at all possible prices.

It is also desirable to think in terms of average costs rather than total costs, as this allows costs to be related directly to prices. Corresponding to the concepts of total cost, total variable cost, and total fixed cost, there are average total cost, average variable cost, and average fixed cost.

The average total cost is the sum of the average variable and the average fixed costs. Average variable cost is derived by dividing total variable costs by output, and average fixed cost is derived by dividing total fixed cost by output. Marginal cost is neither a total nor an average cost but is simply the additional cost incurred as a result of producing an additional unit of output. The marginal and average cost concepts are presented in the following example. Average fixed costs show that fixed costs per unit decline continuously as output increases. Average variable costs decrease, then reach a minimum value, and thereafter increase. The initial decline in average variable cost is due to the fact that, within limits, the more units of variable factors there are, the more effectively fixed factors are utilized.

Output	Total Fixed Cost ($)	Total Variable Cost ($)	Average Fixed Cost ($)	Average Variable Cost ($)	Marginal Cost ($)
1	10	15	10.00	15.00	15
2	10	28	5.00	14.00	13
3	10	39	3.33	13.00	11
4	10	50	2.50	12.50	11
5	10	59	2.00	11.80	9
6	10	67	1.67	11.16	8
7	10	81	1.43	11.57	14
8	10	97	1.25	12.12	16
9	10	115	1.11	12.77	18
10	10	135	1.00	13.50	20

The concepts of marginal revenue (MR), average revenue (AR), marginal cost (MC), average variable cost (AVC), and average total cost (ATC) are given in Diagram B-2. As mentioned earlier, the marginal cost curve is the short-run supply curve for a firm operating in a purely competitive industry. We should qualify this, however: the marginal cost curve represents the supply curve of the firm only above a certain price. If a firm cannot cover its variable costs, it should shut down. No sensible firm would supply any amount of goods at a price below that which would bring in enough revenue to cover variable costs. This can be shown in the diagram. AVC is the firm's average variable cost curve. No quantity will be supplied at any price below OP_1. If the price falls below this point, the firm should shut down. Thus, the marginal cost curve (MC) becomes the supply curve at all prices above OP_1. As long as the price is above OP_1, the firm will continue to operate even if it is

Diagram B-2 Alternative Price Levels, Pure Competition in Short Run

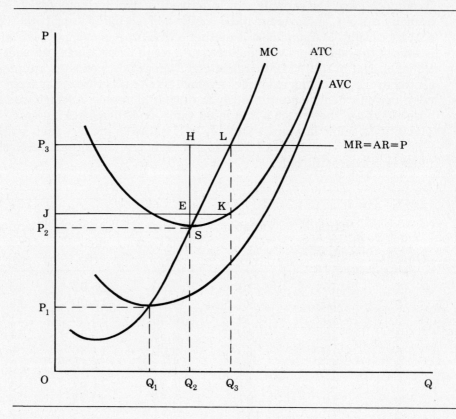

not covering total costs. At prices above this level, it will be more than covering variable cost; it will also be making some return on its fixed investment.

In the diagram, there are three price levels. OP_1 is the minimum price that a firm can receive and remain in business; OP_2 is the break-even point at which the firm would make neither a profit nor a loss; and any point above OP_2 —for instance, OP_3 —is a price at which a firm would make a profit. Using OP_3 as one price, the quantity supplied is OQ_3. At the point L, where MC = MR, profit is maximized and the firm is in short-run equilibrium. At the price OP_3, the average revenue per unit, which is LQ_3, multiplied by the number of units of output, OQ_3, equals total revenue, which is the area of the large rectangle $OP_3 LQ_3$. Similarly, average total cost, KQ_3, multiplied by the number of units of output, OQ_3, equals total cost, or the area of the rectangle $OJKQ_3$. The net profit rectangle is the total revenue rectangle less the total cost rectangle, or the rectangle $JP_3 LK$.

Price and Output Determination—Long Run

In the long run, firms operating under conditions of pure competition can adjust both output and capacity to a given demand and price. In the short run, a firm can adjust output only by changing the amounts of the variable factors of production, but plant capacity remains fixed. In the long run, there may also be a change in the total number of firms in the industry. Assuming that firms are free to enter into and depart from a market, new firms will be attracted to a given industry if existing firms are making an above-normal profit. In other words, if the price is above the short-run average cost, there is an incentive for new firms to enter the industry. Inefficient firms, those sustaining losses, will be eliminated. A long-run equilibrium price is then achieved at the point at which marginal revenue equals not only marginal cost but also the average cost of the firms in the industry. This is possible only at the lowest point on the long-run average cost curve, since this is the only point at which marginal cost and average cost are equal.

Diagram B–3 shows the long-run equilibrium for a firm operating under pure competition. The firm is operating at an output level at

Diagram B–3 Long-Run Equilibrium for Firm under Pure Competition

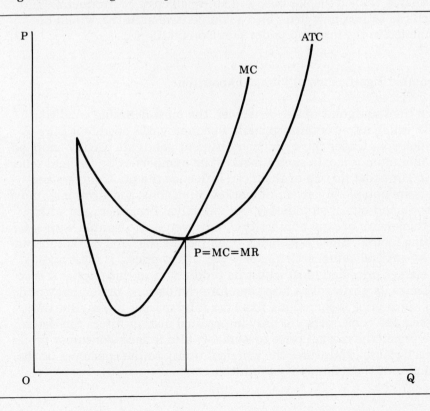

which its average total costs (ATC) are lowest, but all its economic profit has disappeared. Marginal cost (MC), marginal revenue (MR), and price (P) are equal at the equilibrium point. The industry itself is in equilibrium because it has reached a point at which for all the firms in the industry the price just covers their average total cost. There is no incentive for new firms to come into the industry, and each firm will find itself in an equilibrium position. Marginal revenue equals not only each firm's marginal cost but also its average cost. This is possibly only at the lowest point on the long-run average cost curve, since this is the only point at which marginal cost and average cost are equal. Under pure competition, each firm will in the long run produce at the lowest point on the long-run average cost curve.

The long-run equilibrium price can be called a normal price that brings sellers a normal profit—that is, enough profit to keep them from leaving the industry, but not enough to entice other sellers to stop producing other things and shift into this industry. Normal profit may be considered a cost of production, a rate of return on the resources that a firm owns, including the labor of the owner. It also means that the rate of return on all a firm's resources, including internally owned labor and other factors of production, is no greater than can be obtained elsewhere in the economic system. Excess, or economic profit, which is considered to be a surplus over and above all costs of production and which can attract new firms into a competitive industry, would be eliminated in the long run under pure competition.

Economic Significance of Pure Competition

From the standpoint of the consumer, the most desirable condition under which a free enterprise market economy can operate is pure competition. Under this condition different goods are usually supplied at a minimum price. In such a market the numbers of buyers and sellers are so large that no one of them can influence the price; buyers and sellers are completely aware of market conditions; and firms may move freely in and out of an industry. An individual firm operating within the framework of pure competition, however, is confronted with several limiting factors. Since it is such a small part of the total market, it cannot by any individual action in any way affect prices. It must accept the market price and must adjust its production to this price if it is to maximize its profits. The firm therefore can have no price policy of its own, since price is something fixed for it by market forces. But this protects the consumers, for only impersonal market forces can determine price. The market price presumably also reflects consumer preferences, because it measures the marginal utility to the consumer of the final unit of the commodity produced.

In a long-run equilibrium position, price is equal to marginal cost for each firm in a purely competitive industry. An optimum allocation of resources within the industry has been reached. If all industries in the economy were purely competitive, then there would be an optimal use of resources in the entire economy. This would occur because there could not be an excess of profits in any one industry, as new firms would be attracted into it as the margin of profit grew. Wages could not remain higher in any one occupation than in others, for workers would be attracted to the high-paying occupation, with the consequence that the pay level would come more into line with that in other occupations. Consequently, an equality of marginal cost and price in all industries would mean that resources could be used in no better way. No improvement in economic well-being could be obtained by shifting resources from one industry into another. Consumers would be satisfied because their marginal utilities for each of the various products would be approximately equal. In the theoretical equilibrium position, consumers cannot improve their satisfaction by changing any one of their expenditures for goods and services.

The ideal market situation epitomized by pure competition is never achieved, except perhaps approximately in the buying and selling of some farm products. But even in agriculture, farmers have created marketing cooperatives for some crops and have obtained special legislation in the form of price-support and acreage-allotment programs. In retailing, in which pure competition is sometimes approached, retail price maintenance laws, usually referred to as fair-trade laws by their supporters, have prevented price competition. Most other markets are characterized by imperfect competition, in which sellers or buyers have some control over price. In such situations the price policy of one seller depends on the expected reaction of rival sellers. Price wars, the elimination of rival competitors, collusion, and combinations all are possible. Instead of regulating prices, the government may try to enforce competition through prosecution based on antitrust laws.

Pure competition should be regarded as one of several economic models that have been developed to describe a particular structural arrangement within a market economy and to enable economists to predict the consequences of certain changes in variables within that structure. The other models are monopoly, oligopoly, and monopolistic competition. Pure competition is an ideal that can serve as a frame of reference when it is necessary to evaluate whether or not there is viable competition in a given marketplace situation. Actually, there are many different concepts and subconcepts of competition that depart from pure competition. For example, there is the concept of effective or workable competition, which has a pragmatic legal-economic orientation. The economic idea underlying effective competition is that no seller or group of sellers acting in concert has the power to choose its level of profits by giving less and charging more. So competition means different things to different individuals.

MONOPOLY

Pure monopoly, or having only one seller of a commodity for which there are no close substitutes, is a rare market situation. But some of the industries classified by law as public utilities are in approximately this situation, and their prices are regulated by the government. Such monopolies avoid duplication of facilities and achieve the low costs made possible by large-scale production that would not be possible under purely competitive conditions. It is debatable whether this regulation is effective, but it does attest to a deep-seated and well-founded suspicion of the American public of what might happen if it were absent. A monopoly may exist in part because of the decreasing costs resulting from an increased scale of production that reduces the number of sellers in a market or allows a few to agree to avoid price competition. Patents are also the basis for many different monopolies.

A monopolist can fix prices by gaining control of the supply of a given commodity, for the individual firm and the industry are, in effect, identical, and the market demand curve for the industry is the same as the average revenue or sales curve for the monopolist. The demand schedule for the product of a monopolist is the same type as shown in Diagram B-1. There is no supply schedule, for the monopolist has the entire supply. There is no substitute for the product, and so the monopolist need not be concerned with the possibility of consumers shifting to substitute commodities or rival firms. This could be the result of the monopolist's complete control of some strategic raw material or the possession of a specific franchise or patent. The monopolist is primarily interested in regulating supply so as to obtain a maximum profit. Demand and cost of production form the basis for the amount of output. The maximum profit is tied to the quantity sold and the difference between cost and price per unit of output.

Monopoly prices are frequently higher than the prices that would prevail under competitive conditions because a monopolist can sometimes charge different prices to different customers. The individual firm in a purely competitive market can only react to the price set in the market by supply and demand. It need not consider the effect of variations in its output on price, since it is such a small part of the total market. Its average revenue line is horizontal, and it cannot charge different prices to different customers. But the monopolist must examine the effects of pricing policies, for the demand curve for its product, which is also its average revenue curve, slopes downward to the right. This means that a monopolist must consider the effect on the price of changes in its output. A larger output can be sold only at a lower price, the degree to which it is lower depending on the elasticity of demand. If the price is raised, consumers will reduce the amount of the product they purchase, but they cannot shift to substitute commodities or rival producers.

Price and Output Under Monopoly—Short Run

When the objective is maximization of profit, price and output determination under conditions of monopoly follows basically the same rules as those applying to the firm operating under pure competition. The general rule for maximizing profits is usually stated as the output at which marginal cost equals marginal revenue. Net profit for a monopolist depends on the quantity of output sold and the difference between cost and price per unit of output. Operation at the point of greatest difference between cost and price per unit of output may not yield the monopolist the highest total net profit because added sales beyond that point may more than offset the decline in profit per unit. Demand and the cost of production form the basis for the monopolist's choice of output. In more precise terms, profits are at a maximum when marginal costs equal marginal revenue. When the two amounts become equal, further expansion is not profitable. Up to that point, expansion of output adds more to receipts than to costs; past that point it is the other way around. But when there are finite changes in output, marginal cost will seldom exactly equal marginal revenue.

The monopolist's price and output determination is shown in the example below. Remember that in a monopoly, unlike the conditions prevailing under pure competition, the average revenue line is not horizontal; the price declines as the output increases. The demand and average revenue lines are one and the same, sloping downward from left to right. The average revenue column shows the prices at which various quantities of output can be sold, whereas the marginal revenue column

Output	Price ($)	Total Revenue ($)	Marginal Revenue ($)	Fixed Costs ($)	Variable Costs ($)	Marginal Cost ($)	Profit ($)
10	100	1,000		500	483		17
11	99	1,089	89	500	544	61	45
12	98	1,176	87	500	598	54	78
13	96	1,248	72	500	659	61	89
14	94	1,316	68	500	725	66	91
15	90	1,350	34	500	802	77	48
16	85	1,360	10	500	890	88	- 30

shows the increments to total revenue that result from selling additional units of output. In the short run, some costs are fixed and others are variable. In the example, total fixed costs are assumed to be $500, regardless of the volume of output, and total variable costs have been given assigned values.

At all outputs up to the fourteenth unit, marginal cost is less than marginal revenue. The cutoff point is the fourteenth unit, for the production of this unit will add $2 to net profits. At a volume of fourteen units, marginal revenue is $68, marginal cost is $66, total revenue is $1,316, and total costs are $1,225. The difference, or profits over and above all costs, is $91, which is greater than at any volume of output less than fourteen. Beyond fourteen, marginal cost is greater than marginal revenue. To produce the fifteenth unit, the additional cost is $77 and the additional revenue is $34. Profit declines from $91 to $48. The point of maximum profit is at a price of $94 and at a volume of fourteen units.

The same analysis is presented in Diagram B–4, which shows the monopolist's average revenue or demand curve (d), marginal revenue

Diagram B-4 Short-Run Price and Output for Firm under Monopoly

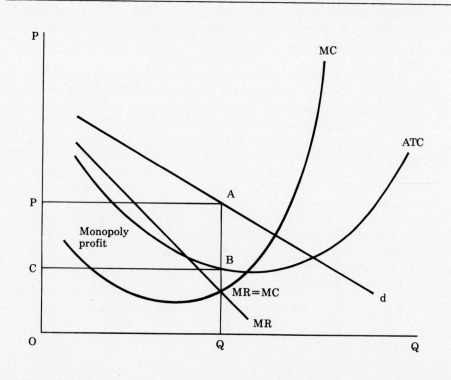

curve (MR), short-run marginal cost (MC), and average total cost (ATC) curves. The marginal cost and marginal revenue curves intersect at a volume of OQ. It would be profitable for the monopolist to expand up to this point, since at all smaller volumes the marginal cost curve lies below the marginal revenue curve. Beyond this point, however, marginal cost rises above marginal revenue. In order to determine the price at which this volume can be sold, it is necessary to use the average revenue curve, which is also the monopolist's demand curve. The average revenue is the price column in the example, and the curve shows the prices at which various outputs can be sold, whereas the marginal revenue curve shows the increments to total revenue that result from selling additional units of output. The price that will maximize profits is OP, the total revenue is represented by the rectangle OPAQ, and the total cost is represented by the smaller rectangle OCBQ. The total profit over and above all necessary costs is represented by the rectangle PABC, the difference between the revenue and cost rectangles.

Monopoly profit is usually higher than that which would prevail under pure competition, as the monopolist has control over supply, whereas the individual firm operating under conditions of pure competition is only one among many, and so it has no control over total output. The individual firm can only react to the price set in the marketplace by supply and demand, but the monopolist can set price and literally hunt for the point on the demand curve at which profit is maximized. Monopoly profits over and above all necessary production costs do not call forth the type of corrective adjustment that would be needed under pure competition. In other words, there is no free movement of resources into and out of a monopoly industry. Typically, output would also be at a level lower than that which would prevail under pure competition.

Long-Run Adjustments

In the short run, the price may be below the average total cost, but this cannot continue in the long run because if it did, the firm would cease operation. If the price is above the average total cost, there will be excess profits, and in a monopoly market there is nothing that can correct this automatically because of barriers to the entrance of new firms. In the long run, a monopoly is able to adjust its scale of operation because all costs are variable, whereas in the short run it can determine the most profitable rate of operation only for its existing fixed and variable factors of production. The most profitable scale of operation in the long run is the one that equates marginal cost and marginal revenue. The monopoly, like the purely competitive firm, has a U-shaped long-run average cost curve; that is, if the firm is either too small or too large, its production cost per unit will be higher than if it is of optimum size. The actual size of the firm will depend on the expected demand for its product. This size may happen to be that at which the cost per unit is minimal, but because the monopolistic firm does not have to compete, it is more likely that the firm will be either too large or too small to minimize cost.

Economic Significance of Monopoly

Pure monopoly, like pure competition, is a rare market situation and should be regarded as a theoretical framework in which to decide regulatory policies. The main defect in a monopolistic market situation is that there is nothing that automatically protects the consumer, as there is under conditions of pure competition. The existence of monopolies and their consequent excessive profits obviously would affect the personal distribution of income in the economy and result in a misallocation of resources. Monopoly prices are frequently higher than the prices that would prevail under competitive conditions because a monopolist can charge different prices to different customers. There are no competing sellers to whom buyers may go in case of price discrimination. Moreover, there is less incentive for a monopoly to organize its plant in the most efficient manner because it may make profits that are greater than in competitive industries merely by restricting supply. Modernization of facilities, experimentation with lower prices and larger output, and managerial incentives may be retarded by the lack of competition. In some instances the monopolist may be unwilling to experiment and expand, even though greater profits are possible.

But in some cases, monopoly prices may be as low or lower than competitive prices. For instance, when the scale of production is much larger and the level of costs is much lower than they would be under competition, a monopoly price may be lower than a competitive price. Furthermore, a greater long-run efficiency of production sometimes may be achieved under monopoly conditions when the economy is highly unstable. A monopoly can operate at a more uniform rate and maintain an inventory to carry it through the changes in demand. Under competition, firms must estimate demand and also their competitors' probable supplies. The accumulation of an inventory is risky, and consequently, many firms may operate beyond capacity at one time and much below capacity at another time. High prices encourage expansion, which may result in very low prices. And very low prices may bankrupt many firms, which will result in very high prices from the firms that remain in business. The average competitive price may very well exceed the monopoly price.

OLIGOPOLY

Oligopoly refers to a market situation in which there are a few sellers of
a differentiated product. Many American industries have oligopolistic
qualities, the steel, automobile, and cigarette industries being examples.
In fact, oligopoly seems to be a characteristic of industries to which
modern methods of production are applicable. The pattern of oligopolistic industries is for there to be a few giant firms that account for one-
half or more of the total industry output, followed by smaller firms that
produce the rest. For example, General Motors and Ford account for at
least two-thirds of the automobile sales by American car manufacturers.
Typical of most oligopolistic industries is mass merchandising, which
means distinguishing a firm's products from those of its competitors by
means of branding and trademarks, and creating a preference for the
brand by means of advertising. Some industries, however, approach pure
oligopoly. Here the firms in the industry produce virtually identical
products. Buyers have little reason to prefer the product of one firm to
that of another except on the basis of price. Examples of industries that
are nearly pure oligopolies are the cement, aluminum, and steel
industries.
   Oligopoly markets have several important characteristics. First, no
one firm can profit by adhering to price competition. For example, if a
firm raises its price and other firms do not follow suit, its sales usually
will suffer. Second, prices are identical or almost identical in oligopoly
markets. Finally, without price competition, firms reach some sort of
agreement, tacitly or otherwise, as to what the set price will be. There
may be a leader, usually the largest firm in the industry, that sets the
price, and the other firms merely follow it. What little competition
there it takes the form of product differentiation. The products of all
firms in an oligopolistic industry are nearly interchangeable, but each
firm's products have their own distinguishing characteristics, real or
fancied. These consist of real differences in quality or design or merely
differences in brand names.

Price and Output Under Oligopoly—Short Run

The basic tools for analyzing price and output under conditions of
oligopoly are the same as those used in analyzing pure competition and
pure monopoly. If a firm seeks to maximize its short-run profits, price
and output will be set at the point at which marginal cost equals marginal revenue. Under oligopoly, the average revenue curve slopes downward from left to right and in general appearance is similar to that
under monopoly. The total sales of a product sold under oligopoly,
however, are divided among a number of firms. The average revenue

curve of each firm, therefore, reflects not only the change in total sales that accompanies a change in price but also the shifts in sales among the various firms resulting from the price change. If one firm reduces its price, this will increase somewhat the industry's total sales, and it will also attract some sales from its competitors. The extent of the shift in sales will depend on the reactions of its rivals to the initial price reduction. Other firms may leave their prices unchanged, reduce their prices by varying amounts, increase sales promotion activities, or introduce product changes. Firms operating under conditions of oligopoly are faced with much uncertainty; instead of a single determinate average revenue curve as there is under monopoly, there is a family of average revenue curves, each indicating a different reaction by rival firms.

The above reasoning means that the very nature of an oligopoly frequently rules out price competition. Firms in oligopoly know that price competition is unlikely to yield any significant gain in either sales or revenue. So each firm is likely to practice some form of product differentiation, such as advertising, to increase the demand curve for the firm's product. The individual firm's profit will be increased, too, because a shift to the right in the demand curve increases the differential between price and average total cost. Economies of scale would affect the part of the cost curve in which the average total costs are still declining. Since there are relatively few oligopolistic firms, any successful product differentiation by one firm will have significant effects on the sales of its rivals. These rivals will seek to offset this by trying to differentiate their own products. In estimating the effectiveness of a new advertising program, therefore, each firm must gauge the likely reactions of its rivals.

Price and Output—Long Run

In the short run, an oligopolist can make a profit or a loss. If its losses continue, the firm will be forced to leave the industry. In the long run, all of the oligopolist's costs can vary, as existing plant facilities can be expanded. Economies of scale can result from decreases in a firm's long-run average total costs as the size of its plant increases. This is, of course, also true of firms operating in the long run under conditions of pure competition or pure monopoly. Those factors that produce economies of scale or decreasing long-run average costs as plant size increases are reduced input unit costs, greater specialization of resources, and more efficient utilization of equipment. Economies of scale shift all short-run cost curves to a lower level as the scale of operations becomes larger.

In the long run, the excess profits of firms operating in an oligopoly market situation can be maintained if there are restrictions on the entry of new firms into the market. Entry into an oligopolistic industry may be restricted in many ways, large capital requirements being one. The automobile industry is an example. Few companies have the resources to enter the industry, which was demonstrated after the end of World War II when the highly successful Kaiser Industries, the maker of various defense products, attempted to capitalize on an increased demand for automobiles by entering the automobile market. Its effort ended in failure. There also may be legal barriers in the form of patents, licenses, tariffs, or franchises, and it also may be difficult to counter the reputations of established firms. If the entry of new firms is restricted, which is likely in a typical oligopolistic situation, the prices may remain permanently above the average total costs, with excess profits both for the individual firms and the industry.

Economic Significance of Oligopoly

The economic and social losses from oligopolists' collusive practices are similar to those connected with monopoly. Output in such industries tends to be restricted; prices are maintained at high levels; and too few resources are employed, when compared with the more competitive areas of the economy. Nonetheless, oligopoly itself does not necessarily contradict the social interest, since it may be based on the economies that can be obtained by large-sized firms. These economies may be so great in relation to the market served that they leave room for only a limited number of firms in an industry. When, however, oligopoly results from the exclusion of new, potentially efficient firms by such means as patent holdings, withholding of needed materials, or any form of collusion, the situation is clearly contrary to the public interest. Even when the small number of sellers can be traced to the economies of scale, this efficiency does the public little good if there is no real price competition to ensure that the prices reflect that efficiency.

In summary, in a free enterprise market economy, theoretically the most desirable goal is pure competition because goods purchased by consumers usually are supplied at a minimum price under these conditions. The forms of competition in the real world, however, are far more numerous than the simple price and output adjustments that occur in the classical model of pure competition. In addition to price, real world competition includes, among others, the variables of product quality, product performance, and product financing and marketing. Business firms' planning and controlling activities are efforts to adjust to external economic and market conditions, including the strategies of rival firms. The use of standard costing, target pricing, market share measurements, and similar practices are common to small and large firms and are part of the competitive process rather than evidences of monopoly power. Competition can occur in oligopolistic industries, and large firms can enable society to benefit from important economies of scale.

Index